OF ANCIENT

John R. Hinnells is Research Professor in the Comparative Study of Religions at Liverpool Hope University, Honorary Professorial Research Fellow at SOAS, University of London and Senior Member of Robinson College, Cambridge. He is author of *Zoroastrians in Britain* (1996) and *The Zoroastrian Diaspora* (2005). His edited works include *The New Dictionary of Religions* (1995/1997) and *A New Handbook of Living Religions* (1996/1998).

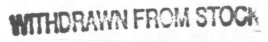

The Penguin Handbook of Ancient Religions

Edited by **John R. Hinnells**

PENGUIN BOOKS

PENGUIN BOOKS

Published by the Penguin Group
Penguin Books Ltd, 80 Strand, London WC2R ORL, England
Penguin Group (USA) Inc., 375 Hudson Street, New York, New York 10014, USA
Penguin Group (Canada), 90 Eglinton Avenue East, Suite 700, Toronto, Ontario, Canada M4P 2Y3
(a division of Pearson Penguin Canada Inc.)
Penguin Ireland, 25 St Stephen's Green, Dublin 2, Ireland (a division of Penguin Books Ltd)
Penguin Group (Australia), 250 Camberwell Road, Camberwell, Victoria 3124, Australia
(a division of Pearson Australia Group Pty Ltd)
Penguin Books India Pvt Ltd, 11 Community Centre, Panchsheel Park, New Delhi – 110 017, India
Penguin Group (NZ), 67 Apollo Drive, Rosedale, North Shore 0632, New Zealand
(a division of Pearson New Zealand Ltd)
Penguin Books (South Africa) (Pty) Ltd, 24 Sturdee Avenue, Rosebank, Johannesburg 2196, South Africa

Penguin Books Ltd, Registered Offices: 80 Strand, London WC2R ORL, England

www.penguin.com

First published in hardback as *A Handbook of Ancient Religions* by Cambridge University Press 2007
Published in paperback under the present title by Penguin Books 2009

1

Set in Utopia
Printed in England by Clays Ltd, St Ives plc

ISBN: 978-0-140-51364-6

www.greenpenguin.co.uk

Penguin Books is committed to a sustainable future
for our business, our readers and our planet.
The book in your hands is made from paper
certified by the Forest Stewardship Council.

Contents

Illustrations

Maps

Tables

Contributors

Philip P. Arnold Associate Professor, Department of Religion, Syracuse University

Jean Clottes Conservateur Général du Patrimoine, French Ministry of Culture

Susan Guettel Cole Associate Professor, Department of Classics, SUNY, Buffalo

Rosalie David Director, The KNH Centre, University of Manchester

Hilda Ellis Davidson Deceased. Formerly Vice-President of Lucy Cavendish College, Cambridge

Benjamin R. Foster Curator of the Yale Babylonian Collection, Department of Near Eastern Languages and Civilizations, Yale University

John R. Hinnells Research Professor, Liverpool Hope University, Honorary Professorial Research Fellow, SOAS, University of London, Senior Member Robinson College Cambridge

David Lewis-Williams Senior Mentor, The Rock Art Institute, University of the Witwatersrand

J. A. North Emeritus Professor, Department of History, University College London

Gregory L. Possehl Professor of Archaeology, University of Pennsylvania

John Rogerson Emeritus Professor, Department of Biblical Studies, University of Sheffield

Edward L. Shaughnessy Professor in Early Chinese Studies, East Asian Languages and Civilizations, University of Chicago

Nicolas Wyatt Emeritus Professor, University of Edinburgh

Introduction

JOHN R. HINNELLS

The ancient worlds fascinate most people. Few are unmoved at the wonder and awe on seeing the Egyptian mummies, the magnificence of the civilizations of the Aztecs and Incas, and the mystery of ancient China. But the ancient world is not important simply because it is interesting; it also helps us to understand later society. Just as conquerors commonly erected their religious buildings on the holy sites of their victims (churches on temples for example), so also ancient beliefs and practices were often absorbed into later culture. In my own native county of Derbyshire, in pre-Christian times wells where water sprang apparently inexplicably from the ground were decorated with pictures made from flowers at the start of spring. Nowadays this ancient custom has been taken over by the church (and later by the tourist trade!). The pre-Christian symbols are replaced by Christian images and the village priest tours the fields blessing the wells and the lands in order to ensure fertility in the growing season. Most religions take over practices and beliefs from ancient local traditions and reformulate them and by appropriating local traditions indigenize the global religion. Ancient religious figures become local saints. That is one reason why one religion takes on a variety of forms around the world. Christianity, Islam and other traditions have been localized in this way. If one is to understand many features of modern religions, one commonly has to study the past.

This book brings together the latest research on the major cultures of the ancient worlds. Each chapter is written by a leading figure in her/his field and the team which produced this book is international, drawn from America, Britain, France and South Africa. Many have pioneered completely new areas or methods of research: for example, the work of Professor Rosalie David when she brought together a team of doctors and scientists to unwrap Egyptian mummies in the Manchester Museum and subject them to advanced medical and a range of scientific tests, or Jean Clottes' discovery of hitherto unknown sites with Palaeolithic cave paintings. New evidence for ancient societies is always coming to light;

some archaeological finds were made by great scholars, for example Marshall's discovery of the Great 'Public Bath' at Mohenjo-daro as discussed and interpreted by Greg Possehl in the chapter on ancient India. New discoveries have sometimes been found accidentally, for example by the farmers working their land and uncovering sites from ancient Ugarit, or a shepherd boy finding the first Dead Sea Scrolls in a cave as discussed by John Rogerson in the chapter on ancient Israel. Alongside these discoveries there are new ways to study the finds, such as the pyramids in Aztec culture. Other chapters offer new ways to approach well-known ancient texts, for example Rogerson's application of Geertz's theories to the study of the Bible. So the study of ancient societies and religions is not static, but rather an ever changing picture. Unfortunately, reconstructing a picture of ancient societies can be like putting together a jigsaw from which many, and important, pieces are missing (to use another analogy), and scholars must attempt to do so without knowing what the final picture should look like. The painstaking task of interpreting ancient sites which are not fully understood, and fragmentary stone tablets as in the case of Ugarit and Mesopotamia, is a labour of love. But the excitement of doing that jigsaw is a major drive behind some of the greatest scholarship in these fields. The work of completing that picture is a vocation for the scholars involved.

The ancient world, while inspiring a sense of awe in its students, also presents particular problems of interpretation. In some cases there are few if any texts (for example the Indus Civilization); in others we have mostly texts with relatively few material remains (as in ancient Israel). In some cases we are heavily dependent on external accounts; for example, although the Aztecs and Incas left magnificent structures, we are heavily dependent on accounts by their Christian conquerors to understand them. The view of some ancient empires is often seen through a veil of presuppositions, such as Christian readings of Jewish scriptures or the perception of ancient Rome, or the new age interest in Druids and Celtic traditions. To what extent can we rely on Herodotus' account of ancient Egypt, or Christian accounts of Icelandic or Aztec religions? The study of other cultures in the modern world raises problems of presuppositions and bias, but at least one can dialogue with, or question, members of living religions. Those who study the ancient world are faced with the problems of interpreting silent stones, or understanding little-known or unknown languages, from another culture and from another age. Modern western writers commonly come from industrialized urban environments. Trying to stand aside from their conditioning in order to understand ancient, often rural, artefacts and writings requires a leap of imagination to attain an empathetic insight, as well as considerable scholarly linguistic and/or scientific archaeological expertise. Some scholars approach ancient cultures with their own agendas; for example an earlier school of biblical critics sought a better understanding of ancient Israel from studying the civilizations of Ugarit and Mesopotamia. Studying some of the great writers of classical antiquity, either in China or Greece, does not prepare us for an understanding of the broad religious practice of the time. Artefacts, structures and texts that withstood the ravages of time are often the possessions and products of the rich and powerful rulers, and may reveal little of the general culture and religion of the ordinary people.

The very term 'religion' is an example of the imposition of a modern western label on the ancient worlds. Many cultures, such as those of Greece, the Aztecs and the Incas, have no single-word equivalent to 'religion'. Separating out a culture's perceptions of god(s) or spiritual forces from its economic, social and political life is not simply difficult, it is misguided. The perception of religion as a matter of private personal belief is a particularly modern, western and rather Protestant idea. Some ancient cultures did have complex 'theologies', but in others 'religion' is more a matter of duty, either to the elders or to the (ultimate) powers, a matter of practice, not of doctrine, a matter of civic and social obligations. But 'religion' is a convenient term, providing it is not taken too narrowly, to look at the ancient worlds' perceptions of their places in the order of things, in understanding their duties, aspirations, fears and not least the remarkably widespread belief in a life after death. The term 'ancient' is also necessarily loose. Whereas Palaeolithic art dates back over three millennia, the Aztec and Inca civilizations were not overcome until some 500 years ago.

How does the scholar proceed in her/his attempts to interpret silent stones, burial sites, paintings on cave walls from truly ancient sites, or unknown languages, markings on seals and tablets, cuneiform and pictograms? Authors in this volume demonstrate how people work at the coalface, or at the cutting edge, of research. They do so in a way that conveys their own excitement with new techniques and new discoveries. The work of the historian is complex. Sometimes important parallels, or guides, may be the beliefs and practices gleaned from ethnographic studies, for example in understanding the culture of the Aztecs and Incas, or the Palaeolithic cave art. What all this implies is that there is rarely, if ever, any such thing as historical 'fact'. There may be physical objects or texts, but the task of interpreting them is subjective. Scholarly views change, in the light of new discoveries, new evidence or different approaches to understanding the evidence. For that reason contributors to this volume were asked to start with a consideration of where each subject stands now, and where the scholarship has come form. They were asked to give an account of the sources, be they literary or archaeological, so that the reader is aware not only of the nature of the evidence, but of how people have approached that evidence. Where the evidence is archaeological or iconographic, or from such artefacts as seals or tablets, these are illustrated in the figures. Authors were asked to supply, wherever appropriate, maps locating the places referred to in the text and time charts to give a visual image of the flow of history, and examples of what they considered central to learning about their subject, from temple plans to practices associated with divination. Each author was allocated 20,000 words, facilitating more substantial accounts than are found in most encyclopaedias. This allocation was made to take account of the importance of providing the reader with an account of the sources which in most subjects include materials not likely to be known to the reader. The obvious examples are the seals and the script of the Indus Valley, and the tablets and archaeological material from Ugarit. Authors were asked, where appropriate, to include a translation (virtually always their own) of some of the key passages of texts – where they occur in their subject – to give the reader a flavour of what to him or her may be 'the new world' of antiquity.

Authors were asked to follow a general structure to their chapters, in so far as this was appropriate for their subject. They were asked: (a) to give a brief review of the histories of their subject, highlighting the presuppositions which have lain behind previous scholarship, and their own; (b) to give an account of the sources used, be they literary or archaeological; (c) to provide a brief overview of the relevant history of the religion or civilization; (d) to include an account of the whole society, so that the chapters are not concerned simply with monarchs, battles and the great writers; (d) to provide an account of myths, beliefs and practices, of belief in god(s) or spirits, and an afterlife, of popular as well as 'official' religion; (e) to bring out, and focus on, what they see as the key feature to understanding of the religion in the culture they deal with (e.g. divination in China). In some chapters this breakdown of material is obvious, in others less so because it is not appropriate, but the broad issues are addressed in every chapter. It is obviously impossible to impose a straitjacket of uniformity on authors, in view of such huge differences between the civilizations covered here. But the difference is not only in the nature of these civilizations but in their considerably different geographical size, such as the relatively small Israel compared with the huge areas covered in the chapters on ancient Europe and China. The nature of the evidence is also very different, from literate Greece and Rome to the wholly iconographic material from Palaeolithic caves.

Writers in general often make certain presuppositions about ancient religion. One is that these religions are necessarily 'primitive', 'simple' or undeveloped. That is not an assumption made by writers in this book. Ancient societies and cultures were often complex. Some of the cultures interacted. Greeks met Egyptians, there was trade between Mesopotamia and the Indus Valley, and Romans encountered the tribes of northern Europe. Some religions were genetically related, notably those of the Greeks, Romans and northern Europeans which derived from a shared Indo-European heritage. Though some were largely cut off from other cultures, notably the Chinese and the Aztecs and Incas, few ancient cultures were in hermetically sealed 'packets'. A form of 'interfaith' activity occurred then as now, sometimes in the form of conquest, but also simply out of interest, for example the Romans' fascination with Egypt, or with identifying the various gods of ancient Mesopotamia and those of other cultures. Scholars of religion wrote, and write, of early religion as 'animistic', that is the belief that spirits animated material objects such as trees or stones. The difficulty with that word is that by adding the 'ism' one implies a more formal, defined movement than is valid. The same is true of the term 'polytheism'. Too often writers have given the false impression of a monolithic phenomenon, where no such single 'thing' existed, for example the term 'paganism' in the Roman Empire. One of the most dangerous suffixes in the English language must be 'ism'! In the nineteenth and early twentieth centuries, scholars assumed that there had been an evolution of religion comparable to evolution in the biological world. That is, they assumed that religion progressed from the crude, from a belief in many gods, to the peak of the evolutionary ladder represented by an ethical monotheism, exemplified in Christianity. It is simply not the case that the more ancient religions were crude and simple. As the chapters on cave art and the Indus Valley show, behind what modern western commentators see as crude drawings, there may well have been a profound understanding of human life. The word 'magic' is another term which is sometimes used uncritically to refer to the belief in the efficacy of prayer made by members of a different religion or culture.

`Although I do not subscribe to the notion that basically all religions say the same thing (for me their very diversity is part of the fascination of the subject), nevertheless in the chapters of this book it is noticeable how widespread some phenomena are: divination, astrology, the veneration of ancestors, the idea of the divine dwelling in material forms on earth, and shamans. Religion and politics are as interwoven in the ancient as in the modern world. Human beings with similar resources and addressing similar problems independently use similar ideas, symbols and solutions. Yet the ancient worlds were different from the modern urban west, and seeing just how and why they are different is part of the intriguing nature of studying religions.

Decisions on what should, and should not, be included were difficult. It would obviously have been artificial and arbitrary to have given a common date line in history since civilizations rise and fall in different eras. Although Judaism is a living religion it was decided to include ancient Israel, in part because of the link with other ancient Near Eastern civilizations (Ugarit, Mesopotamia and Egypt). As a Zoroastrian specialist, I was obviously tempted to include ancient non-Zoroastrian Iran (and maybe in a later edition will do so). But the picture of that civilization is so unclear that reluctantly I decided to omit the subject. Some of the so-called primal religions, e.g. North American Indians, have an enormous history behind them, but we mostly know of them in their living form. It seemed wise to restrict the number of subjects covered in this book so that those which were included could be given a reasonably substantial coverage. Because it is assumed that, however interesting the book is, few will sit down and read it straight through from beginning to end like a novel, what comes first and what is at the end of the book is not significant. But it made sense to start with the earliest period of history for which one can study religion, and the book ends with the civilization that was the last to be destroyed. Within those borders, chapters are grouped according to their interaction, notably the religions of the ancient Near East. As Mesopotamia and the Indus Valley civilizations were in some contact, those two subjects are placed near each other.

Finally a note of personal thanks both to the authors and to the publisher, especially Caroline Pretty, with whom it has been a delight to work, and Kate Brett and the production team at Cambridge University Press who are publishing the hardback edition. I thank Frances Brown for her superb copy-editing, and Dr Mitra Sharafi for help with the bibliographies. I thank all for their patience in the long delayed publication of this book, caused by problems beyond editorial control. It is a pleasure to see such international collaboration come to fruition.

1 Palaeolithic art and religion

JEAN CLOTTES AND DAVID LEWIS-WILLIAMS

Introduction

Towards the end of the eighteenth century, Edmund Burke contemplated the essence of mankind: he wrote, 'Man is by his constitution a religious animal.' In the second half of the twentieth century, we have had other definitions: Man the Toolmaker and Man the Symbol-Maker, the second being a reworking of Burke's feeling that the defining trait of 'man' is in some way or other 'spiritual' or non-material. Whether one adopts a technological, a cognitive or a spiritual definition, the intertwined roots of ur-religion (the hypothetical 'original' religion), the beliefs and practices that preceded what we know today as 'religion', lie deep in prehistory.

The word 'prehistory' is generally applied to the extremely long period that stretches from the origins of humankind, about 3 million years or more ago, to the advent of writing. In some regions, such as the Middle East, writing led to profound social changes many thousands of years ago, while in other parts of the world the impact of writing was not felt until contact with European colonists, sometimes not until the nineteenth or even the beginning of the twentieth century. We are thus dealing with immense periods of time about which – in most cases – we know next to nothing. Unlike some other chapters in this book, this one can draw on neither inscriptions nor texts; nor can its writers question prehistoric people about their beliefs.

'Prehistory' may also be taken to include 'pre-human' hominids. Did the numerous pre-human primates – the australopithecines, *Homo habilis* or, much later, *Homo erectus* – have a religion? Did they consider the world around them other than as a source of food and, if so, how? Researchers have no way of knowing because there is no archaeological evidence that the thoughts of these species went beyond the satisfaction of their immediate bodily needs. This does not mean that they were no more than brutish animals. The chances are that their curiosity about the world, which seems sometimes to have been manifested in their selecting and collecting of stones with strange appearances, may have extended to phenomena and experiences that they could not understand and that seemed to require 'supernatural' explanation. In pointing to this evidence, slight as it is, we do not wish to imply that religion originated in an innate desire to explain the world; there is more to religion than the aetiological explanation allows. Be that as it may, there is not the slightest direct or even indirect evidence of what may be called religious thought until the time of the Neanderthals.

Neanderthals (*Homo sapiens neanderthalensis*) lived in Europe and the Middle East from perhaps 250,000 to 30,000 years ago, the period known as the Middle Palaeolithic. Most archaeologists and palaeo-anthropologists now believe that they were replaced by, rather than evolved into, our own species, *Homo sapiens sapiens*, at the beginning of the Upper Palaeolithic (30,000 to 35,000 BP (Before Present)). For about 10,000 years prior to that time, Neanderthals shared parts of Europe with *Homo sapiens sapiens*.

No rock art can be attributed to Neanderthals. Excavators have found only a few scratched bones or stones, but these cannot be related, even remotely, to religious thought. There is, however, evidence of another kind that has attracted researchers' attention. They buried their dead, or at least some of them did – there is indisputable evidence for only a few burials. When they did bury, as at the sites of La Chapelle-aux-Saints, Le Roc de Marsal, La Ferrassie and Le Moustier in France, Teshik-Tash in Uzbekistan, Kebara in Israel and Shanidar in Iraq, they buried people of all ages, from the 'old man' (about fiftyish) of La Chapelle-aux-Saints to foetuses at La Ferrassie. Both men and women were buried. Occasionally, various objects, such as stone tools and animal parts, were deposited with the bodies. At La Ferrassie, a stone slab with a number of hollowed-out cup-marks was discovered with a three-year-old child. Sometimes traces of red ochre have also been found associated with burials. Even though all this evidence is relatively slight, it still provides a few hints about the Neanderthals: at least some of them may have shown some form of respect for certain of their dead, and the grave-goods could, perhaps, have been a way to help them in the other world.

When did this revolutionary way of thinking about the dead begin? Many traces of 'rites' may have been destroyed by the passage of time. Still, all the absolutely certain Neanderthal burials are relatively recent, between 60,000 and 30,000 BP (Jaubert 1999); we do not know what the earlier Neanderthals did with their dead.

Today there is much debate about just how 'human' the Neanderthals were. New light has recently been thrown on this question by a highly significant discovery in south-west France. In the depths of the Bruniquel cave, in the Tarn-et-Garonne, broken stalactites and stalagmites were piled and arranged in a kind of oval roughly 5 m × 4 m, with a much smaller round structure next to it (Fig. 1.1). The structures themselves cannot, of course, be directly dated, but a fire was made nearby, and a burnt bone from it was dated to more than 47,600 BP. If this date also applies to the arrangement of stalagmites, it puts the structures well within the Mousterian, the local Neanderthal cultural period (Rouzaud et al. 1996). No practical purpose can be suggested for these constructions: the people who made them did not live that far inside the cave, as the absence of the kind of remains so common on habitation sites testifies. The only hypothesis that makes sense is the delimitation of a symbolic or ritual space well inside the subterranean world. The significance of such apparently symbolic subterranean activity will become clear later.

With the advent of our direct, fully modern ancestors, *Homo sapiens sapiens*, commonly called Cro-Magnons in Europe, there are many more clues. The practice of burial was markedly more common in the Upper Palaeolithic than in the Middle Palaeolithic. In addition, 'art' became widespread at the beginning of this period, whether on artefacts (portable art) or on the walls of deep caves and in more open contexts (rock art).

We can now no longer side-step two difficult definitional problems: both 'art' and 'religion' elude clear, universally accepted definition. Common understandings of the words come out of western capitalist and industrialist society and are therefore not universal. We do not wish to become embroiled in an endless debate about definitions, so we simply point out that the boundaries that western definitions impose on 'art' did not (and still do not) exist in small-scale societies, such as those in which the first 'art' and 'religion' were born. 'Religion' is perhaps even more difficult to define than 'art'. Some definitions avoid reference to belief in a supernatural realm and spirit beings; others insist on these features. For our present purposes, we take 'religion' to denote beliefs in supernatural entities and related practices believed to afford contact with those entities. Whether a distinction between 'material' and 'spiritual' was recognized in prehistory is another question altogether. These broad definitions noted, it is perhaps safe to allow that not all Upper Palaeolithic 'art' was strictly 'religious' – even though it is virtually impossible to distinguish between what was religious and what was secular at that time. Nevertheless, the quest for ur-religion is inevitably intertwined with the origins of art.

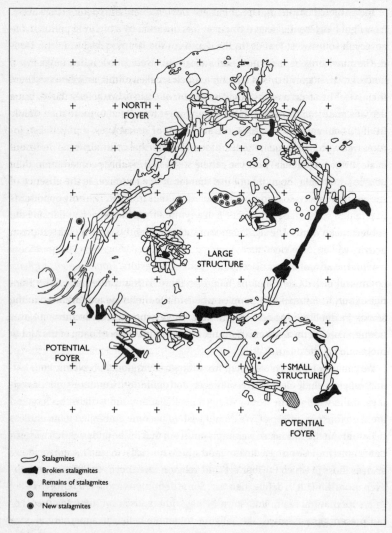

Fig. 1.1. Two probably Neanderthal structures of broken stalagmites found in the Bruniquel cave (France).

Despite such problems, Upper Palaeolithic art gives illuminating clues about its authors' beliefs. European Upper Palaeolithic art covers a long period, from at least 40,000 to 12,000 BP. In this chapter, we keep to it because it provides the best available basis for inferences about early prehistoric religion. We must, however, enter two provisos. The first concerns Palaeolithic religion elsewhere in the world. Australia was peopled by *Homo sapiens sapiens* at least 55,000 years ago, and people there made rock art perhaps as early as 40,000 years ago, certainly from 25,000 onwards. In Africa, the evidence for portable art and possibly for rock art may be of the same order. Researchers know hardly anything yet about Palaeolithic rock art in Asia. The Americas were probably peopled more than 20,000 years ago, though there is debate about this estimate. In the absence of sufficient evidence, we cannot assume that the early religions of those continents were the same as those of Upper Palaeolithic Europe, or that the beliefs held nowadays by indigenous cultures there were handed down unchanged from prehistoric times. Inevitably, researchers are restricted to western Europe, where evidence is complex and abundant.

The second proviso concerns 'late' prehistory. This is a different subject from ours, even in Europe. The peoples who built Stonehenge and other standing stones in the Neolithic and Chalcolithic, those who erected dolmens all over western Europe, the authors of Levantine rock art in western Spain, of the Alpine rock art in Valcamonica (Italy) and Monte Bego (France), or again of the rock art of Scandinavia, may well have had different types of religion(s). Certainly, they had different social systems and economies. We mention them here even though they fall outside of our remit because there is still much work to be done on them.

Rather than skim unsatisfactorily over other regions and 'late' prehistory, we concentrate on Upper Palaeolithic Europe, especially western Europe, where there is the earliest and the most evidence for humankind's ur-religion.

Ice Age societies

A different world

To understand Upper Palaeolithic religion, it is necessary to know how the people of that time lived. Only then can we discern the ways in which their religion articulated with daily life and social relations. Religion was not a 'free-floating', optional extra to society; it was embedded in the social fabric.

The European Upper Palaeolithic lasted for nearly 30,000 years, roughly between 40,000 and 11,000 BP. It ended at the same time as the Ice Age, which had begun tens of thousands of years before. The lower temperatures had caused Europe to look very different from what it is now, with thick and extensive ice caps that covered most of the northern parts of the continent and the high mountain ranges. As a consequence, the level of the sea was far lower, at times 120 m below present-day level, a situation which changed the coast lines, in some regions very markedly. For instance, the entrance to the Cosquer Cave near Marseilles, now under 37 m of water, was at the time when the paintings were made about 5 km inland. Then, in large areas of Europe, instead of thick forests, there were scattered clumps of trees, mostly birches and firs, and the cold, windswept plains were wide bare expanses.

The world in which the Cro-Magnons lived has been reconstructed through analyses of sediments and pollens recovered from peat bogs, from the debris of habitation sites, and also through a study of the fauna of the time. Animals were plentiful to a point which it is difficult for us to imagine because that kind of a world – full of animals, with very few people – has vanished for ever. Trout and salmon were abundant in the rivers; they were occasionally caught, particularly at the end of the Upper Palaeolithic. Huge herds of bison, aurochs and horses grazing in the valleys were consistently hunted, as were reindeer during their yearly migrations, and ibex and chamois among steep slopes and rocks. When the climate warmed up a little, during an interglacial of a few centuries or millennia, deer became more numerous. Among them, a particular genus, called *Megaceros* because of its huge antlers, is now extinct, as are so many other animals of the Ice Age, such as mammoths, hyenas and leopards, woolly rhinoceroses, and cave bears and cave lions 3 m in length, as well as lesser felines.

Ways of life

The ways of life of Upper Palaeolithic people are known through the remains of meals scattered around their hearths, together with many tools and weapons and the debris left over from their making. The people were hunter-gatherers who lived exclusively from what they could find in nature without practising either agriculture or herding. They hunted the bigger herbivores, while berries, leaves, roots, wild fruit and mushrooms probably played a major role in their diet. Their hunting was indiscriminate, perhaps because so many animals were about that they did not need to spare pregnant females or the young. In the cave of Enlène, for example, many bones of reindeer and bison foetuses were found. Apparently, Upper Palaeolithic people hunted like other predators and killed the weakest prey first. They did, however, sometimes concentrate on salmon runs and migrating herds of reindeer.

Contrary to popular beliefs about 'cave men', Upper Palaeolithic people did not live deep inside caves. They rather chose the foot of cliffs, especially when an overhang provided good shelter. On the plains and in the valleys, they used tents made from hides of the animals they killed. At times, on the great Russian plains, they built huts with huge bones and tusks collected from the skeletons of mammoths.

Men hunted mostly with spears; the bow and arrow was probably not invented until the Magdalenian period that came at the end of the Upper Palaeolithic. Tools and weapons, made out of wood or reindeer antlers, often had flint cutting edges. Flint knappers were skilful and traditions in flint knapping were pursued for thousands of years. This continuity means that they must have been carefully taught how to find good flint nodules and how to knap them in order to make knives, burins (chisel-like tools) or scrapers, which could be used for various purposes.

Only a small part of the implements they used has, however, been preserved, and we know little about wooden artefacts, cured hides, clothing and body decoration, except for the stone or bone pendants and beads which they wore. Tool-making traditions changed over time, but very slowly, and a series of Upper Palaeolithic 'cultures', or 'industries', has been defined from flint and bone tool assemblages.

The first fully Upper Palaeolithic culture was the Aurignacian. Then, from around 28,000 BP, the people of the Gravettian culture consistently used a particular sharp elongated flint point, probably as the head of wooden long-shafted spears. The Solutrean culture developed about 22,000 BP. Flint-knapping was then at its best. These people invented a tool – the bone needle – which has kept exactly the same shape for 20,000 years, even if its material has been changed to steel. Magdalenians, from around 18,000 to 11,500 BP, are famous for their portable art, for the invention of the barbed harpoon towards the end of the period, and also for their use of the spear-thrower, a clever device which enabled them to project their spears much farther with deadly accuracy.

Were these changes due to the movement of groups of people from one part of Europe to another, or did inventions spread slowly over vast areas as many specialists believe? Certainly, it is probable that travellers went to far-away places:

perforated sea shells used as pendants have been found far inland on sites belonging to all the cultures of the Upper Palaeolithic. Those travellers carried not only goods to bring back or to exchange but also ideas and myths. At the same time, both goods and beliefs could have been passed from community to community. These are probably the main reasons why Palaeolithic art and religion show a deep overall unity, despite regional and temporal differences.

Some specifics of the art

As we have seen, paintings and engravings are not all in deep caves: some are on open-air rock surfaces. The rituals and the roles of these different locations may (or may not) have been different. Be that as it may, systematically going very far into extensive caves during some periods, particularly in the Magdalenian but also for a long time before (e.g. Chauvet Cave, about 31,000 BP), is a rare phenomenon in the history of humankind, and nowhere except in the European Palaeolithic has it been found to last, as it did then, for more than 20,000 years.

Right from the beginning (i.e. the Aurignacian), the techniques of image-making were fully mastered. True, they were not all 'great artists', but some were outstanding. For example, in the Chauvet Cave, as early as 31,000 BP, they seem to have evolved different means for showing spatial perspective. They also made sophisticated use of shading and captured the expressions of the animals they drew with an astonishing vividness. Such expertise in so many caves of varying antiquity – for example Lascaux (about 17,000 BP) and Altamira, Niaux, Font-de-Gaume, Rouffignac or Les Trois-Frères (all about 13,000 to 15,000 BP) – suggests that the 'artists' were, in some sense, trained. Cave art, at least, was not for everybody. Who, then, made the images? And what did they believe they were accomplishing?

Sources of knowledge

In the absence of writing and oral tradition, the sources of knowledge about pre-historic religion(s) must necessarily be oblique. There are four kinds of evidence.

Material remains

Remains recovered, often but not always, by means of excavations provide evidence for the ways of life of the people who left them. They are mostly the results of actions with practical purposes – or at least which appear so to us – like making fires and cooking meat, or making tools and weapons. Such activities can, however, have a variety of meanings which we have no way of knowing. For example, certain kinds of stone could have been associated with specific social groups and have pointed to highly or lowly valued activities. More obviously, personal adornments, like pendants, shells and beads, could have had an aesthetic value and have been meant to please the eye and add to a person's allure, but they could also have been – indeed probably were – symbols of rank and prestige. They could also have had a concomitant religious significance. In modern western society, a gold cross worn as a pendant may have all of those meanings.

Other material remains seem to have had no practical purpose that we can imagine and were probably motivated by something other than practical necessities, though we must always remember that a distinction between 'practical' and 'non-practical' was probably not clear-cut in Upper Palaeolithic societies. The burials and grave-goods to which we have referred are instances of activities that seem to have gone beyond the purely practical. The earliest evidence for Upper Palaeolithic graves has been found in the Middle East, where anatomically modern bodies were buried with 'offerings' as early as 90,000 to 100,000 years ago at Qafzeh (Fig. 1.2) and Skhul. What had been exceptional during the time of the Neanderthals was now becoming commonplace: indeed, grave-goods accompany *Homo sapiens sapiens* dead as a matter of course. Some sites have extremely elaborate burials. For instance, at Sungir, in Russia, two children were buried with beautiful ivory spearheads, ivory statuettes and thousands of beads. Red ochre was also frequently used. Sometimes a corpse was placed on a layer of ochre; in other instances it was sprinkled with ochre, either over the whole body or more often on and around the head, as at Dolní Vestonice in the Czech Republic (Fig. 1.3).

Of course, disposing of dead bodies may be seen as a necessity. But digging a grave, scattering it with red ochre (which might symbolise blood or life), depositing fine flint or ivory artefacts, reindeer antlers or the leg of an animal near a corpse or on top of it, are different matters altogether. They seem to testify to a belief that a dead person is, in some way or other, still valuable and needs not only 'respect' but also perhaps some kind of 'help' in the form of material goods. Many researchers argue that such practices make sense only if we surmise that the people thought that there was another world to which the dead went. As we have seen, recently discovered Bruniquel arrangements of stalagmites and stalactites seem to make that belief as old as the later Neanderthals,

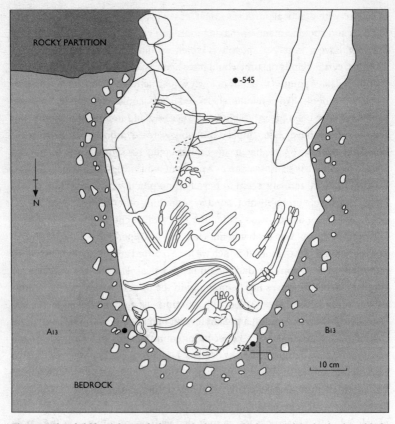

Fig. 1.2. The child burial at Qafzeh (Israel) showing the layout of the body, the added limestone blocks and the offerings. From Vandermeersch 1970.

and as to our own species, it would have been firmly established by the time modern humans reached the Middle East around 100,000 years ago. Belief in a supernatural world to which the dead go can be safely assumed for the Upper Palaeolithic. What forms those beliefs took is a question that we address below.

Portable art was consistently made by those anatomically modern people. They carved and engraved mammoth tusk ivory, bones and reindeer antlers, probably wood, and sometimes stone plaquettes. Many of these objects, such as the plaquettes, seem to have no practical purpose. But when a tool or a weapon is

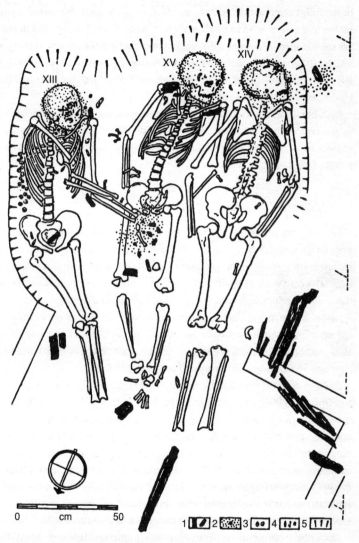

Fig. 1.3. Triple Upper Palaeolithic burial at Dolní Vestonice (Czech Republic). 1: charcoal and stone tools, 2: red ochre, 3: molluscs 4: human and animal teeth and ivory pendant, 5: side of the pit. From B. Klíma.

beautifully carved with a representation of, say, an animal, this sort of art may go far beyond a mere wish to add beauty to it. Some of the finest pieces of portable art are the spear-throwers, implements that enabled their users to cast a spear much farther and with considerably more strength and accuracy than by brute force: the 'magical' power of the spear-thrower could well have been enhanced by the power of the image that it bore.

Both burials and portable art can be dated by their archaeological context and by the radiocarbon technique, which provides firm temporal landmarks and – in the case of portable art – enables researchers to make comparisons with the images found on the cave walls.

The art of the caves and shelters

'Cave art' is a misleading phrase, because Upper Palaeolithic people made engravings and paintings not only in the complete darkness of deep caves, but also in shelters where light could reach the walls and even on cliff faces or boulders, as recent finds in Spain and Portugal confirm. The rituals and the roles of these different locations may (or may not) have been different.

About 350 cave and open art sites are currently known all over Europe, from the tip of the Iberian Peninsula (Andalucia) to the Urals. France has about 160 sites, and Spain nearly as many. The rest are scattered in Portugal, the south of Italy and Sicily, and a few in central Europe and in Russia.

Striking continuities may be discerned throughout the very long period of the Upper Palaeolithic. Whether in the light or in the dark, broadly the same images of animals and geometric signs were made with the same techniques and the same conventions, though exclusively regional and temporal features are certainly identifiable and should not be ignored. For pigment, they used iron oxides for the reds and charcoal or manganese dioxide for the blacks. They made images with their fingers on soft surfaces inside the caves, or finer ones with flint tools on the harder surfaces of walls and ceilings. To explore the deeper caves, they used wooden torches and, later on, grease lamps with a wick.

Upper Palaeolithic artists depicted mostly animals and geometric 'signs'. From among the available animals around them, the image-makers chose to represent the big herbivores which they hunted, especially horses, bison and aurochs, ibex and all varieties of deer. Aurignacians (as at the Chauvet Cave) seem to have favoured the most fearsome species: woolly rhinoceroses, cave lions, mammoths and cave bears. In all periods, birds and fish are only occasionally featured. Some creatures are very rare, like snakes, wolves, foxes and insects. Some animals are 'monsters' that have no counterpart in nature. The choices made have nothing to do with the relative proportions of animal species in the neighbourhood. Significantly, anthropomorphic images are rare, and usually appear deliberately sketchy or as caricatures.

The sun, stars and moon were never drawn, nor the ground line. No mountains, no huts, no natural landscapes, and very few recognizable representations of tools, weapons or personal adornment. Generally, the images were painted or engraved without any obvious reference to one another: explicit 'scenes' are exceptional. Clearly, Upper Palaeolithic art was not intended to give an accurate account of the world outside the caves. Rather, it concerned beliefs entertained by the authors of the images. The image-makers were dealing with specific kinds of interactions between selected parts of the material and the supernatural worlds and with how they could take advantage of forces deriving from those interactions.

This (at this stage perhaps bold) inference brings us to what may be called religious beliefs. It seems to be supported by the two different types of location that are found in the caves. Paintings and engravings are sometimes in small narrow recesses where only one person can crawl (Fig. 1.4). In this case, the images were obviously not meant to be seen by large groups, and we may surmise that, unlike paintings in western art galleries, the act of making them mattered more than the finished product. In other cases, like the Chamber of the Bulls in Lascaux or the Salon Noir in Niaux, the paintings were arranged in vast chambers in a most spectacular way. Here, it was probably not only the act of making the images that was important; they seem to have been meant to impress spectators. These two types of subterranean location are not mutually exclusive: both can be found in the same cave. As we shall see in a subsequent section, they reflect different uses of the chambers and passages, and different rites and ceremonies within a religious and cosmological framework.

One of the consistent and remarkable features of Upper Palaeolithic images provides a clue to the people's attitude towards these different locations. Upper Palaeolithic people, throughout the period, used features of the natural relief in their animal images. Examples of this are extremely numerous. For instance, a concavity in the wall was sometimes seen as the dorsal line of a bison, and the rest of the animal was drawn in relation to it (Niaux). Under the flickering light of smoky torches, people seem to have been looking for animal shapes in the rock surfaces; when they found them, they sometimes completed them. Often, too,

Fig. 1.4. Many figures of reindeer, ibex and bison were engraved in a place where only one person can squeeze in. Les Trois-Frères (France). From Abbé H. Breuil 1952.

they painted animals as though they were issuing from cracks, fissures, recesses or holes, as at Rouffignac and Chauvet.

The remarkable uniformity of the complex of imagery and, especially, the locations of Upper Palaeolithic art, both too often overlooked by late twentieth-century researchers, means that the beliefs which underlay the making of the images probably followed the same general, overall pattern for human groups far distant in space and in time. This point is important because it testifies to a long-standing religion and cosmology that certainly changed regionally and with time but which remained fundamentally the same for more than 20,000 years. In studying Upper Palaeolithic art, researchers need to pay constant attention to both continuity and change; to ignore one or the other, as is common today, is to deny the evidence.

Human activities in the caves

For archaeologists, deep caves have an advantage over shelters and open air sites: if they are not vandalized as soon as they are discovered (Lascaux) or by early modern visitors (Niaux), the chances are that many activities of the people who frequented them in Palaeolithic times may have been preserved (Fontanet, Chauvet, Tuc d'Audoubert; Clottes 1998, 1999). This contextualizing evidence is as important as the images themselves; unfortunately, it has not always been given its due because researchers have concentrated on the 'beauty' of the images and their evolutionary place in art history.

Footprints, handprints and other traces provide valuable information about Upper Palaeolithic visitors to the caves, such as their numbers and their ages. We thus know that very young children, one aged about six in Fontanet and a three-year-old in Tuc d'Audoubert, were taken into the deep caves. Footprints of an eight- to ten-year old boy from a much earlier period were recently found in Chauvet. A number of remains are from what researchers have, rashly, taken to be purely 'practical' activities They include the remains of fires, hearths, torches, and bones left over after meals, as well as 'lost' tools.

Other remains clearly cannot be explained as the result of 'practical' activities. Deposits of objects, such as bear teeth or teeth of other animals, shells, flints or antlers, in small cavities in the walls almost certainly testify to ritual practices. After attention had been drawn to them in some Pyrenean caves (Bégouën and Clottes 1981), such discoveries became common. In the Magdalenian caves of Enlène, Montespan, Troubat, Bédeilhac, Portel, Tuc d'Audoubert, all in the Pyrenees, many small pieces of bone were found forcibly thrust into cracks in the cave wall. Others were discovered in far older contexts at Gargas, one being radiocarbon dated to 26,860 BP ± 460. Very recently, another was found in the Chauvet cave where the dates for the cave art are still older. Again, whatever changes undoubtedly took place, there is strong evidence that similar activities were practised in the deep caves for many thousands of years.

Ethnography and analogy

Some historians of religion have attempted to reconstruct ur-religion by comparative methods that seek to isolate the oldest components of ethnographically recorded religions. To these components they sometimes add what they take to be universal human traits, such as a desire to explain natural phenomena. Archaeologists, on the other hand, have been much less inclined to follow these routes. Some have tried to infer religion directly from material evidence; others have sought relations between material evidence and specific, ethnographically recorded rituals and beliefs. All these approaches, whether of historians of religion or of archaeologists, are fraught with logical problems. Indeed, much unnecessary debate results from a lack of agreement on what constitutes evidence and how explanations should be constructed. An explicit methodology needs to be developed and accepted before interdisciplinary debate can be meaningful.

Today all archaeologists agree that the *Homo sapiens sapiens* populations of 30,000 or 40,000 years ago were anatomically and physiologically the same as we are. They had the same brains and nervous system, the same cognitive abilities as us. What changed drastically over the millennia that succeeded the Upper Palaeolithic was their economic and social conditions and their ways of life. But, during the Upper Palaeolithic, the people remained hunters and gatherers. Though challenged by some researchers, it has therefore been long accepted that when we want to interpret the material remains of Upper Palaeolithic activities we have a much better chance of success if we turn to hunter-gatherer cultures than by trying to apply the logic of western people living in an industrial society. Such cultures have been ethnographically well documented in many parts of the world, in the Americas, in Africa and in Australia.

This concern with hunter-gatherers certainly does not mean that we should take any of those cultures as a model that we can apply directly to Upper

Palaeolithic people. That would be a serious error. Nor should we err, as the earlier European researchers did when they examined 'primitive' arts for similarities with the art of the ancient caves and shelters. If a geometric design in a French cave looks like a hut somewhere in central Africa, it does not necessarily mean that its maker intended it to depict a hut. There are, however, some universals in human ways of thinking, and those can be used, with circumspection, to interpret Palaeolithic evidence. For example, all over the world, deep caves are considered as the realm of the spirits, or of the dead, or of the gods, as a supernatural world parallel to ours yet below it, as a dangerous world to which very few – if any – have access and then only for very precise purposes (Clottes and Lewis-Williams 1998; Lewis-Williams 2002).

Ethnographic analogy can throw some light on the results of people's actions both in the deep caves where they rarely went and in the shelters where they dwelt. Without such analogies, researchers must necessarily fall back on covert and highly misleading analogies with modern western thought and life. But they need to avoid a facile game of 'ethnographic snap' and to explore multiple, not just one or two, analogies that are based on universal links between activities and evidence, what philosophers of science call 'strong relations of relevance'. In brief, 'strong relations of relevance' are causal or other necessary connections between, say, A and B in the ethnographic record. If we find B in the archaeological record, we can infer the presence of A. In this way, ethnographic analogy can extend the range of possible explanations beyond the confines of our own experience. Always, those explanations must 'fit' the diversity of Upper Palaeolithic evidence (Lewis-Williams 1991).

Former understandings of ur-religion

Studies of early religion, as evidenced by Upper Palaeolithic art, have always been to some extent 'of their time'. Despite recourse to ethnographic analogies, explanations have been expressed in the concepts and terms of the historically situated community in which they were formulated. All too often, postulated Upper Palaeolithic religion bears a clear stamp of the researchers' own beliefs – or lack of beliefs. Noting this seemingly ineluctable trammel of circumstances, some late twentieth-century researchers adopt a pessimistic view; for them, early religion is altogether unrecoverable. This is a point to which we return, but we raise it here to acknowledge that explanations are indeed historically situated. That can hardly be disputed. The question is: Are they irredeemably so?

Art for art's sake

In the second half of the nineteenth century, with the scientific community's acceptance of the existence of 'prehistory', and even more after Charles Darwin published his work on evolution, bitter strifes erupted, and scientists found themselves attacked by religious traditionalists. In this disputatious time, anticlerical prehistorians, in particular Gabriel de Mortillet, strongly opposed the idea that Upper Palaeolithic portable art – which had then been recently discovered in caves in the Pyrenees and the Dordogne – could have anything to do with religious sentiments: 'The aim of all those works of art was only to adorn weapons, tools and pendants' (in Delporte 1990: 191). In this view, art was gratuitous and resulted from a powerful, innate drive in human nature to create beautiful things that were not associated with any form of religion.

The 'art for art's sake' theory, as this explanation became known, was abandoned as a global explanation for Palaeolithic art at the beginning of the twentieth century. It was in 1902 that cave art – first revealed in the cave of Altamira (Spain) in 1879 – was belatedly accepted by the scientific establishment. It seemed obvious that people would not have penetrated deep underground simply to make *objets d'art*.

Nowadays, art for art's sake still crops up in various guises. It is, after all, indisputable that many images show what we, at any rate, see as superb aesthetic qualities, but to reason that they were therefore made for purely aesthetic purposes is to be caught in a circular argument. Even today, some researchers infer an 'aesthetic imperative' from the art and then use this supposed universal drive to explain the art.

Sympathetic magic

At the very beginning of the twentieth century the first religious conception of the art was proposed (Reinach 1903). It was to enjoy enormous prestige after the Abbé Henri Breuil and his friend Count Henri Bégouën formalized and popularized it. 'Hunting magic', as it was generally called, was even exported abroad and used to interpret ethnic arts and practices in Africa and America.

Fundamentally, hunting magic was a type of sympathetic, or imitative, magic that was based on a postulated identity between an image and the reality it represented. As a result of tampering with the image one could exercise power over the person or animal that it represented. Imitative and contagious magic (in which actual parts rather than likeness supply the link) were concepts that Sir James Frazer popularized towards the end of the nineteenth century. Frazer believed that religion originated in magic and that it would eventually give way to science.

Taking up such widely current ideas about 'primitive societies', Breuil and Bégouën argued that, when prehistoric 'sorcerers' went into the deep caverns, it was not to create beautiful works of art in remote places which were hardly ever visited. Rather, it was for practical purposes, to help with the basic reality of their lives: essentially, to exercise a form of control over the animals that provided their means of sustenance. From that point of view, only the making of the drawing or the carving was important. 'The representation of an animal was an act valuable in itself. Once it had been accomplished, its immediate result, the drawing, no longer had the slightest importance' (Bégouën 1939: 211). This, it was thought, explained why most paintings and engravings did not seem to have any relationship to one another and could even be superimposed in intricate palimpsests (Fig. 1.4).

Eventually, three types of sympathetic magic were postulated to account for cave art. First, hunting magic was considered to be by far the most important. By representing animals and by marking them with spear-like signs, a sorcerer facilitated their killing. Incomplete animal outlines were taken to mean that the makers wanted to weaken the animals and diminish their defence abilities. Geometric signs were then interpreted as weapons, wounds or traps. Secondly, destructive magic was said to have been used against the most dangerous species, such as bears, lions and rhinoceroses. Thirdly, fertility magic helped to increase the herds of herbivores by representing mating scenes or pregnant females. The few human figures were taken to represent sorcerers or gods, especially when they were given animal characteristics, like those in Les Trois Frères and Gabillou (Fig. 1.5).

Some of these ideas still make sense. Modern ethnology has abundantly shown that most cultures, not only traditional ones, did and still do try to change the natural course of events in order to facilitate daily life. To do this, they resort to magical/religious practices. Trying to avoid catastrophes, to cure the sick, to make rain fall, to enlarge animal herds and to kill them more easily, to restore a lost equilibrium in nature by various means, all this seems to be part of the universals in human thinking. Indeed, the proposition that Upper Palaeolithic people went into the deep caves to perform ceremonies in another more sacred and potent world is a concept far more believable than any other. Inside the

Fig. 1.5. Paleolithic therianthropes, with an association of human and animal features. Top and right: Les Trois-Frères, Left: Gabillou. From Abbé H. Breuil and Gaussen.

caves, their constant use of natural reliefs, the lack of visibility and remoteness of so many of their drawings and their frequent superimpositions do support the idea that each figure was intrinsically important and that the image-makers' primary aim was often its making rather than the end result. This inference does not, however, necessarily imply the existence of sympathetic magic.

Over the years sympathetic magic was criticized and finally abandoned – at least as an all-encompassing explanation – for a number of reasons. Many contradictions were pointed out. If sympathetic magic had really been at the root of Upper Palaeolithic religion and art, one would have expected to find a large majority of animals wounded with spears, many pregnant females and blatant sexual scenes. Also, the most hunted animals should have been the ones most frequently represented. In fact, the existing evidence, such as it has accumulated over the century, is quite different. Animals with weapons or wounds depicted on them are a minority, and pregnant females are nearly as rare as mating scenes. Moreover, there is no correlation between the animals eaten – as evidenced by broken and charred bones on habitation sites – and those painted or engraved in caves. In addition, images like hand stencils, jumbles of indeterminate lines and composite creatures cannot be convincingly explained by sympathetic magic. We have reservations about the logical force of some of these objections; they seem to be of the if-I-were-a-horse variety (if I were a horse this is how I would think about X). The best way to counter the naively simplistic sympathetic magic explanation is to provide a better one.

Totemism

At the beginning of the twentieth century, under the influence of nineteenth-century writers such as James Frazer and the sociologist Émile Durkheim, many researchers were tempted by totemism, as an 'elementary form of religious life' and, putatively, the most ancient (Durkheim in Delporte 1990: 192).

According to this explanation, human groups had a privileged relationship, often a result of supposed descent, with a particular animal or vegetable species that would be its 'totem' (an Algonquian word) and which it would revere. Off and on, the totemic hypothesis has found renewal of favour in various forms with some authors, but it has never enjoyed the success of sympathetic magic. Its appeal is probably due to the representation of so many animal images in cave art, and its lack of success to the oft-quoted fact that one does not find caves devoted to a single animal species (as one would expect in the case of totemism);

instead, the representation of a very limited range of species occurs in most caves. In a totemic society, extending all over Europe and lasting for millennia, there should have been far greater diversity in the themes painted and engraved (Leroi-Gourhan 1964: 147). But this may be another if-I-were-a-horse objection: it is impossible to say that a totemic community should or should not do this or that.

In any event, anthropologists today regard totemism as a highly problematic concept. Certainly, as Claude Lévi-Strauss and other researchers have shown, totemism is much more complex than most students of Upper Palaeolithic art seem to realise.

Structuralism

In the 1960s a new philosophical paradigm seized the imagination of many social scientists; certainly, it could not be termed simplistic or naive. Following the earlier pioneering Marxist writer Max Raphael, Annette Laming-Emperaire and above all André Leroi-Gourhan proposed a structuralist theory to account for the religious practices supposed to have taken place in the painted caves. Their standpoint was different from their predecessors' in so far as they refused to start from an ethnographic hypothesis or to use ethnographic analogy. According to them, an in-depth study of the caves themselves should provide enough evidence to understand the broad outlines of Upper Palaeolithic religion. Details and most probably even some essential aspects of Upper Palaeolithic religion were, they allowed, irretrievably lost.

The 'broad outline', in terms of structuralism, was a set of binary oppositions that could be 'read' so that one opposition (e.g. light : darkness) could be used to talk about another (e.g. good : evil). According to structuralists, such as Lévi-Strauss, this kind of binary and analogical thinking is 'wired into' the human brain.

For structuralists, the cave itself was an essential part in the conceptions of its users. Upper Palaeolithic people did not scatter their drawings randomly; on the contrary, they placed them carefully according to a pre-ordained idea of an ideal 'sanctuary'. They brought to every cave the same mental scheme and applied this to its particular topography. Thus, selected species of animals and particular geometric signs were drawn next to the entrances or at the ends of the galleries, others in recesses and in out-of-the-way passages; importantly, others were placed on large central panels. The varying configurations of the caves delimited areas that were used differently or that had a particular value in themselves: for example, fissures were female, as was the cave itself.

Indeed, the gist of the Upper Palaeolithic binary conception of the world was, for Leroi-Gourhan and Laming-Emperaire, sexual and could be expressed by a simple binary opposition: male : female. They noticed that bison and horses, the most frequent animals represented, were so often pictured side by side that their relationship went beyond the bounds of coincidence. They then postulated that horses and bison constituted a binary opposition that represented the male and female principles, both antagonistically and complementarily. For Leroi-Gourhan, bison were female and horses male; it was the opposite for Laming-Emperaire. Geometric signs were also given a male or female symbolic meaning according to their shapes: 'narrow' signs were male, while 'wide' signs were female. According to these two researchers, male and female animals and signs were combined with the topographic and morphological features of the cave to express a gendered binary conception of the world that lasted for 20,000 to 25,000 years all over Europe.

Both the empirical content and the temporal component of the structuralist theory were severely criticized. As a result, its proponents either abandoned it (Laming-Emperaire) or later expressed reservations (Leroi-Gourhan). The main reason for their doubts was that, while striving towards an apparent objectivity through the use of statistics, the determination of the criteria on which those statistics were based was wholly subjective and sometimes circular. For instance, 'entrances' were often established by proximity to the outside world; at other times, the location of 'entrance' art was established by the species depicted, even though the location was comparatively deep underground. As for the female or male value of animals and signs, was it conceivable that one animal could have as much importance as a dozen of the other sex on the same panel, as Leroi-Gourhan believed? Would the image-makers have pictured a majority of male bison to represent what was interpreted as a female symbol? Would the Upper Palaeolithic practitioners have drawn signs so far removed in appearance from the sexual organs that they were supposed to symbolize?

Leroi-Gourhan was perfectly aware that, rather than an interpretation of Upper Palaeolithic religion, his theory provided an 'excessively extensive framework'. Cave art was 'the expression of concepts about the natural and supernatural organization (which must have been one in Palaeolithic thought) of the living world' (Leroi-Gourhan 1965: 120). The rest was unknowable. We were looking at a theatre, but 'only its scenery has reached us, the traces of actions are extremely scarce and most often incomprehensible. So that we must study an empty stage as though we were asked to reconstitute a play, without having ever seen it, from painted props where a palace, a lake and a forest have been painted in the background' (Leroi-Gourhan 1964: 149–50).

After an initial reaction of conservatism and rejection – as is so often the case with revolutionary theories – the influence of Laming-Emperaire and Leroi-Gourhan was immense. It is still felt today in various ways. For some prehistorians, what was theory and hypothesis has become fact and brooks no discussion, whether it be the structure of the caves or the impossibility of knowledge about religious beliefs and rites. Other followers of Leroi-Gourhan are more interested in looking for structures within panels or in the semiology of the themes (symbols) represented. More positively, most researchers now reject notions of 'primitive thinking' and accept that Upper Palaeolithic thought patterns were like our own, whether they were binary or not.

Still, most modern researchers agree with Leroi-Gourhan's pessimism, though they take it further than he did. This is why they do not try to understand what the images may mean and are satisfied with vague concepts (undefined religion, magic, totemism, the expression of myths, etc.). They confine themselves to empirical work, much of it absolutely indispensable. But they do not tackle the problem of why Upper Palaeolithic people went so far underground to make their paintings and drawings on cave walls.

Ur-religion

So far, we have examined some of the complex evidence for – and the considerable difficulties in the way of discovering – humankind's Upper Palaeolithic religion. Small wonder that earlier writers often fell back on rather vague notions such as 'animism', the belief that the physical world is animated by supernatural powers, or 'fetishism', the worship of inanimate things and animals, or the intellectualists' 'primitive aetiology', baffled 'savages' inventing bizarre supernatural forces to explain natural phenomena, or an original belief in 'souls' and 'spirits' arising from dreams of the dead. Small wonder, too, that today pessimism and, worse, thoroughgoing epistemological cynicism have become de rigueur in some quarters. Fortunately, there are still researchers who do not embrace a priori defeat and believe that the task, daunting though it be, is worth addressing.

For many years an explanation has hovered in the background, undeveloped and insufficiently explored: Upper Palaeolithic religion was in some sense shamanistic. Leroi-Gourhan (1964: 147–8) dismissed these poorly argued suggestions. He exposed the superficiality of comparing photographs of modern shamans with the images of 'sorcerers' in Les Trois Frères or Gabillou (Fig. 1.5), or of finding a simplistic parallel between the bird on a pole in Lascaux and the American Pacific Northwest practice of putting the effigy of a bird on top of a shaman's tomb. He was, of course, correct.

Since those early attempts, others have tackled the problem more thoroughly. Mircea Éliade, for instance, thought that it was no coincidence that many similarities existed between shamanism in the Altai and in the Americas, as 'a certain form of shamanism was probably brought to the two American continents with the first waves of immigrants' (Éliade 1951:267). Shamanism, he argued, was humankind's first religion. Weston Labarre, Joan Halifax and, in particular, Andreas Lommel suggested that some paintings and engravings in Lascaux and Les Trois Frères represent shamans and their spirit-helpers. More recently, Noel Smith (1992) has made the point that some motifs may represent 'vital forces' associated with some form of shamanism.

When early European travellers explored central Asia, they encountered ritual specialists who, in the Tungus language of Siberia, were given the name shaman. As an accident of history, these Siberian shamans came to represent 'classic' shamanism, and Siberia became the 'type site' of shamanism. Later, similar specialists and practices were found in North America, Africa and elsewhere, and the name was extended to those places.

Today, some researchers emphasize differences rather than similarities and question the integrity of 'shamanism' as a category of belief and practice. They see 'shamanism' as a semantic trap. Certainly, there has been much ambiguity and vagueness in the ways that the word has been used. Some writers emphasize ecstatic relations with a spiritual realm to the exclusion of social relations; others downplay the role of altered states of consciousness. Some critics go further and claim that 'shamanism' should not be termed a religion; for them, it is rather a 'configuration' of belief and practice that can be identified in a number of religions. At the same time, there are researchers who believe that the critics have gone too far and that the word still has validity – provided it is carefully defined (e.g. Hultkranz 1996). It is therefore necessary to state clearly what we understand by the word.

Although other societies sometimes have elements of shamanism, we confine our definition to hunter-gatherers and propose ten characteristics of shamanism as it is practised in such societies; elements of shamanism may well appear in other kinds of society, but it is not of them that we speak.

1. Fundamentally, hunter-gatherer shamanism is posited on a range of altered states of consciousness, be they induced by ingestion of hallucinogens, rhythmic driving, such as insistent drumming and dancing, hyperventilation, sensory deprivation, pathological conditions, etc. Dreams, too, should be included here. Such states are often termed 'trance' or 'ecstasy'. Of necessity, they are institutionalized, that is, they have social consequences.

2. Visual, aural and somatic experiences of altered states that are 'wired' into the human nervous system give rise to conceptions of an 'alternative reality' that is frequently tiered. Three tiers are common, but socially complex hunter-gatherers often acknowledge more. It is this sort of cosmology that makes contact with the supernatural realm possible. Cosmology is both enabling and constraining.

3. People with special powers and skills, shamans, are believed to have access to this alternative reality. In some societies, there is one shaman to a community; in others, there are more. Some shamans are politically powerful; others are not influential outside of their ritual performances. The important point is that shamans are intermediaries between their communities and supernaturals. The mastery of ecstasy therefore has important socio-political implications in shamanistic communities.

4. The behaviour of the human nervous system in certain altered states creates the illusion of dissociation from one's body, sometimes known as 'spirit loss' or 'extra-corporeal activity'. Less commonly in hunter-gatherer societies, this experience is understood as possession by external spirits. Possession and extra-corporeal travel are believers' explanations of trance or ecstasy. Shamans use dissociation and the other experiences of altered states to achieve a variety of ends, such as the following (all four are not universally present):

5. Contacting spirits and supernatural entities;

6. Controlling the movements and lives of real animals;

7. Healing the sick;

8. Changing the weather.

9. These functions and entry into an altered state are believed to be facilitated by a variously conceived supernatural power, or energy, that may, in some ways, be likened to electricity.

10. This power is often associated with spirit-helpers (often in the form of animals) who impart it to shamans and assist them in the performance of their tasks. Commonly, shamans encounter their spirit-helper during a 'vision quest'. Whether some shamans may be said to be 'possessed' by such spirit-helpers is a question to be decided for each community individually, though by no means easily so.

It will be clear that this descriptive definition is broad and not tied to any one ethnographically recorded shamanistic community; the restrictive Siberia-centric view should be abandoned. Indeed, given the Ice Age way of life that we have described, it seems likely that Upper Palaeolithic shamanism did not exactly match any specific instance known today. It is essential that researchers remain flexible and do not force ethnography onto Upper Palaeolithic data. Ethnography should bring to light special features of Upper Palaeolithic religion, not obscure them. It should also be clear that a certain amount of fuzziness around the edges – instances that are difficult to categorize as being or not being shamanistic – does not invalidate the central notion. In the old world, hunter-gatherers have religious practitioners who enter altered states to perform tasks such as those we have listed. The widespread occurrence of shamanism results not from diffusionism but (in part) from universal neurological inheritance that includes the capacity of the nervous system to enter altered states and the need to make sense of the resulting experiences and hallucinations within a foraging community.

These three points strongly suggest that there were, in all probability, some types of shamanism in the Upper Palaeolithic. Exactly what form shamans took and what their social status was, and how shamanism changed through the long period of the Upper Palaeolithic are all questions requiring research. Before we attempt to answer them, two methodological cruxes need to be clarified. As we have already had cause to point out, it is uncertainty about an appropriate method of study that inhibits researchers' quest for humankind's ur-religion and, at least in part, induces epistemological cynicism.

The first methodological point derives from the observation that, broadly (and perhaps somewhat unfairly) stated, explanations for religion have been either psychological or social in nature. Psychological explanations include the one that Bronislaw Malinowski developed as a result of his work with the Trobriand Islanders. Faced with death and other crises, he argued, people experience fear and anxiety and then alleviate their tensions by the performance of religious rituals; religion is cathartic. Developing similar notions, Sigmund Freud postulated that feelings of guilt lay at the bottom of religion and that religion usefully assuaged these debilitating feelings (of course, religion also creates a sense of guilt). Like these psychological theories, early sociological theories of religion also had a pragmatist flavour. Their proponents argued that religion is useful because it makes for social cohesion and continuity: religion is the 'glue' of society. Durkheim, one of the great sociologists of religion, rejected the notion that religion could simply be a mistake, arising from a misunderstanding of dreams and trances. For him, religion was like language; it was social rather than personal, and it was learned. He agreed with those who saw totemism as the original religion and went on to argue that the totem – and eventually 'god' – was the tribe made divine. Religion is a system of ideas and rituals that represents to people the society to which they belong. Marxists present this notion in a more sophisticated form. They argue that religion is part of a 'superstructure' that in some ways reflects the socio-economic relations of the 'infrastructure'. At the same time, religion can be part of ideology and mask the true nature of exploitative social relations – the famed 'opiate of the people'.

We shall not discuss the problems that arise from these views. Neither the psychological nor the purely sociological explanations for religion are, in themselves, persuasive. By contrast, the shamanistic account which we are outlining unites psychology and sociology, though our emphasis on the antiquity of the human nervous system and the ways in which it behaves in altered states is in some sense reducing 'psychology' to physiology, or more precisely to neurophysiology. Essentially, the unity of psychology and sociology consists in the way in which each society is bound to make sense of and to socialize the products of the nervous system. That 'taming' of the mind in altered states is always historically and socially situated. The ways in which it happens cannot be predicted from neuropsychology alone. Methodologically, therefore, we need to consider both the behaviour of the nervous system and the social contexts in which this behaviour takes place; there are intricate relationships between the two.

The second methodological point follows on from the first. Having established the broadly conceived behaviour of the nervous system in altered states and the diverse ways in which it is accommodated in foraging societies, researchers need to examine the empirical evidence that has come down to us from the Upper

Palaeolithic. We have every reason to believe: (a) that the people of that period would have had to make sense of altered states within the context of their hunting and gathering economy and social relations and (b) that the human behaviour that this process entailed left physical traces. It therefore remains for us to see if (c) these propositions co-ordinate and explain the diverse and highly puzzling Upper Palaeolithic evidence.

Upper Palaeolithic religion in context

The process of research entails exploring the explanatory potential of hypotheses by allowing them to interact with empirical data. At the same time, we need to intertwine different strands of evidence (empirical, social, psychological, neurological and ethnographic) as we feel our way forward.

We begin this part of our exploration by noting that the overview which we have presented provides clues to what is perhaps the most demanding question posed by west European Upper Palaeolithic art. Whatever they may have done in open sites and with portable art, why did people walk, crawl and climb through deep underground passages and chambers to make images? From the beginning to the end of the period, caves were an important, and to us thoroughly intriguing, context for image-making.

As we address this key question, Upper Palaeolithic religion, society and cosmology come together. All life, economic, social and religious, takes place within and interacts reciprocally with a historically situated cosmology. What, then, can be said about Upper Palaeolithic cosmology?

Ur-cosmology

The widespread shamanistic notion of a tiered cosmology – the level on which people live and spirit realms below and above – probably derives from certain universal experiences of altered states. These include sensations, on the one hand, of rising up and flying, and, on the other, of entering a vortex and passing underground and through water. These experiences are not only recorded ethnographically throughout the world; they are also verified by laboratory research. They are the experiences that, shamans claim, provide access to spirit realms when they enter what we call an altered state. The vortex, or tunnel, experience is perhaps the best known. People report passing through a constricting passage and then emerging into another realm with its own rules of causality and its own beings, animals and monsters. Flight, too, is a commonly reported shamanistic experience from around the world. The path of the shaman through the realms, whether by tunnel or flight, is sometimes referred to as the *axis mundi*. It is variously conceived in different shamanistic societies: it may, for instance, be thought of as a hole in the ground at the back of a shaman's dwelling, a tree, the roots of a tree or, significantly, a cave. These neurologically generated experiences make it highly probable that entry into a cave was, for Upper Palaeolithic people, entry into a subterranean spirit world. A cave in the mind took the human mind into the caves and gave them profound experiential significance.

Further, the sensory deprivation of the utterly dark, silent passages may not only have replicated the vortex; it may also have contributed to the induction of an altered state. Indeed, spelaeologists report experiencing hallucinations while deep underground. For Upper Palaeolithic people, the underground passages and the neurological experience of the vortex may have become inextricably interwoven: 'spiritual' experiences were probably given topographical materiality. For them, entry into a cave was entry into part of the spirit world. Caves afforded close contact with, even penetration of, spiritual nether tiers of the cosmos; they were part of the *axis mundi*.

The images that people made there related to the chthonic world. They were not so much taken underground in people's minds as discovered in the subterranean tier of the cosmos. No matter how realistic they appear to us, the images do not represent 'real' animals that could be encountered in the Ice Age landscape. Rather, they are 'things-in-themselves', spirit-animals 'fixed' by the image-maker. That is why there are the numerous discrepancies that we have noted between the material, above-ground world and the underground images. There was, for instance, no need for a ground line on which images of animals could stand; they were not intended to depict real animals standing on the ground. The hallucinatory images of altered states are often projected onto surfaces, rather like a slide or film show; they 'float', as do the painted and engraved images. The subterranean images do not replicate the material world; they are components of a spirit world.

Searching for power

This understanding represents a major break from the usual way of looking at and admiring Upper Palaeolithic images. It leads on to a feature of Upper Palaeolithic cave art that is difficult to explain outside of the shamanistic hypothesis. The artists frequently and at all periods used features of the rock surfaces on which they placed their images. Depictions are often placed so that a small, seemingly insignificant nodule forms the eye of an animal. Some of these nodules are so insignificant that one suspects that they were identified by touch rather than by sight. Fingers lightly exploring the walls may have discovered a nodule, and the mind, prepared by socially inculcated expectations for the discovery of animals, took it to be an eye. All the image-maker had to do was to add a few strategic lines to complete the spirit-animal.

The importance of natural features is especially clear at Castillo, Spain, and Niaux, in the French Pyrenees. In Castillo, a depiction of a bison has been painted to fit undulations in a stalagmite: the back, tail and hindleg fit the shape of the rock; the image-maker merely added a few strokes to bring the form into sight. But in order to use the rock in this way, he or she had to position the bison vertically. What was important to the Castillo image-maker was finding the bison in the natural features of the rock, not orienting the image so that it would call to mind a real, standing bison. In Niaux, there is a different use of the rock wall. An image-maker added antlers to a dark hole in the rock that looks something like the head of a deer seen face on. The animal so created looks out from the rock; its body is hidden in the realm behind the surface.

Some of the most intriguing images are created by light and shadow and the addition of only a few lines. This technique is far more common than is generally supposed (Freeman et al. 1987: 105). Sometimes an undulation in the rock surface becomes the dorsal line of an animal if one's light is held in a specific position. In Niaux, for example, an image-maker added a bison head, legs, belly line and tail to such a shadow. By moving one's lamp images like these can be made to appear and disappear. An important reciprocality is implied by these images born of shifting chiaroscuro. On the one hand, the image-maker holds the image in his or her power. A movement of the light source can cause the image to appear out of the murk; another movement causes it to disappear. The creator is master of the image. On the other hand, the image holds its creator in its thrall: if the creator (or subsequent viewer) wishes the image to remain visible, he or she is obliged to maintain a posture that keeps the light source in a precise position. Relax, and the image returns into the Stygian realm from which it was coaxed. These 'creatures', or 'creations', of light and darkness point to a complex interaction between person and spirit, artist (or viewer) and image. This may be why some Upper Palaeolithic lamps were embellished with images and signs: light was genesial. Here, we can glimpse something of Upper Palaeolithic religious experience: an interplay of light and darkness, controlled by a human being, bringing a spirit-animal into view. These shadowy images are the earliest evidence for a major symbolic opposition, light : darkness, that runs through so many religions.

What, then, did Upper Palaeolithic image-makers believe they were doing? In some shamanistic societies, such as those of North America, the notion of a vision quest is crucial to becoming a shaman. A North American quester usually repairs to a remote, isolated place, sometimes a high cliff-top, sometimes a cave (Éliade 1951: 50–1; Halifax 1980: 6), to fast, meditate and induce an altered state of consciousness in which he or she will 'see' an animal helper that will impart the necessary shamanistic power. It is a vision, a spirit-animal, that bestows power, not a real animal. Upper Palaeolithic evidence suggests that parts of the caves, especially the deep passages and small, hidden nooks, were places where solitary vision quests took place. In various stages of altered consciousness, questers sought, by sight, touch and light, in the folds and cracks of the rock face visions of powerful animals. It is as if the rock was a membrane between them and one of the lowest levels of the cosmos. The caves were the entrails of the chthonic world; behind their surfaces lay a realm inhabited by spirits and potential spirit-helpers in animal form.

What we have said so far accounts for and co-ordinates five other extremely puzzling features of Upper Palaeolithic art. These features need not be seen as individual puzzles; they are interrelated manifestations of the Upper Palaeolithic psychic and topographic cosmos. First, the walls of numerous caverns were touched and treated in various ways other than image-making. In some sites, such as Grotte Cosquer, finger-flutings cover most of the walls and parts of the ceiling to a considerable height (Clottes et al. 1992: 586; Clottes and Courtin 1996). If we allow that Upper Palaeolithic people believed that the spirit world lay behind the thin, membranous walls of underground chambers and passages, we can begin to understand why they touched and ritually treated those surfaces. The walls were not a meaningless support. They were part of the images, a highly charged context.

The second feature is handprints. Some were made by placing paint on a hand and then pressing the hand against the rock; these are known as positive prints. Negative prints were made by holding a hand, and sometimes the forearm as well, against the rock while paint was sprayed over both hand and adjacent rock. When the hand was removed, a negative print remained. Most accounts of handprints stress the image that remained; perhaps, it is argued, it was an I-was-here sign. We do not deny the importance of the image, but what we have said about Upper

Palaeolithic cosmology and entrance into caves raises another possibility: it was the ritual act of making the print that was of primary importance. When paint was sprayed (by the mouth or through a hollow bone) over the hand, the hand 'disappeared' into the rock. Similarly, when placed on the palm and fingers, the paint acted as a 'solvent', dissolving the hard rock and creating access to the realm behind the surface. Paint was almost certainly much more than purely the technical substance that westerners consider it to be. It probably had its own power, a suggestion supported by some ethnographic accounts of rock painting. The ritual sequence of which the making of handprints was only a part probably began with the collection of the ingredients of the paint, mixing them, taking them ritually underground, and then using the paint for 'sealing' someone's hand into the rock. Whether this sequence was part of a vision quest or another ritual altogether is hard to say.

It is in this context that we should consider the next two puzzling features of the embellished caves. In caves such as Enlène in the Ariège, hundreds of small pieces of bone were thrust into cracks. They are too small to have served any practical purpose. Rather, they are evidence for another ritual that involved penetrating the 'membrane' and making some kind of contact – exactly what we do not know – with the spirit world. Also in Enlène, in the depths of the cave where there are no images, there are a few isolated red dots that were probably made with a finger. Such finger dots are found in many caves. Someone carried paint far underground and then simply made what is for us an insignificant dot. Probably what mattered was not so much the dot that remained but what we cannot see, the whole ritual process of taking powerful paint underground and then, as part of a complex rite, touching the wall of the cave with it. The complexity and diversity of Upper Palaeolithic subterranean ritual activities is becoming clearer.

Finally, there is the juxtaposition in so many shamanistic rock arts of what appear to be 'realistic' depictions of animals and geometric 'signs'. Some researchers have seen these two kinds of image as two related though distinct systems of communication – like text and graphs in a book that say the same thing but in different ways. There is, however, another way of seeing the relationship between the two kinds of images that derives from what we have been saying about shamanism worldwide. In an early stage of altered states, people see what have been called 'phosphenes', 'form constants' and 'entoptic phenomena'. These are incandescent geometric forms – dots, zigzags, crescents, grids are among the most common – that move in the visual field and that are projected onto surfaces, as are the hallucinations of deeper levels of trance. Some shamanistic communities around the world give the various shapes meanings that we could not possibly guess. For the shamanistic Tukano of South America, for instance, an arc or semicircle of parallel lines may represent a rainbow or the Sun-Father's penis (Reichel-Dolmatoff 1978: 32). The Tukano themselves state that they represent what they see in trance. Some, not all, of the geometric 'signs' of Upper Palaeolithic art conform to these shapes. It is therefore possible that some of the 'signs' of Upper Palaeolithic art may have derived, as we argue that the images of bison and so forth did, from the working of the human nervous system in a specific social context. The geometric and the representational images may thus have had their origin in the same source, what was for Upper Palaeolithic people the spirit world. The striking difference between the two kinds of image is a product of our western way of seeing.

Upper Palaeolithic images of bison, horses, mammoths and so forth, as well as the geometric 'signs', must all be seen in a wider context than 'art'. They were not simply 'pictures' but 'things-in-themselves' that were intimately related to diverse rituals and to a cosmos that was, like the medieval Christian cosmos, as much religious as descriptive of materiality. But the Upper Palaeolithic cosmos, still like the medieval cosmos, was not an immutable 'given'; it could be created, re-created and manipulated by people in particular social and political circumstances. Upper Palaeolithic religion was as much social and political as it was psychological.

Building a cosmological religion

Upper Palaeolithic people did not 'process' caves in a rigid, formularistic way according to an inherited and immutable 'mythogram', as Leroi-Grourhan suggested. Rather, they explored and adapted each cave in accordance with its peculiar topography and, most importantly, the particular expression of shamanistic cosmology, social relations and religion that existed at a particular time in a given region. If we wish to move from generalities, with which we must necessarily start, to more specific instances of Upper Palaeolithic religion, we must consider the complex implications of individual caves. To illustrate this point, we examine, very briefly, two topographically different caves, Gabillou and Lascaux.

Gabillou comprises only an entrance chamber, probably at least partially open to natural light in prehistoric times but now part of a cellar, and a straight tunnel that extends from the entrance chamber for approximately 33 m. What remains in the entrance chamber shows that it was embellished with carefully painted images and some 'simpler' engravings. This area may have been a kind of vestibule in which group ceremonies, accompanied by music and dancing, were performed. The images, some of which may have been communally produced, may, in some ritual circumstances, have prepared the minds of selected vision questers for what they were to see at the climax of their initiation. The culturally informed component of deep trance derives from memory, and the novices were being shown not just pictures of animals but re-creations of spirit-animals of the kind that they themselves hoped to encounter.

The tunnel that leads off the entrance chamber was narrow and low-ceilinged in Upper Palaeolithic times, and those who entered it were obliged to crawl one at a time. The images here are engraved, often with a few strokes only. There are no elaborately painted images in the passage, though there are some patches of paint. The comparatively 'simple' execution of the passage engravings implies that less time was spent on them than on those in the entrance chamber. The images are, moreover, strung out along the entire length of the passage. Some sections are slightly more densely engraved than others, but, although some images are overlaid by other marks (said to be 'magical strokes'; Breuil 1952: 311), there is no area of dense engraving. At the very end of the passage, just around a short bend, there is an image of a therianthropic figure. It has a bison head and what appear to be human legs but which may terminate in hoofs (fig. 1.5, lower left).

The use of Gabillou may be compared with that of Lascaux. Unlike Gabillou, Lascaux comprises a comparatively large entrance chamber, the Rotunda (or the Hall of the Bulls), and two narrow passages that lead off it. The curving walls of the Rotunda are embellished with a vast cavalcade of huge animals, aurochs, horses, deer, a bear and a strange 'monster'. Many of these images are so large that one concludes that that they were communally made: the collection of the pigment, mixing it, getting up to the higher surfaces and applying the paint suggest the co-operation of many people. The Axial Gallery, one of the narrow passages that slope down from the Rotunda, is comparably embellished; the images arch over the ceiling and almost encircle the viewer. Evidence for the use of scaffolding has been found here. At the very end of this gallery is the so-called 'falling horse', painted upside down on a low protruding rock so that it cannot be viewed whole from any one position. As one looks down this gallery from the Rotunda, one finds oneself in a tunnel of images that ends in a vortexical swirl created by the 'falling horse'.

The other, longer, gallery is the more varied. After a low, densely engraved and painted section there is a side chamber known as the Apse. Here there are hundreds of engravings as well the remains of painted images. Unlike other parts of the cave the images here are executed one on top of another in a confusing palimpsest. Beyond the Apse, is the richly decorated Nave and, finally, the Chamber of Felines. This deepest part of Lascaux is so small that only one person at a time can fit into it. It is engraved with bold strokes. There are images of felines, a horse head-on and signs. Finally, the Apse is situated over the Shaft, at the bottom of which is the celebrated group comprising an apparently bird-headed anthropomorph, a 'wounded' bison, what may be a bird-headed staff and other images. There is some debate about the location of the prehistoric entrance to Lascaux and as to whether the Shaft was accessible from the Apse in ancient times.

Comparing Lascaux with Gabillou brings out a number of significant points about Upper Palaeolithic religion. We note but a few.

Both caves have chambers where communal rituals probably took place. The images in these areas were probably not the result of individual visions (though they may have been) but rather were socially constructed and served different purposes from those that are in the confined depths of the caves. The caves thus became manipulable social and political templates, as well as entrances into the nether realm: outside was the bulk of the community; in large, richly decorated chambers select groups performed subterranean rituals; in the depths, sometimes squeezed into small alcoves, a few made solitary, more personal and intimate contact with the supernatural world. Those who controlled access to the caves could use them to reproduce, challenge and change social structure by demarcating areas with social significance and by restricting entry into them. Religion was thus reciprocally embedded in evolving social differentiation. The evolution of religion and hierarchical human society go hand in hand (cf. Bender 1989).

Further, in the Apse there seems to have been a determined and sustained effort to place principally engraved images in a single area. The complexity of the superimpositions here suggests that the people who made them were sharing, or desired to share, the acquisition of a special, topographically situated power, and that power was, for reasons that we do not know, located in the Apse. This power was probably related in complex ways to the different kinds of images in the other, topographically, iconographically and socially distinct, areas of Lascaux. By contrast, the separated images in the tunnel at Gabillou suggest that the acquisition of visions there was of a more individual nature. The people of Gabillou did not seek to associate their visions intimately with the visions of others, so they strung them out along the length of the tunnel. The different ways of placing imagery in the Apse and the Gabillou tunnel thus point to different kinds of social relations between vision questers themselves and, by extension, between shamans and the wider community. Importantly, we have clues to variations and developments in the psychology and sociology of Upper Palaeolithic religion.

Not only did the underground realms provide a material context for spiritual experiences. Image-making did not merely take place in the spirit world; it also informed and incrementally created that world. There was a complex interaction between the topography of the caves, mental imagery and historically situated image-making by individuals and social groups that, through time, built up and changed the spirit world both conceptually and materially. Riches (1994) has made the point that religious specialists among the Mountain Ok of New Guinea effect incremental shifts in the connotations of particular symbols. In Riches' apt phrase, the shaman is a 'cosmology maker'. Similarly, as Upper Palaeolithic shamans pursued their personal and group interests, the cosmology that they created and modified (partly by their art) both constrained and enabled social change.

Conclusion

Writing an account, brief or otherwise, of ur-religion is a daunting endeavour. Our holy grail is deep in prehistory; there are no potential informants whom we can consult; little evidence has survived the millennia. Still, despite all the undoubted difficulties, it is possible to glimpse the first emergence of the 'religious animal'. By intertwining diverse empirical data, multiple ethnographic analogies with strong relations of relevance, and the results of neuropsychological research on altered states of consciousness and, finally, applying our results to individual Upper Palaeolithic caves, we can overcome the epistemological malaise that has infected so much present-day research.

We should not ignore the importance of such a task. Whatever Burke's modern critics may think, Man has not lived by bread alone. Symbolic thought and the very ability to conceive of a cosmology lie at the foundation of modern science and technology. In the Upper Palaeolithic caves, we can see that foundation being laid in religious experience inextricably coalesced with social distinctions and knowledge of the form of the cosmos; at that time there was no distinction between religion and science. After the Upper Palaeolithic, humankind extensively developed symbolic thought and separated it off from neuropsychologically informed experiences; knowledge of the cosmos is no longer sought in religious experience.

Bibliography

Bégouen, Comte H. 1939. Les bases magiques de l'art préhistorique. *Scientia*, 4th series, 33: 202–16.

Bégouen, R. and J. Clottes 1981. Apports mobiliers dans les Cavernes du Volp (Enlène, Les Trois-Frères, Le Tuc d'Audoubert). In *Altamira Symposium*, pp. 157–88.

Bender, B. 1989. The roots of inequality. In D. Miller, M. Rowlands and C. Tilley (eds.), *Domination and resistance*. London: Unwin and Hyman, pp. 83–93.

Breuil, H. 1952. *Four hundred centuries of cave art*. Montignac: Centres d'étude et de documentation préhistoriques.

Clottes, J. 1998. *Voyage en préhistoire: l'art des cavernes et des abris, de la découverte à l'interprétation*. Paris: La Maison des Roches.

  1999. *Vie et art des Magdaléniens en Ariège*. Paris: La Maison des Roches.

Clottes, J., A. Beltran, J. Courtin and H. Cosquer 1992. The Cosquer Cave on Cape Morgiou, Marseilles. *Antiquity* 66: 583–98.

Clottes, J. and J. Courtin 1996. *The cave beneath the sea: Paleolithic images at Cosquer*. New York: Harry Abrams.

Clottes, J. and D. Lewis-Williams 1998. *The shamans of prehistory: trance and magic in the painted caves*. New York: Harry Abrams.

Delporte, H. 1990. *L'image des animaux dans l'art préhistorique*. Paris: Picard.

Éliade, M. 1951. *Le chamanisme et les techniques archaïques de l'extase*. Paris: Payot.

Freeman, D., J. G. Echegerey, F. Bernaldo de Quiros and J. Ogden 1987. *Altamira revisited and other essays on early art*. Chicago: Institute for Prehistoric Investigations.

Halifax, J. 1980. *Shamanistic voices*. Harmondsworth: Penguin.

Harner, M. J. (ed.) 1973. *Hallucinogens and shamanism*. New York: Oxford University Press.

Hultkranz, Å. 1996. Ecological and phenomenological aspects of shamanism. In V. Diószegi and M. Hoppel (eds.), *Shamanism in Siberia*. Budapest: Akadémiai Kiadó, pp. 1–32.

Jaubert, J. 1999. *Chasseurs et artisans du Moustérien*. Paris: La Maison des Roches.

Leroi-Gourhan, A. 1964. *Les religions de la préhistoire*. Paris: Presses Universitaires de France.

1965. *Préhistoire de l'art occidental*. Paris: Mazenod.

Lewis-Williams, J. D. 1991. Wrestling with analogy: a problem in Upper Palaeolithic art research. *Proceedings of the Prehistoric Society* 57: 149–62.

1995. Modelling the production and consumption of rock art. *South African Archaeological Bulletin* 50: 143–54.

1997. Agency, art and altered consciousness: a motif in French (Quercy) Upper Palaeolithic parietal art. *Antiquity* 71: 810–30.

2002. *The mind in the cave: consciousness and the origins of art*. London: Thames and Hudson.

Lewis-Williams, J. D. and T. A. Dowson. 1988. The signs of all times: entoptic phemomena in Upper Palaeolithic art. *Current Anthropology* 29: 201–45.

1993. On vision and power in the Neolithic: evidence from the decorated monuments. *Current Anthropology* 34: 55–65.

Reichel-Dolmatoff, G. 1978. *Beyond the Milky Way: hallucinatory imagery of the Tukano Indians*. Los Angeles: UCLA Latin America Center.

Reinach, S. 1903. L'art et la magie à propos des peintures et des gravures de l'Âge du Renne. *L'Anthropologie* 14: 257–66.

Riches, D. 1994. Shamanism: the key to religion. *Man* (N.S.) 29: 381–405.

Rouzaud F., M. Soulier and Y. Lignereux 1996. La Grotte de Bruniquel. *Spélunca* 60: 28–34.

Siegel, R. K. and M. E. Jarvik 1975. Drug-induced hallucinations in animals and man. In R. K. Siegel and L. J. West (eds.), *Hallucinations: behaviour, experience, and theory*. New York: Wiley, pp. 81–161.

Smith, N. 1992. *An analysis of Ice Age art: its psychology and belief system*. New York: Peter Lang.

Vandermeersch, B. 1970. Une sépulture moustérienne avec offrandes découverte dans la grotte de Qafzeh. *Comptes-rendus de l'Académie des Sciences de Paris* 270, series D: 298–301.

Vitebsky, P. 1995. *The shaman*. London: Macmillan.

Winkelman, M. 1986. Trance states: a theoretical model and cross-cultural analysis. *Ethos* 14: 174–203.

2 Ancient Egypt

ROSALIE DAVID

History of scholarship

Ancient Egypt has left the modern world a rich legacy: not only are there well-preserved monuments, artefacts and human remains, but an extensive religious and secular literature has also survived. The following discussion of the religious beliefs and practices will attempt to show how all these sources enable us to understand and interpret ideas and concepts that originated over 5000 years ago (Frankfort 1961; Hornung 1971; Morenz 1973; Shafer 1991). However, it must be stated that even this rich legacy can provide only a partial view of the civilization.

The surviving archaeological evidence is fragmentary, owing on the one hand to environmental and geographical factors and, on the other, to political and cultural practices. Sites in the south of Egypt, better preserved than those in the north because of climatic and environmental variations, have attracted more attention from the excavators. Religious monuments (pyramids, tombs and temples) were largely constructed of stone, so that they would survive 'for eternity', whereas cities, towns and domestic buildings, mainly built of mudbrick, have consequently suffered more destruction. This inequality of evidence profoundly affects our knowledge and understanding of the people's daily religious observances.

It was only after Champollion's decipherment of hieroglyphs 200 years ago that scholars were able to translate and begin to understand the texts. Subsequently, intensive study of the language in all its forms has been required to enable scholars to interpret the inscriptions more accurately. There are, however, still areas which are open to discussion, particularly in connection with the religious texts. This uneven pattern of evidence has resulted in a marked variation in the interpretation and understanding of different periods of Egypt's history.

There are few hard facts in the study of Egyptian civilization, and often only imprecise conclusions can be drawn. In addition, successive generations of scholars have approached the subject with a range of presuppositions. For example, early classical writers who visited Egypt proposed some fantastic explanations for the monuments they saw, while later Christian travellers in medieval and Renaissance times often interpreted the civilization in the context of the Bible.

Today, despite our ability to read the inscriptions with some degree of certainty and although there are vastly improved archaeological techniques, the evidence is still subject to individual bias in its interpretation. Although it is now customary to try to assess the Egyptians within the context of their own civilization and beliefs rather than interpreting them from other religious and social viewpoints, many questions remain unresolved. For example, various explanations have been offered in connection with the 'facts' associated with the biblical Exodus, while the true nature and motives of Akhenaten, as either a 'failed messiah', a 'political opportunist' or a leader who would not have distinguished between religious and secular ideas, continue to inspire lively debate (Redford 1984).

Sources: archaeology and literature

Chronology

Today, the chronology of ancient Egypt is based on the work of an ancient priest, Manetho (see p. 63), and is divided into a series of dynasties. Historians have arranged these dynasties into groups and placed them within major historical periods: the Archaic Period (Dynasties 1 and 2), the Old Kingdom (Dynasties 3 to 6), the First Intermediate Period (Dynasties 7 to 11), the Middle Kingdom (Dynasty 12), the Second Intermediate Period (Dynasties 13 to 17), the New Kingdom (Dynasties 18 to 20), the Third Intermediate Period (Dynasties 21 to 25) and the Late Period (Dynasties 26 to 31). This is shown in the Table 2.1.

Because of the climatic and environmental conditions of Egypt, a wealth of evidence has survived which provides one of the most complete pictures of the development of an early society. The civilization lasted for over 5000 years, and, although evidence is relatively scanty for some periods, the monuments, artefacts and literary sources have survived in a remarkable state of preservation and, in many cases, can be used to interpret the Egyptians' religious beliefs and practices.

Table 2.1 *Chronological table of Egyptian history*

Period	Date	Dynasty
Predynastic Period	*c.* 5000–*c.* 3100 BCE	
Archaic Period	*c.* 3100–*c.* 2890 BCE	I
	c. 2890–*c.* 2686 BCE	II
Old Kingdom	*c.* 2686–*c.* 2613 BCE	III
	c. 2613–*c.* 2494 BCE	IV
	c. 2494–*c.* 2345 BCE	V
	c. 2345–*c.* 2181 BCE	VI
First Intermediate Period	*c.* 2181–*c.* 2173 BCE	VII
	c. 2173–*c.* 2160 BCE	VIII
	c. 2160–*c.* 2130 BCE	IX
	c. 2130–*c.* 2040 BCE	X
	c. 2133–*c.* 1991 BCE	XI
Middle Kingdom	1991–1786 BCE	XII
Second Intermediate Period	1786–1633 BCE	XIII
	1786–*c.* 1603 BCE	XIV
	1674–1567 BCE	XV
	c. 1684–1567 BCE	XVI
	c. 1650–1567 BCE	XVII
New Kingdom	1567–1320 BCE	XVIII
	1320–1200 BCE	XIX
	1200–1085 BCE	XX
Third Intermediate Period	1085–945 BCE	XXI
	945–730 BCE	XXII
	817(?)–730 BCE	XXIII
	720–715 BCE	XXIV
	715–668 BCE	XXV
Late Period	664–525 BCE	XXVI
	525–404 BCE	XXVII
	404–399 BCE	XXVIII
	399–380 BCE	XXIX
	380–343 BCE	XXX
	343–332 BCE	XXXI
Conquest by Alexander the Great	332 BCE	
Ptolemaic Period	332–30 BCE	
Conquest by Romans	30 BCE	
Roman Period	30 BCE–4th century CE	

Archaeological sites (Map 2.1)

Many of the archaeological sites, including the pyramids and temples, have remained partially visible above ground, and were frequently visited by travellers during the Roman Empire and the mediaeval and Renaissance periods. Over the past 200 years, however, excavation has revealed many more sites, and there has also been an extensive programme to clear sand and debris from the tombs and temples, so that the wall scenes and inscriptions have been revealed. This has enabled further study and translation of the inscriptions to be undertaken, thus allowing the ritual use of various parts of the temples to be determined.

Egypt has two main types of archaeological site. There are 'settlement sites' – the villages, towns, cities and fortresses where people lived, which were situated in the cultivated land on either side of the Nile or in the Delta; and the cemeteries (often referred to as necropolis/necropolises) which included royal burial places (pyramid complexes or other tombs) and private (non-royal) tombs or graves for the nobles, officials, craftsmen and peasants.

There were also temples for the worship of the gods and dead rulers. The two main types were termed 'mortuary temples' and 'cultus temples' by Egyptologists of the nineteenth century CE, who claimed that, in the cultus temples, the resident deity was worshipped through regular rituals carried out by the king or high-priest, while the mortuary temples were the locations for rituals performed by the king or high-priest on behalf of the resident deity plus the dead, deified king who had built the temple (so that the living ruler could be carrying out rites for his future, dead, deified form!), together with all the previous legitimate rulers who were known as the 'Royal Ancestors'.

However, more recent scholarship has shown (Shafer 1998) that this division is misleading because it infers that each type of temple was limited to the cult of either a god or a king, and that the Egyptians themselves made a clear distinction between 'cultus' and 'mortuary' temples. It has been argued that the temples should not be divided in this simplistic way, because their functions were too varied and interwoven, and that these names are therefore inappropriate. The term 'cult complex' is now used for all cultic enclosures, but where it is necessary to be more specific, 'royal cult complex' now replaces 'mortuary temple' and 'divine cult complex' stands instead of 'cultus temple'. Generally, the divine cult complex was used for the worship of a god and sometimes of a (usually) living king, whereas in the royal cult complex, the worship of a divine king (usually deceased) was maintained, sometimes accompanied by the worship of another god.

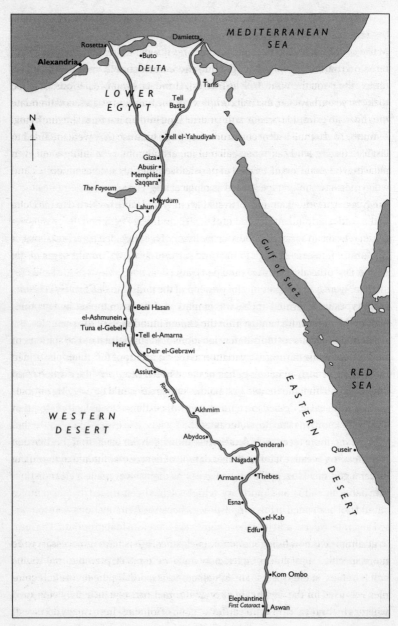

Map 2.1. Egypt showing main sites.

The divine cult complex was always built in the city or town, whereas in some periods the royal cult complex was attached to the king's burial place (as in the pyramid complexes), but at other times was a separate building which might be located some distance from the burial site (for example, the New Kingdom temples built on the West Bank at Thebes). However, even when it was attached to the royal burial place, this cult complex's prime function was to accommodate the rituals that would transform the mortal king into an immortal, divine being.

Tombs and temples were constructed of stone because they were intended to last for eternity, whereas houses, all municipal and military buildings, and even palaces were mainly constructed of perishable materials such as mudbrick and wood, because they were regarded as replaceable.

Egypt had a limited amount of available cultivated land, restricted to the Delta and a fertile strip on either side of the Nile, and this was required for growing crops, rearing animals and housing the living. Therefore, from earliest times, it was deemed necessary to bury the dead outside this area, on the edges of the desert. Here, the environment provided by the heat and dryness of the sand created perfect natural conditions for preserving the tombs, their funerary contents and the bodies of the dead. This was in marked contrast to the settlement sites, which were subject to damage from the annual inundation of the river.

Therefore, because of the different locations of the burial places and settlement sites, and because of the great variation in the durability of the materials used in their construction, archaeology has revealed much more about the tombs and their contents than about palaces, houses and articles of daily use. This imbalance of physical evidence has tended to produce a one-sided view of Egyptian civilization, but, in order to understand the society, it is essential to realize that they were not obsessed with death: it is simply that we have more evidence of their funerary beliefs than about their daily lives because a preponderance of the burial goods have survived.

Artefacts

In addition to the standing monuments, archaeologists have uncovered a wide range of manmade objects (artefacts) which were either placed in the tombs or left behind in the houses. The Egyptians believed that people would require many articles for use in the life after death, and consequently they equipped their graves and tombs with a variety of goods. Some of these were funerary in purpose, and formed part of the beliefs and customs surrounding death and burial, whereas others were everyday items, supplied so that the deceased could continue with the activities he had pursued when he was alive. These objects included pottery, make-up and cosmetic equipment, jewellery, clothing, food and drink, tools, weapons, and toys and games. From them, we gain a great deal of information about everyday life and technology.

The funerary objects also provide evidence of their religious beliefs and customs. By the Middle Kingdom (c. 1900 BCE), democratization of religious beliefs and practices meant that the range and quality of funerary goods for private as well as royal burials were greatly expanded. A major feature of the private tomb was the coffin or nest of coffins that housed the mummified body. These protected the body and also provided a surface on which magical spells (Coffin Texts) could be inscribed, to assist the passage of the deceased into the next world.

There was often an outer, rectangular coffin which contained an anthropoid (body-shaped) coffin. Royalty and the great nobles were sometimes buried in stone coffins, but most examples were made of wood and, depending on their date, were painted either with geometric designs which represented the stylized façade of a palace or house, or with scenes featuring the gods. Some burials were also supplied with a wooden canopic chest which contained four pottery jars (canopic jars) in which the embalmers had placed the preserved viscera (abdominal and chest organs), removed from the body during mummification.

From the Middle Kingdom onwards, a large variety of wooden models were also placed in the tombs. These frequently provided a three-dimensional image of the subject matter represented in the wall scenes in the tombs. There were statuettes of the tomb-owner because, if the mummy were destroyed, it was believed that these could function on his behalf to receive sustenance from the food offerings placed at the tomb. Sometimes there were also statuettes of other members of the family, and groups of servant models engaged in food production and preparation, in order that the deceased owner would be provided with adequate and eternal supplies of bread, beer, meat, fish, fowl and other delicacies. There were models of granaries, breweries, slaughterhouses, and peasants engaged in agricultural work, as well as of the owner's house and garden. Some tombs also included model soldiers to protect the deceased, and figurines of animals, musicians and concubines to entertain him.

A special category of these models were the ushabti (or shabti) figures which, from the Middle Kingdom onwards, were placed in the tombs. These sets each contained hundreds of figurines (possibly one for each day of the year) plus an additional group of 'overseers' to control the ushabtis. They were provided to undertake the manual and agricultural tasks on behalf of their owner, when he entered the kingdom of Osiris (the realm of the dead).

Tombs were also supplied with model boats. Sometimes, only one would be included but wealthy people might have complete fleets. The main purpose of including a model boat was to allow the owner to travel to Abydos, the burial place of the god Osiris, so that he could enhance his chances of resurrection. However, some tombs included model boats for other purposes: there were funerary barques, long-distance boats for travelling on the Nile and fishing boats to supply food. Finally, tombs were also frequently equipped with 'soul-houses'. These pottery model houses had features which reflected contemporary domestic architecture, such as flat rooftops and open courtyards for cooking. In fact they were provided to be used as offering trays in Middle Kingdom tombs. Food provisions were placed on them for the deceased as an alternative to the circular offering tables or rectangular slabs that had been used for that purpose in earlier periods, and from which the soul-houses had evolved.

Much of our information about the funerary customs is derived from the mummified body, and the bandages and protective items that were placed inside the wrappings (Smith 1991). These included the face mask (which was often made of cartonnage – a mixture of gum and linen or papyrus) which protected the face and also provided another locus for the owner's spirit if the mummy and coffin had been destroyed; there were also chest and foot covers which provided protection for those parts of the mummy. The body was enclosed in many layers of linen bandages, between which were inserted the pieces of sacred jewellery (amulets), intended to provide magical and spiritual protection for the owner during his passage into the next world. Amulets are found in a variety of shapes and materials: some represented gods, or sacred symbols or parts of the body, to attract good influences to help the deceased. One special category – scarabs – represented the dung beetle which was regarded as a symbol of constant renewal of life.

Mummification

Since the mid-nineteenth century, the scientific study of Egyptian mummified human and animal remains has added considerably to our knowledge of mummification techniques and funerary practices, as well as disease patterns, diet and familial relationships (David 1999, 2000). These early investigations were important because they established that mummies could be studied scientifically instead of merely being regarded as curiosities, brought back as souvenirs to Europe and America by wealthy travellers who visited Egypt.

Subsequently, scientists and scholars have built on this early research, and there have been radiological surveys of the royal mummies in Cairo, and detailed investigations of the bodies of individual rulers such as Ramesses II and Tutankhamun. Studies of mummies were greatly facilitated in the twentieth century because of the expertise developed by various multidisciplinary teams who have access to a wide range of medical and scientific techniques. In addition, excavation has provided these scientists with a greatly expanded source of human and animal mummies on which to undertake their research.

Since 1973, one team – the Manchester Egyptian Mummy Research Project (David 1979) – has pioneered and developed a methodology for examining mummified remains which has been adopted by many other groups. One of the main aims of this project has been to discover evidence from the mummies about disease, diet and funerary practices. Various techniques have been employed, including radiology, histology, endoscopy, electron microscopy, serology, palaeodontology and DNA studies.

In 1995, the Manchester team established a joint project with the Egyptian Ministry of Health in Cairo, to construct an epidemiological profile of one particular disease, schistosomiasis, by comparing its pattern in ancient and modern times. In order to obtain a wide range of tissue samples for this study, the world's first International Ancient Egyptian Mummy Tissue Bank has been set up at Manchester, to be used as a major resource for studies on this and other diseases. In order to detect if schistosomiasis is present in these minute tissue samples, one particular technique – immunocytochemistry – has been developed and used for the first time as a diagnostic tool in relation to mummified tissue.

In addition to disease studies, this type of research augments knowledge about religious and funerary customs, and the mummification procedure itself. Scientific studies have been undertaken to investigate the use of natron (a naturally occurring chemical compound, found in one of Egypt's dry desert valleys) as a dehydrating agent in mummification, and radiology has proved to be a useful tool to examine the artefacts found inside the mummy bandages.

Radiology can supply evidence about the historical and cultural context of each mummy: radiographs will indicate if resin or natron have been used in the mummification process, and can demonstrate if amulets have been placed between the bandages that encase the mummy. Also, other details such as embalmers' restorations (false limbs, false eyes or subcutaneous packing to enhance the rounded, bodily shape of the mummy) may be detected, and it is usually possible to determine if, during the mummification process, the abdominal and thoracic cavities have been eviscerated and subsequently filled either with linen packages or the returned, mummified viscera.

Generally, scientific studies on mummies add new facts to existing knowledge, and whereas archaeological or literary evidence may present a biased or incomplete picture of life in ancient Egypt, physical facts gleaned from this type of scientific research can provide a more balanced viewpoint.

Religious paintings

During the period when Egypt was under Roman rule (after 30 BCE), evidence from some of the cemeteries indicates that foreign settlers (mainly Greeks and Romans) adopted Egyptian funerary practices (Bagnall 1993). They mummified their dead and encased them in bandages and cartonnage covers, but they now also incorporated panel portraits in the funerary head-piece. These portraits provide almost the only surviving evidence for the study of this type of ancient portrait painting which must have existed in many other parts of the Roman Empire. However, in Egypt, the uniquely favourable environmental conditions and the adaptation of such paintings for funerary purposes ensured their survival here as nowhere else. Each probably represents a realistic likeness of the deceased (in whose lifetime the portrait may have been painted by an itinerant artist). As such they provide a marked contrast to the earlier pharaonic art.

The official, state art of pharaonic Egypt is a major source for the study of religion because it was almost completely interwoven with religious development. This art has survived because the tombs and temples were built of stone. Also, because religious concepts had inspired the form and decoration of these buildings, the scenes which cover the walls of tombs and temples preserve detailed information about rituals, mythology, beliefs and customs.

Wall reliefs in the temples show the rites which were once performed in the various chambers and halls (Fig. 2.1), while mural paintings in the rock-cut tombs of the New Kingdom (which replaced pyramids as the architectural style for royal burials) depict representations from the magical funerary books. These were intended to secure a safe passage for the king when he travelled into the next world. Finally, in the private tombs, mural scenes which represented the daily activities which were once part of the tomb-owner's life on earth were intended to enable him to continue these pleasures in the afterlife.

Fig. 2.1. Temple wall relief of king presenting burning incense before the god, as part of the Daily Temple Ritual.

Religious literature

There is a more profound modern understanding of Egyptian civilization than of some other early societies because we have access to their ideas, thoughts and beliefs through an extensive religious and secular literature. Until Egyptian hieroglyphs were deciphered by the French scholar Champollion in the early nineteenth century, ancient Egypt was regarded as an awesome but mysterious civilization that had produced vast monuments, strange art forms and quaint religious beliefs and customs. Until then, knowledge of the civilization had rested on the accounts of classical writers such as Herodotus, Diodorus Siculus and Strabo, and all travellers and scholars in medieval and Renaissance times continued to rely substantially on these early writings.

Ludicrous conclusions were frequently reached about the significance and meaning of monuments such as the pyramids (which some identified as Joseph's granaries or astronomical structures rather than burial places), or about the correct interpretation of hieroglyphs, which were merely regarded as magical symbols rather than as a writing system which conveyed the syntax, grammar and vocabulary of a language which had been spoken for over 3000 years.

However, once decipherment had enabled scholars to understand and translate the texts, a rich literary tradition was revealed. Archaeology can still only provide a limited and sometimes unbalanced view of a society, whereas literary sources can amplify and sometimes contradict the evidence of the monuments and artefacts. For example, the archaeological data from ancient Egypt give the impression that a belief in continued existence after death was universal and unchallenged, but some of the texts indicate that, in times of social collapse and upheaval, people questioned this certainty. Such writings emphasize the fact that, despite elaborate funerary preparations, no one had actually returned from the realm of the dead to confirm the reality of survival and eternity.

The funerary texts

Some of the earliest and most important religious texts can be traced to the Old Kingdom. Towards the end of this period (Dynasties 5 and 6), the kings' pyramids were reduced in size and quality because of increasing religious and economic pressures. Instead of enjoying the apparent protection of great burial monuments, the kings now chose to rely increasingly on alternative, magical methods of securing their burials and ensuring that they could ascend to heaven where they would be received and accepted by the gods.

The most important of these methods was the inclusion of a set of spells, carved on the walls inside the pyramid (Faulkner 1969). Known as the Pyramid Texts, these form the oldest substantial body of written religious material that has ever been discovered. The texts are inscribed on the interior walls of pyramids of Dynasties 5, 6 and 7 at Saqqara; the first set was discovered by the French archaeologist Gaston Maspero, in 1880. These spells were exclusively intended for royal use, to ensure that the king attained individual immortality, and there is no evidence that they were made available to commoners in the Old Kingdom.

Intended to ensure the dead king's resurrection and ascent to heaven, and to confirm his survival and immortality, the texts refer to various means – wings, steps and ramps – by which the king could reach the sky. For example, in Utterance (Spell) 267 it is stated:

> A ramp to the sky is built for him, that he can go up to the sky on it.
> He goes up upon the incense.
> He flies as a bird, and he settles as a beetle on an empty seat that is in the ship of Re.

With the democratization of religion in the Middle Kingdom, other religious inscriptions were developed for the use of non-royal owners. Known as the Coffin Texts, these spells were inscribed on the coffins, with the aim of assisting the owner to enter the hereafter. They also provided a 'menu' of food and drink so that the owner would receive adequate spiritual sustenance after death (Faulkner 1973–8). One example from the Tomb of Two Brothers at Rifeh shows how such lists were organized:

> A boon-which-the-king-gives (to) Osiris, Lord of Busiris, the Great God, Lord of Abydos, in all his places, that he may give invocation-offerings (consisting of) bread and beer, oxen and fowl, alabaster, clothing and incense, all things good and pure on which a god lives, for the spirit of the revered Nekht-Ankh, born of Khnum-Aa.

During the New Kingdom, the function of the Coffin Texts was largely taken over by the so-called 'Funerary Books', the most famous of which is known as the 'Book of the Dead' (the Egyptians called it the 'Book of Coming Forth by Day'). The spells contained in these books included measures to ensure the resurrection of the deceased and his safety in the next world, and also represented various rituals enacted at the burial and in the subsequent cult. Scenes and inscriptions from these books were used to decorate the interior walls of the rock-cut royal tombs of this period, and were written on papyrus scrolls which could be purchased and placed in the tombs of non-royal owners.

Mythology

Egyptian literature includes a wealth of mythological texts, of which the Cosmogonies (Creation Myths) and the Myth of Osiris are amongst the most significant. The Egyptians believed that creation had been brought about through divine thoughts and words. During the Old Kingdom, when the priests attempted to rationalize the worship of a multiplicity of gods whose cults had come into existence in earlier times, they arranged them into groups or families. Many now had cult centres, and a few cities became places of great religious importance where powerful priesthoods promoted the cults of particular gods, and developed individual theologies.

Each of these included a mythological explanation of how the cult centre's chief god had played a primary role in creating the universe, other deities and mankind. The most important creation myths were established at Heliopolis (the ancient Egyptian Iwnw), Memphis and Hermopolis, and later, in the New Kingdom, the creator role of the god Amun was developed at Thebes. The myths had some common, underlying concepts, such as the belief that creation had occurred on a primordial mound or island that had emerged from the primeval ocean. Each priesthood claimed that the temple of its own god was the location of that actual primeval mound, and so every temple in Egypt came to be regarded as the original 'Island of Creation'. As such, each temple was a place of great spiritual potency where the king or his delegate, the high-priest, could approach the gods to seek benefits for mankind.

The Myth of Osiris explains the background to the success of one of Egypt's greatest deities (Griffiths 1980). Although there are many references to Osiris and his cult in the Egyptian texts, there is no extant account of his myth, and the earliest, and most complete version, entitled *De Iside et Osiride*, is preserved in Greek in the writings of Plutarch (50–120 CE). It describes how Osiris ruled Egypt as an early king and brought the people the benefits of civilization and agriculture. However, because of the jealousy of his brother Seth, Osiris was murdered, his body was dismembered, and the parts were scattered throughout Egypt. After Isis, his sister-wife, had subsequently gathered together his limbs and restored his body, she posthumously conceived his child, Horus, who grew up to avenge his father's death by fighting Seth.

A tribunal of gods finally judged the dispute, and found in favour of Osiris and Horus, with the result that Osiris was resurrected and became the ruler of every living thing on earth, with whom every king of Egypt was identified, while Seth was personified as evil and became an outcast. This mythology was the source from which Osiris' roles developed as god and judge of the dead, expressing his victory over evil and death, and enabling him to promise eternal life to his followers.

The Wisdom literature

This major literary genre, which first developed in the Old Kingdom and continued until the Late Period, provides the earliest written evidence of a code of morals and ethics which expressed a close relationship between the gods and non-royal people (Lichtheim 1973, 1976).

The 'Instructions in Wisdom', which had been authorized by the gods, provided a set of rules and a code of behaviour which were taught to young boys. Usually presented in the form of an address from a wise elder (the king, First Minister or father) to his charges, the texts gave advice on how to advance in society. They were copied as model writing exercises by generations of schoolboys, and emphasized such values as kindness, moderation, and the ability to exercise good judgement, as well as practical attributes such as polite behaviour at table and in other people's houses. For example:

> Do not exalt someone of noble birth
> More than you do the child of a humble man,
> But choose a man because of his actions.
>
> (The Instruction addressed to Merikare)

> If you are a guest
> At the table of one greater than you,
> Take what he gives as it is set before you;
> Look at what is before you . . .
> Don't speak until he addresses you,
> One does not know what may cause offence.
>
> (The Instruction of Ptah-hotep)

Although originally intended as a code of behaviour for the upper classes and a training for future courtiers and officials, in later times the Instructions were developed to include and address the educational needs of middle-class children.

The Pessimistic literature

This particular term is used for a genre of literature which provides a very different insight into the Egyptians' attitudes towards life and death (Lichtheim 1973, 1976). Instead of the confidence exemplified by the funerary monuments and burial goods, these texts question the certainty of immortality and an individual hereafter.

In some examples, the author examines social and religious concepts against the general historical background of the period, and in two famous examples – the 'Prophecy of Nefertiti' and the 'Admonitions of a Prophet' – the texts may well describe the appalling social conditions which occurred as a result of the collapse of centralized government from the end of the Old Kingdom through to the First Intermediate Period:

> I will show you the land in lamentation and distress,
> That which has never happened before has come to pass.
> Men will take up weapons of warfare,
> The land will live in uproar.

(Prophecy of Nefertiti)

In another example, death is seen as the only solution to the agony brought about by social collapse:

> Lo, great and small say 'I wish I were dead,'
> Little children say 'He should never have caused me to live!'
> Lo, children of princes are dashed against walls,
> Infants are put on the high ground.

(Admonitions of a Prophet)

In other texts, an individual crisis, perhaps brought about by social and economic upheaval in the country, sets the background for the author to describe personal doubt and despair. One unique text – 'The Dispute between a Man and his Soul' (which is regarded as a masterpiece in the literature of the ancient world) – takes the form of a dialogue between a man and his soul, and addresses the man's fears and self-doubts. Driven to despair by personal problems and by the social catastrophe of his times, the man longs for death and possibly even contemplates suicide:

> Death is before me today
> As the fragrance of myrrh,
> As when one sits under sail on a breezy day.
>
> Death is before me today,
> As when a man longs to see his home
> When he has spent many years in captivity.

However, his soul (described as a separate entity) strongly opposes this stance, and eventually persuades the man to continue his life to its natural end so that they can eventually share a properly prepared tomb throughout eternity:

> This is what my soul said to me: throw aside lamentation, my comrade, my brother . . . I will stay here if you reject the West. But when you arrive in the West, and your body is reunited with the earth, then I will alight after you rest, and then we shall dwell together.

This profound pessimism, probably generated by the complete collapse of the society at the end of the Old Kingdom, also influenced some of the later funerary hymns or songs which came to form part of the burial service in the Middle and New Kingdoms. These hymns were intended to reassure the deceased tomb-owner and assert the joys of eternal life, but one version (exemplified by the 'Song in the Tomb of Intef') now encouraged the owner to enjoy life while he could, emphasizing its ephemeral nature and the uncertainty of immortality:

> The gods who were before rest in their tombs,
> The blessed nobles too are buried in their tombs.
> Those who built tombs,
> Their places are no more,
> What has become of them?

Other hymns (such as the 'Song from the Tomb of Neferhotep') were later intro-duced to attempt to counteract the scepticism expressed in the Intef song, and to reassure the tomb-owner of the validity of a continued belief in the afterlife. Both hymns continued to be used in the tombs, expressing two different viewpoints and underlining the fact that there was no conclusive or satisfactory answer to the questions relating to eternity and the deceased's attainment of immortality. The

Pessimistic Texts are important because they provide a marked contrast to the archaeological evidence, which stresses certainty in a belief in an afterlife, and also because they represent an invaluable insight into the Egyptians' unresolved self-doubts.

Historical overview

Sources

The history of ancient Egyptian civilization covers the period from *c.* 3100 BCE to Alexander the Great's conquest of the country in 332 BCE. Before this 'Dynastic Period', scattered communities had gradually come together to form two kingdoms; today, this span (*c.* 5000–3100 BCE) is known as the 'Predynastic Period'. After Alexander's conquest in 332 BCE, a line of Macedonian Greeks (the Ptolemies) ruled Egypt. They were descended from Alexander's general, Ptolemy (who became Ptolemy I); with the death of Cleopatra VII, last of this dynasty, Egypt became part of the Roman Empire in 30 BCE, and was subsequently ruled from Rome as a province.

The modern chronology of Egypt is based on the writings of an Egyptian priest, Manetho (323–245 BCE), who compiled a chronicle of Egyptian kings who ruled between *c.* 3100 BCE and 332 BCE, dividing his king-list into dynasties. Although Manetho's records are sometimes unreliable and inaccurate (and have only survived in later sources which include Josephus, Eusebius and Africanus), Egyptologists have accepted his division of reigns into thirty dynasties. A later chronographer added a thirty-first dynasty.

In addition to Manetho's Chronicle, several Egyptian king-lists have survived that preserve partial or damaged evidence about Egyptian chronology. Most of these were inscribed on temple walls, where they formed a key feature in the ritual performed daily in royal cult complexes to honour previous rulers and gain their acceptance for the present king. As such, these were never intended as historical records; they are incomplete and include only the names of rulers who were deemed to be 'legitimate', and had reigned during the period between the reign of the first king and that of the ruler who commissioned the list.

The Predynastic Period (*c.* 5000–*c.* 3100 BCE)

After *c.* 3400 BCE, the scattered communities who had settled in the Delta and the Nile Valley evolved into two distinct kingdoms. The northern kingdom – the Red Land – was situated in the Delta and the northernmost part of the Nile

Valley, while its southern counterpart – the White Land – occupied the Delta and the rest of the Nile Valley within Egypt. One theory (now largely discounted) claimed that it was the arrival in Egypt of a new group of people (the so-called 'Dynastic Race') which led to the first appearance of writing, monumental brick architecture, and the advances in arts and crafts that occurred in *c.* 3400 BCE, but a more recent proposal suggests that these advances were the sole achievements of the indigenous population, which owed nothing to any external influence. However these changes may have originated, it is evident that advances were made in technology and building techniques, and that both kingdoms shared many features of a common culture.

At this period there is already evidence of the social and religious customs which would later develop in the Dynastic Period. A belief in continued existence after death for the individual is apparent in the burial preparations, and there was already a well-established tradition of animal cults. We can also observe the process of syncretism – where the multitude of deities worshipped by the many local communities either merged to create one deity with a range of attributes, or became a family group of gods. Thus, as the villages and towns were amalgamated into larger social and political units, this process was reflected in the corresponding religious developments.

The Archaic Period (*c.* 3100–*c.* 2686 BCE)

As the southern rulers ultimately set out to conquer the northern kingdom, one king – Scorpion – made some military advances, but it was the ruler named Menes in classical sources (either Narmer or Hor-aha) who finally defeated the north in *c.* 3100 BCE and unified the two kingdoms under his rulership. The rulers of this dynasty moved the capital city to Memphis, at the apex of the Delta, and during the first two dynasties they ruled a unified state. They laid the foundations for the political, social and religious organization of the country, and established avenues of national and local government. This period of peace and stability enabled the resources of the country to be focused on the advancement of technology and the arts and crafts; substantial funerary monuments (brick-built 'mastaba'-tombs), constructed to house the burials of the royal family and nobility, are one example of this policy.

The Old Kingdom (*c.* 2686–*c.* 2181 BCE)

The mastaba-tombs were retained for the wealthy classes throughout the Old Kingdom, and most of the population were buried in shallow desert graves,

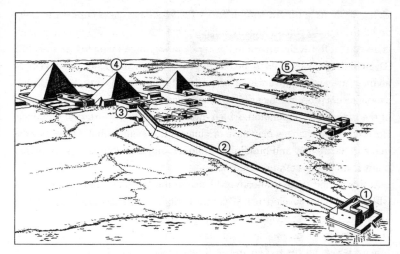

Fig. 2.2. A reconstruction of the Dynasty 5 pyramids at Abusir, adapted from
L. Borchardt, *Das Grabdenkmal des Königs Ne-user-Re*, plate 1, showing the main
elements of a pyramid complex, as exemplified by that of Niuserre, 1. valley building,
2. causeway, 3. mortuary temple, 4. pyramid and sun temple, 5. temple of Niuserre.

as they had been since predynastic times, but early in the Old Kingdom, the
pyramid was introduced for royal burials, epitomizing the first great period of
Egyptian civilization and the gulf between ruler and ruled. Imhotep, the vizier
and architect of Djoser who ruled in Dynasty 3, built the first pyramid at Saqqara.
This was designed as a stepped structure, and was part of an elaborate burial and
mortuary complex.

There then followed a period of experimentation, but by Dynasty 4 the true
pyramid, featuring smooth, sloping sides, had emerged. These pyramids reached
their zenith at Giza, where the famous burial sites of the kings Cheops, Chephren
and Mycerinus were built. These monuments, and the nobles' mastaba-tombs
that surrounded them, were constructed of stone to last for eternity. The pyramid
was probably intended not only to protect the king's body and funerary goods,
but also to provide him with a magical 'ramp' which could be used to gain access
to the heavens. The pyramid form may have represented a sun-ray, and was
probably closely associated with the cult of the sun-god Re.

However, by Dynasty 5, the construction and maintenance of the pyramid
complexes, and the employment of priests and other staff to service them, had
become an economic burden on the royal resources (see Figs. 2.2 and 2.3). Also,

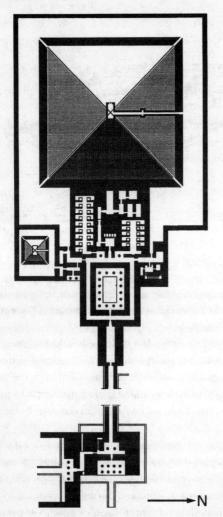

Fig. 2.3. Plan of the pyramid complex of Sahure (Dynasty 5) at Abusir. Adapted from L. Borchardt, *Das Grabdenkmal des Königs Ne-user-Re*, vol. I, plate 16).

as the power of the kings began to decline, the sun-cult became increasingly important, with the result that resources were now directed towards building new sun temples, whereas the size and quality of the pyramids were reduced. Subsequently, the kings sought another means of securing their eternal life by inscribing magical spells – the Pyramid Texts – on the interior walls of their pyramids.

Throughout Dynasty 6, the power of the king and of the centralized bureaucracy steadily declined, exacerbated by economic, political, religious and social factors. The long reign of Pepy II brought the dynasty to an end, and in the following years there was a period of anarchy when centralized government collapsed and Egypt returned to the political conditions of early predynastic times when local rulers wielded power in their districts and fought against each other.

The stability of the Old Kingdom had allowed art, religion and literature to flourish, and the lavish funerary equipment placed in the tombs and the registers of scenes painted on the interior walls of the mastabas provide an indication of the quality of everyday existence for the wealthy and those who served them. The literature that has survived includes not only historical, religious and legal texts, but also an important didactic source – the Wisdom Texts – which provides insight into moral and ethical values.

The First Intermediate Period (*c.* 2181–*c.* 1991 BCE)
During this time of decentralization and anarchy, all the values of the Old Kingdom were overturned. Internal political and social collapse was probably exacerbated by the external threat of Beduin raids and incursions, and many monuments and graves were desecrated and robbed. The countryside was gradually overwhelmed by poverty, famine and disease. The effect of this upon the population and on individuals is probably recalled in a collection of literary works that is now known as the 'Pessimistic Literature'.

This upheaval only drew to a close when a line of local princes at Thebes who carried the family name Mentuhotep were able to exert their power and establish Dynasty 11. They restored some order to Egypt, and arts and crafts again enjoyed a revival. Throughout this period, the power of Memphis, the Old Kingdom capital, had disappeared: the political institutions were no longer centralized there, and the city had ceased to accommodate the major concentration of craftsmen. Instead, provincial rulers were buried in rock-cut tombs in the cliffs along the river, which were decorated with painted wall-scenes and equipped with the tomb goods made by local artists and craftsmen. When the Mentuhotep family seized overall control, it was their own city of Thebes that flourished as the capital, and a new art style emerged as a result of the goods produced there by local artisans.

The Middle Kingdom (1991–1786 BCE)
At the beginning of Dynasty 12, a commoner – Amenemhet I – seized the throne; he was probably the First Minister of the last king of Dynasty 11, whom he

assassinated. Amenemhet I inaugurated another period of great prosperity; he moved the capital north to Lisht, and he and his descendants re-established a firm system of government. Because this dynasty had no royal antecedents, it was necessary to establish an uncontested succession, and thus these kings introduced the concept of co-regency, when the chosen heir joined the king as co-ruler. They also developed positive external policies, restoring dominion over Nubia to the south, by building a string of garrisoned fortresses, and also fostering trading contacts with the Aegean islands, and with the inhabitants of Byblos (on the Syrian coast) and Punt (which had access to the Red Sea coast).

Now, the king no longer held the supreme power he had theoretically enjoyed in the Old Kingdom, and also Re, the royal patron god of the Old Kingdom, did not retain his unrivalled position. Following the collapse of divine and royal power at the end of the Old Kingdom, a new, democratic concept of the afterlife emerged, and the belief that only the king could experience an individual eternity was replaced by the idea that immortality would be available to all believers who could demonstrate pious and worthy lives. This concept was closely associated with the worship of the god Osiris, and it profoundly affected religious beliefs and customs, and funerary practices. The kings continued to be buried in pyramids, but many provincial governors built rock-cut tombs in their own districts in preference to the mastaba-tombs which surrounded the royal burial site.

The Second Intermediate Period (1786–1567 BCE)

This period, which consists of five dynasties, was again characterized by decentralization and decline. Some dynasties with lines of native rulers were contemporary, but in Dynasties 15 and 16 a group of foreign conquerors known as the Hyksos entered Egypt and established themselves as rulers over much of the country. The native princes of Thebes (who formed Dynasty 17) eventually drove the Hyksos out of Egypt into southern Palestine, and then established themselves as the founders of Dynasty 18 and the New Kingdom.

The New Kingdom (1567–1085 BCE)

The Hyksos invasion profoundly influenced and changed the Egyptians' attitude towards foreign policy and colonization. Instead of contact with other countries through trade, they now adopted an aggressive policy, particularly towards Syria/Palestine, in order to prevent any further attempted invasion of Egypt. The New Kingdom therefore became the period of Egypt's empire, when a succession of kings sought to subdue the minor states in Palestine and bring them under

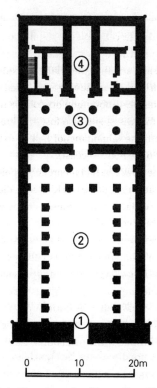

Fig. 2.4. Plan of temple of Amen-Re at Karnak (New Kingdom), showing main elements of a typical cultus temple. 1. pylon, 2. outer court, 3. hypostyle hall, 4. sanctuary. Adapted from A. Erman, *Life in Egypt* (trans. H. M. Tirard), 1971, p. 280.

their own influence. This policy brought Egypt into major conflict with other great powers of the area, the Mitannians and the Hittites, but at its zenith Egypt was able to create and govern the world's first empire, which stretched from the River Euphrates in the north to Nubia in the south.

These military expeditions brought extensive booty back to Egypt, and Amen-Re, the great state god and royal patron of this period, was the major recipient of this vast wealth (Fig. 2.4). Originally the local, family god of the princes of Thebes, in the New Kingdom Amun adopted the additional characteristics of the sun-god Re and, as Amen-Re, became the supreme god of Egypt and its empire in Dynasty 18. However, the god's priesthood at his main temple at Karnak soon acquired such wealth and power that they posed a threat to the king himself, and towards the end of Dynasty 18 (in the so-called Amarna Period) King Akhenaten (Amenhotep IV) took unprecedented and ultimately unsuccessful measures to try to curtail this power.

Throughout the New Kingdom (apart from the reign of Amenhotep IV), Egypt's main religious centre was Thebes. By now, the kings had abandoned the pyramid as a burial place and chose instead to be interred in rock-cut tombs in the Valley of the Kings on the west bank of the river, opposite Thebes. The town of the royal necropolis workmen, known today as Deir el Medina, has provided a wealth of evidence from the archaeological remains and documents discovered in the rubbish heaps, and this has supplied details about their everyday lives, religious customs and working conditions.

The Third Intermediate Period (1085–668 BCE)

Egypt fought successfully against the Hittites in Dynasty 19; they also faced new enemies such as the Libyan tribes who threatened their western front, and the coalitions of 'Sea-peoples' who attacked the Delta in Dynasties 19 and 20, in their search for new homelands.

By Dynasty 21, Egypt's slow but inevitable decline had already begun. The kingdom was now effectively divided, with the kings ruling the north from the city of Tanis while a line of high-priests of Amun controlled the south around Thebes. At Tanis, the royal tombs and treasure discovered by French archaeologists demonstrated the wealth of the rulers even in this period of decline. In Dynasties 22 and 23, rulers of Libyan descent, whose forebears had settled in the Delta, briefly reunited the country, but in Dynasty 25 another line of foreign kings emerged who had originated in a kingdom (Kush) which lay to the south of Egypt. However, although they briefly gained control, they were eventually driven back to their homeland by the Assyrians who invaded Egypt from the north.

The Late Period (664–332 BCE)

After a brief occupation by the Assyrians, another native Egyptian line (Dynasty 26) emerged at Sais in the Delta. There was a short resurgence of former glory, with renewed nationalism and interest in earlier religious and literary beliefs and forms, but soon Egypt was once again under foreign domination, when she became part of the Persian Empire and was ruled as a Persian satrapy (possession) during Dynasties 27 and 31. The overall influence of Assyria and Persia on Egyptian institutions and beliefs was probably minimal, but following the conquest of Egypt by Alexander the Great, ruler of Macedon, in 332 BCE, profound changes were introduced, first by the Ptolemies and then by the Roman rulers who became the absolute governors of the country and its people.

The Greek and Roman rulers nevertheless recognized the need to be regarded as the legitimate rulers of Egypt, in order that they could exploit the economic and political powers this bestowed, and so they were careful to support the traditional state religion by building and restoring the major temples dedicated to the Egyptian gods. There was also a degree of syncretism between Egyptian and Greek religious beliefs and customs, especially in relation to funerary practices, and the state cult of the god Serapis attempted to fuse Egyptian and Greek traditions. However, the general practice was for Greeks and Egyptians to pursue their own separate religious beliefs.

The political and social context

In the Predynastic Period, the communities scattered throughout the Delta and along the Nile Valley were governed by local chieftains. These communities were gradually amalgamated into larger units, either because of the need for mutual co-operation or because one ruler conquered other leaders. This gave the overall community greater protection and enabled co-operation to be developed for schemes of mutual benefit such as irrigation. Nevertheless, each unit remained politically and socially independent and was governed by a chieftain who lived in the main town; the community was supported by the adjacent land. In time, these larger units were themselves drawn into districts which became the 'nomes' or administrative divisions in later periods.

In c. 3400 BCE, two kingdoms came into existence, into which these larger units were now incorporated. The Red Land in the north and the White Land in the south each had its own king, capital city and patron deity. Eventually, in c. 3100 BCE, when the ruler of the White Land conquered the north and unified the country, he established a dynasty which governed the whole of Egypt (Emery 1961: 38–47). Despite this unification, the dualism of the 'Two Lands' remained an important concept throughout pharaonic times, and was retained both as a basis for administering the country and as a strong element in religious symbolism.

During the subsequent Archaic Period (Dynasties 1 and 2) and Old Kingdom (Dynasties 3 to 6), the social structure became firmly established, and this continued, with minor adjustments, until the Graeco-Roman era, when the Ptolemies and the Romans introduced their own systems. The central feature of pharaonic political and religious development was the concept of divine kingship.

The pharaoh

The pharaoh was the king of Egypt; the title was derived from the hieroglyphic phrase per-aa which literally meant 'the great house'. This was the term used for the palace, and was consequently applied to identify the king himself.

The pharaoh was regarded as partly divine and, at least in theory, he was an absolute monarch (O'Connor and Silverman 1995). His role and duties had developed out of those of the early local chieftains, and he was expected to fulfil political, religious, social, military, economic and legal commitments, although in time many of these were delegated to royal officials.

As early as the Archaic Period, the king was identified with the royal hawk-god Horus; throughout his reign, the king was regarded as the incarnation of the god on earth, and after death, when he became Osiris, the divine father of Horus, the Horus title was then passed on to his successor. One theory (although now disputed) is that succession to the kingship passed through the female line, and each king was considered to be the offspring of the chief state god and the previous king's principal queen.

As the son of the god on earth, the king certainly had a unique status which not only emphasized the great divide between himself and his subjects, but also gave him special powers to intercede between gods and mankind. For example, he was responsible for founding and provisioning the temples, and for perform-ing the temple rituals for the gods. In return, he received the kingship from the gods, and had theoretical ownership of the land, its resources and its people. He could dispose of these as he wished, but his actions were subject to the principles of the goddess Ma'at who personified divine balance and order throughout the universe. In practice, he was to a large extent advised and controlled by his coun-sellors and administrators. The coronation ceremony was believed to endow the king with the necessary divine and royal powers to make him an effective ruler, and these were renewed periodically at jubilee festivals.

As a reward for his attention to the gods, the king was assured military supremacy over his enemies, and peace and prosperity for his people. His semi-divine nature also ensured that he would achieve individual immortality after death. In the Old Kingdom, this was a key difference between the king and his subjects, who could only hope for continued existence through their role in assisting the king. Even when religious beliefs became more democratic in the Middle Kingdom, and all believers could expect individual eternity, the king's hereafter differed from that of his subjects. Whereas non-royal persons could expect to pass their eternity in the tomb and in the underworld realm of Osiris, the king would sail in the divine barque, in the company of the gods, forever encircling the heavens.

The queens also played an important part in the royal succession. In the early Old Kingdom and at different periods in Egypt's later history, it was customary for the royal heir to marry his own sister (the Great Royal Daughter) who was the child of the ruling king and his principal queen (Great Royal Wife), but sometimes this did not happen, perhaps because the royal couple did not have a son and daughter who could marry each other. Since the kings were polygamous and there were secondary branches of the family from these minor wives, there was sometimes rivalry and the succession was disputed.

The nobility and officials

In the early Old Kingdom, the nobility consisted of members of the royal family. The king attempted to gain the allegiance of his relatives by granting them the most important positions in the government, and by giving them gifts of royal land and possessions, as well as tombs, burial goods and estates to provide income for the perpetual upkeep of the tombs. However, by the end of the Old Kingdom, the governorships and top administrative posts were increasingly allocated to people outside the royal family, whose support the king now wished to gain.

The country was ruled through a system of local governors who controlled the administrative districts, and were responsible to the king, through his First Minister. This man was effectively the king's deputy, acting as head of the judiciary, chief royal architect and keeper of the state archives. At first, the local governorships had been non-hereditary, to ensure that the king could limit these powers and control the men's actions, but increasingly, the positions became hereditary (a favour bestowed by the king in order to gain the governor's support), and when the centralized administration was weak the local governors were able to seize considerable powers and become virtually independent of the king. This happened during the First Intermediate Period, and even in the early Middle Kingdom the kings needed the governors' support because of their own tenuous right to rule. In the later Middle Kingdom, the political power of the provincial governors seems to disappear, together with their rights and privileges. They were replaced as administrators by a new middle class drawn from the small farmers, craftsmen and tradesmen, and these officials were now directly responsible to the king or First Minister.

The nobles had posed a real threat to royal supremacy since the middle of the Old Kingdom. As his own power waned, this decline in royal supremacy was exacerbated by the king's attempts to gain the nobles' favour and support, by lavishing land and wealth on them. The result, however, was that his own position declined, while the nobles exploited their increased independence. The other threat to the king's supremacy came from the priests but the king was never able effectively to quell their power, and they remained a formidable force.

The officials who supported the government bureaucracy formed an extensive hierarchy who ran the treasury, armoury, granaries and public works. These departments were accommodated within the precinct of the palace in the capital city. This complex also included one of the main residences of the royal family. As well as the centralized bureaucracy, there were also local government departments in the provincial districts. The royal burial area, with its associated temples and cities where the mortuary priests and workers lived, was supervised by its own administration.

Craftsmen and peasants

Below the extensive bureaucracy of officials, there were the artisans and craftsmen. Their most important duties revolved around the production of goods for the tombs. They were mainly organized into communal workshops where associated crafts were practised alongside each other. The capital city was the main centre of activity for these workers, although there were workshops in other towns and localities which each produced its own distinctive style of goods. In some periods, significant schools of art developed in, for example, Memphis and Thebes, where the sculpture and painting exhibited some quite distinctive features (such as the elongated, slender forms of the human figures seen in the Theban style), although in general all works followed the prescribed format for religious art. Some of the larger temples had their own workshops where the ritual objects used in temple worship were produced.

The best artisans were engaged to prepare, decorate and equip the royal tombs. They were housed in purpose-built towns near to the burial site, and some of these, discovered at Giza (Edwards 1985: 282–4), Kahun (David 1997), Tell el

Amarna and Deir el Medina (near Thebes) (Černý 1973), have been excavated. The objects and papyri found at these sites have provided a wealth of information about the living conditions and terms of employment of the royal workmen. The craftsmen made advances in many branches of technology, specifically to improve tomb architecture and tomb goods such as coffins, furniture, clothing, jewellery, pottery and toiletries, but from earliest times they were able to expand this knowledge and expertise to produce domestic and luxury items for the living.

Although the craftsmen were responsible for the skilled work on the tombs, Egypt also required a substantial labouring workforce who could be used at the building sites, to mine gold and to quarry stone. This labour force was drawn largely from the serfs or peasants who comprised perhaps 80 per cent of the population. For much of the year, they worked on the land and produced the food for the whole population. However, they could also be called upon to undertake special tasks for the king (*corvée* duty). In fact, all subjects (regardless of status) were liable for this duty, but wealthier individuals paid substitutes to undertake the obligation on their behalf.

Until a professional army was established in the New Kingdom, the peasants were used by the nobles to fight as soldiers in any military ventures in which the king wished to engage. The peasants also worked in the labour gangs at the royal building sites, particularly during the three months of each year when the inundation flooded the land and made cultivation impossible. In this way, the peasants could be continuously employed: food payments made to them and their families prevented starvation, and their time and efforts were concentrated so that they did not have the opportunity to foment rebellion.

During the period of their employment on the land, they produced enough food to meet their own needs. They were also heavily taxed in kind and this food provided daily sustenance for the whole population and also offerings for the rituals in the tombs and the temples.

Egypt's neighbours

Egypt had little interest in the exploration of lands beyond its borders, except when it was necessary for commercial or trading ventures, or to establish military control over peoples who might otherwise attempt invasion. From earliest times, the Egyptians maintained trading contacts with Byblos on the Syrian coast, to obtain high-quality timber from the hinterland, which Egypt itself lacked. There were also expeditions to Punt, an unidentified region which lay somewhere near the west coast of the Red Sea, in order to trade for myrrh and incense which the Egyptians required for their religious rituals. To the south, they travelled to Nubia (the region which today straddles northern Sudan and southern Egypt), to acquire the granite for their monuments, and also gold, semi-precious stones, and exotic goods such as ivory and ebony from the far south. There were other trading connections with northern neighbours, including Crete and the Aegean islands.

Egypt's contacts with these regions were generally peaceful, but they maintained access to Nubia with the support of military operations. By contrast, their relations with their northern neighbours were primarily diplomatic and commercial until, in the New Kingdom, they began to build and consolidate an empire which at its height stretched as far as northern Syria.

This aggressive policy was introduced to counteract any renewed attempt by foreigners to invade and rule Egypt, after they had expelled the Hyksos, a line of foreign dynasts, in *c.* 1560 BCE. The Egyptians were the first people to establish an empire; loosely based on a confederation of vassal city-states in Syria/Palestine, it was relatively benign and tolerant, particularly with regard to religious beliefs. Nevertheless, the pharaohs led regular campaigns throughout the New Kingdom to reassert their control, and from the Middle Kingdom, prisoners-of-war were brought back to Egypt where they were employed in a number of ways including domestic service and work on building sites.

The role of religion in education, law and medicine

Religion permeated every aspect of life. Many of the functions of the temples were performed by lay priests who spent three months each year in the temples, and the remainder of the time pursuing their careers as scribes, lawyers or doctors. The scribes ('educated men') were responsible to the god Thoth, who had invented writing and was in charge of numbers and the divisions of time. Scribes kept accounts and army records, collected taxes and controlled the law courts, but, most importantly, they composed and copied religious texts in the temple scriptoria, and some held priesthoods and taught students. Education involved training of the character as well as the mind, a concept which is made clear in the Wisdom Texts and other moral compositions that schoolboys were expected to copy out.

Religion also played a vital role in the legal system. It was believed that law had been given to mankind at the time of creation, and Ma'at, who represented truth, righteousness and justice, and the equilibrium of the universe, was the patron goddess of lawyers. The officials of the judiciary were the priests of Ma'at. Some aspects of the legal system, such as the practice of obtaining a verdict by means of an oracle when a god's statue acted as judge, emphasized the influence of religion on the law.

Egyptian medicine contained a mixture of magico-religious and rational treatments which were regarded as equally valid. Specialist doctors were priests of the goddess Sekhmet, and Imhotep, the First Minister of Djoser and architect of the Step Pyramid at Saqqara, was revered as a great physician and the founder of medical science in Egypt. He was later worshipped as god of medicine and healing. Some temples were renowned as centres of healing, long before this became a feature of the Greek tradition. In a sanatorium attached to the Temple of Hathor at Denderah, the mentally ill were accommodated and treated with a form of hypnotic therapy. Temples were also centres where medical training was provided for students.

Religious beliefs and practices

State religion

Religion permeated most aspects of life and death in ancient Egypt. It was practised at state level: the temples were a key feature and the king had an important role as the essential link between gods and men. Even in the Predynastic Period, the living had performed religious rites, but the gods' shrines, constructed of perishable materials, have not survived. The only evidence of them is provided in scenes painted on pottery placed in the graves, and in representations carved on cylinder seals and ebony and ivory tablets. However, in the later periods, stone-built temples provide information about the state cult and rituals.

The temples

Initially, two types of temple developed in ancient Egypt. Solar (sun) temples occurred in Dynasties 5 and 18, and were directly associated with the worship of the sun-god. In Dynasty 5, when the priests of Re (the sun-god) wielded unprecedented power, the kings built six sun temples at Abu Ghurab. These were modelled on the original sun temple at Heliopolis, which has never been discovered. Towards the end of Dynasty 18, during the Amarna Period, special temples were built at Amarna, Thebes and elsewhere for the cult of the Aten (sun's disc). The solar temple tradition may have been introduced into Egypt from elsewhere, but the royal cult complexes and divine cult complexes built in the New Kingdom and later periods were both derived from the predynastic local shrines where community leaders, on behalf of the people, had presented offerings before the resident cult statues.

Eventually, when the Egyptians developed their skills in stone masonry, the fragile construction of the early shrines was replaced with the masonry of the large stone temples, but these monuments retained the same layout and features as the shrines. The most powerful predynastic local leader eventually became king of Egypt, and his local deity became the chief state god. In the temples, the king (or the high-priest as his delegate) acted on behalf of his subjects by offering food and other requirements to the god's statue. This became the basis of the rituals performed in the temples, carried out for the benefit of the state; in return for these offerings, the god was expected to provide the king and his people with success in warfare and ample harvests and wealth (Fairman 1945).

The royal cult and divine cult complexes were built to the same basic layout and had many architectural features in common, since many aspects of their rituals were similar. The divine cult complex was designed primarily to house and protect the god's statue, and had space and accommodation for the rituals which were performed for the resident deity. The royal cult complex included provision for the same rites to be performed for the resident god but there were also locations where the dead, deified ruler who had built the temple was continuously worshipped and received offerings and where, by means of ritual, he could approach all the previous legitimate kings in order to gain their acceptance and approval of his reign (David 1981).

In the Old and Middle Kingdoms, the royal cult complex was attached to the pyramid, but when rulers began to construct rock-cut tombs in the Valley of the Kings at Thebes in the New Kingdom, there was no space there to accommodate any adjacent temples, and so they were now designed as separate units, usually built on the plain between the river and the burial site.

The divine cult complex provided regular sustenance and care for the resident deity through the Daily Temple Ritual, and celebrated the major events of the god's life by the performance of festivals held on occasions throughout the year. This relationship between gods and men, expressed through the king's personal role, formed the basis of Egyptian society, and it was believed that neglect of these duties would bring disaster to Egypt. In the royal cult complexes, in addition to the daily divine ritual, the king's own acceptance and eternal status as a ruler even after death was ensured by the performance of the Ritual of the Royal Ancestors.

The form, layout and architectural features of these temples were established by exact ritual requirements and by the mythology on which the temples were based. The main mythological explanation of the temple was that it was the 'Island of Creation' where life had first come into existence; it was also the 'Mansion of the God' where the god resided, and a microcosm of the universe.

As the 'Mansion of the God', the temple provided a place of shelter, protection and worship, and its design incorporated features found in domestic architecture such as a bedroom (the shrine), a reception area (the hypostyle halls) and storerooms. However, the house plan was modified to accommodate a central processional route. As the 'Island of Creation', the architectural features reflected and symbolically re-created the location and vegetation of the island, providing a place of great sanctity where the god could rest and be approached. Thus, the columns in the hypostyle halls, with their palmiform, lotiform or papyriform capitals and the frieze of plants carved on the bases of the walls, represented the island's vegetation, while the ceiling was decorated to reflect the sky above the island.

The wall scenes inside the temples also had a special purpose (see Fig. 2.1). In some areas, they represented specific events in the history of the building such as its foundation or consecration, or in the reign of its royal founder, such as his coronation. However, in other areas, they precisely indicate the different rituals once performed in those parts of the building. Here, scenes are arranged in horizontal registers on the walls, and provide invaluable information about the sequence of the rites. They always show the king performing the ritual for the god (although usually this was actually undertaken by the high-priest). In the accompanying inscriptions, the title of the rite and the conversation and speeches of the god and king are given. Because of the limitations of wall space, only a selection of the rites appear, chosen from the complete version of the ritual which was originally recorded on papyrus.

Because of the strict mythological and ritual requirements, only minor variations occur in the design and decoration of all these extant complexes, even though they were built at different sites and dates from the New Kingdom onwards. Through the temples and their rituals, the Egyptians sought to use magic as a means of manipulating supernatural forces to influence events on a cosmic scale, and to maintain the balance and order of the universe, thus preventing the return of chaos. The temples, with their special architecture and ritual wall scenes, were regarded as potent locations where these spiritual and temporal aims could be achieved.

The priesthood

The state and local gods had temples and priesthoods whose prime duty was to act as the 'servants of the god' and thus acquire the ability to control the supernatural forces that created and maintained life (Sauneron 1980). It was believed that this gave the priests their supposed power to influence events in life and after death. The priests were therefore essentially 'state magicians', but they had no pastoral role and no duties to preach to the populace. In fact, the temples and their priesthoods played no direct part in the religious activities of the masses. The priests were functionaries who performed the rituals on behalf of the temple deities, and although it was expected that they would display desirable characteristics such as discretion, honesty and fairness, they were not expected to have a religious vocation. Indeed, candidates were usually attracted by the affluent lifestyle and prospects of career advancement that the priesthood offered.

Sometimes, the priesthood passed down in the family, with the son inheriting his father's place, but on other occasions either high-level selections and promotions were made by the king, or a committee of priests would choose a candidate for a vacancy, or a position could be purchased by payment of a fee. Most temple priests were employed on a lay or part-time basis, although from the New Kingdom onwards larger temples were staffed with many permanent priests.

The lay priests in each temple were organized into four groups to undertake the daily rituals. Each group consisted of the same number of priests who served a rotational term of duty of one month, repeated thrice yearly, with a free period of three months in between, when they pursued other careers, often as doctors, lawyers or scribes. They were allowed to marry, and lived outside the temple enclosure when they were not on duty. During their term in the temple, they were required to observe certain taboos regarding food, clothing, worship and sexual abstinence, so that their physical and spiritual purity was ensured when they came in contact with the god's statue or his cult possessions.

In the great temples, there were established hierarchies of priests. The high-priest of Amun at Karnak had extensive political power because he could confer or withhold the god's approval of the royal heir, thus effectively controlling dynastic power. The top priests also advised the king on temple taxation, revenues and building plans, and wielded real political power. The temples also employed lay workers such as clerks, overseers of the estates that the temples owned, and butchers, bakers and florists who prepared the divine offerings. According to one record, the Temple of Karnak employed a total of 80,000 people.

In addition to performing the rituals and educating their students, an important duty of the priests was to compose and copy the sacred texts to perpetuate the divine cult. These specialist priests, who worked in an area of the temple known as the 'House of Life', would discuss and develop the god's mythology and theology, and prepare religious, astronomical and medical texts. Each temple may have been aligned towards a star that was linked to the mythology of the resident deity. However, although the Egyptians made many astronomical observations, they retained the belief that the earth was flat and suspended in the midst of a circular ocean, the upper half of which represented the sky while the lower half was the location of the underworld where the dead dwelt.

The gods

The Egyptian pantheon embraced hundreds of deities whom, on the basis of each god's role and characteristics, Egyptologists have classified under the three main categories of state, local and household gods (Morenz 1973). Originally, in predynastic times, each local community had its own deity, but with the political amalgamation of villages into districts and ultimately into a nation-state, the main gods of the communities were transformed into district gods, and in some cases into deities of national importance and influence.

These became state gods who were worshipped throughout Egypt, although they often retained a strong connection with a particular city or site. The country's external and internal success was accredited to their influence and support, and in each dynasty the rulers would select a particular god as their own royal patron and protector. Some gods, such as the 'creator-gods' Re (whose first centre was at Heliopolis) or Amun (the chief god of Thebes), were continuously included amongst the state gods and were generally worshipped as supreme deities, but in several dynasties the rulers would elevate their own local god as the dynasty's royal patron so that the god acquired a temporary status as a state deity. The gods in this top league usually had temples and cults and were served by their own priesthoods.

Briefly, at the end of Dynasty 18, King Akhenaten elevated the cult of the Aten (sun's disc) to an unprecedented form of monotheism (Aldred 1988). Some of the state gods formed family groups, such as the triad of Amun, his wife Mut and his son Khonsu at Thebes, and the ennead (nine gods) at Heliopolis which included Re. The Osirian triad (Osiris, his wife Isis and his son Horus) was uniquely important, although the worship of Osiris focused on his role as a god of the dead, unlike the other deities who were gods of the living (Griffiths 1980). Although the two centres associated with Osiris – Abydos and Busiris – were great centres of pilgrimage, Osiris did not possess his own temple and priesthood, but was accommodated in the shrines of other gods. The local gods, although they possessed temples and priesthoods at particular sites, never attained permanent national importance, although they continued to be worshipped over many centuries and exerted considerable local influence.

Some deities were worshipped at shrines in the houses and did not receive any temple cults (Černý 1973). Today, these are termed 'household gods', and they played a very important role in the personal religion of the ancient Egyptians. People of all classes addressed their requests and prayers to these gods, rather than to the temple deities, although Amun appears to have had a dual role as both the nation's supreme god and the personal deity of the royal necropolis workforce at Deir el Medina. The household gods most widely worshipped were Bes, a dwarf god with special responsibility for marriage and jollification, and his consort Tauert, a hippopotamus goddess who assisted women in childbirth.

Some gods had special roles. Seth, the wicked brother of Osiris who murdered him and subsequently fought Osiris' son Horus, was found guilty by the divine tribunal in the *Myth of Osiris*. Consequently, he became an outcast, and the personification of evil – the 'devil' of the Egyptian pantheon. Occasionally, famous human individuals were deified and worshipped: King Amenhotep I and his mother Queen Ahmose-Nefertari received a cult from the royal necropolis workers whose village at Deir el Medina had been founded by this king, and Imhotep, the First Minister and architect of King Djoser's Step Pyramid at Saqqara, was later worshipped as the founder of medical science and a god of medicine. The Greeks who became resident in Egypt ultimately identified him with their own god of medicine, Asklepios.

Personal piety

Evidence for popular religion and personal piety comes from literary sources, and from objects discovered at settlement sites, particularly the villages and towns of the royal necropolis workmen. Their deities included those with widespread appeal such as Bes and Tauert, and also some with local associations such as the 'Peak-of-the-West' (the personification of the mountain behind the Valley of the Kings), and the deified rulers Amenhotep I and Ahmose-Nefertari at Deir el Medina (Černý 1973). In this community, there is also evidence of the worship of several foreign gods, including Syrian deities. Elsewhere, at Kahun, another royal necropolis town, some objects and practices (distinctive altar-stands and intra-mural burials of babies within the town) may indicate the presence of religious activities which were related to immigrant sections within these communities.

At Deir el Medina, we can gain a rare insight into one aspect of personal piety, provided by the memorial stelae (inscribed stones) set up by the workmen in some of the offering chapels. In these inscriptions, the men sometimes appeal to the gods for mercy, and confess their sins, in a rare expression of humility, or they thank the gods for their own delivery or that of their family members from illnesses which were believed to be the result of personal transgressions. Impiety and blasphemy were apparently regarded as major sins, and blindness was considered to be a particular punishment for offending the gods. The high level of literacy at Deir el Medina may explain the existence of these texts in this particular location (the men wrote down concepts here that had existed elsewhere in Egypt but were left unexpressed), but an alternative explanation is that these were new ideas, perhaps introduced by Syrian immigrants. For other literary evidence of morality and ethics, the much more formal Wisdom Texts provide our major source.

Another aspect of popular religion is represented by the use of the oracle at Deir el Medina. Here, the priests, chosen from amongst the workmen themselves, had a surprising degree of autonomy, and one of their functions was to hold up the god's statue on front of the petitioner and move it in response to his enquiry. It was believed that, through this oracle, the deified Amenhotep I gave advice on a range of matters including personal and family concerns. The oracle also provided an alternative to unacceptable rulings given on cases presented in the local law courts. Also, the priests participated in local festivals, when the gods' statues were paraded through the town.

At Kahun, there is evidence of the practice of non-state (secular or private) magic (David 1997: 131–41). Local magicians exercised their skills to protect individuals against their fears of sickness, hunger, thirst, drowning, asphyxiation, hostile attack and dangerous animals. Magicians used spells to counteract these dangers, seeking to block out the negative forces which supposedly caused them, and their techniques and healing skills were in widespread demand (Pinch 1994: 76–89). When Kahun was excavated in the 1890s, the house of a local magician was uncovered and found to contain a sacred mask, which was worn to imitate Beset (the female counterpart of Bes), and a set of magical equipment.

The key feature of personal religion in Egypt revolved around the domestic worship carried out in the houses. This was probably often performed in a special, separate area of the house, in front of the god's shrine which held the deity's statue and a selection of stelae. Utensils used in the rituals included offering tables, water jars, vases and braziers. The rites probably copied the rituals performed in the temples of the state or local gods, and involved the presentation of food offerings and libations, and the burning of incense in the presence of the divine statues.

In addition to a deep personal faith and a close relationship with their domestic gods, it is evident that the Egyptians believed that each individual was responsible for the good or evil deeds they performed during life, on which depended their ultimate fate in the next world. This was decided at the Day of Judgement which every person faced at the time of death. The goddess of fate or destiny was present on the Day of Judgement; her name, Shay, meant 'that which is decreed', and she was closely associated with the ram-headed creator-god, Khnum. Shay was also present at each person's birth. The Egyptians believed that individual fate or destiny was established at the time of birth, and ultimately determined the manner of each person's death. Sometimes, fate was also considered to control the course of each individual's life, with its successes and misfortunes, but freedom of action and the flexibility to act for good or evil were also important factors which were weighed and considered at the Day of Judgement.

The Egyptians used hemerology – the determination of lucky and unlucky days – to assist them in achieving desired results throughout life, but this concept was derived from mythology rather than astrology. The Egyptians had a long-established interest in astronomy, and included 'star-ceilings' with charts of the heavens and tables of the nocturnal movements of stars in their tombs and temples. They also devised a calendar which was based on their agricultural year. Astrology was brought to Egypt from Mesopotamia in later times, possibly in the Persian Period (*c.* 450 BCE).

Funerary beliefs and customs

The concept of the personality

The ancient Egyptian concept of the human personality was complex, and directly influenced their ideas of the afterlife. Some elements, such as the individual's name, were regarded as an integral part of the personality, while the body was thought to provide an essential link between the deceased once he had attained his afterlife, and his former earthly existence. The body had to be preserved from decay in order to ensure that a recognizable likeness of the deceased remained in the tomb, so that his spirit could return to his body and thus obtain sustenance from the food offerings placed in the funerary chapel.

Some elements, however, were regarded as immortal and indestructible parts of an individual. The 'Ka' (often translated as 'spirit') was the person's life-force or essential being which, after death, became free and immortal, although it retained a vital link with the tomb and the body. The 'Ba' (usually translated as 'soul') was a force that could travel outside the tomb so that its owner could experience places that he had enjoyed when he was alive. The 'Akh' was another supernatural power which assisted both the dead and the living. In order to allow the deceased tomb-owner to regain his life-force, a special ritual was performed by the priest at the funeral. Known as the ceremony of 'Opening the Mouth', this involved using an adze (a carpenter's tool, rather like an axe) to touch the mouth, hands and feet of the mummy, all the model figurines, and the figures represented in the mural scenes. It was believed that this would animate them to act on behalf of the deceased.

The afterlife

Several different kinds of afterlife were envisaged. The kings were expected to pass their eternity in the heavens, sailing with the gods in the sacred barque. The nobility and middle classes, however, prepared lavish tombs where they planned to spend part of their afterlife. Each tomb was named the 'House of the Ka', and closely followed the layout and design of contemporary domestic architecture: the burial chamber represented the bedroom, the offering chapel was the equivalent of the reception hall, and the storerooms held the owner's goods and possessions. Food and drink were provided for the dead by means of a funerary ritual performed by his relatives, or by a Ka-priest who was paid from the deceased's estate to undertake this obligation. In the event that human agents neglected these duties, a 'menu' of provisions was inscribed inside the tomb, which could be magically activated to ensure eternal sustenance. Essentially, the wall decoration and contents of these tombs were designed to provide a pleasant hereafter for the deceased.

From the Middle Kingdom onwards, democratization of religious beliefs and a new emphasis on the cult of Osiris fostered the concept that everyone, regardless of status or wealth, could spend eternity in the realm of Osiris (Griffiths 1980). This kingdom was situated in the underworld, and the only means of entry was for the individual to perform satisfactorily at the Day of Judgement, when a person's actions during life were assessed. In Osiris' kingdom, each person was allocated a small plot of land, which they were expected to cultivate. The wealthy classes, on the other hand, sought to avoid this duty by continuing to prepare comfortable tombs where they hoped to provide themselves with an alternative eternity. The priests attempted to rationalize and integrate these three concepts of the afterlife, but this was never satisfactorily achieved, and an individual's expectation of eternity continued to depend largely on his status in this world.

Tomb and pyramid development

In the Predynastic Period, the earliest pit-graves housed the burials of community leaders and ordinary people, but in *c.* 3400 BCE a new type of tomb was introduced for the ruling classes. This consisted of a brick-lined substructure underground which housed the burial, and a mudbrick, bench-shaped superstructure which marked the site of the tomb above ground. Because of its shape, Egyptologists use the term 'mastaba' (which comes from the Arabic word meaning 'bench-shaped') for this type of burial place.

By the early Old Kingdom (*c.* 2600 BCE), the kings had started to construct pyramids to house their own burials, but the nobles and officials continued to use mastaba tombs, while the rest of the population were still interred in pit-graves. Burial customs changed again when the Old Kingdom collapsed, and the nobility – to underline their independence and personal power – moved away from the royal burial sites and built their tombs in the cliffs alongside the river, in their own areas of political influence. This practice continued in the Middle Kingdom, even when pyramids were reintroduced for royal burials.

By the New Kingdom, pyramids were no longer used and both royal and private tombs were now located on the west bank of the river, opposite the capital city, Thebes. Expense involved in constructing pyramids and their vulnerability to tomb-robbers had persuaded the kings to build hidden tombs, excavated deep into the natural rock of the area known today as the Valley of the Kings. Nearby, similar tombs were prepared for some queens and princes of the New Kingdom at various sites (Weeks 1992).

These royal tombs consisted of a series of passages and chambers, and were decorated with scenes and texts from the various funerary books, depicting the dangers the royal owner would have to encounter and defeat before he attained eternity. Scattered over the same mountainside were the tombs of the officials and dignitaries of these reigns. Their tombs were also cut into the mountainside: they incorporated an underground burial chamber and an offering chapel above ground, which was decorated with scenes of everyday life and food production, to ensure that the owner would have eternal sustenance and enjoyment in the next world. Despite these lavish precautions, however, both royal and private tombs were robbed extensively in antiquity. The Theban necropolis ceased to be used after Dynasty 20, when the next dynasty moved its capital to Tanis in the north. Here, they built subterranean tombs within the city complex which remained undiscovered until 1939 when Pierre Montet revealed the royal treasure buried there.

Tomb art

Major features of the tombs and temples are the scenes that decorate their walls. In the temples, many scenes represent the rites once performed in special areas of the building, while in the tombs, they represent locations and situations which formed an integral part of the owner's passage to the afterlife and his eternal existence. All these scenes, based on the concept of sympathetic magic, were designed to bring about desired events or results. They were never placed on the walls simply for decoration or even for spiritual inspiration. Because they had this primary function, however, the human figures and objects in the scenes were represented in a way that often puzzles the modern observer, and in order to understand this art it is necessary to study the underlying principles.

Although the Egyptians themselves have left no record of the concepts which underlay their art, the work of a German Egyptologist, Henrich Schäfer, has illuminated our understanding of this subject (Schäfer 1974). He defined two fundamental types of art – 'conceptual' (or 'aspective') and 'perceptual' (or 'perspective'). According to his theory, conceptual art represents the essential character and features of a person or object, whereas perceptual art shows the figure or object from the particular viewpoint or stance of an individual artist. Schäfer claimed that the ancient Egyptians were the most skilful exponents of conceptual art. Prompted by their specific religious requirements to show people and objects 'as they really were', their main aim was to ensure that all the parts of the whole were displayed so that they could be 'brought to life' by magic for the owner's future use.

Tomb equipment

From the Middle Kingdom onwards (*c.* 1900 BCE), because of an increased emphasis on an individual's hereafter, the provision of tomb equipment became a widespread priority, and even the less wealthy now aspired to prepare and equip their burials as extensively as possible. From the Middle Kingdom, there was the nest of coffins, which usually included a rectangular outer coffin and an inner anthropoid ('body-shaped') one; in later times, these were replaced by two or three anthropoid coffins decorated with scenes and spells from the funerary books. Canopic jars and model figurines usually also accompanied the burial.

Symbolism

An important aspect of funerary beliefs and customs was the symbolism associated with death and rebirth. In particular, the symbolism of hieroglyphs as a life-force was emphasized in the tomb inscriptions and funerary texts. Not only were hieroglyphs the means of conveying in writing the syntax, grammar and vocabulary of a contemporary language, but the very act of writing these sacred characters was believed to renew life itself, and to provide the owner of the texts with magical protection and the means to overcome death.

Concerns specific to this religion

Some aspects of religion provide specific and distinctive information about Egyptian civilization. A few key examples are provided here.

The Amarna 'revolution'

One of the most significant events in Egypt's political and religious history occurred towards the end of Dynasty 18. When Amenhotep IV, the son of Amenhotep III and Queen Tiye, succeeded to the throne, he instigated a series of unprecedented changes. He developed the cult of the Aten (sun's disc) into a form of solar monotheism which focused on the worship of the life-force present in the sun. Previously, the kings had each promoted a special royal patron deity who protected their own particular dynasty, but they had never attempted to create an exclusive cult which did not tolerate the existence of other gods, and the state religion had always encompassed a multitude of deities with their own temples and cults.

In the early years of his reign, Amenhotep IV lived with his wife Nefertiti in the capital city of Thebes where he began to promote the Aten's cult, building temples to the god in proximity to the great temple complex of the dynasty's supreme deity, Amen-Re. However, when the king's relationship with the priesthood of Amen-Re began to deteriorate, he took decisive steps to impose his form of monotheism on Egypt. The priesthoods of all other gods were disbanded and the deities' names were expunged from the monuments. The revenues that had supported these cults were now diverted to the Aten. A change of name from Amenhotep ('Amun is satisfied') to Akhenaten ('Servant of the Aten') emphasized the king's allegiance to the new god, and Nefertiti added the new name of 'Nefernefruaten'.

From the evidence of the scenes which once decorated the early Aten temples at Thebes, Nefertiti played a unique and central role – equivalent to that of the king – in the god's cult, exceeding the traditional ritual duties of queens (Smith and Redford 1977). Finally, Akhenaten moved his political and religious capital from Thebes to a new site midway along the Nile which, he claimed, had been selected by the Aten. This virgin site was uncontaminated by association with any other god. Here, the king built the city of Akhetaten ('Horizon of the Aten'), which is known today as Amarna or Tell el Amarna. The royal court, accompanied by the officials, craftsmen and people required to establish a new royal residence and capital now also moved to Akhetaten (Aldred 1988).

The city was constructed over an area of 20 sq km on the east bank of the river, and supplied with food from agricultural land on the west bank. The whole site was delineated by fourteen boundary stelae inscribed with Akhenaten's conditions which related to the establishment and limits of his capital. The city included several royal palaces, administrative quarters, military barracks, a records office (where the famous Amarna Letters were discovered, detailing the royal family's correspondence and relations with contemporary foreign rulers), substantial villas for the officials, and a village which was probably built to house the workmen engaged in constructing the royal tomb, which lay in a distant desert valley, and the tombs of the courtiers and officials, excavated in the eastern cliffs encircling the city. Among the most important features of Akhetaten were the temples dedicated to the Aten which differed markedly from the traditional temples. Instead of the customary dark, roofed buildings with their cult statues, the Aten temples were roofless and had no statues because the sun, the Aten's symbol, was believed to enter the temple to receive the cult offerings.

The cult of the Aten is not described in any one literary source, but inscriptional and archaeological evidence from Amarna and Thebes has enabled scholars to interpret the basic doctrine and beliefs. At Akhetaten, archaeological evidence has been gleaned from the temples and wall-scenes in the courtiers' tombs which depicted the relationship between the royal family and the Aten rather than the owner's expected existence in the afterlife. The famous Hymn to the Aten, inscribed on a courtier's tomb wall, described the main elements of Atenism.

At Thebes, the earlier Aten temples were later dismantled by Akhenaten's successors, and used as infill for new constructions in the Temple of Amen-Re at Karnak. During dismantling of these buildings for a restoration programme of the temple carried out in modern times, archaeologists revealed some 36,000 decorated and inscribed blocks which had once been part of the original Aten buildings. Using a computer, they were able to reassemble the information on many of these blocks, revealing many of the unique and remarkable features which had distinguished the early years of this religious experiment (Smith and Redford 1977).

From the Hymn to the Aten and other sources, it is evident that the god was regarded as the beneficent creator of all living things, including mankind, animals and plants. This creative force was expressed through the light and heat of the sun. The sun's disc (Aten) was the symbol of the god, visible in the heavens to all on earth, while the king himself was regarded as the divine incarnation who shared the deity's nature and acted as sole divine agent and representative on earth. In effect, the king and the god became interchangeable, and the king's power was no longer rivalled by that of a separate priesthood who served another god. The new faith essentially restored the kingship to the pre-eminence it had enjoyed in the early Old Kingdom.

When this historical period was first revealed to modern scholars in the early twentieth century, they regarded Atenism as a 'revolutionary' concept without precedent in Egypt. However, it was not a new invention. The Aten, as the sun-disc representing one aspect of the sun-god Re, first appeared in the Middle Kingdom, but Tuthmosis IV (Akhenaten's grandfather) and his father, Amenhotep III, developed the Aten's cult, although there is no evidence that they attempted to make the god unique or exclusive. It is now recognized that Akhenaten's one truly revolutionary idea was the introduction of a monotheistic concept of the Aten. Other aspects, such as the god's role as a universal god of foreign peoples as well as Egyptians, and his powers as creator, can be identified in earlier religious trends of the New Kingdom, particularly the cult of Amen-Re where they were used to emphasise the god's significance as a unifying force for Egypt's empire.

A style of representation in painting and sculpture (which is now referred to as 'Amarna Art') flourished during this period, and was inextricably linked with the religious developments (Aldred 1988). Characterized by a new emphasis on 'reality', the art portrays the plant and animal life of Egypt with a refreshing naturalism, as expressions of the Aten's creative power. The royal family is also portrayed with a realism and informality not found in the traditional art which was itself an expression of conventional religion. However, the art is particularly notable for its representation of the human figure, grossly exaggerating certain physical features: the elongated face and head and an apparently malformed body with emaciated neck and pronounced breasts and thighs. It has been suggested that these features may be based on the king's own physical condition, perhaps reflecting a glandular disorder, but his body has never been identified (and presumably remains undiscovered), and so this speculation remains tentative. Another equally valid view is that the art is simply experimental, marking a complete break with earlier religious and artistic conventions.

Although the royal family and court promoted and supported the cult of the Aten, there is little evidence that it was favoured by the general population. It enhanced the king's own status and position, but offered no moral philosophy or popular mythology to attract other worshippers. It apparently proposed no alternative concept of an individual hereafter to replace that offered by the cult of Osiris, but seemed to promote the belief that, as in the Old Kingdom, individual immortality could only be achieved through the king's bounty.

It is therefore not surprising that, after Akhenaten's death, his religious innovations did not survive, and following the reigns of his immediate successors, Smenkhkare and Tutankhamun, when there was a partial return to traditional religion, a 'counter-revolution' was pursued during the reigns of Ay and Horemheb. The court returned to Memphis in the reign of Tutankhamun, and Thebes was restored as the country's religious capital, while, under later kings, Akhetaten was finally abandoned.

Akhenaten's motives in promoting Atenism as a form of monotheism have been widely discussed: was he a visionary, prompted by religious ideas to establish a new order, or was he a political opportunist who used this religious upheaval to overthrow the priesthood of Amen-Re and the threat it posed to the power of the kingship (Redford 1984)? Perhaps both played their part in influencing this unique and unrepeated religious experiment.

The tomb of Tutankhamun

Tutankhamun was possibly the son of Amenhotep III by a secondary wife, although it has also been proposed that his father was Akhenaten. He married

Ankhesenamun, the third daughter of Akhenaten and Nefertiti, and succeeded Smenkhkare (who was probably his elder brother) to the throne. His short reign of some ten years was perhaps most notable for the steps he took after the Amarna 'revolution', to restore, at least in part, the worship of the traditional gods. He ascended the throne as a child and, on the advice of his courtiers, began to reverse Akhenaten's policies. He and his wife changed their names from Tutankhaten and Ankhesenpaaten to Tutankhamun and Ankhesenamun, emphasizing their allegiance to the traditional deity, Amun (Amen-Re), in place of the Aten. However, the king's coronation may have taken place at Akhetaten, and during his reign the Aten's cult was probably allowed to continue alongside those of the reinstated traditional deities.

Thebes was once again Egypt's foremost religious centre and, when Tutankhamun died as a young king without any living heirs, he was buried in a tomb in the Valley of the Kings on the west bank opposite Thebes. This tomb, with its virtually intact contents, was discovered in 1922 by Howard Carter, the Egyptologist working on behalf of his patron, Lord Carnarvon.

The discovery and subsequent excavation of this tomb and its treasure have ensured Tutankhamun's fame in modern times. The rarity of a virtually intact royal tomb was also significant because it could provide new information about royal funerary beliefs and customs. The Valley of the Kings housed the burials of most of the rulers (and a few non-royal persons) of Dynasties 18, 19 and 20, and although, so far, sixty-two tombs have been uncovered there, the only largely intact royal burial to be discovered has been that of Tutankhamun (Reeves 1990).

Howard Carter, who had worked as an artist and archaeologist in Egypt for many years, was engaged by the 5th earl of Carnarvon (who had gone out to Egypt in 1903 in an attempt to improve his health), to work at Thebes. When the concession to excavate in the Valley of the Kings became available in 1914, Lord Carnarvon took it, and after the First World War they began to search there, in 1919, for the tomb of Tutankhamun.

The earlier discovery by another archaeologist of a small pit that contained the materials used in Tutankhamun's mummification and the remains of his funerary meal led Carter to pursue his exploration in this area. Starting work on 1 November, he revealed the entrance to the tomb three days later, and discovered that a stone staircase led down from this to an intact sealed doorway. The tomb was opened on 26 November, and although it had been robbed twice in antiquity, most of the contents remained intact; extensive robbery had been prevented here because the rubble from the excavation of a later tomb belonging to Ramesses VI had been piled over the entrance to Tutankhamun's tomb and had hidden it from view.

The four-roomed, stone-cut tomb was very small in comparison with some others in the Valley, and was almost certainly not intended for the king, whose early death was probably sudden and unexpected. There was some evidence of hasty preparation of the tomb and its contents. However, the burial contained a wealth of funerary goods including clothes, jewellery, personal possessions, games, weapons and canopic jars, as well as the three magnificent golden coffins and the gold face-mask which covered and encased the king's mummified body. Carter worked in a patient and meticulous manner over many years to remove, record, clean and restore the vast array of objects in the tomb, which were subsequently taken to the Egyptian Museum in Cairo. A definitive and complete study of the objects is still awaited, although some groups have been published. The tomb has provided unique and unparalleled information about the elaborate funerary customs surrounding the burial of even a minor, relatively insignificant, and short-lived king.

Mummification techniques

Mummification occurred in a number of ancient societies, although it is best exemplified in the human and animal remains of Egypt. In some countries, natural conditions – a hot or cold climate, the dryness of the sand in which the body is interred, or the exclusion of air from the burial – produce the ideal environment for natural or unintentional mummification. Sometimes, these conditions have been intentionally enhanced so that the bodies could be even more effectively preserved for social or religious reasons. The Egyptians took this to extreme lengths by developing and utilising a range of sophisticated techniques that involved physical intrusion in the body and the use of chemical and other agents to preserve the soft tissues. From the visible appearance of the bodies, and in terms of the preservation of the tissue structures as revealed by investigative biomedical techniques, it is evident that the Egyptians achieved the most successful results.

The geography of Egypt created environmental conditions that created natural, unintentional mummies. Because of the scarcity of cultivable land, from earliest times the dead were buried away from the areas required for houses, crops and animal husbandry. They occupied shallow pit-graves on the edge of the desert where the dryness of the sand and the sun's heat combined to desiccate the body tissues before decomposition started.

In *c*. 3400 BCE, advances in building techniques led to the construction of the mastaba tombs for the wealthiest classes. However, because the bodies in these tombs were now enclosed in brick-lined burial chambers, where the heat and dry sand provided by the pit-graves were missing, the bodies rapidly decomposed. By this time, there seems to have been a strongly held belief (accredited in inscriptions of the later periods) that it was essential to preserve the body in a recognizable form so that the individual's spirit could return to it at will, in order to use it to gain spiritual sustenance from the actual food offerings placed at the tomb.

The Egyptians began to experiment with practical ways of meeting this religious requirement. At first, they tried to re-create the shape of the body by encasing it in layers of fine linen which were coated with stucco plaster to emphasize the natural contours. Additional features on the breasts, genitalia and face were moulded and painted onto the form. However, despite this elaborate outer structure, the body still decomposed into a skeletal form underneath the wrappings.

The first evidence of true mummification dates to the Predynastic Period. Hundreds of years later, in *c*. 2600 BCE, the viscera (major abdominal and thoracic organs) of Queen Hetepheres, mother of King Cheops who built the Great Pyramid at Giza, were found in a box in her nearby tomb at Giza. Analysis of these packets confirmed that they had been treated with natron, a naturally occurring chemical substance used by the Egyptians to dehydrate the body tissues. Thus, this find produced evidence that the two main stages of mummification – evisceration and dehydration – were already known and practised.

The word 'mummy' is derived from the Persian or Arabic word 'mumia', which means 'pitch' or 'bitumen'. This is now generally used as a term for a naturally or artificially preserved body where putrefaction has been arrested because the tissues have been desiccated. Originally, however, 'mumia' was the name given to the black, bituminous substance which oozed forth from the 'Mummy Mountain' in Persia which, from medieval times, was credited with special healing and medicinal properties. When this supply became inadequate to meet demand, the vendors sought out an alternative source and, since the preserved bodies of the ancient Egyptians had a bituminous appearance, they assumed that they had similar beneficial properties and sold the tissue as a medicinal ingredient for treatment in Europe. Consequently, the word 'mumia' was also used to describe these Egyptian preserved bodies.

There are no extant literary sources from ancient Egypt that provide a detailed account of the mummification procedure, although religious and ritual references occur in many texts, including the 'Ritual of Embalming' preserved on two papyri of the Roman Period. Also, there are no pictorial records, although some stages in the preparation of a mummy occur on the walls of two Theban tombs. The only detailed descriptions of the procedure are found in the writings of two Greek historians, Herodotus (fifth century BCE) and Diodorus Siculus (first century BCE). From their information, and the evidence provided by scientific studies carried out on the mummies themselves (see above, pp. 54–5), it is possible to reconstruct a fairly accurate picture of the main stages of mummification.

According to Herodotus, there were three main methods which could be selected on the basis of cost. The cheapest method involved the injection of an unspecified liquid via the rectum, followed by treatment with natron. The second method (the one also used for animal mummification) was similar, and included injection of cedar oil via the rectum and treatment with natron.

The most expensive method involved the most complicated procedures. First, the viscera and abdominal contents were removed through an incision made in the flank. The heart was left in situ because it was considered to be the location of a person's intellect and emotions; also, the kidneys were not removed, but no religious explanation is given for this. Next, the body was cleansed and washed, the cavities were packed with bandages, herbs and spices, and the incision was closed. Both the viscera and the body were packed with dry natron to dehydrate the tissues. Natron (a mixture of sodium carbonate and bicarbonate with some natural impurities) was found in natural deposits in the Wadi en-Natrun in Egypt.

After a period of forty days, when the dehydration process was complete, the body was ready for the final application of resins and oils. In some mummies, the preserved viscera were stored separately in special containers known as canopic jars; in others, they were made into packages and reinserted inside the body cavities, or made into one package and placed on the legs of the mummy.

In some mummies, from at least as early as the Middle Kingdom, excerebration was practised: the brain was removed either through a passage chiselled through the left nostril and ethmoid bone into the cranial cavity, or through the base of the skull, or through a trepanned orbit (a window cut through the eye socket). The extracted brain tissue was discarded, but it was never possible to remove all the brain, and accidentally some always remained behind in the cranial cavity. Another development in the mummification procedure occurred in Dynasty 21, when subcutaneous packing (the insertion of mud, butter, sawdust and other materials through incisions made in the skin) was introduced in an attempt to preserve the rounded contours and original appearance of the owner.

The mummification process (which lasted seventy days from the arrival of the body at the embalmer's workshop to its eventual return to the family for burial) continued for some 3000 years, down into the Christian period. Originally introduced for royalty, it gradually became available on the basis of ability to pay, and by the Graeco-Roman period it was widely practised by the middle classes. Poor people continued to be buried in the shallow pit-graves on the edge of the desert.

The richest source for the study of royal mummification practices in the New Kingdom is the bodies of some of the kings and queens which were removed from their original tombs. These had been desecrated by tomb-robbers, and the bodies were reburied in two caches by the high-priests at Thebes in Dynasty 21, presumably in a pious attempt to give these rulers a second chance of survival in the hereafter.

One cache, deposited in the tomb of Queen Inha'pi near Deir el Bahri (on the west bank at Thebes), was discovered by the inhabitants of the nearby modern village of Qurneh. This eventually led to investigations by the Antiquities Service in 1881 and the removal of the mummies to the Cairo Museum. The other cache, buried in the tomb of Amenhotep II in the Valley of the Kings, was discovered by the archaeologist Victor Loret in 1898. Again, the mummies were transported to Cairo, where Professor Grafton Elliot Smith subsequently unwrapped and autopsied them. This work provided the foundation for his definitive study of mummification and funerary practices in the New Kingdom, and several later studies have added further infomation (see above, pp. 53–5).

Animal cults

From earliest times, the Egyptians appear to have regarded many animals as the representatives of a multitude of gods and goddesses who could take the form or some of the physical characteristics of animals. In predynastic times (*c.* 5000–3100 BCE), there were special cemeteries for animals where dogs or jackals, sheep and cows were interred in graves that were separate from but close to human burials. The animals were carefully wrapped in linen or matting covers. In later times, there were large animal cemeteries at special locations such as Bubastis, the cult centre of Bastet, the cat-goddess; Saqqara, where there were necropolises for different animals including ibises, falcons, cows and bulls; and Tuna el Gebel, where vast underground chambers housed the mummified remains of ibises and baboons, the two animals sacred to the god Thoth who was worshipped locally at Hermopolis (Ashmunein).

Animal mummification was widely practised, and it was apparently customary to use the second procedure described by Herodotus. There seem to have been several categories of animals that were mummified and given burials. First, there were the cult-animals attached to the temples, in which the spirit of the divine owner of the temple was thought to reside. These were regarded as alternative forms of the divine cult-statue, and were revered and treated with the utmost respect. When the cult-animal died, it was mummified and buried in an elaborate manner: perhaps the most notable examples are the Apis bulls associated with Osiris which were worshipped at Memphis. They were eventually interred in great sarcophagi in underground tomb-chambers in the Serapeum at Saqqara. Some animals, however, were beloved pets which their owners wished to honour with the provision of a coffin and a burial site. Again, others appear to have been animals bred and raised in compounds near to particular temples which were dedicated to animal deities. These could be purchased by pilgrims, and subsequently sacrificed, mummified and buried in special cemeteries, as offerings to the temple deity.

This veneration of animals because they were closely associated with particular deities permeated Egyptian religion. In the early predynastic villages, when cults were largely localized and unconnected, many deities seem to have been represented in animal or fetish form. As well as the animal burials, animal amulets and statuettes were placed in the human graves, presumably to provide the deceased with the power and strength of particular animals, and to supply a source of food that could be activated by means of magic in the next world. Animal forms also occurred on painted pottery found in the graves, and many of the slate palettes provided as part of the burial equipment were carved to represent animal shapes.

Gradually, in the early dynasties, the gods who were originally shown in an entirely animal form underwent an evolution in which many came to be represented with animal or bird heads attached to human bodies. In the Late Period and the Graeco-Roman era, when Egypt's nationalism was constantly threatened by foreign invasion and occupation, animal cults were promoted as expressions of national loyalty, and some were even adopted by the newly established foreign residents.

It is unclear why the Egyptians continued to accord animals such an important role in religion over such a long period. Some deities may have been given animal characteristics because these animals were feared, and it was hoped that veneration of the god in the animal form might deflect the creature's anger and lessen the danger, whereas other animals were regarded as beneficent allies of mankind, and were worshipped accordingly. Whatever the origin of the animal cults in Egypt, it seems clear that the Egyptians regarded both animals and the representation of animal characteristics as means through which the gods' divinity could be made manifest. The extent to which animal cults were developed and promoted in Egypt seems to have been unique in the ancient Near East.

Egypt's religious legacy

Biblical connections

The history of the Jews and the civilization of ancient Egypt are closely interwoven. There has been much debate regarding certain individuals and events in the Old Testament, as well as the related literary and archaeological evidence.

Egyptian and biblical texts

The main difference between Egyptian religion and Christianity and Judaism is the fact that the former developed around ritual and cultic practices whereas the latter were based on a belief in God's revelation of the truth to mankind, as preserved in the scriptures. However, there are clearly some parallels to be drawn between the Egyptian texts and the Bible, particularly the books of Job, Proverbs, Ecclesiastes, Psalms and the Song of Solomon.

One special example is provided by the Hymn to the Aten, inscribed on a wall in the tomb of the courtier Ay at Amarna, which presents a detailed description of the doctrine of Atenism. Although this hymn incorporated some earlier ideas, it also gave unprecedented importance to the god's unique and exclusive nature, to his role as universal creator, and to the king's position within the cult. Some passages in the hymn show a close resemblance to verses in Psalm 104 in the Bible, although it is unclear if there was direct borrowing between these texts or if they are derived from a lost, common source. The following selection of passages shows a particularly close association of ideas.

Example 1
Psalm 104:14
He caused the grass to grow for the cattle, and the herb for the service of man: that he may bring forth food out of the earth.

Hymn to the Aten
Your rays give sustenance to all fields: when you shine forth, they live and grow for you. You make the seasons to nurture all you have made.

Example 2
Psalm 104:20–21
Thou makest darkness, and it is night: wherein all the beasts of the forest do creep forth. The young lions roar after their prey, and seek their meat from God.

Hymn to the Aten
Every lion comes forth from its den, and all serpents bite. The darkness hovers, and the earth is silent while their creator rests in his horizon.

Example 3
Psalm 104:22–23
The sun ariseth, they gather themselves together, and lay them down in their dens. Man goeth forth unto his work and to his labour until the evening.

Hymn to the Aten
The earth grows bright when you arise in the horizon . . . the Two Lands make festival. Awakened, they stand on their feet, for you have raised them up . . . The entire land goes about its work.

Another example where biblical texts may have been influenced by earlier Egyptian writings is evident in the Egyptian Wisdom Literature and the book of Proverbs. One Wisdom Text – the Instruction of Ptah-hotep – which is attributed to the Old Kingdom, presents ideas which also occur in Proverbs, but the clearest evidence of influence is found in the Instruction of Amenemope, composed in the Ramesside Period (*c.* 1250 BCE), at a time immediately before the date most widely accepted by current scholarship for the Exodus. At this time, the Israelites would probably have been most influenced by Egypt. However, again, an alternative explanation is that both texts may be derived from a common but undiscovered source. A few examples from Amenemope and Proverbs will demonstrate the similarity of these texts.

Example 1

Proverbs 22:24–25

Make no friendship with an angry man, and with a furious man thou shalt not go: Lest thou learn his ways, and get a snare to thy soul.

Amenemope, ch. 10

Do not force yourself to greet the heated man. For then you injure your own heart: Do not say 'greetings' to him falsely, while there is terror in your belly.   (Lichtheim 1976: 154).

Example 2

Proverbs 22: 1

A good name is rather to be chosen than great riches, and loving favour rather than silver and gold.

Amenemope, ch. 6

Poverty is better in the hand of the god than wealth in the storehouse; bread is better with a happy heart than wealth with vexation.

(Lichtheim 1976: 152).

Example 3

Proverbs 23:10

Remove not the old landmark; and enter not into the fields of the fatherless.

Amenemope, ch. 6

Do not move the markers on the borders of the fields, do not shift the position of the measuring-cord. Do not be greedy for a cubit of land, nor encroach on the boundaries of a widow.   (Lichtheim 1976: 151).

Events and personalities

Historical evidence for the biblical Exodus, and for the roles played by Joseph and Moses, has been sought in Egyptian literature and archaeology. There has also been historical comment: for example, the Jewish historian Josephus (first century CE) referred to Joseph and Moses, and the possibility that the Exodus could be identified with the expulsion of the Hyksos by the Theban princes of Dynasty 17 (*c.* 1567 BCE).

According to the biblical account, Joseph was sold into slavery by his jealous half-brothers and sent to Egypt where he eventually acquired great wealth and power. He became vizier and brought his family, the tribe of Israel, into Egypt, where they remained for over 400 years. Joseph achieved great honour and was embalmed and buried in Egypt. However, a later pharaoh coerced the descendants of Joseph's family to work as labourers on building sites. Eventually, they were led out of bondage by Moses, and in Sinai they received God's covenant in the form of the Ten Commandments; finally, they established a new homeland in the region that became known as Israel. Moses, subsequently regarded by the Jews as their great spiritual leader, was the child of Hebrew slaves who had been rescued from the bulrushes by an Egyptian princess and reared as a royal prince. He later defied the pharaoh's refusal to release the Hebrews, and consequently led his people out of Egypt. The Bible recounts how, when the pharaoh attempted to recapture them by force, the windblown waters (probably of the Sea of Reeds) parted briefly to allow the Hebrews to cross, but then engulfed the royal chariot-force who were in pursuit.

Although these events were recorded in some detail in biblical sources and were regarded as key events in the political and religious history of Israel, no reference to them is found in Egyptian sources. However, it is unlikely that the Egyptians would have wished to record a relatively unimportant uprising on the part of their workforce, particularly as, for them, there was an unsuccessful outcome. In this respect, the Egyptian sources do not offer any assistance in fixing firm dates for these events.

A more recent theory has suggested that Joseph may have entered Egypt amongst the groups of Semitic-speaking peoples who established themselves in the Delta and Upper Egypt from the Old Kingdom (c. 2340 BCE) down to the Hyksos Period. It has also been proposed that Joseph could possibly be identified with Yuya, father-in-law of Amenhotep III. However, despite continuing academic debate, the most widely accepted date for the Exodus is during Dynasty 19, when the working conditions of the Hebrews described in the Bible reflect known events in Egypt, when large groups of itinerant labourers (the Apiru), who had lived in the Delta for centuries, were coerced to work on large building projects, and to make bricks for the cities of Avaris and Pi-Ramses.

Although scholars have tentatively identified Merneptah as the pharaoh of the Exodus, a stela was discovered in 1896 CE which Merneptah had usurped from Amenhotep III. The inscription, added on Merneptah's orders, gives details of Egypt's Libyan War and also supplies the only known reference to Israel in an

Egyptian text. Since this proves that Israel was already founded and established by the middle of Merneptah's reign, it is generally accepted that Ramesses II, Merneptah's father and predecessor, was more probably the pharaoh of the Exodus.

The contribution to Hellenistic culture, Christianity and Islam

Egypt and the classical world

Following the conquest of Egypt by Alexander the Great in 332 BCE, when the country was ruled first by the Ptolemies and then as part of the Roman Empire, there were many changes in political and social administration. Because of the large numbers of Greeks who settled in Egypt, profound developments also occurred in religion. At first, Greeks and Egyptians tended to pursue their separate religious beliefs and practices, although state initiatives promoted the establishment of some cults that would unite both peoples and secure the Ptolemies' dynastic claim to Egypt. However, the most important of these gods, Serapis, who was given a Greek appearance but incorporated popular aspects of earlier Egyptian deities, achieved only limited success. The revival of the Egyptian practice of deifying and worshipping certain dead rulers provided an official dynastic cult to justify the Ptolemies' claim to rule Egypt.

The Greek and Roman rulers built and repaired temples dedicated to the Egyptian gods, which, apart from minor architectural variations, continued the tradition of the pharaonic temples. In this way, and by decreeing substantial concessions to the temples, they gained the support of the Egyptian priests and proved themselves to be legitimate pharaohs, able to claim ownership over the land and its people which gave them the right to seize the country's economic benefits.

The Greeks and Romans who became resident in this period adopted Egyptian funerary beliefs and practices, especially the mummification process, a custom which was probably accelerated by intermarriage between Egyptians and the immigrants. This hybridization of beliefs is evident in the new or changed forms of the mummy casings, and particularly in the mummy panel portrait which was now placed over the face of the deceased. Although this use of an image of the human face was Egyptian in concept, the artistic techniques and conventions demonstrated in the panels, which produced realistic likenesses of the owners instead of the stylized representations of pharaonic times, were drawn entirely from the Hellenistic world.

The cults of some Egyptian deities such as Isis, Osiris and Amun were carried by traders and administrators to other parts of the Roman Empire, where they continued to enjoy great popularity because they combined human and divine characteristics and promised individual immortality.

The legacy to Christianity and Islam

Egyptian concepts probably entered early Christian belief through both the biblical Old and New Testaments, and more directly through Egypt's influence on the Hellenistic world. Thus, the divine triads of the pharaonic period and the concept of the Trinity may be associated, while there are probably links between the cult of the Virgin Mary and the Isis cult. Again, basic strands in the mythology of Osiris, such as the cycle of death, rebirth and resurrection, as well as the significance of the Day of Judgement, can be traced in later ideas.

In modern Egypt, although the population is mainly Muslim or Christian, some of the most popular festivals preserve ancient traditions. These include the Festival of Shem el Nessim, when the start of spring is celebrated as it was in the Festival of Khoiakh in antiquity; and the festival of Awru el Nil, a national holiday which coincides with the inundation of the Nile which was feted in ancient times. Similarly, some modern ceremonies reflect ancient funerary practices, when food is taken to the grave by the deceased's family, and subsequently distributed amongst the poor.

Bibliography

Aldred, C. 1988. *Akhenaten: King of Egypt*. London: Thames and Hudson.

Allen, J. P. 1988. *Genesis in Egypt: the philosophy of ancient Egyptian creation accounts*. New Haven: Yale University Press.

Bagnall, R. S. 1993. *Egypt in late antiquity*. Princeton: Princeton University Press.

Borchardt, L. 1907. *Das Grabdenkmal des Königs Ne-user-Re*. Leipzig: J. C. Hinrichs'sche Buchhandlung.

Černý, J. 1973. *A community of workmen at Thebes in the Ramesside Period*. Cairo: Institut Français d'Archéologie Orientale du Caire.

David, A. R. (ed.) 1979. *The Manchester Museum Mummy Project*. Manchester: Manchester University Press.

1981. *A guide to religious ritual at Abydos*. Warminster: Aris and Phillips.

1997. *The pyramid builders of ancient Egypt*. 2nd rev. edn, London: Routledge.

1999. *The experience of ancient Egypt*. London: Routledge.

2000. *Religion and Magic in Ancient Egypt*. Harmondsworth: Penguin.

Edwards, I. E. S. 1985. *The pyramids of Egypt*. Harmondsworth: Penguin.

Emery, W. B. 1961. *Archaic Egypt*. Harmondsworth: Penguin.

Erman, A. 1971. *Life in Egypt* (trans. H. M. Tirard). New York: Dover Publications.

Fairman, H. W. 1945. The consecration of an Egyptian temple according to the use of Edfu. *Journal of Egyptian Archaeology* 32 75–91.

Faulkner, R. O. 1969. *The Ancient Egyptian Pyramid Texts*. 2 vols., Oxford: Oxford University Press.

1973–78. *The Ancient Egyptian Coffin Texts*. 3 vols., Warminster: Aris and Phillips.

Frankfort, H. 1961. *Ancient Egyptian religion*. New York: Columbia University Press.

Griffiths, J. G. 1980. *The origins of Osiris and his cult*. 2nd rev. edn, Leiden: Brill.

Hornung, E. 1971. *Conceptions of god in ancient Egypt: the one and the many*. Ithaca, NY: Cornell University Press.

Lichtheim, M. 1973, 1976, 1980. *Ancient Egyptian literature*. 3 vols., Berkeley: University of California Press.

Morenz, S. 1973. *Egyptian religion*, trans. A. Keep. London: Methuen.

O'Connor, D. and D. Silverman 1995. *Ancient Egyptian kingship*. Leiden: Brill.

Pinch, G. 1994. *Magic in ancient Egypt*. London: British Museum Press.

Redford, D. B. 1984. *Akhenaten: the heretic king*. Princeton: Princeton University Press.

Reeves, C. N. 1990. *The complete Tutankhamun*. London: Thames and Hudson.

Sauneron, S. 1980. *The priests of ancient Egypt*. New York: Grove Press.

Schäfer, H. 1974. *Principles of Egyptian art*, trans. and ed. J. Baines, ed. with epilogue by E. Brunner-Traut. Oxford: Oxford University Press.

Shafer, B. 1991. *Religion in ancient Egypt*. London: Routledge.

1988. *Temples of ancient Egypt*. London: I. B. Tauris.

Smith, G. E. 1991 *Egyptian mummies*. 2nd edn, London: Kegan Paul International.

Smith, R. W. and D. B. Redford 1977. *The Akhenaten Temple Project*, I: *The initial discoveries*. Warminster: Aris and Phillips.

Weeks, K. R. 1992. The Theban Mapping Project and work in KV5. In C. N. Reeves (ed.), *After Tutankhamun: research and excavation in the royal necropolis at Thebes*. London: Kegan Paul, pp. 99–121.

3 Religion in ancient Ugarit

NICOLAS WYATT

Introduction

There is a sense in which no religion dies, unless it be through the extermination of its believers and practitioners and the destruction of its sacred traditions. So long as there is any historical continuity, elements, however transformed in the transmission, will survive into the belief systems of the physical and cultural heirs of the community under examination. This is certainly the case with the religion of Ugarit, whose links with contiguous and subsequent cultures can be so well documented.[1]

The city of Ugarit, rediscovered and excavated continuously from 1929 to the present day at the north Syrian coastal site of Tell Ras Shamra, 11 km north of Latakia (Map 3.1), has yielded more substantial written records than any other in the Levant throughout the ancient (BCE) period, and indeed more than all other sites in Syria, the Lebanon and Israel put together. While this archive is fairly restricted in scope, dating from the Late Bronze Age, from the late fourteenth to the first decade of the twelfth century BCE, its religious contents in particular betray wide influences, and have significant links with later religious tradition, in Greece, the Levant and in particular Israel. The importance of this material is out of all proportion to its limited quantity, and if one archaeological site should be identified as the most significant for the early history of the entire region (including Israel), Ras Shamra has perhaps the best claim. It is on this basis that, in a volume which treats the ancient religions of the major cultures and empires of the ancient world, a chapter is devoted here apparently to the religious tradition of one single city.

While small groups of scholars, mainly in Europe and North America, research in this area, and a larger number take its findings into account in biblical or classical research, it may be regarded so far as the general public is concerned as Near Eastern archaeology's best-kept secret. But Ugarit here represents the whole

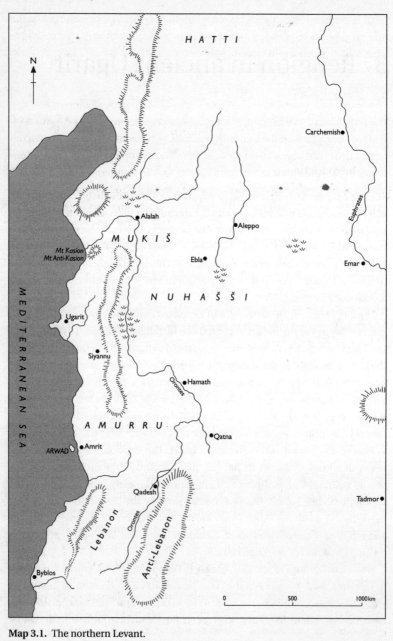

Map 3.1. The northern Levant.

Levantine tradition (neither Egyptian, Anatolian nor Mesopotamian), one of the primary tap-roots of western Asiatic and European culture, during the formative period of the second millennium BCE.

Description[2]

The tell (ancient city-mound, made of the accumulated debris of some 5000 years of occupation on the site) is approximately 20 hectares in area, though the entire city spilled over a larger area and was the metropolis of a small kingdom stretching at its greatest extent from Kassab, on the southern slopes of Jebel el Aqra (ancient Mount Saphon), in the north, by the mouth of the Orontes, to or just beyond the Nahr al Kabir in the south (a river some 4 km south of Latakia), and eastwards to the Awalite range of mountains flanking the Orontes Valley on the west, that is some 2200 square km. At its greatest extent it may have reached about 5500 square km. Neighbouring kingdoms were at times linked to it by treaties, at least one dynastic marriage with the kingdom of Amurru (northern Lebanon) is attested, while Ugarit spent much of its documented historical period walking a diplomatic knife-edge between the demands of Hatti, the Hittite empire of Anatolia, the great power to the north, and Egypt to the south.

Excavation and discoveries

The site was discovered by accident in 1928, when a local farmer struck a limestone slab with his ploughshare. It was quickly identified as belonging to a chambered tomb of a type familiar in early Greece, suggesting a substantial settlement in the neighbourhood. The first excavations revealed a port on the shore at Minet el Beida (ancient Mahadu), and about 2 km to the east, the ancient tell of Ras Shamra was quickly identified as the site of Ugarit.

Tablets were unearthed in the first season at Ras Shamra, in 1929. Texts in a number of languages and scripts were found. Thus a few fragments of Egyptian and hieroglyphic Hittite (the imperial language of Anatolia) were found, and some remains identified as Cypro-Minoan. The bulk of the texts were written in cuneiform writing (made by sharpened reeds impressed on damp clay), comprising Akkadian, Sumerian (languages of Mesopotamia) and Hittite written in syllabic script, and what turned out to be two further languages written in a script of only thirty signs, which was therefore essentially alphabetic in nature. With a rapid decipherment by C. Virolleaud and H. Bauer, these were shown to be

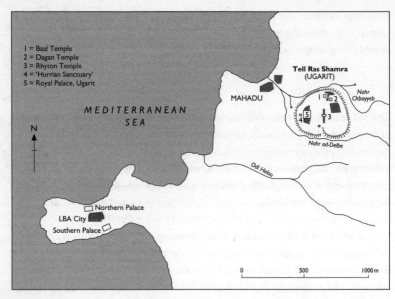

Map 3.2. Tell Ras Shamra and environs.

Hurrian (already known from El Amarna in Egypt, neighbouring Alalakh and Nuzi in Mesopotamia) and a new language subsequently named Ugaritic. The bulk of the written remains from the site are in Akkadian and Ugaritic, with the latter language being most prominent in the religious sphere, internal administration, and royal and private correspondence.

Nature of the site

The tell of Ugarit (Map 3.2) is roughly square in shape, and rises some 20 m above the surrounding terrain. Excavation thus far (in over seventy years!) is still largely in the topmost (Late Bronze Age) levels, though soundings have been made to deeper levels, including one important shaft which reveals settlement on the site going back to the eighth millennium BCE. The site was not resettled on any scale after its final destruction *c.* 1190 BCE, and so the entire Late Bronze city lies fairly close to the surface, where not already excavated. It consists of a well-planned, well-constructed city built almost entirely of stone.

To the north-east, the high point of the tell (the 'acropolis') is the site of two temples of the 'Migdal' (tower) type typical of the Levantine coast, built in massive masonry, with walls up to 3 m thick in parts. The north-westerly of the two is identified as that of Baal (Hadad), the ancient Amorite storm-god, while some 50 m to its south-east stands a temple usually associated with Dagan (encountered as the Philistine god Dagon in the Bible). Both deities had a widespread cult over most of the fertile crescent. In the centre of the city stood another temple, the so-called 'rhyton temple', which is perhaps to be regarded as that of El. This deity, again widely worshipped beyond Ugarit, was treated in pantheon lists and mythology as the father of the gods, the creator, though no creation myth has so far been discovered. A further building identified tentatively as a royal chapel was found among the extensive constructions on the west of the tell, almost a quarter of the entire area being taken up with a series of palaces and their administrative blocks, archives and storerooms. In addition, other sites may represent sanctuaries, and a number of allusions are made in the literary remains to further temples.[3]

The considerable extent of the palaces reveals the fact that Ugarit was a capital city: here was concentrated not only the civil and economic but also the military and priestly administration of the kingdom, with all the complex ritual practices which nurtured community life, supported the royal ideology and maintained the complex diplomatic relationships of a small kingdom.

The king was the titular head of all these departments of state, and was particularly prominent in the ritual life of the kingdom, being represented in mythological texts as divine, an incarnation in the midst of his subjects. In all probability, the ideology we can reconstruct from Ugaritian evidence is probably fairly representative of kingship beliefs in the ancient Levant, and provides analogues to the system already familiar from the larger-scale Egyptian monarchy.

The residential quarters of the city reveal a network of streets and alleyways, paved in stone and with under-street and house drainage systems which must have been an enormous boon in a hot climate, if well maintained. Houses comprised rooms surrounding central courtyards, with evidence of staircases showing that they were often of two or three storeys in height. In most houses, one room was set aside for the family burial vault, which consisted of a mausoleum entered through a staircase going down beneath the floor, and giving onto one or more chambers. Thus the family dead continued their existence in close proximity to their descendants.

Dependencies (Mahadu and Ras Ibn Hani)

Ugarit was at the centre of a wide trading network. Some precious substances, such as amber and lapis lazuli, witness trading connections reaching, if only indirectly, as far as the Baltic and Afghanistan. As a major naval power, its cargo vessels went as far west as Crete, if not Greece, and plied the coast down to Egypt. As evidenced by the range of languages attested (above), it was a cosmopolitan community, open to cultural, artistic and religious influences from a wide area. The port was at Mahadu, a substantial satellite development in the bay of Minet el Beida, while a little to the south-west, on the headland of Ras Ibn Hani, the kings constructed summer palaces, cooled by on-shore breezes, from which further texts have been recovered. A small urban development separated the two palaces.

The archives

The archives have been found in widespread parts of the tell, though naturally enough they were concentrated in particular areas, notably various places in the palace complex, in a house identified as 'the high priest's house' near the Baal temple, in other private residences belonging to important people, and most recently in the house of a high official named Urtenu on the south side of the city. In the description below, I shall concentrate on religious texts. The vast bulk of the religious texts are in Ugaritic, with a smaller number in Hurrian, or bilingual, and just a few in Akkadian. Non-religious texts also provide a considerable amount of incidental information (e.g. in theophoric personal names[4] and the general structure of society) which fills out the picture of the religious documents.

Languages and culture

The earliest levels at Ras Shamra (from c. 6500 BCE) are pre-pottery Neolithic, and from then until the Middle Bronze (c. 2200 BCE), when there was a break in occupation, nothing can be said about the ethnic or cultural aspects of the site. But the king-list (KTU 1.113 rev.[5]) may have listed up to fifty kings, which would take us back to this period in a tradition of a single dynastic line (though this was probably fictitious).

Ditanu (var. Didanu), who features in text KTU 1.124 as a minor underworld god, and in KTU 1.161 (the royal funeral liturgy discussed below) as the eponym of the 'ancient *rpum*', legendary kings antedating the historical king-list, may be tentatively identified with an Amorite king from the Assyrian king-list, while Keret (or Kirta?), the hero (or antihero) of the story bearing his name, and apparently 'king of Khabur', has been tentatively identified with a king of Mittanni (in eastern Syria) of the same name.

The neighbouring kingdom of Amurru to the south was evidently 'Amorite'[6] in cultural terms, and we know from one or two older documents that a king of Ugarit was in communication with Mari, whose last king, Zimri-Lim, actually visited Ugarit in the eighteenth century BCE. There may have been a further break in settlement, or at least breakdown in central government, in the fifteenth century, immediately before the apogee of Ugaritian culture in the Late Bronze Age, when the state disengaged from Egyptian control and became a Hittite vassal-state.

The antecedents of the South Arabian alphabet were known in Ugarit, and the cuneiform alphabet itself may have been modelled on Egypto-Levantine alphabetic experiments. Some traditions, notably the Hauran (southern Syria) geography of text KTU 1.108 and the Galilean geography some have discerned in the *Aqhat* story,[7] also point to wider engagement in the larger region of the Levant. As the polyglot nature of the archives indicates (eight languages are attested), Ugarit as a commercial centre was host to resident communities from Egypt, Cyprus, Hatti (Turkey), the neighbouring kingdoms, Mittanni (eastern Syria) and probably further afield. Thus its lifestyle and the range of cultural contacts, interactions and influences were thoroughly cosmopolitan.

Religion at Ugarit

The religious texts written in Ugaritic constitute the most important evidence for the reconstruction of Ugaritian religion. In view of the paucity of later, first-millennium, textual survivals, they also provide our most important single source of information for the Levant throughout the rest of the ancient period (BCE), though here only cautious inferences may be drawn, since the evidence is no longer direct.

The religion of the city undoubtedly represents the broad nature of the 'national' religion, though the surviving textual information, by its nature as royal and priestly archive material, undoubtedly highlights 'official religion' at the expense of popular and private forms. It may be treated systematically, as is done below. There is always a danger, of course, that an analytical treatment will distort the historical reality. It may for instance err in identifying different literary genres which the ancients may not have distinguished. Or it may, as has undoubtedly happened in the period before detailed examination of the ritual texts was undertaken, lead to misreading or over-reading of the data to be gleaned from the earlier material, in particular the mythological texts. Thus by the incautious use of data from Eusebius (writing in the fourth century CE), who quotes older writers, and comparison with Greek and Hittite material, the erroneous conclusion was drawn that El was deposed by a younger generation of gods. This is now known to be false. Early interpretations, in the fashion of the time, also fairly consistently interpreted 'Canaanite religion' (a biblical category!), within which Ugaritian religion was automatically included, as a 'fertility cult', and explained the myths concerning Baal as allegories of the seasons. In addition, biblical estimates of 'Canaanite religion' as an 'abomination' have persistently coloured some interpretations.[8] So long as we remain alert to the dangers of mis-representation and simplistic reductionism, however, and recognize that each step in the recovery of information from scraps of surviving information is only provisional, a balanced view is possible.

Cosmology

We may begin with a general consideration of cosmology, that is, the imagined structure of the world, as represented in the minds of the theologians of the culture. These would have been the poets who not only preserved ancient beliefs, but consciously or otherwise continually adapted them to changing circumstances, since no theology is immutable.

No formal statement of cosmological beliefs survives, but the following picture may be reconstructed from incidental allusions. The cosmic centre was Mount Saphon. It is clear from geographical lists and other allusions that this essentially mythical mountain was identified with Jebel el Aqra, the 2000 m massif some 40 km north of Ugarit. It was associated above all in the myths of Baal as the throne of this god.[9] An analysis of the texts shows that it was in fact the seat of El himself (head of the pantheon), which was delegated to the sea-god Yam, won in battle by Baal, and then used for his enthronement by Athtar. Thus a number of individual deities were explicitly associated with it (and were theologically linked by this process), and the 'canonical' pantheon list KTU 1.47 identified all the representative deities of the list as 'gods of Saphon'. The mountain lies on the northern horizon when viewed from Ugarit, and evidently formed the focal point of the community's theology, which like all ancient theologies was associated with geographical features, thus sacralizing the national territory.

While specific details are fragmentary, we can with some assistance from the biblical world-view,[10] which shares many features, reconstruct the fuller ideal landscape. From the sacred mountain at the centre stretched out a zone of productive farmland, giving eventually onto the steppe. This in turn merged into desert, and was bounded by the cosmic sea. This ideal world was probably superimposed upon real geography in the practice of the cult, thus validating the real world of experience by its assimilation to the ideal world. This is particularly evident in the rituals surrounding the birth, accession and death of kings, which were couched in the language of the national myths. An interesting instance of this process of superimposition may be seen in the text KTU 1.23 (*The Gracious Gods*), which combines mythical and ritual elements. The former, in the form of a narrative of divine conception and birth, is located at the end of the world, on the shore of the cosmic ocean. But it is related by means of rubrics and hymnic episodes to a ritual taking place in the city, probably in a shrine in the palace.

The pantheon

Lists

Considerable numbers of divine names appear in the Ugaritic texts, in one estimate over 200. While some of these were epithets (over twenty belong to Baal alone), and others are disputed, new ones are continually coming to light, so that the number is gradually increasing. Most pantheons, in the general sense, are *ad hoc* agglomerations, in that they reflect the unplanned developments of history, migrations here, the growth or shrinkage of empire there. Many of the deities are familiar from other regions of the fertile crescent, some were 'imports' from Mesopotamia[11] or even Egypt,[12] while other native figures in turn migrated to these other regions.[13] At the same time, 'pantheons' in a more restricted sense, of organized lists, reflect processes of systematic theological thinking, though it is of course extremely difficult to discern the motives of the priests compiling them.

Three examples of one pantheon list point to the existence of a 'canonical pantheon' (see Table 3.1), a proposal supported by the use of the list in a composite ritual text. A synoptic text is given here in tabular form, which illustrates the theoretical thinking (if so systematic a term is appropriate) lying behind the

Table 3.1 *The 'Canonical Pantheon' at Ugarit (a synoptic version of texts KTU 1.47 and KTU 1.118 (Ugaritic) and RS 20.24 (Akkadian))*

1	**The deities of Saphon**	
	The god of the ancestor	
	El	see text
	Dagan	see text
2	**Baal of Saphon**	see text
	Baal	
	Baal	
	Baal	the personified clouds
	Baal	
	Baal	
	Baal	
3	**Earth and Heaven**	
	Kotharat	see text
	Yarih	moon-god
	Saphon	the sacred mountain
	Kothar	see text
	Pidray	see text
	Athtar	see text
4	**Mountains and Valleys**	
	Athirat	see text
	Anat	see text
	Shapsh	sun-goddess
	Arṣiy	an underworld goddess
	Ishhara	a Hurrian goddess
	Athtart	see text
5	**The gods who help Baal**	
	Reshef	plague-god
	Dadmish	earth-god?
6	**The assembly of the gods**	
	Yam	sea-god
	Censer	
	Kinnar	lyre-god
7	**Kings**	
	Shalem	see text

list. This list bears the heading 'the deities of Saphon' on one of the tablets. As shown in Table 3.1, the text falls into seven natural parts, each with a representative deity, followed by further exemplars of the type. Three sets (nos. 2–4) each comprise seven members, and Saphon, the mountain at the centre of the universe, appears as the fourth (that is, central) member of the central set of three. This group may therefore represent an earlier form of this pantheon list, in which twenty-one deities (three sets of seven) represented the totality of all divine powers, with their geographical symbol, the sacred mountain, as their central figure. This hypothetical earlier pantheon would correspond to the three realms of Greek cosmology ruled over by Zeus (sky), Poseidon (Sea) and Hades (earth).

The enlargement to seven sets gives a list of thirty-three,[14] which is modified in its application in the ritual text KTU 1.148 to thirty. This in turn suggests that the ritual use of a lunar calendar (twenty-nine is too few) may lie behind the enlargement. Certainly, a lunar calendar appears to determine some features of the regular cult, in which new moons, full moons and sets of seven days are particularly important. Further groups of ritual texts betray other routine orders, evidently representing various sub-groups or alternative pantheons of significance for given ritual occasions. Such structures show the essentially symbolic nature of such groupings, which reflect a variety of theological purposes.

With regard to the 'canonical' lists, but similarly with other lists, their theoretical structure is also indicated by the fact that some members are not individual deities at all, but entire classes ('mountains and valleys', 'the gods who help Baal', 'the assembly of the gods') and therefore already theoretical constructions, while the significance of others (and their seeming priority over important gods not appearing) simply escapes us. In addition, while all the main deities attested in the surviving mythological corpus are present, with the striking exception of Mot (see below), several of those featuring prominently in the ritual corpus are not. Furthermore, while all the members of the Ugaritic pantheon listed are evidently identified with Akkadian divine names in the parallel Akkadian text, they represent a specifically Ugaritian list, as distinct from independent Akkadian deities (such as Marduk and Enlil) occurring sporadically in syllabic documents (and therefore familiar to local priests, if not worshipped locally) as well as listed in other Akkadian pantheon lists, and independent Hurrian pantheons given in yet other lists. There is evidently systematic thought in these compositions, but the details remain elusive.

Individual deities

Relatively few deities feature in the mythological texts. This does not necessarily mean that they are the most important, though their relative importance is perhaps indicated by their incidence in other West Semitic contexts, among which the Hebrew Bible constitutes a significant body of evidence from the first millennium, as well as other contexts (such as Egypt during the Hyksos period and afterwards). The briefest details are given here of only a few, on account of space limitations. I give the familiar forms (usually those found in the Bible) together with vocalized Ugaritic forms. To avoid confusion in matters of precedence they are listed alphabetically.

Anat (*anatu*). Goddess of war and hunting. She bears the title *batulatu* ('Virgin'). Of contradictory nature, she is at once tender and erotic in her relation with Baal (who is not formally her consort), and savage and ruthless with the hero Aqhat, who rejects her request for his bow, and is murdered for his pains.[15] In some texts she works in tandem with Athtart (Greek Astarte), and the two goddesses fuse in the first millennium into Atargatis (Lucian of Samosata's famous 'Syrian Goddess'). Her martial role, glorying in slaughter, can be seen from this excerpt from the Baal cycle of myths:

> And lo,
> Anat fought in the valley;
> > she battled between the two towns.
> She smote the people of the sea-shore;
> > she destroyed the men of the sunrise.
> Beneath her like balls were hea[ds];
> > above her like locusts were palms,
> > like grasshoppers heaps of palms of warriors.
> She fixed heads to her back;
> > she attached palms to her girdle.
> Her knees she stee[ped] in the blood of soldiers;
> > her thighs in the gore of warriors.
> With shafts she drove out the old men;
> > with the string of her bow the townsfolk.[16]

She also claims to have killed the primeval monsters associated with Yam (q.v.). The view that Anat was also a 'fertility goddess', or 'goddess of love', is not substantiated by the texts, despite her erotic encounters with Baal. These labels are used altogether too freely and uncritically with West Semitic deities.

Athirat (*aṯiratu*). She appears to be the consort of El, though this is not stated explicitly. She is called 'the Mother of the Gods', who are in turn called 'the Seventy Sons of Athirat'. Her commonest title, *rbt aṯrt ym*, may mean either 'The Great Lady who tramples (or: walks on) Sea', or 'The Great Lady who bestrides (or: measures) the Day'. The first sense would suggest that like Anat she overcomes maritime monsters, while the latter would confirm the view that she is a sun-goddess. The element *rbt* (*rabitu*, 'Great Lady') in the title cited also points to her importance in royal ideology, as will be seen below. Her cult appears to have survived for some centuries in Israel, according to recent estimates of the biblical evidence.

Athtar (*aṯtaru*). The masculine counterpart to Athtart (following), and, like her, probably an aspect of the planet Venus[17] (see also Shahar and Shalem). He appears in the Baal cycle of myths, complaining initially in a fragmentary text at being passed over for the kingship of the gods, but is later selected by his mother Athirat to be enthroned on Baal's throne following the latter's death. He appears to be a mythic type of the king (though the royal ideology of Ugarit also draws on Baalic imagery). Athtar or his avatars Shahar and Shalem live on in Israelite tradition. The former is the subject of the taunt-songs of Isaiah 14 ('Bright One of the Dawn' (Latin *Lucifer*)), while the latter is the ancient patron-deity of Jerusalem (Akkadian form *Uru-Salim*: 'City of Shalem').

Athtart (*aṯtartu*). She is not prominent in the myths, where she appears only alongside Anat except for a brief episode[18] in which Baal sees her out hunting and tries in vain to seduce her. A fragmentary Egyptian myth, however, known as 'Astarte and the Tribute of the Sea' is undoubtedly of West Semitic origin, and hints at a now-lost myth in which Athtart (who is demanded in tribute) may have vanquished the sea (cf. Anat above).[19] Egyptian evidence confirms the impression from the limited Ugaritic evidence that she was also a goddess of war and hunting, and with no basis in Ugaritian tradition for her later reputation for lasciviousness.

An example of her appearance in a ritual text is the following:

> When Athtart-of-the-Window enters the pit in the royal palace, pour a libation into the pit of the chapel of the star-gods.[20]

This evokes a cultic procession, in which the goddess (i.e. her image) was brought, no doubt accompanied by incense and hymns, into a ritual area. It confirms her character as a royal goddess. Such a reference to a cult-image, of which there are many similar in the ritual texts, demonstrates the ancient view that in some manner the deity was identified with the image. This is not to say that the deity's 'reality' was limited to the image, since it could obviously inhabit other images too. But the kind of distinction modern commentators make between deity and image with regard to ancient religions is palpably not one the ancients would have recognized.

Baal (*ba alu, ba lu*). The storm-god, whose title means 'Lord' or 'Master', is also called Haddu ('Thunderer'), and is evidently a local form of the storm-god found as Adad in Mesopotamia, Teššub in Anatolia, Kumarbi in Mittanni and Hadad in first-millennium Syria. Though all these gods were often regarded as distinct, they were frequently explicitly identified in texts, and shared common features in theology, iconography and mythology. Baal is 'Lord of Saphon', the sacred mountain 40 km north of the city, and appears in a number of hypostases (note the six additional 'Baals' in Table 3.1). He is the patron deity of Ugarit (*b l ugrt*, 'Lord of Ugarit') and of its dynasty. As the chief character in the 'Baal cycle' of myths he overcomes Yam and is enthroned as king among the gods, and has a great palace (i.e. his temple at Ugarit) built. But challenged by Mot, god of death, he dies, though he is later resuscitated and confirmed in his royal status. This extensive mythic complex, whose antecedents have now been traced into the third millennium BCE, was at first widely interpreted in a 'seasonal' fashion, as an allegory of the climatic and agricultural cycles of the year. It is better seen, however, as serving two purposes: first as the 'cult-legend' of the Baal temple, narrating its mythic origins; and second as a vehicle for royal ideology, celebrating Baal's patronage of the dynasty and the claims of the poet Ilimilku's patron Niqmaddu III (*c.* 1200 BCE). Thus the narrative of Baal's palace-construction may also have symbolized the Ugaritian dynastic 'house' (cf. the similar play of temple and dynasty in the Bible, in 2 Samuel 7:1–17). Other myths involving Baal are one in which he fathers a son on Anat,[21] another in which he and Anat make love,[22] and the one noted above, where he attempts a seduction of Athtart. In these myths his virility is paramount, so that he is in a sense a 'fertility god', the author of all fecundity. In one damaged text,[23] however, he encounters two mysterious beings in the desert, and dies. In this narrative it appears that his death has an atoning function for the city. In a hymn to Baal[24] his help is invoked in time of military threat to the city.

An example of apparent henotheism is a hymnic excerpt cited twice in the Baal myths:

> Our king is Valiant,
>> Baal is our ruler:
>> and there is none above him!
> We should all bring his chalice,
>> we should all bring his cup.[25]

It should be recognized however that this monarchy is devolved, held by authority of the supreme god El.

Dagan (*daganu*). This elusive deity, whose cult centre was Tuttul on the upper Euphrates, appears sporadically in Ugaritian tradition, apparently as the father of Baal (who is called *bn dgn*, 'Son of Dagan'). The south-easterly of the two acropolitan temples is usually associated with him, though scant evidence for his cult survives. Two stelae apparently invoke him as an underworld deity, perhaps receiving sacrifices on behalf of the dead, if this is what the term *pagru* meant. Some scholars think that he was identified with El, but there is no clear evidence for this. An Akkadian text from Babylon identifies him as Enlil, the Sumerian storm-god.

El (*ilu*). The word *ilu* appears in Akkadian, South Arabian and all the Northwest Semitic languages. It is the oldest term for 'god', and as an individual deity probably denotes an ancient moon-god. In Ugarit he is called 'Creator of Creatures', and 'Father of Man' (i.e. the king as a 'primal man' figure),[26] and despite early attempts to see him as demoted, he is firmly in command of the pantheon, the highest divine authority. He alone can heal a dying king in the *Keret* story, or can procure an heir for a childless king (in the *Keret* and *Aqhat* stories), and he has an intimate relationship with kings, who are his 'sons'. To be sure, since Ugarit was a royal city, and much of its literature was either ideological compositions by the priest and poet Ilimilku or ritual texts dealing explicitly with the king's involvement in the cult, such an emphasis should occasion no surprise. El may conceivably have been more remote in popular religion, though the incidence of his name in theophoric names suggests a great tradition of devotion here too.

In the Baal cycle of myths, it is El's throne that features throughout as the focus of attention. Successively, Yam, Baal and Athtar are enthroned upon it, wielding devolved power. While vigorous action goes on all around him, El sits enthroned and unmoving at the centre of the universe, and to consult him and receive authority, deities travel

> towards El at the source of the rivers,
> amidst the springs of the two deeps.[27]

Here they bow down before him, and he sits, benign and indulgent, and authorizes their every action, such as sanctioning a temple for Baal, or allowing Anat to indulge her penchant for murder.

El is the chief actor in two further myths. In one he begets the gods Shahar and Shalem (the morning and evening stars as royal gods) on the goddesses Athirat and Rahmay, who are the twin hypostases of Shapsh, the sun-goddess. These goddesses are also his daughters, suggesting an older myth of the androgynous creator-deity attested in India and Egypt. In another text, an 'applied myth', the purpose of which is to provide a prescription to cure hangover, El holds a feast in his *marziḥu* (the prototype of a social and religious institution widely attested in the Mediterranean world), where he becomes gloriously drunk, and is carried home by Anat and Athtart, who fetch medicine for him.

El features prominently in biblical tradition, sometimes with epithets (El Shaddai, El Elyon, etc.). He is usually identified explicitly or implicitly with Yahweh, though the book of Hosea tells a different story, regarding the 'false' calves of northern worship as El.[28]

Horon (*ḥawranu*). This god does not have an active role in the mythical texts. He appears in a curse-formula occurring in literary texts. The formula, adapted to each context, reads

> May Horon smash,
>> May Horon smash your head,
>> Athtart-the-name-of-Baal your skull!

He appears to be an underworld deity (perhaps his name means 'the One of the Pit', i.e. the underworld), suitable to be invoked in curses, but also powerful to intercede in dangerous circumstances. In two snake-bite texts either alone or with other deities he heals from snake venom, while in an exorcism ritual he is invoked to heal the victim. In the latter he appears to be the lord of demons. Such contingencies as these texts reflect, common enough in the ordinary life of the people, suggest that he was widely worshipped, and also explain his invisibility in centralized ritual practice and absence from the pantheon lists. It is perhaps of some note that he is also absent from royal funerary texts (e.g. KTU 1.39, del Olmo 1999: 213–17), where his underworld aspects might be considered important. He appears to belong to a popular level of religious practice, while most of our evidence is of the 'official' state religion.

Kothar (*kaṯaru*). Kothar constructs cultic furniture, a palace for Baal, and a bow for Aqhat in Ugaritic literature. As the apotheosis of all technologies, and thus in control of the most pervasive features of culture, he well illustrates the tendency of polytheism to reify in divine personae every aspect of life that is significant, in his case all technological aspects of life. Kothar is evidently a localized form of the Egyptian god Ptah, and is said in the tradition to come from Crete and Memphis. Ptah appears with the epithet *qsr* (= Ugaritic *kṯr*, 'Skilful'). In the Akkadian pantheon lists, Kothar is represented by Ea (in Sumerian

Enki), the Mesopotamian god of wisdom, but the Egyptian influence appears to be predominant here.

Kotharat (*katarātu* [plural]). Similarly, these goddesses, probably seven in number, who are not directly related to Kothar, are concerned with weddings, pregnancy and childbirth, thus having the oversight of the continuity of the generations. They assist at the birth and infancy of Aqhat, and a hymn to the Kotharat is presumably written after a sacred marriage text on the assumption that they are understood to be present at the nuptials of Yarih and Nikkal.[29]

Mot (*môtu*). The only recognizable god from Ugarit who is consistently absent from all the cultic material, and the recipient of no offerings in texts discovered so far, Mot is the personification of death. He is, as it were, a 'theologian's god', rather than the object of worship. He appears from descriptions to be not only the idea of death, but also the personification of the underworld as a devouring mouth into which all go:

> [He extends a lip to the ea]rth,
>> a lip to the heavens,
> [he extends] a tongue to the stars.[30]

Since the gods are stars, the third line of this tricolon implies that the gods too are threatened by Mot. Thus Baal's ultimate victory over Mot, aided by the goddess Shapsh, herself, like Anat and Athirat, a destroyer of monsters, is evidently an affirmation of the values of life and renewal against the threat of annihilation.

Pidray (*pidrayu*). Appearing only fleetingly in the myths as a daughter and consort of Baal, she is probably to be linked to the Greek characters Phaedra or Pandora, the latter like Pidray an underworld goddess. She appears frequently in sacrificial texts, however, and appears to belong to a group of 'royal' deities invoked on behalf of the monarchy.

Rahmay (*rahmayu*). She appears as twin of Athirat in the myth of *The Gracious Gods*, the two goddesses being geminated hypostases of Shapsh. Her name, meaning 'Uterine', is probably to be restored in the following passage, where we read of Yasib, Keret's son, to be born of the new Queen Hurriy, that:

> He will drink the milk of A[thi]rat
>> He will drain the breast of Virgin [Rahmay];
>> The suckling of [goddesses].[31]

She thus appears to have considerable significance in the royal ideology of Ugarit.

Rapiu (*rapi'u*). Absent from the myths, Rapiu is the subject of a liturgical prayer which invokes his protection of the city. He has been identified with various other gods (e.g. Baal or El), but is rather to be seen as the patron of the *rpum*, who are the heroes of the past, legendary kings of yore, and protectors of Ugarit. The *rpum* themselves feature in three very fragmentary texts, evidently arriving by chariot for a funerary feast, and are summoned along with more recent dead kings to welcome Niqmaddu III into the underworld on the occasion of his funeral.[32] An intriguing element of continuity of tradition is found in a hymn to Rapiu, where he is said to be

> The god enthroned in Athtarat,
> The god who rules in Edrei.[33]

The same cities are said in the Bible to be the abode of Og king of Bashan in Deuteronomy 1:4 ('dwelt' may mean 'was enthroned in'), and he is identified as 'the last of the Rephaim (Hebrew *r pā'îm* = Ugaritic *rpum*)' in Deuteronomy 3:11, while Deuteronomy 3:13b is a note identifying Og's kingdom as 'the country of the Rephaim'. (The Hebrew, *ereṣ rᵉpā'îm*, may mean 'the underworld of the Rephaim'.)

Reshef (*rašpu*). As his name ('Pestilence') indicates, Reshef is the apotheosis of disease, an example of an 'evil' god who is invoked as the most powerful antidote to illness. Widely worshipped throughout the Levant, and even in Egypt, he is probably the prototype of the Greek god Apollo. He contrasts with Horon (above) in being of a similar underworld nature, and yet very prominent in the temple rituals. This may be explained by Reshef's involvement in (and Horon's absence from) the small circle of gods who are evidently the patrons of the dynasty, and thus 'royal' gods.[34] This representative role played by Reshef may also account for the absence of Mot from the cult. Identified in the Akkadian pantheon lists with Nergal (the Mesopotamian god of the underworld), he appears to pre-empt Mot's obvious equivalence with Nergal.

Shahar (*šaḥaru*) and **Shalem** (*šalimu*) as twin-gods of the planet Venus, are further royal gods from Ugarit, and according to some a twinned form of the god Athtar. As markers of dawn and dusk, they represent the temporal construction of the day. As a pair, they symbolize the dual nature of kingship, which is prominent in Egyptian thought, but also, on a different mythological basis more akin to the present tradition, persists into the theory of monarchy in medieval Europe.

Shapsh (*šapšu*). The sun is connected with royalty throughout the ancient Near East. In the Semitic world it is originally deified as a goddess. Thus in the

West Semitic world the solar deity is the mythical mother of the king. She shares the title *rbt* (*rabitu*, 'Great Lady') with Athirat. As the source of all light, the solar deity becomes a representation of wisdom, law and justice. Ruling the day, she also conquers nocturnal monsters during her nightly passage through the underworld. This explains her importance in the liturgy for the funeral of King Niqmaddu III. In *The Gracious Gods* Athirat and Rahmay are her avatars.

Yam (*yamu, yammu*). He is most visible as the opponent of Baal. He is initially made king of the gods by El and placed on his (El's) own throne, before Baal wrests power from him in single combat. Though scholars are generally agreed that we have no specific creation myth from Ugarit, we should probably discern in this cycle of delegated kingship (first Yam, then Baal . . .) a narrative account of world-development, in which Yam represents the primeval order and the old gods (cf. the Asuras of India, the Titans of Greece and the Ogdoad of Hermopolis in Egypt) who play their part in origins before ceding place to the gods of the existential world.

Yam is certainly not to be understood, as some have proposed, as the personification of evil. He is perhaps to be identified with Litan (*ltn*), prototype of the biblical Leviathan and Greek Ladon, who encircles the world as the cosmic ocean (see the expression 'Litan the wriggling serpent . . . the writhing serpent . . . Encircler-with-seven-heads', a passage echoed in Isaiah 27:1). As a serpent and the apotheosis of the sea he embodies the ambiguity of the ocean, the vehicle of much of the economic life of a maritime power, yet fraught with danger, and the ultimate symbol of transformation and renewal.

Yarih (*yariḫu*). The moon-god is apparently quite distinct from El, who formerly may have had, but later lost this function. Apart from being the groom in the marriage myth of Nikkal, he is not conspicuous among the deities. Yet Ugarit clearly followed a cultic calendar linked to the lunar month, with its great emphasis on new moons full moons and seven-day periods, so we may suppose that as a controller of time (cf. Thoth in Egypt and Sin in Mesopotamia) he was a god of the first importance in ritual.

It is evident from this brief discussion that there is a certain division of labour among the deities. They are in effect the apotheosis of various cosmological, environmental or cultural realities which impinged directly on the life of the community. In view of the paucity of the evidence, it is well to avoid too great an assumption of restrictive specialization. Those deities of whom we know most (notably Baal and El) tend to universal qualities. Strict specialization belongs to an early phase in theological development, for increasing symbolic associations and a natural inflation in the language of praise tend always to expansion of conception. Estimates that episodes such as El's inebriation (together with all the sex and violence of other texts!) betray the moral bankruptcy of Ugaritian religion are superficial.[35] While still imperfectly understood, the pantheon of Ugarit is sufficiently documented for us to discern a vigorous and effective theological dimension, in which the natural antagonisms and tensions of social and moral life are given expression in myth, and the theology of the pantheon resolves disruptive aspects, reinforcing social values and structures. It is in the nature of evidence from a royal city that the greatest emphasis should be on the role of the king in social and political management. Through the various deities discussed, and the ritual life to be outlined below, the identity, territorial claims and general life of the community were affirmed and sacralized.

Public (state) religion

The aspects of religion dealt with here were public in the sense that they were practised on behalf of the nation: but performed in temple or palace precincts, they were probably not accessible to public view, except when processions traversed the city. The vast bulk of our information about the performance of regular religious practice comes from archives written in Ugaritic and Hurrian. Of this material, most was found in the so-called 'house of the high-priest', between the two acropolitan temples, and the rest in the palace. The so-called 'house of the diviner' yielded a number of model livers and a lung (see below), on which were inscribed readings of various natural or pathological markings on the surface of the organs, interpreted as arcane messages from the gods warning of future events. Various oracular techniques of this kind would be pursued in both public and private contexts.

Royal involvement in the cultus

Royal involvement is amply attested. Rituals were performed both in the various temples around the city and in different parts of the palace, and no doubt in domestic contexts, which would include funeral rites for private citizens. In addition, there are allusions in the texts to ritual processions, or to the gods 'travelling', which refer to images carried in procession, and these probably travelled around the city and to sacred places outside. Many of the texts involve the king as chief officiant, while others are specifically intended to emphasize, reinforce and declare his status as himself one among the gods. We shall deal with ritual in more general terms below. Here our concern is to indicate the king's role. The following example illustrates both his more general priestly function and his more specific ideological role.

While its status as a formal New Year ritual text is open to debate, one important text[36] is obviously of considerable significance in the ritual calendar. The location of the rites is not specified in detail, but appears to have been peripatetic or in different locations on different days of the festival, since it mentions the chapel royal in line 20, the sanctuary of the Mistress of the Great Temples in lines 26 and 37, a spring in line 33, the sanctuary of El in line 38, and the altar of Baal in line 41, while in lines 54–5 the king is returned to his palace. It deals with a series of rites performed through the month of 'First-of-the-Wine'. The beginning of the month (indicated by the appearance of the new moon) is celebrated with the offering of a bunch of grapes as a communion sacrifice to El (line 2).[37] Then in preparation for the climax of the festival on the fourteenth day, the full moon, 'the king is to wash himself thoroughly' on the thirteenth, that is, for the purification to take effect *before* the fourteenth (line 3). On the fourteenth, we read that the king 'sits (i.e. is formally enthroned), being purified, and shall clap his hands and proclaim the day. Subsequently he is to enter the temple' (lines 6–8).

Evidently the royal behaviour symbolizes the way in which the king links the human and divine worlds by his effective actions. (It is in this context that his 'divine' nature, to be noted below, is actualized and made effective.) In the temple he makes offering to the deities, pours libations, and takes offerings of myrrh oil, spiced oil, honey and pigeons to the royal chapel. Subsequently he makes offerings 'into the hole', which is probably to be construed as a pit symbolizing the entrance to the underworld. This suggests, though this text does not state it, some form of communion with the spirits of dead kings (if situated in the palace, this may be the pit envisaged in, and perhaps the location of the offerings in various other texts). The expression *inš ilm* in the text is construed by del Olmo as 'the divine people', whom he regards as 'the divinized ancestors of the dynasty'.[38] These ancestors feature prominently in other aspects of the cult, as will be seen. Among the offerings are fourteen pitchers of wine (line 22), no doubt intended to represent the fourteen days since the new moon.

The structure of text KTU 1.41 is uncertain. But after the detailed treatment of day fourteen, it reverts to the three days ending the first lunar quarter, i.e. days 5–7 and finally day 1 (new moon). Here are detailed a further complex of ritual acts by the king, some of which at least have, it seems, specifically to deal with royal ideology, and the text ends with the formal desacralization of the king, thus freeing him for secular duties. These additional elements are the *kubadu*-offering (line 39),[39] and the use of eight 'dwellings' constructed on the (palace) roof (line 51). The latter may correspond to the *sukkôt* ('booths' or 'tabernacles') constructed in the Israelite feast of Tabernacles (Leviticus 23:33–6, 39–43), but also to the Mesopotamian *akîtu* shrine, in which the king performed the sacred marriage. The former we shall treat below, along with royal funerals and their subsequent elements of cult.

Royal ideology

We have seen the primary importance of the king in the palace rituals. In a sense, of course, the king is *ex officio* the focus of attention on the human side of the cultic programme, the gods being the recipients of cult mediated through him. But his role was far more than incidental. It is as though his formal status was expressed in terms appropriate to the seriousness of his office. The Ugaritic king-list evidently formed some kind of official list. It is uncertain whether the kings were all regarded as sons of their predecessors,[40] though we know this to have been the case with those of the final documented period. On the basis of other ancient Near Eastern king-lists, which were ideological in purpose, we may suppose that a deliberate choice has been made, 'wicked' kings having been perhaps weeded out, so that the present series, however factual or fictitious, represents a 'canonical' list. Respect for the past and continuity with that past, and even the construction of the past, the hallmarks of all religious tradition, are self-evident in such a composition.

Two features of the text[41] are significant. First, the obverse of the tablet contains a liturgical text. Though it is too fragmentary to be interpreted with certainty, it may be the remains of a litany to be addressed to the listed kings as part of a *kispum*-rite,[42] the purpose of which was to affirm social solidarity with the ancestors, and to invoke their assistance in the maintenance of cosmic order. This suggests that dead kings were understood to maintain a benevolent involvement in the continuing life of the community. Furthermore, each royal name in the list is prefixed with the generic term *il* (*ilu*), 'god', or 'divine'. This may have been no more than a polite cliché, meaning 'dead'. In view of the other evidence to be cited, however, it seems more likely that it has some theological content. If del Olmo's interpretation of the *inš ilm* is correct ('the "divine people"'), then the expression occurring in various ritual texts may be a short-hand reference to the membership of the king-list, invoked and given offerings as a group.

Another important royal text[43] has also been interpreted as consisting partly of a *kispum*-rite. What is clear is that as a whole it formed the liturgy for the funeral of Ugarit's penultimate king, Niqmaddu III. This text begins with the summoning of a number of figures, only the final two being among the names from the king-list:

> You are invoked, O saviours of the under[world],
>> You are summoned, assembly of Di[dan].
> Invoked is Ulkan the saviour;
>> Invoked is Taruman the saviour.
> Invoked is Sidan-and-Radan;
>> Invoked is the eternal one, Thar.
>> They have been invoked, the ancient saviours.
> You are invoked, O saviours of the underworld,
>> You are summoned, O assembly of Didan.
> Invoked is Ammithtamtru the king
>> (and) invoked as well is Niqmaddu[44] the king.

The first nine lines here are devoted to persons not appearing in the king-list. The figures cited here are called *rpum*, which may be translated as 'saviours', 'healers' or perhaps 'heroes'. While their status is much debated, the majority view is that they were illustrious dead kings from the remote past, perhaps more legendary than historical, comparable, as minor gods, to the Greek heroes. Keret and Danel[45] may both be among their number. The 'saviours' may, as noted above, be associated with a patron deity Rapiu (*rpu*, sing. of *rpum*). While there is no direct evidence that they were recipients of cult (unless the term *inš ilm* embraced them too), three fragmentary texts appear to envisage them arriving at feasts in horse-drawn chariots, which may be a mythological or liturgical expression for just such participation. At any rate, the *rpum* appear to link deceased kings to the pantheon in some indeterminate way. The god Rapiu himself is the subject of a hymn (noted above) addressed to this patron of deified kings (or a collective into which they all enter) on the occasion of a king's descent into the underworld to join his ancestors.

There is also evidence from the *Keret* story which has a direct bearing on the status of the living king. While as king of Khabur he may not represent the same royal ideology, the probability is that his story is meant precisely to express a number of aspects of Ugaritian royal ideology. I have argued that the story has been pressed into service by Ilimilku, the royal scribe, in order to bolster the claim to the throne of Niqmaddu III. Keret is said to be *bn il* ('son of God'), which could mean one of two things (or both at once): a *bn il* was a member of the genus 'god', so that it is tantamount to saying that Keret is divine; at the same time, in mythological usage, it meant 'son of El', as though it was the high god who was directly involved in the paternity of the king (rather as in Egypt). This more powerful sense is supported by the fact that El in turn is referred to as *ab adm*, 'Father of Man', where the 'man' is the 'primal man' (or 'Adam' figure) incarnate in the king himself. Echoes of such language can be discerned in Psalms 2, 8, 19 and 110 and elsewhere in the Bible, suggesting that both cultures, Ugaritic and Israelite, are attesting a similar royal ideology. Further elements common to the two ideologies will be seen below. The same familial language implying a divine status is to be discerned in the allusion cited above to Yasib, Keret's son, as being suckled by goddesses.

All in all, there is evidently a considerable body of circumstantial evidence for regarding the king as in some way 'divine'. Is it possible to elaborate on this? The king was obviously a fully human person in so far as he lived and died like a man, begot sons, fought, might be deposed and so forth. Furthermore, in the palace rituals, he performed the role of chief priest. But it is precisely here that, as we have noted, he acted as intermediary between the divine and human realms. We may go further, and say that the language deliberately used of him indicates that he was somehow supposed to participate in both realms, and in both orders of being. He was thus both human and divine. It is perhaps important also to distinguish between the temple cults performed regularly with or without the king's presence, and those performed in the palace complex. If the latter had any distinct rationale (as distinct from a mere domestic duplication of the temple rituals) it was surely to sacralize and confirm the reality of the monarchical order, represented by the king. When he took part in a procession of divine images, it is as though he himself was regarded as one of them, and indeed, if the analogy of Egyptian cult is valid, the cult offered to images was precisely modelled on that offered to the king. Thus their efficacy and importance was as much validated by association with the king, as was his by association with them. We may even postulate that the ritual purification of the king at the beginning of ceremonies, and his desacralization at the end, which are repeatedly prescribed in the ritual texts, were formal ritual means of imposing on him divine and human status respectively. He would thus be a 'god' only during the performance of the royal cultus. This is further reinforced when we consider the deliberate linking of the king to the mythological order, as will be seen in the next feature.

In dealing with the ritual of the month of First-of-the-wine above, we noted the possible allusion to a *kubadu*-rite (line 39). This brings us to another interesting aspect of royal ideology, where evidence from various quarters allows the tentative reconstruction of a feature of Ugaritian theory and practice. The *kubadu*-rite was first identified at Emar on the Euphrates. It appears there in a number of contexts in the NIN.DINGIR ('Lady of the god') installation rites of the high-priestess of the storm-god. It consisted there of the ritual processing of an axe, and possibly of other weapons. Perhaps to be related to this rite was an analogous one from Mari, further down the Euphrates. This was alluded to in an oracle delivered to King Zimri-Lim, ironically the last king of the city:[46]

> Thus speaks Adad . . .
> I have brought you back to the throne of your father, and have given you the arms with which I fought against Tiamat. I have anointed you with the oil of my victory, and no one has withstood you.

This short text is profoundly important, as the key to a great mythic and ritual nexus pervading Near Eastern culture, as we shall see below. In the present context the significant feature is its use of weapons in the cult. Now a further ritual composition from Ugarit, while not explicitly identifiable as a *kubadu*-rite text, may be alluding to the symbolism behind it. This passage invokes the gods to protect Ugarit, and bases its confidence in their goodwill by an appeal to sacred weapons:

> By the divine spear;
> By the divine axe;
> By the divine mace;
> By the divine *dtn*-weapon . . .[47]

Since the ritual texts operated within a context where the presuppositions of this material were simply taken for granted, we should not expect any explanation, and the absence of the term *kubadu* (see n. 40) from the context is not crucial one way or another in interpreting it. We shall see in a mythological context that it was given a far clearer expression, though again without formal explanation.

In view of the storm-god being the focus of the ritual in Emar, and Adad (i.e. the local storm-god) being the source of the oracle and its mythic allusion in Mari, it is perhaps significant that one of Baal's epithets at Ugarit is *ly qrdm* in a number of passages. This may be construed in two ways, as 'Mightiest of Heroes' or as 'Mighty One of the Axe'. I am increasingly inclined to the latter interpretation in view of the comparative evidence noted here. The Mari text also indicates that the significance of the myth presupposed a kind of identification of the king with the god: as the god was victorious in the great act of bringing order to the world by victory over the forces of chaos, so would the king continue to do in his historical military campaigns.

A final aspect of royal ideology, so far as the king was concerned, which is of some interest concerns the nature of royal burials. The ritual material will be noted below. Here I want to draw attention to some comparative evidence, where the Ugaritic and biblical materials provide reciprocal elucidation. This is a text dealing with royal mortuary rites performed in the month of Gannu (*yrh gn*). The term *gn* means 'garden'. A short section deals with the eighth day:

> (To be offered) on the eighth (day of the month) Gannu: [a lu]ng and fourteen ewes, and seven heifers, and an entire fish stew in the Garden. And a response is given in the Garden.[48] Then the king shall be desacralized.[49]

The 'garden' was evidently a part of the palace complex of buildings and lands in the western zone of the city, and constituted the royal cemetery. The recipients of the sacrifices listed here were the chthonian gods of the rest of the text, among whose number were the *inš ilm*, the 'divine people', that is, the deceased kings. These were now among the underworld gods, buried in the cemetery, and themselves recipients of sacrifices and available for consultation through necromantic rites. The sacrifices appear to have been part of a process of enquiry, to judge from the phrase 'and a response is given', which suggests some divine sign that the offerings are acceptable, or perhaps a response to some question put to the gods, or more likely the *inš ilm* as ancestors.

In the pantheon list discussed above, set seven, it will be recalled, begins with *mlkm*, 'Kings'. This is another collective term for deceased kings who are now divine.[50] The expression 'Garden' as the burial place of the kings of Ugarit suggests two intriguing connections. First, within Ugaritian tradition there is a passage in the Baal myth where the god, now dead, and presumably ready to be buried, is sought in a remote place by Anat's messengers. They tell her that

> We travelled to [the ends of the earth],
>   to the edge of the abyss;
> we came to 'Paradise' the land of pasture,
>   to 'Delight', the steppe by the shore of death.
> We came upon Baal fallen to the earth[51]

and she subsequently goes to fetch his body for burial. The place described is at the end of the world, a place of intersection of the world above and the world below.[52] Second, the kings of Judah were routinely buried 'in the king's garden' (*gan hammelek*), where the expression denotes a specific area within the palace complex, and may allude not to living kings, but to dead ones, perhaps seen collectively as 'Melech' (subsequently often distorted to 'Molech'). Not only is this place to be identified in tradition with the Garden of Eden of Genesis 2–3, where post-biblical tradition has the ante-diluvian patriarchs buried, but Jesus is buried there in the Johannine tradition. This appears to be cognate with Ugaritian tradition.

The royal ideology also concerned the person of the queen. No queen of Ugarit is so designated, but the dowager queen of Amurru, whose daughter, the queen of Ugarit, was the subject of vicious divorce proceedings, was consistently referred to in the correspondence as *rabitu*. We have seen this as an epithet, 'Great Lady', used of the sun-goddesses Athirat and Shapsh. It appears that the queen was seen as mystically identified with the sun-goddess in giving birth to the king. We have noted (see further below) that *The Gracious Gods* text gives the mythic account of the birth of the royal gods Shahar and Shalem to El and Shapsh. This text constitutes a 'sacred marriage' tradition in the sense that it appears to give a theological version of the actual marriage and reproduction of the royal couple. A further allusion to a sacred marriage, this time apparently between the king and the goddess Pidray (daughter-wife of Baal in theological terms), may be present in the opening lines of the following text:

> On the nineteenth day the bed of Pidray is made ready for the installation of the king.[53]

This appears to link the king ideologically with Baal, a feature already noted in this discussion. This text has been interpreted as part of the enthronement rites for a new king, but this remains uncertain.

Myths and other 'ideological' literature

We have noted a number of mythological texts, and compositions of similar kind, in discussing the deities. The material thus far discovered can represent only a fraction of the mythic traditions of an ancient community, and presumably many of the gods listed above who have no apparent myths lack them only because of the hazards of survival or non-survival of records. The overwhelming bulk of religious tradition from the following millennium in the Levant is entirely absent, owing at least in part to the abandonment of clay tablets written in cuneiform in favour of parchment, papyrus and other less durable media for writing. All that remain are a few monuments in stone, and allusions in classical authors.

Baal myths

Seven tablets[54] appear to preserve a string of narratives concerning the god Baal, which for all the gaps (about 50 per cent) allow a tentative sequence as follows. El, as lord of the pantheon, enthrones Yam as king among the gods. Baal is bound and placed under his throne. Kothar hands him weapons, with which Baal kills Yam, and takes his place. Baal then goes to Anat and the two set about obtaining El's permission to build Baal a palace.[55] When this is finally achieved, Baal holds a great inaugural feast. He omits to invite Mot, who then invites Baal to dine with him (i.e. to be his meal!), and Baal goes down into the underworld. Athtar in turn is enthroned in Baal's stead, coming down to earth to rule. A restored Baal then fights Mot, and the inconclusive struggle is brought to an end in favour of Baal by Shapsh, the narrative concluding with a hymn in her honour.

The meanings of this mythic series have been much debated. By and large interpretations fall into two types, the 'fertility cult' or 'seasonal' interpretation, and all the others, which vary between historical accounts to various forms of political theology. The former approach was immediately offered by the first interpreters, in accordance with the climate in early twentieth-century scholarship, culminating in the systematic treatment of de Moor,[56] in which the author attempted to correlate the mythic episodes with ritual practice throughout the 'agroclimatic year'. The other approaches see the cult of Baal and the aetiology of his temple-foundation as the chief theme. I have proposed that one of the reasons for Ilimilku's editing of this traditional material was to offer a legitimization of Niqmaddu III, or perhaps to celebrate his marriage to a Hittite princess.

More fundamentally, the conflict myth of Baal versus Yam falls into an ancient pattern, probably of Amorite origin if not even older, attested over a millennium previously in Eshnunna (near Babylon), with Babylonian, Assyrian, Marian, Hittite, Ugaritic and biblical versions, in addition to Greek, Iranian and Indian offshoots. All these versions sanctify the conduct of war as the re-enactment of the primordial divine conflict. The recently discovered text from Mari cited above involves a ritual in which the weapons given to the king are explicitly identified as those used for divine victory in the myth. Thus one of the implications of other allusions to and tellings of the myth, its appropriation by various monarchies, and its ritual dimension, is evidently the legitimization of military activity.

Theogony myths

Two texts from Ugarit, on the surface very different, contain versions of a theogonic tradition, in which El fathers twin sons on his wife, who is geminated for the occasion. In one, *The Devourers*, which harnesses the myth to a redemptive ritual and in which the offspring are devouring monsters, El's wife-wives, who are also his daughters, are called respectively 'Talish handmaid of Yarih' (thus hinting at El's lunar origins) and 'Dimgay handmaid of Athirat'. In the other, *The Gracious Gods*, in which the offspring are Shahar and Shalem, the morning and evening stars, it is Shapsh, the sun-goddess, geminated into the forms of Athirat and Rahmay, who not only are El's daughters, now his wives, but who also address him as 'mother', thus attesting his androgynous nature. As a number of scholars have argued, these myths have close biblical analogues, and their explicitly royal nature is apparent, as myths of the divine conception of the king.[57] This is not immediately apparent from the Ugaritic texts, but the latter is an interesting combination of mythical and ritual elements, which is located in the palace, in the presence of the king and queen, and thus fairly transparently points to royal births as bringing hope and salvation to the nation.

Dealing with sun, moon and stars, it is also the subject of recent enquiry into astral aspects of Ugaritian religion. While there is nothing like the amount of information available from Mesopotamia, we read in various texts that the gods of Ugarit were 'stars', and we have seen the significance of the sun and moon. Here is an important dimension awaiting further research.

Keret

The two extended stories in verse from Ugarit (in addition to the Baal myths) associated with the poet Ilimilku are intrinsically interesting as ancient literature, but also betray strong ideological elements, as we might expect with an author working in the service of a king. The *Keret* story shows evidence of a reworked folktale, in which a king who has lost a wife and seven children (or according to others, seven wives) is instructed by El (the patron of kings, as noted above) to wage war on Pabil, king of Udum, demanding his daughter Hurriy in marriage. She will be blessed, and will bear fourteen children to Keret, and even the youngest will be equally blessed as the first-born. All goes according to plan, except that on the way to Udum, Keret makes a vow to Athirat goddess of Tyre, which he then fails to fulfil. The angry goddess makes him ill. As he lies dying, El fails to persuade other gods of the council to heal the king, and finally himself creates a healing goddess who restores Keret. Meanwhile, however, the king's impetuous son bursts in and demands that his father, unable to fulfil the duties of a king, abdicate in his favour. Keret curses him. Since this curse presumably (just as a blessing would) redounds down to the youngest daughter, Keret is back where he began. The wheel of fortune has turned full circle.

From a religious perspective the story is full of interest. It illustrates a number of important theological points. It shows the close relationship (of father and son, noted above) between El and the king. It shows the unquestioning obedience required of one under divine instruction. No room here for reflection, or the weighing of pros and cons! When Keret has entered into the second relationship, as a votary of Athirat (already a sin, since it interrupts his duty to El), it shows the terrible danger of treating such a serious undertaking lightly. In contrast to the practical benefits of a blessing in ancient thought, it shows the terrible power of a curse. Finally, it illustrates the intriguing theological tension in a pantheon, when different divine powers work against each other.

Aqhat

While the story line of *Aqhat* is on the surface entirely different, it explores some of the same issues as *Keret*. Danel is a king without a son. With a tablet probably lost before the surviving opening of the narrative, we can only speculate on whether any previous children had died. He spends a week in ritual activity in a shrine, and at the end of it we see the gods deliberating in council. Baal asks El to see to Danel's problem, granting him a son who will perform all the appropriate ritual and social duties a son performs for his father. Aqhat is born, and Kothar appears with a composite bow fit for a hero. The goddess Anat no sooner sets eyes on the bow than she determines to have it. Her powers of persuasion do not work with the rather gauche young Aqhat. Even an offer of eternal life merely draws a sarcastic response. At this point she goes to El and demands vengeance. El gives her a free hand. With a mercenary assistant Yatipan, she plots Aqhat's death. They will both hover among a flock of falcons over Aqhat, and Yatipan will swoop down and kill Aqhat with a blow. Thus it happens, and Anat immediately mingles a savage revenge on Aqhat's corpse with a maudlin complaint that she did not even get the bow! Aqhat's remains are devoured by the mother-falcon. Eventually the bleak news is brought to Danel, who retrieves his son's remains and buries them, and goes into mourning for seven years. His daughter Pughat, more practically, seeks vengeance, and the last tablet unfortunately breaks off with her, disguised perhaps as Anat, plying an already somewhat befuddled Yatipan with strong drink . . .

What theological points does this narrative offer? The list of filial duties is recognized as offering an important insight into the routine performance of private religion. Danel is to be blessed

> so that he may beget a son in his house,
>> a scion in the midst of his palace.
> He shall set up the stela of his ancestral god,
>> in the sanctuary the cippus of his kinsman;
> into the earth sending forth his dying breath,
>> into the dust protecting his progress;
> he shall shut the mouths of his slanderers,
>> he shall drive away those who are ill-disposed towards him.
> Taking his hand when he is drunk,
>> supporting him when sated with wine;
> he shall serve up his share in the house of Baal,
>> and his portion in the house of El;
> he shall plaster his roof on a muddy day,
>> he shall wash his clothes on a filthy day.[58]

Here we see the paramount importance of a first-born son in the performance of his father's funeral obsequies. But his duties include a general protection of his father's honour and person, practical support in delicate moments, participation in family ritual duties, and basic house repairs and domestic chores. The text has all the hallmarks of a traditional summary of the demands of filial piety.

Perhaps the most contentious issue in *Aqhat* is the role of Anat and the theological assessment of her nature. She has been described as a spoilt adolescent and as illustrating the moral bankruptcy of a debased religion. Charges of immorality have also been levelled against El and other members of the pantheon (which de Moor has called 'the pantheon of disillusion') on account of this apparent laissez-faire theology. Such judgements miss the point, as noted above, failing to recognize the symbolic nature of the gods, and their role in representing issues of human freedom and responsibility. Polytheism works on a pragmatic basis, balancing human aspirations and ideals against the harsh realities of life where life-expectancy was probably around thirty, and from childbirth on one survived, or failed to survive, drought and famine, disease and poverty, tyranny and war, in equal measure, though these curses of human life were also balanced by blessings of peace and plenty, rich agriculture and productive family life. Theology's task, then as now, was to offer a rationale to this pitiless assault and its puzzling contrast with the happier aspects of life, and to balance these external forces with human aspirations and values. Polytheism's answer was to deify every aspect of human experience.

Anat, the nubile maiden who is a quite unpredictable mixture of ruthlessness and tenderness, lust and hate, embodied to a powerful degree the exigencies of war, its strange combination of the love of comrades and the savagery of the battlefield. No wishful thinking here! But each deity contributed to an overall divine economy: from the full perspective of the pantheon Anat and the horrors she represented were tempered with the lust for life of her brother Baal, lord of Ugarit, and the benign oversight of father El, who sat immovably at the centre of all things.

Shorter compositions

Some shorter compositions have already been noted above. Others of interest and the subject of detailed study are the following.

Three tablets known as the '*Rpum* texts'[59] narrate the coming of the *rpum* on horse-drawn chariots to a feast. We have noted the connection of the *rpum* with deified kings, and the existence of a patron or collective figure called Rapiu (*rpu*). The present texts are perhaps mythic or even hymnic fragments accompanying royal funeral or *kispum*-rites.

The poem of *Nikkal* tells the myth of the courtship and marriage of Nikkal (a Hurrian derivative of the Sumerian goddess NIN.GAL) and Yarih, though his name probably translates Kušuh, the Hurrian moon-god. After the ceremonies, the tablet concludes with a hymn to the Kotharat. The tablet may have constituted part of the liturgy for a wedding or for childbed rites.

There is a fragment describing a goddess fighting a dragon (the sea) and 'binding it in the heights of the Lebanon'. This echoes an episode in the Baal myth in which Anat claims to have killed various monsters, as well as the Egyptian myth of Astarte and the Sea, but the present goddess is not identified. This may perhaps be a myth of the origin of the constellation Draco.

We have a hymn to Baal, describing him reclining on his mountain. It is an interesting amalgam of transcendent and immanent deity, the mountain half-compared with, almost half-identified with the god:

> His head is magnificent,
>> His brow is dew-drenched.
>> his feet are eloquent in (his) wrath.
> [His] horn is [exal]ted;
>> his head is in the snows in heaven,
>> [with] the god there is abounding water.
> His mouth is like two clouds [   ],
>> [his lips] like wine from jars,
>> his heart [   ] ...[60]

Evidence of this kind is frequently cited as indicating Baal's role as a fertility-god. He certainly is in control of environmental and climatic conditions, but the imagery here serves rather as a metaphor for divine majesty and transcendence. The mountain on which the deity reclines is his throne, the omphalos, Mount Saphon.

The obverse of one tablet is a typical ritual text, giving part of a cultic calendar involving the king's duties. On the reverse is a hymn to Baal as protector of the city in time of war. It is in the typical form of a vow, stating what is required of the deity in the form of a condition, followed by what is offered in response:

> If you will drive the strong one from our gate,
>> the warrior from our walls,
> a bull, O Baal, we shall dedicate,
>> a vow, Baal, we shall fulfil:
> a male animal, Baal, we shall dedicate,
>> a propitiation we shall fulfil,
>> a feast, Baal, we shall prepare.
> We shall go up to the sanctuary of Baal,
>> we shall walk in the paths of the temple of Baal.[61]

The word translated here as 'a male animal' (reading *dkr) is damaged, and has alternatively, but less plausibly, been read as *bkr, 'first-born', which would be the only clear evidence so far for human sacrifice in Ugaritian religion.[62] One of the ivory bed-panels suggests the ritual killing of captured kings (see Fig. 3.4), while KTU 1.3 ii 5–30, quoted in part above, contains a double battle scene in which

Anat slaughters her victims. The second episode has been interpreted as the ritual aftermath of war. But whether these reflect actual religious practice or mythological figures remains uncertain. Where human sacrifice is clearly attested (as in Israel and Moab), it is a last resort in times of personal or national crisis. More commonly, as in the translation above, 'votive gifts' in response to a divine favour are usually forms of animal sacrifice, or the dedication of stelae, statues, precious metals or, at Ugarit, ships' anchors, appropriate to a maritime culture.

Ritual

A considerable variety of ritual texts has been discovered, mostly in Ugaritic, with a few in Hurrian. Del Olmo's study[63] provides a typology for the texts. He distinguishes between records, prescriptive rituals and recited rituals. The distinction is important in terms of understanding the amount of information that is to be gleaned from texts that are often succinct to the point of obscurity. The ritual texts merely list victims and other offerings, giving details of time and place. No theory of sacrifice may be discerned, and the actual richness of the cult, with hymns, the playing of instruments and ritual dancing must be left to the imagination. A pale echo may be discerned in the following passage, which addresses Rapiu,

> Whom men hymn and honour with music
>> On the lyre and the flute,
> On drum and cymbals,
>> With castanets of ivory,
> Among the goodly companions of Kothar.[64]

No calendar or list of months has survived from Ugarit. But the month names are known, and their order apart from two, and it is evident from surviving texts that it was normal to have monthly ritual programmes. These survive in the following instances: First-of-the-wine Hiyyaru and 'Garden'. The latter two months appear to have placed considerable emphasis on rituals involving the royal dead.

Religion and economic life

This is an area in which research has barely begun, and which will repay further study. The temple cults of ancient cities must have had a considerable economic impact, which is best documented in Egypt, with extensive accounts of taxation levied on the temples' behalf and extensive storage and warehouse facilities. With their fairly substantial personnel, their evident involvement in government, and consequent land-holdings and agricultural activities, the priesthood obviously had a vested interest in a system in which commodities (livestock, cereals, oil, wine, precious metals, woven products and so forth) were circulated through the economy by means of the cultic process.

The number of animals offered in a single day would vary with the importance of the ritual context. But days of significance, generally quarter-days, with an emphasis on new and full moons, and the periodic festivals, no doubt related to the mythic traditions of individual deities (though no specific information on this count is so far available), would undoubtedly have larger numbers of victims.

The following figures are taken from a selection of tablets:

(1) The Day of Atonement (KTU 1.40). The text is seriously damaged, though its original form can be largely reconstructed, because of its repetitive character. It identifies only six victims, two bulls, two rams and two donkeys. But these are the most significant, and form a series of climaxes to each successive stage. We may suppose a number of preparatory offerings before the final stages.

(2) The rituals of the month of First-of-the-wine, on day 14: fourteen rams, thirteen ewes, one lamb; one bull, twelve heifers; eight birds (unspecified), one pigeon (but how many times?); in addition, seven unidentified items (damaged text: perhaps further animals), a jar, thirty chalices and cups (or their contents?), a libation, fourteen pitchers of wine, myrrh oil, spiced oil (probably olive oil), honey and flour.

(3) Unspecified palace rituals. Text KTU 1.43 is substantially damaged, but two sections allow a fairly continuous reading:

> When Athtart-of-the-Window enters the pit in the royal palace, pour a libation into the pit of the chapel of the star-gods.
>
> Offerings: a robe and a tunic, a *ušpġ*-garment; gold, three (shekels according to the) commercial (weight); a ram, an ox and three sheep as communion-sacrifices, seven times to the gods, (and) seven times to Kothar.
>
> Subsequently the two Gathru-gods come into the royal chapel. A shekel of gold to Shapsh and Yarih; to Gathru a shekel of refined silver; a muzzle and a lun[g] to Anat; a shekel of gold to Shap[sh and Ya]rih; to Gathru two [shekels of] refined [silver]; a muzzle and a lung [to Anat]; [   ] temple, an ox and a ram.

If we quantify the items mentioned here, they amount to a libation, a robe, a tunic, an *ušpġ*-garment; five shekels of gold, three shekels of silver; fourteen bulls, fourteen rams, forty-two sheep (ewes); two muzzles and two lungs (or 'pair of lungs', presumably from one of the victims listed).

(4) The royal funerary cult in the month Hiyyaru. There is some damage to one end, and so important dating aspects may be missing. But taking the requirements of day 18, on the reverse, as continuous with the text of the obverse, for the sake of argument, we have the following results: unspecified amounts of gold and silver; fifteen rams, forty-one ewes; eleven bulls; three birds and one lung (or pair). The origins of some victims, or their prior preparation ('one white ewe, perfumed', obv. 1.2) are mentioned.

Since such texts are often damaged, and those found represent only a fraction of any complete record, it is not possible to build up an absolute figure for consumption, so these are merely random indications of the kind of turnover involved. In any case, each shrine would have its own regular cultic programme, in addition to important and periodic state rituals. But the principles involved are apparent, and we may in any case add the votive stelae, the votive anchors (appropriate to a maritime city), temple timberwork and fabrics, general artistic input, and masonry, construction and repair work, to envisage a substantial body of staff directly or indirectly involved in running an urban temple complex.

At times specific herds are mentioned as the source of individual victims. Ili-milku, the scribe of the literary texts, is identified at the end of the Baal cycle of myths as 'diviner, chief of the priests, chief of the temple herdsmen'.[65] This reference not only indicates the variety of responsibilities one official might have – and Ilimilku was also court poet and theologian, to judge from his compositions – but shows that ritual and managerial roles might be combined, and that temples had a direct involvement in the provision of their livestock requirements.

No information is forthcoming from Ugarit, but the common practice of buying meat in urban markets which had come from temple slaughterhouses, which gave rise to problems for religious susceptibilities among Jews and Christians, suggests that sacrifice could also be viewed as part of the production system for food for the population. This was certainly a likely system, as otherwise the figures cited above could be viewed as a flagrant waste of resources. It is likely that part of the rationale of sacrifice was an incorporation of the gods into the human food-supply system (offering them commensality), so that their continued acceptance of offerings was construed as an endorsement of the 'ritual-industrial complex'.

Again, there is no evidence for financial management from Ugarit, but biblical passages such as 1 Kings 14:25–26, 15:16–19, 2 Kings 12:18–19, 14:8–14 etc. indicate that the throughput of gold and silver bullion effectively made of temples the banks of the ancient world. Deposits were laid in trust with the gods in the form of votive offerings and regular ritualized contributions to the treasury, as in the texts cited above, to be drawn on in time of economic need. The use of such resources by enemy kings was an early form of bank-robbery! More seriously, the taking of booty in turn freed up such resources by bringing them back into circulation. This form of analysis is not intended to be reductionistic: it is important to recognize just how pervasive religion was in the ancient world, so that many categories of social structure and function now treated as economic in nature formed part of the religious praxis of antiquity.

Omens and oracles

An important aspect of religion is the way in which it deals with the problem of the human experience of time. As a species we are probably uniquely aware of time, its flow, the notions of 'past' and 'future', and our inevitable mortality. An interesting starting point for this discussion is the issue of orientation. In all cultures we may speak of a 'canonical orientation', meaning the position adopted in relation to the cardinal points. In all Semitic cultures, as in many others, the primary orientation was, as the term 'orientation' suggests, towards the east. The vocabulary used for the cardinal points (*qdm*, 'east', *aḥr*, 'west', *smal*, 'north', *ymn*, 'south' in Ugaritic) also served to denote the flow of time (*qdm*, 'past', *aḥr*, 'future') and the moral dimension associated with handedness (*smal*, 'left hand', and ideas of moral doubt and the 'sinister', *ymn*, 'right hand' and ideas of the auspicious and the good).[66] What this evidence indicates is that people 'looked' into the past, with the future an unknown quantity behind them. The past provided the paradigms for religious and social behaviour: myth and tradition alike were 'given', and one observed and honoured patterns established in tradition, by the gods and the ancestors.

At the same time, the future remained a concern. If the gods and the ancestors had provided guidance for the present, they must have also provided for future contingencies. This logic invited the scrutiny of ritual contexts to see what clues had been provided. The most elaborate form was in the examination of sacrificial material. The internal organs (omenta) of animals provided the omens of the future. Ugaritian practice here was evidently in the Mesopotamian tradition.

A number of clay model livers have been found at Ugarit, together with one instance of a lung. The priests butchering sacrificial victims would note odd features, inflamed lobes, prominent blood-vessels, and so forth, on the surface of the organ. The actual coincident occasion of royal deaths, battles, storms, famines, and other such crises, were linked in their minds with these features, and a literature grew up in which such 'signs' were taken as divine warnings of future events. What sounds at first an entirely irrational procedure was in fact entirely rational, since the warnings could be used for evasive action. The crucial thing, in terms of religious psychology, was that it gave a sense of control over events, rather than being merely at the mercy of events.

The contexts of the interpretations of these model organs remain opaque. Inscriptions 8–10 on the model lung involve goats, appear to belong together, and read as follows:

[   ] a woman they shall take a goat [   ].

If the city is captured then death (*mt*: or 'the man' i.e. the enemy king) will attack the population.

(In) the temple a citizen shall take a goat and (the future) will be seen from afar.

These may be early examples of the substitutionary atonement ritual attested in Israel in Leviticus 16 (the Day of Atonement scapegoat ritual). A similar early version has been found at Ebla, in central Syria, and Hittite practice is analogous. If the connections are established, the wide incidence of the ritual points to considerable antiquity behind the theory. The present example suggests a general strategy that might be employed to deal with any unknown future contingency.

Birth deformities in animals or children were also seen as signs for the future. Two tablets deal with animals, while another, in a fragmentary state, covers human malformations. Natural portents, such as lunar, stellar and solar eclipses and the like, the perceived influence of the evil eye and without doubt many other natural occurrences, to judge from Mesopotamian parallels,[67] were all treated with extreme circumspection.

Personal religion

Since Ugarit was a royal city, and most of its archives come from palaces, temples or the houses of priestly or administrative people, we have little direct insight into personal piety, and the everyday religious practice of ordinary people. We catch glimpses, as in the list of filial duties in *Aqhat*, and the evidently representative nature of some texts, where perhaps a congregation joined in the singing of hymns or was present at some of the main rites such as the Day of Atonement. A number of kinds of material provide further information of a minimal kind. Thus personal names, as usually in the ancient world, were commonly of theophoric construction, that is, containing a divine name attached to a verbal or epithetal element. Thus *abršp* (Abi-Rašpu) means 'Reshef is my father', while *b lytn* (Ba alu-yatana) means 'Baal has given (me/him/her)'. While these would tend to run in families, they originated in personal experiences (particularly childbirth) and tend to reflect instinctive reactions to a safe birth. Some private correspondence survives, and though most of this is between officials, or to or from members of the royal family, it still betrays common religious clichés. A common formula is *yšlm lkm ilm tġrm tšlmkm*, or some variation: 'may it be well with you; the gods give you good health'. A similar expression occurs typically in a letter written in Akkadian by Abušgama to the Intendant of Amurru:

> Greetings to you! May the gods of Amurru, the gods of
> Ugarit and the gods of the king your lord keep you well!

Various artefacts of a religious kind survive, from large stelae portraying deities, probably votive gifts to temples, to small amulet-plaques representing goddesses, perhaps worn as charms round the neck, and cylinder seals, found in their thousands throughout the ancient Near East, which frequently illustrate some mythical or ritual scene, and were worn as amulets as well as marks of identity.

Sickness and health

A number of texts from Ugarit deal with medical conditions. We have noted text KTU 1.114 (El in his *marziḫu*) as a cure for hangover, and the *Nikkal* text as relating to weddings, or childbirth with its attendant dangers. One tablet contains a spell for curing the effects of snake-bite, in which eleven different deities are invoked in vain, a twelfth, Horon, an underworld god, being able to effect a cure by means of the application of tamarisk, no doubt as the paradigm of what healers did to the accompanying recitation of the text. There are two further snake-bite texts, indicating that here was a common contingency dealt with by ritual-medical means. Incantations used for exorcism have also been found.

One treats a possessed adolescent, or, in the view of some, a case of impotence. Another appears to deal with a paediatric complaint.

Death, funerals and kispum (= pagru?) rites

We have already touched on aspects of this in discussing royal ideology above. Evidence for belief and practice concerning death in other parts of Ugaritian society is found in the numerous family vaults located under the floors of most houses, as well as those in the palaces, at Ugarit, Mahadu and Ras Ibn Hani. Of corbelled construction with dressed stones, the burial chamber sometimes in the form of a simple oblong chamber but sometimes with secondary chambers, was reached by a stair descending from ground-floor level. A certain amount of funerary deposits, pots, jewellery and so forth, were found, though these gave no indication of beliefs among ordinary people. The episode in the *Aqhat* story during which Anat negotiates for the bow is instructive. Here is her final offer and the hero's response:

> 'Ask for life, O hero Aqhat:
>> ask for life and I shall give (it) you,
>> immortality and I shall bestow (it) on you:
> I shall make you number (your) years with Baal:
>> with the son of El you shall number months.
> "Like Baal he shall live indeed!
>> Alive, he shall be feasted,
> he shall be feasted and given to drink.
>> The minstrel shall intone and sing concerning him".'
> [And she] said to him:
>> 'Thus shall I make Aqhat the hero live!'
> But Aqhat the hero replied:
> 'Do not deceive me, O Virgin,
>> for to a hero your deceit is rubbish!
> Man, (at his) end, what will he receive?
>> What will he receive, a man (as his destiny)?
> Silver will be poured on his head,
>> gold on top of his skull,
> [and] the death of all I shall die,
>> and I shall surely die.'

The contrast with the *Gilgamesh* epic is interesting. There it is the hero who aspires to immortality, while the goddess Siduri counsels acceptance of a more limited destiny. Here it is the goddess who offers a life like that of a god, while Aqhat rejects this as preposterous. Tradition teaches him something altogether more down to earth! It is perhaps significant that Ilimilku can *conceptualize* 'eternal life': here is the germ of a new dimension of human experience. But Aqhat, though a prince who might look forward in due course to the divine status of a former king, and membership of the *mlkm* and *inš ilm*, if not the *rpum*, accepts only a minimalist interpretation of human destiny. The allusion to silver and gold, if this is the meaning of an obscure crux, is probably to death masks of the early Greek pattern. It is possible that the text reflects a new development in Ugaritian beliefs, since Baal is significantly used as the object of comparison. Where his mortality (and subsequent restoration to life) is used for a comparison in the *Keret* story, it is with a view to validating royal ideology, as noted above. So the same form of argument may be in evidence here. As this text suggests, there appears to have been a wide incidence of speculation throughout the ancient world about various possibilities of a post-mortem existence.

As to ritual practice with regard to funerals, we have several pieces of evidence, beginning with the funeral text cited above, all of a royal nature. This is the liturgy for the funeral of Niqmaddu III, penultimate king of Ugarit. A number of dead kings, including the (legendary?) *rpum* (see above) are summoned to attend, and are presumably understood to gather in the tomb-entrance, where they will form a ghostly guard of honour to the dead king as he is lowered into his vault, and thus 'goes down into the underworld'. The goddess Shapsh is invoked, apparently in her underworld role of guide of the dead, and then Niqmaddu himself is directed to go down to his ancestors. Seven offerings are made on his behalf, and a blessing is pronounced on his successor King Ammurapi and on the city. The text appears to be the actual liturgy, but may be merely an outline, other elements, such as *kispum*-rites for the dead kings, being understood to form the first part of the proceedings. It is impossible on present evidence to determine how far this may represent more general conceptions about the destiny of commoners. Other texts however, are, associated with aspects of communication with the underworld, and with communication with the dead (as in the *kispum*-rites noted above). Thus one text invokes Hurrian deities at a royal funeral, while others also relate to royal funerals, and the *Rpum* texts undoubtedly constitute some mythic or even hymnic aspect of the *kispum*-rites (above). There was thus a considerable emphasis on the continuing importance of kings after their death, as they remained potent for the continued welfare of the living. Whether the elaborate domestic arrangements for the interment of the dead within the home are to be construed as pointing to similar family cults, possibly centring on the collective figure 'the god of the ancestor', the first member of the 'canonical' pantheon list, remains unknown, and we have already noted ambiguities concerning beliefs.

We also have a number of passages which describe mourning. Two mythological passages narrate the reaction of El and Anat respectively on hearing the news of Baal's death. The first reads as follows:

> Then the wise, the perceptive god,
>> went down from his throne:
>> he sat on his footstool.
>> And from his footstool
>> he sat on the ground.
> He poured the ashes of affliction on his head,
>> the dust of grovelling on his skull.
> For clothing he put on a loin-cloth.
> His skin with a stone he scored,
>> his side-locks with a razor,
> he gashed cheeks and chin.
>> He ploughed his collar-bones,
> he turned over like a garden his chest,
>> like a valley he ploughed his breast,
> He lifted up his voice and cried:
> 'Baal is dead!
>> What has become of the Powerful One?
> The Son of Dagan!
>> What has become of Tempest?
> After Baal I shall go down into the underworld.'[68]

It is striking to find this human response attributed to the head of the pantheon. What is here presented as a potential cosmic dissolution perfectly reflects the emotional despair felt by mourners, but at the same time the acceptance as significant for the mourner of the fate of the dead. It also provides a paradigm for the human ritual response to death. A ritual self-abasement is followed by a self-burial rite, the putting on of a mourning garment (a symbolic shroud?), with self-laceration and the cutting of the hair. The fact that such practices were forbidden in biblical law (e.g. Leviticus 19:27–28) is an indication of their pervasive use.

Elaborate mourning for Keret is envisaged in the *Keret* narrative, probably, even allowing for some literary hyperbole, reflecting actual practice:

> Like dogs shall we howl at your tomb,
>   like whelps at the entrance to your burial chamber?
> Yet father, how can you possibly die,
>   or will your burial chamber be given over to howling
>   on the part of women, O my wretched father?[69]

Similarly, wailing women and self-lacerating men spend seven years mourning Aqhat. Mythic account and ritual practice are designed intuitively to give form as well as expression to grief, thus effecting the acceptance and healing process.

Iconography

Seals

Mention has been made of cylinder seals, small amulets, stelae and so forth. The former categories, while obviously produced in workshops according to accepted stylistic and iconographic canons, represent more popular forms, as being cheaper to produce. They are very diverse in type. The seals cover a huge range of designs, of many variations on traditional themes, so that they borrow many foreign forms, just as distinctive Syrian forms themselves become popular elsewhere. The latter group are more significant, and a fine example is the motif of the 'weather-god on two mountains', showing an armed deity, accompanied by various animal forms, striding along with each foot on an adjacent mountain peak. Examples of this have been found from Egypt to Anatolia from the eighteenth century onwards. The mountains in question are probably to be identifed as the twin peaks of Jebel el Aqra (Mount Saphon, known in Latin as Cassius and Anti-Cassius).

Stelae

The most imposing of these is undoubtedly the so-called 'Baal au foudre' stela, discovered in 1932 (Fig. 3.1). The upper pair of wavy lines has been interpreted as representing the body of the serpentine Yam, on whom the victorious Baal strides in triumph. This is analogous to the two mountains of the cylinder seals, since the mountain is undoubtedly identified with the cadaver of the sea-god.

Fig. 3.1. The 'Baal au Foudre' stela from Ugarit.

The style illustrates the importance of Egyptian influence in Syrian art of the Middle and Late Bronze Age: wearing the Egyptian kilt, the god strides forward, wielding a fenestrated axe in his right hand, and a cedar trunk which ends as a spear in the left. The diminutive figure in front of the god is the king, enrobed in a ritual garment as often portrayed in iconography, and probably described in the opening lines of *Aqhat*.

Figurines

Small figurines in clay or bronze have been found in a number of Levantine sites, conforming to widely attested patterns. From Ugarit come a number of small gold amulets in the form of plaques up to about 10 cm in length, showing a female figure, with pronounced pubic triangle. These are usually supposed to relate to the 'fertility cult', and may have symbolized nubility and fecundity for young women, or were invoked to gain the maternal, protective attention of the goddess. Bronze figures of deities may have been in use as devotional images in domestic contexts. More substantial, though still surprisingly small, are cult images. A gilded bronze of a bearded male figure wearing the Egyptian *Atef*-crown is usually identified as El. The same iconography occurs on a small stela showing El enthroned and blessing the king beneath the winged disk of the sun-goddess, while in the building immediately north of the 'rhyton temple' was found a small stone figure of El on a throne (Fig. 3.2). This was probably the cult image, housed in the shrine. Sockets allowed the addition of arms, perhaps held in gestures of power or benevolence, or holding symbols (thus the stela just noted has El holding up one hand in blessing, while the other holds the ritual cup of blessing). An Atef-crown, derived from Egyptian art where it was worn by Osiris, was probably placed on it during the cult.

Ivories

A number of items in ivory have been found in Ugarit. The most significant are undoubtedly the series of panels forming a bed-head, perhaps belonging to the king, or even used for the sacred marriage. Twelve panels were surrounded by a frieze of plants and moving animals. The panels themselves seem to be devoted primarily to royal ideological motifs. Royal figures are shown in various hunting, military or cultic contexts. The motif of the dual nature of the king is represented by a winged and robed goddess with cow's horns and sun-disc (i.e. Shapsh), suckling two boys (Fig. 3.3). They stand fully clothed on either side, her arms protectively round their shoulders. A variation on the Egyptian smiting motif (Fig. 3.4) shows the king clutching a kneeling enemy and thrusting his eyes out with a sword.

Ugarit and its legacy in the external world

As we noted at the beginning, aspects of religion often outlast a culture, living on among émigrés or through general cultural influence. The continuing influence

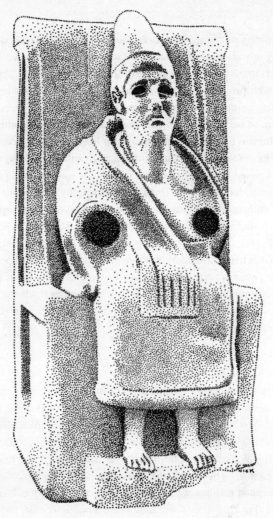

Fig. 3.2. Stone statuette of El from Ugarit.

of Ugarit would certainly inform any discussion of Phoenician religion, that is the religion of the Levant in the first millennium BCE, though this is so poorly documented by direct sources throughout its history that Ugarit remains the primary source, though belonging strictly to its prehistory. In addition, its impact may be discerned in two areas in particular, Greece and Israel.

Fig. 3.3. Suckling goddess from the ivory bed-head from Ugarit.

Greece

We have noted sporadic connections between Ugaritian thought and similar ideas in Greece. It is increasingly recognized that Greek religious thought and practice (and in particular its mythology) owes a profound debt to the ancient Near East at large. This is scarcely surprising, quite apart from early trading and

Fig. 3.4. Smiting panel from the ivory bed-head from Ugarit.

diplomatic links, since Ionian Greek settlements were always directly open to influences from the Anatolian hinterland, and Hittite culture and its inheritors filtered a wide range of Near Eastern ideas. It is probably fair to say that when their prehistories are examined there are few Greek deities who can be described as exclusively Greek, or even exclusively Indo-European. Some oriental dimension or quality is usually to be discerned. Generally studies have noted links over the wider ancient Near Eastern area, but Ugarit played its part in the mediation of ideas. We have noted a possible prototype of Apollo in the plague-god Reshef, and of Perseus and Andromeda in Baal's fight with Yam (see note 19). The latter may also underlie Hesiod's myth of the conflict between Zeus and Typhon (to which name cf. Saphon). Aqhat (killed on Anat's orders) has been seen as lying behind Actaeon (killed on those of Artemis), and Baal's consorts have been seen as underlying the Greek tradition of the three Graces.

Israel

The relationship of Israelite religion to the older world of Ugaritian thought has been much debated. Many scholars have been at pains to minimize the connection, though this varies from claims of little debt at all to insistence that Israel wholeheartedly rejected all the 'pagan' traditions whose antecedents we discern at Ugarit. The reality is infinitely more complex than this.

To begin with, to understand Iron Age Israelite religion it is not sufficient to read the Hebrew Bible. Biblical scholarship increasingly recognizes in the biblical texts, particularly the 'historical' ones,[70] not simply an account of events in Palestine during the first millennium BCE, but a lively critique and revaluation of all its traditions. The new is highlighted and validated in contrast to and rejection of the old. Secondly, it is clear that whatever its own status as historiography, any text has a history, in that it originates in a historical context. Thus in spite of all its own agendas, the Bible reflects all kinds of cultural and religious debts, and its own prehistory may be recovered by judicious analysis of the texts.

We have noted above a number of similarities between Israelite thought, as reflected or criticized in the Bible, and Ugaritian thought and practice. These are so numerous that it is fair to conclude that the two cultures are intimately connected. We even noted that the geography of the traditions of Og king of Bashan occurs in identical wording in an Ugaritic text. Numerous obscurities in the biblical text make sense when viewed against external evidence from the Near Eastern world, and Ugarit is the primary source for such comparisons.

Among all the recent publications which have followed up the various clues relating in particular to Bronze Age antecedents, and links with the Ugaritian evidence, often with surprisingly informative results for the real history of Israelite religious ideas, we may cite just one example, the dictionary edited by K. van der Toorn and colleagues.[71] This offers a huge range of discussion and bibliographies on the numerous deities met with in the Bible. These comprise, among many others, all the main figures of the Ugaritian pantheon. There has been increasing interest in particular in the Ugaritian goddess Athirat, and her Israelite counterpart Asherah, subject of several recent studies noted above. It is now generally conceded that the Israelite goddess was the consort of Yahweh, and evolved into the later figure of Wisdom. The royal significance of Athirat in Ugarit, as mother of the king, is paralleled in a similar ideology concerning the Israelite Queen Mother.

While many of the biblical allusions to 'Canaanite' religion are characterized by caricature and black propaganda, there is a real debt to it. That there is an element of continuity is an unavoidable conclusion to any comparative study. Israelite religion is, after all, from a phenomenological point of view, part of the 'Canaanite' religion of the first millennium. In so far as the biblical texts judged this religion and found it wanting, they may be deemed to corroborate this view.

Notes

1. See pp. 149–54.
2. For the most recent treatment see Yon 2006.
3. Anat (KTU 1.3 ii 17–18); El (KTU 1.119.14); Horon (KTU 1.124.6, if correct reading). 'KTU' (*Die Keilalphabetische Texte aus Ugarit*) is the standard reference system for texts written in the Ugaritic language. A selection of the most important religious texts is available in translation, with commentary, in Wyatt 2002, to which references are made in this chapter.
4. That is, personal names which contain a divine name, a very common form in the ancient Near East. These are explained below, p. 143.
5. The references given in the body of this chapter to KTU text-numbers (see note 3) may be read in translation, with commentary, in Wyatt 2002.
6. This term is used to denote features of West Semitic language and culture, particularly as occurring in Mesopotamian contexts. The 'Amorites' who

appear in Mesopotamian documents were tent-dwelling pastoralists, and the first names in the Assyrian king-list are those of 'kings who lived in tents'. 'Amurru' means 'West (Country)', and the city of Mari on the Euphrates 'West (City)'. The term 'Amorite' occurs in the Bible, where it has become a reference to the pre-Israelite inhabitants of Palestine (though cf. Ezekiel 16:3, 45!). Amorite as a language was closely related to Ugaritic.

7. See pp. 134–6.

8. It is worth noting that human sacrifice (of adults and children) is not attested at Ugarit, but appears to have been endemic in Israelite religion.

9. The Greek name of the twin-peaked mountain was *Kasion*, its two peaks being distinguished in Hellenistic and Roman times by the dual Latin names *Cassius* and *Anti-Cassius*. The element *Kasion* looks suspiciously like a transcription into Greek of the West Semitic word for 'throne' (Ug. *kasi'u*, Heb. *kissē'*, *kēs*), a view supported by a late name for the latter peak *Anti-Cassius* (Ugaritic *Nanu*), *Thronos*, which evidently translates the name.

10. J. Rogerson draws attention to the complex problems of biblical interpretation in his chapter below. My allusions to biblical tradition are made in full recognition of his discussion and the cautions it advises. It is important to distinguish the historical conditions of, say, the pre-monarchical period, which can be tentatively reconstructed by reading between the lines of the books of Judges and First Samuel, and taking full account of archaeological and other evidence, from the Bible's own account of this which presents it as religious anarchy and a falling-away from 'true Mosaic religion' as a result of interaction with 'Canaanite' religion. There is some serious mythologizing at work in such a presentation.

11. E.g. Nikkal, a Hurrianized form of the Sumerian goddess NIN.GAL ('Great Lady').

12. E.g. Kothar, a form of Ptah of Memphis.

13. The West Semitic deities Baal (identified with Egyptian Seth), Reshef, Athtart and Anat became prominent during the Egyptian Second Intermediate Period (of Hyksos rule in Lower Egypt), and later in the nineteenth dynasty. Ramesses II had a particular devotion to the goddess Anat.

14. This is one of the numbers of the gods cited in Yajñavalkya's account of the Vedic pantheon from India (*Bṛhadāraṇyaka Upaniṣad* 3.9.1–2). I suspect that a calendrical application, presumably based on the ritual division of the lunar month, may have applied here, as above.

15. The *Aqhat* story, KTU 1.17–19.

16. KTU 1.3 ii 5–16. This illustrates the general construction of Ugaritic poetry, which uses the principle of parallelism, stating ideas in successive cola in couplets (bicola) or other combinations.
17. The South Arabian god of the morning star is Ashtar. A cuneiform version of the later 22-letter South Arabian alphabet has been found in Ugarit. The extent to which the stars were worshipped at Ugarit remains unclear. See below, p. 133.
18. KTU 1.92.
19. This myth also bears a passing resemblance to that of Perseus and Andromeda, whose Semitic antecedents are generally recognized.
20. KTU 1.43:1–3.
21. KTU 1.10.
22. KTU 1.11 (cf. 1.13:29–36).
23. KTU 1.12.
24. KTU 1.119.
25. KTU 1.3 v 30–4, 1.4 iv 43–6.
26. See pp. 126–31.
27. KTU 1.3 v 6–7 etc.
28. See NEB translation of Hosea 8:6, 'for what sort of a god is this bull?' Or better 'for who is bull El?' 'Bull El' was one of his titles at Ugarit.
29. KTU 1.24.
30. KTU 1.5 ii 1–3.
31. KTU 1.15 ii 26–8.
32. KTU 1.161; cf. Isaiah 14:9–21, which parodies the funeral of a Mesopotamian king, and is evidently familiar with the same theological tradition.
33. KTU 1.108.2–3.
34. On the 'patron' gods see del Olmo 1999: 58–60, where he draws attention to small groups of gods appearing regularly in royal rituals. He distinguishes them as 'patron gods', 'underworld gods', 'dynastic gods' and a small group of the 'great gods'.
35. This point is discussed further at pp. 134–6.
36. KTU 1.41.
37. This may be compared with the biblical narrative in Numbers 13:17–24, where 'in the season for early grapes' the Israelite scouts bring back a vine branch as a sign of the agricultural potential of the land.
38. Del Olmo 1999: 88–9.

39. The *kubadu*-rite ('honouring'?) involved offering sacred weapons to the gods, symbolizing the divine victory at creation, which was recapitulated in the king's military victories.

40. Arhalbu (who apparently died without issue) was succeeded by his brother Niqmepa VI.

41. KTU 1.113.

42. This Akkadian term was the equivalent of Ugaritic *pgr* (*pagru*), offerings to the dead recorded, for instance, on two funerary stelae from Ugarit.

43. KTU 1.161, a royal funeral liturgy.

44. This would have been Niqmaddu II, not III, the subject of the present obsequies. The number of kings of this name remains a problem.

45. See their stories below, pp. 133–6.

46. Zimri-Lim's reign was brought to an end by King Hammurabi of Babylon.

47. KTU 1.65.

48. Text *bgn*: or 'from the Garden', if this is to be construed as a reply from the underworld to an oracular enquiry.

49. KTU 1.106.18–23.

50. The Bible records both 'Milcom' (Heb. *mlkm*) as the national god of Ammon, and 'Molech' (also referred to as 'Moloch') (Heb. *mlk*) as an underworld deity receiving human sacrifice. In both instances we may be dealing with a deliberately distorted account of 'Kings', i.e. the dead kings of Ammon and Judah respectively, who are invoked with sacrifices for oracles. Cf. Saul's invocation through a medium of Samuel's ghost (Heb. *ᵉlōhim*, 'god') in 1 Samuel 28.

51. KTU 1.5 vi 3–9, Wyatt 2002: 126.

52. Baal's death and restoration are compared elliptically to a king's death and restoration in the *Keret* story (KTU 1.16 iii 2–4). This deliberate literary connection, by the same author, Ilimilku, reinforces the associations made here.

53. KTU 1.132.1–2.

54. KTU 1.1–6. KTU 1.2 (as generally numbered) appears to be two separate tablets.

55. The same words in Ugaritic denote a palace or a temple.

56. De Moor 1971.

57. Biblical tales such as Genesis 16 (Hagar and Ishmael), Genesis 19:30–8 (Lot and his daughters and the birth of Ammon and Moab) as well as the various Psalms noted above and a number of other passages.

58. KTU 1.17 i 25–33.
59. KTU 1.20–2.
60. KTU 1.101.5–9.
61. KTU 1.119.28–33.
62. Cf. note 8 above.
63. Del Olmo 1999: 17–19.
64. KTU 1.108,3–5.
65. It is possible that these titles belonged to Attanu, Ilimilku's teacher and mentor. The syntax of the text is uncertain.
66. The terms *qdm* and *aḫr* also refer to the body ('face' and 'back' respectively). Thus it is the placing of the body in a specific direction that allows the extrapolation of the means of organization of space, time and the moral dimension. Similar extensions of body terms apply to the external world in Akkadian, Sumerian, Arabic, Hebrew and Sanskrit.
67. The best general treatment is Blacker and Lowie 1975.
68. KTU 1.5 vi 11–25.
69. KTU 1.16 i 2–5, 14–19.
70. I would not include the 'patriarchal' narratives of Genesis, or for that matter any of the so-called historical material of the Pentateuch, as *prima facie* historical material. It is largely pure fiction, and reflects the mythic account of the origins of a religious community (the Jews) and a tendentious account of all the internecine conflicts which went into its making. Some scholars would tend to apply this principle to the entire corpus. The present consensus (if one dare talk of *consensus* in this area!) outside conservative academic circles would tend nowadays to lower the dates of most biblical historiography to the fifth century BCE or later. The immediate historical context of the texts is therefore the 'post-exilic' world, rather than the time of the monarchy itself. This is not to deny the survival of older traditions embedded in our sources.
71. Van der Toorn et al. 1995, 2nd edn 1999.

Bibliography

I have restricted entries here to useful bibliography for the lay reader in English. See also the bibliography in Watson and Wyatt 1999 for publications down to early 1999, and references to all monograph series, periodicals devoted to Ugaritian studies and other bibliographical resources.

For entries on the various deities, including many references to Ugaritian material, see also D. N. Freedman (ed.), *Anchor Bible dictionary*. 6 vols.,

New York: Doubleday, 1992, and K. van der Toorn et al. (eds.), *Dictionary of deities and demons in the Bible*. Leiden: Brill, 1995, 2nd edn 1999.

Binger, T. 1997. *Asherah: goddesses in Ugarit, Israel and the Old Testament*. Sheffield: Sheffield Academic Press.

Blacker, C. and M. Lowie 1975. *Ancient cosmologies*. London: Allen and Unwin.

Brooke, G. J., A. H. W. Curtis, and J. F. Healey (eds.) 1994. *Ugarit and the Bible: Proceedings of the International Symposium on Ugarit and the Bible, Manchester, September 1992*. Münster: Ugarit-Verlag.

Curtis, A. H. W. 1985. *Ugarit (Ras Shamra)*. Cities of the Biblical World. Cambridge: Lutterworth.

Day, J. 1985. *God's battle with the dragon and the sea: echoes of a Canaanite myth in the Old Testament*. Cambridge: Cambridge University Press.

Handy, L. K. 1994. *Among the Host of Heaven: the Syro-Palestinian pantheon as bureaucracy*. Winona Lake: Eisenbrauns.

Korpel, M. C. A. 1990. *A rift in the clouds: Ugaritic and Hebrew descriptions of the divine*. Münster: Ugarit-Verlag.

Lewis, T. J. 1989. *Cults of the dead in ancient Israel and Ugarit*. Atlanta, GA: Scholars Press.

de Moor, J. C. 1971. *The seasonal pattern in the Ugaritic poem of Ba lu according to the version of Ilimilku*. Neukirchen-Vluyn: Neukirchener Verlag; Kevelaer: Butzon and Bercker.

del Olmo Lete, G. 1999. *Canaanite religion according to the liturgical texts of Ugarit*. Bethesda, MD: CDL Press.

Pardee, D. 2002. *Ritual and cult at Ugarit*. Atlanta, GA: Society of Biblical Literature.

Parker, S. B. 1997. *Ugaritic narrative poetry*. Atlanta, GA: Scholars Press.

Penglase, C. 1994. *Greek myths and Mesopotamia: parallels and influence in the Homeric hymns and Hesiod*. London: Routledge.

Smith, M. S. 2002. *The early history of God*. Grand Rapids, MI: Eerdmans; Deerborn, MI: Dove.

    2001. *The origins of biblical monotheism: Israel's polytheistic background and the Ugaritic texts*. Oxford: Oxford University Press.

Walls, N. 1992. *The goddess Anat in Ugaritic myth*. Atlanta, GA: Scholars Press.

Watson, W. G. E. and N. Wyatt (eds.) 1999. *Handbook of Ugaritic studies*. Leiden: Brill.

Wiggins, S. A. 1993. *A reassessment of 'Asherah'*. Kevelaer: Butzen and Bercker; Neukirchen-Vluyn: Neukirchener Verlag.

Wyatt, N. 1996. *Myths of power: a study of royal myth and ideology in Ugaritic and biblical tradition*. Münster: Ugarit-Verlag.

    2002. *Religious texts from Ugarit*. London: Continuum, 2nd edn.

Wyatt, N., W. G. E. Watson and J. B. Lloyd (eds.) 1996. *Ugarit, religion and culture: Proceedings of the International Colloquium on Ugarit, Religion and Culture, Edinburgh, July 1994*. Münster: Ugarit-Verlag.

Yon, M. 2006. *The royal city of Ugarit on the tell of Ras Shamra*. Winona Lake: Eisenbrauns.

Supplementary reading

Cornelius, I. 2004. *The many faces of the goddess: the iconography of the Syro-Palestinian goddesses Anat, Astarte, Qedeshet and Asherah c. 1500–1000 BCE*. Fribourg: Academic Press; Göttingen: Vandenhoek and Ruprecht).

Feliu, L. 2003. *The god Dagan in Bronze Age Syria*. Leiden: Brill.

Greene, A. R. W. 2003. *The storm-god in the ancient Near East*. Winona Lake, IN: Eisenbrauns.

Watson, W. G. E. 2003. Daily life in ancient Ugarit (Syria), in R. E. Averbeck, M. W. Chavalas and D. B. Weisberg (eds.), *Life and culture in the ancient Near East*. Bethesda, MD: CDL Press, pp. 121–51.

Wyatt, N. 2005a. Epic in Ugaritic literature, in J. M. Foley (ed.), *A companion to ancient epic*. Oxford: Blackwell, pp. 246–54.

    2005b. *The mythic mind: essays on cosmology in Ugaritic and Old Testament literature*. London: Equinox.

    2005c. *'There's such divinity doth hedge a king': selected essays of Nicolas Wyatt on royal ideology in Ugaritic and Old Testament Literature*. London: Ashgate.

4 Mesopotamia

BENJAMIN R. FOSTER

Introduction

Sources

Mesopotamian religion includes certain beliefs and practices of the Sumerians, Akkadians, Assyrians, Babylonians and other peoples who lived at various times in different parts of ancient Mesopotamia, the region corresponding roughly to modern Iraq, from the fourth through the first millennia BCE. The history and cultures of these peoples were mostly forgotten during the early Christian era, save for brief historical narratives of famous kings and cities in the Hebrew Bible, in classical authors such as Herodotus, Diodorus and Josephus, and in scattered excerpts from a lost book by Berossus, a Babylonian writing in Greek in the third century BCE. Beginning in the nineteenth century CE, with the discovery and excavation of ancient Mesopotamian sites and decipherment of Mesopotamian languages such as Sumerian and Akkadian, European and American scholars identified texts, objects and architecture as religious in nature. They used these to reconstruct ancient Mesopotamian religious beliefs and practices in the absence of any continuous or living tradition from ancient times to the present. Inevitably the intellectual concerns of successive generations of scholars, their personal religious commitments and their individual stances, such as piety, scepticism or anticlericalism, had their effect on agendas of research and modes of presentation of Mesopotamian religion in modern studies. Many scholars of an earlier generation took for granted, for example, a higher degree of religious preoccupation and expression among 'ancient Oriental' or 'Semitic peoples' than among other ancient peoples such as the Greeks and Romans, but generalizations on this order are no longer the basis for serious research. Some scholars imagined, for example, that the priesthood was primarily responsible for preserving culture, while others claimed that priests resisted change and

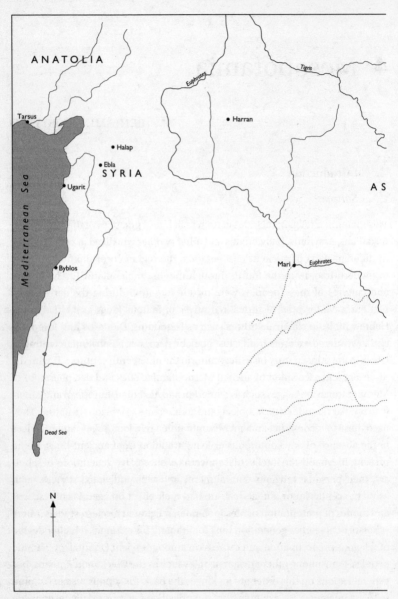

Map 4.1. Early Mesopotamia.

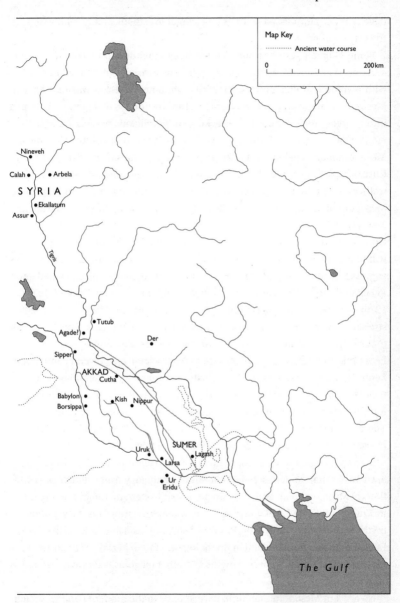

Map 4.1. (*cont.*)

development, suppressed writings unacceptable to them, and generally stood in the way of progress.

Pioneering studies of Mesopotamian religion tended to be comprehensive, such as that by M. Jastrow (1898, partially revised German edition 1912, with a volume of illustrations, 1912). Its fundamental thesis was that ancient Mesopotamian religion derived from local animistic cults that grew and merged into a larger, more complex interlocking set of religious practices and beliefs. Similar views were set forth by R. W. Rogers (1908) in a volume that treated Mesopotamian religion as a sort of prelude to Judaism, itself a prelude to Christianity. E. Dhorme (1945, not available in English) wrote a concise and well-documented descriptive study. The most influential writer in English on Mesopotamian religion was Thorkild Jacobsen. He developed a view that ancient Mesopotamian religion derived from a person's sense of the 'other' in the natural world around him, leading to feelings of fear and awe. People perceived active will in natural events, processes and phenomena. This sense of the other was expressed, using metaphorical terms, in myth and theology and was acted upon in cult and ritual. We have a comprehensive presentation of his views (Jacobsen 1976) and a later summary statement of his work (Jacobsen 1987). Bottéro (2001) stressed spiritual values and a phenomenological rather than a schematic, theoretical approach; for a summary of its main theses see Bottéro (1992: 201–31). Economic and ritual aspects of Mesopotamian religion are presented by Oppenheim (1977), professing disdain for a historical approach to the subject. He contributed a brief but suggestive essay to a collection edited by Ferm (1950: 65–79). A more detailed, primarily bibliographical survey was offered by Römer (1969). There are numerous technical studies of aspects of Mesopotamian religion in the scientific literature of Assyriology, but few of them are in English.

Many presentations of Mesopotamian religion rely on retellings of ancient literary works that modern scholars classify as mythology. Authoritative presentations of Mesopotamian and other ancient Near Eastern mythologies were made in Kramer (1961 and 1969), as well as in a major treatment of Mesopotamian mythological texts jointly with Bottéro (1989, not available in English). Recent English translations of Akkadian mythology are found in Dalley (1989) and Foster (1996). Important Sumerian myths and other religious texts are translated in Jacobsen (1987).

No ancient Mesopotamian term corresponds to the modern concept of 'religion', nor is there any ancient scripture, systematic treatise or general description of religious belief or activity from any period of Mesopotamian history. This means that definition of Mesopotamian religion can at best be only a modern mode of selecting and interpreting ancient writings and material culture using modern humanistic categories for which there may not have been ancient counterparts. Although the Mesopotamians recognized certain matters as 'pertaining to the gods', a distinction between religious and secular matters may not have been always fully comprehensible in the context of Mesopotamian culture.

History

Because this was before the invention of writing about 3300 BCE, evidence for Mesopotamian religion is derived from burials, architecture and artistic and utilitarian objects, including figurines, reliefs, seals and ceramics. The presence of grave-goods in prehistoric burials, for example, suggests belief in some sort of existence after death. Statuettes of women with exaggerated torsos, breasts or genitalia suggest an emphasis on fertility and procreation. The earliest sanctuaries were single-roomed, clay and timber structures not much different from dwelling houses. These had a niche in one wall, where the deity was situated, perhaps in an image or symbol, with an offering table in front of the niche. In the marshes of southern Sumer the earliest built sanctuaries may have been of woven reeds, but still in the form of a human residence.

The Sumerians are the earliest identifiable population of Mesopotamia, though there is evidence for other peoples besides them. Sumerian urban culture was originally centred in the southern third of the floodplain of the Tigris and Euphrates rivers. By the end of the fourth millennium, Sumerian settlements and colonies had spread north, first to Akkad (the region around present-day Baghdad), then as far as what was later Assyria, with outposts in the Upper Euphrates Valley in northern Syria and in Anatolia (see Map 4.1, and chronology, Table 4.1).

Among the characteristics of late fourth- and early third-millennium Sumerian urban culture was gigantic investment of labour and resources in the construction of sanctuaries and related buildings. An early sanctuary at Uruk, for example, was constructed on a massive irregular mudbrick platform rising about 14 m above its foundations. On top of this platform stood a building about 22 × 17.5 m, with a central chamber running its full length, approached by staircases around the platform. Yet this sanctuary was only one of several in the city, another being nearly half as large again with stone foundations. The Uruk sanctuary buildings

166   Benjamin R. Foster

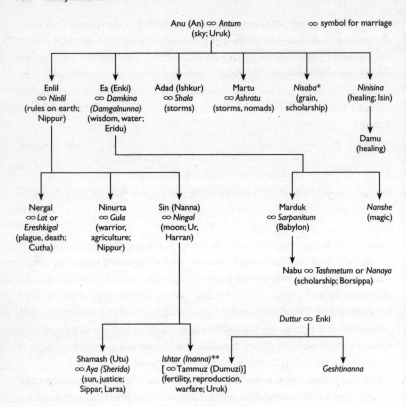

Key:
Anu = Akkadian name, (An) = Sumerian name of deities with two names
Female deities in italic.
* An alternative tradition makes *Nisiba* a daughter of Enki
** An alternative tradition makes *Ishtar* a daughter of Anu

Fig. 4.1. Pantheon of Principal Mesopotamian deities.

were in some instances decorated with tens of thousands of stone and baked clay cones dipped in colours then inserted horizontally in the walls to form polychrome patterns. Temples were further decorated with recessed niches, reliefs, carved stone basins and other, more perishable and valuable, elements now lost, such as reedwork, weaving and metalwork. Religious art of the end of the fourth millennium shows an important male figure in a distinctive fringed garment who

Table 4.1 *Chronology of Mesopotamian civilizations*

BCE	Mesopotamian civilization	Religion
6000	Local cultures in north, first settlements in south	
5000–4000	Villages and towns, subsistence economy	Small sanctuaries like houses, deities aspects of nature with cosmic functions?
4000–3000	Growth of cities, especially Uruk; Sumerian colonization of Euphrates Valley to north; writing, monumental art and architecture; economy based on management and redistribution of surplus	Huge temples at Uruk, deities in human form with superhuman powers?
3000–2300	Semites in Akkad, Sumerians in Sumer, rival city-states and leagues, development of kingship, palaces; at Lagash, attempts to create a theocratic state ruled by king; old Sumerian culture	Articulation of formal pantheon where each major Sumerian city was home to a different Sumerian god
2300–2100	Sargonic dynasty unites Sumer, Akkad, upper Tigris and Euphrates, south-western Iran into an empire based in Akkad	Identification of Sumerian and Semitic deities, deification of reigning king, lavish royal patronage of temples
2100–2000	Dynasty at Ur controls kingdom in Sumer and Akkad built from remains of Sargonic Empire	Sumerian religious literature, first construction of ziggurats
2000–1500	Amorite settlement in Mesopotamia, Amorite city-states from Aleppo to Uruk; formation of Babylonian culture in Sumer and Akkad and Assyrian culture in Assyria; Period of Hammurabi, civilization of Mari, Old Assyrian city-state	Beginnings of Babylonian religious literature; pantheon narrows to small group of leading gods in supreme control: Anu, Enlil, Ea, mother goddess, growing importance of personal god
1500–1100	In Assyria, Hurrian rule, then emergence of Assyrian nation-state (1350–1076); in Babylonia, Kassite rule; era of nation-states and internationalization of Babylonian culture; palace economies sustained by professional military elite	Decrease in number of gods with parallel increase in older divine names considered by-names of major deities; tendency towards emergence of a single dominant god, such as Marduk in Babylonia and Assur in Assyria, but continuity with Sumerian past

(cont.)

Table 4.1 (*cont.*)

BCE	Mesopotamian civilization	Religion
1100–900	Collapse of nation-states in western Asia, growth of Aramean culture in north Syria and Mesopotamia	Few sources available
900–612	Assyrian Empire unites Mesopotamia, Syria-Palestine, conquers Egypt; time of Assurnasirpal, Sennacherib, Esarhaddon, Assurbanipal; Assyria destroyed by Medes	Claims for universal rule of one deity, such as Marduk and Assur, henotheism, continuity with past
612–539	Babylonian empire takes former Assyrian territories; time of Nebuchadnezzar and Nabonidus	Archaizing religious literature; theological speculation based on philology, such as minute analysis of divine names
539–330	Under Persian rule, Babylonia is prosperous and cosmopolitan centre of a vast empire from the Nile to Central Asia	Persian patronage of Babylonian temples, some destruction in times of civil unrest, continuity with past
330–130	Babylonia prospers as centre of Hellenistic empire of Asia; time of Alexander the Great and Seleucid rule in western Asia	Last flowering of native religious culture in Sumerian and Akkadian
130 to Christian era	Gradual disappearance of Mesopotamian civilization; Euphrates loses position as cultural axis of Mesopotamia and becomes frontier between Rome and Parthia; decline in prosperity and population of Babylonia	Local worship of some Mesopotamian deities, such as Nabu, Nanaya, Assur, under Parthian rule

may have exercised both religious and secular authority, though the traditional term 'priest king' for this mysterious figure has been abandoned.

From about 3500 BCE on, the fundamental element in every Mesopotamian temple was the cult chamber or cella, with a niche for the divinity in one side. In some small temples, this chamber constituted the entire structure; in others, there was an anteroom. More palatial structures included one or more court-yards, sometimes with subsidiary rooms along their sides. In some cellas the niche was on the short end of the chamber; these are referred to as 'long room' temples. In others, the niche was on the long side of the cella; these are referred to as 'broad room' temples. Some temples were of the 'bent axis' type, meaning that one entered the cella from the side then turned ninety degrees to see the niche. In others, the niche was often already visible from a doorway to the outer court or anteroom. These elements vary by time and region and have been intensively studied by architectural historians to determine their source and course of development (Frankfort 1996). After the end of the third millennium, many larger temples included an independent temple tower, called a ziggurat. These had several stages and a chapel on the top accessible by stairways. Their terraces may have been planted with trees and decorated with symbols such as bulls' horns but the significance of these is uncertain. These towers rose high above other buildings in Mesopotamian cities. Mesopotamian urban centres of the second and first millennia had many large and small temples. In sixth-century Babylon, for example, there were at least fifty temples and a thousand or more smaller chapels, images and altars throughout the city.

Written sources for Mesopotamian religion begin in the mid-third millennium BCE. From these it is clear that polytheism, or worship of many gods, was the first outstanding trait of Mesopotamian religion. From later times the names of over 2000 deities, male and female, in various Mesopotamian and non-Mesopotamian languages are recorded. Although the Mesopotamians recognized certain deities as more important than others, they did not exclude any deities, foreign or native, by considering them false or imaginary. A second outstanding trait of Mesopotamian religion was the belief that major gods resided in specific sanctuaries built for their service by human beings, in which the gods were present in more or less anthropomorphic form. Many of these sanctuaries were located at important Sumerian cities, such as the temple of Enki at Eridu, of Inanna at Uruk, or of Nanna, the moon-god, at Ur. Others, like the sanctuary of the birth-goddess at Kesh (a Sumerian cult centre, location unknown), were apparently in rural areas. Sometimes two important gods had their sanctuaries in the same city. An, the sky-god, and Inanna, goddess of procreation, both had major temples at Uruk, while there were major temples of both Ninurta and Enlil at Nippur. Linking these deities into families and generations became part of the cultural and political commonality of the various Sumerian city-states of the third millennium, whereby they shared accounts of the god's family relationships, their interactions, rivalries and heroic deeds. The Sumerians deemed their cities the centre of the universe, with the great gods of the universe actually resident within them.

The northern half of Mesopotamia was inhabited by peoples speaking Semitic languages, unrelated to Sumerian. The Semitic peoples of Mesopotamia shared both a bilingual cultural community with the Sumerians and a broad common cultural and linguistic heritage with other Semitic peoples across the Near East. Sumerian- and Semitic-speaking cultures interpenetrated and converged into a bilingual unity. By the middle of the third millennium BCE, syncretism or iden- tification of Semitic and Sumerian deities had begun, for example Semitic Adad or Addu, god of thunderstorms, was identified with Sumerian Ishkur; the sun- god of the Semites, Shamash, was identified with the sun-god of the Sumerians, Utu; Semitic Ea, god of wisdom and magic, was identified with Sumerian Enki; and Sin, the moon-god of the Semites, with Sumerian Nanna (see Fig. 4.1). Since most of the evidence for these deities comes from periods after identification or syncretism had taken place, it is often difficult to identify the characteristics of the originally separate deities combined in them.

With the development of political institutions such as kingship in the Sumerian city-states of the third millennium BCE, as well as among the Semitic peoples of northern Mesopotamia, the gods tended to be reinterpreted as kings, queens, courtiers, military officers, advisors and messengers, along the line of human royal courts (Jacobsen 1976: 75–91; Bottéro 1992: 212–15). This tended to over- shadow their older functions as gods of nature in the village and pastoral societies of earlier times, though these were not forgotten entirely. Astral deities, such as the sun, the moon or the planet Venus, became kings or queens of heaven and were systematized in later times through astronomy and astrology. A few gods, such as Assur, at home on the bend of the Tigris river where the city Assur was to grow, were apparently deities resident in a specific locality (*numen loci*), without a broader function in nature. The chief of the Sumerian pantheon, Enlil, at home in his sanctuary at Nippur, is usually said to be a god of wind or air (van Dijk 1971: 462–3; Jacobsen 1987b: 453–4), but this is debatable.

During the last quarter of the third millennium BCE, the Sargonic, or Akka- dian Empire, based in Akkad, but extending to Syria and Sumer under unified rule, hastened and refined the syncretism of Sumerian and Semitic religions. An Akkadian princess, Enheduanna, composed Sumerian hymns to the temples of Sumer and in honour of Ishtar and the moon-god (Hallo 1997: 518–22). By the beginning of the second millennium, Sumerian was disappearing as a living language and independent culture in the face of Akkadian, and thereby acquired an academic character favoured by small circles of the highly educated. An influx of peoples from northern Syria, called Amorites, brought new religious ideas and practices to Mesopotamia and closer cultural connections with the peoples living along the Middle and Upper Euphrates than before. Babylonia became the new term for the former Sumer and Akkad, reflecting the increasing importance of the city Babylon. In this period certain deities, such as Marduk, god of Babylon, and Nabu, god of nearby Borsippa, gained prominence. Non-Mesopotamian traditions, such as a battle of a hero god with the sea, a story of Syrian origin, entered Mesopotamia.

After the mid-second millennium, Mesopotamia was divided into nation-states that elevated certain local deities, such as Marduk and Assur, into national deities, alongside foreign deities (such as Kassite Shuqamunu), imported by non-Mesopotamian dynasties ruling in the land, including the Kassites and Hurrians. As the great gods seemed increasingly remote from the affairs of people not in positions of authority or prestige, belief in a personal, protective, intercessor deity expanded (Jacobsen 1976: 145–64). An Akkadian prayer to a personal god expresses both the personal and remote aspects of divinity (Foster 1996: 627):

> O my god, who created my name,
> Guardian of my life, producer of my progeny,
> O angry god, may your heart be calmed,
> O angry goddess, be reconciled with me.
> Who knows where you dwell, O my god?
> Never have I seen your pure standing place or sleeping chamber.

Thoughout the second and first millennia, the deities of such centres as Assur and Babylon were often associated with political and military activities, becoming in some instances gods of conquest and empires, 'commanding' the subjugation of other peoples. However, Mesopotamian religion was not forcibly imposed on conquered areas. When in turn Mesopotamia was conquered by an outside people, the Persians, in the sixth century BCE, the national gods of the Babylonians and Assyrians began to diminish in stature with the decline of their cities' and nations' political importance. At first the Persian rulers respected Mesopotamian sanctuaries and cults, but in times of rebellion and political turmoil some important sanctuaries were damaged or destroyed and never thereafter rebuilt. Few Mesopotamian deities, among them Nabu and Nanaya, outlived the period of Hellenistic rule in Mesopotamia (fourth to second centuries BCE), except when identified with Syrian or Graeco-Roman deities (for example, Adad = Jupiter Dolichenus, Ishtar = Astarte). By the time of the incorporation of Mesopotamia into the Parthian Empire in the first century BCE., the traditional Mesopotamian gods had disappeared forever, except in isolated enclaves such as Assur and Uruk.

Pantheon

The many and the particular

The individual Mesopotamian recognized the existence of numerous gods, including deities foreign to his land and culture. In devotional expression and name-giving, where personal piety was expressed, he tended however to stress the importance of only one or a few deities, elevating the chosen one above the others in the rhetoric of his praise and attention, such as in the following addresses to the sun and moon respectively (after Foster 1996: 635, 665):

> O Sun, king of heaven and earth,
> Lord of truth and justice,
> Lord of the greater gods, lord of the lesser gods,
> Whose assent no god can change,
> Whose command cannot be transgressed . . .
> O Moon, shining radiant god, luminary of heaven,
> Firstborn son of Enlil, foremost one of Enlil's temple,
> You reign as king of the universe,
> You set your throne in the shining heavens.

So too villages, towns or cities typically recognized one deity, or a small group of deities, as paramount in that locality, though at the same time they claimed universal dominion for the local deity and recognized the dominion of other gods (Bottéro 2001). Certain groups, such as pastoralists, farmers, hunters or fishermen, and certain professions, such as soldiers or woodworkers, may have favoured certain patron deities, but there is little evidence for this.

Systematization

With the broadening horizons of exchange, colonization, conquest, formation of leagues, city-states, nation-states and empires, ancient Mesopotamian theologians organized deities into pantheons, that is, constructs that were intended to order systematically numerous Mesopotamian gods (Lambert 1975). As early as the middle of the third millennium BCE, Sumerian lists of gods were compiled, arranging the deities into tribe-like hierarchies, with the elder gods first, then their children. In the early lists, the chief gods were An, the sky-god, and Enlil, the chief god living on earth. Later Sumero-Akkadian lists of the early second millennium formed the basis for a large, systematic list called An (in Sumerian) = Anum (in Akkadian). This listed the various names of a given deity, those of the spouse, then their children with their families and retainers, then the retainers of the parent couple. This included nearly 2000 names of deities. Some lists added explanations of the gods' functions and attributes. Documents such as these show how Mesopotamian scholars constructed a pantheon, or overarching hierarchy of the gods of Mesopotamia.

Pantheons were organized in several ways. One ranged gods in large groups or generations. Thereby certain primeval deities were recognized, at least in literature, but there was no active cult or mythology for these deities, who were considered alive but remote. Primeval deities included, for example, pairs of gods mentioned at the beginning of the Babylonian Creation Epic, such as Lahmu and Lahamu, Anshar and Kishar, but there were no temples to these gods nor prayers addressed to them. A second, related technique constructed genealogies whereby some deities were the spouses, children or descendants of others, visualized in human, or anthropomorphic, form. For example, in one tradition, the sky-god An (= Anu) was the father of the moon-god, Nanna (= Suen), who was in turn the father of the sun-god, Utu (= Shamash) and the planet Venus, Ishtar. Yet all of these gods were considered contemporaries and tended to differ in relative importance rather than relative age. According to a third technique, deities were assigned specific areas or regions of the cosmos, such as An (= Anu) in heaven, Enlil on earth, and Enki (= Ea) in the subterranean fresh waters. Since these gods were considered resident in their earthly sanctuaries and were also of universal dominion, they had, in effect, three positions, geographical, social and cosmic. A fourth technique was syncretism or identification of originally distinct deities, from different places or cultures. Thereby Sumerian Inanna was equated with Ishtar of the Semites, and Ningirsu, local god of the city Girsu in Sumer, was equated with the better-known Ninurta of Nippur, one of Sumer's principal cities. Considerable variation in the pantheon is found in different periods and places, so Fig. 4.1 is only approximative. Some deities were ranked numerically by Mesopotamian scholars in that they wrote numerical substitutions instead of spelling the gods' names. In this approach, Anu was given the highest number, 60 (the basis for Mesopotamian sexigesimal mathematics), as most important; Enlil 50, Enki 40, Sin 30, Shamash 20, Ishtar 15, Girra 10, and Adad 6, though variations occur. How or when these numerical values were assigned is unclear. Use of the numeral 30 to write the name of the moon-god, referring to the number of days in the lunar month, seems to antedate the general practice of numerical substitution for divine names, so may have inspired it. The other numerals would therefore have been derived by analogy on the basis of the deities' relative importance.

Modern researchers tend to group Mesopotamian deities according to broad functions in nature: weather-gods (Adad), agricultural deities (Nisaba, Ninurta), gods of livestock (Sumuqan), or, in Mesopotamian fashion, gods of certain parts of the cosmos, such as netherworld deities (Nergal, Ereshkigal). Other scholars group gods based on their relationship to human activities and concerns, such as birth-goddesses (Mah), healing deities (Ba'u, Gula, Ninkarrak); gods of magic (Asalluhi, Marduk), scholarship (Nabu, Nisaba), warfare (Ishtar, Zababa), divination (Shamash, Adad). Mesopotamians, while not referring to such categories in the abstract, followed a similar process in their tendency to identify deities assignable to these categories. A further division of the ruling gods was the recognition of two large sub-groups, greater (Anunna) and lesser (Igigi) gods. It is not always clear what the distinction between these groups may have been. In Akkadian texts of the later periods, the Anunna-gods ruled in the netherworld and the Igigi-gods in heaven, but this may be a secondary development. During the early second millennium, a leading group of three emerges among the great gods: Anu (= An), Enlil and Ea (= Enki) who seem to have exercised the most effective power in the universe. By the end of the second millennium, individual national gods, such as Assur and Marduk, were said to dominate the other gods. As the number of distinct deities diminished through time, the number of names assigned to the remaining deities increased. Marduk, for example, was assigned the names of various originally independent gods in the Babylonian Epic of Creation (Lambert 1990).

Pantheons based on these ways of organizing the gods could be local and universal at the same time. They provided a means for ranking some deities in status ahead of others, based on human politics or cosmological speculation. Moreover, the pantheon included gods of human social relations, productive capacities, and other activities and achievements. Thereby human activities were incorporated into a cosmic unity that did not distinguish religious concerns from non-religious concerns so clearly as in modern societies with a sense of secular and sacred. In later periods there are isolated instances of henotheism, that is, describing certain individual gods as aspects or even bodily parts of a more important god, as in this hymn addressed to the Babylonian deity Marduk (Foster 1996: 598):

> Sin is your divinity, Anu your sovereignty,
> Dagan is your lordship, Enlil your kingship,
> Adad is your might, wise Ea your perception,
> Nabu, holder of the tablet stylus, is your learning.

Although there were ideas of a supreme deity, who might gain power over the other gods by valour or by divine election, there was never a sense of exclusion of other deities, such as characterized later monotheistic religions.

Individual deities

The highest-ranking deities formed the cosmic triad of Anu, Enlil and Ea, with sometimes a mother-goddess of equal rank. Anu was the sky-god, remote from human concerns, with little mythology, and few prayers or hymns addressed to him. His major sanctuary was originally Eanna at Uruk, but this later became sacred to Ishtar as well, so Anu and Antum lived in another building nearby, the Bit Resh or 'chief household'. An elaborate late second- or first-millennium Sumerian poem explains that Anu promoted his daughter Ishtar to rule with him as 'queen of heaven', but the circumstances of her presence in Anu's sanctuary are not clear. There was a second sanctuary of Anu at Der, a town in the foothills of the Zagros, and a joint temple with Adad at Assur. His spouse was Antum, mentioned in magical and astrological texts as well as in offering lists of the late periods, but she seems to have been replaced as spouse by Ishtar in many periods, at least in the active cult.

Enlil was the major god on earth, with executive power in both heaven and earth. He held the 'tablet of destinies' that controlled powers in both spheres. His sanctuary, as at Nippur in northern Sumer, was called Ekur, 'Mountain-House'. His name was sometimes used as a general term for 'supreme deity'. In Assyria, he was identified with the god Assur as 'Assyrian Enlil'. In the Babylonian Epic of Creation (Foster 1996: 350–401), his powers, or 'Enlilship', are given to Marduk, the Babylonian national deity. In the myth of Anzu (Foster 1996: 458–81), a monstrous bird steals them while Enlil is bathing but they are recovered by Ninurta, Enlil's son. Enlil was usually portrayed as harsh or indifferent to the human race. His consort was Ninlil (Assyrian 'Mullissu'), who was also honoured as the spouse of the god Assur.

Enki, Akkadian Ea, was the god of subterranean fresh water, wisdom, the arts and magic. He was instrumental in creating the human race and was usually beneficent to people. He was known for his tricks, devices and elaborate rhetoric, and for his role in ongoing human culture, civilization and religion. His sanctuary was the E-absu or 'House of the Watery Depths' at Eridu, in southern Sumer. His spouse was Damgalnunna; the Babylonian Epic of Creation makes him the father of Marduk.

Wives of major gods were not usually seen as exercising individual power but were often called upon to intercede with their husbands and to placate their wrath in tender moments. The second-ranking group of gods were the astral deities, the moon, the sun, and the planet Venus as morning and evening star. Sin, Sumerian Nanna, the moon, had major sanctuaries at Ur in Sumer and at Harran in southern Anatolia. He was a god of virtue and fair-dealing, protecting the homeless, the wayfarer, widows and orphans. His spouse was Ningal, known as Nikkal in Aramaic and at Ugarit in Syria. Observation of the moon was essential for determining the Mesopotamian calendar and lunar eclipses were usually bad omens.

Shamash, Sumerian Utu, the sun, was a warrior deity among the early Semitic-speaking peoples, with an interest in trade and commerce. Later he was primarily a god of justice, guardian of oaths, contracts, business, law and legal practice. He was important also as a god of truth in divination, which was often understood as a kind of judicial appeal. His daily course across the sky allowed him to see far and wide to the remotest places; no miscreant was beyond his rays. His major sanctuaries, called the E-babbar 'House of Radiance', were at Sippar and Larsa in northern Babylonia. His spouse was Aya, goddess of the dawn.

Ishtar, Sumerian Inanna, or Venus, was the sister of the sun and daughter of the moon (at Uruk and Nippur daughter of Anu). She was a complicated figure embodying love, sensuality and reproduction (characteristic of Inanna), as well as strife and warfare (characteristic of Ishtar, see Harris 1991). Her major cult centres in the north were at Assur, Nineveh and Arbela, where she was honoured as a goddess of warfare; in the south at Uruk, as a goddess of sex and procreation. Aspects of her cult at Uruk, including self-mutilation, prostitution and sexual role reversal, were looked upon with revulsion by some Mesopotamians. As a goddess of battle, she had a major sanctuary at the city Agade, in northern Babylonia, called the E-ulmash (meaning uncertain). Under the name Anunitum, 'Battle Goddess', she was honoured at Sippar. She was a patron deity of the Sargonic dynasty, which created the first empire in Mesopotamia, and was said to have loved the Sargonic kings. In fact, the period of the Sargonic kings, with their capital at Agade, was sometimes referred to as the 'Reign of Ishtar'. Some Sumerian poetry portrays her as a girl falling in love for the first time, with Dumuzi (= Tammuz), a god of shepherding. Some Akkadian poetry emphasizes variously her beauty, sensuality and interest in the needs of women. Other literary texts, such as the Epic of Gilgamesh (Foster 2001), portray her as harsh, violent, vindictive, profane and sexually insatiable. Although some theology assigns her a husband and child, she was not normally reckoned as a mother-goddess and did not have such clearly structured family ties as other Mesopotamian goddesses.

The next major group of gods was comprised of gods of nature. These included the fire-god Girra (Sumerian Gibil), often invoked in magic to destroy evil; Nusku was also a god of fire and torchlight. Ninurta was a god of vegetation and a warrior-god. In Assur he was venerated as a god of warfare and the hunt. As son of Enlil he avenged his father when the monstrous bird Anzu stole his father's powers. His spouse was Gula, a goddess of healing. He was early identified with Ningirsu, a god of the Lagash region, and Gula with Ba'u, Ningirsu's spouse. Ningirsu and Ninurta had an especially rich mythology in Sumerian, important elements of which were borrowed into Akkadian and later assigned to Marduk in the Babylonian Epic of Creation. Adad, Sumerian Ishkur, was god of thunderstorms and flash floods. In Mesopotamia, he was mostly considered destructive, because storms were often harmful to irrigation works and agriculture. He was also a god of divination. In Sumer his major sanctuary was at Enegi, near Ur, in the north at Assur, Calah and Ekallate, and further west at Halap (modern Aleppo). His spouse was Shala, possibly a name of non-Mesopotamian origin. As the weather-god Hadad or Addu, Adad was better known in Syria than in Mesopotamia.

Gods of the netherworld included Nergal, king of the realm of the dead, and his spouse Ereshkigal. He was also a god of plague. His main sanctuary was the E-meslam, 'House of the Warrior of the Netherworld', at Cutha, in northern

Babylonia, where he had a different spouse, Laz. He was sometimes equated with Erra, a god of violence, warfare, pestilence and 'scorched earth'.

Among other gods of particular importance was Assur, the national god of Assyria, at home in the city Assur on the Tigris. With the expansion of Assyria into an imperial power beginning in the fourteenth century BCE, the god Assur was increasingly identified with warfare and empire-building. The Assyrian king officiated as his high-priest at his principal sanctuary, the E-hursagkurkurra, 'Mountain House of All Lands', apparently an expansion of Ekur, the name of Enlil's temple at Nippur. Assyrian theologians, in response to the Babylonian Epic of Creation, attempted to identify Assur with Anshar, a primeval deity, but the cult of Assur remained confined to Assyria itself and her military outposts. His spouse was Ninlil (Mulissu), or Sherua, a goddess of the dawn.

Marduk, the national god of Babylon, may originally have been a storm deity. Through syncretism with Asalluhi, a god of magic, son of Enki, he became a god of healing and magic and took over many functions of Ea. His main sanctuary was the temple Esagila at Babylon, a vast complex with a temple tower that was one of the largest structures of Mesopotamian antiquity. Marduk's spouse was Sarpanitum, originally referring to a town near Babylon and the poplar tree, but later etymologized as 'creatress of seed'. Their son was Nabu (Nebo), whose major sanctuary was the Ezida, 'House of Truth', at Borsippa, south of Babylon. Nabu was a god of wisdom and literate scholarship. His cult enjoyed considerable prominence in Assur after the mid-second millennium. In the late periods Nabu took over some of the names and functions of his father Marduk. His spouse was Tashmetum, a goddess of favourable attention to prayers and petitions, also Nanaya, a goddess of warfare and reproduction whose cult survived in Mesopotamia into the Christian era.

Tammuz (Dumuzi) is usually explained as a youthful god of shepherding or of the date palm. Sumerian love poetry dwells on his adolescent courtship of the youthful Inanna; he was shallow and impetuous, she passionate and sensuous. Despite the efforts of his loving sister, Geshtinanna, he was killed and sent off to the netherworld, to be mourned thereafter by the human race. Some scholars consider him a vegetation deity or god of fertility who was considered to have died in the hot summer months but returned in the spring, but this is doubtful. Others claim that he was a historical personage who was later worshipped as a god.

Mother-goddesses were largely known for their role in creation of the human race and supervision of birth. These included Nammu, Aruru, Mami, Ninmah,

Ninhursag and Belet-ili, 'mistress of the gods'. Deified natural features included the river-god, important in judicial ordeals, resorted to when other means of ascertaining truth failed. The accused jumped into the river and if he came out safely was deemed vindicated. Many people considered themselves as having a personal god or goddess, without a name but referred to as 'god' or 'goddess'. This deity was supposed to look after a person's interests and to intercede on his behalf with more important deities. A few letters addressed to personal deities express reproof and regret that the deity has not been more effective in this role.

Divine images, symbols and attributes

The major Mesopotamian deities were worshipped in the form of anthropomorphic images and also in the form of specific symbols such as animals, plants, implements or abstract shapes. For example, the crescent was the symbol for Sin, the seven-pointed star for Ishtar, the sun-disk for Shamash, the lightning bolt for Adad, the horned cap for Anu or Enlil, the hoe for Marduk, the plough for Ningirsu, the flowing vase for Ea, the bull for weather-gods, the lion for the warlike Ishtar, the staff with turban for Inanna or Ishtar as a fertility goddess. Certain objects associated with gods, such as weapons and musical instruments, were individually deified and accorded offerings (Selz, in Finkel and Geller 1997). Gods also had standards or emblems that could be carried from place to place to represent their presence. In literature, gods were often described as holding specific objects, such as a sceptre or a tablet stylus, representing their functions. In astrology and astronomy, gods were associated with specific planets, stars and constellations, for example Marduk with the planet Jupiter. Many gods and goddesses had specific monsters or beasts associated with them, such as a bull with Anu, a lion with Ishtar or a snake dragon with Marduk.

Mythology

Properties of divinity

Although the gods were visualized in anthropomorphic form, with human emotions and physical needs and desires, important distinctions set the gods apart from humanity. First, they had transcendent divine powers in the universe, over other gods, and over human lives and institutions. Second was the gods' sublime position in an ordered universe, in which divinity could be expressed in terms of rank and precedence. Sublime power and position inspired fear, trembling and speechlessness in the presence of a god (Jacobsen 1976: 3–5; Bottéro 1992: 210). Divinity was furthermore revealed by a radiant brightness, not as of heat but as of a gem-like sheen, blinding, pure and holy. This was sometimes seen as separate from the divine being, worn like a brilliant garment or headgear, or set about the features as glories. In art, this property could be represented by brightly coloured inlays on the surface of figures, or rosettes or stars sewn on textiles. In poetry, this concept was expressed by words meaning awe-inspiring radiance and sublime purity.

A distinctive aspect of Sumerian religious thought was the concept called 'me', literally 'is'. This was an individual, differentiated, abstract power that defined and controlled both divine attributes and attributes of human civilization (van Dijk 1971: 440–2). Thus there was a 'me' of individual gods, temples and lands, and of human institutions, states and accomplishments such as kingship, wisdom, music, old age or carpentry. According to the Sumerian myth of Inanna and Enki, Enki controlled these but Inanna got them away from him by getting him drunk then taking them as gifts proffered in his intoxicated state, which he regretted when sober (Farber, in Hallo 1997: 522–6). The concept of 'me' did not carry over into post-Sumerian times, though there was an Akkadian concept called 'parsu' which referred to the dynamic existence of gods and temples.

Birth and death

A further property of divinity was immortality. In narratives about divine deeds, gods were understood to be born of the intercourse of male and female parents. There is reference to their being nursed as infants but no further indication of a sense of their education, training or personal development. Rather, as in the case of Marduk in the Babylonian Epic of Creation, the gods were born with full powers, knowing how to use weapons, understand magic words and so forth. As with Ninurta, a hero god, younger gods were expected to honour, obey and avenge slights to their parents. Having achieved a certain maturity, the gods stayed that way and did not age, though one and the same god could be portrayed as a youthful hero or as a sublime sage with magical, in preference to physical, prowess.

Gods could die, but only at the hands of other gods. Some died in battle or were executed for offences against higher gods. For example, the rebel god, Aw-ila, in the Story of the Flood (Foster 1996: 160–203 and below, pp. 184–5, 187) was executed to punish the uprising of the lesser gods against the great gods, but his spirit lingered on in the newly created human race, palpable as the human pulse. His flesh and blood were used to make the first human and his will may have given the human race its rebellious or wayward spirit. The execution of Kingu, leader of the attacking army of gods and monsters in the Babylonian Epic of Creation, was modelled on this episode, but Kingu was there (falsely) accused of suborning Tiamat, mother of the gods, to kill her children (Foster 1996: 350–401).

Gods in their dwellings

Just as a great king might exercise wide dominion in the world but needed to sleep and eat, so too the Mesopotamian gods were ascribed universal dominion but had physical, social and aesthetic needs that their human subjects were created to serve (Oppenheim 1977: 183–98). Thus temples of the gods were at first houses then palatial structures where the god ruled as a householder and dignitary (Oppenheim 1961: 158–69). The god's house was provided with sleeping quarters, audience chambers, storerooms and dining halls in which choice foods were served and music performed. There were gardens for the god's enjoyment and dalliance. Their homes were appointed in luxurious style with works of art, commemorative inscriptions and treasuries of offerings, gifts and valuables. The gods travelled to visit other gods and entertained each other with feasts accompanied by speeches and heavy drinking. Like any good householder, the gods were concerned with the stewardship of their domains. The Sumerian goddess Nanshe, for example, is described in a hymn as searching out fraud and embezzlement in her household accounts (Jacobsen 1987a: 131; Heimpel in Hallo 1997: 526–31).

The gods were understood to be physically present at will in an image (Hallo 1983) that was dressed and adorned with special clothing, jewelry and headdresses. Destruction of the image or its removal by an enemy was a disaster for the community, demanding a theological explanation: the deity was angry with his city or her people, even if no cause for this anger could be established, and had forsaken both the image and the community. Return of an abducted image was a moment of jubilation and renewal of patriotic feeling, as when the lost statue of Marduk was returned from its captivity in Elam by the Babylonian king Nebuchadnezzar I (twelfth century BCE). Some Mesopotamian authors speculated on the relationship between an object produced by human craftsmanship and a universal cosmic power, asserting, as in the Epic of Erra, that the image was primeval and the craftsmen uncanny, with later human counterparts permitted by the gods to make repairs (Foster 1996: 765). However, reports of theft of divine apparel or jewelry suggest that not all Mesopotamians were awed by images of the gods.

Works and deeds

Whereas Mesopotamians believed that the gods controlled all events and processes in the universe, Mesopotamian literature preserved narratives of surpassing deeds of individual gods. One narrative pattern involved a warrior-god who defeated a monster, often when other gods had tried and failed or were too frightened to attempt the quest. The victor was then acclaimed hero or even leader of the other gods. The opposing monster may have been a gigantic serpent or dragon, a monstrous bird or a mythologized volcano. In the latest version of this story, the Babylonian Epic of Creation (Dalley 1989: 228–77; Foster 1996: 350–401), the monster was Tiamat or the sea, primeval mother of the younger gods, a portrayal said to be of Syrian origin, as the sea was of lesser importance in Mesopotamian thought than in Syria. This narrative type is sometimes understood as a Mesopotamian justification for absolute rule as necessary to ward off outside threats.

Other narratives of divine deeds include construction of natural features of the landscape such as mountains or watercourses, or the erection of barriers, fortifications or cities, as well as the initiation of human cultural and political institutions. For example, a Sumerian poem describes how the god Ninurta reconstructed the bed of the Tigris river along the foot of the mountains (after Jacobsen 1987a: 252):

> (In those former days) the Tigris river did not rise splendid,
> It did not flow directly to the sea,
> It did not carry fresh (irrigation) water . . .
> (The god Ninurta) made a bank of stones against the mountain,
> These hovered before it, like drifting clouds on outstretched wings.
> He set this to be a barrier before the land, like a great wall,
> . . .
> And the mighty waters ran along these stones.

Crediting the gods with human achievements, such as instituting magic or monarchy, lent these human affairs prestige, antiquity and validity because Mesopotamians considered antiquity of human institutions a proof that they were favoured by the gods.

Cosmology

In literature and magic spells, Mesopotamians referred to the beginnings of the world. The various accounts were quite different, so there was no one story that should be considered standard or universally accepted. The most comprehensive and ambitious of the accounts of creation, contained in the Babylonian Epic of Creation, refers to a time before the present generation of gods in which there were two waters, male and female, commingling with no distinct separation. Rather than the 'chaos' which it is often considered, this combination was dynamic and productive, yielding several pairs of older gods, male and female, and ultimately a much larger number of younger gods, on whom the narrative focuses. The successive generations of gods were progressively stronger and greater than the preceding ones, suggesting that the Mesopotamians visualized a dynamic past development of their universe, culminating in a present order that was stable and unchanging (Foster 1996: 350):

> When on high no name was given to heaven,
> Nor below was the netherworld called by name,
> Primeval Apsu was their progenitor,
> And matrix-Tiamat was she who bore them all,
> They were mingling their waters together,
> No canebrake was intertwined nor thicket matted close.
> When no gods at all had been brought forth,
> None called by names, none destinies ordained,
> Then were the gods formed within these two.

The Babylonian Epic of Creation ascribed to Marduk, god of Babylon, the reorganization of the cosmos into the form the Babylonians knew it, including the motions of the stars, a firmament above the earth, rivers and mountains of the earth, the phases of the moon, and so forth. Since this account dates only to the second half of the second millennium BCE and presupposes a cosmos centred on Babylon, there is no reason to assign it universal validity in Mesopotamia. The poem appears to contain a variety of earlier materials worked into a coherent narrative.

The universe was visualized as circular, with a firmament below heaven and a corresponding surface above the netherworld. Some speculative texts proposed several layers in the cosmos (Lambert 1975). In any case, heaven was so remote from earth that the land was not visible to a human observer who had risen so high, such as the mythologized king Etana, who flew up to heaven on an eagle, or the sage Adapa, who was summoned to heaven after interfering with the wind. In later periods, heaven and netherworld were thought to be organized like urban earth, with gates, defences, and large residences for the gods containing reception areas, sleeping quarters, baths and other amenities.

Above and below

Despite the basic tripartite division of the cosmos into heaven, earth and nether-world, Mesopotamian literature often referred to a bipartite division, 'above and below', in which 'below' or 'earth' may have included both the earth inhabited by humans and the netherworld, the two visualized as a unit opposite heaven. Earth had a five-part division: heartland (Mesopotamia, called 'the land') and the four cardinal directions, constituting 'inhabited territories', or the 'four quarters' (Babylonian 'edges') of the earth. Beyond these lay oceans in all directions, in some cases separated from the inhabited world by mountain ranges. Far in the west, according to the Epic of Gilgamesh (Foster 2001), lay 'the waters of death', which separated the land of the living from a remote place where the survivor of the deluge, Utanapishtim, lived with his wife. Mesopotamian literate culture generally viewed urban areas as safe, civilized and inhabited by gods. The inter-vening steppe was inhabited by wild animals and demons. Except for the sun, even the gods did not visit remote, uninhabited spaces.

End of the world

Mesopotamia offers little evidence for a belief in a future end of the world. The only clear reference to this occurs in a third-century BCE work in Greek by Berossus, reputedly a Babylonian priest. He stated that the earth was in dan-ger of ending in fire or flood when the planets were gathered in a straight line in the constellations Cancer or Capricorn. No earlier Mesopotamian reference to this belief has been identified, so its authenticity as a native Mesopotamian tradition is disputed. Although there are references to good and bad times and to the impermanence of political power in any one city or dynasty, these changes were described not as cyclical but as the result of divine favour or disfavour to individual rulers or their cities. The Mesopotamians viewed the world in which they lived as different from that of very ancient times, which were separated from the more recent past by the flood. The Mesopotamians believed that the flood would not recur; therefore, in effect the end of the world had already taken place. They expected the world to endure in the form they knew it, despite individual triumphs and destructions of cities and states. Since the flood had shown that the human race was essential to maintain the living standards of the gods, the gods might reduce the human population through plague or famine, but would never again attempt to eliminate it entirely.

Gods and the human race

According to the Babylonian Flood Story, the gods created the human race in order for it to maintain them in a comfortable and luxurious living standard. In this account, the first human was made in collaboration by the birth-goddess, Mami or Nintu, and Enki, god of wisdom. They took a piece of clay, kneaded it with divine spittle, then mixed in the spirit, flesh and blood of a slain rebellious god (Foster 1996: 168):

> They slaughtered Aw-ilu, who had the inspiration [for the revolt against
>   the gods], in their assembly.
> The [birth-goddess] Nintu mixed clay with his flesh and blood.
> That same god and man were thoroughly mixed in the clay.
> For the rest of time they would hear the drum,
> From the flesh of the god the spirit remained.
> It would make the living know its sign,
> Lest he be allowed to be forgotten, the spirit remained.

To sustain the human race, birth, maturity, marriage and procreation were instituted. Later, when the population had grown too great, celibacy, infertility, still birth and social restrictions against childbirth for certain groups of people were imposed on the human race.

This was not the only Mesopotamian story of how human beings were created. In a Sumerian account, the god of wisdom produced various experimental but defective human beings until a satisfactory human was brought forth (Kramer 1961: 68–70). In another Sumerian creation story, human beings grew from the earth after Enlil struck it with a pickaxe. Then he handed them the pickaxe and they set to work (Farber in Hallo 1997: 511–13). In the Babylonian Epic of Creation, Enki/Ea's role in creating the human race is subordinated to Marduk, who is said to have had the original idea for it (Foster 1996: 383):

> I shall compact blood, I shall cause bones to be.
> I shall make stand a human being, let 'Man' be its name.
> I shall create human kind.
> They shall bear the gods' burden that those may rest.

Humans in Mesopotamian thought were differentiated from animals in that they ate prepared foods, such as bread and beer, in preference to uncooked wild plants and water. Humans, unlike animals, wore clothes and treated and adorned their bodies with alien substances, such as oils and cosmetics, and cut their hair, rather than letting it grow to a natural length. Humans were different from gods in that they had inferior mental and physical powers and had limited lifespans. What some later peoples deemed human characteristics, such as an immortal soul, language, social organization and use of implements, seemed to the Mesopotamians to be developments of human potential rather than distinguishing features of the race.

Treatment of humanity

Although human justice was said to be pleasing to the gods, a gift of the gods, or of divine nature or origin, the Mesopotamians did not expect that their gods would necessarily treat them, their subjects, justly. The gods could be alternately protective and cruel, sustaining or harmful. The gods might reward good behaviour or they might be exploitative, indifferent or capricious, as in this characterization of the Babylonian god Marduk (Foster 1996: 309):

> His scourge is barbed and punctures the body,
> His bandages are soothing, they heal the doomed.
> He speaks and makes one incur many sins,
> On the day of his justice sin and guilt are dispelled.

Gods might take a sudden affection to a human; at least, certain kings sometimes claimed that this happened to them, guaranteeing their success as rulers. Gods might have long-standing individual friendships with humans, such as the sages Adapa and Atrahasis enjoyed with Enki, god of wisdom, but these were exceptional instances.

Gods were expected to punish human wrong-doing, but this could not be relied upon. More than one Mesopotamian text reflects upon divine justice and wonders if proper service of the gods really promised a better human life or afterlife or if divine favour simply came or went without predictable patterns of consequences (Foster 1996: 796):

> God does not block the progress of a demon.
> A father hauls a boat up a channel,
> While his firstborn sprawls in bed.
> . . .
> What has it profited me that I knelt before my god?

The deluge

A major defining event in the Mesopotamian view of the history of the human race was the deluge, known in several Akkadian versions (Foster 1996: 160–203; George 1999: 88–95; Foster 2001: 84–9). This was considered a one-time, universal flood that changed human history forever. Although the Mesopotamians believed that certain familiar human institutions, such as living in cities, building temples and rule by kings, antedated the deluge, at the same time they believed that the correlation of biological and calendrical time was different before the flood from thereafter. Before the deluge, human beings lived immensely long lives, in some versions with long childhoods and adulthoods, in others with long adulthoods only. The flood was sent by the gods to diminish the human population of the world when their noise and clamour became intolerable to Enlil. So effective was the deluge that the human race was nearly wiped out, save for a flood hero, called Atrahasis or Utanapishtim, in Sumerian Ziusudra, who, at the urging of his friend Enki, built a boat, took on family and livestock, and was thereby saved from the catastrophe (Foster 2001: 85):

> Wreck house, build boat,
> Forsake possessions and seek life,
> Belongings reject and life save!
> Take aboard the boat seed of all living things.

The gods soon repented their deed in the face of devastation and hunger, so allowed the human race to repopulate, but with certain natural controls on productivity, and a normal lifespan of up to eighty years. The survivor of the flood was given immortality and removed to a location far beyond human existence, at the 'sources of the rivers'.

Death and the afterlife

Death in Mesopotamian religious thought did not mean the total extinction of the individual, only of the physical self and of those qualities of a person that made him productive and attractive to other human beings (Bottéro 1992: 268–86). A recognizable winged spirit, resembling a dove, passed to the netherworld. This was a dreary, sombre domain ruled by a pitiless hierarchy of deities and demons. There the spirit languished, often in hunger, thirst and misery, unless family or friends remembered to leave offerings of food and drink for the spirit to partake of and prayed for the spirit's rest and contentment (Foster 1996: 403):

> Dust is their sustenance and clay their food,
> They see no light but dwell in darkness,
> They are clothed like birds in wings for garments,
> And dust has gathered on the door and bolt.

A Sumerian poem recounting a visit to the netherworld refers to the dependence of the dead upon the living (Foster 2001: 141):

> Did you see the ghost of him who has no one to make funerary offerings?
> I saw him. He eats table scraps and bread crusts thrown into the street.

Ghosts and spectres of the dead could trouble the living, sometimes for no apparent reason, sometimes because they had not been properly interred or were discontented because of some human action or neglect. The city Cutha, in northern Babylonia, was considered the city of the dead and the centre of the cult of death.

The netherworld was organized like an earthly or heavenly kingdom, surrounded by walls with seven gates (Lambert 1990). A popular Mesopotamian poem (Dalley 1989: 163–81; Foster 1996: 410–28) told how the netherworld had once been ruled by a queen alone, Ereshkigal, but that she eventually found a husband, Nergal or Erra. In one version of the story, he forces himself into the netherworld by violence and threatens her into submission. In another, he breaks her loneliness and sexual frustration with a passionate relationship that finally results in their marriage. The gods of heaven and netherworld, separated, according to the Babylonian Epic of Creation, into two groups of 600 each, could not visit each other, though they could exchange messengers. Even the great gods feared the netherworld, which barred countless human dead from swarming onto the earth to devour the living in their eternal, unsatiated hunger.

The dead entered the netherworld naked and relinquished all hope of returning to life. How their ghosts escaped to plague the living is not clear. Various Mesopotamian stories told of human beings who learned what happened after a person died. In one, the Sumerian hero Enkidu volunteered in a fit of bravado to go down to the netherworld to retrieve a favourite athletic object of the king, Gilgamesh. This was apparently a stick and a ball or puck that had fallen down there at the pleas of the people who were oppressed by the violent game that made use of them. The losers resented Gilgamesh's bullying tactics in the game. Enkidu recognized his relatives and saw certain distinctions among the dead: heroes were treated better than common folk, for example, and stillborn children had a sort of play area with miniature furniture. He barely escaped alive and forgot in the stress of the moment to bring back the objects (Foster 2001: 129–43). Much later, an Assyrian dignitary described a vision of the netherworld that included an array of monsters, composites of humans and animals in shape. He, like Enkidu, recognized a dead spirit, but fled in an ecstasy of terror and grief, narrowly escaping permanent confinement (Foster 1996: 715–22):

> He darted out into the street like an arrow and scooped up dirt from alley and square in his mouth, all the while setting up a frightful clamor, 'Woe! Alas! Why have you ordained this for me?'

Mesopotamians honoured the dead of their families with a regular ceremony of remembrance and offering. Dead and sometimes even living kings were accorded divine honours and observances in special sanctuaries. Rulers and other powerful people could be buried in lavish tombs with grave gifts, perhaps more as a splendid way of dying than out of hope that they would need such gifts in the afterlife. Some Sumerian rulers had chariots, animals and even court attendants buried with them; Assyrian queens might be buried with their finest jewelry. Clay or metal vessels might hold food, drink and cosmetics. Burial might be in vaults in royal palaces, under the floor of homes (especially for children) or in cemeteries outside the city. Graves were not marked on the surface, so far as is known, and funerary inscriptions, naming the deceased or invoking blessings upon them from future descendants or passers-by, were very rare. One literary text describes an excavation to open an ancient tomb and the horrible shock the investigators felt when they beheld and reflected on the fate in store for them (Foster 1996: 436).

One of the major literary achievements of ancient Mesopotamia, the Akkadian Epic of Gilgamesh (George 1999; Foster 2001), tells the story of Gilgamesh, king of

Uruk, who sought immortal life. This was based on older Sumerian poems about various episodes in Gilgamesh's life. In the epic, Gilgamesh's beloved friend, the wild man Enkidu, dies as the result of an expedition to achieve eternal fame for Gilgamesh by slaying a distant monster and cutting down a great tree. Terrified of dying himself, Gilgamesh abandons all in a desperate quest to find the survivor of the flood, Utanapishtim, to ask him his secret of immortality. Gilgamesh eventually reaches Utanapishtim after unexampled heroism and hardships, not to mention the timely intervention of several kind-hearted women, but learns that his hope is vain – Utanapishtim was granted immortality for surviving the flood, but this was a one-time event that would not be repeated for Gilgamesh's sake. Neither he nor any other human being had any hope of achieving immortality. This poem was popular in learned circles; manuscripts have turned up throughout Mesopotamia, and from Syria and Asia Minor, dating to a time span of 1500 years.

There was no Mesopotamian paradise, no return of the soul in another body for another life, no judgement, and no sense that death might eventually end in a final consummation. Some Mesopotamians responded to this outlook by suggesting that the good for a human being was to enjoy life, love, family and vitality while they were within reach, for even a modest life was better than a grand death, as a tavern keeper advises Gilgamesh (Foster 2001: 75):

> When the gods created mankind,
> They established death for mankind,
> And withheld eternal life for themselves.
> As for you, Gilgamesh, let your stomach be full,
> Always be happy, night and day.
> Make every day a delight,
> Night and day play and dance.
> Your clothes should be clean,
> Your head should be washed,
> You should bathe in water,
> Look proudly on the little one holding your hand,
> Let your mate be always blissful in your loins,
> This, then, is the work of mankind.

Demons, ghosts, monsters, protective spirits

In addition to the gods, the human race and animal life, Mesopotamians recognized divine classes of beings, mostly harmful to the human race, which could be described as demons, often with human shapes but hideous or distorted features (Black and Green 1992). Most demons were not individuals with personal names, but belonged to a class or type, like a wild animal, referred to by general term: 'lurker' 'snatcher' or the like. An exception was Lamashtu, an evil goddess expelled from heaven who pursued the human race, causing infant death, disease and unhappiness in family life (Foster 1996: 850):

> She touches the bellies of women in labor,
> She yanks out the pregnant woman's baby
> . . .
> She roars like a lion,
> She keeps up the howling of a demonic dog.

Demons might lurk in unfrequented spots to attack the unwary or might sneak into people's homes, like serpents through crevices, to work their will. They might physically seize upon a person, clutching, twisting or hitting him, to cause pain, sickness and dysfunction such as paralysis, mumbling speech or twitching. They might startle or terrify a person by strange noises or sensations, or rob them of vitality, beauty, energy or health by hostile staring and malevolent stalking. They could attack animals as well, silently dogging their footsteps to bring lameness, fever or distress upon them. Demons had no emotions and needed no rest, sleep or sustenance (Foster 1996: 833):

> They are drifting phantoms,
> They take no wife, they beget no son,
> They know neither sparing of life nor mercy,
> They heed no prayers or entreaties.

Some demons were ghosts of a person's family or ghosts of people who had never enjoyed a fulfilling life, such as familial or conjugal love or sexual satisfaction. These were thus doomed to harass a happier humanity in their perpetual discontent. Human beings could protect themselves from demons through the intervention of a beneficent guardian spirit through prayer to the individual deity who was supposed to be concerned with their welfare, and through rituals and magic that could harm the demon, or drive or entice it away (Foster 1996: 832):

> Make the evil eye cross seven rivers,
> Make the evil eye cross seven canals,
> Make the evil eye cross seven mountains.
> Take the evil eye and tie its feet to an isolated reed stalk.

Monsters were visualized as composite creatures, made up of elements of bulls, lions, serpents, birds of prey, bisons, fish and human beings (Black and Green 1992). Mesopotamian art was highly successful in representing organically credible composite beasts. Literary descriptions of monsters are known, including, for example, men with heads or limbs of lion, fish, scorpion, bull or bison, as well as various kinds of dragons. Although most were harmful and terrifying, some could be beneficent to the human race, so that images of them were used to protect major public buildings, such as the royal palace or temples, from outside harm. The Babylonian Epic of Creation describes how Tiamat, mother of all the gods, formed monsters as part of an army to kill her offspring, the younger gods. In general, however, demons and monsters were taken for granted as part of the universe with which weaker humans had to contend. Demons and monsters could be defeated and killed by hero gods. They were seen as a frightening and baleful presence that one hoped to avoid wherever possible.

Protective spirits were sometimes personified human qualities, such as talent, ability to succeed and the instinct for self-preservation. These were referred to as Lamassu and Shedu (Oppenheim 1977: 198–206). Images of Lamassu were placed near the entrance of ceremonial buildings to protect the occupants of the building from harm. These spirits were not prayed to specifically, but were supposed to be vigilant to protect a person's interests, health, professional advancement and similar concerns.

Religious institutions in human society

The temple was constructed as the personal residence of the deity, the divine family and divine servants and was often described as a physical link between the world of the gods in heaven and the world of the human race on earth. A Sumerian hymn expresses this as follows (after Jacobsen 1987: 380):

> House, great tiara thrust up into the sky,
> House, rainbow thrust up into the sky,
> House, whose lordly tiara is worn in innermost heaven,
> Whose foundation is set in the depths below.

Within the temple were living quarters for its permanent human residents, including priests and priestesses, administrators, and dependent workers and slaves. Some priests and administrators lived in their own homes, often in a superior residential area near the temple complex. There were some public areas of the temple, such as courtyards and gardens, where anyone could approach the deity with regular offerings, individual prayers, petitions and gifts. Other areas, such as the cult chamber, were accessible only to certain members of the temple staff, such as priests or temple workers.

Temples were usually the largest and most imposing structures in a community, symbolizing its wealth and success (Kraus 1990). Babylonian temples often controlled important economic resources, such as arable land, livestock, precious metals, timber and other commodities. Temples could therefore act in the community as proprietors, investors and employers, numbering among their personnel privileged and educated members of the community of free citizens, who might serve as priests or other professionals, as well as outcasts of society, who performed menial tasks. Temples could lease out land and livestock to entrepreneurs, for in some areas, such as Uruk in the middle of the first millennium BCE, the temples owned enormous tracts of land, thousands of head of livestock and extensive orchards. From the end of the third millennium on, temple resources were increasingly managed by agents of the king, but the temples still retained ultimate ownership. Northern Mesopotamian temples could act as banks, making loans or advancing resources to speculators or those in need.

As an important emotional and spiritual focal point of the community, temples provided divine sanctions for human activities where recourse to the divine was called for. Oaths to establish truth and to promise adherence to the terms of contracts and treaties might be administered in the temple or in the presence of divine symbols. Temples provided social services, such as maintenance and employment for the destitute and handicapped or the children of poor families who might otherwise find no productive place in human society. Some people, especially children, might be given as a pious act to a temple or dedicated to work as servants to a god often in times of personal or economic distress. Temples might serve as a community storehouse and treasury for the safekeeping of valuables and important records. Temples attracted the services of a literate, specialized elite. At the early second-millennium cities of Ur and Nippur, for example, members of the temple staff operated private academies in their homes to teach Mesopotamian learning to the future ruling class of the community, at the same time inculcating the values and common experiences of management and leadership. There is no evidence that temples maintained schools of their own.

In second- and first-millennium Babylonia, the custom grew of buying and selling prebends or allotments of temple offices, offerings and income, sometimes in minute shares. Perhaps the buyers of such shares in temple offices gained economic benefits or perhaps they sought prestige by participating in an important urban establishment. Perhaps too temples needed to convert some of their prerogatives to cash. The temples were supported by the income from their own resources, by a regular tithe or temple tax levied on the population, including the king, and by regular deliveries of food, livestock and other commodities provided by the king. Individuals could make gifts as the result of vows or in gratitude for some success, such as a commercial venture. Kings presented temples with monuments commemorating their deeds. Many of these were open to public inspection in temple courtyards and stood as an important statement of royal ideology. Construction, adornment and restoration of temples was a fundamental duty of monarchy throughout Mesopotamian history.

In second-millennium Babylonia, some temples, such as the temple of the sun-god at Sippar, included residential complexes for sequestered women of local wealthy families. These have sometimes been compared to the cloisters of the Christian world. The women, called *naditu*, 'fallow', often owned substantial property through inheritance, which they increased through long, active careers in business, using agents. Being married to the deity, they took no human husbands and bore no children, apparently lest they alienate important wealth from the paternal family. However these women sometimes adopted younger cloistered women or sons to care for them in their old age and willed to their adopted children their well-furnished homes in the temple complex and their often valuable estates, to the chagrin of the paternal family. There is no evidence that these women played any sacerdotal role, nor is it clear whether or not they could leave the cloistered complex at will.

Priesthood

A broad class of professional people approached the gods directly. In the late third and early second millennia, major male gods had a high-priestess and female gods a high-priest. At the Sumerian city of Ur, for example, the high-priestesses of the moon-god were women of royal birth who served the god for their entire lives. Letters and poetry attributed to these women show their high social importance, deep religious feeling and impressive educations. They lived in a residential complex within the temple and officiated at rites as the chief and closest human being to the divinity. In later Babylonia, high-priestesses are less well known and some gods, such as Marduk, had only a high-priest. In Assyria, on the other hand, the king acted as high-priest of the principal god Assur, representing the Assyrian community to its god. The king wrote formal accounts of his deeds addressed to the god Assur in letter form, perhaps read aloud to members of the government. Assyrian deities other than the god Assur seem to have had their own priesthood.

Large temples had an elaborately articulated hierarchy of cultic personnel, such as performers of laments and penitential prayers, purifiers and other specialists. Some of these were literate and in some temples they were part of a controlling family group. These were allowed to enter inner areas of the temple and were entitled to income and support from the offerings to the deity. The temple staff included many people who were not specialists in cultic matters, such as shepherds, cooks, doorkeepers, courtyard sweepers, and others who participated in the day-to-day operations of the large building complex and estate. In the first millennium, major temples had gangs of slave workmen in addition to dependent and handicapped people who worked in the orchards and gardens. Some temples sustained women without husbands or paternal family connections. The role of these women in society is not clear. Some may have worked as midwives or taken care of orphan children, while others may have engaged in prostitution, but there is little evidence for this. Their status as temple dependants might be indicated by distinctive ways of dressing their hair, but this is uncertain.

Dozens of titles of temple officials from various periods are known. In the first millennium, there is reference to a kind of collegium of priests, as well as to an assembly of the temple staff and other free citizens which adjudicated non-capital offences, such as theft of temple property, assault, public drunkenness and improper liaisons with temple women. In later Babylonia, large temples included a royal steward to represent the king's interests in the temple economy, and the king could lease out large areas of temple land to entrepreneurs on his own volition.

Prophets and oracles

Outside the ranks of regular temple staff, particularly in the Syrian city of Mari during the early second millennium BCE, there is ample reference to prophets and ecstatics who spoke directly on behalf of the gods (Durand 1988: 377–452). Some of these people, both men and women, went into a trance-like state and recounted visions, along with the speech of the gods. Others seem to have had their prophetic state induced by the administration of beverages. Their utterances tended to be brief, in poetic language, and focused on affairs of state and matters affecting the king (Foster 1996: 213–14):

> They will put you to the test with a revolt. Watch over yourself! Set in position around yourself trustworthy servants whom you love, so they can watch over you. You must not go anywhere by yourself! But those men who would put you to the test, I [the goddess Anunitum], will deliver these men into your power.

The veracity of prophetic speech was checked by divination. The spoken prophecies normally lacked the ethical content associated with the biblical prophecies and often exhorted the king to take care of himself and to beware his enemies. A few instances of gods responding in written form to prayers and petitions are also known from northern Mesopotamia. Prophecy seems to have been more characteristic of the northern Semitic-speaking world than of Sumer or even Babylonia.

In Assyria in the first millennium, oracles from a god or goddess were addressed directly to Assyrian kings, promising them protection from their enemies (Parpola 1997). Like the prophecies from Mari, these could make use of striking figurative language and tended to be intimate addresses to the ruler. How these were delivered is unclear, perhaps through ecstatics or through voices heard by the king when he was in the sanctuary (Foster 1996: 712–13):

> Fear not, Assurbanipal, I [the god Nabu] will give you long life, I will entrust fair breezes with your spirit. This, my eloquent mouth, will ever bless you among the great gods.

Celebrations of religion in human society

Devotion

Mesopotamian devotion is best known from personal names, many of which contained the names of gods, together with a prayer or statement of praise or blessing: 'O-Sin-Accept-My-Entreaties', 'My-Ear-Is-Listening-for-Aya', 'My-God-Is-Like-My-Father', 'Ishtar-Is-Gracious', 'I-Saw-Her-Greatness', 'Assur-Is-My-Trust'. Analysis of personal names shows that although many gods were known in the pantheon, far fewer occurred as elements in name-giving. Deities appearing frequently in names included Ishtar, Sin, Shamash, Ea, Marduk, Assur and Nabu. Certain gods' names were found in certain regions, such as Dagan on the upper and middle Euphrates, but less commonly in Babylonia; or Anu, the use of whose name greatly increased in Late Babylonian Uruk. The name of the local city-god, such as Marduk in Babylon, tended to predominate in names of that region.

Short expressions of piety, such as blessings, were standard in salutations but were less frequent in the body of letters, for example, so it is difficult to gauge their importance in common speech outside of formulas of politeness. Short prayers can occur in the inscriptions on mundane objects such as cylinder seals, especially during the second half of the second millennium BCE. Impressions of these seals were used to indicate ownership, authenticity and authority in documents, fastenings of doors, packing materials and the like, so the prayers may have been more conventional than deeply felt expressions of devotion.

Rituals, observances, offerings, festivals

Formal service to a deity entailed specific rites and rituals, both spoken and performed. These commenced in a state of ritual purity achieved by washing or 'lustration' and sprinkling the floor with clean water. Formal actions included burning incense, making food offerings and libations, scattering flour, making gestures with the hands, facing in certain directions, or laying out objects, such as pieces of cloth, twigs or dishes. Some rituals called for fabrication of objects such as figurines, normally of clay or paste, and manipulating them. Many rituals were long and complicated, requiring considerable preparation, memorization of prayers and spells in Sumerian and Akkadian, and careful performance by trained specialists.

A fundamental principle of divine service was regular and extensive consumption of commodities by the gods in the form of food, sacrifices and offerings. At Uruk in the first millennium, for example, major gods were served two major and two minor meals a day. The divine diet might include, at different times and places, cooked meats and fish, vegetables, salt, baked goods such as breads, dairy products such as cheese and butter, beverages such as beer, ale and wine, and sweets such as honey and sweet cakes, accompanied by recitations, music and aromatics. The table was ritually set and cleared and the priests, sometimes the king, officiated. There were also banquets on festival occasions.

A festival called 'akitu', known already in the third millennium, may originally have been associated with the equinoxes. The city-god left his city in procession, sojourned briefly in a special building outside the city walls, then returned in triumphal procession again. By the first millennium, this festival was associated with the new year, which occurred in the spring. Local versions of its elaborate rituals are known from Assur, Babylon and Uruk, mostly from tablets dating after the seventh century BCE. The new year's ritual from Babylon, for example, began with washing by the officiants, opening doors to the temple, fabrication of figurines to be ritually beheaded on the sixth day of the festival, and recitation of prayers. On the fourth day the Babylonian Epic of Creation was recited. Towards the end of the festival, the king participated, laying down his sceptre before the god Marduk. The officiating priest slapped the king's face and pulled his face to the ground by the ears, while the king spoke words of submission to Marduk and his temple. Later the king was slapped again. If tears came to his eyes, this was considered a favourable omen. No one knows if this ceremony was ever fully carried out as described or if many kings submitted themselves to these indignities. The high point of the festival remained the procession of the god, which moved through richly decorated streets on an established route from the festival house to his sanctuary (Cohen 1993: 400–53).

Abundant documentation attests to sacrifice of live animals. For some rituals these were carefully selected by age, fatness, diet, sexual experience, state of their horns, colour and so forth. Cattle and sheep were most often used for this purpose. These were slaughtered by a professional slaughterer in the ceremony and the carcass divided among temple personnel according to specific rules. Victims could be offered in gratitude, as substitutes for divine punishment or for divination purposes. In divination a question was posed of the gods of divination, such as Shamash and Adad; then after a vigil the animal was slaughtered and the entrails, gall bladder and liver were examined for certain marks or configurations of ominous significance (Oppenheim 1977: 206–27).

There were regular and free-will offerings presented by private citizens, administrators and the king. These included agricultural products, livestock, clothing and valuable objects of wood, metal and stone. Individuals were supposed to set aside for the gods on some occasions portions of their own meals; it was considered an affront to the gods to eat these. First-fruit offerings celebrated the harvest and yield of livestock. Thank offerings for vows and ventures were also made, such as model ships for the successful completion of commercial voyages. In addition to consumption as food or gifts, various commodities were burned, such as incense, to draw the attention of a god to prayer about to be made, for example. Some temples had a basket or box for small, free-will donations made as an act of virtue.

Individual gifts of objects, such as bowls, stands, weapons, furniture or statues to the gods were common practice at all periods. Many were expensive objects engraved with a prayer for the dedicant's life or with a statement of the name of the dedicant and a record of his donation. Some dedications add the name of a ruler or patron. Dedications by both men and women are known. Royal dedications were usually more lavish, for the presentation of which poetry and formal commemorative inscriptions were commissioned. In early second-millennium Babylonia, when years were named in honour of a major event of the preceding year, numerous year names commemorated art objects, weapons, sculpture and major pieces of furniture prepared for gods, temples or the priesthood.

Formal verbal expressions of piety and religious feeling are found in numerous prayers in Sumerian and Akkadian. Prayers may contain petitions for a favour, reminding the deity of a deed of a loyal servant, or they may express contrition for evils done and obligations not met. Sometimes specific evil deeds are alluded to, but more commonly the petitioner professes to be unaware of the cause of the deity's anger against him (Foster 1996: 670–1):

> I do not know what wrong I have done,
> I do not know what sin I have committed,
> I do not know what abomination I have perpetrated,
> I do not know what taboo I have violated!

Prayers usually contain praises for the divinity, stressing the god's power, valour, position of leadership among the gods, and sometimes the god's merciful nature as well. Some prayers conclude with a promise, not for better behaviour, but for glorification of the mighty deed the god has done in forgiving the petitioner and removing the punishment for his sins. Some prayers conclude as well by asking for the benevolent intercession of the god's wife or of other gods. Occasionally prayers were written out in letter form; others were evidently spoken or performed. Goddesses were generally considered potentially more forgiving than gods. Prayer to the gods on ritual occasions often had a tone of appeasement, sorrow, hope and penitence. The dominating mood was one of formality and anxiety. For rituals involving an all-night vigil, a special type of prayer addresses the beings of the night sky and reflects on the loneliness and solemnity of the occasion, when the rest of the community is asleep.

Hymns of praise were composed for numerous major gods, including stars and planets. These were intended to be sung by single voices and by choruses. Some manuscripts make allusion to performance with brief notations such as 'Its antiphon' but nothing is known of the performance techniques or even what musical instruments were used. In addition to praise of the divinity, some hymns may contain petitions for the city or the reigning king. Some hymns contained narratives of the god's deeds or allusions to cultic changes, such as exaltation to new status. Others were so general in nature that the same hymn could be used for different gods. In the second millennium BCE, elaborate hymns up to 200 lines in length combined different styles and compositions about a deity into large, composite works that are sometimes called 'literary' or 'great' hymns. Whether or not these large texts had a liturgical use is not known. A distinctive form of praise for female deities was the hymn of self-praise, in which a goddess sings of her beauty, valour, lofty responsibilities, learning and other accomplishments (Foster 1996: 486–94). Hymns, like personal names, invoked only a small number of deities within the larger pantheon, scarcely thirty out of many hundreds, with preference to the more important ones, such as Ishtar, Marduk, Sin, Shamash and Nabu.

Letters and other records occasionally refer to rituals and observances that private people or families might perform, but their purpose and procedure are mostly unknown. Some of these included honouring the dead of the family, expressing hope or thanks for good health and happiness, seeking the cause of some misfortune or seeking to avert portended evil. Such rituals might require the purchase of materials not commonly found in the home. Calendars of favourable and unfavourable days include simple rituals anyone could perform.

From the late third millennium, a vivid picture of the rituals carried out, over many days, for the consecration of a new temple is provided by the temple hymn of Gudea of Lagash (Jacobsen 1987a: 386–444). A few major rituals from the late periods are known in some detail, such as for the Babylonian new year's festival, and rituals for the reconstruction of a temple, the putting into cultic service of certain objects such as statues, weapons or musical instruments, and the cleansing of impurities from the person of the king or from the temple precincts.

In a ritual scholars call the 'sacred marriage', the king had intercourse with a woman, perhaps a priestess, representing a goddess (Kramer 1969). The poetry celebrating this ritual suggests that it took place in the early spring to guarantee fertility in the land. Any male offspring of such a union could be heir to the throne and claim divine parentage. The hymns of this ceremony show that it was carried out with the joy and solemnity of a royal marriage. It is best known from sources dating to the end of the third and the beginning of the second millennium BCE, with scattered allusions to it in later periods.

In a ritual known as the 'substitute king', a ruler sought to avoid misfortune presaged in omens by setting a substitute, perhaps a condemned person, on the throne for a limited period, who bore the misfortune or was killed if he was still alive at the end of the period (Bottéro 1992: 138–55). The seventh-century Assyrian king Esarhaddon, for example, dressed as a farmer for this ritual, and official letters were directed to the 'farmer'.

Public festivals and processions occurred at regular intervals throughout the year. In some, the whole community participated, dressed in holiday clothes and watching a procession of the god's image through the streets or by boat through a canal on a ritual journey to another sanctuary. The image was splendidly attired and the mood seems to have been one of display and exhilaration. Some festivals included athletic events in honour of a god or goddess, dancing, and dramatic performances. Others entailed consumption of special seasonal or holiday foods. For most of these occasions, little is known beyond their names and the general idea that they were in honour of certain deities. These festivals were provided for in the calendar, which was based on a lunar year of twelve months, but included extra days from time to time in order to keep the calendar in accord with the seasons. For religious sanction of occasions not on the calendar, belief in favourable and unfavourable days and propitious weather conditions led to the construction of hemerologies and menologies, that is, calendars or tables of good and bad occasions for business, journeys and family activities, and for state events, such as military campaigns, as well as important ceremonies such as parades and coronations.

Ethics, piety

Mesopotamian literature did not hesitate to present the gods in ways that would be discreditable to human beings, such as being deceitful, intoxicated or irrational. These portrayals need only mean that the Mesopotamians did not expect their gods to be more ethical than they, only more powerful. At the same time, ethical and moral behaviour was considered honourable for a human being, likely to win favour from the gods just as among the human community. Religious ethics included honesty and fairness, truthfulness, and generosity towards less fortunate members of society. Some ancient texts elaborate on these themes, discussing at length such matters as perjury, fraud in business, abuse of power, theft and sexual licence, asserting that these would be punished by the gods in due season, but acknowledging, in some instances, that such punishment did not always occur. For most people, religious duty and piety consisted of regular libations and food offerings, prayer, observance of holy days and festivals, holding prescribed rites, teaching dependants reverence and worship, and not invoking the name of a god lightly or falsely. Neglect of these matters could result in divine displeasure or punishment (Foster 1996: 312–13):

> Like one who had not made libations to his god,
> Nor invoked his goddess with a food offering,
> Who was not wont to prostrate, nor seen to bow down,
> From whose mouth supplication and prayer were wanting,
> Who skipped holy days, despised festivals,
> Who was neglectful, omitted the gods' rites,
> Who had not taught his people reverence and worship,
> Who did not invoke his god, but ate his food offering,
> Who snubbed his goddess, brought her no flour offering,
> Like one possessed, who fogot his lord,
> Who casually swore a solemn oath by his god:
> (I was unjustly punished like such a man).

Scepticism, impiety

Mesopotamian written tradition did not admit openly expressed doubt as to the very existence of gods, for to most people the existence of gods was self-evident in the powers of nature and the endurance of human institutions. Doubt in the likelihood of punishment and reward for human conduct was openly expressed, for experience showed that bad people could prosper and righteous ones suffer. Some authors lamented that the rich and powerful were held up as good examples, no matter what their behaviour, while the poor could be disdained as outlaws solely because of their poverty (Foster 1996: 797):

They fill the oppressor's strongroom with refined gold,
They empty the beggar's larder of his provisions.
They shore up the tyrant whose all is crime,
They ruin the weak, they oppress the powerless.
. . .
Solemnly they speak well of a rich man,
'He's a king,' they say, 'he has much wealth.'
They malign a poor man as a thief,
They lavish mischief upon him, they conspire to kill him.

Some authors responded to the question of whether or not the gods were just by asserting that suffering and redemption from suffering were simply two sides of a god's power, not dependent on justice at all. Others insisted that everyone who suffered misfortune must have done some evil sometime, even if he was unaware of it, and that everyone who committed a misdeed would eventually come to grief, thus justifying moral behaviour. One cynical writer remarked that he could train his god to follow him around like a dog making tiresome demands upon his master (Bottéro 1992: 251–67).

Impiety and sacrilege were sometimes committed by enemy kings who violated sanctuaries in warfare. A Sumerian inscription from Lagash, for example, accuses the king of Umma, a nearby city, of sacrilegious behaviour, as does an Akkadian poem about an Elamite ruler who violated the sanctuary of Enlil at Nippur. When Mesopotamian kings violated foreign sanctuaries, they sometimes felt the need to justify their actions, as when the eighth-century Assyrian king Sargon II explained his looting of the temple of the Urartian god Haldi, which was located somewhere in eastern Anatolia.

Impiety and violation of taboos in private life were sometimes considered signs of incipient insanity. The Epic of Erra develops the theme of sacrilege in describing a society that had thrown off all restraints and was bent on self-destruction through murder, violence and looting. According to this poem, violence developed its own uncontrollable momentum, destroying good and evil alike and bringing havoc upon palaces, hovels, temples and private homes. This in turn forced the gods to curse and forsake their cities in revulsion at the atrocities of their inhabitants. To the author of the Epic of Erra, impious acts could be symptomatic of collective insanity and he was deeply concerned as to how such social madness could develop in a world supposedly controlled by sage-like deities (Foster 1996: 782):

He who did not die in battle will die in the epidemic,
He who did not die in the epidemic, the enemy will plunder him,
He whom the enemy has not plundered, the bandit will murder him,
He whom the bandit did not murder, the king's weapon will vanquish
    him.
He whom the king's weapon did not vanquish, the prince will slay him,
He whom the prince did not slay, a thunderstorm will wash him away,
He whom the thunderstorm did not wash away, the sun will parch him.

Applications of religion in human society

Destiny

Mesopotamian thought was preoccupied by destiny, a belief that a person's success or failure in life was ordained at birth, even written on a tablet in the netherworld. Because a person's destiny was already decided at birth, his future was in fact his past. Destiny was not directly controlled by the gods but seems to have been understood as impersonal necessity, a hidden given, or a fact in the course of accomplishment. The gods did, however, vouchsafe to observant human beings glimpses of their destinies, long and short term, either in response to questions or through random sights, sounds or actions of potentially ominous significance. Knowledge of one's destiny opened the way to its modification or evasion if the prognosis seemed unfavourable (Rochberg-Halton 1982; Maul in Abusch 1999: 123–9). While one could not significantly change unfavourable character traits or propensities to failure or such a universal destiny as death, certain likelihoods of destiny such as health, happiness and prosperity might be revealed in signs and portents that could be evaluated by a specialist and divine assistance sought to enhance or alter them.

Divination

Divination in a broad sense was the Mesopotamian science of discerning destiny, divine will and intention behind observable phenomena (Bottéro 1974; Oppenheim 1977: 206–27). Almost anything had potentially positive or negative significance towards understanding a person's destiny: the regular motion of the stars and planets; exceptional celestial occurrences such as meteors or eclipses; atmospheric and meteorological variations; activity of human beings and animals; physical characteristics and placement, normal or abnormal, of inanimate objects, plants and other living things; accidents and common occurrences in human life. Specialists in interpretation of these prognoses used such techniques as historical coincidence (what occurred in the past when a certain omen was seen), analogy and contrast (up, down; left, right; pointing towards or away from) to add up a balance of positive and negative tendencies in the evidence, as in the modern technique of handwriting analysis.

The two basic approaches of divination were observation of random phenomena (such as objects lying in the street) or causing phenomena in the hope of a response to a specific question (pouring oil on water, sacrificing a sheep to examine its entrails). Both required specialized training and consultation of large collections of written omens. The consultation was expensive so was available only to those who had means to pay for it. Some phenomena, such as eclipses or monstrous births, were thought to be significant for public life, with portents for the stability of government and the well-being of the king, so were reported to the royal court along with other local news for evaluation by experts. Other types of omens, such as chance sounds or peculiar behaviour of domestic or wild animals, might apply to the person who experienced them, so he could seek professional assistance in interpreting them. Private letters only occasionally refer to consultation with diviners, though literary texts often do, so it is hard to know how important divination was in the life of ordinary citizens. Diviners were not priests but scholars learned in an intellectual endeavour. They sought to develop systematic tools to understand the present and future through observation, study and verification of findings. The arts of the diviner were therefore at the crossroads of human and divine coexistence, seeking to pass from the one to the other sphere by rational means.

Magic

Belief in and practice of magic flourished in the environment of Mesopotamian religious belief and practice (Abusch 1999). The magician accepted the existence of non-human powers and beings that could be invoked and used by humans. Magic words, for example, possessed in themselves the power to bring about a desired consequence: success in love or business; warding off human hostility, slander, threats, anger and unwanted feelings and desires. Often the magic words were said to originate with a god of magic, not the human speaker.

Magic words and rituals could work against more powerful threats such as sorcery, hidden misdeeds of the past, false or unfulfilled oaths, ghosts, demons, and evils of unknown origin. One common technique was to identify the evil as closely as possible, then to bring against it positive forces of a beneficent god such as Ea, Marduk or Asalluhi. More elaborate magical procedure entailed rituals carried out by specialists, such as exorcists, to identify and get rid of the affliction. Signs of affliction might include mental or bodily illness, loss of vitality, sexual dysfunction, alienation, feelings of anxiety or persecution. These might suggest the agency of gods, demons, ghosts, or all of them, which had to be identified and dealt with. Rituals might include symbolic washing off of impurities, burning, or interring evil in symbolic form and using magic words to ensure that the evil itself suffered the same fate as the symbol of it.

Exorcists, like diviners, were not priests so much as professionals who specialized in identifying and removing causes of human complaints through mostly magical means. In the case of illness, besides magic formulae and rituals, rational means such as pharmacopoeia, psychiatry, manipulation, poultices and dressings could also be used, thereby combining the practice of medicine with the arts of the magician. Here too religion, magic and human existence intersected to a degree that the activity cannot always be consigned to one or another category. They form rather a continuum between the sphere of human beings and the sphere of the gods that training, practice and skill could bridge.

Innovation and reform

Innovation in Mesopotamian religion was usually presented in symbolic terms that can be difficult to evaluate in modern times. A lengthy Sumerian poem, 'The Exaltation of Ishtar', refers to the elevation of the cult of Ishtar at Uruk over that of Anu, in which Anu joyfully promotes her to the status of queen of heaven. No one knows how or why Ishtar's cult gained prominence at Uruk. Perhaps too the cult of Ninurta originally dominated at Nippur, but was displaced at an unknown date by the cult of Enlil, who was called his 'father', although many scholars believe that the cult of Enlil was in fact original to Nippur.

Certain rulers, such as the sixth-century BCE Babylonian king Nabonidus, took pride in reviving ancient and forgotten religious practices. This shows that the cult changed over time and that certain practices were abandoned. He is also known for an abortive effort to promote the cult of the moon-god Sin, as a personal preference, at Babylon. This caused considerable resentment and was later transformed into a biblical legend of a mad Babylonian king, but there confused with Nebuchadnezzar II, Nabonidus' better-known predecessor. The Sargonic king Naram-Sin (late third millennium BCE) stated in an inscription that the grateful citizenry of his city, Agade, asked to have him made a god along with the other leading gods of Mesopotamia, but deification of living rulers was not a common practice. Another ruler, Urukagina (or Uruinimgina) of Lagash, commemorated his change of ancient practices, claiming that they were made with divine approval. He stated that he turned over various properties to the gods and that he had changed certain fees, obligations and practices, but the significance of his reforms is disputed.

Mesopotamian religion and the Bible

Mesopotamian religion has been of interest to biblical scholars since the discovery in 1872 by George Smith of a flood story in an Assyrian tablet. This proved that non-biblical ancient Near Eastern documents contained material directly pertinent to the Bible. To some thinkers, the uniqueness and integrity of the Bible could therefore no longer be maintained. Leading philologists, especially in Germany, such as Hugo Winckler, Hermann Gunkel, Heinrich Zimmern and Friedrich Delitzsch, staked out different and sometimes contradictory positions in what became known as 'Pan-Babylonianism' or the 'Astral-mythological' school. The basic tenet of this group was that the civilization of Israel was essentially Babylonian in origin, including its religious ideas, such as monotheism. Winckler, for example, argued that Joshua, Saul and David were actually Babylonian astral deities. Zimmern went on to suggest that Marduk was a forerunner of Jesus. Peter Jensen, a distinguished Assyriologist, argued that Abraham, Jesus and John the Baptist, for example, were borrowed from Babylonian mythology and that the Gilgamesh epic, to him a kind of astral saga, was the basis for the New Testament and the Koran. Outside of Germany more moderate positions were taken, but still implying a strong cultural and religious dependency of Israel upon Babylonia. The extravagant claims of the Pan-Babylonianists eventually collapsed and are not taken seriously today.

A broader and more moderate view held that Babylonia was part of the ancient Near Eastern context of the Hebrew Bible (Lambert 1988). Committed Christian and Jewish scholars, for example, often put the Bible first, so to them ancient Near Eastern 'parallels' helped to clarify or even 'prove' the validity of the Bible because they were independent witness to biblical passages. Mesopotamian studies, especially in the United States, became effectively an adjunct of biblical studies. In the period 1880–1940 the majority of leading American scholars in the discipline were Protestant clergymen, very much interested in possible biblical connections. To some scholars, such as W. F. Albright, the 'biblical world' came to include the whole of the ancient Near East. There was therefore no need to separate Mesopotamian studies from biblical studies; they were aspects of the same agenda. In this spirit, Albright could entitle one of his most popular books *From the Stone Age to Christianity* (Albright 1940). According to this, Mesopotamian religion was a 'preparatio' for the more profound religion of Israel, itself a preparation for Christianity. Today, because of the accumulation of new material, a panoramic grasp of the languages and civilizations of the ancient Near East such as Albright enjoyed is impossible to attain, but Albright's fundamental approach remains influential, especially among conservative Christian scholars.

Each new discovery of cuneiform tablets elicits a wave of publications asserting biblical 'parallels', many of them uncertain and farfetched, even when a millennium or more may have elapsed between the tablets and the relevant portion of the Bible. The biblical scholar M. Dahood, for example, saw parallels betwen the Bible and cuneiform tablets from Ebla in northern Syria, which date to approximately 1300 years before the kingdom of David. E. A. Speiser insisted that the 'patriarchal age' of the Bible was reflected in tablets from Nuzi in northern Mesopotamia (early fourteenth century BCE), although most of his analogies have been discarded in recent years. The discovery of prophetic documents at Mari (eighteenth century BCE) attracted much discussion, as did comparison of ancient treaties with the biblical covenant.

A subtler interconnection between the worlds of the Hebrews and of the Babylonians was provided by what might be called 'Pan-Semitism', the idea that the Semitic peoples had certain innate mental and emotional characteristics and limitations in common that conditioned their religious values. A concise statement of this view, which is traceable, for example, to the works of the influential French thinker Ernest Renan, will be found in S. A. Cook's contribution 'The Semites, Temperament and Thought' in the *Cambridge Ancient History* (1924), chapter V. Cook held that Semitic thought was verbal rather than visual, emotional rather than systematic or speculative, and so could not have created such a grand astral system of beliefs as the Pan-Babylonianists had imagined underlay modern Christianity, Judaism and Islam. To Pan-Semitists, Greece, with its alleged superior visual and speculative thought, albeit comparatively shallow religion, was as essential to understanding Christianity as was Judaism. Scholars wrote of the 'Hebrew' and the 'Greek' element in Christianity and European culture. The Pan-Semitists bracketed Judaism, Islam and Babylonia as 'Semitic' in type, but not Christianity. This left the place of the Sumerians in the equation Babylonian = Semitic difficult to define. The early twentieth-century historian Eduard Meyer, for example, therefore argued that the Semites were the original inhabitants of Mesopotamia and the Sumerians were later invaders, thereby maintaining the originally 'Semitic' character of Mesopotamian civilization. In the period after World War I, some scholars tried to distinguish 'Sumerian' from 'Semitic' thought in Mesopotamian culture. Thus discussion of the relations between Babylonia and the Bible proceeded in an atmosphere charged with faith, scepticism and anti-Semitism.

Some scholars of Mesopotamia sought to declare independence from biblical studies in the 1930s, insisting that Mesopotamia be studied on its own terms, even in isolation, but for most people the main interest of Mesopotamian religions lies in their historical interest and comparison with ancient Greece and the Bible. Studies regularly appear on the Near Eastern background of Greek mythology and culture. Some, such as the work of Cyrus Gordon, are strongly critical of a perceived tendency of Classicists to assume that Greece stood alone in the eastern Mediterranean and was not significantly influenced by Near Eastern (or 'Semitic') peoples (Gordon 1965).

With respect to the Bible, the 'contextual approach', advocated by scholars such as William W. Hallo, makes both comparisons and contrasts, recognizing the autonomy and interdependence of ancient Israel and Mesopotamia (Hallo 1997). This steers a middle course between the extremism of the Pan-Babylonianists and of those who would build a fence around the Bible and claim that Israel was somehow exempt from the dynamic influences of Mesopotamia, the greatest cultural centre in Western Asia during the first millennium BCE. No serious student of the Bible can ignore Mesopotamian civilization, but the religious experiences of both Mesopotamia and the Hebrews have to be understood in their own terms before they can be profitably compared or contrasted.

Bibliography

Mesopotamian studies is an international discipline with much important scholarship on religion published in French, German and Italian. Although every effort has been made to favour English-language sources here, a few essential works in French and German must be included.

Abusch, T. and K. van der Toorn (ed.) 1999. *Mesopotamian magic: textual, historical and interpretive perspective*. Groningen: Styx Publications. Excellent volume of essays, useful for the general reader.

Albright, W. 1940. *From the Stone Age to Christianity: monotheism and the historical process*. Baltimore: Johns Hopkins University Press; London: Oxford University Press. Classic statement of his integrative approach to the religions of the ancient Near East.

Black, J. and A. Green 1992. *Gods, demons and symbols of ancient Mesopotamia: an illustrated dictionary*. London: British Museum Press; Austin: University of Texas Press. Useful reference work for many topics connected to religion.

Bottéro, J. 1974. Symptômes, signes, écritures. In J. Vernant (ed.), *Divination et rationalité*. Paris: Éditions du Seuil, pp. 70–197. Best study of Mesopotamian divination in all its branches.

   1989. *Lorsque les dieux faisaient l'homme: mythologie mesopotamienne*, Paris: Gallimard. Translation and comments on Sumerian and Akkadian mythology.

   1992. *Mesopotamia: writing, reasoning, and the gods*, trans. Z. Bahrani and M. Van De Mieroop. Chicago: University of Chicago Press. Collection of essays on diverse topics, some pertinent to Mesopotamian religion.

   2001. *Religion in ancient Mesopotamia*, trans. T. L. Fagan. Chicago: University of Chicago Press. Sensitive and penetrating study of Mesopotamian religion.

Cohen, M. 1993. *The cultic calenders of the ancient Near East*. Bethesda, MD: CDL Press. Comprehensive survey, with reference to biblical connections.

Dalley, S. 1989. *Myths from Mesopotamia*. Oxford: Oxford University Press. Excellent translation and comments on Assyro-Babylonian myths.

Dhorme, E. 1945. *Les religions de Babylonie et d'Assyrie*. Paris: Presses Universitaires de France. Classic study still well worth consulting.

Durand, J.-M. 1988. *Archives épistolaires de Mari*, I/1: *Archives royales de Mari XXVI*. Paris: Éditions Recherches sur les Civilisations. Contains the best and most authoritative study of prophecy from Mari, replacing all previous works on this subject.

Edzard, D. 1965. Mesopotamien, die Mythologie der Sumerer und Akkader. In H. Haussig (ed.), *Mythen in Vorderen Orient*. Stuttgart: Ernst Klett Verlag = *Wörterbuch der Mythologie* I, pp. 19–139. Very useful compendium of information on Mesopotamian religion in condensed form.

Ferm, V. (ed.) 1950. *Ancient religions.* New York: The Philosophical Library (originally published as *Forgotten religions*). Contains chapters on Sumer (Kramer) and Assyria and Babylonia (Oppenheim) now mostly out of date.

Finkel, I. and M. Geller (eds.) 1997. *Sumerian gods and their representations.* Groningen: Styx Publications. Collection of essays on Sumerian religion, intended for the specialist.

Foster, B. 1996. *Before the Muses: an anthology of Akkadian literature.* 2nd edn, Bethesda, MD: CDL Press. Translations and notes on Assyro-Babylonian mythological texts, as well as hymns, prayers and other texts of importance to the study of religion. Third and revised edition 2005.

(ed.) 2001. *The Epic of Gilgamesh.* New York: W. W. Norton and Co. New translations of Sumerian, Akkadian and Hittite Gilgamesh with critical essays.

Frankfort, H. 1996. *The art and architecture of the ancient orient.* 1st edn, Hardmondsworth: Penguin, 1971. New Haven: Yale University Press.

George, A. 1999. *The Epic of Gilgamesh: a new translation.* London: Allen Lane. Authoritative translation of the epic and its Sumerian forerunners.

Gordon, C. 1965. *The common background of Greek and Hebrew civilization.* New York: W. W. Norton & Co. Controversial, pioneering study stressing the cultural debt of ancient Greece to the Near East.

Hallo, W. 1983. Cult statue and divine image: a preliminary study. In W. Hallo, J. Moyer and L. Purdue (eds.), *Scripture in context,* II: *More essays on the comparative method.* Winona Lake, ID: Eisenbrauns, pp. 1–17.

Sumerian religion. *Journal of the Institute of Archaeology of Tel Aviv University, Tel Aviv,* Occasional Publications 1, pp. 15–35.

Hallo, W. and K. Younger (ed.) 1997. *The context of scripture: canonical compositions from the biblical world.* Leiden: E. J. Brill. Compendium of numerous ancient Near Eastern texts, including important Sumerian religious texts, translated into English.

Harris, R. 1991. Inanna-Ishtar as paradox and a coincidence of opposites. *History of Religions* 30: 261–78.

Heidel, A. 1951. *The Babylonian genesis.* 2nd edn, Chicago: University of Chicago Press. Although the translations are out of date, Heidel's discussion of biblical parallels to Mesopotamian creation stories gives a good example of a conservative Christian approach.

Jacobsen, T. 1976. *The treasures of darkness: a history of Mesopotamian religion.* New Haven: Yale University Press. Major integrative study of Mesopotamian religion.

    1987a. *The harps that once* . . . New Haven: Yale University Press. Important anthology of Sumerian literature in translation, including myths and other religious texts.

    1987b. Mesopotamian religion. In M. Éliade (ed.), *Encyclopedia of religion.* New York: Macmillan; London: Collier-Macmillan.

Jastrow, M. 1898. *The religion of Babylonia and Assyria.* New York and London: Putnam's. One of the first comprehensive presentations of Mesopotamian religion, widely used by later authors, now antiquated.

Kramer, S. 1961. *Sumerian mythology: a study of spiritual and literary achievement in the third millennium B.C.* Revised edn, New York: Harper and Row. Though outdated in many respects, a lively presentation of Sumerian mythology for the general reader.

    1969. *The sacred marriage rite: aspects of faith, myth, and ritual in ancient Sumer.* Bloomington and London: Indiana University Press (revised, expanded French edition, *Le mariage sacré à Sumer et à Babylone*, trans. J. Bottéro. Paris: Berg International, 1983).

Kraus, F. 1990. *The role of temples from the third dynasty of Ur to the first dynasty of Babylon*, trans. B. Foster. Monographs on the Ancient Near East 2 fascicle 4, Malibu.

Lambert, W. 1975. The cosmology of Sumer and Babylon. In C. Bleecker and M. Loewe (eds.), *Ancient cosmologies.* London: Allen and Unwin, pp. 42–65. Concise, authoritative survey.

    1988. Old Testament mythology in its Near Eastern context. *Vetus Testamentum Supplement* 40: 124–43.

    1990. Ancient Mesopotamian gods, superstition, philosophy, theology. *Revue de l'Histoire des Religions* 207: 115–30.

Nemet-Nejat, K. 1998. *Daily life in ancient Mesopotamia.* Westport, CT and London: Greenwood Press. Good introductory book for the general reader; ch. 9 is on 'Religion'.

Oppenheim, A. 1961. The Mesopotamian temple. In G. Wright and D. Freedman (eds.), *The biblical archaeologist reader* I. Garden City, NY: Anchor Books, pp. 158–69.

    1977. *Ancient Mesopotamia: portrait of a dead civilization.* Revised edn completed by Erica Reiner. Chicago: University of Chicago Press. Excellent, sometimes capricious chapters on Mesopotamian religious belief and practice.

Parpola, S. 1997. *Assyrian prophecies, State Archives of Assyria* IX. Helsinki: Helsinki University Press.

Porter, B. 2000. One god or many? Concepts of divinity in the ancient world. *Transactions of the Casco Bay Archaeological Institute* 1. Contains two essays on Assyrian concepts of divinity

Reallexikon der Assyriologie. Berlin: De Gruyter (in progress). Contains full information on Mesopotamian deities and other religious topics, with bibliography, and some important articles in English.

Rochberg-Halton, F. 1982. Fate and divination in Mesopotamia. *Archiv für Orientforschung* 19: 363–71.

Rogers, R. 1940. *The religion of Babylonia and Assyria, especially in its relations to Israel.* New York: Eaton and Main. Antiquated forerunner to Albright.

Römer, W. 1969. Religion of ancient Mesopotamia. In G. Widengren (ed.), *Historia religionum: handbook for the history of religions* I: *Religions of the past.* Leiden: E. J. Brill. 115–94.

Van Dijk, J. 1971. Sumerische religion. In J. Asmussen and J. Laessøe (eds.), *Handbuch der Religionsgeschichte* I. Göttingen: Vandenhoeck and Ruprecht, pp. 431–96. Difficult reading for the non-specialist, but filled with original ideas and interpretations of key Sumerian religious concepts.

5 Ancient Israel to the fall of the Second Temple

JOHN ROGERSON

Historical and methodological perspectives

Introduction

The major source for information about the religion of ancient Israel is the Hebrew Bible, referring to twenty-four books written in Hebrew from roughly the ninth to the second century BCE and accepted as Holy Scripture by Jews. Additional information comes from books not found in the Hebrew Bible, but included in the Greek Septuagint (a translation of the Hebrew Bible and other texts, begun in the third century BCE), such as the books of Maccabees. An important contribution is also made by the findings of archaeology, including the Dead Sea Scrolls.

That scholars possess an extensive literature by way of original sources for ancient Israel's religion is, at first sight, an advantage. On further inspection it turns out to be a disadvantage, for the following reason. For much of recent western history the Bible has been regarded as an infallible source of information for the origin of the universe and the earliest history of the human race, not to mention the religion of ancient Israel. In parts of the world where biblical criticism has not touched new and younger churches, the Bible is still regarded in this way. If the Bible is believed to be infallible, the task of describing ancient Israel's religion becomes simple. For the period covered by the Bible all that is needed is for its contents to be outlined with modern readers in mind. Unfortunately for this simple task, scholars working in universities and church academies have, over the past 200 years, studied the Bible like any other book. The result has been that a radically different picture of ancient Israel's religion has been proposed compared with that presented in the Bible. Not surprisingly, this has not been welcomed in circles where the Bible has been, and is still, regarded as infallible; and critical scholars are often accused of being unbelievers whose aim is to

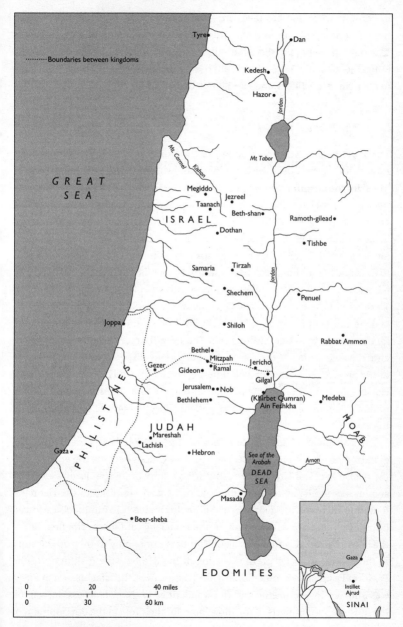

Map 5.1. Ancient Israel.

undermine what God has revealed. This is not a charge that can be discussed here. To put the matter in perspective, however, the picture of ancient Israel's religion as presented in the Bible will be outlined, followed by the reasons why critical scholarship has proposed alternative reconstructions. The present state of the matter in biblical studies will then be indicated.

The biblical picture

The Bible begins with the creation of the universe and of the human race. Although Genesis 1 uses the common Hebrew word *'elohim* meaning 'God' or 'gods' for the creator rather than the name YHWH, which is the specific name of the God of Israel, it is implicit in Genesis 1 that it is the God of Israel who is the creator, and in Genesis 2 the name YHWH is added to that of *'elohim* producing, in the standard English translations, the compound name LORD God. The opening chapters of Genesis describe various acts of human disobedience in regard to God, and of inhuman behaviour towards other humans. A universal flood (the biblical traditions have much in common with other flood stories from ancient Mesopotamia; see Rogerson and Davies 1989) destroys all but the family of Noah and the animals preserved by him in the ark, but the attempt at a new beginning for the human race after the flood fails. The story of Israel's religion begins when, after the destruction of the Tower of Babel and the dispersal of the human race into separate countries with their differing languages, God calls Abram[1] to leave Haran in northern Mesopotamia and to migrate to a country where God will multiply Abram's offspring and make them a blessing for the other peoples of the world.

The remainder of Genesis describes the fortunes of Abra(ha)m's family. His grandson Jacob is renamed Israel and his twelve sons become the ancestors of the twelve tribes of Israel. The highly artistic story of Joseph, Jacob's eleventh son, moves the Israelites from the land of Canaan promised to the Hebrews' founding ancestors to Egypt, where they multiply greatly in numbers, are forced into slavery and are delivered under the leadership of Moses. The first half of the book of Exodus, and the book of Numbers, containing as they do the story of the Exodus from Egypt, the crossing of the Red Sea, the institution of the Passover Festival to commemorate God 'passing over' the Israelites when Egypt was afflicted by the plague and the wanderings in the wilderness are among the most important parts of the Bible, both for their role in the development of biblical ethics and for the part that they play in present-day Judaism.

For forty years Moses leads the Israelites from Egypt back to the promised land, stopping on the way at Mount Sinai, where God reveals the laws that will govern Israel's civil and religious life. Aaron is consecrated as priest, and he and his descendants are entrusted with the performance of the rituals and sacrifices that will remove ritual defilement and enable Israel to be a holy people before God. These founding laws and institutions are contained in the books of Exodus through to Deuteronomy.

Already in the book of Numbers it is related how the Israelites began to occupy that part of the promised land east of the River Jordan. The book of Joshua describes the occupation of the land west of the Jordan under the leadership of Moses' successor Joshua. This is described as a united campaign of the tribes, who, following Joshua's death, occupy the areas allocated to them by Joshua. No leader comparable to Moses or Joshua arises in the following period. Occasional leaders, called judges, are inspired by God to deliver the people from subservience to various neighbouring nations. According to the book of Judges, it is God who is responsible for allowing the Israelites to become subservient, as a way of punishing them for turning to other gods. The last of the nations to become Israel's overlord is the Philistines, and the Philistine threat has consequences which are as significant for the religion of Israel as is the Exodus, the Passover and the law-giving at Sinai. Out of the Philistine threat develops the institution of Israelite kingship, whose greatest representative, David, secures Jerusalem as his people's capital, and whose son, Solomon, builds the first temple.

Following Solomon's death, the kingdom splits into a larger, northern kingdom of Israel (the present-day Bethel and Samaria hills, the Jezreel valley and Lower and Upper Galilee), with various capitals including, ultimately, Samaria, and a smaller, southern kingdom of Judah, with its capital Jerusalem ruled by the descendants of David. The books of Kings, which record the history of the two kingdoms, devote more space to Israel than to Judah, and interpret obedience to God in terms of loyalty to God's chosen sanctuary in Jerusalem. On this view, the entire northern kingdom, Israel, exists in defiance of God's will and all its kings are evil. Yet Israel is also the location of prophetic groups fiercely loyal to God, who become actively engaged in resistance to their kings. Noteworthy in this regard are Elijah and Elisha, accounts of whose exploits extend from 1 Kings 17 to 2 Kings 10. Kings of Judah have a better chance of being faithful to the Jerusalem sanctuary; yet even some of them are condemned for allowing worship to be carried on at so-called high places – what the biblical writers see as places of pagan offerings outside Jerusalem.

The books of Kings show the two kingdoms struggling to survive against stronger neighbours: Syria, Assyria and Babylon to the north and east and Egypt to the south. The northern kingdom, Israel, eventually falls to the Assyrians (722/1 BCE), the southern kingdom, Judah, to the Babylonians (587 BCE). In both cases, Israelites are deported; in the case of Judah the first temple is destroyed. These disasters are interpreted as the fulfilment of prophecies given in the name of God by prophets from the eighth century onwards, whose words are recorded in books of the Bible bearing their names. Well known are Hosea, Amos, Micah and Isaiah (chs. 1–11) who lived in the second part of the eighth century, and Jeremiah and Ezekiel, who lived in the seventh to sixth centuries.

The only glimpse of conditions during the period when Jewish leaders were deported into exile in Babylon is given by Ezekiel, and it is such a small glimpse as to amount to nothing. The silence is broken only by the book of Ezra, which records that Cyrus, the Persian ruler (who defeated the Babylonian Empire in 540), issued a decree encouraging the Jews to return to their own land and to rebuild the temple in Jerusalem. The books of Ezra and Nehemiah, and the prophecies of Haggai and Zechariah (chs. 1–8) cover what we know on modern chronology to be the period 540 to roughly 420 BCE. They record the building of the Second Temple (completed *c*. 515) and the missions of Ezra and Nehemiah (458–420). The latter find Jerusalem in a dire state physically and religiously, and institute reforms designed to recall the people to the observance of the law given at Sinai. With these books, the biblical account of Israel's religion ends, and the story is taken on by books such as 1 and 2 Maccabees. They tell of the attempt by the Seleucid King Antiochus IV to proscribe Judaism (in 168/7) and of the resistance offered by the Hasmoneans, the family of Mattathias of Modein, led initially by Judas Maccabaeus. Material provided by the Jewish historian Josephus (37/8–100 CE) supplements the books of Maccabees, and takes the story through the Roman occupation (from 67 BCE) to the final destruction of the Second Temple by the Romans in 70 CE

Readers will have noticed that the brief outline just given is a continuous story with little actual information about Israel's religion. This has been deliberate, because the Bible is to a large extent a long story which relates how Israel was chosen by God, and how it suffered changing fortunes throughout its history depending on whether or not it was faithful to the laws revealed by God. Certain central themes emerge from the story, of course: Israel as the people chosen by God, and delivered by him from slavery in Egypt; Jerusalem as the sanctuary chosen by God at which his people should offer sacrifice and worship; Moses as the lawgiver and Aaron as the ancestor of the priestly families; David as the chosen king whose descendants will rule in Jerusalem and from whose line will come a future deliverer. The Bible also indicates that the Israelites often turned to other gods, such as the god of the storm, Baal, and that Israelite rulers did not uphold justice in the land. From the Psalms, and books such as Job and Ecclesiastes insights can be gained into the personal piety of devout Israelites, including their attempts to understand why the wicked often prospered and the faithful suffered. Books such as the Wisdom of Solomon and Ecclesiasticus (the Wisdom of Jesus ben Sirah) show Judaism adopting Greek ideas and concepts.

What is found in books such as the Psalms, Job, Ecclesiastes, Wisdom of Solomon and Ecclesiasticus has not been radically affected by critical scholarship. What has been affected is the overall story of Israel's religion as related above, and with it have come new and radical ideas about the origins and development of Israel's faith – ideas which continue to change in the light of new research and archaeological discoveries. The course of these critical challenges must now be charted.

The critical reassessment

The Bible has always been studied critically, if 'critically' is understood to include judgements based upon human scientific knowledge and the need to make sense of the Bible as a whole. The statement in the Hebrew text of 1 Samuel 13:1, that Saul was one year old when he began to reign, was not taken literally by ancient interpreters, contradicting as it did both knowledge about human growth and development and other parts of the Bible that indicated that Saul had a son, Jonathan, who was probably in his late teens when Saul became king. The literal impossibility of 1 Samuel 13:1, and many other contractions, was well known to Jews and Christian interpreters of the Bible from at least the second century CE (see Rogerson 1998: ch. 1). However, methods were found of harmonizing them, in the belief that an infallible book could not contradict itself. The critical reassessment that led to a new reconstruction of Israel's religion came about because scholars stopped harmonizing contradictions, and used them as a means of probing behind the picture of Israel's religion as presented in the Bible.

The fundamental contradiction that opened the door to the critical reassessment was that between the command in the book of Deuteronomy that Israelites should worship God at only one sanctuary and should destroy all other

Table 5.1 *Chart of conjectural composition of books of the Bible (including Apocrypha)*

People and events		Books
~~Second period 650–540 BCE~~		*First period 1900–650 BCE*
Slavery in Egyptian		
Exodus		
Israelites in Canaan	1250	
Early monarchy	10th–9th cents.	Temple and court administration records
Ahab king of Israel	873–53	compiled in Jerusalem and Samaria
Prophetic revolution of Jehu	841	
David king in Jerusalem		Eighth century
Assyrian destruction of Samaria	722	Collections of materials that will become Hebrew Bible Oracles of Hosea, Amos, Micah
Second period 650–540 BCE		Seventh century
Josiah's reforms, Jerusalem centre of worship	622	First drafts of Deuteronomy, Jeremiah, Nahum, Zephaniah
Babylonians invade Jerusalem	597	Sixth century
Destruction of Jerusalem temple	587	Jeremiah works collected, Ezekiel, Isaiah 40–55,
Jewish leaders exiled in Babylon		Habbakuk, Haggai, Zechariah 1–8, 9–50, 56–66;
Cyrus, king of Persia defeats Babylonians and releases the Jews	540	work on Israelite history, Deuteronomy, more Psalms, Lamentations
Jerusalem temple rebuilt	515	
Third period 540–50 BCE		Fifth century
Alexander defeats Persians	333	Pentateuch (Genesis–Deuteronomy), Joshua–2 Kings, Proverbs all nearing final form, Ezra,
Judah part of Greek Empire		Nehemiah, Jonah (?), Ruth (?) composed
Seleucide rule of Israel	200	Fourth century
Antiochus IV persecutes Jews	168	Chronicles, Malachi (?), Zechariah, Song of
Maccabean revolt	153	Songs, Job, Ecclesiastes, Esther composed
Masada synagogue		
Roman rule in Judah	63	Third century
Herod 'the Great' becomes king	37	Isaiah 24–9, Enoch 1–36, 72–92,
Parthians temporarily occupy Jerusalem	34–32	Ecclesiasticus, rest of Enoch, Wisdom of Solomon
Romans occupy Jerusalem	67 CE	First century
Destruction of 2nd Jerusalem Temple	70 CE	3 and 4 Maccabees, Tobit, Judith, Baruch, Prayer of Manasseh, 2 Esdras, Dead Sea Scrolls

sanctuaries (Deut. 12:2–14) and the information in 1 Samuel that leaders such as Samuel offered sacrifices at various sanctuaries or places, including Mizpah (1 Sam. 7:9), a city in the land of Zuph (1 Sam. 9:5, 11–13) and Gilgal (1 Sam. 11:14–15). In the story of David, David goes to the sanctuary at Nob where he and his men are given holy bread to eat (1 Sam. 21:1–6). The problem created by this contradiction is that, according to Deuteronomy, the law of the single sanctuary was given by Moses, in which case either Samuel or David was unaware of the law, or deliberately broke it. In the book of Amos the Israelites are criticized because they offer sacrifices at Bethel and Gilgal but oppress the poor (Amos 4:1–5). The accusation that their sacrifices are insincere is a powerful one; but Amos could have brought a more powerful argument – that Moses had explicitly forbidden any sacrifices except at the single sanctuary (which was Jerusalem in Amos' time). The reason why Amos did not use this argument is that he was not familiar with a law of a central sanctuary, not out of ignorance, but because no such law existed in his day (the second half of the eighth century BCE).

The central point of the critical reassessment came to be the date of the book of Deuteronomy, and the following position received widespread critical acceptance by the end of the nineteenth century. Deuteronomy, with its demand that sacrifice should be offered to God only at one sanctuary, was written in the seventh century BCE and was the basis for the reformation of Josiah, king of Judah, in 622 (2 Kings 22:3 to 23:25), in which all sanctuaries other than the Jerusalem temple were destroyed. The stories in 1 Samuel, which indicate that there were many legitimate Israelite sanctuaries, reflect a period prior to Josiah's reformation. Further, the fact that Samuel offered sacrifices at various sanctuaries even though he did not belong to the priestly tribe of Levi or the house of Aaron (he belonged to the tribe of Ephraim, 1 Sam. 1:1) indicates that it was not always the case that only the descendants of Aaron could offer sacrifices to God.

Bound up with the critical reassessment was the theory that underlying the books of Genesis to 2 Kings were four documents (or, according to other scholars, streams of tradition) that were called J (because of the use of the divine name YHWH or JHWH in German, the J in German being pronounced as Y), E (because of the use of the divine name *'elohim*, God) and P (because of the presence of material relating to priesthood and ritual), and D. According to this theory, J and E were written in the ninth to eighth centuries, D was largely the book of Deuteronomy, and P was written after the exile.

A three-stage theory of the development of Israelite religion was widely accepted, in the following terms:

First period (1900–650 BCE)

Proto-Israelite families or clans migrated from northern Mesopotamia to Syria/Palestine. Their religion was a 'clan' religion in which God was not tied to a particular location but travelled with the clan and could be worshipped at whatever sanctuary the clan came to. The clans were polytheists but had a special relationship to a particular manifestation of the deity. They used the common Semitic designation 'El (God) for God. There was no established priesthood, and leaders of clans offered sacrifices. Sacrifices were offered at times of crisis (e.g. before battles), to express gratitude and devotion, and were believed to establish communion with God and fellowship within the clan or family.

The events of the Egyptian slavery, exodus and journey to the promised land gave rise to the belief that the God of the Hebrews is named YHWH (thought to have been pronounced Yahweh). It is unlikely that Moses instituted the laws and the priestly and sacrificial institutions attributed to him in Exodus, Leviticus and Numbers. He probably did promulgate some form of the Ten Commandments which were kept and carried in the Ark of the Covenant.

The occupation of Canaan brought the Israelites into contact with a settled, agricultural people (the 'Canaanites') whose fertility religion based upon the storm-god Baal proved to be attractive to ordinary Israelites. 'Pure' Yahwism was upheld by ecstatic prophetic groups led by men such as Samuel, Elijah and Elisha who involved themselves actively in political matters. Later, this role was taken on by the so-called writing prophets: Hosea, Amos, Micah and Isaiah (mainly chs. 1–11) in the eighth century. These prophets were the creators of the ethical monotheism of ancient Israel. They condemned the worship of other gods and they demanded, in the name of YHWH, that kings and those in power should uphold and support the poor and needy. They threatened, if these things were not done, that YHWH would punish his people by delivering them into the power of their enemies.

Second period (650–540 BCE)

An attempt to consolidate the teachings of the prophets into a practical programme of legislation led to the production of a first draft of Deuteronomy, probably during the reign of Manasseh (698/7–642). The writers were court officials influenced by prophetic teaching. Because sanctuaries outside Jerusalem had led ordinary Israelites to worship the pagan deities associated with them, the destruction of these sanctuaries was enjoined, and a single sanctuary promoted. This had practical consequences. Provision had to be made for the support of the YHWH priests who served at the condemned sanctuaries and the Passover had to be redesignated as a national festival held at the single sanctuary. Previously, it had been a local festival centred upon the homes of families (Deut. 16:1–7; 2 Kings 23:21–23). The laws of the 'Book of the Covenant' (Exod. 21:1 to 23:19) dating from the first period had to be reformulated to take account of the centralization of the sanctuary.

The work began (and continued during the exile) of revising the story of Israel in the light of centralization. This particularly affected the books of Kings, whose rulers were judged to be good or evil according to whether they had suppressed worship at sanctuaries other than Jerusalem.

The main prophets of this period, Jeremiah, Ezekiel and Deutero-Isaiah (in Isa. 40–55), proclaimed a full-blooded monotheism, by maintaining that other gods did not exist, and that in events such as Cyrus' defeat of the Babylonian Empire God was using even a non-Israelite ruler to work out his (God's) plans for Israel and the nations (Isa. 44:28, 45:1–7).

Third period (540–50 BCE)

The great shock of the destruction of the Jerusalem temple in 587 and the experience of exile led to a profound shift in Israelite religion away from the freedom and plurality of the first period to a much greater rigidity. The urgent need to avoid a repetition of the destruction of the temple, a destruction, according to the prophets, brought about by God as a punishment for disobedience, led to the attempt to impose upon all Israelites the holiness laws appropriate to the priests. Rituals and sacrifices designed to remove defilement from among the people were prescribed, and the Israelite community increasingly became a theocracy, that is, a religious community ruled by priests and governed by divine law. The Bible began to assume the form familiar to present-day readers, with its claim that the priestly and sacrificial ordinances had been given by God via Moses after the exodus. According to the critical reassessment, these were post-exile innovations. When the Jews became part of the empire of the Greek rulers of Syria (the Seleucids) in 200–198 BCE, and Antiochus IV attempted to outlaw Judaism, he was opposed not only by the family of Mattathias, but by 'Hasideans, mighty warriors of Israel, all who offered themselves willingly for the law' (1 Macc. 2:42). These were the representatives of those in Judah whose devotion to the Jewish law indicated the progress of Jewish religion towards the Pharisaism of the last century before the Common Era, and the successors of the Pharisees after the fall of Jerusalem in 70 CE, the founders of Rabbinic Judaism. However, the Hasideans and their successors were not the only strand of late Judaism. The Sadducees represented the aristocratic and priestly families of Jerusalem, and denied belief in resurrection. On the other hand, thanks to contacts with the Zoroastrianism of the Persian Empire, Jewish religion developed dualistic and apocalyptic ideas, which were expressed in books such as Enoch and Daniel. These saw the world as a battleground between the human forces of good (Israel helped by God) and the forces of evil (the other nations), as well as between supernatural angelic forces led respectively by the Archangel Michael (Dan. 12:1) and Satan (under that and various other names). There is also the development of belief in life after death (cp. Dan. 12:2–3).

Assessment of the critical reassessment

What has been attempted in the above paragraphs is a summary of the critical position often associated with the name of the German scholar Julius Wellhausen (see its statement in Smith 1881) that commanded widespread support by the end of the nineteenth century. Many features of this position remain intact today; in other regards it needs to be revised. For example, the discovery of the Dead Sea Scrolls from 1947 to 1967 has entirely altered our knowledge of the last two centuries before the Common Era, while some of the archaeological discoveries and new theories of recent times pose challenges to the critical reassessment that are almost as radical as the challenge posed by the critical reassessment to the traditional biblical picture. The justification for outlining the essentially nineteenth-century critical reassessment is that it has become the basis for all subsequent critical work on the religion of ancient Israel; and in a rapidly changing academic discipline it remains, in spite of its defects, a logical and coherent theory around which discussion can be organized.

Twentieth-century refinements

Two refinements of the critical reassessment proposed in the first half of the twentieth century owed their existence to social anthropology. The first, classically expressed by Oesterley and Robinson (1930), assumed that Israelite religion passed through the stages of animism and polytheism before reaching monotheism, and it searched the Bible for evidence of survivals of animism (belief in spirits associated with high places, wells, trees, etc.) and polytheism. The latter is not hard to find, for example, in the Psalms: 'The Lord is a great God, and a great King above all gods' (Psalm 95:3). For the former, reference can be made to the oaks (sacred trees) at Mamre (Gen. 14:13) or the sacred stone upon which Jacob dreamed a dream about heaven (Gen. 28:11, 18). This is a method that would be regarded as highly questionable today (see Rogerson 1978: 34–6), but makes the assumption that all religions have developed in similar ways, and that Israelite religion was no exception.

The second refinement, drawing upon anthropological theory of the 1920s, assumed that there had been a uniform culture pattern that covered the ancient Near East from Mesopotamia to Egypt, including ancient Israel. Representatives of this theory included S. H. Hooke and Sigmund Mowinckel (see Rogerson 1978). If this was so, then it would be necessary to look for features of the religion of this pattern in the Bible. Because, it was believed, texts deriving from Babylonia best described this religion, attempts were made to reconstruct from the Bible an elaborate ritual of new year celebrations or of royal coronations in ancient Israel, based upon these rituals in Babylon. According to this reconstruction, the Israelite king was believed to be quasi divine. At the new year and/or his coronation he played a leading part in re-enacting a sacred drama, in which he engaged the forces of chaos. An initial defeat, in which he was subjected to ritual humiliation and death, was followed by resurrection and a sacred marriage. His victory ensured stability and agricultural prosperity for the coming year/reign, and part of the ceremony may have included the reading of an early draft of the creation account of Genesis 1. The so-called royal psalms were especially appealed to in this connection, and the first line of Psalms 93, 97 and 99, usually translated 'The Lord reigns' or 'The Lord is King', was rendered 'The Lord has become king.' The meaning was that God's Kingship had once more been established following the new year/coronation ceremony.

Like the first refinement, the second would probably find few supporters among present-day scholars. In a revised form, however, it commands widespread acceptance. The revised form assumes that, in the official religion of Jerusalem, there was an annual or periodic ceremony in which God's covenant with the house of David was celebrated and renewed (Kraus 1966). The ceremony included a re-enactment of David's bringing of the Ark of the Covenant from Kiriath-jearim to Jerusalem (2 Sam. 6:1–19). The Ark of the Coverant was a portable shrine containing the two tablets of the Ten Commandments. As the Ark was solemnly placed in the temple, trumpets were blown and it was proclaimed that the God of Israel was king of all nations (cf. Ps. 47:5–9). A priest or cultic prophet then rehearsed the conditions of the covenant between God and the house of David:

> One of the sons of your body
> I will set on your throne.
> If your sons keep my covenant
> and my testimonies which I shall teach them,
> their sons for ever shall sit upon your throne.
>
> (Ps. 132:11–12)

The importance of the refinements is that they appealed to general theories of religion as described in social anthropology and sought to apply them to the religion of ancient Israel. Whether or not they were successful, they highlighted the fact that it is impossible to describe a religion without making certain assumptions. The traditional position outlined above (pp. 216–18) assumed that God had communicated his will directly to Moses. The critical reassessment worked with an essentially unilinear model, in which two phases followed an initial phase. Oesterley and Robinson were representatives of those using an evolutionistic model of religions, while advocates of the role of divine kingship in ancient Israel had adapted a diffusionist model.

The present chapter, similarly, cannot avoid making certain assumptions; but before these are outlined it is necessary to consider briefly a recent, and radical, proposal about the history of ancient Israelite religion, by Niehr (1990). Niehr's subtitle expresses clearly his aim: *Alttestamentlicher JHWH Glaube im Kontext syrisch-kanaanäischer Religion des 1. Jahrtausends v. Chr* (Old Testament belief in YHWH in the context of Syrian-Canaanite Religion of the First Millennium BCE). Niehr argues that in the religion of Syria/Palestine two phenomena occur. First, the high god 'EL, known for example from the Ugaritic texts, disappears, while second, the storm-god Ba'alshamen increasingly assumes the functions of the high god. Niehr's case is that precisely the same phenomenon occurs in the Hebrew Bible, and that YHWH increasingly assumes the functions of a high god in the course of the first millennium BCE. As boldly stated, this does not sound radical; but it has radical implications for understanding how biblical texts should be handled when reconstructing ancient Israel's religion. Two examples can be given.

Psalm 91 begins 'He who dwells in the shadow of the Most High, who abides in the shadow of the Almighty, will say to the LORD, "My refuge and my fortress; my

God, in whom I trust.'" In these two verses four divine names occur: Most High (Hebrew *'elyon*), Almighty (Hebrew *shaddai*), LORD (Hebrew YHWH) and God (Hebrew *'elohim*). It is normally assumed that *'elyon* and *shaddai* are survivals from a polytheistic past and that they have been assimilated in Israel's monotheistic religion to become epithets for YHWH. Indeed, it has become almost a commonplace that *'elyon* was the name under which God was worshipped in Jerusalem before the city was captured by David. The basis for this view has been the reference in Genesis 14:18–19 to 'Melchizedek king of Salem' (taken to be Jerusalem) who was 'priest of God Most High' (Hebrew *'el 'elyon*). According to this interpretation, Melchizedek was the priest-king of Jebusite (i.e. pre-Israelite) Jerusalem, whose god was *'elyon* or *'el 'elyon*. Niehr turns this theory on its head by arguing that *'elyon* occurs only in post-exilic texts in the Bible (six times alone in Daniel and four times in Daniel following 'God'!), and in the Pseudepigrapha and the Dead Sea Scrolls. *'Elyon* is therefore not a survival from Israel's earliest contact with Canaanite culture but a title used in post-exilic texts in order to describe YHWH as the 'Most High', i.e. the highest God. Further, the fact that *'elyon* occurs in texts that contain themes drawn from Canaanite mythology[2] indicates that the writers of the Hebrew Bible drew upon Canaanite mythology in order to claim that YHWH was the highest God.

This argument destroys at a stroke the two refinements mentioned at the beginning of this section. For the attempt to describe Israelite religion in evolutionary terms it was necessary to regard the use of divine names such as *'elyon* as remnants of polytheism. Niehr argues that the use of these divine names is a literary device in post-exilic literature to express the absolute supremacy of the one God. The divine kingship theory likewise used mythological themes, especially in the Psalms, as evidence that there had been sacred dramas centred around the king in pre-exilic Jerusalem. According to Niehr, such themes were part of the language deliberately used by writers to express the absolute supremacy of YHWH in the post-exilic period, when there was no longer a king.

The second example from Niehr concerns his view that in the late post-exilic period biblical writers often deliberately used non-monotheistic language because monotheism was so well established that polytheism and mythology offered no real challenge to it. He writes of a 'literary paganism', instances of which can be found in texts such as Proverbs 9:1–3a, 5 and Song of Songs 8:6ff.

Niehr has deliberately adopted a comparative 'history of religions' approach, and assumed that developments that can be observed in the religion of Syria-Canaan of the first millennium BCE provide a model for understanding the development of ancient Israelite religion. Whether or not his view is accepted – and it is carefully and impressively argued – what is demonstrated is that the reconstruction of Israelite religion is more complex than even the critical reassessment had recognized.

This complexity is increased by recent literary and archaeological research in Hebrew Bible studies which is promising to redraw the map of the discipline. The critical reassessment assumed two things: first, that for the period from the Settlement of the Israelites in Canaan onwards (i.e. from *c*. 1250 BCE) the books of Judges to 2 Kings contained a basically reliable account of Israel's history, a history which could be critically reconstructed with the help of extra-biblical sources. Secondly, the critical reassessment assumed that some of the sources used in Judges to 2 Kings could be dated to the ninth to eighth centuries BCE. Both of these assumptions have been challenged in recent scholarship.

Recent archaeological findings suggest that the northern kingdom, Israel, and neighbouring kingdoms such as Moab, Ammon and Edom did not exist significantly until the ninth century BCE, and that Judah did not become a state until the eighth century. It is beginning to be questioned whether the Solomonic gates and walls found at Megiddo, Hazor and Gezer did in fact date from Solomon's time. A minimalist view of Jerusalem's history (Auld and Steiner 1996) argues that the city had not been occupied for some centuries prior to David's capture of it. All this puts a large question mark against the Hebrew Bible's view of a small Davidic and Solomonic empire in the tenth century BCE incorporating the neighbouring kingdoms of Damascus, Ammon, Moab and Edom. The publication in 1993 and 1995 of the so-called 'house of David' inscription found at Dan produced fierce argument between scholars who accepted a critical version of the biblical picture and those who did not. The former argued that the inscription showed that David had indeed established a dynasty that had controlled territory as far north as Dan. The opponents argued that the inscription did not refer to the house (dynasty) of King David.

The truth may lie between the two extremes. While claims that David could have controlled large areas of territory embracing Damascus, Ammon, Moab and Edom are unlikely to be true, the possibility remains that he was capable of defeating the rulers of key cities, and of thereby making a claim on their kingdoms, even though this did not amount to controlling their territory. The idea that rulers exercise total sovereignty over areas enclosed by borders is a modern one (Giddens 1985: 52–3). Nonetheless, even the mediating position proposed here entails that the biblical material must be read with a good deal of caution.

The second revolution in recent biblical studies is the tendency to date in the post-exilic period books or sources that were once dated in the pre-exilic period. A case in point is the so-called Yahwist, an author or tradition among whose stylistic trademarks is the use of the name YHWH. In the mid-twentieth century he was confidently identified as a sort of historian who, working in the tenth to ninth centuries, was responsible for producing an account of Israel's fortunes from the time of Abraham to that of David or Solomon. Today, the Yahwist's work is increasingly dated to the post-exilic period, i.e. sixth to fifth centuries BCE. This, if correct, has profound consequences for the critical reassessment; for this reconstruction depended crucially upon the contrast between the many sanctuaries mentioned, for example in 1 Samuel, and the command of the single sanctuary in Deuteronomy. On the assumption that 1 Samuel could be dated to the tenth/ninth centuries and Deuteronomy to the seventh century, it was possible to use these sources, as dated, as evidence for two distinct phases in Israelite religion. If, however, 1 Samuel was composed after the exile (Deuteronomy has also been dated to the post-exilic period) it is no longer possible to juxtapose the information contained in these books so as to produce two distinct phases.

The assumptions of the present chapter

Two main assumptions will be made in the thematic treatment of ancient Israel's religion below. The first is that, when allowances have been made for recent archaeological and literary research, a reasonably coherent general picture of Israel's history can be reconstructed as the basis of biblical and other material, at least from the ninth century onwards. The names of a number of kings of Israel and Judah are attested in extra-biblical sources, including Omri, Ahab, Jehu, Pekah, Hoshea, Hezekiah and Jehoiachin (see Rogerson 1999b). Events are also attested in extra-biblical sources, such as the invasion of Palestine by the Egyptian Sheshonk I in *c.* 925 BCE (1 Kings 14:25–27), the destruction of Samaria in 722/1 by the Assyrians, and the capture of Jerusalem by the Babylonians in 597 and the destruction of the temple a decade later. Josiah's reform in 622 BCE also seems to be confirmed by the iconographic evidence gathered by Keel and Uehlinger (1992) that shows that Judahite high officials of that period banished all forms of pictorial representation from their seals. Also, there can be no doubt that Judah passed from Babylonian to Persian hegemony (540 BCE), that Alexander's defeat of the Persians (333 BCE) brought Judah into the sphere of Greek influence, and that Judah was first part of the Greek empire of the rulers of Egypt (323-200/198), then of Syria (from 200/198) and finally a part of the Roman Empire (from 63 BCE). That these epochs had an effect on Israelite religion cannot be doubted, and account will be taken of them where appropriate.

The second main assumption will be that the most appropriate model for describing Israel's religion in all its phases is that proposed by Geertz (1964). This classic study of the religion of Java charts the interactions between the religions of various groups in a small town in east central Java under three headings: *abangan, santri* and *prijaji. Abangan* is roughly folk religion, including belief in spirits, sorcery and magic. *Santri* is the observance of Islam, also with political activities, and subject to internal reformist movements designed to produce a purer Islam. *Prijaji* is found among the former members of the aristocracy and bureaucracy. It derives from court etiquette and is an amalgam of artistic practice and Hindu-Buddhist mysticism. Geertz sums up the three types of religious practice as follows:

> *Abangan*, representing a stress on the animistic aspects of the over-all Javanese syncretism and broadly related to the peasant element in the population; *santri*, representing a stress on the Islamic elements of the syncretism and generally related to the trading element (and to certain elements in the peasantry as well); and *prijaji*, stressing the Hinduist aspects and related to the bureaucratic element – these, then are the three main subtractions I shall describe.
>
> (Geertz 1964: 6)

Geertz's model has the advantage, for use with ancient Israel, of avoiding the unilinear model of the critical reassessment, and it also enables religion to be seen as a phenomenon related to labour and class divisions. Geertz also shows how religion has both a uniting and a disrupting role to play in a society. It needs to be pointed out, of course, that Geertz's scheme has not escaped reassessment as a description of the religion of Java (see most recently, but on the whole positively, Beatty 1999). Ultimately, no one scheme can adequately describe the complicated facets of a religion deeply embedded in a society or its sub-cultures.

Taking Geertz's model to ancient Israel, I would distinguish three levels of belief and practice: popular Yahwism, prophetic Yahwism and official Yahwism. Popular Yahwism, probably practised by the peasantry, was a syncretistic religion which included divination, necromancy and fertility beliefs. Never to the fore in the Bible, for the obvious reason that it is only mentioned in order to be condemned, it is nonetheless a significant factor, and one attested to by archaeological discoveries such as statuettes and seals (although the latter were hardly the property of the peasantry!). Passages such as Deuteronomy 18:10–12 and Isaiah 8:19 indicate what must have gone on in popular Yahwism:

> There shall not be found among you any one who burns his son or his daughter as an offering, any one who practises divination, a soothsayer, or an augur, or a sorcerer, or a charmer, or a medium, or a wizard, or a necromancer. For whoever does these things is as an abomination to the LORD. (Deut. 18:10–12)

> When they say to you 'Consult the mediums and the wizards who chirp and mutter', should not a people consult their God? (Isa. 8:19)

Prophetic Yahwism was probably a peripheral factor socially in ancient Israel, but one which was highly significant in shaping Yahwism as it is presented in the Bible. From the evidence of 1 Samuel and the books of Kings (whether they are dated early or late), prophetic groups lived on the margins of society and may even have tried to adopt alternative lifestyles. One group, not unconnected with prophetic groups, was the Rechabites, who refused to build houses, plant vineyards or drink wine (Jer. 35:1–11; cf. 2 Kings 10:15, 23). At the time of Josiah's reformation (622 BCE) prophetic groups seem to have become allied to some members of the Judahite aristocracy and bureaucracy. At any rate, the latter were strongly supportive of prophets and their ideals. An unanswerable question is whether prophets such as Amos, Hosea, Micah and Isaiah worked as individuals or whether they were the leaders of schools of disciples (Petersen 1981). Much recent work on prophetic books implies that there were prophetic schools.

Towards the end of the Second Temple period prophecy seems to have been assimilated into official Yahwism. However, the group that lived at Qumran, and produced at least some of the Dead Sea Scrolls, could be described in terms of prophetic Yahwism. They lived on the margins of society in the Judean desert, they were sharply critical of official Judaism to the point of rejecting it altogether, and they adopted an alternative lifestyle with the intention of embodying the ideal Israel.

Official Yahwism took several forms, and included an openness to artistic, musical and literary products of an international nature. The comparison with Geertz's *prijaji* is interesting here; for whatever is made of the claim that Solomon composed 3000 proverbs and 1005 songs (1 Kings 4:32) or that the men of (king) Hezekiah copied the Proverbs of Solomon (Prov. 25:1), it constitutes evidence for an aesthetic and intellectual component in official Yahwism that was open to international influence. The statements in Ecclesiastes 2 that the author (who claims to have been a king, even if this is a fiction) had made parks, gardens and forests, all watered by pools, and had constructed fine houses and had employed singers, also points to an aesthetic element in the outlook of the aristocracy.

Official Yahwism no doubt took two distinct forms during the so-called divided monarchy. In Jerusalem, Yahwism centred upon God's covenant with the house of David; and if there was a historical David, the likelihood is that his was a soldier's religion, with YHWH as a warrior who assisted him in his battles. The official Yahwism of the northern kingdom, Israel, was more pragmatic, and also susceptible to powerful opposition mounted by the prophetic groups that operated in the north. Under Omri and Ahab, it was convenient, for the purposes of international trade and alliances, to promote the worship of the Canaanite storm-god Baal along with that of YHWH. The so-called prophetic revolution of Jehu in *c.* 841, when an army commander, Jehu, was impelled by prophetic groups to overthrow the dynasty of Omri and Ahab and to destroy the prophets of Baal, was an attempt to make official Yahwism conform to prophetic Yahwism (2 Kings 9:1 to 10:30). The dynasty of Jehu, if not its ideals, endured for nearly a century; and when the northern kingdom was destroyed by the Assyrians in 722/1 BCE the northern prophetic groups probably migrated to Judah, where their presence and activity brought about a fundamental change in the Jerusalem form of official Yahwism. The distinctive beliefs of the northern prophetic groups, centred upon the traditions of the exodus, combined with the ideology of God's covenant with David to produce the official Yahwism under whose aegis the Bible reached the form in which it appears today.

Beliefs and practices

YHWH and the gods

YHWH, his consorts and other gods in popular, prophetic and official religion

The origin of the name YHWH is unknown. According to biblical tradition (Exod. 3:13–15, 6:2–3) the name was revealed by God to Moses prior to the deliverance of the Israelites from slavery in Egypt. In Exodus 3:14 the name is connected with the verb 'to be' in Hebrew in a passage variously translated as 'I am who I am' or 'I am what I am' or 'I will be what I will be.' The fact that the name cannot be associated with any object in the natural world had often been noted. At Exodus 33:19 and 34:6 there are other expositions of the meaning or significance of the name:

> And he (God) said 'I will make all my goodness pass before you, and will proclaim before you my name "The LORD"; and I will be gracious to whom I will be gracious, and will show mercy on whom I will show mercy.'
>
> (Exod. 33:19)

> The LORD passed before him (Moses), and proclaimed, 'the LORD, the LORD, a God merciful and gracious, slow to anger, and abounding in steadfast love and faithfulness, keeping steadfast love for thousands, forgiving iniquity and transgression and sin, but who will by no means clear the guilty, visiting the iniquity of the fathers upon the children and the childen's children, to the third and the fourth generation'.   (Exod. 34:6–7)

Scholarship of the critical reassessment period looked for the origin of YHWH among the Kenites, on the basis of Exodus 3:1–6 and 18:1–12. In these passages there is mention of Moses' father-in-law, Jethro, described as a priest of Midian. It is while looking after Jethro's flock that the name YHWH is revealed to Moses, and on Moses' arrival in the Sinai desert following the Exodus, he is greeted by Jethro, who offers sacrifices to God. The mention of the Kenites as being descended from Moses' father-in-law (here called Hobab) in Judges 4:11 gave rise to the theory that the Kenites were a YHWH-worshipping clan among the Midianites from whom Moses learned the name (Rowley 1950: 149–54).

Modern critical scholars will find it difficult to accept this kind of argumentation, which treats Exodus 3 and 18 as historical sources for the thirteenth century BCE. Interest has been aroused, however, by the occurrence of the phrase 'Yhw in *Shasu*-land' in texts from the time of the Egyptian Amenophis III (1391–1353 BCE), and Yhw has been tentatively identified with a sacred mountain or mountain-god in the region of Seir or ancient Edom (Knauf 1988: 46). There are also biblical traditions that speak of YHWH 'coming' from Seir, as in the 'Song of Deborah':

> LORD (i.e. YHWH), when you went out from Seir, when you marched from the region of Edom, the earth trembled . . .   (Judg. 5:4; cf. Ps. 68:7–8)

The biblical references at least testify to the belief, among some Israelites, that YHWH 'came' from the region of Edom, although the origin of the name is

234 John Rogerson

less important than what was believed about YHWH. The earliest non-biblical reference to YHWH in connection with (the northern kingdom) Israel comes in the Mesha Inscription, found in Transjordan and dated to the first half of the ninth century BCE. It reads (lines 17–18), 'I took from there (Nebo) the [vessels] of YHWH' (Pritchard 1955: 320). It indicates that the northern kingdom, ruled by Omri (c. 885–874 BCE) who is named in the inscription at lines 4 to 5, had outposts in Transjordan with holy places where YHWH was worshipped.

Much interest has been aroused by the discovery, in 1975/6, of two inscribed jars at Kuntillet-ajrud, a kind of caravanserai 50 km south of Kadesh-barnea in the Negev. Dated about 800 BCE, they were evidently written and painted on by travellers (Renz and Röllig, 1995: 48–50) and among the inscriptions are references to 'YHWH of Samaria', 'YHWH of Teman' and 'YHWH and his Asherah'. These references introduce us to popular conceptions of YHWH.

For the travellers who stopped at Kuntillet-ajrud YHWH seems to have been a local deity worshipped in Samaria and Teman (in the south of Edom) and possibly believed to accompany travellers on their journeys. The reference to 'YHWH and his Asherah' has provoked much discussion, centring on whether Asherah was a goddess, a female consort of YHWH, or a sacred pole or tree that represented Asherah. At present, the balance of evidence favours the latter view because in ancient Hebrew (on all the evidence available) it is not possible to add a suffix meaning 'his' to a proper name such as Asherah. The worship of the fertility pole or tree is strongly condemned in the Bible (1 Kings 15:13), which is a good indication of its probably widespread practice.

In the Elephantine papyri (written from a Jewish colony near Aswan, downstream from the first cataract of the Nile, towards the end of the fifth century BCE) the God YHW (yaho) is mentioned along with two male deities and the female deity Anathbethel (Pritchard 1955: 491). Whether the latter was a consort to YHW or whether the other deities named were worshipped by non-Jews cannot be determined.

When using the Bible as evidence for worship of other gods in ancient Israel it is not always easy to distinguish between popular and official Yahwism at some periods; indeed, there may have been occasions such as during the reign of Manasseh (698–642 BCE) when there was little distinction. Also, if local sanctuaries wanted to cater for 'local' needs as well as supporting official Yahwism, they may well have been 'pluralistic' in what they offered. However, the distinction between popular and official Yahwism is an important one to maintain.

We are on safest ground for popular religion with Jeremiah 44:15–19 and Ezekiel 8:14, according to which there were women who worshipped the 'queen of heaven' (possibly some form of the Babylonian goddess Ishtar, or a sun-goddess) and Tammuz, a fertility-god. Amos (5:26) accuses the 'the house of Israel' of worshipping Sakkuth and Kaiwan, gods which have been connected with the cult of Saturn. Another god referred to in Jeremiah 32:35 and elsewhere is Molech, evidently a Canaanite god of the underworld to whom people offered human sacrifice in the valley of Hinnom near Jerusalem (Day 1989). And of course there is abundant evidence of the worship of the storm-god Baal at popular and official level. That YHWH was also worshipped at a popular level is indicated by extra-biblical texts such as the Lachish ostraca, messages written by Jewish soldiers on pieces of broken pot and sent to Lachish during Nebuchadnezzar's invasion of Judah in 588 BCE (Pritchard 1955: 322), although nothing can be said about the form that such worship took.

Prophetic Yahwism was characterized by what has been called 'YHWH-alone' devotion (Lang 1983) and was nationalistic in the sense that Israel (Judah) was believed to stand in a special relationship to YHWH and was therefore expected to display unalloyed loyalty to him. Yet prophetic Yahwism also sees the YHWH–Israel relationship in a universal context. YHWH does not exist merely for Israel's benefit, and YHWH will deliver Israel into the hand of its enemies and will let the temple be destroyed, if necessary, in order to punish and restore the people. This view leads necessarily to the idea that YHWH controls the destinies of other nations as they impinge upon Israel (or Judah). Isaiah 10:5–11 summons Assyria to the be rod of YHWH's anger against his people; Jeremiah 27:6 describes the Babylonian king Nebuchadnezzar as YHWH's servant, whom all the nations will serve. Isaiah 44:11 and 45:1 (dated to the mid-sixth century BCE) describes the Persian conqueror Cyrus as YHWH's shepherd and anointed (the Hebrew word for Messiah).

The claim that YHWH has universal power over the nations is also found in what is probably not the direct descendant of prophecy, but what is treated here for the sake of convenience under the heading of prophetic Yahwism, namely, Apocalyptic. In the book of Daniel there are stories in which Nebuchadnezzar (Dan. 4:1–37) and Darius, the sixth-century king of Persia (Dan. 6:25–28), acknowledge that the God of Israel is the Most High God. This literature also contains a significant difference from the prophetic viewpoint, in that the world has become a battleground between supernatural forces of good and evil whose struggles affect human nations. Nations are therefore no longer instruments used by YHWH to discipline Israel. They represent malign forces ranged against Israel, which only God and his heavenly servants can protect. This view is strongly represented in the Dead Sea Scrolls, where the community, representing the true Israel, the sons of light, finds itself ranged against a whole panoply of supernatural and human evil from which only God can ultimately deliver it.

Official Yahwism, as already pointed out, took different forms in the northern and southern kingdoms, until the two forms were united after the fall of Samaria (722/1). Both forms could be syncretistic. Ahab (c. 873–853 BCE), king of Israel, is described in 1 Kings 16:31–32 as serving Baal, building an altar and temple for Baal, and making an Asherah. Indications of the extent of syncretism in the official Yahwism of Jerusalem can be seen in the account of Josiah's reform (2 Kings 23:1–14) and the abominations in the Jerusalem temple which Ezekiel saw in a vision (Ezek. 8:1–18).

On the other side, names or titles of other gods were taken into official Yahwism and used as synonyms for, or instead of, YHWH, in order to indicate his universal power. These included 'elyon (Most High), shaddai (Almighty) and the general Semitic terms 'el and 'elohim.

A specific name found in official (and prophetic) Yahwism is YHWH tseva'ot, usually translated as 'LORD of hosts', and associated with the Ark of the Covenant (Num. 10:35–36, 1 Sam. 4:3–4), which seems to have symbolized the warlike presence of YHWH among his people. The 'hosts' of the title were the earthly and heavenly armies of Israel, in accordance with the belief that the powers of heaven fought on Israel's side (Judg. 5:20: 'From heaven fought the stars, from their courses they fought against Sisera' [Israel's enemy in the battle]). The title was a specifically Jerusalem title.

The openness of official Yahwism, the Yahwism of the aristocracy and bureaucracy, to international influences is well illustrated by the figure of wisdom in the book of Proverbs. In Proverbs 1:20–33 Wisdom addresses her readers/hearers, urging them to seek her counsel. In Proverbs 8:22–36 she claims that YHWH created her before anything else, and that she enjoyed an intimate relationship with him, which is one reason why her teachings should be taken seriously. The Wisdom figure in Proverbs probably pre-dates the passing of Judah under Hellenistic influence after 333, BCE and is derived from international wisdom teaching known from Egypt and Babylonia. After 333, however, the figure of wisdom was no doubt influenced by Hellenism, and she plays a major role in the Wisdom of Solomon (probably written in Alexandria 100–50 BCE) and the Wisdom of Jesus ben Sirach (Ecclesiasticus), written around 190–180 BCE.

A notable feature of official Yahwism as the Second Temple period comes to a close is the absence of the name YHWH in extant Hebrew texts. The non-biblical texts among the Dead Sea Scrolls use '*EL*, and in some biblical manuscripts written in the square Aramaic script the name YHWH is written in an adaptation of the Phoenician script. This no doubt reflects an avoidance of writing or pronouncing the name YHWH out of respect.

YHWH's attributes

The process by which YHWH became the highest god in prophetic and official Yahwism involved taking over functions that were associated with other gods in the neighbouring religions. These included fertility (Baal), and creation and the maintenance of justice (the sun-god). YHWH is also appealed to in the Psalms as God of healing. That the popular religion (and some kings!) found it difficult to apply this lofty monotheism in practice is evident from the condemnations of pagan practices in the Bible.

The passages cited above from Exodus 33:19 and 34:6–7 stress mercy, graciousness and steadfast love as primary attributes of YHWH. Steadfast love (Hebrew *hesed*) is a word used almost exclusively in connection with YHWH in the Old Testament. It contains the sense of loyalty, reliability and inexhaustibility (the New English Bible renders it as 'unfailing love') and it expresses YHWH's determination to be true to the covenants made with Israel come what may. Three other key terms associated with YHWH are 'glory', 'name' and 'holy'.

'Glory' (Hebrew *kavod*) is a synonym for the divine presence in all its mysterious awesomeness. In Ezekiel the 'glory of YHWH', meaning the divine presence in the temple, removes itself from the temple prior to the temple's destruction by the Babylonians in 587 BCE (Ezek. 11:22). In the prophet's vision of a restored temple, the 'glory' returns (Ezek. 43:1–5). However, the prophet also sees a vision 'of the likeness of the glory of the LORD' (Ezek. 1:28) and a description of this is given in chapter 1 in terms of wheels, living creatures, fire and lightning.

'Name' theology is found in the book of Deuteronomy and in the books of Kings and is closely associated with the divine presence in the temple, as in the phrase 'the place (i.e. sanctuary) which the LORD your God will choose, to make his name dwell there' (Deut. 12:11). 'Holy' is best taken to mean 'that which belongs to'. What is holy is God's property, and it can only be approached with awe and reverence, and not without danger (cf. 2 Sam. 6:6–7). Only properly consecrated priests of the priestly family, and only if they are without blemish as human beings (Lev. 21:16–24), may present sacrifices to God. A derived sense of 'holy' is 'ritually pure'. If Israel is God's special property then it, too, must be ritually pure; and one aim of the laws in Leviticus and Numbers is to extend to the whole people the regulations of ritual purity that originally only applied to priests. In Deuteronomy the emphasis is upon the purity of the land of Israel, and the belief that it can become defiled by evil moral action, such as an unavenged murder. Rituals for purifying the land in such a case are prescribed (Deut. 21:1–9). When the Bible says that YHWH is holy (cf. Isa. 6:3; Lev. 21:8) the claim ranges across a wide spectrum of meaning, from awesome otherness through moral rectitude to ritual separatedness.

Angels, demons and the Satan

YHWH is not a solitary figure in the Bible. Although he absorbed the functions of other deities he presided over a heavenly court and employed angelic beings to carry out his will. Towards the end of the Second Temple period the angelology and demonology become more developed.

If it is possible to take stories from Genesis, Exodus, Joshua and Judges as expressions of popular Yahwism, in the sense that such stories would need to correspond to the expectations of readers/hearers of these stories, the following points can be made. YHWH was believed to operate on earth by means of angelic messengers in human form, about whose real nature there was sufficient obscurity to make it difficult to tell that they were not humans. Genesis 18 begins with the statement that YHWH appeared to Abraham by the oaks of Mamre. The narrative continues with an account of three men who visited Abraham, and whom Abraham took to be important travellers who needed this hospitality. As the story continues, one of the three men appears to take on the role of YHWH, while the other two, explicitly called angels in Genesis 19:1 (in Hebrew the word means 'messenger') go on to Sodom. Here they are entertained by Lot, whose hospitality arouses the curiosity of the men of Sodom who insist that the visitors should be brought out of the house in order that they might know (i.e. sexually abuse) them. In Genesis 32:22–32 Jacob, prior to his reunion with his brother Esau, wrestles with a mysterious figure who is first described as a man (v. 24), who then displays supernatural power (v. 25) and who finally tells Jacob that he has been wrestling with God (*'elohim*).

In Joshua 5:13–15, prior to the battle of Jericho, Joshua is met by a man who describes himself as 'commander of the army of YHWH'. Gideon is also confronted by a divine messenger in Judges 6:11–24. Although the text describes him as 'the angel of YHWH', Gideon carries on a normal conversation with him, and only becomes aware of the status of his visitor when the latter produces fire from a staff. The parents-to-be of Samson have a similar visitation in Judges 13:2–23, which the woman describes in the following words: 'A man of God came to me, and his countenance was like the countenance of the angel of God, very terrible' (Judg. 13:6).

In those stories the angels are not named. The book of Tobit, on the other hand, written around 200 BCE, features an angel who is indistinguishable from a young man, and who is named Raphael. He plays a much fuller role in the story of Tobit than the angels in the incidents mentioned above, and presumably represents the stage in popular religion in which the angelology had become more developed.

Prophetic Yahwism was in particular the locus of the belief that YHWH presided over a divine court. The form of prophetic oracle known as the messenger formula expressed this particularly powerfully. In secular diplomacy, a king would send a message to another king by speaking to his ambassador as though he were actually addressing the other king. The formula was stereotyped and included surveys of past dealings between the kings. Its climax would come with the words 'Therefore, thus says X the great king to Y.' The ambassador would then go and repeat verbatim in the presence of the other king what he had heard his own master say.

The prophets adopted the messenger formula for their own declarations to monarchs and people, and when their oracles reached the words 'Therefore, thus says YHWH' they spoke as though they had been standing in the heavenly court, hearing a message from YHWH which they were now bound to speak verbatim to whomever the message was intended for. Accounts of prophetic visions in the Bible draw on the idea of the prophetic presence in the divine court. Micaiah ben Imlah relates a conversation in the divine court dealing with how Ahab might be lured to his death (1 Kings 22:19–23), while Isaiah heard the voice of God saying to his court, 'whom shall I send, and who will go for us?' (Isaiah 6:8). The book of Jeremiah claims that true prophets are the ones that have stood in YHWH's council: 'For who among them [the false prophets] has stood in the council of the LORD, to perceive and hear his word . . .?' (Jer. 23:18).

There are other passages that indicate a belief that YHWH had apportioned the care of various nations to angelic members of the divine court, reserving Israel for his own special attention. The classic statement is in Deuteronomy 32:8–9:

> When the Most High (*'elyon*) gave to the nations their inheritance,
> when he separated the sons of men,
> he fixed the bounds of the peoples according to the number of the sons
>   of God.
> For the LORD's portion is his people,
> Jacob his allotted heritage.

In Psalm 82 it is likely that God condemns the angelic beings responsible for the fortunes of other nations, because they have not upheld justice and protected the weak: 'You are gods, sons of the Most High (*'elyon*), all of you; nevertheless you shall die like men' (Ps. 82:6–7). The occurrence in both passages of *'elyon* is noteworthy. It is difficult to know whether this material represents prophetic or official Yahwism, except that the emphasis on justice in Psalm 82 is characteristic of prophetic Yahwism.

In what can be dated with some confidence as late books, a developed angelology and demonology is apparent. In Daniel (second century BCE) there appear the named angels Gabriel (8:16) and Michael (10:21). Tobit (*c.* 200 BCE) adds Raphael (5:4) and 2 Esdras 4:1 (100 CE) adds Uriel. Before the developed angelology and demonology are discussed however, it is necessary to comment upon popular belief in malevolent powers.

For ancient Israelites, as for other peoples of the ancient Near East, regions beyond the confines of ordered social life were the haunt of malevolent powers. Ruins were particularly to be feared, and it is no accident that oracles concerning ruined Babylon and desolated Edom in Isa. 13:9–22 and 34:8–14 contain references to satyrs and to Lilith (Isa. 34:14 where RSV has 'night hag'). Satyrs were goat-like demons; Lilith was a female demon prone to attack women in childbirth and men who slept alone (Handy 1992: 324–5). A more sophisticated version of this kind of superstition is found in the book of Tobit (3:18), where there is a demon Asmodus who killed the seven husbands of Sarah before she could have intercourse with them. In Exodus 4:24–26 there is possibly a survival of the same belief. We are told that YHWH met and tried to kill Moses but was prevented from so doing when his wife Zipporah cut off her son's foreskin and touched Moses's feet (i.e. penis) with it. Whatever this strange and difficult passage may mean, it seems to retain a popular superstition about demonic powers attacking human beings. If the mysterious figure of Azazel in Leviticus 16:8, 10 is a demon representing the forces of chaos and disorder to whom the scapegoat is made over, then this is another instance of popular superstition, albeit one which left its mark on official Yahwism.

Although new and radical views about the relative dating of biblical books may ultimately affect what immediately follows, the following stages in the development of demonology in ancient Israel's religion have traditionally been delineated. (1) A 'classical' period indebted to the ethical monotheism of the prophets in which YHWH was held to be responsible for everything that happened, whether good or evil (cf. Amos 3:6, Isa. 45:7). (2) A transition period in which a Satan figure (the Hebrew verb *satan* means 'to be an adversary') begins to emerge, gradually taking on increasingly sinister and independent features. In Job 1:6–7 the Satan is a member of YHWH's heavenly court, and although he afflicts Job with great misfortune and personal suffering, this is only with YHWH's permission. In Zechariah 3:1 Satan has taken on a definite accusing role, and he is rebuked by YHWH. (3) The 'ethical dualism' of the late Second Temple period, familiar also in the New Testament and especially the Dead Sea Scrolls, in which Satan (or Melchiresha, Belial, Beliar, Mastema – the chief of the evil angels has various names; see further Newsom 1992: 253) exercises power over the world with the help of evil angelic assistants. In the Dead Sea Scrolls the world is divided into the 'sons of light' (members of the Qumran community) and the 'sons of darkness' (the rest of the world) who are ruled respectively by the Prince of Light and the Angel of Darkness (IQS III 20f in Vermes 1997: 101). However, the Angel of Darkness has limited power over even the 'sons of light', who can obtain help from God and his Angel of Truth and who wait for the time when God will destroy all falsehood for ever (IQS IV, 18f). This kind of 'ethical dualism' is also presupposed in the New Testament, where the angels Gabriel (Luke 1:19, 26) and Michael (Jude v. 9, Rev. 12:7) appear and where there is war between good angels led by Michael and bad angels led by Satan (Rev. 12:7–9). The light/darkness dualism is particularly strong in John's Gospel, where there is also a reference to the defeat of the 'ruler of this world' (John 12:31). It is possible to see the influence of Zoroastrianism here (Hinnells 2000: 29–92).

In a fragmentary text from cave 11 at Qumran (11Q13 in Vermes 1997: 500–2) the role of Michael as leader of God's angels and destroyer of the angels of darkness is taken over by Melchizedek. The text is a commentary on the Jubilee law of Leviticus 25, and Psalm 82 in which God judges the gods appointed over the nations. The leader of the evil angels is called Belial, and the text mentions the theme of the rebellion of the evil angels against God, a theme often linked to

Genesis 6:1–4 (the 'fall' of the sons of God who desired and married the daughters of men). On a certain day after nine or ten Jubilees (Jubilee is a period of fifty years), Melchizedek will destroy Belial and his angels and bring comfort to those faithful to God. It is interesting that in the New Testament the figure of Melchizedek is used to enable the Letter to the Hebrews to interpret the ministry of Jesus in terms of priesthood (referring back to Ps. 110:4).

Israel and the nations

Election and covenant

That Israel (and Israel when represented by Judah) stands in a special relationship to YHWH is presupposed throughout the Bible, and is the Israelite version of the general belief in the ancient Near East that nations stand under the patronage of their gods. Expressions of the view that YHWH had appointed other divine beings to look after other nations at Deuteronomy 32:8 or Psalm 82 have already been noted. In popular and much official Yahwism this no doubt amounted to the view that YHWH should concentrate on ensuring the prosperity of the nation and its members and should not be too sensitive to corruption, injustice and occasional disloyalty. Prophetic Yahwism took a less relaxed view, and proclaimed a YHWH who not only would not tolerate corruption, injustice and disloyalty among his people, but who would allow them and their land to be destroyed by other nations as a punishment for their action. Even the reason for YHWH favouring Israel was qualified, according to the prophetically inspired Deuteronomy 9:4–6:

> Do not say in your heart . . . 'It is because of my righteousness that the LORD has brought me in to possess this land . . . The LORD your God is not giving you this good land to possess because of your righteousness; for you are a stubborn people.'

On the other hand, prophetic Yahwism invoked the theme of a parent's love for a child, to stress that, come what may, YHWH would never surrender his special relationship with Israel (Hos. 11:1–9; Isa. 46:3–4, 49:15).

Various covenants between God and other parties are recorded in the Bible: between God, and Noah and his descendants and other living creatures (Gen. 9:8–16), God and Abraham and his descendants (Gen. 17:1–8), God and the Israelites who had escaped from Egypt (Exod. 24:3–8), God and the house of David (2 Sam. 7:11–16). Of these, that between God and Israel as set out in the book of Deuteronomy is the most significant, and it probably follows the general pattern of vassal treaties known from elsewhere in the ancient Near East of the first millennium BCE.

Vassal treaties bound lesser nations to greater nations. They contained a historical prologue describing the background to the treaty, stipulated the obligations of the lesser party to the greater party, detailed grim consequences that would follow if the vassal proved to be disloyal, and called upon gods and powers of nature to be witnesses to the treaty (for an example see the Vassal-Treaties of Esarhaddon, king of Assyria 681–669 BCE in Pritchard 1969: 534–41). All of these elements, the last with the omission of other gods, can be found in Deuteronomy: historical prologue (4:44 to 11:32), Israel's obligations to YHWH (12:1 to 26:19), descriptions of blessings and curses that will follow obedience or disobedience (28:1–68), the summoning of heaven and earth as witnesses of the covenant (30:15–20). The Ten Commandments (Exod. 20:1–17, Deuteronomy 5:6–21) also contain elements of the pattern: they begin with a reminder that YHWH delivered the Israelites from slavery in Egypt (i.e. the historical prologue), they demand absolute loyalty to YHWH ('you shall have no other gods before me') and they set out obligations for Israel to observe. Whether parts of the Bible actually used treaty forms that were current in the ancient world at the time is disputed, but likely. It is incontestable that there are similarities between the way in which great rulers gave legal expression to the loyalty required from vassals, and the way in which parts of the Bible formulated YHWH's claim upon Israel's loyalty.

Israel's failure to observe the covenant is a feature of the books of Kings and of Jeremiah and Ezekiel, and prepares the way for the mention of a new covenant (Jer. 31:31–34; cf. Ezek. 36:24–32). The idea of a new covenant was taken up by the Covenanters of the Dead Sea Scrolls (see Vermes 1997: 67–72). In the Damascus Document (a medieval text discovered in Cairo in 1896–7 but fragments of which have been discovered at Qumran: see Vermes 1997: 125–56) the Covenanters were said to have entered into a New Covenant in the land of Damascus (CD VI, 19, Vermes 1997: 132). Whether 'Damascus' is to be taken literally or not, the community members believed that they constituted the new Israel. An annual covenant renewal ceremony was held during the feast of weeks (Pentecost) at which new members were admitted and existing members renewed their commitment. The task of community members was to study, interpret and obey the laws of God contained in the Jewish scriptures. Penalties, including expulsion, were prescribed for any member who broke the community's rules, and admission seems to have been a process that involved several years of trial membership.

Other nations as servants of YHWH

'He has not dealt with any other nation; they do not know his ordinances.' This claim in Psalm 147:20 could well create the impression that other nations occupied a very minor second place in Israel's world-view. This would be a mistake. The Bible has many surprising things to say about other nations, at any rate in the non-apocalyptic literature. (The apocalyptic literature, for example parts of Daniel, sees foreign nations as hostile forces ranged against Israel, forces that will be punished and judged by God.) A feature of the three major prophetic books (Isaiah, Jeremiah, Ezekiel) is a section of oracles against foreign nations (Isa. 13–19, Jer. 46–49, Ezek. 25–32). Amos has two chapters devoted to the same (Amos 1–2), while Nahum (in its final form) is an oracle against the Assyrian capital Nineveh.

The oracles against the nations are largely expressed in terms of judgement; but they also claim that YHWH is active in their affairs. For example, the oracles against Babylon in Jeremiah claim that YHWH is bringing the kings of the Medes against Babylon (Jer. 51:11) while in Jeremiah 46:13 Egypt is warned about what Nebuchadnezzar, king of Babylon, is about to do in Egypt. The oracles claim that YHWH is active in the disasters that are befalling nations, and that he is working out his judgement upon them. In this, of course, they are faring no better than Israel, which is also the object of oracles of judgement throughout the prophetic literature, and which is punished by God by means of nations such as Assyria (Isa. 10:5) and Babylon (Jer. 32:28).

The attitude of YHWH to members of other nations and their religion is sometimes surprisingly generous. A Moabite woman Ruth is the heroine of the book of Ruth and is described as an ancestor of David, while the book of Jonah, perhaps not without some irony, casts the citizens of the Assyrian capital of Nineveh in the unlikely role of people who repent immediately they hear Jonah's warning of impending disaster. In 2 Kings 5:17–18, the Syrian commander Naaman, who has been cured by Elisha of leprosy, utters a noble speech in which he begs YHWH for pardon when, in performance of his official duties, he is required to accompany his master the king to the house of the god Rimmon. For his part, Naaman wishes to acknowledge no God other than YHWH. In Amos 9:7, the prophet claims that YHWH brought not only Israel out of Egypt, but also the Philistines from Caphtor and the Syrians from Kir. Biblical claims about YHWH's special relationship with Israel have to be read in the light of YHWH's involvement with the other nations also.

The religious consciousness of Israelites

Creation and cosmos

The best-known account of creation in the Bible is in Genesis 1; and it is often claimed that there is a second creation account in Genesis 2:4b–25. This claim is wrong on two counts: Genesis 2 is an origins story, i.e. a story that presupposes the existence of the world, and which seeks to account for features within it. Second, the complete creation narrative runs from Genesis 1 to Genesis 9, albeit with the insertion of material from another source or sources. Only in Genesis 9 is the world known to humans reached. That of Genesis 1, in which animals and humans are vegetarians (Gen. 1:3a) is the world as God ideally intends it. The actual world is thus a compromise world, and the vegetarian world reappears in prophetic visions of a re-created cosmos (Isa. 11:1–9, 65:17–25). The story of the flood (Gen. 6:5 to 8:19) describes the destruction of the created world of Genesis 1, as the forces which restrain the destructive waters above and below the heavens are released (Gen. 7:11).

This destruction of the created world by means of releasing the powerful waters points to the heart of the Hebrew Bible's idea of creation, that of order. In Job 38:4–41, YHWH's unanswerable questions to Job stress the theme of order. The sea has powerful limits (Job 38:8–11), dawn happens at God's command (38:12–15), light has a definite source, while there are storehouses where snow and hail are kept (38:22). The stars and the clouds operate only at God's behest (38:31–8).

Creation does not only involve the order of the natural world, however. It includes the human moral order, and disorder in this area can affect the order in creation. This is most clearly seen in Genesis 4:1–16, where Cain's murder of his brother Abel affects the earth. 'When you till the ground, it shall no longer yield to you its strength' (Gen. 4:12); but the reason for the destructive flood is also human wickedness. The link between the moral order and the created order is also implied in 'covenant' passages in which the fertility of the land is linked with Israel's obedience to YHWH's commandments (e.g. Deut. 28).

The foregoing can be loosely described as the view of prophetic Yahwism. Official Yahwism, as found in the book of Proverbs, was probably more oriented to the view that the universe was a 'moral universe' in which there were built-in mechanisms that brought advantage to those who practised virtue and thrift, or disadvantages to the lazy and devious. There is also to be found here the belief that wisdom was present at the creation and that she assisted YHWH (Prov. 8:22–31).

In Sirach (Ecclesiasticus) the wisdom present at creation begins to be identified with the Mosaic law (Sirach 24).

In the apocalyptic literature, especially the Dead Sea Scrolls, the world which God has created is also not what he ideally intends. It is a battleground between angels of light and darkness. Yet this situation is under God's control and will be resolved in God's favour. It profoundly affects the present lives of humans, however, especially those of members of the community (Vermes 1997: 74).

Consciousness of sin and evil

Because the Bible included the moral order in the overall order which is creation, and saw a connection between moral and natural disorder, it has much to say about sin and evil. This is all, however, at the pragmatic level. There is no theorizing about the origin of evil, and certainly no doctrine of 'original sin' as developed in Christian theology. The stories of human disobedience and inhumanity in Genesis 3–6 are descriptive, as are the important narratives in Exodus and Numbers, which describe the constant rebellions of the Israelites who have been delivered from slavery in Egypt. Passages such as Jeremiah 31:31–4 and Ezekiel 36:24–27 which envisage a new covenant written on human hearts, and led by a new spirit, are to humanity what the paradox of Genesis 1–9 is to creation – a statement that the human race is both created by YHWH and prone to rebellion, pride and inhumanity.

It is no surprise that the existence of moral evil should encourage the kind of speculation about the origin of human fallenness that is found in the Christian doctrine of 'original sin'. One line of development, based upon Genesis 6:1–4, is the belief that watcher angels 'fell' by being attracted sexually to human women. This led to the existence of angels opposed to God who then corrupted the human race. The 'fall' of the watchers is mentioned in the Ethiopic book of Enoch (69:6) and in the Damascus Document associated with Qumran (CD ii, 18, in Vermes 1997: 129). It is also possibly implied in the oft-quoted verse from Wisdom of Solomon 2:24: 'through the devil's envy death entered the world, and those who belong to his company experience it'.

In 2 Esdras (also known as iv Ezra) 7:116 [sic], written c. 100 CE as a Jewish response to the destruction of the Second Temple, the view is found that Adam's disobedience brought dire consequences for his descendants.

Theodicy and scepticism

If there is speculation in the Bible about the paradox of belief in one supreme creator God and the existence of human disobedience and inhumanity, it is to be found in the areas of theodicy and scepticism. To the question 'why do the righteous suffer and the wicked prosper?' one answer, given in Psalm 37, is that this state of affairs is only temporary: 'I have not seen the righteous forsaken or his children begging bread' (Ps. 37:25). A more sophisticated answer is attempted in Psalm 73. It is only when the psalmist goes to the temple that he is assured that God's justice will ultimately prevail, and this assurance is supported by one of the few glimmers of the possibility of an afterlife in ancient Judaism: 'you guide me with your counsel, and afterward you will receive me with honour' (Ps. 73:24). Other answers to the question range from outright disregard of YHWH (Ps. 14:1, 94:7) or, in popular religion, in turning to other gods who might grant what YHWH had been unable to achieve (Jer. 44:15–25).

The most elaborate discussion is in the book of Job. YHWH allows the Satan, who is a member of the heavenly court, to destroy Job's wealth and to bring about the death of his children, but Job will not reproach YHWH. Three (later, four) friends arrive who attempt to persuade Job that God is just, and that Job must have committed an enormous crime against God to have merited such punishment. Their tactics include appealing to divine revelation (4:12–21) and to the wisdom of bygone ages (8:8–10). Job is reminded that he is a mere mortal who cannot fathom God's ways (11:7–12), and his honesty and integrity are called into question (22:6–11). For his part, Job maintains that he has done nothing to merit the scale of disaster that has befallen him, and he calls upon God to let him put his case which, he is sure, God would judge fairly (23:1–7). When YHWH finally addresses Job out of a whirlwind he makes no attempt to answer Job's complaints, and on the face of it, his questions to Job about whether Job was present at the creation of the universe seem to support the arguments of the friends that mere human knowledge cannot fathom the ways of God. Yet God vindicates Job and criticizes his friends (42:7–9). The outcome seems to be that Job has been right to maintain his integrity; and he experiences YHWH's transcendence in such a way that he can say that his whole understanding of reality has been transformed (42:1, 5–6).

Another exploration of these themes is in Ecclesiastes, probably written towards the end of the fourth century BCE. Qoheleth (as the self-styled author is called in Hebrew) is candid not only about the injustices of the world (4:1–3) but about the apparent purposelessness of much life, which he describes as 'vanity'. The created order exhibits only the recurrent cycles of nature (1:2–11), human life is largely constrained by events over which humans have little control (3:1–8) and life will end in the weakness and infirmity of old age (12:1–8). The main positive contribution that can be made in this situation is for humans to enjoy what God has given them (2:24–26).

Job and Ecclesiastes, for all their individualism, are close to official Yahwism, with its more international concerns. The name YHWH is never used in Ecclesiastes, and in Job comes only in the prologue (chs. 1–2) and in ch. 38 when YHWH addresses Job from the whirlwind. (The text may have had several authors or editors, and the prologue and epilogue may be later compositions. This does not affect the teaching of the book taken as a whole, however.) All the dialogues in Job use divine names other than YHWH. Also absent from Job and Ecclesiastes are references to Israel's election. Nonetheless, the two books presuppose God's absolute sovereignty in the universe. Their honest questionings add an important dimension to the spectrum of ancient Israel's religion, and one that is absent from the prophetic and apocalyptic traditions, with their certainty that YHWH or God is fully in control of all that happens in the life of nations.

Conceptions of afterlife and eschatology

How people cope with actual deaths and how they theorize about death are two different things, and this section will be concerned with the latter. Given the distinction that is being made, however, between popular, prophetic and official Yahwism, it should be noted that the Hebrew Bible prohibits, and therefore provides evidence for, elements of a 'cult of the dead' in ancient Israel. These implied customs include making cuts in the flesh on account of the dead (perhaps to provide blood for the spirit of the deceased, cf. Lev. 19:28), defiling oneself for the sake of a dead person (Lev. 21:11) and offering the tithe or part of it to the dead (Deut. 26:14). On the other hand, Jeremiah 16:6–7, apparently without any condemnation, describes various mourning rites, including some of those that are prohibited in the texts just quoted.

The belief of official (and presumably prophetic) Yahwism was that the dead went to Sheol, a cosmic underworld that was linked to the graves in which people were placed. In Sheol there was a shadowy existence which, according to some texts, excluded any form of contact with God (Psalm 88:10–12). On the other hand, the writers of Job (Job 3:17–19) and Ecclesiastes (Eccles. 3:18–20) could gain a certain comfort from Sheol. For Job, Sheol was a place where prisoners would no longer hear the voice of the taskmaster and where the slave would be free from his master. For Ecclesiastes Sheol ended the opportunity that the powerful had to oppress the weak, and it indicated that, in respect of their final destinies, humans had no advantages over beasts. It is noteworthy that neither

Job nor Ecclesiastes had recourse to the afterlife in trying to explain the success of the wicked in the world, unless there is a glimpse of an afterworld in Job's exclamation that God himself will act as his *Go'el* (his kinsperson who upholds his cause, cf. Job 19:25–27). Texts that push the standard view just outlined to its limits and beyond are found in Psalm 139:8, where the psalmist states that even if he tries to flee from God by going to Sheol he will find God there, and incidents such as the taking of Enoch and Elijah up to heaven (Gen. 5:24; 2 Kings 2:11–12). Both stories use the Hebrew verb 'to take' in the sense of being taken to God, and the occurrence of this verb in a similar sense in Psalms 49:15 and 73:24 (translated as 'receive' in both cases) has been seen as evidence for a strand of belief according to which fellowship with God established in this life cannot be broken by death.

The impulse towards belief in an afterlife, possibly helped by contact with Zoroastrianism, seems to have come from the crisis of 168/7 to 164 BCE, when Antiochus IV proscribed Judaism and some Jews were martyred for their faith. Daniel 12:2–3 seems to envisage a limited resurrection (of Jews?), leading to 'everlasting life' for some and 'shame and everlasting contempt' for others. Another late passage (Isa. 26:17–19) ends with the exclamation 'Thy dead shall live, their bodies shall rise.' The Isaiah passage probably influenced the Thanksgiving Hymn from Qumran (IQH xi in Vermes 1997: 259–60) which has been thought to attest a similar belief in resurrection at Qumran. More recently, a fragment called the 'Resurrection fragment' (4Q521 in Vermes 1997: 391–2) has been published which contains the line 'For He will heal the wounded, and revive the dead and bring good news to the poor.'

In the Judaism influenced by Greek thought, the idea of the immortality of the soul is found, and it also helps to explain the problem of the suffering of the innocent and the prosperity of the wicked. The Wisdom of Solomon describes life as seen by the ungodly (Wisd. 1:16–20). This includes deliberately oppressing the weak and disposing of the righteous man, 'because he is inconvenient to us and opposes out actions' (Wisd. 2:12). The ungodly are mistaken (Wisd. 2:21–24) and the souls of the righteous are in the hand of God (Wisd. 3:1). The righteous will condemn the wicked and will stand in confidence at the final judgement (Wisd. 5:1–14), after which they will enjoy eternal life (Wisd. 5:15–23). More complex schemes concerning the fate of humans after death can be found in 2 Esdras 7:75–101, according to which there will be seven orders or ways of punishment and of reward for the unrighteous and righteous respectively, or Enoch 22 in which Sheol is divided into various sections in which the dead wait for the final judgement, and enjoy comfort or punishment depending on how they have lived their earthly lives.

An incident in 2 Maccabees 12:39–45 indicates belief in atonement for the dead. Following a particular battle, Judas Maccabaeus and his men discover that some of their fallen comrades are wearing 'sacred tokens of the idols of Jamnia', that is, protective pagan amulets derived from popular religion. The death of these warriors may have been due to this disobedience to the law (cf. 2 Macc. 12:34–42), but given that they had died fighting for God's cause, Judas organizes a collection of money to be sent to Jerusalem to provide for a sin offering for them. As the writer comments, 'if he were not expecting that those who had fallen would rise again, it would have been superfluous and foolish to pray for the dead' (2 Macc. 44).

Ancient Israel's eschatological beliefs were bound up with the gap between the world as it was and the world as it should be ideally, if it were the work of YHWH. In prophetic Yahwism an important theme is that of the 'day' of YHWH, a day on which the whole world would witness the awesome splendour of YHWH's judgement; a day on which all that was proud and lofty would be brought low (Isa. 2:12–21; Zeph. 1:2–18; Amos 5:18–20). Other prophetic visions concern what will happen 'in the last days'. According to one vision (Isa. 2:22–24; Mic. 4:104) Jerusalem will become the place from which God's law will be proclaimed for all nations. The nations will go up to Jerusalem and 'beat their spears into pruning hooks'. Other visions look to a covenant for Israel written on human hearts (Jer. 31:31–34; Ezek. 36:24–27), or to the creation of a new heaven and a new earth, in which the original vegetarian creation is re-established (Isa. 65:17–25; cf. Gen. 1:30). Yet other visions are conceived in terms of the coming of prophetic or royal figures in the pattern of Moses (Deut. 18:15) or David (Ezek. 34:20–24) or Elijah (Ezek. 4:5–6). The Psalms look forward to the 'coming' of God to judge the earth, a judgement that will be accompanied by rejoicing by the forces of nature (Ps. 96:11–13).

The social and formal expression of Israelite religion

Sanctuaries, temples and the temple

'The local sanctuaries were the centres of all Hebrew life. How little of the history would remain if Shechem and Bethel, the two Mizpahs and Ophra, Gilgal, Ramah and Gibeon, Hebron, Bethlehem, and Beersheba, Kadesh and Mahanaim, Tabor and Carmel, were blotted out of the Old Testament!' (Smith 1881: 235). Unfortunately, in the Bible as we have it, strenuous attempts were made either to blot these sanctuaries out of the text, or to discredit what went on at them, from the point of view of later orthodoxies. Nowhere is the tension between popular religion and prophetic religion as great as in regard to sanctuaries and temples, with official religion vying with both as occasion demanded. Yet many stories afford glimpses of popular religious practices which, if the recent tendency to date such stories to the post-exilic period is correct, must have persisted well into the Second Temple period.

The story of Jacob mentions a sacred stone (Hebrew *matzevah*; the setting up of such stones is roundly condemned at Deuteronomy 12:3, 16:23!) which Jacob set up and anointed as a sign that the place was 'the house of God' (Gen. 28:18). Pillars (using the same Hebrew word) are also mentioned in the story of Moses (Exod. 24:4) as having been set up when the 'book of the Covenant' was ratified. Such visual markers of the presence of the deity are well known from excavations in the ancient Near East. Portable symbols of the divine presence, in the form of 'household gods' (Hebrew *teraphim*), are mentioned in the stories of Jacob (Gen. 31:33–35) and David (1 Sam. 19:16), while in the book of Judges a certain Micah sets up in his house both teraphim and an ephod (possibly an object used for divination) and installs a priest to minister at his shrine, which apparently also includes a graven image (Hebrew *pesel* – forbidden in the Ten Commandments at Exodus 20:4!) and a molten image. Although the word 'ephod' is the same Hebrew word as for the garment to be worn by the high-priest (Exod. 28:4) it is presumably a different object, and in the story of Gideon (Judg. 8:27) the ephod which he makes from a vast quantity of gold is, in the view of the text as we have it, a snare which leads Gideon and his people away from God. In the story of Abraham, God appears to him 'by the oaks [or terebinths] of Mamre', and it is arguable that these trees were a sacred grove associated with the divine presence (cf. Isa. 1:29) rather than simply indicators of a location.

Sanctuaries were often sited upon hills, so that going to the sanctuary involved mounting up the sides of hills or sets of steps (cf. Jacob's dream at Gen. 28:12). In this way the idea of divine transcendence was mediated, and such sanctuaries were called 'high places'. Various cult objects were sited in or close to sanctuaries, apart from obvious cultic furniture such as altars and their accoutrements. The Ark of the Covenant resided successively at the sanctuaries of Bethel (Judg. 20:27), Shiloh (1 Sam. 3:3) and finally Jerusalem. There is mention of the 'lamp of God' at Shiloh (1 Sam. 3:3), 'the bread of the Presence' at Nob (1 Sam. 21:6) and bull images at Bethel and Dan (1 Kings 12:28–29). The latter are condemned by the text as we have it, and there are doubtless links between the story of Jeroboam setting up the bull images at Bethel and Dan and the story of the Israelites making and worshipping the golden calf in Exodus 32. However, it has been argued that the bull images served as the throne of the invisible YHWH and that they earned prophetic and, later, official disapproval because of their possible identification as fertility symbols. Hezekiah is reported to have broken in pieces a bronze serpent to which the people burned incense, and which was said to have been made by Moses (2 Kings 18:4).

The Solomonic temple contained, in addition to the usual cultic furniture, two pillars (not *matzevot*) called Jachin and Boaz. While these names have not been satisfactorily explained, the function of the pillars was probably to convey a sense of grandeur and transcendence, given their height (some 26 feet 6 inches) and their circumference (some 17 feet 6 inches). Together with a molten sea standing upon twelve oxen, stands with panels portraying lions, oxen and cherubim and standing upon wheels, and ten lavers of bronze (1 Kings 7:21–39), the two great pillars were part of an architectural assemblage designed to convey the splendour and mystery of the house of God.

For much of its history, the first (Jerusalem) temple was a royal sanctuary, serving the needs of the official cult, as opposed to the local sanctuaries which served the needs of popular religion. As such, the Jerusalem temple reflected the ups and downs of Judah's political life. Ahaz is reported to have installed an altar copied from one he saw in Damascus when he paid homage to Tiglath-pileser III of Assyria in around 733 BCE (2 Kings 16:10–16). Josiah removed from it the vessels made for Baal, Asherah and the host of heaven, as well as horses and chariots dedicated to the sun that stood at the entrance to the temple (2 Kings 23:4–12).

The attempted centralization of worship in Jerusalem by Josiah from 622 BCE had the effect of making the Jerusalem temple into a national sanctuary. This had profound implications for the personnel of the local sanctuaries that were closed down, and it had the effect of making the Passover (see p. 254 below) a festival that could only be celebrated in Jerusalem (Deut. 16:1–7). No doubt the centralization was a device for securing greater control over affairs in Judah; but it was also an attempt to bind the nation closer to the one God, YHWH, who could only legitimately be worshipped at the one sanctuary. From now on, the Jerusalem temple played a key role in the theologizing of Judaism. Books such as Joshua, Judges and 1 and 2 Kings were edited from the standpoint that faithfulness to the one sanctuary was identical to exclusive loyalty to YHWH. Kings and their subjects were judged to be either righteous or evil according to whether or not they were loyal to the one sanctuary.

Following the temple's destruction in 587 BCE it became a site towards which those who were in exile prayed (1 Kings 8:27–30; Dan. 6:10). Hopes for its restoration became a vehicle for eschatology. The closing chapters of Ezekiel envisage a restored temple that will be appropriate to a people who will have received a new heart and a new spirit (Ezek. 36:26). The temple will be fitting for a holy and transcendent God, and its appearance will differ from that of the first temple (Ezek. 43:6–9; see Allen 1990: 229–35 for a description and plan of the temple as conceived by Ezekiel). By describing a temple different from the Second Temple (rebuilt and completed *c.* 515 BCE) the Qumran community indicated their rejection of official Judaism. The Temple Scroll (11QT, Vermes 1997: 190–219) fills a gap in the biblical record by purporting to be the instructions of God to Moses about the building of the Jerusalem temple, and the organization of its personnel and festivals (see below, pp. 256–7 and 283–6). 'Its criticism of the current temple are . . . articulated in a unique fashion, not as prophetic revelation in the manner of Ezekiel, but as divine revelation to Moses – actually in direct imperative speech to Moses, as part of the Torah' (Maier, 59; German edn 67). Because of the sometimes fragmentary nature of the text the exact reconstruction of the Qumran temple is disputed (see Maier 1985: 58–70; German edn 68–76). What is clear, however, is that architectural descriptions became a potent method for sectarian definition. It has been argued that the same consideration played a part in the origins of Christianity, and that part of the programme of Jesus and his followers was a rejection of the Jerusalem temple (Chilton 1992).

By the time of the Dead Sea Scrolls and the beginning of Christianity, Judaism had had to develop forms of worship, especially in the diaspora (i.e. Jews living outside Palestine), that did not require the temple and its services. It is usually supposed that the synagogue was developed during the post-exilic period to meet this need, although the earliest actually surviving synagogue, that at Masada, dates only from the first century BCE at the earliest. Literary sources, however, suggest that the synagogue was a well-established phenomenon by this time, although the term 'synagogue' can refer to a group of people or a building, and no doubt covered these and other forms of activity/space devoted to prayer, worship, study and education.

Religious calendars and festivals
Calendars, like temples, can become institutions that are used to shape and control a nation's religious life. They can also become the means whereby a dissident group expresses its rejection of an official cult.

It is generally held that the oldest calendar in the Bible is the so-called ritual decalogue of Exodus 34:17–26, dating perhaps from the early monarchy (i.e. tenth–ninth century BCE). Prominent in this 'decalogue' is the following calendar: seven days of unleavened bread are to be observed in the month of Abib (March) as well as the feast of weeks (i.e. the wheat harvest) and the feast of ingathering (of the fruit harvest) at the year's end (i.e. autumn). These are three harvest festivals: the barley harvest (unleavened bread), the wheat harvest (in May/June) and the fruit harvest (September). It has often been pointed out that Passover is not mentioned in connection with these festivals (although it is referred to in Exodus 34:25 in another context) and that the command to all males to appear on these three occasions before YHWH does not specify that this should be at the single sanctuary. The calendar in the 'ritual decalogue' is thus assumed to date from a period when males were required to go to a local sanctuary on the occasion of the three harvest festivals.

In the course of time, Passover was linked with the feast of unleavened bread and the whole timetable was elaborately set out in connection with stipulations about temple offerings and sabbath rests in Numbers 28 (see also Lev. 23). It is generally held that what had originally simply been agricultural festivals were progressively officially observed as commemorating Israel's deliverance from Egypt. Passover was linked to the barley harvest celebration of unleavened bread, while the wilderness wanderings were associated with the autumnal fruit harvest, which was called the festival of booths or tabernacles (see Lev. 23:33–43). Later Judaism associated the festival of weeks with the giving of the law at Mount Sinai, although this connection is not explicitly made in the Bible. Leviticus 23:26 adds in the Day of Atonement.

This is the official calendar. However, there are glimpses in the Bible of other, popular, festivals, as well as indications of how the harvest festivals were celebrated in the popular religion. Judges 21:19–21 mentions a yearly feast of YHWH at Shiloh at which the 'daughters of Shiloh' came out of the vineyards to dance. It can be inferred from the context that this was an autumnal harvest celebration at which future wives were chosen. A connection between barley harvest celebrations and marriage can also be inferred from Ruth 3:1–13, where Ruth indicates her willingness to marry Boaz by lying at his feet on the threshing floor. 1 Samuel 1:3 mentions an annual pilgrimage to Shiloh by Elkanah and his two wives in order to offer sacrifice, while 1 Samuel 20:18 indicates that the new moon was an occasion for an important festival. Jonathan warns David that he will be missed if he does not attend, even though his life is in danger from Saul's attempts to kill him. The excuse offered on David's behalf is that he has been required to attend a yearly sacrifice organized by his family (1 Sam. 20:6, 29). In the story of Elisha (2 Kings 4:11–24), the prophet promises the Shunammite woman that she will have a boy. When the boy later dies, the woman commands her servant to summon the prophet. The Shunammite's husband is puzzled that the prophet is being summoned, since it is neither 'new moon nor sabbath'. This latter quotation confirms that the new moon was a time for popular celebration; the reference to the sabbath is intriguing, since it can hardly be the weekly sabbath that is being referred to, or if it is, it is clearly envisaged in the story that its observance requires the presence of a holy man. This is a far cry from the sabbath as a day of no work.

The weekly sabbath rest was the most distinctive feature of the Israelite calendar, and all attempts to trace its origin to another people from whom the Israelites borrowed it have failed. Whether the sabbath *day* was derived from the sabbath *year* (Exod. 23:10–12) or vice versa is not clear, but a strong case can be made for seeing both ordinances as originating in the attempt to create 'structures of grace', that is, practical arrangements that would prevent the exploitation of slaves, and which would provide food for the poor. The principle of the sabbath year, that the land was to remain fallow and that the poor and wild animals should eat what grew of itself, was extended to cover the remission of debts in the seventh year (Deut. 15:1–6; this is the most likely interpretation of a partly obscure regulation) and the restoration of land to its original owners in the Jubilee Year (the forty-ninth or fiftieth year, i.e. after seven sabbatical years) in Leviticus 25.

Scholars have found hints of other official festivals such as a festival every year or seventh year of the reading of the law (Deut. 31:10) and an annual (or periodic) celebration of the bringing of the Ark of the Covenant to Jerusalem and God's covenant with the house of David (cf. Ps. 132, 24, 47). No treatment of the calendar and festivals can be exhaustive in a brief chapter.

The publication in 1977 of the Temple Scroll from Qumran has revealed a Jewish calendar from the first century BCE that appears to have differed radically from what had come to be the calendar for the Jerusalem temple of the time (see 11 QT cols. 13–29 in Vermes 1997: 192–200; the whole calendar is set out in Maier 1985: 71–6). Whereas the official calendar worked on a lunar year of 354 days with the addition of a thirteenth lunar month every three years or so, the Qumran calendar used a solar year of 364 days, one in which each festival would occur on the same day of the week each year. A similar calendar is known from the books of Enoch and Jubilees. This entailed that major festivals would more often than not be observed at different times at Qumran, compared with Jerusalem.

This not only divided the communities but indicated the Qumran belief in the illegitimacy of the Jerusalem cult. The Qumran calendar also interpreted certain biblical texts about how festivals should be celebrated, differently from 'official' Judaism, and added festivals of wine, oil and wood gathering not known from the Bible (see Yadin 1985: 84–111).

It has sometimes been argued that Jesus also used an 'irregular' calendar and celebrated the Passover 'illegally'. According to the Temple Scroll 14 Nisan fell on a Monday/Tuesday, which is at odds with Christian tradition that Jesus celebrated the Passover/Last Supper on a Thursday evening. If Jesus was using a different calendar it does not appear to have been that from Qumran.

Priesthood

In the developed religion of the Second Temple period, as found in books such as Leviticus, Numbers and 1 and 2 Chronicles, priesthood is a sophisticated institution which regulates access to God in matters of sacrifice and purity. The latter includes making the priests responsible for diagnosing the skin complaint misleadingly called leprosy in many translations, and for deciding when sufferers from this complaint had been cured (Lev. 14). In the developed system, all priests are sons of (i.e. descended from the family of) Aaron, and they are headed by a high-priest. There is also the priestly tribe of Levi (to which Moses and Aaron belonged) whose members perform ancillary duties in the temple, working as officers and judges, gatekeepers and musicians (1 Chron. 23:4–5). Scholars are generally agreed that, in the pre-exilic period, Levites (members of the tribe of Levi) were probably priests at the local sanctuaries of YHWH and that they were reduced in status as a result of the centralization under Josiah in the late seventh century, and the destruction of the temple and its reordering after the exile. It is also widely believed that the office of high-priest is a post-exilic innovation designed to take the place of the monarchy, which did not survive the disruptions of 587 BCE. Certainly, the high-priesthood eventually became so important politically that the Seleucid kings (the Greek rulers of Syria from the late fourth century and of Palestine from 200 BCE) were prepared to accept bribes in order to displace holders of an office meant to last for life. Jason ousted his brother Onias III around 170 BCE by bribing Antiochus IV (2 Macc. 4:7–10) only to be outbid and displaced three years later by Menelaus (2 Macc. 4:23–29). Later, the Maccabees (the sons and descendants of Mattathias – see 1 Macc. 2) assumed the high-priesthood. Jonathan, the second Maccabean leader (161–143 BCE) became high-priest in 153, the post having been vacant since around

160 BCE. Herod the Great (37–4 BCE) appointed and deposed a whole series of high-priests between 35 and 23 BCE. It is widely held that one of the reasons for the founding of the Qumran community was to preserve the true priesthood, following the deposition, and later murder, of Onias III. The community certainly came to be led by priests who claimed to be 'sons of Zadok', thus claiming legitimate descent and priesthood from the (high-)priest of David's reign (cf. 1 Kings 1:32–40).

In these later centuries in which the high-priesthood had become a position of power and intrigue, many Jews, especially in the diaspora, had developed their religion in the direction of interpreting the Bible and using it to regulate worship and daily life. Thus, priesthood had become peripheral. Before the exile the situation was much more pluralistic, if books such as Genesis, Judges and Samuel can be taken to give information about this period. Heads of large families such as Abraham offered sacrifice (Gen. 22:13) and priesthood was not confined to the tribe of Levi. Samuel, who was an Ephraimite, exercised priestly functions (1 Sam. 7:9) while David is also said to have offered sacrifices (2 Sam. 6:18), perhaps inheriting the priestly role of the Jerusalemite kings prior to his capture of the city (but see above, p. 217). From the story of Hannah and Eli (1 Sam. 1) it is evident that priests at local sanctuaries exercised a pastoral role, and scholars have interpreted the Psalms in such a way as to suggest that priests offered comfort to individual worshippers who were in distress, and played a crucial role in national celebrations such as coronations (see also 2 Kings 11, where the priest Jehoiada plays the key role in deposing Queen Athaliah and in installing Jehoash as king).

Prophecy

As the division of Israelite religion into official, prophetic and popular religion in this chapter indicates, prophets played a major role in the shaping of Israelite religion. Because their importance has been indicated in other sections where appropriate, this section will confine itself to the institution of prophecy, if there was such a thing. Certainly, the editors of the Bible into its present form thought that there was such a thing as prophecy, but this view conceals the diversity of the phenomenon and the unanswered questions that it raises.

In what have traditionally been taken to be 'early' books of the Bible, prophets appear as groups living out alternative lifestyles on the edges of society, under the leadership of figures such as Samuel, Elijah and Elisha (1 Sam. 19:18–24; 2 Kings 2). They engage in ecstatic behaviour and intervene in the political affairs of the nation (1 Sam. 10:1, 16:1–13; 2 Kings 9:1–13). It is also clear that there were court prophets, whose role was to predict, and therefore hopefully ensure, success for the king (1 Kings 22:5–12).

From the eighth century there appear the misleadingly called 'writing prophets', Amos, Hosea, Micah and Isaiah of Jerusalem, who are a diverse set of individuals. Isaiah appears to be a court prophet while Micah, from the provincial Judahite town of Moreshah, is bitterly critical of Jerusalem and its temple. Amos describes himself as a herdsman and denies that he is a prophet in the professional or conventional sense (Amos 7:14–15). Recent scholarship has suggested that these were not isolated individuals but the heads of groups of disciples.

The flowering of 'prophecy' was from the eighth to the sixth centuries, with figures such as Jeremiah, Ezekiel and the authors or originators of Isaiah 40–55 and 56–66 being worthy successors to the eighth-century prophets. After the exile, perhaps because of the greater institutionalization of Israelite religion, prophets became rarer, and were even regarded with alarm, as in Zechariah 13:2–3: 'I will remove from the land the prophets . . . And if any one again appears as a prophet, his father and mother who bore him will say to him, "You shall not live. For you speak lies in the name of the LORD".' By this time, 'prophecy' had become a literary phenomenon, with much attention devoted to the editing of the prophetic books into their extant form. The creative and almost subversive contribution of prophecy was taken over by apocalyptic (see p. 246), whose role was to provide comfort to a beleaguered and oppressed Israelite people.

Resources for the practice of religion

Sacrifice

In the popular and official religion of ancient Israel sacrifice was an important element. Prophetic religion, on the other hand, was often critical of sacrifice, even to the point of saying that it was offensive to God. Although it is not easy to disentangle the history and uses of sacrifice from the priestly perspective that dominates the treatment of the subject in the Bible in its final form, the most common types of sacrifice in popular religion were probably the whole burnt offering, the 'communion sacrifice' and offering of first-born animals and of first fruits.

The whole burnt offering, in which an animal was entirely burned on the altar, was made at times of great importance such as prior to going to war (1 Sam. 13:8–12) or to celebrate the return of the Ark of the Covenant from the Philistines

(1 Sam. 6:14–15). 'Communion sacrifices' (the usual translation is 'peace offer-ings', cf. 1 Sam. 11:15) were probably sacrifices in which the animal was shared by the worshippers and participants as a kind of sacred meal designed to strengthen the bonds between those taking part. 'Communion sacrifices' were offered when Saul was made king (1 Sam. 11:15) and in addition to the burnt offering prior to battle (1 Sam. 13:9), and presumably they were also the sacrifices at family sac-rifices (1 Sam. 20:6, 29) and at city sacrifices (1 Sam. 9:12). Offerings of first-born animals or their equivalent (Exod. 34:19–20) and of first fruits (Exod. 34:26) were a means of thanksgiving, and also an expression of hopes for continued material blessing. Popular practices that are condemned include offering the blood of a sacrifice with leaven and boiling a kid in its mother's milk (Exod. 34:25–26). No satisfactory explanation for the rationale or reason for prohibiting the latter practice has yet been advanced.

In Israel's priestly religion, sacrifices existed almost entirely to deal with ritual rather than moral offences. This comes as a surprise to those who approach the Bible from a Christian perspective, in which Christ's death on the cross is believed to enable moral offences to be forgiven, and is seen as a fulfilment of Old Testament sacrifice. In fact, moral offences had direct penalties in biblical law. Murder, adultery, blasphemy, apostasy, abuse of parents and certain types of theft were all offences for which the penalty was death. Damages to persons or property required the guilty party to restore what was damaged with interest. Whether or not the penalties were always carried out (e.g. in the case of adultery) the point was that no sacrifice was prescribed for them.

The ritual offences for which sacrifices operated had the effect of cleansing an offender either from uncleanness (e.g. women from menstrual or birth-giving blood: Leviticus 12:11–18, 15:19–30), men from bodily discharges, including semen (Lev. 15:1–18, 32–33), or from contact with death (Lev. 11:39–40, 21:11). Sacrifices also enabled boundaries between the sacred and the everyday to be crossed, as when priests were consecrated and took part in an elaborate 'rite of passage' from lay to priestly status (Lev. 8). A 'rite of passage' similar to that of priestly consecration was prescribed for a cured 'leper' in order to enable a person to cross the boundary from outside the sphere of ordered social relation-ships, to which 'lepers' were banished, to within that ordered sphere (Lev. 14).

The idea of the crossing of boundaries was also at the heart of the 'Day of Atonement' ritual in Leviticus 16, in which a goat over which the high-priest had confessed 'all the iniquities of the people of Israel, and all their transgressions, all their sins' (Lev. 16:21) was led from the sanctuary, through the people into the wilderness, the sphere of chaos and disorder outside ordered human relationships, to be abandoned there. The reference to Leviticus 16:21 may appear to contradict what was said above about sacrifices dealing mainly with ritual, not moral offences. But the purpose of the Day of Atonement was to deal with inadvertent, unknown breaches of ritual and cultic prescriptions, as well as guilt in cases where murderers had gone undetected. The concern to deal with guilt in the case of an unsolved murder is indicated in Deuteronomy 21:1–9 in which there is a sacrificial ritual prescribed for any city that is nearest to a man found in open country who has been murdered by an unknown assailant. The purpose of the ritual is to 'purge the guilt of innocent blood' from the midst of the people.

Another important element in the sacrifices of ancient Israel was the regular sacrifices offered to God in the temple, each morning and afternoon (Exod. 29:38–42) as well as on the occasion of great festivals such as Passover, weeks and booths (Num. 28:1 to 29:39, and see p. 254). If these regulations were carried out, and were not simply ideals, the demand upon animals and upon the wood to burn them (one animal would require the wood of one small tree) would have been enormous in a tiny country not best fitted to provide either vast flocks and herds or abundant trees.

How far the sacrificial cult as elaborated in parts of Exodus, Leviticus and Numbers was actually carried out, and whether it impinged upon ordinary people, is hard to say. In the late Second Temple period, Jews living close enough to Jerusalem to fulfil at least some of the requirements about males appearing before YHWH three times a year did go up to the temple. For many others, this was impossible on a regular basis.

The prophetic denunciation of sacrifice is most strongly expressed in Isaiah 66:3:

> He who slaughters an ox is like him who kills a man;
> he who sacrifices a lamb like him who breaks a dog's neck;
> he who presents a cereal offering like him who offers swine's blood;
> he who makes a memorial offering of frankincense, like him who blesses an idol.

Other condemnations of sacrifice occur at Hosea 6:6 ('I desire steadfast love and not sacrifice, the knowledge of God, rather than burnt offerings'), Amos 5:25, Isaiah 1:12–17 and Jeremiah 7:21–26. Also, Psalms 50:7–15 is critical of sacrifice, while Psalm 51:16–17 proclaims:

> For thou hast no delight in sacrifice;
> were I to give a burnt offering, thou wouldst not be pleased.
> The sacrifice acceptable to God is a broken spirit;
> a broken and contrite heart, O God, thou wilt not despise.

Sacrifice in ancient Israel served many different needs, was understood in many ways, and provoked varying responses.

Hymns, prayers and sacred texts

An important part of the religious life of a people are the liturgies, including the hymns and prayers, which shape their identity and self-understanding. Central to the Bible in its final form are the themes of the delivery from slavery in Egypt and the occupation of the promised land and the giving of the law. The first was celebrated annually in the Passover, a festival whose origins are obscure, but which was certainly observed as a national festival from the late seventh century BCE. Its significance is well expressed at Exodus 12:26–27: 'When your children say to you, "What do you mean by this service?" you shall say, "It is the sacrifice of the LORD's passover, for he passed over the houses of the people of Israel in Egypt, when he slew the Egyptians but spared our houses".' At the Passover, the story of the deliverance was rehearsed, accompanied by the eating of the Passover lamb. Deuteronomy 26:5–9 contains another summary of the story of the Exodus and the settlement in the promised land, as part of the ceremony of offering the first fruits at the sanctuary. There are also indications that, at the autumnal festival celebrating the fruit harvest, there was a commemoration of the episode of the wilderness wanderings after the Exodus (Lev. 23:39–43).

The best-known prayer in Judaism is the Shema, beginning with the words 'Hear (Hebrew *sh^{e}ma'*), O Israel, the LORD our God, the LORD is one' (Deut. 6:4). As used traditionally in Judaism this prayer is a combination of three passages, Deuteronomy 6:4–9, 11:13–21 and Numbers 15:37–41, and this combination and use probably date from the late Second Temple period. In Deuteronomy 6 the words are a command to the Israelites to show exclusive loyalty to YHWH by learning, absorbing and teaching the words of the law, which are the basis of a covenant between YHWH and his people. In other words, the law has become scripture – a sacred text authoritatively declaring God's will. These liturgies, centred around the events of the Exodus and possession of the land and the giving of the law, are the high-point of the attempt of prophetically led official religion to shape and control popular religion, and they certainly provided the general framework of Judaism in the Second Temple period.

What other resources were available? It has often been suggested that many of the Psalms in which an individual expresses his (or her – cf. 1 Sam. 1:9–18) distress originated in ready-made compositions that worshippers could use when they went to a sanctuary. This raises the question whether such worshippers could read, and how the texts would be used by illiterate worshippers, i.e. did they learn them, helped by a priest? Although there is no direct proof for this suggestion, it is a reasonable one, and indicates further contact between popular and official religion in times of crisis.

In what are probably the later parts of the Bible, the editors have attributed prayers to characters in the narrative, prayers that are indicative of the piety and resources available to worshippers. Some prayers, e.g. those of Jacob (Gen. 28:20–22) and Hannah (1 Sam. 1:11), take the form of vows and promises. Hannah prays: 'O Lord of hosts, if thou wilt indeed look on the affliction of thy maidservant, and remember me, and not forget thy maidservant, but will give to thy maidservant a son, then I will give him to the Lord all the days of his life, and no razor shall touch his head.' 1 Kings 8:12–53 and Daniel 9:4–19 contain long prayers that deal with the fortunes of the nation, while Jeremiah contains passages which imply a personal religion of intense self-questioning and even doubt (Jer. 15:15–18, 17:14–18, 20:7–18).

The Dead Sea Scrolls contain a scroll of thanksgiving hymns (1QH in Vermes 1997: 244–300) as well as Songs for the Holocaust (i.e. whole burnt offering) of the Sabbath (4Q 400–407, 11Q 17, Masada 1039–200 in Vermes 1997: 322–30). The latter are songs sung by angelic beings on the first thirteen Sabbaths of the solar year. The former, although said to be inspired by the biblical Psalms, are highly individual and remarkable compositions, witnessing to the diversity and creativity of the many strands of ancient Judaism. A quotation from Hymn 12 lines 29–33 (Vermes 1997: 265–6) can form the conclusion to this chapter:

> But what is flesh (to be worthy) of this?
> What is a creature of clay for such marvels to be done,
> whereas he is in iniquity from the womb
> and in guilty unfaithfulness until his old age?
> Righteousness, I know, is not of man,
> nor is perfection of way of the son of man:

to the Most High God belong all righteous deeds.
The way of man is not established
except by the spirit which God created for him
to make perfect a way for the children of men,
that all His creatures may know
the might of His power,
and the abundance of His mercies
towards all the sons of His grace.

Notes

1. Gen. 17:5; God in making a covenant with him says your name shall not be Abram but Abraham for the father of a multitude of nations have I made thee.
2. *'Elyon* presides over a heavenly court: Deut. 32:8; Isa. 14:13ff; Ps. 82:6; Dan. 7:18, 22, 25, 27; he dwells on the holy mountain, where the gods assemble: Isa. 14:13ff; Ps. 46:5; 87:5; he is the creator of heaven and earth and opponent of chaos: Gen. 14:19, 22; Ps. 18:14–18; he represents the sun-god, who upholds justice: Ps. 9; 46:5ff; 50; 57.

Bibliography

Allen, L. C. 1990. *Ezekiel 20–48*. Word Biblical Commentary 29. Dallas: Word Books.

Auld, G. and M. Steiner 1966. *Jerusalem I: From the Bronze Age to the Maccabees*. Cities of the Biblical World. Cambridge: Lutterworth.

Beatty, A. 1999. *Varieties of Javanese religion: an anthropological account*. Cambridge: Cambridge University Press. Contains a critique of Geertz, see below.

Chilton, B. D. 1992. *The Temple of Jesus: His sacrificial program within a cultural history of sacrifice*. Philadelphia: Pennsylvania State University Press.

Day, J. 1989. *Molech: a god of human sacrifice in the Old Testament*. University of Cambridge Oriental Publications 41. Cambridge: Cambridge University Press.

Geertz, C. 1964. *The religion of Java*. New York: The Free Press. A classic anthropological monograph which provides the model adopted in this chapter; but see also Beatty.

Giddens, A. 1985. *A contemporary critique of historical materialism*, II: *The nation-state and violence*. Cambridge: Polity Press. A sociological account of the difference between traditional and modern nation-states.

Handy, L. K. 1992. Lilith. In D. N. Freedman (ed.), *The Anchor Bible dictionary* IV. New York: Doubleday.

Hinnells, J. R. 2000. *Zoroastrian and Parsi studies: selected works of John R. Hinnells*. Aldershot: Ashgate.

Keel, O. and C. Uehlinger 1992. *Göttinnen, Götter und Gottessymbole: neue Erkentnisse zur Religionsgeschichte Kanaans und Israels aufgrund bislang unerschlossener ikonographischer Quellen*. Freiburg: Herder Verlag. An account of Israel's popular religion on the basis of iconographic materials.

Knauf, A. E. 1988. *Midian: Untersuchungen zur Geschichte Palästinas und Nordarabiens am Ende des 2. Jahrtausends v. Chr*. Abhandlungen des Deutschen Palästinavereins. Wiesbaden: Otto Harrassowitz. An archaeological monograph relating to one of ancient Israel's neighbours.

Kraus, H.-J. 1966. *Worship in Israel: a cultic history of the Old Testament*. Oxford: Blackwell; trans. by G. Buswell of *Gottesdienst in Israel*. 2nd edn, Munich: Kaiser Verlag, 1962.

Lang, B. 1983. *Monotheism and the prophetic minority*. Social World of Biblical Antiquity Series 1. Sheffield: Almond Press. An account of the origins of ancient Judaism in a prophetic YHWH-alone movement of the ninth to eighth centuries BCE.

Maier, J. 1985. *The temple scroll: an introduction, translation and commentary*. JSOTSS 34. Sheffield: JSOT Press; trans. R. T. White from *Die Tempelrolle vom Toten Meer*. Uni-Taschenbücher 829. Munich: Ernst Reinhardt, 1978.

Mazar, A. 1990. *Archaeology of the land of the Bible 10,000–586 B.C.E*. New York: Doubleday.

Newsom, C. A. 1992. Angels. Old Testament. In D. N. Freedman (ed.), *The Anchor Bible dictionary* I, pp. 248–53. New York: Doubleday.

Niehr, H. 1990. *Der höchste Gott: alttestamentlicher JHWH-Glaube im Kontext syrisch-kanaanäischer Religion des 1. Jahrtausends v. Chr*. BZAW 190. Berlin: De Gruyter. A pioneering monograph arguing that ancient Israel's religion developed in the same way as that of Syria with a single god (YHWH for Israel, Ba'alshamem for Syria) gradually and increasingly becoming the high and supreme god.

Oesterley, W. O. E. and T. H. Robinson 1930. *Hebrew religion: its origin and development*. London: SPCK. An example of a now-superseded way of using anthropology in reconstructing the religion of ancient Israel.

Petersen, D. L. 1981. *The roles of Israel's prophets*. JSOTSS 17. Sheffield: Sheffield Academic Press. Uses role-theory to understand the prophets.

Pritchard, J. B. (ed.) 1955. *Ancient Near Eastern texts relating to the Old Testament*. Princeton: Princeton University Press.

(ed.) 1969. *The Ancient Near East: supplementary texts and pictures relating to the Old Testament*. Princeton: Princeton University Press. A standard collection of texts in translation from ancient Egypt, Syria/Palestine, Persia and Mesopotamia relating to ancient Israel.

Renz, J. and W. Röllig 1995. *Handbuch der althebräischen Epigraphik I*. Darmstadt: Wissenschaftliche Buchgesellschaft. The most recent scholarly edition of ancient Hebrew inscrpitions outside the Bible.

Rogerson, J. W. 1978. *Anthropology and the Old Testament*. Oxford: Blackwell. A pioneering monograph about the use of methods drawn from social anthropology.

1998. *Beginning Old Testament Study*. 2nd revised edn, London: SPCK. An elementary introduction to the academic study of the Old Testament.

1999a. *An introduction to the Bible*. Harmondsworth: Penguin Books.

1999b. *Chronicle of the Old Testament kings: the reign-by-reign record of the rulers of ancient Israel*. London: Thames and Hudson.

Rogerson, J. W. and P. R. Davies 1989. *The Old Testament world*. Cambridge: Cambridge University Press. A standard introduction to the history and literature of the Old Testament.

Rowley, H. H. 1950. *From Joseph to Joshua: biblical traditions in the light of archaeology*. Schweich Lectures 1948. London: London University Press.

Smith, W. R. 1881. *The Old Testament in the Jewish Church*. Edinburgh: A. and C. Black. Perhaps still the best introduction to the so-called Wellhausen hypothesis of the history of ancient Israelite religion and sacrifice that was proposed in the late nineteenth century and has influenced biblical scholarship ever since.

Vermes, G. 1997. *The complete Dead Sea Scrolls in English*. London: Allen Lane.

Yadin, Y. 1985. *The Temple Scroll: the hidden law of the Dead Sea sect*. London: Weidenfeld and Nicolson.

6 Greek religion

SUSAN GUETTEL COLE

An introduction to recent scholarship on Greek religion

Greek religion is not a subject that the Greeks themselves would have recognized. Religion was not an abstract category, and the language had no generic term to identify it. Action was more important than ideas. Ritual acts accompanied almost every human activity, but piety could be measured only by being visibly displayed action. Men and women performed rituals to demonstrate expectation of divine response, but people did not have to enter a sanctuary or visit a temple to recognize the power of the gods. Because attention to the divine was a constant concern, and because ritual was almost always a social event, evidence can be found in any ancient source. Information is embedded in the works of ancient poets, philosophers, dramatists and orators, as well as in the works of artists and the architectural remains, inscriptions and the debris of daily life turned up by the archaeologist's spade. We often find important information where we least expect it.

The scholarship on Greek religion has always concentrated on basic questions, such as the problem of origins, the nature of divinity, the relation between myth and ritual, and the connections between Greek ideology and other belief systems of contemporary Near Eastern cultures. In the eighteenth century scholars tried to make Greek religion look like Christianity; in the nineteenth close attention was paid to literary sources that identified the Greek belief system as unique; by the early twentieth century the invention of ethnographical research had convinced some classical scholars that Greek religion was a fascinating collection of 'primitive' responses to a confusing and unstable environment. In the twentieth the pendulum swung between sober collection of evidence and speculation about universal patterns of ritual.

The work of Walter Burkert has focused discussion on all of these broader issues, inspiring a revival of interest and a new awareness of the importance of ritual in the ancient Greek experience. On the whole, attention has moved from a mid-century concern for individual members of the divine family (Otto 1965 on Dionysos, for instance) or the entire divine pantheon (Guthrie 1950) to description more thoroughly grounded in the varieties of evidence. Marcel Detienne and Jean-Paul Vernant (1989) have interpreted ritual as an expression of culturally determined patterns of thought. Some scholars notice the way in which rituals for the gods also reflect relationships of power between rulers and the ruled (Price 1987). Many look for patterns noticed by anthropologists in other societies (Bremmer 1983, 1999 and Seaford 1994). Others have broadened the definition of religion itself to embrace the acts of surreptitious ritual violence that Greeks directed at each other in the form of curses and love charms as well as rituals and devices for personal protection (Faraone and Obbink 1991; Gager 1992). New discoveries continue to introduce new subjects for debate. Discovery of the charred remains of a papyrus text at Derveni in 1964 has inspired a new interest in theogony and esoteric doctrine, and discussions of eschatology must now take into account the new evidence from texts inscribed on gold tablets found in the graves of followers of bacchic Dionysos.

Publication of new material evidence has raised questions about methodology, and experts from many fields now contribute to the discussion. Systematic publication of new archaeological and epigraphical material has facilitated regional studies of local cults, for example the work of Madelene Jost (1985) on Arcadia, Albert Schachter (1992) on Boeotia, and Fritz Graf (1985) on Ionia, but the volume of material has also raised expectations. Christiana Sourvinou-Inwood (1995), by bringing together discussions of image, material evidence and text, emphasizes the necessity of a unifed approach for interpretation of the evidence. Pauline Schmitt Pantel's work (1992) on the social meaning of banqueting demonstrates the importance of a thematic study of the epigraphical evidence for a diachronic approach to the social context of ritual. At the same time, literary sources continue to provide a base for intensive studies of particular themes, like those of Robert Parker (1983) on pollution and Simon Pulleyn (1997) on prayer, books that illustrate the ritual procedures considered necessary for securing the attention of the gods. Other approaches to ritual concentrate on sacrificial procedure or the system of supplying the sanctuary with animal victims (for instance, Jameson 1988, 1991).

General studies continue to inform. Syntheses are provided by Simon Price (1999), Robert Parker (1996), Jon Mikalson (1983, 1998), Louise Bruit Zaidman and Pauline Schmitt Pantel (1992), and P. E. Easterling and J. V. Muir (1985). A good

Map 6.1. The ancient Mediterranean.

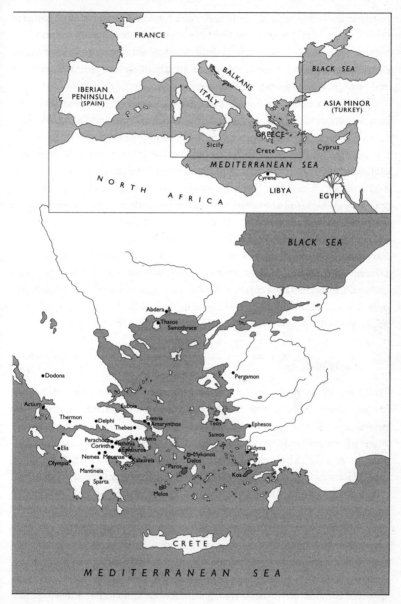

Map 6.1. (*cont.*)

introduction to the basic issues is to be found in Jan Bremmer's *Greek Religion* (1999), a survey of the recent bibliography organized thematically to introduce readers to the new scholarship. Richard Buxton's volume, *Oxford Readings in Greek Religion* (2000), collects important articles of the late twentieth century and provides a different point of departure.

Group projects and conference proceedings are also good indicators of the range of current controversies. For the archaeological evidence, Susan Alcock and Robin Osborne (1994) present a collection responding to François de Polignac's theory about the relation of the organization of sacred space to the development of the ancient Greek city-state. N. Marinatos and R. Hägg (1993) have collected a series of articles on the physical remains of Greek sanctuaries. Susan Blundell and Margaret Williamson (1998) have brought together a collection of articles on gender and religion. Robin Hägg's collections of conference proceedings of the Swedish Institute at Athens have brought the archaeological evidence to international attention. *Kernos*, an international journal devoted to the study of ancient Greek religion, reports extensively each year on new scholarship around the world. From this brief survey it is clear that what we call 'Greek religion' has provided a new focus for lively discussion involving all branches of the field. It is unlikely that the productive stream of new scholarship will dry up soon.

Early history

The history of Greek religion is by and large the history of the Greeks themselves. During the Bronze Age (3000–1000 BCE) there were two distinct cultures in the Aegean area, Minoan (not Greek), located on Crete and some southern Aegean islands, followed by the Mycenaean (definitely Greek), extending from the mainland through the Cyclades as far east as the coast of Asia Minor. On Crete in the second millennium BCE Minoan religious ritual was organized around several palaces, large unwalled complexes that functioned as regional political centres. In each region the local palace was associated with sanctuaries on mountain peaks and in natural caves, usually at the outer reaches of the territory. There are indications that the Minoans, who spoke a language unrelated to Greek, practised a form of animal sacrifice. The imagery of animals, especially bulls, dominates the Minoan arsenal of decorative patterns. Representations of actual ritual, however, are rare, and possible remains of sacrifice ambiguous. Surviving ritual equipment is usually considered more appropriate for libation (pouring liquid offerings) and donations of agricultural products than for animal slaughter.

On the Greek mainland during the Mycenaean period, sanctuaries in mountains or caves were almost unknown. The Mycenaeans who brought the Greek language to the mainland (about 1900 BCE) practised forms of ritual organized around the local ruler's residence. Unlike the open Minoan palace, the typical residence of a Mycenaean leader was located on a height overlooking its territory and enclosed within a heavily fortified walled complex. Separate spaces or buildings for ritual have been identified only at Mycenae and on the islands of Keos and Melos. Clay tablets inscribed in an early form of Greek list items appropriate for sacrifice, suggesting that the Mycenaeans practised animal sacrifice. The tablets also record the names of divinities, about half of which can be associated with gods and goddesses worshipped later by the Greeks throughout the Aegean area. The others do not appear among the known Greek divine names of the next millennium. That there was continuity of religious practice between the Mycenaeans and their later Greek descendants is not to be doubted, but the content and structure of Mycenaean practice and the means of its transmission are nevertheless still difficult to reconstruct.

The early Greek *polis*

The Iron Age began in the Greek Aegean in about 1000 BCE. The early centuries of the first millennium witnessed many changes in the Mediterranean area. In Greek areas after the destruction of Mycenaean palaces and the decline of the palace economy, populations scattered, local leaders multiplied, and durable written records came to an end. Considerable changes in social structure and political organization in the Greek lands of the Aegean contributed to innovations in ritual patterns. Smaller, dispersed agricultural communities replaced the centralized bureaucracies of the Mycenaean period; local landholders competed for political leadership; and religious ritual, no longer centralized around the residence of a chief, was beginning to be organized around sacred spaces sprinkled throughout the countryside. Two contrasting influences can be detected, one internal and the other external. Internally, veneration of prestigious local heroes encouraged a fierce allegiance to home and land. Distinctive forms of ritual for dead heroes at the sites of ancient Mycenaean tombs inspired legends that integrated local myths with the extended epic tradition. Externally, contact with the hierarchically organized empires of Egypt and Mesopotamia, Phoenician traders, and the mixed populations of Cyprus, Syria and Palestine broadened the experience of Greek travellers and emigrants and contributed to changes for those who remained at home. Increased access to a cultural context that emphasized myths of regeneration, distinctions between pollution and purification, a methodology for divination, and rituals grounded in sympathetic magic had an effect on Greek developments. Adapted to the institutions of the growing communities of the Aegean, some of these practices and ideas would be incorporated into the ritual of the early Greek city-state, the *polis*. At the same time innovations in architecture, sculpture and metalwork contributed a new material context for Greek rituals that emphasized the community rather than the authority of an individual ruler.

By the eighth century BCE space for public worship was recognized as belonging not to a ruler, but to a god. The gods themselves were now the guardians of surplus wealth and mediators of competition on the human level. Wealth, once collected and displayed in the palace of a Minoan leader or deposited in the tomb of a Mycenaean ruler, would now be shared with the gods and exhibited in their sanctuaries. Specially designated sacred space was therefore systematically reserved for the gods. Sanctuaries of the gods were strategically placed where worshippers needed them, whether within core settlements, out in the cultivated lands of the city, or even at the borders of the community's territory. Public space set aside for the interaction between human and divine would be used to display the gifts that recognized and testified to divine support.

Dividing the cosmos

The Greeks assumed that the earth itself was shared with the gods. Stability and continuity in support of human endeavour therefore required divine approval. In the Homeric *Iliad* (usually dated to the eighth century BCE), the natural divisions of a divided universe are explained in terms of a political agreement between three major gods: Zeus, Poseidon and Hades. Zeus is allotted the sky, Poseidon the sea and Hades the world of the dead, with the earth itself ruled in common by all three. A negotiated agreement had become a model for human behaviour. In the human realm, communities defined themselves by rituals that recognized divine power. The organization of the local city-state, *polis*, depended on the support of the gods. Special features of the landscape were associated with particular divinities. Zeus, as authoritative father of gods and human beings, was reached on the mountaintop because he was the god who controlled the weather and sent rain. Demeter was the divinity of cultivated crops, Dionysos the god of fruits of the vine and woody plants (often located in the transitional space between plains and mountain), Poseidon the god of the sea, and Artemis, as divinity of the hunt, haunting the furthest boundaries. Nymphs were associated with the sources of water needed for growth and fertility, and Pan represented the raw animal energy of those who lived beyond the borders of the community.

Divine partition of territory reflected the patterns of division resulting from the founding of new cities and the establishment of settlements at home and abroad. Consolidation of local populations in a town centre (*astu*) became a characteristic pattern as Greek cities were founded along the coasts of the Black Sea and the coastal areas of southern Italy and Sicily. Colonial foundations imitated the rituals of their founding cities. New cities and old shared a system of religious ritual and a common family of gods, but new settlements also responded, each in its own way, to the influence of local indigenous populations.

Some communities believed that their people had always occupied the same piece of land and that the local divine hierarchy was bestowed later. The Athenians claimed that their ancestors were born from the land itself. They explained the status of Athena, goddess of the acropolis, by the myth of an ancient contest with Poseidon, decided by vote of a population already in residence. When Poseidon offered a gushing salt spring and Athena an olive tree, the people chose Athena as supreme divinity. This story recognizes the economic advantage of the olive, eventually Athens' primary export, but some versions of the myth find fault with the outcome because women were allowed to vote. The myth may also reflect a tension between those who made a living from the land and those who made a living from the sea. Athena's original name at Athens was the adjectival form, Athenaia, 'the Athenian goddess', a form that suggests a god named for a city, not a city named for a god.

Other communities claimed to remember migration from abroad and believed that their gods had discovered their city for them. The people of Kolophon on the coast of Asia Minor maintained that the gods themselves had marked out their territory and founded their sanctuaries. Still others, for instance the Thebans, were able to combine both traditions. Their foundation myth described how Kadmos came from the land of the Phoenicians, slew a monster on the site of Thebes and planted the monster's teeth to 'grow' the ancestors of the people who populated the land. Colonial cities, on the other hand, derived status from claiming foundation at the command of an oracle of Apollo at Delphi. In truth, the Greeks continued to be migratory throughout their history, and frequent movement, even of whole city populations, was a feature of the culture. Foundation myths were subject to revision; tradition was not permanent. The activities of war, travel associated with energetic commerce, and the experience of living close to neighbours of different cultures all contributed to a flexible system, responsive to innovation. Nevertheless, all who considered themselves 'Hellenes' (the term the Greeks used to identify themselves as a group) paid homage to the same family of the gods.

The regional sanctuaries

Greek-speaking communities throughout the Mediterranean recognized the paternal supremacy of Zeus, the conventions of animal sacrifice, the rituals of warfare, and the same great 'international' sanctuaries. The most important sanctuaries were those for Zeus at Olympia and for Apollo at Delphi and on Delos. In addition to these comprehensive centres, regional sanctuaries, such as those of Apollo at Kalapodi, Thermon and Didyma, the sanctuary of Zeus at Dodona, and the sanctuaries of Hera on Samos and in the Argolid exercised more than a strictly local attraction. Political ties between cities were strengthened further when in the seventh and sixth centuries athletic contests at Olympia and Nemea (for Zeus) at Isthmia (for Poseidon) and at Delphi (for Apollo) brought together representatives from many cities on a regular basis.

International and regional sanctuaries provided neutral space for interaction between city-states, because the gods were believed to protect the institutions that encouraged peaceful interchange. Athletic contests imitated the competition of warfare, but were performed in the context of ritual designed to emphasize co-operation instead of violence. The truce that legitimated the festival at Olympia was under the protection of Zeus, the same god who also sanctioned the truce that concluded war. Weapons captured by victors and dedicated in his sanctuaries testified to his protection and support. Sanctuaries that sponsored great regional festivals attracted a clientele that reached far beyond the local constituency. New Greek cities in Sicily and southern Italy in the west joined their Peloponnesian rivals in competition at Olympia, and the wealth of these new cities was shared with the sanctuary by means of dedications deposited with the god. The most prominent of these cities demonstrated their accomplishments by constructing in the sanctuary their own treasury houses (*thesauroi*) to exhibit the fine gifts they had consecrated to Zeus.

The Ionian cities of the Aegean area celebrated together with festivals honouring Apollo at Delos. In the north the Phocians joined other communities in mutual support and competition at Delphi. They were organized with other communities on the mainland into an amphictyony, a regional league organized around a sanctuary. An important Peloponnesian amphictyony also operated in the Saronic Gulf around the sanctuary of Poseidon on the island of Kalaureia, where Peloponnesian communities, although competitive rivals at home, could meet together offshore at the neutral island site. Although the early years of the Greek city-state were a time of intense military and political competition, communities derived mutual strength from shared rituals. The institutionalized games and the sacrifices and processions sponsored by the regional sanctuaries encouraged co-operation. All recognized the authority of Apollo and Zeus, mediators of dispute and champions of law and stability.

Apollo and Zeus supported order and political organization. In recognition, many cities inscribed their earliest laws in sanctuaries of Apollo, sometimes cutting the text directly into the wall of the temple itself. Inscriptions on stone implied permanence, and the authority of Apollo gave authority to the laws. Cities also deposited revenues in the temples of their gods. At Thasos, in the early fifth century, a series of laws about street maintenance illustrates the importance of the sanctuaries to civic administration. Fines were collected in three different ways – by Apollo Pythios and the *polis*, by the *polis* alone, and by Artemis Hekate and the *polis*. Earlier, fines had been paid in their entirety to a god. Thasos in the 460s was a town in transition between a system that relied on the representatives of principal deities to collect fines and a civic system organized to maintain public funds. In the period of transition the city and its gods shared responsibility. Early Greek myth and poetry represented the gods as irresponsible and quarrelsome, but in the give and take of community life the gods were needed to keep order and to legitimate the political and judicial institutions that maintained each community.

Behaviour and belief

Greek literature preserves many contradictory claims about the gods. At Olympia a statue of Zeus with a thunderbolt in each hand stood to warn visitors and athletes of the terrible punishment for anyone who broke an oath. Yet the statues of athletes fined for cheating lined the path into the stadium. A character in a fifth-century Athenian tragedy could even claim that the gods were merely human inventions, designed to frighten people and to keep them from doing, saying or even thinking anything wrong. Greek sanctuaries were crowded with the dedications of pious believers, objects given in return for a god's protection, but when the philosopher Diagoras visited Samothrace and saw the many thank-offerings and plaques dedicated by those saved from shipwreck, he was quick to observe that there would have been many more if those who drowned could have left them, too.

These examples illustrate some of the problems in interpreting the evidence for Greek beliefs about the gods. Families and individuals prayed for the attention of the gods at critical points in the life-cycle; traditional rituals involved the gods in projects both private and public; and cities maintained a complex calendar of public sacrifices and religious festivals. Understandably, most people were careful not to challenge what they accepted as the divine order. On the other hand, as cities grew and poets began to raise philosophical issues, both poets and philosophers offered criticism of popular conceptions about the gods and even mocked some ritual practices. Usually tolerated by the flexible authorities of the new city-states, this habit of self-examination indicates a pronounced difference between Greek communities and the more rigidly organized hieratic systems of their neighbours to the east. Greek poets and philosophers constantly tested prevailing habits and popular assumptions without, however, arousing serious doubts about the system itself. The general population accepted the patterns of worship and traditional belief, called *ta patria*, 'ancestral rites', or *ta nomizomena*, 'what is customary'. Although Xenophanes (who wrote after 500 BCE) finds fault with traditional myths about the gods, and Heraclitus (*c.* 500 BCE) criticizes the Greek habit of praying to statues, these early philosophers are complaining not that people were too serious about the gods, but that they were not serious enough.

Xenophanes and Heraclitus were not punished for criticizing the system, nor did their criticism change that system. Intentional insult to the gods and deliberate lack of reverence (*asebeia*) was actionable and punishable, but impiety was usually defined in terms of actions, not ideas. *Asebeia* was associated with direct harm to sacred things or sacred rites. The concept included offences such as damaging or stealing sacred property, violating a person protected by right of sanctuary, or disclosing the content of the secret rites. There was no monolithic entity called 'religion'. Nevertheless, although the Greeks were not especially reverent people, the life of the community was organized by ritual, and the community itself derived strength from recognizing and participating in a shared system of ritual practice.

Religion was concerned not so much with belief or strong personal feeling, but with the public performance of traditional actions that recognized the gods and their divine power. Ritual almost always required a social act. What mattered most was the expected traditional gesture, made in the right way, at the right time. By and large people ignored the intellectual challenge of poets and philosophers and continued to assume that their livelihood, health and success depended on the good will of the gods. Even Heraclitus dedicated his philosophical writings in the temple of Artemis at Ephesos. For the population at large, traditional rituals reinforced confidence in the belief that the security of the community required the attention of the gods. Communal rituals represented the group acting as one and invited the gods to participate in human endeavour. Conversely, failure to perform a communal ritual properly could put the entire community at risk.

When Athenian jurors voted to put Socrates to death in 399 BCE, they apparently felt the weight of this risk. The charge of impiety covered two matters: that Socrates had failed to worship the gods the city worshipped and that he had introduced new gods. The case against Socrates had been brought for political reasons, but the official charges represent concerns consistent with traditional fears of the public. The enemies of Socrates were able to convince the jury that Socrates did not worship the gods the city worshipped. In accepting this argument, the jury erred. Xenophon tells us that Socrates participated regularly in public ceremonies and behaved in public no differently from anyone else. However, once the jury accepted the implications of the charge, execution was inevitable. The risk to the city of being obliged to share with Socrates any punishment incurred by an alleged offence to a divinity was too great.

Piety and reverence, *to hosion* and *eusebeia*, required giving everyone, mortal and immortal alike, their due. Sacrifice was one way to fulfil obligations to the gods; making a gift provided another. No one wished to offend a god or risk the anger of a divinity. Public ritual involved the whole community, and everyone was expected to follow established procedures and to demonstrate by their actions respect for the gods. The philosophers who found fault with religious practice did not themselves turn away from ritual. Democritus, the philosopher who invented atomism, was reluctant to die at the time of the Thesmophoria, a series of rituals celebrated by women for Demeter. These ceremonies required participants to maintain a special level of purity. Democritus considered the rituals so important that he is said to have succeeded in postponing his death for three days because he did not want his sister, who would have been polluted by his death and funeral, to miss them.

The flexible system of the individual Greek city-state, administered by the many instead of by the one or the few, depended on the public recognition of social obligation. The strength of this concept is illustrated by the story in Euripides' sole surviving satyr play, *The Cyclops*. In this play, Odysseus and his men, shipwrecked in the wilds of Sicily, come upon the cave of a solitary Cyclops. They expect to be received according to the rules of hospitality (*xenia*) recognized by gods and men. The Cyclops, a one-eyed monster who recognizes neither the gods nor the standards of civilized life, disappoints their expectations and goes so far that he even ignores the temple of his own father, Poseidon. He says that he pays no attention to the thunderbolts of Zeus, and claims that he does not need to sow crops or sacrifice because,

> the earth brings forth grain, grass to feed my flock, and these animals I sacrifice to no one except to *me*, to the gods not a bit, but to the greatest divinity of all, to my stomach. To chug-a-lug and gobble up food for a day and to cause oneself no pain, this is Zeus for men of good sense. As for those who established the laws that complicate people's lives, I say, let them go weep.   (Euripides, *Cyclops* 332–40, translation by the author)

The Cyclops promises Odysseus a fire to warm him, salt from Poseidon to flavour his meal, and a bronze pot to clothe him, but Euripides' audience knew that Odysseus had to work fast to escape. He was not going to receive a meal, but if he stayed, would become the meal himself.

The Cyclops, who lives in isolation and acts only on his own behalf, violates all norms of community. The procedures of collective ritual, on the other hand, emphasized the group, created opportunities to involve the gods in collective decisions, and recognized the responsibilities of honour. The competitive ethic of epic warrior society and the emphasis on competition in both athletic and political arena were balanced in the developing city-state by a ritual system that recognized obligation to the suppliant, protected the rules of hospitality, and required those with more than average resources to subsidize public ritual and public festivals for the many.

The history of the ritual institutions of the Greek *polis* was to some extent the result of translating the norms of heroic society, based in epic poetry on competition between individuals, into the institutions that emphasized collective identity and the collective power of a more broadly defined group of male actors. In the political world of the Greek *polis*, individual achievement remained important, but individual achievement could be demonstrated only in the context of the community. Respect for the suppliant, in Homer granted to an individual by a ruler, was broadened in the era of the *polis* to include respect for anyone in a sacred space. Swearing oaths remained a means of sealing a contract between two individuals, but in the more complex world of the *polis*, representatives of the city could swear oaths on behalf of the entire community. Likewise, an individual could curse an enemy or rival, but the ritual specialists of the community could protect the population by issuing a curse in the voice of the whole.

Any individual could make a pilgrimage to a great and distant sanctuary, but those who were invested with the responsibility of representing their city enjoyed a special status. Cities could delegate representatives to sacrifice, pray or seek an oracle on behalf of the population at home. Representatives of the community whose task it was to witness sacred rites for the sake of fellow citizens at home were called *theoroi*. These were officials appointed to 'see' the rites for the sake of others and to make sacrifices on behalf of all for the security and welfare of their city. Individual states may have claimed political autonomy but, in fact, all cities strove for recognition in the rituals of the great regional sanctuaries. True autonomy was possible only when everyone recognized the same institutions of oath, truce and curse. Representatives from any city could engage in competitive discourse at the great sanctuaries because they were protected by ritual. Protection was necessary whether it was a matter of putting questions of public policy to oracles, competing for a city's honour in athletic events, making war, negotiating treaties, or making dedications on behalf of an entire population.

Defining the sacred

The world of the Cyclops is a world without boundaries, a world without social obligations, and a world without gods. It turns the world of the *polis* upside down. Greek religious ideology recognized three categories of existence, the dead, the living and the immortal. This division is reflected in the popular cosmology of a tripartite universe with separate realms for the living, the dead and the divine. Expectation of death divided humans from the gods. The gods were *hoi athanatoi* (the immortals) or *hoi makares* (the blessed), who in Homeric poetry could move at will between the divine realm and the earth. This mobility was recognized in the early Greek *polis* by the division of public space. Untouched by death, the gods required a special space in the human realm, where they could be reached by human ritual. The land was imagined as divided into those places where normal human life could be lived and those places specially marked, where there was the possibility of encountering divinity. The sanctuary (*to hieron*, 'the sacred space') was a space marked off, a *temenos*, a space 'cut off' from normal human life because it was a space for the gods. To reach the gods or to enter a sacred space a person had to be pure (*hagnos)* or purified (*katharos)*. Because the gods did not share in all human physical processes, bodily functions were kept separate from sanctuaries. Humans had to be 'pure' or 'purified', 'cleansed' to engage in a ritual relationship with a divinity. Anyone contaminated by defilement (*miasma*) was filthy (*miaros)* or dirty (*bdeleros)*. The gods avoided death because death or contact with a corpse was also polluting. For this reason, cities kept cemeteries outside the city wall. Communication with the gods required observance of routine rules for purity, because any worshipper who was not purified, *ou katharos*, could compromise sacred space and spoil any ritual act in progress.

The Greek language had no specialized religious vocabulary, but several key terms were used to define human relationships with the gods and the obligations of the individual to the community. The terminology of piety stressed living in accordance with both divine and human rules. The term *hieron*, 'sacred', was a versatile word, used in the singular to refer to both the sanctuary and the sacrificial victim, and in the plural (*hiera)* for the ritual acts, sacrifices, prayers and libations performed in honour of the gods. The priest, *hiereus*, or the priestess, *hiereia*, officiated in sacrifice with the assistance of specialists, especially the *mageiros*, who was slaughterer, butcher and sometimes even cook. Priests and priestesses performed a variety of official duties. Gender of attendants was usually, but not always, matched to the gender of the divinity.

Other key adjectives meant one thing when applied to gods and another when applied to humans. *Hagnos* used of humans meant 'pure', but when used of gods described their effect on humans. The term *hosios*, 'pleasing to the gods', meant 'sanctified' or 'consecrated' when used in relation to the gods, but 'acting according to the rules of human behaviour' when applied to human concerns or human actions. *Hosion kai dikaion*, 'piously and rightly', was a common expression to describe an act performed in accordance with human laws: by making communal obligation a concern of the gods, the city-state strengthened its authority. In the plural *hiera kai hosia* (*hosia* coupled with *hiera)* could refer to correct ritual behaviour and the correct treatment of other human beings because treating other people appropriately and justly was pleasing to the gods.

No single word meant 'pious'. The Greek language made a distinction between piety, *to hosion* (openly demonstrated) and respect or reverent feeling, *eusebeia* (experienced internally). The abstract term *eusebeia* encouraged both appropriate ritual behaviour and the right relationship with the gods, but also included the sense of having the right relationship to the family, the city and the dead, as well as maintaining the right relationship with friends, strangers and suppliants. The range of the semantic field is clear from a remark of Aristotle (philosopher, fourth century BCE), who describes its opposite, *asebeia* ('impiety'), as 'being out of tune with the gods and lesser divinities' and also with the dead, one's parents, and one's fatherland.

Temples and sacred places

Some places acquired their sacred nature simply by virtue of what they were, a particularly beautiful grove of trees, a secluded cave or a cool spring within the city walls or out in the country. Athenians worshipped Athena on the acropolis, Pan in caves, Zeus Ombrios (Zeus of the rain cloud) on mountaintops and the Semnai Theai, 'Revered Goddesses', at Kolonos in a grove so charged with special power that no one was supposed to enter. But a space could also be made sacred by an act of consecration that established a boundary to set the site off from everyday life. A sanctuary (*to hieron*) was such a designated space, with or without buildings. Such space did not need a temple to be recognized as sacred.

Special rules separated activities in a sanctuary from the activities of everyday life. Boundary stones (*horoi*), a wooden fence, a stone wall, ritual installations or a text displayed at the entrance indicated the boundary between the space where normal human life was lived and the area set aside for communication with the divine. The earliest inscriptions marking the boundaries of sacred areas were simple inscriptions of a single word, *horos* (boundary) or a simple phrase, 'boundary of the sanctuary' (*horos tou hierou*). More complicated signs with detailed texts came later. These inscriptions preserve a variety of rules. The conditions most often stipulated for caution include very recent sexual intercourse, recent attendance at a funeral, contact with childbirth, the wearing of certain clothing and the eating of certain foods. Any of these could be considered polluting. The most frequently mentioned and probably the most consistently recognized concerns were contact with the dead and participation in a funeral or contact with or the experience of childbirth. Special vessels filled with pure spring water, *perirrhanteria*, stood at the entrance to a sanctuary to mark the transition between open space and sacred space. Worshippers could demonstrate the purity that made them eligible for collective ritual by sprinkling themselves with the pure water. This reassuring gesture guaranteed the state of purity necessary for taking part in the group ritual. Sprinkling with pure water was an important signal, not only to the gods but also to other worshippers. No one wanted to engage in ritual with someone who was not qualified. A polluted individual threatened the entire group.

The typical Greek temple provided a central enclosed space (*cella*) to display the cult statue of the divinity. Temples usually faced east, so that the statue of the divinity faced the door, the main altar and the rising sun. A high stone altar, which the Greeks called *bomos*, usually stood in front of the temple. The altar was the focal point of the sanctuary because this was the place of sacrifice, where direct contact with divinity was possible.

The temple itself was a place to visit and honour a god, but usually not a place for communal worship. Frequency of access depended on the divinity and the local rules. Statues were of two types, archaic images called *xoana* (usually carved in wood and small and light enough to be carried or transported in procession), and large statues in stone that could fill the interior space of the *cella*. The most expensive of these were made of fine marble, with exposed feet, forearms and hands in ivory, and the eyes in precious stones. In addition to the cult statue of the divinity housed in the temple, other statues could be found outside in the open air. These could represent the divinity, other divine attendants, or priests and priestesses who has performed the obligations of a term of service to the god. By the late fourth century BCE, under the influence of Macedonian custom, statues of rulers and special benefactors were also erected in sacred areas.

Developed sanctuaries were embellished not only with temples, but also with any of a number of outbuildings and constructions. These could be such structures as treasuries (erected by individual cities to display public dedications), residences for priests and ritual attendants, altars, dining rooms, the grave of a local hero or heroine, a stoa (an extended, rectangular building with a columned porch on its long side), or exhibition halls to display the votive gifts and dedications testifying to the divinity's generous dispensations. Greek temples could be of any size and were constructed of a variety of building materials. The earliest temples, ninth and eighth centuries BCE, were of wood and mudbrick. Limestone temples were an innovation of the seventh century BCE . Marble, introduced for the first time at Delphi in the sixth century, became a mark of status and prestige in the fifth. As stone began to be used everywhere, temple size increased. By the end of the Persian Wars (479 BCE), at least sixty-one large temples in stone had been built in Greek communities. The most magnificent of these were located on the margins of the area settled by Greeks – to the west in Sicily at Selinous and Akragas, and to the east in Ionia on Samos, at Ephesos and at Didyma. The magnificence of a city's temples was a statement of prestige rather than a record of piety.

Of the sixty-one known examples of large stone temples, forty-two can be associated with a particular god. In the late archaic and early classical periods Apollo, with eleven, was the divinity with by far the most large stone temples. Hera was runner up with five, and Poseidon and Athena, with four each, were tied for third place. Zeus enters the list in only three of the forty-two examples, and Artemis in only two. Demeter, who had hundreds of small, local sanctuaries, simple with only modest structures, was honoured with size only in the far west. Artemis, who later had as many as 175 sanctuaries in the Peloponnese alone, in the early fifth century was honoured with a large stone temple only at Corcyra and Ehesos. Ares is noticeable by his absence, as are Dionysos and Aphrodite. Ares did not have many temples because, as the god of war, he was not very popular. The other two, universally recognized because their gifts included sensual and sexual pleasure, do not seem to have inspired monumental temples in the archaic and classical periods at all. Public worship of Dionysos was centred on the theatre, and Aphrodite's sanctuaries were usually modest. Hestia, rarely personified, was worshipped in the form of the public hearth and permanent fire of the *polis*. The number and size of a divinity's temples is not an indication of importance. There were other ways to recognize the gods.

The gods of the *polis*

Each *polis* had its own contingent of divinities, some dwelling in the countryside and others at the town centre. When people prayed, they began with an invocation that located the divinity in a particular place or at a particular cult site. It was important to match the divinity to the request, and it was also necessary to know where to find a god. In a crisis, one could call on all possible candidates for help. When the dramatist Aeschylus (525–456 BCE) represents the women of Thebes under siege, he shows them praying to all the gods of the *polis* for protection. These women call their gods 'the fortress-protecting gods of the land' and name them as 'Zeus, Pallas Athena, Poseidon, Ares, Cyprian Aphrodite, Apollo Lykeios, Hera, Artemis and Ogkas [a local Theban hero]'. At Selinous in the fifth century, after a local victory, citizens inscribed on the wall of one of their temples a vow of thanks to 'Zeus, Phobos, Apollo, Poseidon, the Tyndaridai [Castor and Pollux], Athena, Demeter Malophoros, Kasipatea, and all the other gods, but especially Zeus'. It is easy to see why Zeus and Phobos were so important. Zeus was considered the leader and Phobos, whose name means 'fear' stood for the terror the soldiers of Selinous had inspired in their enemy. The people of Selinous recognized all of the local gods because it was unwise to deprive a divinity of credit where credit might actually be due.

None of the divinities addressed at Selinous is associated specifically with the last defence of the city, its wall. Gods were more likely to be connected by function to natural features of the landscape, not to physical features of the built city. Gods might be considered residents of a city, but except for Hestia, whose name actually means 'hearth', individual deities were rarely identified with a particular architectural feature. One exception is the gate of the citadel. At Athens in the second century BCE the travel writer Pausanias encountered Hermes Propylaios (Hermes of the main gateway), Hekate Propylaia (Hekate of the main gateway) and Artemis Epipyrgidia (Artemis on the Tower). In town, the gods took on the responsibilities of citizenship. At Athens Athena was still Athena Polias, goddess of the acropolis heights, and Zeus was still Zeus Polieus, god of the high citadel, but the two also became Athena Boulaia and Zeus Boulaios, because now they also protected the deliberations of the Council (*Boule*). Gods still protected the landscape: Demeter the fields, Artemis the territorial boundaries, Poseidon the sea, Zeus the tops of mountains, and Pan the uncultivated wild areas. Even the borders of Attica were recognized by the institutions of the city. In the fourth century, when the young men of Athens swore the oath that made them ephebes (citizen soldiers in training), they swore to defend their weapons, their comrades, all things *hiera* and *hosia*, and concluded their statement with the land itself:

> and I shall not hand down a diminished fatherland, but one increased in size and strength as far as I am able and [working together] with the assistance of all . . . I shall also honour the ancestral sacred rites. The witnesses [to this oath] are: the gods Aglauros, Hestia, Enyo, Enyalios, Ares and Athena Areia, Zeus, Thallo, Auxo, Hegemone, Herakles [and] the boundaries of my fatherland, and the wheat, the barley, the vines, the olives, the figs.   (translation by the author, following Fornara)

In this oath, which may be older than the inscription of the fourth century BCE that preserves it, the boundaries of the *polis*, invoked as witnesses, were just as vital to the city-state as the crops that fed its people. Aglauros and Hestia were worshipped by the *polis* at its centre, Aglauros in a cave on the east slope of the acropolis, and Hestia in the nearby *prutaneion*, the building that sanctified political unity. Ares, Athena Areia (Warrior Athena) and Zeus Areios (Warrior

Zeus) were defenders of the city. Thallo ('Blooming') and Auxo ('Increase') were concerned with the crops and human reproduction, Hegemone was 'leadership' personified, Herakles represented the special prowess a soldier needed to fight successfully in battle, and Enyalios, and Ares represented the martial fury that turned farmers into fighters.

Each *polis* organized its sanctuaries, whether those in the city or the country-side, in its own way. Topography, politics and geographical conditions all played a role, but any local pantheon could be revised. Eretria, Mantineia and Thasos, three different city-states, illustrate three different ways of organizing local divinities. Eretria, settled in the eighth century BCE, was spread out around a central public space (*agora*) near the natural harbour. The grave of a local hero, unnamed, was prominent in the early town, but located some distance from the *agora*. A small, hairpin-shaped temple to Apollo, early focus of the *agora*, was eventually replaced by successively larger structures on the same site as the town developed. Apollo protected the institutions of the city; Demeter protected agricultural production and the reproductive capacity of the city's women. A small temple of Demeter, called 'Thesmophorion' in honour of Demeter's great-est and universal festival, the Thesmophoria, stood on the hill overlooking the town centre, aloof from the settlement. Demeter Thesmophoros was important to the city, but her sanctuary was modest, her rites reserved for women and not to be seen by men's eyes. Artemis, equal in status to her brother Apollo, had her own temple outside the town, near the frontier of Eretria's territory in the area of the old Mycenaean site at Amarynthos. Here a river ran into the sea, creating the combination of water sources that seem to have been considered ideal for a sanctuary of Artemis. For Eretria, the sanctuary of Artemis at the extremity of her territory was just as important in defining the interests of the *polis* as the gods at the centre. The treasury of the city was eventually kept at the sanctuary of Artemis, and her festival, the Artemisia, became one of the major annual celebra-tions of the city. The ceremonial procession in honour of Artemis connected her sanctuary to the town, where Apollo and Artemis, with their mother Leto, were the divinities by which the *polis* swore its collective oaths. These three divinities were also represented on the stone reliefs that decorated the city's important inscribed documents.

Mantineia, an old community in the central Peloponnese, had a very different environment. Cut off entirely from the sea, the territory of Mantineia was sur-rounded by mountains and positioned squarely on the only direct route through the Peloponnese between Argos and Sparta. The relationship of the plains to the mountains and mountain passes influenced the placement of Mantineia's sanctuaries. In the archaic period the population was concentrated around a shallow hill whose name, 'Ptolis,' indicates an ancient fortified citadel. As the population grew, the Mantineians moved about a kilometre south and fortified a new town site, complete with central agora. Even when the town moved, however, the gods retained their old places in the countryside. A grove of Demeter lay in the plain near the old village of Nestane; Poseidon Hippios (inland, a god of earthquakes and horses) had his sanctuary at the edge of a mountain; Dionysos and Black Aphrodite shared a sanctuary in the foothills; and to the north the Mantineians celebrated festivals at a major sanctuary of Artemis shared with neighbouring Orchomenos. Mantineian heroes and heroines included Herakles, Penelope, Arkas (son of Kallisto), and the local heroine, Antinoë. When Pausanias visited in the second century CE, he found Asklepios sharing a temple with Leto, Apollo and Artemis, and in town, Zeus Soter (Zeus Preserver), Zeus Epidotes (Zeus the Generous), Zeus Keraunos (Zeus the Thunderbolt), Zeus Kharmon (Zeus Rejoicer), Zeus Eubouleus (Zeus of Good Advice), Hera and the Dioskouroi. Demeter and Kore, with an eternal fire, seem to have been outside the town. Pausanias identifies the public hearth of the city, Hestia Koine (Common Hearth), with a circular hearth at the grave of Antinoe.

The Mantineians had accumulated an impressive group of divinities, but the process was gradual. Asklepios could not have been worshipped in Arkadia until the late fifth or early fourth century BCE, and other divinities noticed by Pausanias in the second century CE could not have been important in the Peleponnese before the Roman period. Pausanias calls attention to a temple of Aphrodite Summachia, 'Aphrodite of the Alliance'. The goddess is described with an epithet that recognizes Aphrodite's support for the Roman victory at Actium in 31 BCE. Nevertheless, the Mantineians also remained loyal to the worship of the ancient local Peloponnesian Athena Aleia, and they kept their own 'Black' Aphrodite (said to be so named because she identified night as the best time for sex). Nevertheless, Mantineians were flexible enough to acknowledge Roman power by recognizing an Aphrodite friendly to Romans. They even connected another local Aphrodite to the Roman myth of Aeneas. Finally, at the time of Pausanias' visit, a place had already been reserved for the emperor Hadrian's boyfriend, Antinoos, only recently recognized as a hero after his early death.

Thasos, an island in the northern Aegean colonized from Paros, had her own unique history. Like her mother-city Paros, the town of Thasos was a harbour town on an island. Both cities were grape growers and wine producers, both were fortified, and both had sanctuaries both inside and outside the city wall. The original colonists had brought three things to Thasos from Paros: sacred fire, the images of their gods (*amphidrumata*), and the special sacred objects necessary for replicating their hometown rituals in the new city. These two cities shared a tradition of transplanted rituals and images, similarities in local topography and a similar economic base, but they did not have identical ritual histories.

The list of divinities at Thasos included Zeus, Apollo, Artemis, Athena (called Poliouchos, 'she who holds the city'), the Charites (the Graces), Peitho (Persuasion), Demeter, Kore, Eileithyia (goddess of childbirth), Herakles, Hera, Poseidon, Dionysos, Hermes, Pan and the Dioskouroi. Demeter had extra-mural sanctuaries on both islands, and Herakles, Dionysos, the Dioskouroi, the Charites, Hermes, Eileithyia and Artemis Polo appear on both lists. Similarities end here. First, local heroes seem to have traded places. Thasian Archilochos, son of the Parian founder, had a *heroön* (heroic shrine) in the agora at Paros, and the Parian military leader Glaukon was accorded heroic honours at his grave in the agora at Thasos. At Thasos Artemis had her temple inside the city wall near the agora, while at Paros she was located in the Delion, a sanctuary of her brother, Delian Apollo, outside.

Thasos was unusual in that the city had a double acropolis. Athena Poliouchos occupied one peak and Apollo Pythios the other. Apollo's epithet associates him with Delphi, not with Delos as at Paros. No temple site has been identified with Athena in the town of Paros. Herakles was recognized in both towns, but the Phoenician Herakles in the Thasian agora, as described by Herodotus (historian, fifth century BCE) is unique. Finally, influence did not always travel from the older to the younger community, as tradition maintained. Thasos was a source of inspiration for her own mother-city when Artemis Polos (Artemis who wears the *polos*, a high-crowned hat), who had been introduced into Thasos from Thrace to the north, moved from Thasos to Paros.

At Thasos the fortification wall represented the physical integrity of the city. Thasos could be maintained in warfare even when cut off from its vineyards on the mainland, as it was when under siege by the Athenians under Kimon in the 460s. The people of Thasos guarded their city with a symbol that could be classified as a form of magic. At one of the highest points reached by the citadel wall, near the very top of the acropolis itself and not far from the temple of Athena Poliouchos, a striking image protected a vulnerable section of the wall. Carved on a large block of the wall from the lintel, two giant eyes stare straight ahead, creating the dangerous and aggressive, direct and head-on gaze believed capable of paralysing whoever dared to face it. The relief itself is a rare surviving example of protective magic on behalf of the entire community. Dedicated by a man named Parmenon, the image was placed to frighten attackers and freeze them in their tracks. The giant eyes gazing out over the approaches to the city were placed there as a first-strike defence against invaders.

Demeter was located just outside the Thasian wall, a typical position for her sanctuary in Greek colonial cities both east and west. At Thasos Demeter's little sanctuary overlooked the harbour. Pausanias describes how the priestess of Demeter, the *parthenos* Kleoboia, arrived by boat from Paros with the basket containing Demeter's sacred objects on her lap. The women of Thasos gathered in this sanctuary for the annual Thesmophoria, the festival celebrated throughout the Greek world by the wives of citizens to prepare the way for the autumn planting of grain and to guarantee the community's harvest the next summer. Near the Thesmophorion was an open precinct with several modest altars belonging to the Thasian *patriai*, the traditional hereditary groups into which the citizens were divided. An inscription indicates that at the sacrifice for Athena Patroie, women were allotted sacrificial meat (480 BCE). The altar of Demeter and the altars of the *patriai* belonged together because both encouraged family continuity in the context of the *polis*.

Ritual acts

The Cyclops in Euripides' play did not need to sacrifice because he did not recognize the gods. For the Greeks, on the other hand, human endeavour of any sort required communication with the divine. Animal sacrifice provided the most impressive means of gaining the attention of a god. Every performance of ritual slaughter underlined the division between human and animal, and every act of sacrifice attempted to bridge the division between human and divine. There were often special requirements for participation. Gender, status, kinship, residence, political affiliation, administrative assignment and profession were some of the categories that defined eligibility. Eating together emphasized unity, whether the group was the family, the *deme* (local residential unit), the tribe, the *phratry* (male kin group) or the *polis* at large. Sacrifice connected the community with the gods, but it also reiterated the social order, confirmed group identity and provided opportunity for celebrating important relationships.

The philosopher Theophrastos (fourth century BCE) lists three reasons to sacrifice to the gods: to honour them, to fulfil an obligation of exchange and to gain benefits. Every act of sacrifice was a transaction. In exchange for worship or honour (both of which were represented by the Greek word *timē*), even the gods owed something in return. Likewise, when a prayer or request was answered, worshippers offered a gift of thanks, and often dedicated a tangible object in a sanctuary where others could see it.

There was no comprehensive term for animal sacrifice in Greek. The word 'sacrifice' in English suggests an act of renouncement, of giving up something important or valuable in exchange for a god's attention. In the case of most Greek sacrifices, however, very little was actually given up to the gods. The word *thusia*, the term most commonly translated as the noun 'sacrifice', had no connotation of giving something up. It referred to the very specific activity of the fire turning meat and fat into smoke. The gods, who did not eat food, did not need meat, but they did demand recognition in the form of the smoke that rose naturally to the sky. Smoke represented the purified part of the animal, indicated human attention and homage, and was the only thing that reached the gods. It was the human participants who ate the meat. Where the victim was an edible animal, the main result of the ceremony was a high-protein communal meal.

In a story about the invention of sacrifice, the poet Hesiod (late eighth century BCE) explains why the gods did not receive the edible portions of the animal. In a challenge to Zeus, Prometheus wrapped a thighbone in shining fat, so that Zeus would choose the most attractive, but least edible portion. He out-tricked himself when he tried to trick Zeus, because Zeus understood what Prometheus was up to and chose the inedible portion anyway. Prometheus was therefore severely punished because he had tested a god. For punishment, he was sent to the ends of the earth, fastened to a cliff, and had to submit to an eagle (the bird of Zeus) feeding on his liver.

The story about Prometheus indicates a certain ambivalence about the institution of animal sacrifice. Menander (Athenian writer of comedies, fourth century BCE) makes fun of the uneven distribution of meat and calls those who sacrifice thieves:

> For them, incense and cake, that's called 'piety', that's all the god gets, placed on the fire . . . and as the tail and the gallbladder burn, the parts that aren't edible, they gobble down the rest themselves.
>
> (Menander, *Duskolos* 447–53; translation by the author)

A portfolio of sacred actions framed the killing of the animal, the division of meat and the serving of the meal. The major ingredients required for sacrifice included the animal, pure water, barley (and cakes), wine and wood. Cattle, sheep, goats and pigs were the animals normally used in sacrifice, sheep being the most common, but cattle (because they were the most valuable and therefore the most expensive) the most prestigious. Other items, for instance the special cakes, liquids like milk or honey, or an animal for preliminary sacrifice (*prothusia*) were also possible ingredients, depending on the deity and the occasion. A libation of liquid (*sponde*), often wine, might be included in a series of actions, or it could stand alone. The plural of the word for libation, *spondai*, was the word for 'truce' because a truce required mingling libations from both parties.

A typical sequence of events can be reconstructed by comparing the major sacrificial scenes in the *Iliad* and the *Odyssey*. First the animal was prepared for slaughter while attendants brought pure spring water in a special bowl or pitcher and barley in a basket. Those officiating washed their hands and sprinkled barley. After the barley was scattered, the leader marked out the altar by sprinkling around it the pure water and more barley. Then he prayed and cut some hairs from the forelock of the animal before throwing them into the fire as a first offering. This act was followed by a libation of wine and sprinkling of barley into the fire and by a stroke of the axe to stun the animal. The attendants pulled the head of the animal back so that the slaughterer could cut the throat with a knife.

At the moment when the slaughterer cut through the neck of the animal, any women present raised the *ololuge*, a ritual cry that announced the animal's death. Restricted to women, the *ololuge* marked the moment as special and called attention to the deed. The animal was then lifted up, so that the blood could run out and life could leave the flesh. The carcass was singed and skinned, the meat divided, and a thighbone wrapped in fat. The thighbone and fat, the portion for the god, were burned on the altar. The culminating event of the ritual was a communal meal shared by the group for whose benefit the rite was performed, but the rest of the meat could not be prepared for the meal until the gods themselves were satisfied. The inner organs of the animal, called *splanchna* (lung, heart, liver, kidneys and spleen), were roasted on sticks over the fire and distributed to the group. These were consumed first, and the meat itself was either roasted or cooked in a stew pot. Ritual eating always remained central to the experience of visiting a sanctuary. As a result special buildings with rooms designed to accommodate reclining banqueters became a standard feature of sanctuary architecture.

Some kinds of sacrifice were associated with situations of such risk that the flesh of the animal could not be eaten. Examples are *sphagia* (slaughter where the blood of the animal had special meaning), holocaust (complete consumption of the animal by fire) and oath sacrifice (where pieces of the animal were treated in a special way). The Spartans on military campaign, when leaving the boundaries of their own territory and crossing into the territory of an enemy, performed *sphagia* at the frontier. For this occasion, the neck of the animal was cut and the blood flowed into the ground. On the battlefield itself the Spartans did not begin to fight until a professional seer had slaughtered a young female goat to Artemis Agrotera (Artemis of the Wilds), examined the internal organs and decided that the time and place were appropriate for battle. Offerings to the dead, in particular offerings to heroes, constituted another category of powerful actions. Human in life, heroes in death rarely attain the status of a god. Herakles, his mortality burned away in his death by fire, was an exceptional hero who could also be called *theos*, 'god'. Asklepios was another. As intermediaries between gods and humans, heroes were assumed to have protective powers, and their graves were recognized as special sites. Offerings to the dead were delivered at the grave in liquid form: water, wine, honey, milk or blood. If in blood, the animal was slaughtered on the spot and the head held down so that its blood could flow directly into the ground to reach the hero buried below.

Literary descriptions of actual sacrifices and sacrificial calendars are selective in what they include. There is no clear pattern that isolates rites for a hero from rites for a god, or even the rites of Homeric Olympians from the rites of divinities below the earth. Different kinds of rites could be combined together into a single event. In the case of oath sacrifice there was a broad list of procedures from which any particular series of actions could be constructed for a specific ritual occasion. In oath sacrifice it appears that the gender of the animal matched the gender of the agent. Parts of the animal (testicles, if male) were cut up. A male swearing what was called a 'great' (solemn) oath stood on cut-up body parts and uttered a curse promising self-destruction if the oath were forfeit. Females were asked to swear an oath when the paternity of their child was an issue. Herodotus says that when the mother of the Spartan king Kleomenes swore an oath about Kleomenes' paternity, she held the meat of the animal in her hands. The remains of the carcass had to be destroyed, burnt entirely in holocaust or thrown beyond the borders of the city's territory, in the mountains, at a crossroads or into the sea.

Holocaust was not uncommon, but consumption by fire of an animal otherwise suitable for eating would have wasted scant protein resources and was therefore reserved for special circumstances. When required as preliminary to another rite, holocaust might indicate a special form of purification. For example, in a list of procedures on Kos the piglet consumed in holocaust for Zeus Polieus prepared the way for the multiple sacrifice that celebrated the union of the island's three tribes. At Sikyon a sacrifice to Herakles combined *thusia* and holocaust and recognized Herakles as both god and hero. First a lamb was slain, the thighbones were roasted on the altar and the meat divided, but only part of the meat was eaten in the normal way because the rest had to be consecrated to the hero in holocaust.

Women participated directly in sacrifice only in limited and specific rituals and, it appears, only when those rituals did not include men. A *mageiros*, the specialist in charge of killing the animal, presided over sacrifice even where women worshipped alone. Vase paintings depicting a woman holding a knife for butchering are rare. Sanctuary regulations and ritual calendars authorize rites where women feasted at their own celebrations without men. At the Thesmophoria, always off bounds for men, fasting preceded the feast that concluded a ceremony designed to encourage an abundant food supply. Banquet menus included bread, cakes, cheese and meat, especially roast pork and pork stew. Other rites without men mentioned in sacrificial calendars and dedications include sacrifices to Dionysos and Semele in the Attic *deme* Erchia, rituals at Thasos to Athena Patroe, and the sacrifice to Demeter Chloe at Mukonos.

Prayer and the expectation of reciprocity

Some Greek words used to describe ritual behaviour or ritual gesture had a double meaning. The common word for prayer was *euche*, but the verb 'to pray' (*euchesthai*) could also mean 'to proudly publicize'. In a prayer to a god, therefore, the line between making an appeal and making a proud assertion was thin. Although, as Pindar (poet; fifth century BCE) says, gods and men belong to different categories, it seems that the Greeks did not need to prostrate themselves before divinities. They addressed their gods standing, face up and right arm extended. Free women and girls (in comedy, also slaves) sometimes kneeled to pray, but women kneeled only in critical situations or when the request had to do with the family.

Formal prayers had three parts: invocation of a divinity (identified precisely with specific epithets); justification or argument (including reminder of past worship); and finally, the request itself (explicitly stated). Most extant examples of any length are from poetic texts. The one most frequently cited is the first prayer in the *Iliad*, addressed to Apollo by his priest, the Trojan Chryses, who wants the Greek leader, Agamemnon, punished for insolence:

> Hear me, god of the silver bow, you who protect Chryse and sacred Killa and rule Tenedos with your power. If ever I roofed a temple pleasing to you, if ever I burned for you the fat thighs of bulls or goats, fulfil this wish for me: may the Danaans pay for my tears with your arrows.
>
> (*Iliad* 1.37–42; translation by the author)

Comic parodies, in all likelihood based on well-known formulas, are frequent. In the *Thesmophoriazusae*, a comic play by Aristophanes (writer of comedies in the late fifth and early fourth century BCE), the women pray to Athena, invite her to their festival and ask for peace. Their invocation of Demeter and her daughter, Kore, although it lacks a specific request, nevertheless preserves the 'if ever' reminder used in Chryses' prayer. This formula indicates a continuing relationship with the two goddesses as well as the expectation of their response. The prayer itself constitutes an urgent request that the two goddesses be present to witness and therefore recognize and honour the ceremonies their worshippers are about to perform:

> And come, O Goddesses, kind and generous, to your sacred grove, where you illuminate with your torches the sacred rites, an immortal vision not permitted for men to see. Approach, come, we entreat you, O most powerful Thesmophoroi! If ever before you came when called, come now, too, we implore you, to us here.
>
> (Aristophanes, *Thesmophoriazusae* 1148–58; translation by the author)

Choral performances at festivals or in a sanctuary often set the stage for a divinity's epiphany by issuing an invitation sung in verse. Hymns were prayers set to music. Other forms of prayer were normally not sung. The several different words for prayer, *euche*, *ara*, *lite* and *hiketeia*, are not interchangeable. *Ara* could mean 'prayer', but it could also mean 'curse'. *Litai* were urgent requests made in situations of crisis, and *hiketeiai* were formal requests of supplication made only by those in truly desperate circumstances to someone obliged to respond.

All forms of prayer emphasized the necessity of catching the divinity's attention, inviting the divinity's presence and prompting the divinity's good will. If sacrifice was a transaction, prayer was the verbal counterpart that made clear the obligations on both sides. It was the expectation of an exchange of gifts that kept the relationship with a god alive. The Greek word *charis* (in English 'grace', or better, 'reciprocal generosity') covers both sides of the process. If part of a prayer was like a public declaration (reminding the god that the worshipper deserved attention), then the response to a god's generosity in granting the request was commendation or praise. A Hellenistic hymn to Serapis on Delos contains the phrase 'We praise the gods because they bestow worthy *charis*.' In a dialogue by Plato (philosopher, 428–347 BCE), Socrates suggests to Euthyphro that sacrifice was the same as making a gift to a god and that prayer was the same as making a request. Euthyphro agrees, but in fact both acts could occur together and the god's action in granting a request could be considered reciprocation for the gift implicit in any sacrifice.

Prayers were appropriate in any context and could be offered at the beginning of any project. For individuals a prayer might be spoken at the dawn of a new day or at the beginning of the farming season. The gods could be invited to aid in any undertaking. People prayed for help in love and in war, for successful crops, for children, or simply for good fortune. Prayers were also routinely offered on important public occasions, at the opening of a meeting of the assembly or the council, and at the beginning of dramatic festivals, athletic contests and military campaigns. Prayers could request favours for friends and harm to enemies. The official prayer spoken at the beginning of every meeting of the Athenian assembly included a curse against traitors and enemies of the people.

Sacrifice and prayer belonged together, but prayer did not require sacrifice, and even prayers accompanying sacrifice could be quite simple. Some expressions, where a wish made with a single word involved a god in its fulfilment, were in fact abbreviated prayers. Free people could give orders to a god; a slave could only make a wish. The prayers of slaves lacked formal structure and were expressed as wishes. Free people, on the other hand, had no qualms about addressing a god with a command in the imperative mood. Moreover, when slaves prayed, they prayed without sacrifice. In situations where a slave is depicted accompanying a family in sacrifice, that slave is present as a member of the household to provide domestic service, not as a direct participant or recipient.

Women could pray at home, even silently, and women could offer prayers in the context of a festival of their own. In group sacrifice, however, their prayers were probably important only in those rituals where they themselves had a designated role. On the whole, women played a supportive but minor role in any sacrifice where a male was present. As we have seen, their only act of agency was the ululation at the moment of the animal's death. This high-pitched, reverberating cry vibrating deep in the throat called attention to situations of crisis just past.

Women cried the *ololuge* in jubilation at the moment of a birth, in sorrow at the moment of death, and at a sacrifice to emphasize the instant of the kill.

Menander's *Duskolos*, staged in 317 BCE, ends in a marriage, and the groom's mother spends almost the entire play in prayer and sacrifice to Pan and the Nymphs. These are the divinities associated with the local spring where the bride will fetch the water for her wedding ceremony at the end of the play. As in this play, women prayed even to male divinities, but the issues of their concern are primarily the issues of family life, that is, personal health, successful childbirth, the health of family members, the well-being of children, and even the well-being of farm animals ('Elpis, daughter of Andronikos, prays a prayer and makes a vow for the sake of the mule', in an inscribed Greek prayer from Lydia). Males were concerned about such issues, too, but they were also active in a wider sphere and had broader interests and more opportunities to represent the community in fulfilling the obligations of public ritual.

Votive gifts

When a prayer was answered and a request granted, the gods expected thanks. People could express their gratitude in the form of a sacrifice. In another play of Menander the announcement of a marriage inspires a character to sacrifice a pig to mark the occasion. Worshippers also dedicated gifts to the gods. Permanent tokens of thanks to the gods survive as reminders of ritual performed or as thanks for gifts received. When dedicated in fulfilment of a vow, such gifts are called votives. These objects are the tangible records of a complex system of exchange between human and divine realms, a form of exchange that assumed mutual reciprocity between gods and human beings. Thousands upon thousands of such gifts are found in sanctuaries everywhere. Gifts range from elaborate, specially commissioned statues and reliefs to the modest ceramics mass-produced in local workshops. Donations created such clutter that sanctuaries often had to have special rules to regulate display.

A dedication could record a ritual act, service to a divinity or a positive response to a prayer. Some were merely ornamental, others were real tools or miniature models of real tools. From these we can often identify the occupation or accomplishments of the donor. Soldiers dedicated arms and armour captured in battle, craftsmen dedicated their tools, athletes dedicated their athletic equipment, and women dedicated their jewelry and the products of their weaving, as well as their loom weights, distaffs and spindles. Other votives, in the form of reliefs and

simple ceramic or metal vases and figurines, represent ritual or objects significant for cult. Reliefs depict the dedicator in an act of ritual. Figurines in bronze or
inexpensive terracotta represented the god, the worshipper or the animal victim.
The rich variety of the extant votives makes it difficult to classify dedications. The
wealthy dedicated buildings and statues and commissioned objects made from
valuable materials. Ordinary people were more likely to dedicate mass-produced
votive reliefs, ceramic figurines or simple objects of daily use. Freedom of choice
was limited only by means. Although local sanctuary officials could regulate the
display of votives within the sanctuary, the choice of an individual dedication
was up to the donor and not controlled by sanctuary personnel or local governing bodies. For this reason the record of votive practice offers the possibility of a
glimpse into the interests, concerns and anxieties of ordinary people.

Plato reminds us that people dedicated gifts in both prosperity and need, and
says that those in need, especially women and sick people, were most likely to
make dedications. The epigraphical evidence shows that women usually targeted
female divinities, but that when they chose to honour a male divinity, that divinity
was more likely to be Dionysos or Asklepios than any other. Asklepios presided
over the physical health of individuals, and special concerns for women's health,
especially with regard to fertility and the risks of pregnancy and childbirth, are
strikingly evident in the dedications and testimonies of women at his healing
sanctuaries.

From patterns of gift giving, we might infer that some divinities were worshipped primarily by men (Zeus, Poseidon, Ares); others by both men and women
(Apollo, Artemis, Athena); and still others almost exclusively by women (Demeter, Kore, Hera). Categories, however, are not always neatly drawn. The evidence
is by and large archaeological. The variety of dedications is more limited at
sanctuaries of female divinities, where the most common objects are ceramic
female figurines, woven clothing, weaving tools, jewelry and bronze mirrors
(both miniature and full size), and animal figurines. Women worshipped female
divinities that protected children. Such divinities were called 'kourotrophic'
(child-nourishing). Female divinities also protected men. More than 100,000
votive lead figurines, both male and female, found in the sanctuary of Artemis
Ortheia at Sparta, indicate that she was a goddess for both.

The material remains of votives and dedications can correct distortions of
the poets. Material remains can also raise problems of interpretation. Hera is
a good example to consider. This goddess is a puzzling figure. Although her
rituals emphasized marriage, the female life-cycle and athletic competition, the

literary sources represent her as a jealous wife, an incompetent mother and an annoyance to the hero Herakles. Yet, she has a Mycenaean pedigree, important sanctuaries and a long history of receiving substantial dedications in the Argolid, at Perachora and on Samos. In the Argolid Hera received thousands of small items reflecting ritual (miniature offering tables, 1500 miniature ceramic pots of many shapes, and bronze and terracotta animal figurines) plus many items associated primarily with women (2800 bronze dress pins, 2000 knobbed straight pins, a considerable amount of other forms of jewelry and thirty bronze mirrors). Of 2865 terracotta figurines in the Argive Heraion, 85 per cent were standing or seated females representing her worshippers. Argive Hera received no weapons (although one of the prizes at her games, for men, was a bronze shield), but Hera at nearby Perachora enjoyed armour, weapons and iron spits, in addition to jewelry (miniature rings and pins) and seated and standing females in terracotta. Material remains, especially the dedications, establish that Argive Hera was not a template for Hera elsewhere.

Divination and oracles

The habit of regular communication with the gods encouraged the expectation of direct response. That response could take many forms. For example, in some cases of animal sacrifice, before the meat for eating was cooked, the tail of the animal was burned on the altar. The way it curled, the direction it turned, and how it moved while burning, were all carefully observed in order to determine whether the sacrifice was propitious. The conditions of inner organs could be considered an important indicator of divine will. Professional seers (*manteis*) studied the colour, character and shape of the liver and gallbladder to discover clues to divine intention. Specialists also looked for signs in the flight of birds; the content of dreams; unusual natural phenomena (eclipse of moon or sun, thunder or lightning on a clear day); or climatic disaster (drought, famine or plague). The Greek practice of hepatoscopy (scrutiny of the liver of a sacrificial victim) shared many parallels with Mesopotamian practice, and in this and other kinds of divination the religious traditions of Akkadian and Babylonian cultures must have provided the original model.

Cities retained professional seers to take omens when leaders had to make important decisions at times of extraordinary risk. Situations of risk included founding a new city, deciding to make war, crossing the boundaries and leaving the territory of the *polis* on campaign, or making a significant legislative or administrative decision. The Greek word for seer was *mantis*, a word connected with an ancient word for 'know'. The reputation of the seer was highest in the archaic period. Even in the mid-fifth century, when Perikles sent the professional seer Lampon to give advice to the founders of an Athenian colony in southern Italy, the office of *mantis* was still a respectable position. By the fourth century BCE, however, the craft had become so debased by imitators who sold prophecies for cash that those who sought advice from a *mantis* could be considered to be excessively superstitious.

The reputation of oracular sanctuaries was very different. An oracle was a message in a god's voice delivered (usually) through a human medium as the result of a specific request from a private or public enquirer. Questions were usually framed to provoke a simple positive or negative answer. Apollo's sanctuaries at Delphi in the middle of the Greek peninsula and Didyma on the coast of Asia Minor were both great oracular centres. Apollo was also associated with many small, local oracular shrines in places like Boeotia, a territory riddled with the springs, caves and fissures in the earth believed to be sources of the god's direct address. Zeus was the god of prophecy at the important oracular site at Dodona. Female intermediaries were associated with both Delphi and Dodona, but male prophets delivered the messages from Apollo at Didyma. In Greek Asia Minor, local traditions also supported a form of prophecy delivered by female prophets whose title was 'Sibyl'.

Procedures differed. For Apollo, purification preceded consultation, and at Delphi questions put to the Pythia (the priestess who delivered the god's response) could produce a text. Responses were ambiguous and, like riddles, constituted puzzles to be solved. Responsibility for interpretation belonged to the enquirer, not to the god. In the archaic and classical periods cities throughout Greece and even foreign dynasts consulted the oracle at Delphi. Representatives of cities and foreign rulers put questions before the god not so much to discover the course of future events as to confirm the viability of a policy or plan already under discussion. The prestige of the oracle in support of legislative decisions was connected to Apollo's authority as expert in the procedures for purification, as well as to his reputation for support of law and the process of legislative deliberation.

Dodona is another story. Located in a distant valley deep in Epirus, the oracle of Zeus at Dodona had the reputation of great antiquity. Priests called 'Selloi' went barefoot with feet unwashed. Zeus himself, possibly represented by the great oak tree that grew in his sanctuary, was attended by three priestesses and accompanied by doves. Ancient traditions differ in the precise details. Just how responses were delivered is not divulged; some believe the god's will was interpreted from the rustling of the oak leaves, others from the cries of the doves. Enquiries were inscribed on small lead tablets, written by the petitioners themselves. Dozens survive, still rolled or folded just as they left the inscriber's hands. Apparently Zeus could understand the contents without unrolling the tablets. Requests are simple and framed so that the god could respond with a positive or negative sign. The form is usually, 'Is it better for X to do Y?' The simplicity of the procedure did not diminish the oracle's reputation. The god at Dodona was consulted by cities and kings on matters of public policy, by individuals on issues relating to profession, business deals and petty crimes, and, most touchingly, by men concerned about marriage, children, family welfare, the fertility of their wives and the paternity of their children.

Delphi was not above politics. At the time of the Persian invasion of Greece in 480 BCE, the neutrality of sanctuary administrators was compromised by expectation of a Persian victory. When representatives of the Athenian leader Themistokles sought an oracle to help Athenians choose a viable defence policy, the first reply of the Pythia was pessimistic. Her reply indicated certain destruction for the Athenians and advised flight. As Herodotus tells the story, the Athenian emissaries were so upset by this response that they put their question to the Pythia a second time. Herodotus' version of the second response of the Pythia, representing as a possibility the successful fulfilment of Themistokles' plan to abandon the city and rely on the Athenian fleet for victory, sounds very much as if it were composed not before, but after the defeat of Persia at Salamis.

> No, Athena cannot appease great Zeus of Olympus with many eloquent words and all her cunning counsel. To you I declare again this word, and make it as iron: All shall be taken by foemen, whatever within his border Cecrops contains, and whatever the glades of sacred Cithaeron. Yet to Tritogeneia shall Zeus, loud-voiced, give a present, a wall of wood, which alone shall abide unsacked by the foemen. Well shall it serve yourselves and your children in days that shall be. Do not abide the charge of horse and foot that come on you, a mighty host from the landward side, but withdraw before it. Turn your back in retreat; on another day you shall face them. Salamis, isle divine, you shall slay many children of women, either when seed is sown or again when the harvest is gathered.
>
> (Herodotus 7.141; trans. D. Grene)

Delphi could clearly be influenced by political events. The oral tradition that preserved the Pythia's responses was open to interference, and the reputation of the oracle could be tarnished by playing favourites. Although later Greeks assumed that the height of Delphic influence was reached in the archaic period (before 480 BCE), the sanctuary continued to thrive and to be embellished by expensive dedications later, throughout the Hellenistic and Roman periods. In the second century CE, Plutarch regretted that the spring associated with the voice of Apollo seemed to have dried up, but the oracle itself did not cease to function. Responses were no longer always delivered in verse. Nevertheless, the attention of Nero in the first century and of Hadrian in the second indicates that Delphi's reputation still remained high.

Oaths: calling the gods to witness

Early Greek society was a society without written contracts. Oaths sanctioned agreements between individuals, between the individual and the community, and, at higher levels, between communities. At Athens citizens swore oaths to mark important stages in their lives. Young men swore the oath of the ephebes when undertaking military training, and fathers swore an oath of paternity when introducing a son to his phratry. An oath was required whenever a man made the transition from private status to public responsibility. Magistrates swore an oath when they assumed office, and jurors swore an oath before serving in trials. Lykouros (orator, fourth century BCE) said that oaths held the democracy together, and Isokrates (orator, fourth century BCE) makes it clear that piety required not only respect for the gods, but also respect for oaths. Oaths could be an object of fun on the comic stage and elsewhere, but even Thucydides (Athenian historian, fifth century BCE), although he did not believe in oracles, recognized loyalty to oaths and respect for sanctuaries and suppliants as fundamental to the code that made social stability possible.

To illustrate the importance of keeping a promise Herodotus quotes an oracle delivered at Delphi to Glaukos, a Spartan who told a lie to avoid returning a sum of money he had held in trust on oath. The Pythia replied in very harsh terms, describing the irrevocable penalty for breaking an oath. She said that the child of Oath was nameless and relentless, without hands or feet. This monster would pursue the perjurer and destroy forever his house and family line. In the end Glaukos suffered exactly what the Pythia described. Herodotus tells the story to demonstrate the tradition of Delphic authority in shaping standards for behaviour. Any oath involved a god and every oath implied a self-curse if it were broken. A man without descendants was a man who would not be remembered in family cult, a man whose family and ancestral gods died with him. Glaukos failed in his duty as a father and failed in his duty as a citizen because in the eyes of the city it was the citizen's duty to preserve the fatherland (*patris*) and the altars of the gods.

Civic rituals

Every *polis* had its own collection of deities, every city centre was adorned with the sanctuaries and altars of its own divinities, and each *polis* had its own calendar of festivals. One of the Greek words for 'festival' was *heorte*, a word that connoted festivity, pleasure and relaxation. Months were named for traditional civic festivals and the year followed a cycle that recognized major divinities. At Athens seven days of each month were set aside for sacrifices to Agathos Daimon ('Good Demon'), Athena, Herakles, Hera, Aphrodite, Artemis, Apollo, Poseidon, and the local Athenian hero, Theseus. Almost half of the days in the Attic year were targeted for a special celebration or sacrifice. Religious festivals provided the only interruption of the civic calendar, vacation from business responsibilities or break from the work schedule of the agricultural year.

Funerals and festivals provided one of the principal opportunities for young men to see young women in public, but it is not absolutely clear that women regularly attended all great public festivals. Aristophanes' Strepsiades bought a tuppenny cart for his son at the Diasia, a festival of Zeus, but we hear nothing about fathers taking their daughters. Females participated in some events designated for males, but only to perform a specific, limited ritual function. In such cases sexual status and sexual purity were strictly regulated. At the Dionysia the only female in the procession was the young girl who carried the basket of ritual objects required for sacrifice. Inscriptions that commemorate such service are careful to indicate status because basket carriers had to be a *parthenos* (unmarried). Few scholars believe that women attended the theatre in Athens, but we do not even know that females were welcome in the crowds that lined the streets for the rowdy rituals of the parade that preceded the dramatic events.

Most cities began their year as closely as possible to the summer solstice, which corresponded roughly with the conclusion of the grain harvest. At Athens the solstice also marked the beginning of the annual term of office for most city magistrates. Here the festival called Dipolieia ended the year and set the stage for the year's new administration. The celebrations, honouring Zeus Polieus, god of an open precinct high on the acropolis, had two parts: celebration of the first field ploughed (the Field of Hunger behind the *prutaneion*) and a ritual dilemma resolved in the *prutaneion* with a trial for murder after the ox was killed in sacrifice. Bouzyges, in Athenian myth the first man ever to plough a field, was represented in the first part by an official who uttered a series of curses as he walked up and down the furrows. His list represents the reverse of the Cyclops' priorities. Condemning those who did not respond to social obligation, he cursed those who refused to share water, those who refused to share fire and those who refused to give directions to the lost.

Sacrifice of the plough-ox could be staged as a murder, because the plough-ox, a working animal, was an unusual victim for sacrifice. Moreover, he was tricked into assenting to his own death when he bowed his head to eat the grain placed on the altar. The sacrifice where the 'murder' took place and the trial in the *prutaneion* complemented each other because each event made a claim for the values of collective procedures. The ploughing of the field in conjunction with the public curses demonstrated that successful agriculture depended on fulfilling communal responsibility. The gods encouraged successful agriculture only in a city whose citizens, unlike the Cyclops, understood civic responsibility and the importance of judicial solutions for dealing with violence.

The ominous events of the Dipolieia were dispelled by its optimistic conclusion. This conclusion prepared the way for the competitive environment and public festivities of the Panathenaia, the celebration that set the new year on its way. The Panathenaia began with a procession. Images of Athena's myths were woven into a new robe presented to the goddess and displayed like a sail on the cart that carried it through the streets. The *arrhephoroi*, young girls in service to Athena on the acropolis, and the *ergastinai*, the girls who wove the robe, marched in procession together with the ephebes, officials, priests, priestesses and representatives of the population to the acropolis. There, in the presence of the Twelve Gods, they presented the new robe to Athena. People came from all over Attica to see the procession and to attend the athletic, nautical, musical and poetic competitions that followed. Athena's priests and assistants had to work all day slaughtering the cattle to prepare the sacrifices and provide the meat for the banquets consumed by Athenian citizens, who feasted with their neighbours in small groups throughout the centre of town.

The power of dreams

Physical health in this world was more important than spiritual healing in preparation for the next. People turned to several divinities when challenged by illness or disability, but the specialist was Asklepios, son of Apollo. This god's major site was Epidauros, where he seems originally to have been a hero associated with the god Apollo Maleatas. In the late sixth century BCE Asklepios had only an altar and one small building, but by the fourth he was honoured with a full-fledged temple and cult statue. The expansion of the sanctuary at Epidauros together with Asklepios' elevation from hero to god (*theos*) reflects his special appeal and wide popularity.

A reputation for success explains the success of Asklepios. For a fee, sanctuaries of Asklepios offered treatment that included purification, sacrifice, seclusion, therapeutic bathing and incubation. At Epidauros petitioners slept in the sanctuary in hopes of dreaming about a visit from the god. Thank offerings in the form of tablets depicting a scene from treatment, carved in stone or painted on wood, were displayed in the sanctuary. From these images and from local oral tradition sanctuary administrators constructed a series of narratives about successful cures. An anthology of such narratives was recorded on large stone tablets displayed prominently in the sanctuary. Many of these narratives share a common structure. The typical pattern includes sleeping in the sanctuary; seeing a vision in a dream; recognizing the god; having an experience with snakes; undergoing violent, but painless, surgery; and in the end, achieving health. In the following example the god is represented by one of his sacred snakes:

> A man's toe was healed by a snake. He was in a terrible condition from a malignant ulceration on his toe. During the day he was carried out of the *abaton* (a restricted area in the sanctuary) by the servants and was sitting on a seat. He fell asleep there and then a snake came out of the *abaton* again. When the man woke up, he was well and he said he had seen a vision: it seemed to him that a good-looking young man had sprinkled a drug over his toe.   (*Inscriptiones Graecae* iv² 121.113–19; trans. L. LiDonnici)

It was important to acknowledge the god's attention:

> Hermon of Thasos. He came as a blind man, and he was healed. But afterwards when he didn't bring the fee for the cure, the god made him blind again. Then he came back and slept here, and the god restored him to health.   (*Inscriptiones Graecae* iv² 122.7–9; trans. follows that of L. LiDonnici)

According to the official account inscribed on stone, Asklepios and his sacred snake were transported to Athens by chariot from Epidauros in 420/19 BCE. The god and his sacred snake were received at Athens by a certain Telemachos, who paid for the landscaping when the city established a sanctuary for the god.

The episode illustrates what was needed to establish a new god at Athens: a sponsor willing to negotiate with officials; a clientele to lobby for space for a temple; and an assembly of citizens predisposed not only to the god's advocates, but also to the god himself. Procedures for receiving a new god were as complicated as the procedures for naturalizing new citizens. Officials managed festivals, but authority for decisions about cult matters lay with the assembly, and all decisions about civic ritual, such as the sacrificial calendar, the upkeep of sanctuaries and the regulation of priests and priestesses, were subject to public debate and confirmed by vote.

Asklepios represented for Athenians the possibility of health for individuals. The arrival of Asklepios at Athens on the heels of the plague earlier in the 420s suggests to some that he was brought to Athens because residents were concerned about the ravages of this disease. Epidemics, however, were not a speciality of Asklepios. Plague belonged to Apollo, who as Hekatebolos (Far-Shooter) or Apotropaios (Averter) could both inflict plague and take it away. Asklepios was more concerned with ordinary chronic conditions and disabilities. Moreover, he did not treat cities; he treated individuals. His sanctuaries profited from public awareness of the new approach of Hippocratic physicians. Sanctuary procedures incorporated professional medical techniques and imitated the contemporary Hippocratic emphasis on attention to symptoms and the individual case history. By combining an attractive and generous divinity with the pleasant surroundings of his sanctuaries and the personal attention of his staff, the administrators of his sanctuaries developed rituals that inspired confidence and attracted a wide clientele.

Asklepios was not the only divinity recognized for offering remedies. Tiny body parts of gold, electrum and ivory, dating as early as the late eighth to the middle of the seventh century BCE, have been found in deposits at the temple of Artemis at Ephesos. Ceramic models of body parts dedicated to a healing god had become common by the fourth century. They are found throughout mainland Greece (including Thrace) and the Aegean islands and occur as well at Pergamon and Ephesos. Offerings seem to cluster by type. Eyes for Demeter, breasts and vulvae for Artemis and Aphrodite, and male genitalia for Asklepios indicate a certain symmetry, but there is no evidence that individual sanctuaries specialized in particular diseases. At Corinth, the collection includes ceramic heads, ears, eyes, tongues, chests, arms, hands, fingers, legs, feet, hair and thighs.

A series of inventories from the sanctuary of Asklepios at Athens provides a check on actual deposits. These inventories list items of gold and silver to be melted down by the sanctuary. Body parts displayed at the Athenian Asklepieion included heads, ears, faces, eyes, jaws, mouths, body trunks, hearts, breasts, arms, hands, fingers, male and female genitalia, and legs. The inventories also list reliefs, crowns, ritual equipment, coins, jewelry, medical equipment and personal items, such as drinking vessels, cooking utensils and little boxes for cosmetics. On the whole the inventories record a higher proportion of dedications from women than from men. Women dedicated most of the jewelry and a higher proportion of body parts. Males dedicated most of the equipment associated with priestly service (ritual vessels, crowns and medical instruments) because, as administrators of the sanctuary, they made ceremonial dedications at the conclusion of service. As far as limbs and organs are concerned, men and women made dedications for themselves and occasionally for other members of their families. Men made dedications for their wives, fathers and mothers for their sons or children, and once a mother and grandmother joined together in making a dedication on behalf of a child.

A concern for reproduction and the health of women and children is evident from both votives and inscriptions. Women dedicated most of the votives concerned with reproductive problems, and in the narratives recorded at Epidauros female sterility is a serious problem. Petitioners, however, were on the whole more likely to be male than female, and male bodies suffered from a wider variety of medical problems. When we compare the inventories that list donors, we can see that males were treated for injury, blindness, paralysis, lameness, lice, kidney stone, tuberculosis, hepatitis, infection, pleurisy, indelible tattoos, headache, arthritis, dyspepsia and gout, while females were brought to the sanctuary for reproductiove disorders, in particular, prolonged or false pregnancy or sterility, and dropsy, tumour, infection, blindness and tapeworm.

Healing sanctuaries continued to be a growth industry after the fourth century and were so popular that evidence for temples of Asklepios became a reliable measure of the spread of Hellenism in Asia Minor in the Hellenistic period. Although direct attention to the individual client might go some way to explain this phenomenal development, the construction rate of new sanctuaries for Asklepios was everywhere dependent on city sponsorship. At Erythrai in the second quarter of the fourth century BCE, the city passed legislation to retain for the *polis* the privilege of the first sacrifice at a festival for Asklepios. In other cities Asklepios became the major divinity in the Hellenistic period. This is true at Kos (home of one of antiquity's great medical centres), where Asklepios and his sanctuary were the focus of an annual festival attended by *theoroi*, representatives from cities throughout the Greek world. The festival of Asklepios at Kos was so popular that it eventually rivalled even well-established Pan-Hellenic festivals at Delphi and Olympia. Elaborate facilities for guests, dormitories for those awaiting dreams, large facilities for therapeutic bathing and theatres for entertainment are among the improvements added to sanctuaries of Asklepios in the Hellenistic period. Asklepios may have been a god who served individuals, but his sanctuaries were sponsored and maintained by cities.

The life-cycle

The cycle of life from birth to death was organized by a series of rituals to mark important transitions. Some ceremonies stressed the completion of an earlier stage, others emphasized transitions to the next. Many of these rituals were the responsibility of the family. Local customs varied, but gods were often involved, and the city had an interest in the cycle, whether of rituals that eased a child into public responsibility or of the procedures by which the dead were reconciled to the grave.

Birth

Birth, as the first transition, was a time of danger for the mother as well as the child. A woman in childbirth was considered to be especially polluted, even able to pollute others. This means that she herself could not enter a sanctuary or approach the gods in ritual or supplication until she had waited from ten to twenty-one days for the pollution to dissipate. During this period rituals for the newborn were the responsibility of the family. An infant, *brephos* (the same word also means 'foetus'), was not considered a member of the family until recognized by the father. The first few days were a period of stress for most infants, and Aristotle tells us that babies were not named immediately. Families waited to assess the infant's chance for survival. To join the family the child was carried around a hearth in the house in ceremonies called *amphidromia* ('rites of running around'), similar to the reception at the hearth that brought a new slave or new bride into the household.

When an infant was named (on the fifth or tenth day) the chosen name could indicate a tie to a local god. Personal names based on expressions compounded with the name of a god were common. Such names are called theophoric names. Because he was protector of young boys through childhood and adolescence,

Apollo was the god whose name most parents used. Apollodoros, a very popular name, meant 'gift of Apollo', and Artemidoros meant 'gift of Artemis'. 'Apollonius', 'Demetrius' and 'Dionysius' were all adjectival forms of a divine name. Others, Diogeiton ('neighbour of Zeus'), Pythogeiton ('neighbour of the Pythian god, Apollo') or Athanogeiton ('neighbour of Athena'), all indicate that the family lived near a sanctuary. Theophoric names were not so much an indication of personal devotion as a sign of Hellenic identity. Claiming a god's protection seems to have made parents feel more secure.

Rituals of maturation

Political status and paternity were a concern of the city and a concern of the gods. Every year, the adult males of the community met in small groups consisting of the extended male kin group. These groups were called *phratriai* (phratries). In Athens during the Apatouria, a three-day festival for Apollo, each phratry held its own meeting. Members gathered to announce recent births, to recognize the maturity of sons ready for membership, and to hear young adult members announce the names of their brides. Fathers of children born in the past year offered a sacrifice (*to meion*) to introduce new sons to the group. By accepting the sacrifice, the phratry acknowledged paternity and provided an important contribution to family coherence and community stability. Fathers of sons who had reached adolescence offered the *koureion*, a second sacrifice that marked a boy's application for membership. The father's oath accompanied this ritual. Phratry members voted on the application, and if rejected, the animal for sacrifice was simply led away. On the third day of the Apatouria a new cycle of paternity began when the young male members about to marry offered the *gamelia* to announce their marriage and thereby legitimate the union in the eyes of the kin group. The celebrations in the phratries provided an important opportunity for young males to join their fathers in ritual, to become acquainted with their extended male kin, and to learn the rituals they would be expected to perform when they assumed the responsibilities of adulthood. The Apatouria was considered to be a time of pleasant festivity, and those who offered sacrifices were expected to provide a holiday meal for the membership.

In Attica Zeus Phratrios and Athena Phratria received the sacrifices in the phratry. For other male rituals, Apollo was often the model for young males preparing for citizen status. As Apollo Patroos, he was recognized at several levels. Originally attached to institutions of the *genos*, the name for the exclusive hereditary groups limited to males of the oldest and most prestigious families, his jurisdiction was broadened as the citizen body grew. For the phratries, Apollo Patroos validated the individual paternal line. For the city of Athens, as father of their mythical ancestor, Ion, he ratified for citizens membership in the Attic family. Candidates for public office had to give the names of parents and grandparents, to report the location of their Zeus Herkios (Zeus of the courtyard, protector of the household), and to locate their Apollo Patroos and their family's graves. Apollo Patroos was invoked when magistrates took the oath because he was witness to family status and family continuity.

An early stage in the male life-cycle was under the jurisdiction of Dionysos. He was the god whose gift of wine, properly used, encouraged commensality. An important ritual introduced very young boys about three years old to the drinking of wine. Called 'Pitchers' (Choes), this ceremony took place each year on the second day of the three-day Anthesteria, the festival in February when the wine of the year before was tasted for the first time. Toddlers were wreathed with flowers and given tiny pitchers filled with watered wine. The child's first official taste of wine was offered in a controlled setting and marked his first entry into male society. The ceremony was still celebrated in the second century CE, the date of an inscription listing the Choes with three other important stages of life: birth, military training (*ephebeia*) and marriage.

At about eighteen years of age an Athenian male was registered in his father's *deme*, the smallest division of the citizen body, but only after scrutiny by the city council (*boule*). Those eligible for service as ephebes were taken to the *prutaneion*, the building that sheltered the communal hearth of the entire *polis*. Here they were introduced to the city's hearth and sacred fire. Next they advanced to the sanctuary of Aglauros at a cave on the east slope of the acropolis, where they swore the oath of the ephebes (see above). Aglauros, daughter of an early king of Attica, was worshipped as a heroine, and her sanctuary probably marks the birthplace of Erichthonios the mythical king born from the earth who was progenitor of all Athenians through his daughter, Kreousa. Athena had presided over his birth, just as she presided over the people of Athens. When young men swore the oath to take up the responsibilities of citizenship, they laid claim to a common identity that made all citizens members of one Attic family. The induction of the ephebe began at the centre of the city and gradually moved outwards, as the youths were formally introduced to the boundaries of the territory, replicated at the city wall by the sanctuary of Artemis Agrotera, just outside. Artemis' epithet means that she was Artemis of the 'wilds', goddess of the fringe area at the outer limits of the city's political reach.

Artemis, Hera, Demeter, Athena and Aphrodite presided over the lives of young girls. Artemis, the goddess most widely associated with the female maturation process, was especially popular in the Peloponnese. Elsewhere, in particular in the Argolid, at Elis, on Samos and probably at Poseidonia, Hera took first place. Artemis was a permanent virgin, but Hera, worshipped in the Argolid as virgin, wife and widow, represented the complete female life-cycle. To assure divine protection young girls danced and sang hymns for Artemis in choruses throughout the Peloponnese. In Attica they played the part of bears in the *arkteia*, a festival where their dance separated them from the first stage of childhood and prepared them for the next. Girls wove textiles and dedicated them to Kore in Lokroi; to Hera on Samos; to Artemis in Attica and Boeotia. They did this to glorify a goddess, but also to demonstrate their achievement of the skills that would make them good wives and mothers.

Goddesses who presided over the rituals of the female life-cycle often required attendants who had to be unmarried and sexually pure. In the case of Artemis, such attendants imitated the status of the goddess and also served as example for all the girls of the city. Young women had to know Artemis before they could come to know Aphrodite. Myths of Artemis, where young women are punished severely for pre-marital sexual experience, demonstrate the consequences of arousing her anger. Death in childbirth was explained by her arrows. A fourth-century inscription from Cyrene shows how important Artemis could be for the welfare of the *polis*. The people of Cyrene recognized that if Artemis was not satisfied with the rituals performed by the young women of the city, the whole population would suffer. They consulted Delphi and received an oracle that validated local procedures for protecting young women as they married and anticipated their first child. This law isolates three important stages: before marriage (although the text is uncertain), at the time of marriage and in pregnancy. Detailed instructions for performing rituals for Artemis are laid out and penalties assessed for any young woman who failed to comply. The city took an interest in the health of its young women because the risks of neglect threatened everyone.

Weddings and funerals

Weddings and funerals were family affairs, but gods were invoked at several points in the proceedings, and divinities protected specific aspects of the process. The divinities associated with weddings and marriage included Apollo and Artemis (associated with transitions), Zeus and Hera (whose marriage was a model), Peitho (goddess of persuasion) and Aphrodite (who represented sexual arousal). Except for the announcement of marriage at the *gamelia*, most of the ceremony was centred on the bride herself, because she was the individual for whom marriage required the most significant change. For her, the wedding was both a physical and a social transition.

Before the ceremony the bride had to be purified by a ritual bath. The water came from a local spring especially designated for such occasions. The dozens of fragmentary miniature *loutrophoroi*, vases for carrying water for ritual baths, found in the waters of a copious spring in a cave near Athens represent the full-sized pitchers used by local brides for the ritual. The deposits identify this as the designated spring for the local *deme*. The purity of the bride, called 'nymph' from her wedding day until the birth of her first child, was emphasized by the purity of the spring, guarded by divine nymphs. Other items found in the cave include dolls, dedicated by the bride who no longer needed the toys of child-hood. Terracotta figurines representing Eros, Aphrodite, Pan, Silenos and a satyr, found together with ordinary female figurines in the same place, were also dedi-cations. These recognized the bride's new sexual responsibilities. The water from the communal spring purified the bride and prepared her for her reproductive responsibilities in marriage.

The main event of the ceremony was the procession that carried the bride from her parents' home to the home of the new husband. The procession openly displayed the new union before neighbours who might be called upon later to witness that it had taken place. Friends and family accompanied the wagon that carried bride and groom, singing the wedding song to Hymen, a divinity of marriage, and shouting the ritual (and ribald) cries that were supposed to keep bad spirits at bay, encourage sexual success and promote the successful fertility both families anticipated. The bride, who was veiled during the transition, did not reveal her face until just before she untied her belt, the act that represented the gift of her body to her husband. The untying of her belt was under the protection of Artemis Lusizonos (Artemis who 'loosens belts'), the same Artemis who would protect the young wife when she untied her belt again to deliver her first child. On the next day her parents brought gifts, and her mother offered sacrifice to Hera, the goddess identified with the keys of marriage.

Serving the dead

The last transition was the transition of death. Greeks thought of death as sep-aration of the living self, in Homer the breath, in later writers the soul, from the body. Death itself was considered polluting. Because the body without the soul could not be purified by any ritual, even the funeral was a source of pollution for participants. Funerals, like weddings, had several stages. Women presided over the activities most charged with pollution. They washed the body, supervised the laying out (*prothesis*) of the corpse, and participated in the laments and other rites of mourning within the home.

Separation from the living was represented by the procession (*ekphora*) to the cemetery, the public event that announced the death to the community. This procession imitated the invisible journey of the soul or 'image' (*eidolon*) of the dead person from this world to the next. Cities, careful to minimize exaggerated public expressions of family prominence or influence, resented excessive public displays of personal wealth and uncontrolled gestures of mourning on the part of the women of the family. Female participation in public funeral ritual, especially the *ekphora*, was considered to be problematical. Therefore, only women closely related to the dead person could take part. Cities often passed legislation to limit the number of women that could be seen in public at a family funeral. The traditional laments delivered by female relatives and close friends of the deceased, well known from epic and dramatic poetry, were curtailed in the *polis* and, if performed at all, had to be confined to the home.

Burial of the corpse or its cremated remains satisfied the claims of the dead on the living. For those lost at sea or others whose bodies were unrecoverable, families provided an empty tomb. Offerings were made to the dead at the gravesite on the third and ninth days after the funeral, and on the thirteenth day the family closed this stage of ritual obligation with a meal that reconstituted the family as a unit. Other ceremonies at the gravesite would follow every year, on the anniversary of the death. Completion of all customary rites secured the corpse in the grave, and the dead in the underworld, because once received by the gods of the dead, Hades and Persephone, the dead could not return.

Wearing amulets, making spells and cursing competitors

Devices for rituals of protection were well known in Greek literature. Hermes gave to Odysseus the plant called *molu*, to keep Circe from turning him into a hog; Demeter knew a plant to protect babies from sudden infant death; and people wore amulets to avoid trouble and achieve success. Women wore amulets to encourage conception, and Athenian mothers shielded their babies from harm with amulets in the form of the snake that had protected the infant Erechtheus. Mothers who attached amulets to their babies' clothing had good reason to fear infant death. Powerful spirits roamed the earth, spirits like Gello, said to kill virgins and new babies, or Mormo, who ate her own children, and Lamia, ready to kill any child. Some people did not believe in amulets, but even the great Athenian leader Perikles, well known for his preference for philosophy and natural science, when on his deathbed, allowed the women of his family to hang an amulet around his neck. Educated males may have been contemptuous of such practices, but the impulse to seek special protection from danger was accepted by the society as a practical strategy. Soldiers converted their shields to protective amulets by decorating them with representations of fierce monsters designed to frighten the enemy. The owl on Athenian coins, with its threatening full frontal stare, made each coin a protective amulet for the entire city.

Greek religious practice also includes a dark corner of personal rituals secretly performed to compel an oblivious victim. Such rituals included writing love charms to force a beloved from the arms of another or scratching a curse on a lead tablet to destroy a competitor in law, business, athletics or politics. Individuals at all levels of society participated in such practices. Writing a curse while reciting it aloud increased its effectiveness, insured that it would not be forgotten, and, what is more, enabled its conveyance to the underworld, where the deities who could carry out the terms were to be found (for example Hermes Chthonios, Persephone, Hades and the Erinyes, spirits of revenge). The preferred messenger for transmission was a young person recently, but untimely dead, an *ahoros*. A message deposited in the grave of one who had died too soon accompanied the wraith straight to the underworld.

The general opinion about such rituals is not favourable. Perikles was embarrassed by his amulet, and Plato shows nothing but contempt. In ancient literature, women are held responsible for most of the trouble, but in fact, when extant examples of actual practice are considered, most known practitioners are male. Two issues aroused suspicion. One was secrecy, the other was acting alone. Spells and curses cast by the individual in solitude, without an audience, for personal gain and directed at a victim without warning or explanation were considered problematical. Such tactics were not only antisocial, they were unfair. Some rituals delivered in secret, however, differed very little in intent and method from public rituals designed to secure protection for the whole city. The giant pair of eyes on the city wall at Thasos, its gaze aimed to paralyse attackers, was displayed in public because it protected the entire city. At Teos and Abdera public curses were proclaimed at the greatest annual festivals. Pronounced on behalf of the city by a magistrate speaking to the entire citizen population, these official curses clarify the difference between a public and a private curse. The public curse at Teos threatened destruction for anyone who interfered with the local grain trade or any individual who tried to cast spells against the many. What was at stake was not the casting of spells (for what else is a public curse?) but doing so alone, secretly, on the sly and, even more terrible, targeting 'the many'.

Fear of the negative consequences of unofficial spells indicates the depth of the belief in the potency of any spell. For this reason the *polis* retained the institution of the public curse, an instrument invoked especially in periods of crisis. At Athens, on the eve of a major military expedition during the Peloponnesian War, almost all the protective statues standing before the doors of private homes and public buildings in Athens were destroyed. The entire city was in uproar. Those held responsible were convicted on a charge of impiety. As an indication of the seriousness of the crime, conspirators were publicly cursed by all the priests and priestesses of the city. One priestess is said to have refused to participate, claiming that she was a priestess who performed prayers, not curses. We do not hear much about public cursing after the classical period, but private cursing, although never officially approved, persisted throughout antiquity, leaving behind for us a twisted trail of bizarre texts scratched on lead, papyrus and scraps of broken pottery.

The shifting topography of the dead

The journey to the underworld was the final separation. There was little common opinion about conditions, but everyone knew that once the last boundary was crossed, there would be no return. Families sought to complete all rites securing a dead relative in the grave in order to create a firm boundary between the land of the dead and the land of the living. There were, however, few fixed features to define that boundary. Poets describe water to be crossed, some even mention a gate, but the geography of the underworld was under constant revision, landmarks were altered by every poet who attempted a description, and even though some groups claimed esoteric knowledge about what lay beyond, there was little agreement about content.

Epic poetry knew the underworld as a gloomy place under the earth. For narrative reasons, Homer's dead can hear and speak, but sometimes only when they have drunk blood; they can be seen but not touched because they are only witless images, *eidola*, of their former selves. Both Homer and Hesiod describe a place of darkness associated with punishment. For Hesiod, it is a place of confinement for the rebellious Titans. For Homer, it is the corner where Sisyphos, Tantalos and Tityos endlessly labour. Both poets also hint at another possibility. Homer tells of an Elysian Field, far in the west, a place for the special dead, where there is neither punishment nor tedium. Structurally, this place beyond the waters of Okeanos seems equivalent to what Hesiod calls 'Islands of the Blessed', a place whose name implies that only those close to the gods can reach it.

The first hint of the possibility of preparing for something better comes at the end of the *Homeric Hymn to Demeter*, probably composed in the sixth century BCE, where those who have seen the rites of Demeter, therefore *olbioi*, 'blessed' (also 'rich' or 'happy'), are distinguished from those who must go down to the misty darkness. For the first time there is a hint of the possibility of dissolving the difference between the gods and the dead. That possibility is associated with annual rituals for Demeter and Kore, begun at Athens and concluded at Eleusis. By the classical period Eleusis was the home of *mysteria*, 'mysteries', rituals that could not be described or discussed, but which were available to all who spoke Greek, male and female, slave and free. Eleusis became a new kind of Pan-Hellenic sanctuary, dominated by Athens, but open to individual Greeks from elsewhere who wished to share in the possibility of this special blessing. The temple of Demeter at Eleusis was unlike any other in the Greek world. Built to enclose Demeter's secret rites, it had columns on the inside to support a roof that enclosed a space large enough for a large group to worship. The building had no cult statue, and its only separate room was the interior, windowless space where the Hierophant (priest who 'shows the sacred things') kept the sacred objects. The base of the temple was cut directly into the living rock, with the risers for candidates cut into the stone on three sides. Here initiates stood as spectators. We are still in the dark about the content of the ceremony and the precise details of the blessing, because those who 'saw' the rites were never to tell what they had seen, heard or been shown.

In Pindar and Plato the contrast between the *olbioi* and those who go down to the misty darkness is much more dramatic than the comparison in the Homeric Hymn. For Pindar, the dead are judged and separated into two groups: those who must pay a penalty and those, only a few, who having kept their oaths need not suffer. After completing three cycles of earthly life free from injustice, the just may walk the road of Zeus to the Island of the Blessed, a place of light, flowers, pleasant breezes and clear water. Plato also predicts two pathways, a journey and a judgement, but he makes the goal consonant with his own philosophical theories, correcting not only flaws of the new popular notions about the afterlife, but flaws in the way life itself was lived.

The journey after death is also a theme for tiny, inscribed gold tablets found buried with corpses throughout the Greek Mediterranean. The inscriptions describe a journey through a landscape bordering the land of the dead and a choice the soul must make. Some even give advice on how to address the gods of the dead. The gold tablets give hints of a widespread network of freelance ritual specialists sharing in an oral tradition of esoteric poetry. The gold tablets are souvenirs of a special ritual experience and they serve as a badge of membership in a privileged group. The god who protects this group is Bacchic Dionysos; by experiencing his special rites, the worshipper becomes *bakchos*, a status shared with the god himself. On the journey to the land of the dead the inscriptions remind the soul of the experience of those rites because the soul must choose between the water of Forgetting and the water of Memory in order to reach its special destination. Whoever drinks the water of Memory will walk the sacred road of the blessed together with other *bakchoi* and *mystai* (initiates).

The ceremonies of the *polis* emphasized collective ritual, but the gold tablets focused on the individual. Evidence for private esoteric *mysteria* in the classical period is scarce. Practitioners must have been discreet. With the Bacchic mysteries there comes a new emphasis on privacy, choice and personal goals. While the goal of the secret ritual pertains to the next life, the experience suggests the possibility of aspiring to new forms of ritual identity and new definitions of achievement in this one.

The gold tablets, like the case histories published at Epidauros, and the curse tablets everywhere, are signs of new ways of ritual communication in the fourth century BCE. Popular literacy has had an impact on religious practice and religious experience. Reading a text where a god gives instructions encourages the reader to become a direct participant in his own rituals. Narratives of personal experience and the recitation of performative utterances creates illusions of the possibility of power. The texts on gold, the narratives at Epidauros and the inscribed competitive curses everywhere are working texts, potent in themselves. Reading them now, we can experience a miracle cure, curse a rival in politics, an opponent in litigation or a competitor in a race. We can even approach the waters of Memory and ask to take a drink.

Bibliography

Alcock, S. and R. Osborne 1994. *Placing the gods: sanctuaries and sacred places in ancient Greece.* Oxford: Oxford University Press.

Blundell, S. and M. Williamson 1998. *The sacred and the feminine in ancient Greece.* London: Routledge.

Bremmer, J. 1983. *The early Greek concept of the soul*. Princeton: Princeton University Press.

1999. *Greek religion*. Greece & Rome, New Surveys in the Classics 24. Oxford: Oxford University Press.

Bruit Zaidman, L. and P. Schmitt Pantel 1992. *Religion in the ancient Greek city*. Cambridge: Cambridge University Press.

Burkert, W. 1977. *Greek religion*. Cambridge, MA: Harvard University Press.

1983. *Homo necans*. Berkeley: University of California Press.

1992. *The orientalizing revolution: Near Eastern influence on Greek culture in the early Archaic age*. Cambridge, MA: Harvard University Press.

Buxton, R. 2000. *Oxford readings in Greek religion*. Oxford: Oxford University Press.

Detienne, M. 1977. *Dionysos slain*. Baltimore: Johns Hopkins University Press.

1994. *The gardens of Adonis: spices in Greek mythology*. Princeton: Princeton University Press.

Detienne, M. and J.-P. Vernant 1989. *The cuisine of sacrifice among the Greeks*. Chicago: University of Chicago Press.

Easterling, P. E. and J. V. Muir 1985. *Greek religion and society*. Cambridge: Cambridge University Press.

Faraone, C. A. and D. Obbink 1991. *Magica hiera: ancient Greek magic and religion*. New York: Oxford University Press.

Gager, J. G. 1992. *Curse tablets and binding spells from the ancient world*. New York: Oxford University Press.

Graf, F. 1985. *Nordionische Kulte*. Rome: The Swiss Institute in Rome.

Guthrie, W. K. C. 1950. *The Greeks and their gods*. Boston: Beacon Press.

Hägg, R. 1996. *The role of religion in the early Greek polis*. Stockholm: The Swedish Institute.

Hägg, R., N. Marinatos and G. C. Nordquist 1988. *Early Greek cult practice*. Stockholm: The Swedish Institute.

Jameson, M. H. 1988: Sacrifice and animal husbandry in classical Greece. In C. R. Whitaker (ed.), *Pastoral economies in classical antiquity*. Cambridge: Cambridge University Press, pp. 87–119 (Cambridge Philological Society, Suppl.; v. 14).

1991. *Sacrifice before battle*. In V. D. Hanson (ed.), *Hoplites: the classical Greek battle experience*. London and New York: Routledge.

Jost, M. 1985. *Sanctuaires et cultes d'Arcadie*. Paris: J. Vrin.

LiDonnici, L. R. 1995. *The Epidaurian miracle inscriptions: text, translation, commentary*. Atlanta, GA: Scholars Press.

Marinatos, N. and R. Hägg 1993. *Greek sanctuaries: new approaches*. London: Routledge.

Mikalson, J. 1983. *Athenian popular religion*. Chapel Hill and London: University of North Carolina Press.

1998. *Religion in Hellenistic Athens*. Berkeley: University of California Press.

Otto, W. F. 1965. *Dionysos: myth and cult*. Bloomington, IN: Indiana University Press.

Parker, R. 1996. *Athenian religion: a history*. Oxford: Oxford University Press.

1983. *Miasma: pollution and purification in early Greek religion*. Oxford: Oxford University Press.

Polignac, F. de 1995. *Cults, territory, and the origins of the Greek city-state*. Chicago: University of Chicago Press.

Price, S. 1987. *Rituals and power*. Cambridge: Cambridge University Press.

1999. *Religions of the ancient Greeks*. Cambridge: Cambridge University Press.

Pulleyn, S. 1997. *Prayer in Greek religion*. Oxford: Oxford University Press.

Schachter, A. 1992. Policy, cult, and the placing of Greek sanctuaries. In A. Schachter and J. Bingen (eds.), *Le sanctuaire grec*. Entretiens sur l'antiquité classique 37. Geneva: Foundation Hardt, pp. 1–57.

Schmitt Pantel, P. 1992. *La cité au banquet*. Rome: École français de Rome.

Seaford, R. 1994. *Reciprocity and ritual*. Oxford: Oxford University Press.

Sourvinou-Inwood, C. 1995. *Reading Greek death*. Oxford: Oxford University Press.

Van Bremen, R. 1996. *The limits of participation: women and civic life in the Greek East in the Hellenistic and Roman periods*. Amsterdam: C. Gieben.

Van Straten, F. T. 1995. *Hiera kala*. Leiden: E. J. Brill.

Vernant, J.-P. 1980. *Myth and society in ancient Greece*. Sussex: Harvester Press.

7 Religions in the Roman Empire

J. A. NORTH

The study of Roman 'paganism'

The study of Roman pagan[1] religion as a separate subject does not go back before the early nineteenth century. In its relatively short history it has been dominated by a small number of ideas that have sometimes been seen as almost beyond challenge. The keynote was set from the very beginning as a story of 'decline'. The idea was that the religion of the very earliest Romans was closely adapted to their needs but that for one reason or another its development was stunted, so that it became progressively more and more stultified and ritualized and remote from the needs of the worshippers. Proof of all this was thought to come from the last generation of the Republic for whom religion had become nothing more or less than a meaningless set of rules. These could be freely exploited by anybody who wished to, as the source of useful political manoeuvres or for any other advantages, without thought about the gods and goddesses who were supposedly the objects of the worship.

By the end of the nineteenth century this view had become well established as an orthodoxy. At that date the great handbook of Georg Wissowa enshrined a certain approach to the subject. The book is a mine of information about the religious institutions of Rome and still provides the fullest and safest source for such information; but it is organized in a legalistic framework that implies a vision of the system in which it parallels the constitutional law so much admired at the time. Mommsen's authority lay behind this approach, since he saw religion as the least interesting area of Roman life. To some extent, this view was modified at the turn of the century by new approaches, which began to take seriously theories of human history tracing the evolution of a series of stages, beginning from simple societies and going through stages of increasing complexity. The early stages were modelled on the views of anthropologists of the time about the starting point of this evolution; but it was not at all difficult to adapt existing views to the later stages, and to see stagnation and decline as once again the factors that prevented Rome from following the correct evolutionary path. The same basic view of the character of Roman religious experience was thus being recycled in a modern form, compatible with the anthropology of the period (Wissowa 1912; Scheid 1987; North 1997).

The most powerful and long-lasting part of this theory was best elaborated by Warde Fowler in Oxford. He argued that there were various clues that suggested a period of Roman history in which the Romans had established worship and even some of their characteristic institutions, but had not yet acquired gods and goddesses in any recognizable form. Varro, the great antiquarian writer of the late Republic, believed that for many decades the Romans made no images of their deities; the implication seemed to be that at this stage they worshipped spirits inherent in natural phenomena such as springs or fire. This ancient evidence fitted with the idea that animism was the first form of religion in all societies, so the Romans were starting out on the normal evolutionary route. The theory seemed to be confirmed by two arguments: first, that the Roman gods never developed family relationships or personalities of their own and consequently that the Romans had no mythology of their own; secondly, that a word in Latin, *numen*, seemed to correspond exactly to the spirits that early man was supposed to have worshipped. The Romans were now fitted out with the early history that the theory would have predicted. The real Roman religion was the religion of the *numina*, which had of course no personality, form or kin, because they were the powers of natural forces. The whole apparatus of pagan religion had to be borrowed from more developed peoples: images from the Etruscans, myths from the Greeks (Warde Fowler 1911; *RoR* I: 10–18).

In the course of the middle decades of the twentieth century, many variations of this basic scheme were explored, but the most radical revision of it was pioneered by the most controversial religious historian of the time. This was Georges Dumézil, the leading exponent of the claimed mythology and theology of the Indo-Europeans. His theory of the threefold structure of ideology traced back, at least in theory, to the society (supposedly divided into three classes, kings/priests, warriors and producers) as well as the mythology of the original Indo-Europeans. The theory was based not just on Romans, but on a comparison of many different ancient and later societies; but the ideology was inherited by many different peoples, Celts and Germans as well as Persians and Indians. The Roman version was just another example. There is a great deal about this which is highly controversial and puzzling today, as it was already in the 1930s,

320 J. A. North

Map 7.1. The Roman Empire in 27 BCE.

Map 7.1. (*cont.*).

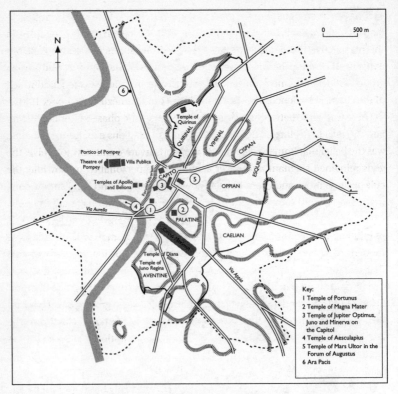

Map 7.2. Major Roman temples in the first century BCE.

not least the medium through which Dumézil thought his ideology was passed down from generation to generation. But, even if the details are rejected, there can be very little doubt that many Roman linguistic forms were shared with other Indo-European speakers. Both the names of many Roman gods and the words for god and goddess themselves are Indo-European. If so, then the gods themselves must have come to Latium when the Romans and Latins first arrived and cannot have been developed in Latium itself, as the theory of the *numina* required.

As for the missing mythology of the Romans, Dumézil believed that he had found that also. Roman deities do not have characteristically Roman stories told about them; but Roman kings and queens do have a whole body of narratives, regarded by the Romans themselves as history, not myth. Romulus and Remus, Numa and the other early Roman kings on Dumézil's view preserved the otherwise lost ideology of the Indo-Europeans.

So again the Romans emerge not as a people who evolved their own unique religion on their own soil, but as a branch of the Indo-European family of peoples. In this perspective, the idea of a pre-deistic phase of development loses all plausibility. By the time these theories were appearing, however, the theory that all human groups follow the same evolutionary pattern had been abandoned; and much of the classical evidence had been questioned too (Dumézil 1970; Belier 1991).

There was a link between the theory of the predeistic phase of Roman history and the idea of decline as the keynote of Roman religious experience. The link was the belief that Roman religion was very conservative and slow to evolve: the gods remained stagnant and never acquired true personality; meanwhile, the cult became more and more bogged down in ritualism and legalism. At core, there was a deeply Roman tradition, typical of a practical, unimaginative people, which failed to respond to changing conditions and became less and less capable of fulfilling the needs of the people. Many aspects of Roman religious life were thought to provide confirmation of this hypothesis. For instance, it was said that religion was simply exploited by politicians for their own ends; that new cults were imported in a desperate effort to revive a failing system; that Romans' belief in the gods and goddesses was undermined by the growth of scepticism. Well-known incidents such as the struggle between Cicero and Clodius in the last years of the Republic were interpreted on the assumption that their motives were entirely political and that the religious issues were a mere excuse for the manoeuvring.

It is important to remember that this picture can hardly be supported by any direct evidence. Our sources are on the whole very reluctant to commit themselves at all on such issues as the motives on which participants acted. The Greek historian Polybius, a visitor to Rome in the second century BCE, does indeed speak of religion as a necessary way of maintaining morale and good order; but his point is that the Romans still had a useful religious tradition of this kind, while the Greeks had irresponsibly dissipated theirs. Perhaps the most direct evidence comes from the orator Cicero, who has a good deal to say about religion, including a philosophical dialogue (*On divination*) in which two speakers, Cicero and his brother, put the case for and against belief in the sending of signs by the gods for the benefit of humans. The end of the dialogue suspends any final decision, leaving that step to readers. But at least the issues have been placed before the reader – issues that might seem to be fundamental to religion (*RoR* II: 13.1b; 13.2; Beard 1986).

So far in this section, we have seen an essentially negative account of Roman religion dominating all views about it. But very little of this negativity is really to be found in the source material. There certainly were Romans who thought that the negligence of their leaders had allowed some of their inherited institutions to be forgotten or omitted. Both Cicero and Varro say something of this kind. But in general what the Romans and their foreign visitors tell us is that the Romans were and continued to be the most religious of peoples, the most scrupulous in the maintenance of their civic rituals: it was precisely their piety that had led directly to their conquest of the known world. If some of them lamented the loss of rituals it was because their preservation was so highly valued.

In recent years, a new way of perceiving this history has been worked out, reversing most of the assumptions on which the old views were based. It would be wrong to say that this is universally accepted or that all its supporters hold identical views. But there has been a general trend to recognize that in many respects the traditional picture of Roman religion has been constructed not on the ideas of the Romans themselves, but on judgements about the proper character of religion that are essentially anachronistic and derived from modern parallels. For example, it has often been argued that the introduction of new gods represented a progressive weakening of the true religious tradition of Rome – repeated attempts at revival that always failed. But in fact the Romans introduced new rituals and cults throughout their history and quite clearly saw this as a source of strength and pride, not of failure.

Again, the relationship of politics and religion has been seen as a clear sign that religion was virtually dead, only useful as a trick to be used by politicians in need of a cynical manoeuvre. In this case as well, it is now argued that this interpretation rests on a misunderstanding of the long-term relationship between religion and politics, which had at all dates been deeply implicated with one another. The priests had their own duty to interpret the sacred law; so, they must always have been open to the charge that they were abusing this privilege in their own political interest. We have no reason to think that this raised new problems in the late republican period, though at that time the political struggle was at its most intense and perilous, as conflicting groups and conflicting leaders such as Caesar and Pompey used every means they could of protecting their own power and diminishing that of their enemies. In all ways, the gloves were off and religion was involved in the political upheaval, as it was in all other aspects of the life of Rome. But it is quite clear that the participants almost all took the religious issues very seriously, just as they did the political issues (*RoR* I: 114–40; Scheid 2001).

The result of this shift of outlook is that a reassessment is now due of many aspects of religious life and literature in this period. The fundamental change that has taken place is the recognition that common sense and guesswork are not good guides to this area of life. The religious ideas and actions of the ancients cannot be understood without a recognition that they were profoundly different from our own. It is from this point that future research must begin; this survey assumes that this approach is the right one to use at least at this stage in our understanding of the religion of the Romans. There are, however, quite fundamental problems of interpretation, which originate from the very nature of the information about Roman life that has survived to our time. It is therefore from the sources that we should begin.

The sources

The character of the evidence available to us is a critical determinant of what can be said and not said about the religion or religions of this period. At some points the tradition narrows to a fragment of what would be necessary to understand the character of Roman religious life. At others it seems adequate at least to establish the general character of pagan religion. There are, however, always problems of interpretation; and even when particular sources seems to throw light on the problems, they need to be considered in the light of the religious situation as whole. Nothing causes greater misunderstanding than taking particular fragments of evidence out of their context and assuming that they can be properly criticized in the light of twenty-first-century common sense and of our ideas about religious life today. It always has to be borne in mind that the assumptions of pagans about the most fundamental issues are quite different from ours.

The first question that arises in discussing the sources is to specify what is to count as evidence about religion and what is not. In the Rome of the fifth and fourth centuries BCE at least, the religious and political activities of the Romans are thoroughly intertwined so that every action has its ritual attached to it; every campaign is interspersed with consultations of the gods, sacrifices to them, celebrations in their honour and so on. In the Roman conception at least, the actions of men and women involve a divine aspect at every stage. By the same token, it is not easy to distinguish religious buildings from secular ones, since every household contained its shrine and its sacred objects and was the location of certain rituals. The converse of this proposition is that there was no purely religious organization to which the population of Rome belonged; they were not members of any church and had no option to change religious affiliation. Their religious life was embedded in the city and its activities. The only separate religious organizations were the priestly colleges, whose membership consisted of members of the ruling elite. (For these, see below pp. 344–6 and Table 7.3).

The result of this situation is that the possible evidence for religious life is enormous and very varied: historical texts are full of information about religion in action; coins are covered with religious symbols; many inscriptions are records of religious dedications; the archaeology of Italy tells us of sanctuaries, temples, sacred groves and burial areas everywhere; the literature of Rome, especially in the Augustan Age, has much to say about ritual actions, about the gods and also about magical procedures; the art both of Rome and of the Empire in general produces images of sacrificers and of sacrificial equipment in large quantities, but also bas-reliefs of many other ceremonies – triumphs, the lustration of military camps, state sacrifices and so on. Under the Empire the mix becomes if anything richer as time goes by: not just evidence of Christianity and a mounting library of Christian literature and debate, but also the reflections of successive Christian apologists on the character of pagan life and the pagan tradition; and a mass of evidence about the various new cults that became common throughout the cities of the Empire, perhaps most dramatically the evidence of Mithraism, known to us primarily through the decoration of the grottoes which were its hallmark and which survive in quite large numbers. (See *RoR* II.12.5.)

The first period for which we have a quantity of evidence sufficient to ground an account of the structure and practices of religion is the last century or so of the Republic. It would not be true to say that we are wholly ignorant of what went before this, but we are very largely dependent on the sources of the first century BCE for everything that went before. The two surviving historians Livy and Dionysius of Halicarnassus both lived in this period and were themselves reconstructing early history from inadequate data. They very largely reflect the ideas and aspirations of their own period, believing as they did that the early years of Rome were an ideal age of piety, such that later generations could scarcely hope to emulate. They provide us mostly with the myths preserved into later periods, not records of historical truth. By the middle Republic, we have more solid ground to rest on; but the fact remains that archaeology is the best hope we have of acquiring any reliable idea at all of the religion of early Rome. The most solid achievement so far is to have established that the Rome of the sixth century BCE was far from being an unsophisticated or isolated community, but in the mainstream of western Mediterranean life in close touch with Greeks, Etruscans and Carthaginians. This in itself shows that we need to be thoroughly sceptical about the continuity of the Roman tradition.

There is yet another very sharp contrast between the record we have for the third and second centuries BCE and that for the first century BCE. By the first

Table 7.1 *Chronology of Roman history*

Date	Event	Periods	Personalities
753 BCE	Varro's date for the foundation of Rome, Romulus and Remus	Regal period, down to 509	King Numa, founder of the religion?
509	First magistrates of the Republic	Republican period, 509–31	Junius Brutus, the first consul of Rome
390	Capture of Rome by the Gauls		Camillus, saviour of Rome
338	Abolition of the Latin League	Expansion of Roman control of Italy, 338–264	
264–241	First war between Rome and Carthage		
218–201	Second war between Rome and Carthage		Hannibal of Carthage Scipio Africanus
from 200	Roman wars in the east	Roman Empire in east	
133	Agrarian reforms; conflicts in Rome		Tiberius Gracchus, tribune of the plebs
91–83	War by Italian allies against Rome	All Italians gain citizenship	
81–79	Sulla dictator – reforms of political system		Sulla as dictator
66–61	Eastern wars	Period of Cicero's career	Pompey's campaigns in the east
58–49	Conquest of Gaul		Caesar's campaigns
59	Deal between Pompey, Caesar and Crassus	First triumvirate	
49	Civil War between Caesar and Pompey		Death of Pompey
44	Caesar assassinated	Series of Civil Wars, till 31 BCE	

(*cont.*)

Table 7.1 (*cont.*)

Date	Event	Periods	Personalities
31	Defeat of Antony and Cleopatra at Actium		
31 BCE to 14 CE	Augustus as ruler (*princeps*), worship of the Emperor established; wide expansion of Empire	Principate (first century BCE to third century CE)	Lifetime of Livy, Virgil, Ovid
c. 30 CE	Crucifixion of Jesus		Pontius Pilate, Prefect of Judaea
54–68	64 CE, first persecution?	Reign of Nero	Death of Paul in Rome?
98–117	Conquest of Dacia; war against Parthia	Reign of Trajan	113 CE Pliny's letter about the Christians; Tacitus historian
161–180	Attacks on frontiers begin	Reign of Marcus Aurelius	Marcus' *Confessions*
198–217	Extension of citizenship to all free inhabitants of the Empire	Reign of Caracalla	Dio Cassius historian
235–284	Wars in north and east, period of instability	Third-century 'crisis'	
284–305	Rule of four Emperors; final persecutions; reform of Empire	Reign of Diocletian and colleagues	
312–336	First Christian Emperor; first legislation favouring Christians	Late Empire; reign of Constantine	Eusebius' *History of the Church*
378–395	Laws against pagan practices	Reign of Theodosius I	Ammianus Marcellinus historian

century, we have extensive contemporary writings, including letters and even memoirs, as well as a great deal of literature. But this is true only from the age of Cicero onwards: earlier, the record is very much more distant and formal; but it does contain a great deal of methodical information, preserved by the early chronological historians. The bad fit of these two kinds of record contributes to the impression that the late republicans were far less careful in their maintenance of regular rituals; but in this case it is very probably the record not the reality that changes so dramatically. On the other hand, with Cicero we have for the first time a set of various sources giving us different visions of religious or non-religious life. This is the first period in which religion itself became a topic of discourse: first, in the writings of antiquarians, who lovingly collected the details of clothes, traditions and books of the priests and other religious officials; secondly, in philosophical discussion, including books that survive by Cicero *On the nature of the gods* and *On divination*. The impact of these debates is a subject of lively argument. Did they undermine belief and weaken the religion as a whole? Or did they rather create a debate that strengthened and developed the theology of paganism (Beard 1986)?

One very clear theme in this period, repeatedly mentioned, is the belief, clearly widespread, that the religion of Rome was badly neglected and that the gods and goddesses were betrayed in the last few years of the republican period and in the years of civil war that followed (49–45; 43–31 BCE). The civil wars were the gods' punishment for their neglected temples and rituals. This theme was literally a god-send to the propagandists of the new regime set up by Augustus and his supporters in the years after their victory over Antony and Cleopatra in 31 BCE. They could set themselves up, and duly did, as the revivalists of a religion in decline. Augustus is credited with the restoration of temples, the reinstitution of lost priesthoods and the revival of forgotten rituals. There is no doubt that some of this was real enough. But in large part, it was the loving antiquarians of the late Republic who had created the possibility of revivalism, by showing the traditions that had lapsed. With the benefit of hindsight, it is not difficult to see that this is all largely a misunderstanding; but it clearly had a powerful influence at the time.

Amongst the most important sources we have for religious attitudes are the works of the historians of the early Empire, particularly Livy writing on the Republic, but also Tacitus on the earlier Emperors, and indeed the poets, especially Ovid who provides us with a version of the Roman calendar for the months of January to June, including his thoughts about many of the major festivals of the year. A great deal of this writing is not very reliable as an account of the origins of the various institutions; but it does tell us a great deal about the ideas and assumptions of the early imperial years, in which the authors themselves lived. Roman historical writing, however, needs to be interpreted with care and imagination. At first sight, it seems to say little, and that little rather formal and remote; but this reticence is the characteristic style of the period, which does not easily see the gods and goddesses as causing events directly. There are few miracles or epiphanies. But the narrative in fact interweaves human and divine contributions and one of Livy's themes is the care with which the great men of the past concerned themselves with signs from the gods and rituals. He reinforces the message that religious care goes with imperial success (Liebeschuetz 1967; Miles 1995; *RoR* I: 5–12).

Pagan writing is marked not only by an oblique attitude to the working of the divine, but also by a very limited range of topics on which religious writing seems ever to have existed. There are very few discussions of the significance of rituals – even of sacrifice, the basic ritual of the whole cycle; there is virtually no discussion at all of the character of priesthood. Antiquarian writing gives details of the ceremonies, clothes and proceedings of priests; philosophic writing discusses the existence of gods and of communication with the gods; but these writings are essentially external debates, not internal exegeses of the character of pagan religion. The priests themselves certainly had books, which they guarded in their colleges and which were the basis of their judgements. It may be that some of this material found its way into the antiquarian writers. But the evasiveness that marks historical writing also affects all other forms of religious discourse. One consequence of this is that many critics have seen moribund religion in what was actually guarded and reverent expression.

Another consequence is that there is a sharp and critical contrast between the verbal expression of pagan religion and the discourse that arrives with the evolution of Christianity. Religious language becomes far more direct. Christian writers have no such hesitation in speaking of the divine or in attributing the causes of events to divine intervention. They also engage in a debate about the exact character of the deity or rather of his incarnation in Jesus Christ. Soon enough there are creeds and explicit debates on matters of theology. In one sense, of course, all these new types of text are invaluable to the historian, providing a tool that had been missing; but the fact that such explicit texts do not exist for earlier periods should not be seen as an accident. The silence reflects what pagans thought it appropriate or not appropriate to speak of. We have to look with care at more reticent texts to see what they are thinking.

There is another consequence of the rise and elaboration of Christian writing for the historian of pagan Rome. Christian writers have among their concerns the maintaining of a polemic against pagan practices and ideas. Leading Christian writers such as Lactantius (*c.* 240 to *c.* 320 CE) and Augustine (354–430 CE) give a good deal of space to the subject; and lesser figures such as Arnobius of Sicca in North Africa (third century CE) devoted whole works to this project. To a modern judgement, they set about this task with a will, but with a very odd set of tactics. They almost wholly ignore the pagan religion of their own day; and give as their examples practices drawn from the works of long-dead first-century BCE antiquarians, such as Varro and Verrius. Their generous quotations from these works provide invaluable information about the republican cult, but it is all selected to illustrate the absurdities of Roman cult practice as seen by later Christians. Their ridicule is hard to escape when the information is transferred from their texts into the collections of antiquarian fragments. So their bitter jibes not only helped weaken pagan religion in their own day, but also served to obscure its significance from modern interpreters (Liebeschuetz 1967: 252–77; Feeney 1998; North 2000: 76–85).

The history of the Romans

Our knowledge of the regal period of Roman history is limited by the fact that the sources were composed by authors living in a quite different age with little or no continuity of written tradition. The authors whose works we possess (Cicero, Livy, Dionysius of Halicarnassus) lived in the first century BCE and the sources they had available dated back only another century or so before their own time. There is sharp disagreement between historians as to whether these traditions are reliable guides to the general character of early Roman society, or whether they should be treated as Roman myths and only the archaeology of the early period regarded as evidence of history. Certainly the list of kings and their traditional dates must be a construction; it is quite incredible that seven kings should between them reign for two and a half centuries. But the accounts of the later kings do suggest that Rome was in the sixth century BCE open to a range of foreign influences, from the Etruscans to the north of them, from the Greeks of southern Italy, from Carthaginians with local trading links and, above all, from their Latin-speaking neighbours. The archaeology of the period supports the view that Rome was by this time an important town of central Italy and that it did indeed have widespread foreign contacts.

In particular, there is good reason to believe that the Latins from the archaic period onwards acted not as a number of quite separate states, but as a community with shared religious traditions and rights. Every Latin had the right to trade and inter-marry in any Latin state and also to migrate and take on the full citizenship of the host state. The Latins also acted in concert down to 338 BCE to set up new Latin communities, or colonies. The detailed history of this 'Latin League' and the question of whether it was dominated by Rome or whether Rome was simply a member like the others are all still much debated; but it seems a safe conclusion that the later Roman willingness to expand their citizenship outside the city and its immediate territory, first to adjacent areas and finally to the whole of Italy (in the first century BCE) and the whole Empire (in the third century CE), can be traced back to these open boundaries of the regal and early republican years.

It is a striking fact that the Romans' own accounts of their kings, of which the earliest are in Cicero's *Republic* and Livy's *History*, are quite positive in their assessment of them. The kings are represented as each contributing to the development of the Roman constitution and their social and religious institutions. Numa contributes the religion, Servius Tullius the organization of the army and the popular assembly, and so on. The only exception is the last king, Tarquin the Proud, who is represented as a tyrant and finally expelled, defeated and disgraced. The Tarquins had strong connections with the Etruscan cities, especially with Tarquinii and Chiusi, and they have sometimes been regarded as foreign rulers imposed on Rome by Etruria, so Tarquin's expulsion becomes the freeing of Rome from alien rule. This is, however, very far from certain, since Rome keeps its own language and traditions. It seems much likelier that Etruscan influence on Rome was a matter of both belonging to a common central Italian culture. At least, the grandest and most important temple in Rome was the triple temple of Jupiter, Juno and Minerva on the Capitolin Hill (Map 7.2): this became a symbol of Roman-ness, despite the fact that its building was attributed to the Tarquins (Cornell 1995; *OCD*[3] 1322–5).

Neither the date nor the detail of the end of the monarchy can be established, but it seems clear that other Italian cities too expelled their kings and created new civic institutions around the beginning of the fifth century BCE. The Romans thought that certain principles guided the Republic from its inception; we may suspect that in fact these were the product of slow growth later retrojected. They were the popular election of the magistrates for each year; the sharing of power between equal office-holders; and the guiding control of the senate, consisting of life-members who had served as magistrates. In essence this is the system that we do find operating in the third to first centuries BCE. It is then clear that one of the functions of the system was to ensure that no excessive concentration of power could be acquired by any individual or family. The rules were gradually elaborated to make this division of authority more comprehensive: office could only be held for one year, repetition of the highest office (the consulate) was rationed so that you could hold it only at a fixed age and only once every ten years. But although these practices may date back to the earlier Republic, the rules were only formalized in the second century BCE and reflect the thinking of that period.

In the early republican period, our sources tell of a conflict between patricians and plebeians, the so-called 'struggle of the orders'. Patricians were members of a specific group of clans (*gentes*) and their status was still remembered and still went with birth even in the late Republic. Plebeians are said to have included everybody else, but especially the common people, the soldiers of Rome. Patricians are said to have claimed a monopoly of office and power; but lists of office-holders suggest that this was never completely established and that it became less and less true as time went by. Meanwhile some plebeians seem not to have been poor men at all, but landholders and men of substance. By the middle Republic, the patricians and the rich plebeians had sorted out their differences and ruled together as an elite of wealth, basing their power on keeping control of office-holding and hence of the senate (Cornell 1995).

This plebeio-patrician oligarchy dominated a highly successful period in which Roman power was gradually extended first through southern and central Italy, in the late fourth and third centuries BCE; then after a great struggle with the Carthaginians, in the third century BCE, to new areas in the western and eastern Mediterranean, second century BCE. The formation of an empire in the familiar sense was a slow, even reluctant process; the Romans conquered irresistibly, but were in no hurry to set up systems of rule or to administer their new territories. In the very late Republic (91–44 BCE) and in the age of Augustus (31 BCE – 14 CE) both conquering and reorganizing went ahead methodically for the first time and by the early Empire the whole Mediterranean area and much territory beyond were incorporated in a unified system of rule (Beard and Crawford 1999; and see Map 7.1, for the situation in 27 BCE).

From the age of Augustus onwards, it is conventional to speak of the Emperor and the Empire, but this is confusing for several reasons: first, the Empire (in the sense of the area ruled by Rome) had very largely been created in the republican period (during the third to first centuries BCE) not in the Empire (in the sense of the period when Emperors ruled), though the reign of Augustus himself did see a dramatic increase in its size, including the conquest of the whole of eastern Europe (see Map 7.1); secondly, the title of the ruler at this date was not Emperor (*Imperator*) at all, but 'first citizen' (*princeps*), so that historians often refer to this period as the 'principate', opposing this to the 'dominate' in the late Empire period; thirdly, the regime itself sought to deny that there was a new constitution or that the old republican system had been abolished, emphasizing rather the continuity of their rule with that system.

In formal terms indeed there was little change, at least during the age of Augustus himself; the elections and the passing of laws were still the work of the assemblies of the people; the annual magistrates were still called by the same titles and notionally had the same tasks to perform; the governors of the provinces were still drawn from the ranks of the senators and ex-magistrates; the senate still met and retained, in fact enhanced, its powers. Not only that, but the new regime was only too anxious to parade its devotion to the ancestral ways of the Romans and to revive ancient practices and rituals as well as ancient moral standards, as understood by contemporaries.

All this was in a sense a blind to obscure the fact that Augustus and his successors had seized the real power from the people and from the other members of the old republican oligarchy. However, it is also true that much continued as before: the Roman people had even less control; many of the same families were powerful, and the land-owning classes continued to exercise the real power in the state and individuals of that class still commanded the armies and ruled the provinces. There had certainly been nothing to be called a revolution in the modern sense of the word. The main superficial difference was that one or two families could now dominate all the other families of the ruling group, as they could not under the republican system. In fact, however, as the historians make very clear to us, the Emperor had huge power in Rome over his court and over the senators as individuals; he controlled their careers and even their lives; his private wealth was enormous, his public powers extensive, he was the governor of the major military provinces and so the commander of the legions and other forces (*OCD*[3] 1327–9; Zanker 1988).

The Empire (geographic) was still divided into provinces as before, some of them ruled directly by proconsuls, others by the Emperor as a proconsul himself through officers (called *legati*) that he appointed. It is important to note that this body of senior administrators was quite small, one governor with a small staff for each province with no sign of any substantial force of administrators either attached to him or established in the provincial cities. His task was largely to command whatever forces were in the province; to tour the major cities hearing the most important legal cases; and to supervise the collection of taxes. The Emperor did make other appointments from amongst non-senators to manage his own estates and concerns and to organize the provincial finances directly. Essentially it seems that the Romans made no attempt, at least in the early Empire, to run an administration themselves (*OCD*³ 1329–30; Goodman 1997: 100–10).

The Empire as Augustus set it up was astonishingly stable for more than two centuries after his death. There were of course revolts in different areas, and persistent problems, not least with Jews living in Palestine or in the diaspora; but Roman customs and city planning, the Latin language and even Roman gods spread widely in the western half of the Empire and had some influence in the east, where Greek continued to be the most visible culture. Many other cultures (Celtic, Spanish, North African) survived alongside the dominant Greek and Roman ones, but so far as we can tell, there are few occasions when local culture formed the basis for revolt. At the same time, the Roman ruling elite showed few signs of divisions except when the succession to the Empire was unresolved, as it was in 68/9 CE after the death of Nero and 192 CE after the death of Commodus. Throughout these years the Roman Citizenship, which had already been extended to all free men living in Italy by the end of the Republic, continued to be widened, partly through the emigration of citizens into the provinces, partly through grants to auxiliary troops on their discharge from military service, partly by grants to particular individuals or communities. Finally, almost all free inhabitants of the Empire obtained citizenship by decree of the Emperor in 212 CE.

The middle of the third century CE, from 235 CE onwards, saw the collapse of the stability and security that the Empire had previously assured for its inhabitants. Outside peoples broke into the Empire and at least on some occasions defeated the once invincible legions of Rome. Emperors changed with great speed and there were usurpers constantly seeking to overthrow the current ruler; areas of the Empire east and west seem to have escaped from the control of Rome at least for some time and one Emperor suffered the humiliation of being captured by Persians on the eastern frontier. Recent research, however, has become sceptical about the extent and seriousness of this so-called 'crisis': some areas (e.g. Egypt) seem to have escaped any problems and the impact of the troubles seems to have been variable across the Empire. It now seems over-simplistic to call this an 'age of anxiety' and, even if in some respects or some places there were serious problems, to make any causal connections between these troubles and the rise of Christianity.

Certainly, after the 280s CE there was a strong recovery, the restoration of stability and a period of sustained cultural achievement in many spheres. The imperial regime perhaps became more centralized and bureaucratic than before and the Emperor more remote and authoritarian than before. On the other hand, for quite long periods (284–312 CE and the end of the fourth century CE) the Empire was divided and the foundation of a new capital in the east (at Constantinople, modern Istanbul) presaged the permanent division of the Empire into western and eastern halves. The most spectacular change of all (whether or not it derived from the 'crisis' of the third century) was that the Emperor Constantine (312–336 CE) abandoned the policy of supporting paganism against the Christians. It is unknowable whether or when he in truth converted to Christianity himself, but he certainly removed the legal limitations from the Christians and began the process of giving them support and privilege. By the end of the fourth century CE, it was the Christians who were beginning to persecute the pagans rather than *vice versa* (Lane Fox 1986; *RoR* I: 364–88).

Society and economy

The Roman Empire was quite largely, but not entirely, organized by cities. In the east these were often old foundations with a long history of civic life and their own traditions as to how to run themselves and to worship their own gods and goddesses. They were also already accustomed to coping with imperial structures. In some ways, they still organized themselves as free communities within the Roman Empire, electing their own officials, passing their own decrees and holding their own ceremonies and festivals in vigorous competition with one another. Of course, Roman governors and imperial agents set limits to their freedom of action. When the cities conferred honours on their leading citizens, it was often for their services to the city's fostering of a good relationship with the ruling power of Rome (Garnsey and Saller 1987: 34–40).

In at least parts of the west, there was no such tradition of urban life and the Romans responded, in much of Spain, Gaul and the newly conquered areas of central and eastern Europe, by the creation of new cities to serve as administrative and political centres and the base of activities for the local elite class. Both east and west, this process goes hand in hand with the slow spread of Roman citizenship and lesser sets of rights for new foundations. Roman administration was entirely dependent on these local leading men, since the actual imperial administration involved tiny numbers of Roman officials from the senatorial order or from the *equites*, the members of wealthy non-senatorial Roman families. There was almost no Roman bureaucracy to back up the governor and his aides. The local families were responsible for their cities, providing the membership of the councils that ran them, and for the collection of taxes both local and payable to Rome, which they guaranteed from their own resources. They were the crucial link between the governor and the local population. We know them best from eastern decrees voting them honours and listing their services and benefactions to the local communities. We also meet them as local councillors (*decuriones*) in much later imperial legislation.

The importance of cities does not of course mean that most inhabitants of the Empire were dwellers in built-up areas. Only a handful of cities had a huge population (Rome's is estimated at 1 million in the early Empire), and the great bulk of the population of the Empire must have been engaged in food production, often on very small farms, with no chance of doing more than keeping themselves and their children alive, living in the countryside attached to villages or other small settlements. But the 'city' in the ancient sense consisted both of the built-up area and of its associated villages; the free peasants, living in the countryside, had some share in the political rights of the city. Some areas did not fit this pattern; there were large estates owned by the Emperor and run by his officials; and Egypt had its own more centralized system, in which cities developed only slowly.

While food for their own families may have been the dominant interest for many, the archaeology of the Empire leaves no room for doubt that there was a great deal of trading over quite long distances. Partly, this will have been moving basic foodstuffs, either to the great cities, where there must have been major markets, or to compensate for shortages in particular areas, especially grains, which give variable crops from year to year. Luxury goods and precious metals were also moved over long distances, as were slaves for slave-markets. It may be tempting to write off trade as only affecting the wealthy elite; but it is in fact clear that trading activity was profitable and that it played an important part in the economy of the Empire as a whole. Large numbers of people will have made their livelihoods by sea-faring and trading, or supporting these activities. To sum up, the Empire provided some areas of unchanging stability, but also elements of mobility and change. It is clear that the Mediterranean in the context of Roman peace provided the means for regular movements of ships and goods, but also of people. Where the trade went, communities of foreigners began to settle and they took with them their own traditions and religious practices. This movement of population must have been a vital factor in the religious history of antiquity, pagan, Jewish or Christian (Garnsey and Saller 1987: 43).

Throughout the Empire, slavery was legal and widely practised in the Graeco-Roman world at all dates. Many slaves were engaged in household or personal duties and, while great households had large numbers of such retainers, it is clear that slave-owning did extend below the level of the very rich. In some industries, particularly mining and agriculture, there were large numbers of slave-workers living on estates or in barracks; but again quite small farmers often possessed at least one slave to work on the farm. So slavery should be seen as a basic part of the social structure of antiquity and we hear little or nothing of any effective protest against it, either by free observers commenting or by the slaves themselves rebelling.

It is a subject of great debate amongst historians whether or not there is major historical change in the institution over the years of Roman power. One view is that there was an enormous development towards large slave-manned enterprises in the third and second centuries BCE as a result of the expansion of Roman power both east and west. The ruling class made huge profits at this point, which they invested in land; slaves were cheap because of the number of prisoners of war available on the battlefields. Roman landowners thus made their money from agriculture and from other forms of production. It is a corollary of this view that the profits of these enterprises diminished in subsequent centuries as the provision of slaves became more expensive. The decline of slave-holding accompanied the decline of the Empire more generally. All aspects of this narrative, can be challenged; but it is clear that the late republican period saw very large numbers of foreign slaves in Italy and that the prosperity of the land-owning classes was dependent on their labour (Hopkins 1978).

It is characteristic of Roman as opposed to Greek society that the slave of a Roman citizen became a Roman citizen when manumitted; this seems to have happened very frequently for various reasons, but perhaps primarily because the offer of eventual freedom motivated hard work on the part of the slave. The ex-slave himself did not at once enjoy full citizen rights and had to perform some duties for his former owner. But his descendants were full citizens, often taking the name of their ancestor's owner and continuing to be his or his descendants' clients. These rights were somewhat limited by Augustus, evidently aiming to stop the flow of foreigners into the citizenship. All the same, the class of ex-slaves is extremely prominent in our records. They are frequent whenever we have inscribed lists of the members of clubs or of minor local officials; they are frequent among those who record their religious dedications in fulfilment of vows; they appear setting up both their own tombstones and those of their patrons and former masters. The likeliest explanation of their prominence in these contexts is that recording your own activity in this way was an important part of establishing yourself as part of the free Roman community. It is not that they were necessarily more active or pious than citizens with an older claim in the city, but that they had a greater interest in leaving a written record of their new-found status.

Again here, the picture to be found is a mixture of stability of institutions, but mobility of people and ideas. Through force and exploitation, large numbers of people were taken from their homes and resettled in the west, first as slaves and then as freedmen. The evidence bears witness clearly enough to their struggles to be accepted as part of the pattern of Roman life; but they must also have brought with them connections with the culture of their lost homelands and not least their religious traditions.

The legal systems in operation across the Empire were variable: the Romans did not try to impose their own system everywhere and it is therefore wrong to generalize too much in this area. But as time went by, the Roman legal system, which applied to Roman citizens, came to be more influential, especially amongst the well-off. The Roman family placed all legal power in the hands of men, in particular in the hands of one man – the *paterfamilias*, who was the oldest surviving male in direct line of ascent. So a man's *paterfamilias* would normally be his father, unless the father's father (grandfather) was still alive. If your father's father was still alive, then your father was in the same position as you, i.e. under the authority of grandfather. When the *paterfamilias* died, his children, male and female alike, inherited and became independent; but there was a difference: a son would become *paterfamilias* to his own children; a daughter was either subordinate to her husband or had to have a tutor, legally responsible for her, often a brother (Gardner 1986; Garnsey and Saller 1987: 126–47).

These legal rules sound very impracticable to operate, since even adult sons were made dependent on the father: they could not take on obligations or contracts of their own and the father had the right to make them marry or divorce and even (theoretically) to put them to death. In practice perhaps, there were ways in which more freedom of action was possible than the law seemed to allow.

Modern demographic studies also suggest that, given the normal expectation of life in pre-industrial societies, only a small percentage of sons would have had living fathers for much of their adult lives. But the structure of the Roman *familia*, which included not just family members but slaves and freedmen as well, set up the authority of the eldest male over the whole group; and the *familia* was in sense a religious group with its own cultic traditions and responsibilities, also in the charge of the *paterfamilias*.

In the religious life of Rome we find reflected both the authority of the male members of society and the importance of the family as a unit of society. Women are to a certain extent excluded from cult activities, not least in the public arena. There are almost no female priests; women seem to take no part in ritual processions; and only a very small number of the old festivals seem to make any room for them. They appear occasionally firmly placed in a family role as mother or aunt but especially as child-bearer. They are not eligible for any positions of authority. It has been argued that they were formally excluded from taking part in the ritual of sacrifice, but current research challenges this view. To the absence of women from public religious life there was one major exception, though that was a very significant one. The Vestal Virgins, the female priests of the cult of Vesta, were six women recruited as children of six years old and committed to the preservation of their virginity and the service of the goddess for thirty years. They were concerned with a very wide range of cults and rituals and it is clear that the security and health of the whole community depended on the maintenance of their duties. They had to keep the sacred fire on the hearth of Vesta burning at all times. In periods of extreme danger, the city sometimes turned on them and accused them of unchastity, evidently seeking to blame them for the crisis. If found guilty they were buried alive at the limit of the city. In some theories, they were originally the daughters of the old kings of Rome, so that their relationship to the fire and the hearth echoed the duties of the ordinary household. The theories are more attractive than reliable. Important though the Vestals may have been, they were no more than a single exception to the general exclusion of women from public positions of authority or power in the public life of Rome. Some women in the late Republic and early Empire did achieve personal power and influence, but this did not change the basic rules by which social institutions operated (Ross Kraemer 1989; Scheid 1992).

The strength of male domination within the family and the recognition that the family was a powerful social institution throughout this period sets the stage for much of the conflict that arises over religious issues in this period. The customs of paganism essentially reinforced and supported the established order. When religions arose that sought to convert, that is to detach individuals from their family context and make them look to new groups for their religious ideas and practices, conflict was nothing if not predictable.

The religion of the Roman people

Much of the practice of Roman pagan religion seems at first sight deceptively familiar to us: the conceptions were much the same – there were deities, prayers, vows, sacrifices, festivals, sacred persons and sacred spaces. There was a constant need to consult the deities about what should happen or be done and much the same acceptance that prayers might be answered or not answered, but that the pious must maintain their devotion even when the situation was at a low ebb. There was also a distinction between proper devotion to the gods and excessive concern about them, for which the Roman term was superstition. A good deal of the vocabulary is the same too: *superstitio, religio, sacrificium*. But such parallels can be deeply deceptive. It is all too easy to think, without thinking too much, that the Romans had a religion just like modern ones, that we can coin a word 'pagan-*ism*' and it will mean the same as *religio* does for the Romans. But modern religions are systems of belief and systems of morality, while *religio* seems only to concern the institutions and practices of religious life. Not of course that the Romans lacked beliefs or morality, but their religious system did not explicitly connect a set of rituals with particular ideas and beliefs.

This leaves the interpreter with a particularly delicate task to perform. We must not assume that the religion of the Romans occupied the same social or imaginative space in their lives as do modern religions for modern believers. All too often, judgements have been made based on the absences from pagan religion: the absence of guidance and comfort, the absence of spiritual development, the absence of emotional appeal or the absence of a promise of a life after death in Roman *religio*. There is of course some truth in all these observations, but they should be seen as implying not deficiencies in pagan-ism, but either that religion had nothing to do with these particular areas of experience or expectation, or that these expectations did not exist. Still less can we assume that pagans saw these as deficiencies and were therefore awaiting or wanting a new religion. In other words, the interpreter has to respect the otherness of pagan religious life.

The gods and goddesses of the Roman people were literally without number. There were some high gods and goddesses, with complex different functions and rituals – Jupiter, Juno, Apollo, Mars, Diana – who were consistently important in all periods. They were, however, not formed into a pantheon, but they certainly did have areas in which they specialized. Mostly they were shared with other Italian communities, especially Mars who was important throughout Italy, not just where Latin was spoken as by the Romans, but also in the areas of southern Italy where the language was Oscan, as for example by the Samnites. It is clear that these deities were very early on identified with corresponding Greek ones, and these identifications remain constant over time. So far as we can tell, there were few local myths that belonged to the Roman gods and no tradition that they had family relationships like Greek gods. They borrowed Greek stories and it is often these that we meet in later poets.

There were then innumerable grades of lesser gods. Some were specific to one particular place or one natural process, for example the growing of crops. Some were identified with what might be seen as human products, such as Terminus who was the boundary marker of the farm. Specific deities were the patrons of the household and the farm, especially the Lares and Penates, and were worshipped in individual families. Other gods were associated with a specific moment in the calendar of festivals and never occur except in that single annual ritual moment. Some gods seem not to receive worship in the city, but belong to the countryside or the wilds. Some are revealed and defined by a single spot and a single moment in history (Table 7.2 and see *RoR* I: ch. 2.)

New gods were discovered or introduced at most periods of Roman history. Romans had a strong sense of the Roman-ness of the gods of Rome, but no sense that they should constitute a closed list or that newcomers would not be welcome. Gods are sometimes introduced from abroad, as the healing god Aesculapius from Greece in 296 BCE or Magna Mater (Cybele) from Asia Minor in 207 BCE; or tempted out from enemy cities and offered cult by the Romans; or identified with the many personifications recognized by the Romans in the course of the third–second centuries BCE. This preparedness to experiment and innovate continued in the imperial period, not least in the inscribed records, preserved in large quantities, of a priestly group called the Arval Brethren, where we still find a constant process of adaptation and development.

This all raises some problems for the understanding of the whole situation. In many ways the Roman religious tradition was and had to be deeply conservative: it placed huge emphasis on the accurate repetition of religious rituals – even the smallest aberration led to a repeat performance (*instauratio*) of the whole; the rituals were supposed to have been handed by the religious founder Numa Pompilius, the second Roman king (traditional dates 715–673 BCE), to the first of the Roman priests; so the Roman religious order depended fundamentally on the retention of this revealed ritual practice. In many cases, we do not know how

Table 7.2 *Gods and goddesses of the Romans*

Latin name	Greek name	Area of major activity	Roman festival
Aesculapius	Asklepios	Curing of illness	
Apollo	Apollo	Health; prophecy	Ludi Apollinares (July)
Liber Pater	Dionysus/ Bacchus	Wine, ecstatic possession	Liberalia (17 March)
Ceres	Demeter	Corn	Cerialia, Ludi Ceriales (April)
Diana	Artemis	Marginal areas	
Dis Pater	Hades	Death and the underworld	Secular Games, at century-long intervals
Fortuna	Tyche	Fortune, luck	
Juno	Hera	Goddess of the state; protector of childbirth	
Jupiter	Zeus	First god of the state, warfare	Ludi Romani (Sept.), Ludi Plebeii (Nov.)
Magna Mater	Cybele	Fertility; ecstatic dance	Ludi Megalenses (April)
Mars	Ares	War; protection of agriculture	Salian dances (March, October)
Mercury	Hermes	Business, commerce, communications	
Minerva	Athena	Skilled crafts	Quinquatrus (19 March)
Neptune	Poseidon	Water, transport by sea	Neptunalia (23 July)
Quirinus		Identified with Romulus	Quirinalia (17 Feb.)
Saturn	Chronos	?	Saturnalia (17 Dec. etc.)
Venus	Aphrodite	Charm, seduction, mediation between humans and deities	
Vesta	Hestia	The hearth	Vestalia (9 June)
Vulcan	Hephaestus	Metalworking	Volcanalia (23 Aug.)

the apparent opposition between conservatism and innovation was reconciled in practice; but part of the answer must lie in the Romans' tendency to see as the revival of some ancient practice or forgotten deity what we might prefer to call an innovation. Thus, for instance, the Magna Mater, apparently a strange and foreign goddess, turns out in Roman poets to be the goddess of Troy, and so an ancestral power re-accepted. In any case, the reality for the historian must be innovation, even when contemporaries could not or did not accept it as such (North 1976; Beard 1994).

The Romans from a very early date had a rich variety of priestly groups (*collegia* or *sodalitates*) with defined and specialized functions (see Table 7.3). These seem always to have been responsible for choosing their own members and for keeping their own records and lists of members, though their numbers seem to have been fixed and changes were made by state legislation not by the colleges themselves. The duties of the groups varied widely, from officiating or performing at a single occasion in the calendar (as the Luperci on 15 February – the Lupercalia; see Table 7.3) to taking general responsibility for a whole area of religious activity (as the *fetiales* take responsibility for the rituals of declaring war and making treaties). Four groups (*pontifices, augures, quindecimviri, septemviri*) were regarded as the major colleges and their affairs were controlled by law in the late Republic, while others remained under their own control.

All the priests had some ritual duties to perform and it might be assumed that originally they were primarily ritual officers. By the late Republic and later, when we have reliable information, they presided over the rituals and carried out symbolic actions, but had many assistants who carried out the killing of victims and the watching of birds on their behalf. The priests themselves, at least in the most important colleges, were almost all leading men of the political oligarchy; in many cases we know the priesthoods they held – Cicero and Mark Antony were *augures*, Caesar the *pontifex maximus*. Members of the top families of the ruling elite often took these priesthoods at an early age, before they had become senators and started on their political careers.

The role in which we know them best and can see them at work through the surviving sources is not as religious agents, but as religious advisors. The state's main religious agents were in fact the high magistrates (consuls and praetors), who held the sacrifices, formally consulted the gods/goddesses and took vows to them binding the state to future actions. The priests appear as helpers and advisors, dictating the formulas to the magistrate; or else as experts on the religious law (the *ius divinum*). They kept books which contained (or were supposed to contain) the rituals and the precedents from earlier rulings on points of religious

Table 7.3 *Roman priests*

Name	Number	Duties	Other
Augures (Augurs)	3; 9 (300 BCE); 15 (81/80 BCE); 16 (Caesar)	Seeking divine approval or disapproval by divination through birds. Defining sacred space	Hold office even if exiled
Pontifices (Pontiffs)	?; 9 (300 BCE); 15 (81/80 BCE); 16 (Caesar)	Advice to senate/citizens on religious law; responsible for rituals, sacrifices etc.	Head is *pontifex maximus* (after Augustus, always = reigning Emperor)
Virgines vestales (vestals) (members of pontifical college)	6	Cult of Vesta, inc. sacred hearth; ritual duties in many festivals	Full-time presence, special privileges, dress etc; must preserve virginity and sacred flame
Flamines (flamens) (members of pontifical college)	3 major; 12 minor	Priests of specific gods/goddesses	Flamen of Jupiter has special taboos, restrictions. All major flamens have political restrictions
Rex sacrorum (king) (member of pontifical college)	1	Carrying out the religious rituals of the king, after the fall of the monarchy	Prohibited from politics
Quindecimviri sacris faciundis	2; 10 (367 BCE); 15 (81/80 BCE); 16 (Caesar)	Charge of and consultation of the Sibylline Books	Responsibility for foreign cults in Rome
†Septemviri epulones	3 (196 BCE); 7 (81/80 BCE); 10 (Caesar)	Organize ritual meals for gods at Games	
Fetiales	20	Ritual conduct of war and peace	
Salii	2 groups of 12	Warrior-priests, sing and dance for Mars in March and Oct.	
Luperci	2 groups	Ritual run at Lupercalia (15 Feb.)	
Fratres Arvales	12	Ritual for goddess at grove outside Rome	Renewed by Augustus, known from records in the imperial period
Sodales Titii	?	Ritual functions	Little known

*Priests were elected by the Roman people between 104 and 81 BCE and again after 63 BCE.
† This college was introduced in 196 BCE, the only such innovation in the republican period.

law. It was in this capacity that the senate when faced with religious decisions consulted the priests. Even here, however, the final decision lay not with the priests, who only gave a statement as to the rules of the sacred law, but with the senate itself; only they could produce action, even though they followed the priests' advice (Beard and North 1990: 17–31).

The origins of this complex system of priesthood must go back to very early times, but in the form we actually meet it in the second/third centuries BCE it is clear that it expresses in religious terms the dominant theory of the republican era. Power over religious matters in the state was distributed as widely as it could be: the priesthoods themselves had rules that prevented more than one member of any family from joining any particular college and any individual from joining more than one college; meanwhile the religious issues concerning the state were divided between the colleges so that none had a monopoly of advice. It is true that the *pontifex maximus* had great authority, but in no sense was he or anyone else the head of the system. The significance of this system became dramatically apparent as soon as the Republic broke down and the new emperor almost at once appropriated all the priesthoods of any significance and also became permanently the *pontifex maximus* (Gordon 1990).

The ritual of sacrifice is a key to the whole religious order of the Romans. Sacrifices were involved in all the main festivals and occurred before any military action or in any celebration of victory. Images of sacrifice are to be found not just when sacrificial events are recorded as on bas-reliefs, but also when sacrificial instruments are depicted regularly as artistic motifs. The imagery of a monument such as the Ara Pacis – whose primary references are to victory, peace and the glory of the ruling dynasty – is in fact full of sacrificial elements. Meanwhile, under the Empire, the image of the sacrificer, presented as a magistrate with his toga pulled over his head pouring incense from a saucer onto an altar, became virtually the monopoly of the reigning emperor, a familiar expression of his power (Gordon 1990: 202–19).

The ritual was quite elaborate and governed by rules that had to be respected and an order of events to be followed. The victim had to be selected in relation to the god or goddess to whom the sacrifice was to be addressed, in terms of its sex, age and colour; it had to be brought willingly to the altar of the appropriate deity, and sanctified by placing wine and meal on its head (this element was called the immolation (*immolatio*)); a prayer had to be spoken, naming the deity for whom the victim was intended. The killing had to be instantaneous and the monuments show us how in the case of a large victim the animal was stunned by a blow from a mallet, while a knife was simultaneously slipped into its neck. Any struggle or escape by the victim was very unpropitious. The next stage was the extispicy, the inspection of the entrails by a diviner; at its simplest this confirmed that the sacrifice was acceptable, but more explicit interpretations could be sought and given. Then, when the sacrifice had been confirmed, the carcass was elaborately butchered and the entrails returned to the gods, together with their particular share of the meat. The rest was cooked on the spot and eaten at a feast by the participants; alternatively at least some of the meat found its way on to the meat market (*RoR* II: ch. 6).

The Romans are remarkably silent on the significance of this ritual to them. We have no interpretation at all from a believing Roman, only one from a Greek observer and one from a third-century CE Christian convert (Dionysius of Halicarnassus; Arnobius, *Against the Gentiles* Book VII). Some aspects can be clearly established: the victims were almost invariably farm animals, and were normally eaten – and it may be that a sacrifice gave much of the population their only opportunity to eat meat at all. The effect of the sacrifice must have been to identify the separation, but also the interaction, of men and gods – sharing in the ritual and even sharing in the food, but in food carefully divided between them. It is relevant here that the Romans regularly brought out their gods and goddesses from inside their temple-homes and offered them meals. The second clear point is that there were communications between humans and deities implicit in the ritual programme: the behaviour of the victim and the state of its entrails indicated the acceptance or otherwise of the gods; humans communicated verbally by prayer, but also symbolically by the choice of victim, by the conduct of the ritual, by the offering of the deity's share. Finally, the whole procedure was informed by the skills and knowledge of the participants on which success of the transaction depended.

In many ways, the most important evidence we have about the religious history of Rome comes from a set of records, mostly though not exclusively preserved on stone, and mostly dating from the age of the first emperor, Augustus (31 BCE–14 CE). They provide us with quite elaborate calendars of Roman religion, mainly as it was in the republican era, though with some more recent anniversaries noted. These calendars in their fullest versions encode a great deal of information not just about religious festivals, but about the legal status of different days and the organization of time in relation to public life. Days are given individual markings, showing whether the popular assemblies could meet, the courts sit and so on. All these matters fell within the responsibility of the college of *pontifices*. Some sets of calendars also have attached notes explaining the entries and probably derived from the work of Roman scholars of the late republican period.

The calendars seem to reveal a distinction between festivals marked in capital letters and those, seemingly added to the calendar at a later date, in smaller letters. The capital-letter festivals seem to represent some older stage of the calendar's history: they do not, for instance, include the different sets of games (*ludi*) which became important later on and which are mostly recorded as introductions of the republican period; again, the great gods of the later period do not have festivals of their own, whereas many gods and goddesses, later completely obscure, do. So, the calendars provide us with another example of the pattern of slow change and adjustment of Roman religious life, even in a document intended to reflect an unchanging annual rhythm. The copies of this calendar, widely distributed under the rule of Augustus, must show what importance was attached to the religious tradition as a marker of what it was to share a Roman identity, as all Italians were by the late Republic supposed to do, since they had all received the citizenship of Rome during the preceding century (Wallace-Hadrill 1987).

When it comes to the interpretation of these festivals, we have a quite rich tradition to turn to – especially a poetic account of the calendar written by the Augustan poet Ovid (43 BCE–17 CE) and covering the first six months of the year, but also including scattered writings derived from the antiquarian tradition of the late republican period. At one time this body of material was methodically scoured to see whether it could tell us about the earliest periods of Roman history; scholars today often regard that as a misguided search, but use the same material to assess the religious attitudes of the writers' own period. The results are surprising: what characterizes the tradition is the variety of different interpretations of the same festivals that emerges. Ovid in particular is proud to display a number of different views: sometimes he calls them Greek, sometimes Italian, sometimes they contradict one another, sometimes they are compatible. Ovid does not declare his choice among the possibilities he expounds. The view now being argued is that Romans did not expect their festivals to have a fixed canonical meaning. The rituals were thought of as never-changing, but evidently the meaning for those experiencing them was not fixed, at least over any period of time. We can prove this clearly in a handful of cases: for example, the Parilia is celebrated as a festival of shepherds, but later as the Birthday of Rome. If this is right, then the later commentators, like Ovid, are simply echoing the range of possible meanings that participants would have attributed to them at the time.

At least for most of the festivals, there was no established myth or exposition that fixed meanings or even limited the formation of new meanings (Beard 1987).

Divination was an area to which the Romans gave a good deal of attention and on which they prided themselves for their care and concern – at least as remembered from the time of their ancestors. Late republicans tell us that originally nothing was done, no action attempted, without a prior consultation of the gods. Various priests (*haruspices*, *quindecimviri*, *augures*) were involved and could give advice, though in this case as in others, it was the magistrates not the priests who carried out many of the rituals on the state's behalf. At least so far as our records go, the most prominent feature of this activity was not so much foretelling the future as communicating warnings and advice as to which deities needed to be offered sacrifices or piacular offerings. Even if, as is quite possible, our sources deliberately play down the prophetic elements and play up the pious fulfilling of ritual obligations, it was undoubtedly a major part of the diviner's job to identify the deities and the ceremonies needed (MacBain 1982; *RoR* II: ch. 7).

The Romans distinguished between signs for which the diviner asked (*impetrativa*) and those that the gods sent on their own initiative (*oblativa*), warning of dangers to the state. The most distinctive form of warning was the prodigy (*prodigium*), whole lists of which are recorded, particularly by Livy for the middle to late Republic. To judge by these lists, a prodigy could be any event that the Romans judged to be outside the normal course of nature. Some of them we should classify as miraculous (for example the raining from the sky of blood, milk or stones), but many were natural or at least believable events: the birth of deformed animals, the intrusion of wild animals into urban space, lightning striking buildings and even natural disasters such as earthquakes and floods. They do all tend to involve the transgressing of some boundary, seen by the Romans as natural and they all imply the need for placatory action.

The senate was the authority that dealt initially with all prodigies; they sought the advice of the specialists in the particular field and followed their advice. Measures taken to deal with prodigies generally consisted of rituals, but all the priests sometimes produced at least generalized warnings. There was nothing unacceptable about prediction as such, and on formal occasions such as the declaration of a war the diviners (*haruspices*) did predict victory and expansion of the frontiers. The augurs were responsible for consultations either before action in the city or before campaigns and battles. They sought the answer to straightforward questions of consent or denial; without consent the action could not or should not proceed. There was, however, no question of the gods guaranteeing victory or success in advance. It seems a more useful approach to say that the gods and goddesses were seen as a part of the community, sharing in the activities and at least normally supporting the Romans in whatever they did. But their support could not be taken for granted: it was earned by the care and skill of the priests and magistrates. The Romans succeeded because they were so scrupulous in the execution of the *religio* the gods required (Liebeschuetz 1967; Scheid 2001).

In the republican period, there was no question that contemporary human beings could ever cross the dividing line between the human and the divine. Only in the mythical past were they aware of Romans who had become gods. In the very late Republic, this line started to be blurred, as increasingly superhuman honours began to be conceded to the great generals who were conquering the known world – Pompey and, most of all, Caesar. All the same, in Rome itself, living men did not receive divine honours even in the imperial period; but this was not true of the provinces, where the living Emperor could be and was the object of a full cult.

In Rome itself, there was a quite elaborate ceremony that developed in the course of the first century CE, in which, after orations in praise of the dead Emperor and a parade involving the members of the elite of Rome, his body was ritually burned on an elaborate pyre and his soul, symbolized by the flight of an eagle, ascended to the heavens. This ceremony only took place after the senate had recognized that he had become a god; some emperors were never so recognized at all, apparently because the senate disapproved of their rule. In their life-times, a careful ritual distinction was maintained between the dead divine emperors (the *divi*), to whom sacrifice was offered directly, and the living ruler, who received no sacrifices for himself, only for his *genius* (inherited spirit?). The *divi* themselves were very prominent in the space of the city as much of the new temple building was in their honour, including some of the grandest temples ever built in Rome (Price 1984, 1987; *RoR* I: 253).

These careful distinctions applied apparently only inside Rome. Everywhere else, sacrifice took place, though sometimes it is recorded as *for* rather than *to* the Emperor. There was no direction from the centre, so the cult was organized and devised in the various regions and cities of the Empire. But temples to the Emperor, or to him together with the goddess Roma, games in his honour, priests of his cult and so on, all were to be found throughout the provinces. Cities competed in devising festivals in his honour more spectacular than those of their rivals. Statues and images of him abounded in the cities (*RoR* I: 348–63).

There is no doubt that all this is important, but it is also important not to get the new cult out of proportion. The new gods in no sense replaced the old ones: they did not become the recipients of prayers or vows, or play any role in the private lives of the citizens. They did not offer cures or help with childbirth. Their place was in the public arena. It is also a mistake to think that this was in any sense a new religion different from traditional paganism: it fitted neatly into the pattern of the multiplicity of gods and goddesses worshipped in the vast areas of the Empire, offering no challenge to the belief in the old gods. Modern interpreters have often found the whole phenomenon deeply problematic; ancient commentators sometimes found it a suitable subject for wit, but few ancients seem to have protested or refused to participate apart from the Christians, for whom it was used as a test of their commitment.

The Romans had a clear sense that the dead needed to be remembered and honoured and there were annual festivals to achieve this. At the festival of the Parentalia, which occupied nine days in February, offerings were brought by families to the tombs or graves of their families outside the walls of the city. The next day after the end of this period was a time of reunion and reconciliation amongst the living members of the family. It was an obligation of those who inherited an estate to maintain the *sacra* of the family, that is to ensure that the rituals for the ancestors were properly carried out. All this implied that there was a sense of the continuing existence and power of the dead, at least in the mass if not as individual personalities. Families – at least elite families – also kept a memorial of their ancestors in the form of wax masks, likenesses that lived in the atrium of the house; at noble funerals these masks were worn by actors dressed in the triumphal or magisterial robes of the dead man as part of the procession that followed the corpse. Imperial funerals were later modelled on this ritual. This implies that the family as a unit was conceived as developing its glory over time. It does not imply any concern with the individual's survival of death.

In the second festival, in the middle of May, the dead were conceived in a different way and called *lemures* (hostile spirits); the ritual was intended to placate them and keep them away from the living. Ovid in his *Fasti* connects this ritual with the violent death of the founder Remus, killed by his own brother Romulus; this may not be entirely reliable, but it does suggest that the idea underlying the festival concerned the restless ghosts of those who had been abused. At least, the evidence suggests that the two festivals expressed opposite visions of the dead, at peace or not at peace. (For the calendar, Table 7.2; Scullard 1981: 74–6, 118–19.)

It is usually argued that a concern with the individual's survival of death origi-nated in the period of the Empire, partly under the influence of Greek philosophy, partly in the so-called mystery cults and in the context of Christianity. This is all highly questionable in the case of the mysteries. At least in the case of pagans, however, it seems certain that there was a widespread debate of which peo-ple were aware; tombstones quite regularly assert the dead person's rejection of the idea of survival, worked so as to imply that others do believe in it. The dead must in this case have been carrying on an argument familiar among the living. Here as elsewhere we must never forget the limits of the subject under discussion: 'paganism' as such had no explicit beliefs or doctrines that were cod-ified, debated or challenged as such; individuals of course had their thoughts and doubts, but in earlier Rome such ideas would have had no consequences, good or bad, because the question of leaving the religion and joining a different one did not arise. It was only with the emergence of religious alternatives that the nature of such religious issues became transformed.

Religious change in the Roman Empire

In some respects the pagan religion of the Romans can be described, as in parts of the previous section, as if it was a timeless unchanging system. This is to some extent misleading: as we saw above (pp. 342–4), the introduction of new cults was a regular event. More significantly still, the city's whole religious life was in fact adjusted quite dramatically to the realities of power in the state: we know enough, for example, to be certain that the religion of early Rome was built around the position of the king; that in the religion of the late Republic, the location of authority within the system had become fragmented so that power was shared between the senate, the popular assemblies, the many priests of different kinds and the magistrates of the particular year; and that by the end of Augustus' reign (14 CE), there had been such radical restructuring that the Emperor can be said not only to be the head of the state religion but to be reorganizing the whole cult around his house, his family. All religious decisions seem to come to him; he has become almost the only human to be depicted in the act of sacrificing to the gods; and his own status has risen almost to that of a god himself. The Emperor in many ways plays the role of guaranteeing Rome's relationship with the gods that once had been shared between the whole ruling elite. In some ways, this religious transformation is the most important change of all in the period of the establishment of the new monarchy.

These were of course radical changes, and they would have horrified Cicero's contemporaries had they lived to see them; but a far deeper transformation of religious life was in progress that affected not just the public life of the Empire, but the experience of all its inhabitants. The religion of Rome before 1 BCE, like that of many cities of the ancient world, was an inherent part of the city's life and activity. The individual assumed a certain religious place derived from his or her family, trade or dwelling and participated more or less actively in the festivals and ceremonies of the state, many of which had both central and domestic rituals associated with them. It is an oversimplification to say that this was a religion of ritual alone; but the specific nature of the individual's ideas or beliefs was not an issue, as long as he or she conformed to a normal pattern of behaviour. That does not mean that some were not sceptical and others pious; but such variations had no consequences in terms of provoking persecution or of converting from one religion to another. There were no alternative religions to which one could convert at the time.

Four hundred years later, the social location and significance of religion had changed radically. By this time, a range of religions (Judaism, Christianity, paganism), cults (Mithraism, the Isis cult) and sects within religions (Arianism, Donatism, Orthodoxy) were competing for members. The notion of competition should not be exaggerated here: there was a great deal of peaceful co-existence and mutual tolerance as well as conflict. We know of families in which some members were Christian, some pagan; and we know of cities where there seems to have been no real violence for long periods. What is beyond all doubt, how- ever, is that individual members by birth of one religion often converted to a different religion as a result of a change of conviction. The option to do so now existed and individuals – as well as whole families – made use of it. This is logi- cally implied by the fact that Christianity started as a tiny group (in the 30s CE) and grew, very slowly at first, over the course of three centuries. In this period, in each generation the Christian groups must have contained a high percentage of converted pagans. The mixing of paganism and Christianity will have happened both externally between the rival groups and internally in the minds and hearts of the converts (Lane Fox 1986; North 1992; Hopkins 1998; *RoR* I: ch. 6).

One approach to the question, and a traditional one, is implied by concen- trating more on events internal to pagan life and less on the competition with new religions. Two trends have been very much emphasized in the past: the first was the rise to major importance of mystery cults; the second was a supposed trend towards monotheism, which allegedly predisposed pagans to accept a

Judaeo-Christian outlook. Both these ideas have formed part of a coherent scheme of staged development starting from polytheism, passing through mystery cults and belief in the afterlife, then through monotheism to the final culmination in Christianity. The scheme was essentially a (brilliant) nineteenth-century construction and is no longer defended or defensible, though its assumptions may still be powerful.

One problem with the scheme is that the elements that are supposed to represent 'progress' were in fact already present in religious life long before the Roman Empire in both Greece and Italy. The mystery cults, for instance, clearly went back in their basic structure at least to the early Greek society of the sixth century BCE and the idea of monotheism was discussed and highly influential also in early Greek thought. The Stoics believed in worshipping the gods and goddesses, but they saw them only as aspects of the single divine principle, the *logos* – the rationality inherent in the nature of the universe. In some sense, both mystery cult and philosophical ideas about a single deity may be seen as anticipations of what happened in later history, but it is also entirely clear that both could co-exist for very long periods in a pagan and polytheist environment. Neither the existence of the mysteries nor the possibility that all the gods should be seen as a unity proved fatal to pagan practice over hundreds of years. What is needed is a demonstration that some quite new factor arose in the imperial period and that its emergence caused the collapse of polytheistic ideas (Burkert 1987; Turcan 1996; *RoR* II: ch. 12).

The particular mysteries that were most prominent in these years were those of Isis, claiming to have originated in Egypt; of Attis and Cybele from Asia Minor; of Bacchus, immediately from Greece, but originally from further afield; and of Mithras from Persia. In every case, there is some substance in the claimed origin, but also a substratum of the older Greek mysteries. Perhaps, the eastern connections resulted from real contacts with the east or easterners; perhaps, it was no more than a veneer of easternness, derived from reading or learning. Mysterious wisdom was known to be a possession of the ancient eastern civilizations and the cults must have derived prestige from the association as well as natural supporters among the descendants of easterners living in the west. The cults did have some elements in common: they all had a mystery only revealed to the initiate at a ceremony; they all seem to have offered a personal experience of the divine and some contact with an experience of symbolic death and rebirth. But, beyond these basic points, they had very different ideas and systems (Burkert 1987).

The cult of Mithras, for instance, excluded women from its groups, whereas the other cults did not. It also had its own special appeal to two groups of people: soldiers in the frontier zones and freedmen in Rome and in Ostia (the port of Rome). On the other hand, there is little evidence that it had any importance among the elite groups of Rome, even though leading Romans played their parts in the cult when on the frontiers. The main evidence about the cult's character has to be inferred from the decoration and imagery of Mithraic shrines or caves, which were the characteristic meeting-places of the cult, where cult-meals were probably held in honour of the god. There is also a plentiful and varied tradition of sculpture, including the scene of bull-slaying by Mithras himself. There is hardly any written evidence about the ideas of the cult's adherents from their own point of view; and even Christian writers, so loquacious about paganism in other contexts, tell us little in this case. We know that there was an elaborately structured system of grades, so that the individual group member would have undergone a series of initiations starting out under the grade of 'raven' and moving up through five grades ('male bride', 'soldier', 'lion', 'Persian', 'sun-runner') to become finally a 'father'. Each of these grades was under the protection of a planet, including the sun and moon, starting from Mercury and finishing with Saturn. These grades, and the movements of individuals through them, must have been controlled by theories about the universe and about the connections between stars and human experience on the earth. The individual ascent through the seven grades must have reflected the soul's progress through the stars. It seems clear that they were combining in a very original way the old idea of the mystery cult and up-to-date ideas about the stars and the universe. The details are all very controversial and it is far from certain that the same theory was being applied in all the parts of the Empire (Beck 1988; Gordon 1996).

The Isis cult is in marked contrast in many respects. Women played a major role, though perhaps not so dominant a role as has sometimes been suggested. The goddess and her rituals were widely disseminated throughout the Empire and she had many public temples, festivals and processions in her honour, often as part of the official religion of the cities. Isis herself claimed that she was the queen above all and that she incorporated all the other deities of the Roman world. The evidence of the cult is plentiful, including a whole temple and its ritual equipment preserved at Pompeii. In the case of Isis, the mysteries cannot have been such a central element of the cult as they were in Mithraism; it is hard to judge even whether they were the highest aspiration of the goddess' most devoted worshippers. We have many inscriptions recording individual devotion to the cult, but only one sustained text giving an account of an initiation; that text is the last section (Book XI) of Apuleius' famous novel *The Golden Ass*. The hero Lucius, who has spent most of the novel bewitched into being an ass, is finally saved by the goddess and in his gratitude seeks initiation into her mysteries. Apuleius does no more than hint at the rewards on offer to the initiate: Lucius' everyday life is certainly transformed – he moves to Rome, becomes a successful lawyer and joins an Isiac group in their devotions. The novel is discreet, witty and even teasing, but it presupposes a rich religious life based on the group of initiates and a priest who offers spiritual guidance. For Lucius at least, his gratitude to the goddess, guided by her own appearance in his dreams, demands his passionate devotion to her worship (Burkert 1987; *RoR* II: 12.4).

In many ways, the most paradoxical cult of all was that of Attis, the shepherdboy-god from Asia Minor. He was part of the circle of Cybele, the Great Mother Goddess, who loved him and mourned his loss. She was identified with the Magna Mater, to whom the Romans built a temple after the Hannibalic War (218–201 BCE); we know from a cache of statuettes under the platform of the temple that Attis came to Rome at the same time as the Magna Mater. The mystery cult of Attis seems, therefore, to have developed under the protection of the Roman state itself, at the very moment when the Bacchic cult was being destroyed by the same authorities. Attis in myth was the beloved of the goddess, and died as a result of his love. He was, at one stage of the modern debate, thought to be a clear example of the god whose death and rebirth symbolically foreshadowed the death and rebirth of his mortal followers. The evidence for this seductive interpretation is all too flimsy: in one version of the myth, the goddess in grief at Attis' death begs Jupiter to save him for her; Jupiter does what he can, but the result of his efforts is that Attis remains incorruptible but incapable of movement – except that he can wiggle his little finger. The myth is not a guarantee of afterlife, but a parable about the limitation even of the gods' control over fate (Sfameni Gasparro 1985; *OCD*[3] 213).

In all these cases, it is far from clear whether the initiate received benefits in this world or the next or both; also, whether the afterlife was an important issue for the cults' adherents. If these cults did provide a bridge from civic religion to new forms of religion, as has often been thought, they do so not so much in their doctrines, or in the quality of religious experience, as in their structure. They consisted of people who had chosen membership of this particular group and undergone a ritual that provided a link between the members of the group. But the commitment seems less than total and there is no real sign that the initiates cut themselves off from the worship of other gods. To judge by the evidence of archaeology, the Mithraists at least allowed other gods within their sanctuaries. The people of the mysteries had some quality of experience in common, but they were far from being a people apart.

The beginning point and the end point of the slow process of religious change are both clear. The journey between them is too badly documented for there to be much confidence in any detailed account of what was happening. The easy story would be to see the arrival of Christianity as the sole cause of the change; but in fact there are many other factors to be assessed. First, in many cities of the diaspora there was a Jewish community before the time of Christianity, which would already have offered an alternative religion; it is true that there is no evidence that these Jewish groups sought to make full converts, but all the same Gentiles sometimes attached themselves voluntarily to Jewish synagogues. Secondly, amongst pagans as well there were developments towards at least an elective element in their religious lives. Again long before the emergence of Christianity, the Bacchic cult in Italy was condemned by the senate and persecuted: the surviving decree shows that it was the articulated structure of the Bacchic cells that the senate was set to destroy. The Bacchic cult did not apparently involve such a complete rupture from pagan practice as did Christianity two or three centuries later. But it is sobering to reflect that the treatment of the Bacchists had in fact been more not less violent and methodical than the later persecution of Christians (Goodman 1994; *RoR* I: 91–8).

Christianity emerged into the awareness of pagans as a variant version of Judaism, not as a new religion at all, and it is probable that in its very early days there was much confusion as a result. What is more, the earliest followers of Christ did not form a single coherent group; it took many decades, even centuries, to create a unified orthodoxy, with a single church organization and doctrine, and orthodoxy at all dates had variant views to contend with. Already in the Acts of the Apostles, a central theme is the potential split between those (apparently based in Jerusalem) who wished to keep the new movement within Judaism and those who wished it to expand to include Gentile converts. There were, of course, fundamental differences between Christians and traditional Jews, but it is hardly surprising if pagans took time to understand these (Meeks 1983; Kyrtatas 1987).

One fundamental difference was that, unlike the Christians, the Jews living in the cities of the Roman Empire maintained their own traditions very much as did other ethnic groups, Egyptians, Syrians in the west or Italians in the east. Their religious activities may have attracted others to join with their practices, but the

Jews seem not to have sought converts, while joining Egyptians or Syrians did not involve abandoning the traditions of your own city or community. Another difference that developed quite quickly was that those who joined the Christians acquired a special name: Jews were Jews because their ancestors were Jews; most Christians were Christians because they had decided to be. It is important to see that this was a critical moment of change. However, there were similarities as well: both Jews and Christians rejected the gods – all the gods. For this reason, Christians in the east were for a time called simply 'atheists'. For different reasons, neither group would participate in pagan sacrifices. On the other hand, Gentile Christians did not maintain the dietary rules or the practice of ritual circumcision that made Jewish customs such a talking-point among hostile pagans.

From a pagan point of view these developments have quite dramatic implications. For the first time pagans as such found themselves under serious challenge. Traditionally, the pagans have been seen as very ill-equipped to face such a challenge, because they were supposedly facing a crisis caused by their religion's long slow decline into inanition. Modern views have on the contrary detected major areas of vigorous pagan activity: partly, these are in the area of the mystery cults and the development of Mithraism; partly, it is in the life of the great oracles in the east, where records of them survive long into the imperial centuries, implying a commitment nobody would have expected; partly, it is the reformation of pagan thoughts and pagan philosophy in the third and fourth centuries. What we can see clearly is that the opposition between pagans and new forms of religion slowly forced the pagans to redefine their own position. They became by force of circumstances a single religion and an alternative to Christianity; this must be the process by which 'pagan-ism' was finally invented.

Part of that process of redefinition was the persecution of the Christians, the parading of those who chose to deviate from the pagan version of civic life. Our information about this comes mostly from later Christian sources, especially martyr-acts, which had a specific role in the memorializing of its saintly heroes and heroines by the later church. These are not the best sources for establishing what really happened. But we have enough information to see that there were persecutions and that an apparatus of suppression did exist; but it is also clear that this was employed only very erratically and that it was no part either of the imperial authorities' purpose or of the real activity of governors to conduct a methodical suppression by searching out the Christian groups and eliminating their activities. The Emperor Trajan declared precisely that they should *not* be sought out, but should be brought to trial only if denounced by persons who declared their names and hence took responsibility for the denunciation. This policy will have meant that persecution took place only when Christians came into conflict with the civic authorities. Only in the third century CE did persecutions begin to take on a more imperial aspect and even then it is not clear how far this was a considered decision (*RoR* I: 236–44).

The key to understanding the progress of Christianity may well lie in events in the cities large and small throughout the Empire. It is clear that cities had come to contain groups both of Jews and of Christians who were at odds with the sacrificial cult that lay at the centre of pagan civic religion. We get glimpses of this plurality, but we have all too little information of how it worked in practice. Did the Jews and Christians attend the regular pagan festivals and thus reconcile themselves formally with pagan opinion? Or did they simply absent themselves and live their own separate lives? Both groups seem to have contained members who were socially and economically successful; at least, it is certain that not all their members were drawn from the excluded groups of society and some scholars have argued that from the beginning they included members of high status. It is very hard to maintain that they were secret and separate.

In the case of Jewish communities in particular, there is some evidence of visible separateness. In some cities, synagogues were built in central, even prominent, sites. Those who attended them must have been known to the community as a whole. These seem to have included pagans, who had not converted but were informally attached to the communities, and sometimes even Christians – to judge by the attacks on their backsliding by their bishops. An inscription from Aphrodisias, a notable city in Asia Minor near the west coast of Turkey, shows us a situation of a Jewish community which seems to be far more integrated into civic life than we would have predicted. It is evidently maintaining at least some parts of a Jewish tradition; but it has as patrons and supporters a number of local people, some of whom declare that they occupy prominent positions in the city itself, serving on the city's council. The implication seems to be that this community at least was thoroughly accepted and even supported at an almost official level (Lieu et al. 1992: 19–21).

It may be argued that the crucial change should be looked for not simply at the level of religion in the cities, but more generally in the life of the cities themselves and their relationship to the whole Empire. Pagan religion was a matter of large numbers of local traditions – rituals, festivals, myths, gods and goddesses – which overlapped with those of their neighbours but thrived on local enthusiasm and commitment. Like everything else in the Empire, this activity depended heavily on the commitment of the local wealthy classes; innumerable inscriptions from the early imperial period show how they were responsible for funding and organizing the religious life of their co-citizens.

In the later period, particularly during and after the third-century troubles (235–84 CE, see pp. 335–6 above), the flow of information about such benefactions comes to an end. There are no more inscriptions from the cities of the Empire detailing the devotion of the civic elites to the cities in which they lived. At the same time, legal sources contain much material on the controversial issue of excuses for avoiding local duties. What this suggests is that local elites, whose members had once been committed to their own communities, were now avoiding these local obligations and devoting themselves instead to the service of the central government and its bureaucracy. This change of attitude was not at all the result of events in the religious sphere, but it would have had dramatic effects on the religious sphere. If the local backers of pagan activity were abandoning it and transferring their enthusiasms elsewhere, then it would not be surprising if the effect was to encourage Christian groups to become more active and to find it easier to make converts. This is no more than one possible theory, but it does have suggestive power and needs to be tested in terms of the surviving record in individual cities and communities (Rives 1995).

Note

1. The term 'pagan' (*paganus*) originally meant country-dweller, rustic, and was apparently used by the early Christians as an unfriendly term for those who had persisted in the old pre-Christian religious ways. We do not know where or why this usage began, but it was adopted by modern writers and is today the established usage in the writing of ancient history. Some contemporary writers have preferred to use 'polytheism' and 'polytheist'; but, at least when writing about earlier periods, this is definitely misleading, since it implies that the Romans thought that having many gods was what defined their religion. They did not. They believed that there were many different gods and goddesses and that all sensible people from all over the world recognized that simple fact. Only when in competition with Jews and Christians in late antiquity, were they forced to acknowledge that the number of gods had become a major issue of contention. In many other contexts today, the word 'pagan' either has become a pejorative term for religions of which the speaker disapproves, or else refers to religious movements of the current age which are distinct from, even if in some way similar to, the religions of the Graeco-Roman world. Perhaps a replacement of the term would be desirable

for these reasons, but none is available at the moment that would not be more misleading still.

Bibliography

Beard, M. 1986. Cicero and divination: the formation of a Latin discourse. *Journal of Roman Studies* 76: 33–46.

1987. A complex of times: no more sheep on Romulus' birthday. *Proceedings of the Cambridge Philological Society* 213, n.s. 33: 1–15.

1994. The Roman and the foreign: the cult of the 'Great Mother' in imperial Rome. In N. Thomas and C. Humphrey (eds.), *Shamanism, History and the State*, pp. 164–9. Ann Arbor, MI.

Beard, M. and M. H. Crawford 1999. *Rome in the Late Republic: problems and interpretations.* 2nd edn, London.

Beard, M. and J. A. North (eds.) 1990. *Pagan priests.* London:

Beard, M., J. A. North and S. R. F. Price 1998. *Religions of Rome.* 2 vols., Cambridge (= *RoR* I and II). Historical account in vol. I; collected sources in vol. II. Currently the authoritative account in English.

Beck, R. 1982. Mithraism since Franz Cumont. In H. Temporini and W. Haase (eds.), *Aufstieg und Niedergang der römischen Welt.* Berlin: pp. 2002–2115.

1988. *Planetary gods and planetary orders in the mysteries of Mithras.* Études Préliminaires aux Religions Orientales 109. Leiden.

Belier, W. W. 1991. *Decayed gods: origin and development of Georges Dumézil's idéologie tripartite'.* Leiden.

Burkert, W. 1987. *Ancient mystery cults.* Cambridge, MA and London. The standard account, emphasising continuity with the Greeks.

Cornell, T. J. 1995. *The beginnings of Rome: Italy and Rome from the Bronze Age to the Punic Wars (c. 1000–264 BC).* London.

Davies, J. P. 2004. *Rome's religious history: Livy, Tacitus and Ammianus on their gods.* Cambridge.

Dumézil, G. 1970. *Archaic Roman religion.* Chicago.

Feeney, D. 1998. *Literature and religion at Rome: cultures, contexts and beliefs.* Cambridge. A pioneering account of the relation of ritual to Roman poetry.

Gardner, J. F. 1986. *Women in Roman law and society.* London and Sydney.

Garnsey, P. and R. Saller 1987. *The Roman Empire: economy, society and culture.* London.

Goodman, M. 1992. Jewish proselytizing in the first century. In Lieu, North and Rajak 1992: 53–78.

1994. *Mission and conversion.* Oxford.

1997. *The Roman world, 44 BC–AD 180.* London and New York.

Gordon, R. 1980. Reality, evocation and boundary in the mysteries of Mithras. *Journal of Mithraic Studies* 3: 19–99; repr. in Gordon 1996.

1990. The Roman Empire. In Beard and North 1990: 177–255.

1996. *Image and value in the Graeco-Roman world.* Aldershot and Brookfield, VT.

Gradel, I. 2002. *Emperor worship and Roman religion.* Oxford.

Hopkins, M. K. 1978. *Conquerors and slaves.* Cambridge.

1998. Christian number and its implications. *Journal of Early Christian Studies* 6.2: 185–226.

1999. *A world full of gods: pagans, Jews and Christians in the Roman Empire.* London.

Lane Fox, R. 1986. *Pagans and Christians.* Harmondsworth and New York.

Kraemer, R. S. 1989. *Her share of the blessings: women's religions among Pagans, Jews and Christians in the Greco-Roman world.* New York and Oxford. A wide-ranging study of the role of women in ancient religious life.

Kyrtatas, D. J. 1987. *The social structure of the early Christian communities.* London and New York. An important work on early Christianity.

Liebeschuetz, J. H. W. G. 1967. *Continuity and change in Roman religion.* Oxford.

Lieu, J., J. North and T. Rajak (eds.) 1992. *The Jews among pagans and Christians in the Roman Empire.* London and New York.

MacBain B. 1982. *Prodigy and expiation: a study in religion and politics in Republican Rome.* Collection Latomus 177. Brussels.

Meeks, W. A. 1983. *The first urban Christians: the social world of the Apostle Paul.* New Haven and London:

Miles, G. B. 1995. *Livy: reconstructing early Rome.* Ithaca, NY and London.

North, J. A. 1976. Conservatism and change in Roman Religion. *Papers of the British School in Rome* 44: 1–12.

1990. Diviners and divination at Rome. In Beard and North 1990: 51–71.

1992. The development of religious pluralism. In Lieu, North and Rajak 1992: 174–93.

1997. The religion of Rome from monarchy to principate. In M. Bentley (ed.), *Companion to historiography.* London and New York, pp. 57–68

2000. *Roman religion.* Greece and Rome, New Surveys in the Classics 30. Oxford.

Oxford Classical Dictionary 1996, ed. S. Hornblower and A. Spawforth. 3rd edn, Oxford and New York (= *OCD³*).

Price, S. R. F. 1984. *Rituals and power: the Roman imperial cult in Asia Minor*. Cambridge. The best modern treatment of the worship of emperors.

1987. From noble funerals to divine cult: the consecration of Roman Emperors. In D. Cannadine and S. Price (eds.), *Rituals of royalty: power and ceremonial in traditional societies*. Cambridge, 56–105.

Rives, J. B. 1995. *Religion and authority in Roman Carthage from Augustus to Constantine*. Oxford.

Scheid, J. 1987. Polytheism impossible; or, the empty gods: reasons behind a void in the history of Roman religion. In F. Schmidt (ed.), *The inconceivable polytheism*. History and Anthropology 3. Paris, pp. 303–25.

1992. The religious roles of Roman women. In P. Schmitt Pantel (ed.), *A history of women: from ancient goddesses to Christian saints*. Cambridge, MA, pp. 377–408.

2001. *Religion et piété à Rome*. Paris. An original and thoughtful essay on the character of Roman religious life.

2003. *An introduction to Roman religion* (English translation by Janet Lloyd). Edinburgh.

Schultz, C. E. 2006. *Woman's religious activity in the Roman Republic*. Chapel Hill, NC.

Scullard, H. H. 1981. *Festivals and ceremonies of the Roman Republic*. London.

Sfameni Gasparro, G. 1985. *Soteriology and mystic aspects in the cult of Cybele and Attis*. EPRO 91. Leiden.

Turcan, R. 1996. *The cults of the Roman Empire*. Oxford.

Wallace-Hadrill, A. 1987. Time for Augustus: Ovid, Augustus and the *Fasti*. In M. Whitby et al. (eds.), *Homo Viator: classical essays for John Bramble*. Bristol and Oak Park, IL, pp. 221–30.

Warde Fowler, W. 1911. *The religious experience of the Roman people from the earliest times to the Age of Augustus*. London. Still interesting as a turning point in thought on the subject.

Wissowa, G. 1912. *Religion und Kultus der Römer*. Handbuch der Altertumswissenschaft v.4. 2nd edn, Munich. Not replaced as a hand-book on the details of the Roman state religion, but only available in German.

Zanker, P. 1988. *The power of images in the Age of Augustus*. Ann Arbor, MI. Creative work on the relation of art, literature and religion in the making of the Augustan regime.

8 Ancient Europe

HILDA ELLIS DAVIDSON

There was a rich diversity of religious beliefs throughout ancient Europe, the land-mass stretching from the Atlantic Ocean to the mountains of the Caucasus. The peoples about whose beliefs and religious practices we know the most are the Greeks and Romans in southern Europe, but we also have some knowledge of the early religion of the Celtic and Germanic peoples in the north-west. They were made up of many separate tribes, and some penetrated at various times into southern and eastern Europe. Their religion was not centrally organized, and was preserved in oral tradition, but archaeology and the study of later literature have added considerably to our knowledge.

Early Europe

The inhabitants of Europe whom the Romans viewed as barbarians consisted of small tribal groups, ruled by petty kings and warrior leaders. Consequently their history is confused and complicated, and there were no major religious centres in pre-Roman times influencing large areas of Europe. The tribes fought with one another, made alliances and formed larger groups from time to time, and a number came under the domination of Rome. When the Roman Empire collapsed there was considerable movement of peoples, and larger permanent kingdoms were established (Map 8.1). Some Germanic tribes penetrated into Italy, and Rome itself was taken over in the last part of the fifth century, to be ruled by Theodoric the Ostrogoth from 493 to 526. The Franks obtained possession of Gaul, and the Anglo-Saxons settled in England. Most of the Celtic peoples in continental Europe, in Gaul and in the west and north of the British Isles, were converted to Christianity by the fifth century CE, and the Germanic kingdoms a little later, but in the north the conversion of Scandinavia was not complete until well after 1000 CE.

Table 8.1 *Chronology of ancient Europe*

End of major Ice Age in northern Europe	*c.* 9000 BCE
Raising of Stonehenge	*c.* 2800
Raising of Avebury	*c.* 2500
Bronze Age in northern Europe	*c.* 1500–500
Flag Fen	*c.* 1350–950
Roman invasion of England	*c.* 43 CE
Patrick's mission to Ireland	*c.* 456
Period of Germanic expansion (Migration Period)	third to sixth centuries
Settlement of Anglo-Saxons in England	from *c.* 400
Augustine brings Christianity to Kent	597
Sutton Hoo ship burial	*c.* 625
Oseberg ship burial	*c.* 835
Period of Viking expansion (Viking Age)	*c.* 780–1070
Settlement of Iceland	from 870
Anskar's mission to Denmark	849
Olaf Tryggvason begins conversion of Norway	995
Christianity accepted in Iceland	1000

In northern and eastern Europe the Finns, Balts and Slavs have left little record of their early religious beliefs and myths. Some figures of Slav gods have survived, and there is evidence for worship of deities and spirits associated with the natural world before the introduction of Christianity into Russia in the tenth century. There is much to be learned from folksongs, oral poetry, chants recorded at local ceremonies and descriptions of fertility customs in Russia and among the people of the Caucasus such as the Ossetes. Records survive of the religion of the Old Prussians, a Baltic people conquered in the thirteenth century by the Teutonic Knights, and of pre-Christian traditions among the Saami people of Lapland, some of whom were not converted until the eighteenth century. However, the material as a whole is fragmentary, with little definite recording of myths, and so is hard to interpret with confidence.

Scandinavian mythology

The richest body of evidence comes from Scandinavia and above all from Iceland, settled from Norway in the late ninth century CE. Christianity was not formally accepted there until 1000 CE, and the Icelanders took great pride in their history

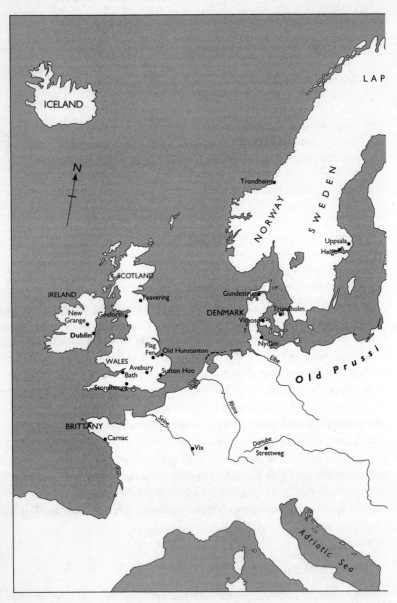

Map 8.1. Northern Europe (showing places mentioned in text).

Map 8.1. (*cont.*)

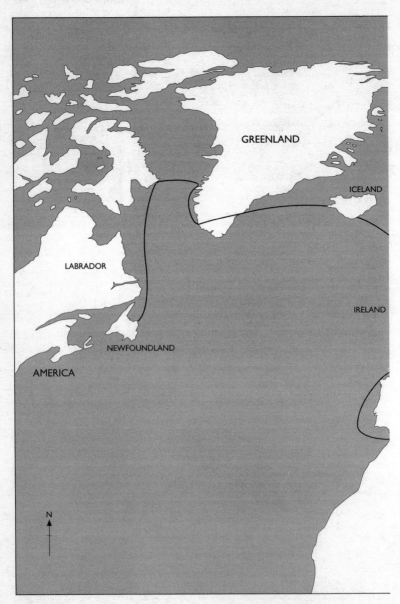

Map 8.2. Viking expeditions: trading, raiding, exploration and some settlement, eighth to eleventh centuries CE.

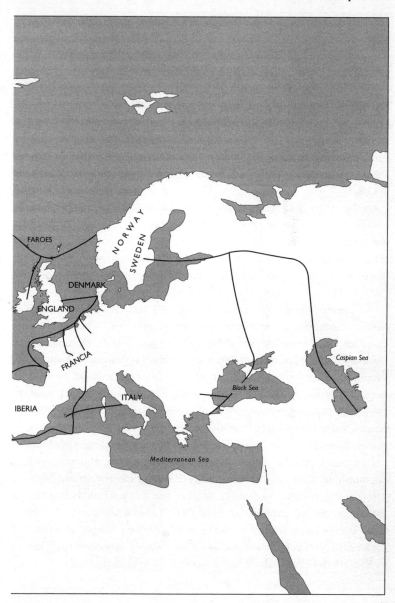

Map 8.2. *(cont.)*

and traditions. Myths, legends, poems and accounts of the independent state which they founded were recorded as soon as they learned to write following their conversion, and they even preserved some mythological poetry from the pre-Christian period. Moreover a gifted writer, Snorri Sturluson, who although a Christian was neither a monk nor a cleric, set out to record mythological lore in the early thirteenth century, since he feared that the old poetry would cease to be understood. He wrote with wit, eloquence and enthusiasm, quoting many passages from early poems, so that young poets could be familiar with the old tales and understand mythological allusions. Snorri was both a historian and a poet, although also an active participant in politics, which resulted in his assassination in 1241.

Another writer in Denmark at about the same time as Snorri was the learned Saxo Grammaticus, writing in Latin in an elaborate style. Although he had little sympathy with the old beliefs, he used some of the tales to enrich his account of the early history of the Danes, and to illustrate his ideas about the duties of kingship. He was also a gifted story-teller, and has preserved some accounts of Otherworld adventures and encounters with supernatural beings.

We have versions of many early myths from Old Norse literature, mostly composed in Iceland. Some short poems go back to the pre-Christian period, although their complex style makes them difficult to interpret. These were composed by Icelandic *skalds* (professsional poets), many of whose names we know. A different style of poetry is preserved in the manuscript collection of poems from the *Codex Regius*, known as the *Poetic* or *Elder Edda* to distinguish it from the *Prose Edda* of Snorri Sturluson. These are either narrative or riddling dialogue poems, and they are divided into two sections, one on gods and the other on heroes. There are later prose additions by an editor, but the identity of editor and poets remains unknown. The manuscript was written in the thirteenth century, but individual poems clearly vary in date. One of the most important, *Völuspá*, telling of the creation and destruction of the world of gods and humankind, is thought to have been composed about 1000 CE. Some additional information about the gods is found in the opening section of *Heimskringla*, an account of the kings of Norway by Snorri Sturluson. There are also legendary sagas known as 'Sagas of Old Times', which contain some pre-Christian material.

Germans and Celts

The Scandinavians were related to the Germanic peoples from central Europe, who were neighbours of the Celts. In the first century CE, Celts and Germans were speaking languages related to those of a number of other peoples in Europe and part of Asia, extending as far as India. These had all developed from an earlier language which we call Indo-European, spoken in Eurasia about 6000 years ago (Table 8.2). There is still vigorous debate as to the Indo-European homeland, and claims have been made for Anatolia, the Pontic-Caspian steppe and southern Russia, while there is as yet no final agreement as to how Indo-European developed into so many later languages, including Latin, Slavonic, Iranian and Sanskrit, as well as those of the Celtic and Germanic groups. The question is relevant for the study of early religions in Europe, since it has been claimed that some of the widespread myths go back to Indo-European times.

The Celtic peoples occupied large areas of central and western Europe from about the fifth century BCE, and moved as far east as Galatia (Map 8.3). Although no Celtic literature survives from continental Europe, there is a rich body of early poetry and prose from Ireland and some from Wales which, although composed in Christian times, preserves some early myths and traditions. There is also much splendid art in stone and metal from Celtic areas surviving from pre-Roman times. While the main structure of the early mythology of the Celtic and Germanic peoples in Europe has been lost, much scholarly work on literary texts from the British Isles has thrown light on individual myths and early gods and goddesses. Moreover, discoveries made in the course of the twentieth century archaeology have led to a fuller understanding of cults and symbols.

Much of our knowledge comes from provinces taken over by the Romans, who often gave local deities Roman names, and set up altars or memorials to them. This happened in England after it became a Roman province in the first century CE. Later it became part of the Germanic world when the Anglo-Saxons settled there, but since the settlers soon adopted Christianity little of their earlier religious beliefs has been recorded. For Germanic religion in central Europe we rely chiefly on Roman writers such as Tacitus, Julius Caesar and Dio Cassius. They were accepted as reliable evidence in the eighteenth and nineteenth centuries, but are now subject to question, since it is felt that we may have been misled into seeing both Celtic and Germanic religion through Roman eyes. The Romans tended to assume that each deity concentrated on one particular field, such as warfare or fertility, but those of the Celts and Germans appear to have been more complex in their nature than Roman writers indicated.

As archaeological discoveries increased, certain types of art in early Europe came to be identified as Celtic. The so-called Hallstatt culture flourished about

Table 8.2 *Development of Indo-European language*

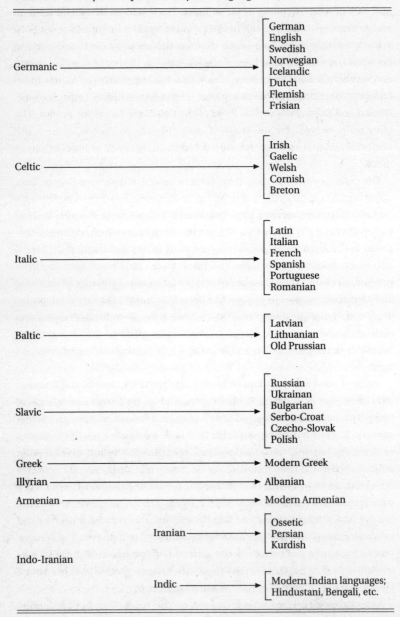

Germanic	German English Swedish Norwegian Icelandic Dutch Flemish Frisian
Celtic	Irish Gaelic Welsh Cornish Breton
Italic	Latin Italian French Spanish Portuguese Romanian
Baltic	Latvian Lithuanian Old Prussian
Slavic	Russian Ukrainan Bulgarian Serbo-Croat Czecho-Slovak Polish
Greek	Modern Greek
Illyrian	Albanian
Armenian	Modern Armenian
Indo-Iranian — Iranian	Ossetic Persian Kurdish
Indo-Iranian — Indic	Modern Indian languages; Hindustani, Bengali, etc.

the eighth century BCE, and was held to be Celtic after the huge cemetery by Lake Hallstatt was excavated in 1846. Later Celtic art was defined as La Tène, after a site in Switzerland dating from about 100 BCE, where many precious objects had been thrown into the water. The La Tène period is held to have begun about 500 BCE, when a new style of winding, twisting patterns appeared on stone and metalwork. Foliage, spirals and tendrils were linked with Mediterranean motifs, and there was powerful, realistic treatment of animals and birds. This style continued to develop in Christian art in Celtic areas of the British Isles, and is found on carved stone crosses and in illuminated manuscripts.

Discovery of the mythology

When Jakob Grimm wrote his preface to *Deutsche Mythologie* in 1844, he expressed regret that so little work had been done on Celtic material. Irish manuscripts were then virtually inaccessible to scholars, and tales from the Irish sagas and from Wales and Scotland were seen as rude and barbaric, even though a romantic interest in the druids developed in the eighteenth century. However, by the early years of the twentieth century the early literature of Ireland was viewed differently, as the result of the work of a group of writers which included the poet Yeats, and the brilliant translations of many tales and legends by Lady Gregory. An interest in early myths now became part of the national movement for the independence of Ireland.

Similarly a new interest in the Germanic past was kindled in the nineteenth century as a result of the work of the Grimm brothers, who began collecting folk-lore and folktales, believing that these preserved traces of pre-Christian myths and legends. Jakob Grimm continued to work on early language, folklore and beliefs all his life, and his four volumes on Germanic mythology were produced between 1883 and 1888. He used little Scandinavian material, except for com-parison, since he felt that this was already accessible to scholars. Serious study of early religion in Scandinavia had begun in France and England a century ear-lier, when the Danish king Christian VII engaged the French scholar Mallet to write a history of Denmark in his own language. Mallet's introduction contained an account of 'the primitive worship of the northern nations', and in 1770 an English translation of this was made by Bishop Percy with his own notes and commentary. He had already published 'Five pieces of Runic poetry translated from the Icelandic language' in 1768. About the same time the poet Thomas Gray composed two verse translations of Old Icelandic poems, *The fatal sisters*

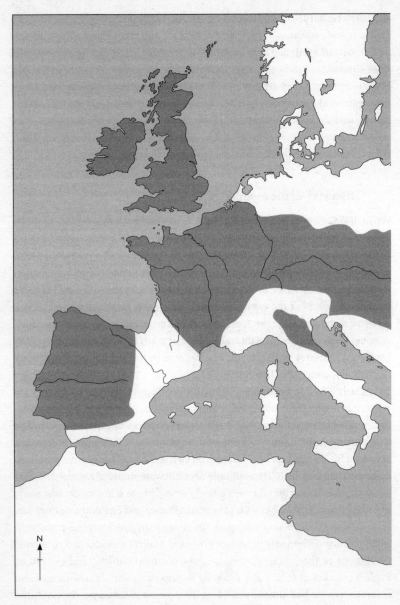

Map 8.3. Expansion of Celtic peoples by the third to fourth centuries BCE.

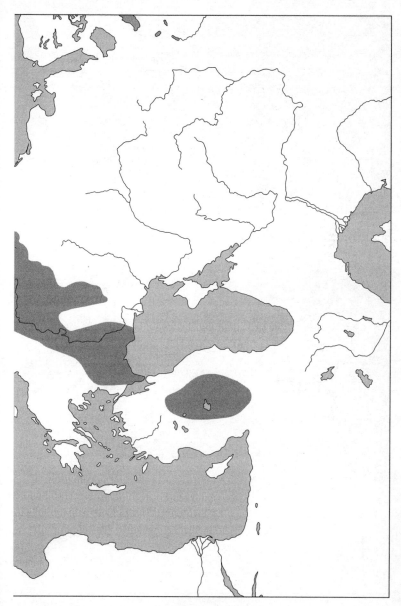

Map 8.3. (*cont.*).

Map 8.4. Expansion of Germanic peoples, first to fifth centuries CE.

Finns

Balts

Slavs

Langobards

Goths

r o g o t h s

Map 8.4. (*cont.*).

and *The descent of Odin*, although his comments show that he knew little of the mythological background.

In the course of the nineteenth century a series of good translations of verse and prose from Old Icelandic were made by such scholars as George West Dasent (from 1842 onwards), Benjamin Thorpe and E. E. J. Powell. Richard Cleasby began work in Copenhagen on an Old Icelandic–English Dictionary, and after his untimely death this was continued by the Icelandic scholar Gudbrand Vigfusson, and was published by the Clarendon Press in 1869. English poets were stirred by the Norse myths; Matthew Arnold published *Balder dead*, a narrative poem, in 1855, based on Mallet's account of the myth of the god's slaying, and William Morris' long epic poem, *Sigurd the Volsung and the fall of the Nibelungs*, appeared in 1875 and won much acclaim. This tells the story of the legendary hero favoured by the god Odin, who slew a dragon and gained a great treasure but met with an early death.

The poet and artist William Morris began to study Icelandic with Eirikr Magnusson in 1858, and their partnership was to have an enormous effect on Norse studies. Magnusson, the son of a poor Icelandic parson, came to England to help with the production of an Icelandic New Testament for the British and Foreign Bible Society. He proved an inspiring teacher, and Morris became fascinated by the Old Icelandic sagas and poems, brought out a series of English translations of the prose sagas in a pseudo-medieval style, and visited Iceland to study the background of the tales.

The operas of Richard Wagner, beginning with *The Nibelungs* in 1848, aroused an even greater interest in Norse mythology. He based them on the German version of the story of Siegfried (corresponding to the Norse Sigurd the Volsung), preserved in the medieval *Nibelungenlied*, a long courtly epic of the late thirteenth century. However, Wagner had also read some of the Icelandic material in translation, and brought the northern god Odin with the Valkyries who served him, together with the troublemaker Loki, into his series of operas making up the cycle of *The Ring*. The splendid productions of Wagner's operas gave a new significance to the old myths, since he used them to express his aspirations for a stronger national identity for Germany.

Early myths were also revived and associated with a new spirit of nationalism in Finland, where Elias Lönnrot published the *Kalevala* in 1835–49. This is a long epic poem made up from verse narratives, chants and laments collected and recorded by him in remote parts of the country. Although this work has been pieced together and contains no coherent mythology, there are many

supernatural characters and tales of Otherworld adventures to be found in
it.

In seeking to establish the nature of ancient religion and mythology in northern
Europe, it is necessary to take into account the effect of later creative artists
and writers who were inspired by the early myths from the eighteenth century
onwards. They have helped to shape our perceptions of the religious beliefs of
the past, and our attitude towards them. Interest in the Celtic druids has resulted
in various attempts to revive them from the eighteenth century onwards. They
were believed to have been the builders of Stonehenge and to have possessed
deep secrets of ancient wisdom. Then came the claim of Edward Williams (whose
bardic name was Iolo Morganwg) in the last quarter of the century that the bards
of Glamorganshire had preserved the wisdom of the druids virtually intact, and
he forged documents to prove this, based on some knowledge of early Welsh
literature. He succeeded in linking a druidical court of 'Bards of the Island of
Britain' with the Welsh National Eisteddfod, and so brought new vigour into a
declining institution. Many wild publications appeared, and the Ancient Order
of Druids was set up in London in 1781. Numerous modern Druid Orders have
since sprung up in Europe, Australia and America, including some for women.
Competing bodies of modern druids have met at Stonehenge on ceremonial
occasions from the late nineteenth century onwards, particularly at dawn on
Midsummer Day, although recently such meetings have been limited to small
groups because of possible damage to the stones.

Attempts to re-establish the pre-Christian Nordic religion came much later,
but there have been increasing attempts to do this since the 1950s. The Pagan
Federation was founded in London in 1971, and is a co-ordinating body linking a
number of pagan groups. Such groups are very varied, and flourish in the United
States, particularly in California. Some call themselves Odinists, and attempt to
follow the traditions of the group of Scandinavian gods and goddesses preserved
in the early literature of Iceland, while in Iceland the group styling themselves
the *Asatruarmenn* (Believers in the *Æsir*) was officially recognized as a sect in
1973, aiming to restore the ancient religious rituals of the ninth century there.

In addition we have the varied groups in England who call themselves Wicca.
Their claim to represent a genuine revival of pre-Christian religion rests largely
on the work of the Egyptologist Margaret Murray, who in her old age became
convinced that the people persecuted for witchcraft in northern Europe were
members of the 'Old Religion', which continued underground until the end of
the Stuart regime in the seventeenth century. This was further strengthened by

the novels and books of Gerald Gardner, a retired colonial civil servant, in touch with various groups working with magic, who started a somewhat disreputable museum of witchcraft in the Isle of Man. His claims for the origins of Wicca show little knowledge of historical sources and are based largely on the theories of Margaret Murray. As Ronald Hutton points out in his description of the new paganism, the weakness of such claims is that the distinction between religion and magic is ignored, since the fundamental idea of witchcraft, that of raising a supernatural power in order to achieve what is desired, differs fundamentally from what we know of the worship of the deities of pre-Christian Europe.

The increasing interest in new paganism, claimed to be a revival of the beliefs held before the coming of Christianity, is partly based in a desire to escape from a materialistic and cynical age and to win back the ancient lost wisdom which earlier peoples are assumed to have possessed. There is, however, a deep-seated reluctance to gain more knowledge about the lost faiths and rituals. This was shown in 1999 in the violent emotional protests made against the decision of English Heritage to remove from the sea at Old Hunstanton in Norfolk the central inverted free trunk with remains of the circle of timbers surrounding it which was discovered there. Removal was carried out to prevent its inevitable destruction and to discover more about its character and the way in which it had been set up. Both archaeologists and protesters cared intensely about this unique monument from the pre-Christian past, and the pity is that this resulted in hostility rather than co-operation.

Many of those seeking to revive the early religions concentrate on the ancient worship of the goddess, which has a strong appeal to feminists, and has been strengthened by the devoted studies of Maria Gimbutas. Others seek to identify the fragmentary beliefs known from pre-Christian Europe with the teaching of old and well-established religions such as that of Ancient Egypt, Hinduism and Tibetan Buddhism, and also with native American beliefs. Workshops for the study of shamanism and attempts to revive its practices in the present day and make use of them for healing and the solving of psychological problems have been set up by the Scandinavian Center for Shamanic Studies in Denmark.

The various groups who seek to rediscover the wisdom of the ancients tend to turn towards nature religion, and some link their ideas about the pre-Christian religion in very early times with earth mysteries. The idea of early prehistoric sacred sites linked by straight lines goes back to the nineteenth century, but the work of Alfred Watkins on the Old Straight Track in the 1920s, and that of John Mitchell, who wrote *The View over Atlantis* in 1968, gave this new impetus; the 'ley lines' proposed by Watkins came to be viewed as magnetic paths for spaceships bringing extra-terrestial visitants, and also as a source of divine energy. The theories of Alexander Thom and Euan MacKie, who claim that the measurements of prehistoric monuments show that early priests possessed advanced knowledge of astronomy and mathematics, are not generally accepted by prehistorians, but have encouraged those looking back to the Neolithic period as a time of mystical wisdom.

A further source of new pagan material has come from folklore, which from the time of the Grimms has been regarded as a rich source of information about pre-Christian beliefs. While some traditions may go back far into the past, further work by folklorists has shown that many are of comparatively recent origin, perhaps deliberately introduced by local antiquaries. As with early literature and place-names, it is necessary to proceed here with caution, investigating each individual problem with an open mind, as Jakob Grimm himself advocated.

In the lively interest in the beliefs of the long past which flourishes in society today, there is both promise and danger. We need to realize how the approach to the pre-Christian religion has varied in different periods, and to take this into account in any estimation of its nature in ancient Europe.

INTERPRETATION

The medieval viewpoint

Apart from rare exceptions like the gifted Snorri Sturluson, medieval writers who described the northern deities and retold the myths were usually monks. Their normal reaction was to view such gods as demons battling against Christ, and delighting to lead mortals astray. Snorri countered this by arguing that after the Flood as recounted in the Bible men forgot the creator god, but continued to feel that some major power must have created the world. They gave various names to this power, one of which was Odin, the leader of the northern deities. This approach allowed Snorri to consider the beliefs of his forebears sympathetically, without condemnation. He thought too that the concepts of some gods might be based on admiration for famous leaders of the heroic past, leading poets and storytellers to regard them as divine figures. Saxo Grammaticus, who did not approve of the 'heathen' gods, also felt that they may have developed out of powerful men of the past, perhaps sorcerers who came to be regarded as divine.

The theorists

From the beginning of the Christian era, then, we can discern changing attitudes to the earlier myths. In the early nineteenth century, Jakob Grimm knew that the old Germanic religion was linked with that of the Scandinavians, and in an early preface of 1844 he made claims for its richness. However, rather than putting forward theories as to its origins, he set out to assemble and arrange relevant material. In his preface to *Deutsche Mythologie* he objects to 'the mania of foisting metaphysical or astronomical solutions on but half-discovered historical data', an enlightened attitude which gives enduring value to his work.

Other scholars, unlike Grimm, were determined to find some prevailing theory to explain and provide a basis for the fragmentary evidence for cults and deities in Europe. In the second half of the nineteenth century, a vigorous debate went on for years between the German scholar Max Müller, lecturing on philology and early Indian religions at Oxford, and the Scottish historian and journalist Andrew Lang, who concentrated on new evidence provided by anthropologists. Both were prolific writers and eloquent debaters, with bodies of devoted followers. Müller had discovered links between the names of classical deities of Greece and Rome and those preserved in Sanskrit in the Vedic literature of India. He traced such names as Zeus and Jupiter back to an Indo-European form **dyeus pate*, and believed that this proved belief in an early deity known as 'Father Sky' worshipped by those speaking the Indo-European language. He claimed that all mythology was based primarily on the sun which dispelled the darkness and caused fertility, while other natural phenomena might also play a part. Some of his followers preferred to stress the importance of the storm wind or the fire of the lightning.

One example of such an approach was an interpretation of the Anglo-Saxon epic poem *Beowulf*, in which the hero overcomes the monster Grendel who lurks in the barren wastes and makes attacks on the hall of the Danish king. This was claimed to be based on the power of the life-giving sun to overcome the dangerous mists of the fens and marshes. Similarly the Irish scholar Thomas O'Rahilly, whose work on *Early history and mythology* appeared in 1946, saw one outstanding character after another in the Irish tales as representing the sun-god with his flaming sword. This god he regarded also as the guardian of the lightning, while other heroes played the part of the youthful god fated to destroy him. One weakness of solar mythology was that scholars failed to agree over the identification of possible solar deities. O'Rahilly hailed the one-eyed god Balor as the sun god, and the powerful god Lug as his youthful adversary, but other Celtic scholars such as Eleanor Hull and Sir John Rhys believed that Lug with his shining face and his hero son Cú Chulainn developed out of earlier sun-gods.

Scandinavian mythology offered further problems, since the leader of the gods, Odin, had none of the characteristics of a solar deity. The god who possessed the hammer of the lightning was Thor, the thunder god, corresponding to the Germanic Donar, god of the sky, while the god whose name was thought to be linked with that of Zeus, the Greek sky-god, was a different deity, the Germanic *Tiwas*. He was remembered in Scandinavia as Tyr, the god who bound the wolf which threatened the gods.

Max Müller's doughty opponent, Andrew Lang, had very different ideas about the origin of early European myths. He believed that they simply developed out of earlier forms of culture, such as may still be found among so-called primitive peoples in remote parts of the world. While Müller explained the tale of the Greek god Chronos devouring his offspring as based on the drying up of clouds by the sun, Lang accounted for it by the practice of cannibalism in early societies. In *Myth, Ritual and Religion*, published in 1887, he strove to show how many strange and barbaric features in the myths could be paralleled by customs surviving in various parts of the world. Lang was much influenced by E. V. Taylor and the evolutionists, who claimed that religion developed from very primitive beginnings. Müller however had a higher opinion of the intelligence of early peoples, believing them capable of metaphorical and poetic ways of thinking. Their imaginative descriptions had in many cases, he felt, been taken literally, through what he called 'the disease of language'. Lang was eventually forced to concede some ground, because it was impossible to deny the concept of a European sky-god, but his evolutionary approach became the generally accepted one when it was further developed by Sir James Frazer in *The Golden Bough*.

Frazer was a classical scholar who collected an immense amount of evidence from anthropologists and folklorists, although he himself did no fieldwork and was something of a recluse. He was able to go further than his predecessors in discerning underlying patterns in widely scattered evidence, and was to have an enormous influence in the first half of the twentieth century. His first two books, based on classical material, appeared in 1890, and he then extended his range to include Germanic and Celtic myths and the folklore and customs of his own time. He viewed religion as an inevitable but limited stage in human development, developing into ritual through the activities of cunning magicians. He believed it must be gradually rejected as scientific explanations were discovered for the mysterious phenomena of the natural world, and myths to him were early misguided attempts to explain such mysteries.

He was greatly influenced by the German scholar Wilhelm Mannhardt, who had collected beliefs and customs in Germany and surrounding countries associated with plants, trees and the growing of crops. Mannhardt saw the basic source of inspiration in early religion in Europe as the death of vegetation in winter followed by the growth of new life in the spring, fostering belief in spirits of the trees and the corn. In the past such beliefs resulted in human and animal sacrifice, which he thought had left a mark on many customs associated with seed-time and harvest. Much of his evidence was adopted by Frazer in *The Golden Bough*. Frazer also believed that early kings were ritually sacrificed and replaced by young successors in order to maintain the land's fertility, and that this had a profound influence on European myths.

Such theories attracted extremists like Lord Raglan, for whom the ritual death of kings formed the basis of all myth. Margaret Murray, a distinguished Egyptologist who after retirement became interested in the study of witchcraft in Scotland, took up such ideas in the 1920s. She became convinced that many Anglo-Saxon, Norman and later kings of England who died violent deaths had been ritually sacrificed in this way, through the activities of members of an underground religion. On the other hand the so-called 'Myth and Ritual school', partly developing from Frazer's work on early myths, resulted in valuable insights into the religions of the Near East, and S. J. Hooke and E. O. James produced a number of important studies on myth from the 1930s onwards. Hooke viewed myth as the spoken part of ritual, the words uttered possessing the efficacy of an act. The importance of kingship rituals in both Scandinavia and Ireland makes such studies relevant for the better understanding of pre-Christian religion in north-western Europe.

Fresh approaches

The question of myth was further developed by other scholars who reacted against Frazer's theories. In 1917 Rudolf Otto had claimed in *Das Heilige* that religion arose out of an independent form of experience for which he used the term 'numinous'. A Romanian scholar, Mircea Éliade, who later worked at Chicago, studied general patterns in religion over a wide area of the world as Frazer had done, but with very different results. He held that myths were intended to reveal how the world and the activities of society came into being, and that they were the means of re-creating such beginnings. The sacred centre, of great importance to both Celts and Germans, represented for each community the place where the work of creation began. Éliade's main contribution was to show how various powerful symbols throughout the world have been taken at different times to represent divine power. He was influenced by the work of Jung, who claimed that echoes of early myths in dreams showed the importance of archetypal symbols, which have survived into our own time.

A more ambitious scheme for the interpretation of myths was that of the French scholar Claude Lévi-Strauss, who claimed to use a more scientific approach. He advocated the structural analysis of myths, since these, like languages, are made up of units which need to be broken down if we are to comprehend them. To do this successfully, he advocated that all available versions of a myth must be brought together, in order to discover the 'true form', a daunting task even in the age of the computer. However, in spite of obvious difficulties, this approach has helped us to interpret mythical material, revealing the importance of polarity and contrast, and has established also the power of creative thinking possessed by what used to be called primitive peoples, which Frazer had denied.

Perhaps of more relevance for the study of Celtic and Germanic mythology than these general theories of myth is the work of Georges Dumézil, beginning in the 1920s. He concentrated on religious concepts derived from the Indo-European peoples, and placed the main gods of such peoples into three categories, which he traced back to ancient India and ancient Rome. The first of his three functions for divine figures was that of the ruler, controlling magico-religious power and law. The second was that of the warrior, employing physical force, while the third was concerned with the fertility of the earth and of living creatures. In the first class he placed the Scandinavian gods Odin and Tyr, and in the second Thor, who protected the gods with his hammer, while the group of gods and goddesses known in Scandinavia as the Vanir, including Njord, Freyr and Freyja, were in the third. This approach can be used to explain certain problems in the northern myths, for instance the mysterious conflicts said to take place in the beginning between two groups of deities in both Scandinavia and Ireland. However there are difficulties in applying Dumézil's theories to the Scandinavian gods. Thor was indeed the champion of the divine world, like Indra, but he was also the god of law, and associated with the fertility of earth and water, while Odin, certainly a ruler and expert in magic, was essentially a warrior-god, inspiring armies and supporting royal power.

As for the Celtic gods, it is now recognized that individual deities were many-skilled, and cannot be fitted into neat categories like the deities of ancient Rome.

This was pointed out by Marie-Louise Sjoestedt in her book *Dieux et héros des Celtes*, published in 1940, which provided new and valuable insights into the study of Irish myths. She also expressed doubts as to whether any clearly defined Celtic religion ever existed to unite the people as a whole, and the same might probably be said of the religious beliefs of the Germanic peoples. However, Dumézil's theories are of value because they have introduced new patterns to be applied to myths and deities, and helped us towards a fuller understanding of the religious needs of different sectors of society.

Dumézil somewhat neglected the goddesses, whom he at first grouped together with fertility gods in his third section. By 1970 however he had come to the conclusion that there was one powerful goddess related to the gods of all three functions, linking and reconciling them. There has been renewed interest in the cults of the early goddesses in Europe during the last half of the twentieth century. The American archaeologist Maria Gimbutas has argued eloquently for the existence of an early matriarchal society in south-eastern Europe, in which the mother-goddess was supreme. She believes that this was destroyed by the incursions of Indo-European warrior tribes who worshipped a powerful sky-god, and has attempted to establish this by a wealth of iconographical evidence, interpreting symbols in early art.

Meanwhile an increasing number of scholars such as Bruce Lincoln and Jan Puhvel have sought to trace back certain myths to the religion of the Indo-European peoples in early times. They claim that certain powerful motifs found in medieval literature in various parts of Eurasia, such as the theft of the mead of inspiration and its recovery, may go back to a very early date. There are striking parallels between myths in cultures which lie far apart, such as that of the destruction and rebirth of the world and the human race in ancient Iran and in Scandinavia in the Viking Age. It is very difficult to determine whether such resemblances are due to the preservation of ancient traditions in certain areas, or to later contacts through travel and trading and the movements of peoples, and much work remains to be done on such problems.

It will be seen that varying theories of the origins of myths found in ancient Europe have inspired scholars and won popular support for a while, until it gradually became apparent that the latest theory did not after all offer a completely satisfying picture of early religion. As the sagacious Charlotte Burne pointed out in 1901 in a review of Frazer's *Golden Bough* in *Folk-Lore*, the fate of the solar mythologists should teach us that there is no master key to the study of ancient religions which will unlock every door. Hopes of finding a neat pattern into which all the evidence will fit, so that former theories can be rejected as completely invalid, have been doomed to disappointment. A preferred method now is to proceed by way of detailed studies of individual myths and the cults of separate deities, endeavouring to discover their history and significance. Scholars such as Hector Munro Chadwick in the first half of the twentieth century and Jan de Vries a little later have, like Jakob Grimm, continued to study the field of early religion in northern Europe with an open mind, without the urge to construct one comprehensive theory to explain it all, and in this way much progress has been made.

EVIDENCE

The written sources for early religion in Europe were for the most part recorded in Christian times, and are not necessarily trustworthy. Throughout the twentieth century there was increasing reliance on archaeology and early art for the interpretation of religion, a record without words, but left by those whose beliefs and customs were based on an earlier world picture. It can tell us much of the religious beliefs and practices of those whose language is unknown to us, although it may not be easy to interpret the message aright. Every major archaeological discovery results in lengthy and often acrimonious disputes as to the dates and significance of the finds, while much valuable evidence has been lost in the past when only what interested the excavators was kept, and no full records were made. Much damage has also been done by careless treatment of unexpected finds. However, archaeological evidence has certainly helped to build up a better understanding of the lives of early peoples, offering new and practical insights into the nature of religious cults. One valuable though disconcerting characteristic of new discoveries is that they tend to contradict previously held assumptions, and require new ways of thinking. The excavation of sacred sites and graves has proved particularly illuminating for our understanding of the religion of ancient Europe.

Sacred sites

In the course of the major Ice Age, around 15,000 BCE, we have the rich cave paintings at Lascaux and other sites in southern France and northern Spain, with skilful and surprisingly sophisticated portrayal of the animals hunted (see chapter 1 above). Evidently ritual practices went on in caves difficult of access and cut off from the light. In Scandinavia no settlement was possible until the ice receded, about 9000 BCE, and then many animal carvings were made on the rocks, together with a few figures shown dancing or in movement, which have been thought to represent priests or shamans. Diagrammatic figures of animals carved on the rocks in Scandinavia during this early period, with what appears to be a life-line running through their bodies, are in keeping with shamanic practices among hunting peoples in later times.

For the Neolithic period in north-western Europe there are a number of sacred places marked by rings or groups of megalithic stones, of which Stonehenge and Avebury in southern England are outstanding examples. Stonehenge is now dated towards the end of the third millennium BCE, and Avebury a little later, about 2500, and there is evidence for monuments of a similar kind in wood. Widely differing claims as to the identity of their builders and the purpose of such huge monuments have been put forward from medieval to modern times, including persistent attempts to link them with the druids who belong to the Roman period, thousands of years later. This shows how difficult it is to interpret sacred sites when no records are available. In the 1960s claims were made that such monuments show considerable knowledge of astronomy and geometric skill, although these have not won general acceptance. The purpose of the long avenues of megalithic stones set up near Carnac in Brittany also remains unexplained.

A more recent discovery of what may have been an important sacred centre in the Late Bronze Age in eastern England is that of Flag Fen near Peterborough, discovered by Francis Pryor in 1982, just before the area was developed as an industrial site. Here vast quantities of timber have been preserved, used to create an artificial island in a lake, and there was a long avenue from which offerings were dropped into the water. More evidence for religious practices of the Bronze Age in about 1000 BCE may be discovered here as excavations continue.

From the early Celtic period in Europe a number of enclosures have been excavated which appear to have been used for sacrificial rites, such as that at Libernice in the Czech Republic. Some of these remained in use over a considerable period, and a site at Courney-sur-Aronde near Compiègne in northern France was kept up from the third century BCE to the fourth century CE. Such centres reveal traces of both human and animal sacrifice, as well as offerings of weapons and ornaments, and they were sometimes converted into temples after Roman occupation of the area. Uley Bury in Gloucestershire is an example of a sacred place in Britain in use for as long as eight centuries; here there were votive deposits and burials, while a shrine was added in the Roman period.

Offering places in peat bogs have been excavated in Denmark and northern Germany. Here there is evidence for human and animal sacrifices, and large quantities of weapons and armour have been found which appear to have been offerings after victories in battle; there are allusions in Latin literature to both Celts and Germans making extravagant offerings of war booty in thanksgiving to the gods, in fulfilment of earlier vows. An early example from the Bronze Age from Denmark is a great war-canoe laden with battle equipment found at Hjortespring, which had been dragged to the offering place and pelted with flints. There is a site from the Roman period at Vimose, and these are later ones at Nydam and Kragehul, Haderslev (dating from the fourth century) and Illerup (from the fifth). Offerings of a different kind were found at Thorsbjerg and at Skedemose on the Swedish island of Öland, such as gold neck ornaments, locks of women's hair, and farm implements, and may have been made to a goddess or to fertility powers rather than to a god of batttle. At Skedemose, where what was once a lake was carefully excavated from 1959 onwards, there was evidence for fires and feasting on the shore, and the remains of the food, including bones of slaughtered animals, had been taken out in boats and dropped into the water.

Great temples were rare among the Celtic peoples, but some elaborate remains survive from Entremont and Roqueperteuse in southern France, where the Celts were under Mediterranean influence in the third century BCE. At Entremont there was a sacred way lined with impressive life-sized figures seated cross-legged, and there was evidence for the preservation of human heads, confirming literary accounts from classical sources of the customs of the Celts. Temples were also set up in sacred places in Gaul and Britain during the Roman occupation. There were a number at the sources of rivers associated with healing, like that of the goddess Sequana at the source of the Seine, or by hot springs, like that of Sulis Minerva at Bath. Such sanctuaries were often dedicated to Celtic goddesses, and they attracted crowds of pilgrims, who left offerings and votive figurines, and sometimes recorded curses against those who had robbed or injured them.

In general, however, remains of temples have not survived, since both Celts and Germans held ceremonies in the open air, or used small wooden shrines likely to vanish without trace. One important site from the early Anglo-Saxon period, excavated by Brian Hope Taylor in the 1970s, is a group of halls from Yeavering in Northumberland, and one of these appears to have been used for sacrificial feasts before being abandoned after the acceptance of Christianity in the seventh century. Here the skulls and bones of many slaughtered oxen had been preserved.

Disposal of the dead

Graves from the pre-Christian period have proved an important source of information, not only because of treasures buried with the dead, but also for the evidence of ritual and symbolism in funeral ceremonies which they provide. Unfortunately many outstanding graves were opened early and treated with scant respect. An example of wanton destruction is a unique burial of the Bronze Age in a huge mound near Kivik in Sweden, opened by two farmers in 1748 looking for treasure, who destroyed everything except stones on which scenes of ritual and strange symbols were carved. The great tombs of the megalithic period, some of which held many skeletal remains and seem to have been connected with a cult of the ancestors, have lost any grave-goods they may have held long ago, although some stones found in them bear figures and symbols. In Brittany there are stylized female figures with breasts and staring eyes, wearing necklaces, thought to represent guardian goddesses of the dead, while there are elaborate patterns of concentric circles and spirals from the great graves of the Boyne Valley in Ireland.

In Celtic areas there are a number of rich wagon graves, dating to around the early fifth century BCE. The body was usually placed in a wagon, presumably used for the funeral, with the wheels removed. One remarkable burial of this type was discovered at Vix on the upper Seine in 1953. A woman of about 35 lay in the wagon, wearing a diadem and supplied with splendid jewellery, and among the grave-goods there was an enormous jar or crater of the kind used for mixing wine and water at feasts. It has been suggested that this was an offering at a local shrine where she was priestess.

From the end of the pre-Christian period there are two exceptional examples of ship graves from Anglo-Saxon England and Norway which have provided a wealth of grave-goods. One is from Sutton Hoo in East Anglia, dated to the early seventh century CE, and the other from Oseberg in southern Norway, from the ninth century CE. Both are thought to have been prepared for persons of royal rank, and careful excavation and preservation of the contents have revealed how elaborate pre-Christian funerals could be. At Sutton Hoo no trace of a body remained, but the mound is thought to be a grave or memorial to King Redwald of East Anglia, who reigned 599–625, and who although officially a Christian is said to have continued to worship the old gods. The ship was loaded with regalia worthy of a king, splendid weapons, valuable dishes and vessels for feasting, and means for preparing meals, as well as treasures appropriate for a royal hall. Some of the ornaments and weapons bear symbols known to be associated with the cult of the Germanic god Wodan, though there are also objects bearing Christian symbols. One possibility is that Redwald was given Christian burial elsewhere, while his royal treasures were placed in an impressive ship which could hold forty rowers, and buried in a mound after the custom of his ancestors. Other graves holding ships or boats in the vicinity show that ship burial was established in East Anglia at the end of the pre-Christian period.

In the Oseberg ship buried in a great mound in the kingdom of Vestfold in Norway, two women had been laid on beds, a sign of rank, and it is thought that one was a queen of Vestfold, and possibly also a priestess of the goddess Freyja. This might account for the opening of the mound not very long after the burial, and the deliberate damage done to much of the grave furniture, while one of the bodies was removed, leaving only a few bones behind. Many wooden objects in the grave were preserved owing to the composition of the soil, and some were of superb workmanship. As well as the beds there were an elaborately carved processional wagon, some carved sledges which must have been used at the funeral, and a quantity of wall-hangings which have been partially restored. These are of great importance because of the scenes and figures woven and embroidered on them, including representation of a great funeral procession, in which supernatural beings take part, and scenes of battle and religious ritual. While many problems concerning these great ship burials remain unsolved, they offer a wealth of religious symbols for us to study, and possible clues for a better understanding of the picture of the Otherworld held by those who planned and carried out the funeral ceremonies. There were great cremation funerals too, in Scandinavia in the Viking Age and in Germany and Anglo-Saxon England, and in some of these a ship formed the funeral pyre We have an eyewitness account of such a funeral among Scandinavians trading in Russia in 921 CE.

The Anglo-Saxon epic poem *Beowulf* begins with an impressive account of a dead king sent out to sea in a ship loaded with treasures, and it is often assumed that the use of ships and wagons in graves was based on a belief in the journey of the dead to another world. Reasons for their use, however, may have been more complex. A wagon used at a funeral might have been buried with the dead as an essential part of the ceremony, while a ship could be sacrificed as a status symbol, or a boat in more humble graves used as a convenient substitute for a coffin or as material for a pyre where wood was scarce. Another possible reason for use of a ship was that this was a recognized symbol for the Vanir deities in the north, associated with the gods Njord and Freyr and the goddess Freyja, and seems sometimes to have represented the journeying sun. The fact that it is a moving symbol of departure and separation, often encountered in dreams, might be one reason for its long popularity in funeral rites in Norway and Sweden, where travel over water was a familiar part of life.

As well as separate graves of the rich and powerful, many inhumation and cremation cemeteries have been excavated in different parts of Europe. In Anglo-Saxon England, where evidence for the pre-Christian religion is limited, much work continues to be done on cemeteries belonging to the period of early settlement. Decoration on cremation urns includes symbols evidently associated with the dead and perhaps with certain deities. There are figures of birds, horses and boars, as well as axe-heads and what may be lightning symbols. Increasing study of these, and also of the arrangement of graves and the use of earlier ones for secondary burials, adds to our knowledge of funeral ritual.

Examples of animal and occasionally of human sacrifice, and the practice of placing food and drink as well as cherished possessions in the graves, continue to be recorded as more cemeteries are found, and the growing impression which we receive is that ideas about the fate of the dead were less naive and more complex than was formerly imagined.

Ritual objects

Certain objects included in graves appear to have ritual significance, while other ritual items have been buried as offerings, thrown into water or hidden away in time of danger. The famous 'Sun Chariot' from the Bronze Age, 60 cm in length, was found buried at Trundholm in Denmark, broken into fragments. This consists of a bronze disk set on wheels, covered in gold plate and elaborately decorated on one side, together with a bronze horse to draw it (perhaps one of an original pair), and the disk is thought to represent the sun. There are records also of finds of small human figures in bronze, dating from the Danish Bronze Age (c. 1600–500 BCE), though few have survived. They seem to have formed part of ceremonial groups, and include a kneeling figure who may represent a driving goddess, found together with a serpent. A group of this kind arranged on a wheeled platform was found in a grave of the seventh century BCE at Strettweg in Austria. This is made up of a number of naked human figures, both male and female, grouped around two stags, with a much larger figure thought to represent a goddess in the centre, holding a bowl on her head.

An outstanding ritual vessel from Denmark is a great silver bowl, known as the Gundestrup Cauldron, found in a peat bog in Jutland in 1891. A series of panels had been torn off the bowl and placed inside it. Those from the outside represent four male and three female busts, assumed to be divinities, while the plates from the inside show elaborate scenes which have provoked much speculation. One shows a horned human figure sitting cross-legged beside a stag, a boar and a serpent, while on another a towering male figure is apparently putting a smaller one into a vessel, and alongside are marching or riding warriors and men playing trumpets. On the base of the bowl there is a vivid picture of a bull-slaying. Certain features, such as the form of the trumpets, the neck-rings of the deities, and realistic portrayal of animals such as the stag, belong to Celtic tradition, but there are other figures which are Mediterranean in style or have been thought to come from further east. Some believe that the bowl was made in Gaul, and others that it came from the area round the Black Sea. There has been much argument about its date, a favoured estimate being the first century BCE.

Another Danish treasure from about the fifth century CE was a pair of magnificent drinking horns covered with gold plates, on which were depicted small figures and scenes which appear to represent cult practices. These were found at Gallehus in the seventeenth century, but were unhappily stolen in 1702 and melted down by the thief. The horns have been reconstructed from contemporary drawings.

Iconography

The pictures on the Gundestrup Cauldron and the Gallehus horns take us into the realm of iconography. Some representations of what may be divine figures survive from early times in Scandinavia. Most carvings on the rocks from the Neolithic period are of animals, but in the Bronze Age there was a striking change. An enormous number of carvings, mostly in western Sweden, show small stylized figures of men and women who seem to be engaged in ritual practices, and who are accompanied by symbols and motifs such as sun-disks, ships, footprints, ploughs, weapons and animals. There are also larger figures which may represent deities, holding ships or spears. Some human figures appear to have bird or animal heads, and there are groups which have been thought to represent a divine marriage. The carvings are widely scattered, but remarkably consistent in character.

Supernatural beings may also be represented on amulets, such as brooches or pendants. A large number of round gold 'bracteates', hanging ornaments imitated from Roman medallions about the size of an old penny, were produced in Scandinavia from the fifth to the seventh century CE. The medallions had shown the head of the Emperor, or scenes representing victory, and these were transformed into lively and fantastic figures and symbols by the northern craftsmen. Such bracteates were evidently worn for luck and protection. A classification system was produced by Mackeprang in 1952, and since then Karl Hauck has done further extensive work on the bracteates. He believes that many show symbols associated with the Germanic god Wodan, and some scenes from northern myths such as the death of Balder or the wolf biting off the hand of the god Tyr.

There is also a series of pictures on tiny pieces of gold foil, found buried in the earth, although these were placed not in graves, but usually in the foundations of buildings. Nineteen were discovered under the medieval church of Mære at Trondheim in Norway, believed to have been built on the site of a pre-Christian temple, and another set at Helgo in Sweden under what may have been a sacred centre. The pictures on the pieces of foil are of a man and woman facing one another, sometimes embracing or with a piece of foliage between them, and this has been taken as a symbol of marriage between the fertility deities known as the Vanir, associated with fruitfulness and prosperity. Individual examples found together vary in style, and they may have continued to be deposited in one place over time.

Symbols which may have been linked with the gods, such as staring faces, have been recognized on Anglo-Saxon brooches. Creatures such as ravens, wolves and boars, known to be symbols of the warrior gods, were used to decorate weapons, shields, helmets and ornaments in Anglo-Saxon England and Scandinavia, and there are more elaborate figures of dancing warriors armed with spears, sometimes linked with animals. In the Viking Age small hammers in honour of the god Thor were worn, possibly as rivals to the Christian cross, and some from Sweden are elaborately decorated to show the terrible eyes of the god, and symbolize his struggle with the World Serpent.

More detailed scenes are found on memorial stones of various kinds, which show figures of gods and goddesses. Such carvings are found in areas which came under Roman influence, such as Germany, Gaul, England and the Netherlands. Anthropomorphic figures of deities in the Roman manner are shown on altars and votive stones, or as statues or figurines, often with Latin inscriptions. Native deities are often identified with Roman ones, such as Jupiter, Mars or Minerva, with the native names also given, and this is a valuable source of information about local Celtic or Germanic deities.

Many different local gods are represented as Mars, while Mercury may be identified with the Celtic Lug or the Germanic Wodan. We find many lively representations of Epona, the Celtic goddess associated with horses, adopted by the Romans as a goddess of cavalry regiments. Groups of mother goddesses, often three in number, are found in both Germanic and Celtic areas. The position was complicated when soldiers in the Roman army dedicated stones to their own native deities in the countries where they were stationed, but many undoubtedly adopted those they found in the new locality. Simple native shrines were sometimes rebuilt as elaborate temples attracting crowds of pilgrims, as happened at Bath.

From Scandinavia we have many memorial stones, usually commemorating the dead. These add considerably to our knowledge of the myths when they show scenes which resemble accounts given in much later literary sources. There is a rich collection of such stones on the island of Gotland, and a number from northern England and the Isle of Man which date back to the time of the Norse settlement there. Some of the scenes from early myths are found on Christian crosses, perhaps intended to mark the contrast between the old faith and the new; on a cross at Andreas in the Isle of Man, for instance, the god Odin is shown being swallowed by the wolf beneath one of the arms of Christ's cross. Some representations are very close to accounts in the Icelandic poems of the god Thor fishing for the World Serpent. This was clearly a well-known and important myth, since we have carvings depicting it from Gotland, Denmark, Sweden and northern England, which cover a period from the eighth century to the late tenth or eleventh and show that the myth existed in a stable form over several centuries.

Splendid carved stones were raised to commemorate the dead on the island of Gotland, and these were originally painted in bright colours, and can be as much as 10 m high. The earliest stones are dated to the fifth or sixth centuries CE, and may have been inspired by Roman tombstones from Europe seen by Gotlanders on their voyages. Some have a great whirling disk on them, with two smaller disks probably representing the sun and moon, and in stones from the Viking Age from the eighth century onwards a ship was often added. This could have been a status symbol, since many Gotlanders owned ships, or a symbol of the journey to the next world. Another type of journey is depicted on stones showing a rider met by a woman who offers him a drinking horn. This appears to represent a dead hero greeted by a valkyrie when he arrives at Odin's hall Valhalla after death in battle, as described in tenth-century funeral poems. Sometimes the horse has eight legs, which identifies it with Sleipnir, the steed used by Odin when he travelled between the worlds.

Names and titles

In addition to evidence of early deities gained from art and literature, some information may be obtained from place-names and personal names, as well as from names and titles of the deities themselves. The study of place-names is an exacting discipline, and many interpretations accepted by earlier scholars as proof that a deity was worshipped in a certain area have now been rejected. The work of Margaret Gelling on evidence from Anglo-Saxon England and of Karl Hald in Denmark has considerably reduced the number of places thought to be named after pre-Christian deities, through rigorous checking of earlier spellings.

There are a few Wodan names in England, such as Wodnesborough in Kent, but in Denmark Odin, the Scandinavian equivalent of Wodan, is seldom represented, and Odin names are totally lacking in Iceland. Some English place-names are derived from Thunor, the thunder-god, and Thor names are frequently found in Scandinavia, as are names derived from Freyr and Njord. Tyr names are rare in Norway and Sweden, but there are numerous Ti names in Denmark. The distribution of names raises many problems. One suggested explanation for the survival in England of names of some Anglo-Saxon deities is that the places called after them were outside the area controlled by the local ruler, and so the names failed to be suppressed at the time of the conversion.

Names indicating a holy place, such as *hof* in Iceland, *hörgr* in Scandinavia and *hearg* in Anglo-Saxon England, also provide valuable evidence. Among the Celtic peoples worship of the god Lug in pre-Roman times is indicated by places named after him, such as Lyons, previously Lugudunum. Many places in Ireland are named after supernatural beings, although these are sometimes due to later folk traditions, as in the case of the Paps of Anu (a local goddess) given to two rounded hills in Kerry.

Personal names are often based on those of deities. The great preponderance of Thor names in Iceland gives some idea of the god's popularity there, and similarly in west Norway, from which many Icelandic settlers came. Something may also be discovered from animal names such as Bjorn (bear) and Ulf (wolf), which can be associated with traditions about shape-changing and berserks.

Divine names and titles are clearly of great importance, although they tend to raise problems rather than solve them. While some interpret the name of the Celtic god Lug as 'shining', 'brilliant', others have derived it from a Celtic word for 'raven'. A stock epithet applied to him, 'of the Long Arm', could either be based on his famous spear, or indicate rule over a wide territory. A powerful god would possess many titles, and as many as seventy have been listed for Odin in Old Norse litertature, included God of the Hanged, Greybeard, Roadwise (*Vegtsamr*) and Masked One (*Grimnir*).

Clearly there are various different ways to discover more about pre-Christian cults and deities and conceptions of the Otherworld, but no one clear method which will quickly reveal their nature. We must make good use of them all if we are to understand vanished cults and beliefs, while realizing that we must be basically dependent on written sources to build up a reliable picture of the religion and myths of ancient Europe.

RELIGIOUS BELIEFS

Indications of religion in Europe begin with fragmentary evidence from the hunting and gathering peoples during and after the Ice Age. But of the beliefs of the early peoples who inhabited Europe in the Neolithic period and the Bronze Age we in fact know little. We do not know what language they spoke and have only vague ideas about the gods they worshipped. Their religion is likely to have been a shamanic one, like that of later hunting peoples in northern Europe and Asia. The shaman, through help of guardian spirits and the ability to send out his own spirit while his body lay in a trance, was held to visit the Otherworld and so gain hidden knowledge. Men and women with shamanic powers acted as healers and counsellors, and helped to find the animals needed for food. It seems probable that in this early period the peoples of Europe worshipped supernatural guardians of the wild, both male and female, who controlled the animals they hunted and had to be treated with great respect. The concept of a powerful hunting goddess is thought by some to have been one of the earliest religious beliefs held in northern Eurasia.

The great megalithic graves which spread northwards over Europe in the third millennium BCE suggest that, as communities led a more settled existence, dead ancestors became increasingly important. There is some indication that bones of the dead from individual families and clans were brought together to be placed in the great stone tombs, and venerated by their descendants. In some graves in Brittany and elsewhere carvings indicate a belief in a powerful goddess who guarded the dead. Leading rulers were now able to establish great sanctuaries like Stonehenge and build impressive tombs like those at New Grange in Ireland, and the placing of some of their monuments appears to indicate observation of the sun, moon and stars.

Since established communities with sacred centres now practised agriculture, a god of the sky became increasingly important. The sun not only caused the crops to grow, but along with the moon provided a way to keep account of time. The symbol of the sun-disk was persistently carved on the rocks by peoples of the Bronze Age in Sweden, and seems to have been carried in procession, from the evidence of rock carvings depicting cult activities. In the Bronze Age we first find figures which seem to represent supernatural powers, both among the rock carvings and also in the form of bronze figurines. The carvings indicate considerable emphasis on ritual and symbolism, and appear to have been executed by members of a heroic, aristocratic society. Some have thought that these people of the northern Bronze Age were early speakers of Indo-European, which afterwards developed into many different national groups of languages, including that of the Romans, while German scholars of the early nineteenth century regarded them as the direct ancestors of their race.

The sky-god

Once we reach the Viking Age, extending from about the late eighth to the end of the eleventh century CE, we have some knowledge of the cults of the gods worshipped in northern Europe and of the myths told about them. From literary material from Scandinavia and Iceland we learn of a company of divine beings dwelling in Asgard, always under threat from their enemies, the frost giants from Jotunheim. In the Viking Age the god of the sky was not depicted as a sun-god; he was Thor, guardian of thunder and lightning, and owner of the hammer which was the lightning weapon. Thunor was the god of the early Anglo-Saxons remembered in English place-names, and Donar that of the continental Germans, and these were presumably gods of a similar kind, while the Celts had a thunder-god Taranis, and the Slavs one called Perun. Thor is known to have been worshipped with particular enthusiasm in western Norway and Iceland, and many people bore names such as Thorstein or Thorgunna, while numerous places were called after him. His worshippers appealed to him for safe voyages and good weather, for prosperity in the local community and the rule of law.

Thor plays a prominent part in the surviving myths, pictured as a powerful, red-bearded figure, possessed of an invincible hammer forged by the dwarfs, as well as a belt and gloves which gave him enormous strength. He drove across the heavens in a wagon drawn by a pair of goats, and its rattle caused the noise of thunder on earth below. Like the Hindu god Indra, with whom he has something in common, Thor had a tremendous appetite, impressing even the giants by his capacity for food and drink. Some of the myths about him are comic ones, like the tale of how he went disguised as a veiled goddess into the world of the giants to discover his stolen hammer, but the terror which his mighty power evoked as well as the warm affection in which he was held can be sensed in tales of his exploits. The gods would have been at the mercy of the giants without his hammer to protect them, and men and women turned to him for support. Since he governed the sky from which came wind and rain, he brought fertility to the land, and could give protection from storms at sea. His hammer was worn as an amulet to protect from evil and danger, as Christians wore the cross, and was depicted on memorial stones with an invocation committing the dead to his keeping. It seems also to have been used to hallow marriages, and to mark acceptance of a newborn child into the community.

Appeals were made to Thor when a difficult decision had to be reached, and his image was set up not only in shrines of the gods but also in places where assemblies were held and law meetings took place, since he was the guardian of law and order. The arm-ring on which oaths were sworn was said to be kept in his shrine, and the Icelandic Assembly opened on his day, Thursday, which replaced the day of Jupiter in the Roman week. The oak tree was sacred to Thor, and there are accounts of sacred oaks being cut down by Christian missionaries in Germany and Scandinavia, while a wood sacred to Thor outside Dublin was destroyed by the Christian king Brian Boru in 1000 CE. There are many allusions to Thor's temples in the Icelandic sagas, and families coming to settle in Iceland might bring with them pillars sacred to Thor from the shrines left behind in Norway, throwing these into the sea to let Thor choose the place where they came ashore, so that the new home could be set up there.

Myths about Thor are for the most part concerned with his victories over the giants who threatened the gods. Sometimes he made visits to Jotunheim, and some of the earliest skaldic verses deal with this theme. One famous journey was to the realm of the giant Geirrod, when Thor was without his hammer, but he slew the giant and his two evil daughters by breaking their backs on the rocks. Snorri Sturluson also relates a sophisticated tale of Thor's visit to the hall of the giant Utgard-Loki, where he and his companions were outwitted in various contests by deceiving magic, although the power of the god terrified the beholders. Thor also fought a duel with the giant Hrungnir, who made his way into Asgard, and on several occasions appeared with his hammer just in time to despatch some troublesome intruder.

The most famous myth about Thor, however, tells how he went fishing with an ox-head for bait, and hooked the terrible World Serpent which lay in the depths of the sea encircling the earth. This achievement is remembered in Icelandic poems and also depicted on stones of the Viking Age earlier than the literary sources, while some of Thor's hammer amulets are decorated with symbols of the god and the serpent. In the story as we have it, the terrified giant in the boat with Thor cut the line as the fearful head of the monster emerged from the waves, so that it sank back into the sea, but this may originally have been a creation myth in which the sky-god overcomes the monster of the deep. Early poems contain allusions to many giants and giantesses slain by Thor whose tales have been lost.

The war-god

Although Thor is a dominant figure among the Scandinavian deities, he does not rule the divine kingdom of Asgard. This is the function of Odin, who plays a major role in the poems and myths. He was held to bring magic power, eloquence and the gift of poetry to his followers, to grant victory in battle to those he favoured, and to decide the fortunes of kings and warrior leaders. Unlike Thor, he was not concerned with law and justice, and indeed was regarded as a deceiving power, ultimately forsaking his followers and treacherously condemning them to death in battle; he was also a deliberate stirrer up of strife. Odin was regarded as the ancestor of kings, as was his counterpart Wodan in Anglo-Saxon England, whose day was Wednesday. Odin's symbols were the eagle, the raven and the wolf, and these were used to adorn weapons, shields and royal treasures, as well as the spear, which was his own chosen weapon. His mighty spear Gungnir was said to be used to provoke conflict, and he could hurl it to decide victory or defeat.

In Scandinavian sources, Odin's insistence on final defeat for his greatest heroes was said to be due to his need of them to defend the gods when their enemies entered Asgard. He welcomed great warriors to his Otherworld hall, Valhalla, the hall of the slain, where dead kings and champions lived a warrior's life of feasting and battle. Odin himself was a constant wanderer, seeking hidden knowledge, and in particular the secret of his own fate in the final conflict which he knew must come at Ragnarok. He journeyed between the worlds on his eight-legged horse Sleipnir, or appeared as an old, one-eyed man in a hood or a broad-brimmed hat, stirring up strife between kings. He could also take on other shapes, sometimes flying as an eagle through the air or crawling through narrow openings as a serpent. Like Thor he sometimes visited the giants, but this was in search of information about the past or future, and his method of overcoming them was to defeat them in riddle contests, a favourite theme of Icelandic poems. He was said to be one-eyed because he had sacrificed an eye in return for hidden knowledge.

In one poem, *Hávamál*, Odin is also described as sacrificing himself on the World Tree, pierced with a spear, in order to obtain knowledge of the runic symbols which he passed on to his followers. Runic letters were used for inscriptions and for divination, to bring healing or to cause injury, as well as providing magical protection and luck. Runic lore was associated with Odin, as was the gift of eloquence and the power to compose poetry, and one of the best-known myths is that of his recovery of the mead of inspiration from the giant who had gained possession of it. The poems tell of his many names, and of his skill in magic, as well as his power over the fates of kings. He could help warriors in battle, and the binding and unbinding of fetters, the hurling of spears and resistance to battle panic were held to be under his control. He was said to instruct young heroes, granting them gifts such as swords, armour and fine horses. Above all he could give men ecstasy in battle, so that his chosen followers, the berserks, were free from fear and believed themselves impervious to wounds. Odin was served by supernatural women, the valkyries, who rode through the air, carried out his commands by ensuring victory or defeat as he willed, and conducted the distinguished leaders of armies to his realm when they fell on the battlefield.

Odin could visit the underworld when he needed to consult the dead, and the Germanic Wodan worshipped by the continental Germans appears to have been mainly an underworld deity. However the eagle symbol, perhaps borrowed from the Roman emperors, linked him with the sky as well as with the depths. He was also said to have a seat high in the World Tree, from which he could look out over all realms, while his two ravens also journeyed far and brought him tidings. As depicted in the Viking Age he is a complex figure, and because he was worshipped by aristocratic warriors many myths concerning him were taught to young men and recited in royal halls, so that they have survived into later times, while many memorial stones bear scenes of heroes arriving in Valhalla. Those raised in Gotland from the eighth to the tenth century CE, as well as funeral poems describing kings entering Valhalla, indicate the importance of the warrior-god among the ruling classes. It was rare, however, for either people or places to be named after Odin, and in Iceland, where there was no king to rule them, people turned increasingly to Thor.

Evidently the cult of a warrior-god was important before the Viking Age, to judge from the extravagant sacrifices of war equipment, horses and even warships which have been found in the peat bogs of Denmark from the early centuries of the Christian era. The identity of such gods before the cult of Odin was established in Scandinavia, however, is not easy to determine. One of them may have been Tyr (earlier *Tiwaz). The single myth which survives about him tells how when the wolf Fenrir was reared among the gods, only Tyr was bold enough to feed and care for him. A magic chain was forged to hold him which could not be broken, but the wolf refused to have it round his neck unless someone would put a hand in his mouth as a pledge that he would not remain a captive. Tyr was the only one willing to do this, and he lost his hand, but Fenrir was fettered and fated to remain so until Ragnarok, when he would break loose and devour Odin.

The powers of fertility

Odin, Thor and Tyr belonged to the race of the Æsir, but there was a second group of deities known as the Vanir, to which the god Njord and his son and daughter, Freyr and Freyja, belonged. Freyr was a powerful god in Sweden, and although the Vanir deities were associated mainly with peace and plenty, he was regarded as the supporter of the Swedish kings in warfare. His boar symbol was said to protect the lives of warriors, and was worn as a crest on early Anglo-Saxon and Swedish helmets, while the kings of Sweden in the period before the Viking Age apparently possessed great helmets like boar masks.

Njord, Freyr's father, was a god associated with ships and with seas and lakes, which in Scandinavia were an important source of food. One myth about Njord tells of his marriage with Skadi, a giant's daughter, but they afterwards parted because she could not bear to live near the sea and he hated the mountains which were her domain. The widespread custom of burying the dead in boats and ships, or of using a ship as a funeral pyre, may possibly have had links with the Vanir. Freyr himself possessed a wonderful ship which could sail against wind and tide, while other symbols associated with him were the horse and the boar. Sacred horses were said to have been kept in his sanctuaries, and Freyr and Freyja possessed a golden boar which ran across the heavens and descended below the sea at night, evidently associated with the sun. There are accounts of worshippers of Freyr setting up temples to him in Iceland, and the sagas preserve memories of rivalry between his cult and that of Odin.

Freyr, like Odin, was closely linked with kingship. He was said to have been the first ruler of Sweden, and to have been represented by the kings who succeeded him. The Danes had a similar tradition of a series of kings called Frodi, renowned for their prosperous reigns. Sometimes their bodies were borne round the land when they died to bring fertility, and sacrifices were made at their burial mounds, as in the case of Freyr. The impression left by these somewhat confused traditions is that the kings reigning at Uppsala were regarded as successors of Freyr, and there is no doubt of the importance of royal ancestors in their burial mounds in the sacred centres of their kingdoms in the early Viking Age, believed to bring prosperity to the realm. This concept seems to have preceded the idea of the king journeying to Valhalla to dwell with Odin after death.

The goddesses also belonged to the Vanir, although some who made marriages with the gods were said to be daughters of giants. There is no doubt of their power and importance, and there were halls sacred to them in Scandinavia, even though comparatively little information has come down to us in the mythical literature, mainly composed by men for a male audience. The two leading goddesses were Freyja, the sister and perhaps also the bride of Freyr, and Frigg, queen of heaven and wife of Odin, and it is possible that these are two different aspects of the same great goddess. Other lesser figures such as Idun, who guarded the golden apples giving the gods perpetual youth, and Gefion, who ploughed round a tract of land in Sweden and then dragged it to Denmark to form the island of Zealand, may again possibly be representations of the same goddess, functioning under different names in separate localities.

The literary sources have a good deal to tell us about lesser beings who might be seen as linked with the Vanir, since they could bring fertility to flocks and herds and to the earth, and a covenant made with such local powers would bring good luck and prosperity in hunting and farming. There were guardian spirits attached to certain families, and land spirits, male and female, dwelling in rocks and stones and hills. These were said to be encountered by the early settlers who came to Iceland, who found that they would give counsel in dreams and bring good fortune if their favour could be won. There are references too to the Norns, female spirits akin to the goddesses who determined the destiny of the individual at birth, and to the 'following ones' (*fylgjur*) which accompanied human beings through life, sometimes in female and sometimes in animal form. Such supernatural beings must be recognized as part of the religious background of the Viking Age, together with the more complex figures of the major gods and goddesses.

Enigmatic gods

There are other figures said to dwell in Asgard of whom we know little, but who may have been prominent in earlier times. Mimir is said to guard the spring of wisdom, and there is an allusion in a poem to Odin sacrificing an eye in return for a drink from Mimir's well, although this may possibly be a borrowing from Irish tradition. Another mysterious character is Ull, called God of the Shield, after whom places in Scandinavia were named, who may have been one of the Vanir. Another is Heimdall, called the White God, whose keen ears could catch the faintest sound, who sat guarding the bridge into Asgard ready to blow his horn if any danger threatened the gods. He is called the son of nine mothers, apparently giantesses connected with the sea, and in one of the poems of the Edda, *Rígsthula*, he appears as Rig, the progenitor of the various classes of society: thrall, farmer and jarl. This is another myth which has been thought to show Irish influence.

Heimdall was the sworn enemy of Loki, one of the most enigmatic inhabitants of Asgard, who appears in many myths. He was a frequent companion of the gods, although sometimes he is represented as a giant, and he supports the giants when they attack the stronghold of the gods at Ragnarok. The monsters who threaten the safety of Asgard, the World Serpent and the Wolf, together with Hel, the sinister goddess ruling the realm of death, are all said to have been begotten by Loki.

In the myths Loki appears mainly as a trickster, whose pranks brings trouble to the gods and arouse their anger, as when he cut off the hair of Thor's wife Sif, or helped a giant to steal the golden apples which kept them young. However he always finds a way to save himself by some ingenious plan to put things right, helped by his ability to change shape and become bird, animal or fish at will. He persuades the dwarfs to make new hair of gold for Sif, and flies in the shape of a hawk to retrieve the goddess and her apples from the giant, while when Thor's hammer is stolen it is Loki who masterminds Thor's journey to Jotunheim disguised as Freyja in order to recover it. When the gods were threatened by a giant building a wall for them round Asgard, Loki took on the shape of a mare and lured away the giant's horse which was assisting him, so that the builder failed to fulfil his contract and was killed. The result of this was the birth of Sleipnir, Odin's wonderful horse with eight legs, and indeed the dubious exploits of Loki often resulted in enormous benefits to the gods, and the creation of some of their greatest treasures. But he did not retrieve the situation after he caused the death of Balder, Odin's son, and the gods took vengeance by binding him under a rock beneath snakes which dropped poison on him from above, there to remain until Ragnarok. The figure of the bound Loki with his wife beside him appears to be depicted on the Gosforth Cross in Cumberland.

Balder is another puzzling figure, who is called the son of Odin, but whom the Danish historian Saxo represents as a human hero. Snorri describes him as the fairest of the gods, and it is indicated in the Edda poems that Odin knew that threats to Balder's life would mark the beginning of the final catastrophe. As Snorri recounts the myth, Balder's mother, the goddess Frigg, took oaths from all living things and even inanimate ones that they would never harm him, but she neglected to include the mistletoe. Through the malice of Loki a blind god, Hother, another obscure character in Asgard, flung a dart of mistletoe at Balder in sport, and slew him. Snorri then gives an elaborate account of Balder's funeral, attended by all the gods, and tells how a messenger was sent to the kingdom of Hel, the goddess of the dead, to bring him back to Asgard. Hel agreed that he should return if all on earth, including inanimate things, wept for him, but once again Loki intervened, taking on the form of an old giantess who brusquely refused to lament over Balder's death. While the tale is in keeping with myths of a slain fertility-god in other religions, there is no convincing evidence of worship of Balder as a god in Scandinavia or Germany, and we do not know the source from which Snorri derived the powerful myth of his death, or that of the ride to Hel to rescue him.

The world of the gods

The mythological geography associated with gods and giants is well developed in Old Norse literature. In the centre of the nine worlds inhabited by various races of beings, including the people of earth, stood the World Tree, the ash Yggdrasil, and around this and beneath its roots were grouped the different worlds, although their names and exact positions are never clearly specified. Hel, the world of the dead (since Valhalla was reserved for kings and heroes), lay under its roots, while others appear to be high above, and Asgard, the world of the gods, is said to be reached by a rainbow bridge running across the heavens. The concept of a tree which rises through a series of worlds is found in northern Eurasia, and forms part of shamanic lore, possibly based on the Pole Star in the centre of the heavens. An eagle was said to perch on the World Tree, and a serpent to twine round its roots, while Odin had his seat high among the branches and could look into all worlds. Odin was said to have hung from the tree, pierced with a spear, as a sacrifice in order to discover the secrets of runic magic.

Jotunheim, the realm of the frost-giants, could be reached from Asgard, but the journey was long and difficult. So also was the route to Hel, the kingdom of death. There are graphic descriptions in the poems of the vast expanses between the worlds, over mountains and across rivers. There was also a second realm of the gods where the Vanir lived, Vanaheim, and it was said that at one time there was a war between the two races, although they afterwards concluded a truce and dwelt together in Asgard.

Since most of our literary evidence comes from late in the Viking Age or after its close, there are many gaps in our knowledge of the earlier beliefs, and the cult of Odin is the one of which we hear most. But it seems as if the community of the gods was a well-established feature in Germanic religion. They were honoured as a group at the main religious feasts, which all were expected to attend, and several deities are mentioned together in oath formulas. In the poem *Völuspá* we have a convincing picture of the gods sitting in council together and establishing order in the world, and three are mentioned as joining together in the creation of humankind, after the earth was formed from the body of a dead giant Ymir. Tacitus in the first century CE refers to the Germans appealing to the gods as a group.

At the regular religious feasts dividing up the year, ale or mead was hallowed to the gods, and there was a sacrificial killing of either a boar, a bull or a stallion to provide a feast for the gods and the community. This however did not prevent an individual from adopting a particular god or goddess as guardian and protector, and raising a shrine on his land to worship the chosen deity. Christianity for many meant adopting Christ in this way, without rejecting other gods preferred by one's neighbours. The Scandinavian kings gave special worship to Odin or Freyr, and worshippers of Freyr or Thor continued to support their cults after they moved to Iceland, raising shrines to them there.

There was no highly organized priesthood, and when a king was present it was he who took the leading part in the ritual at the feast, or else the local chieftain, as in Iceland, where he might well also have been the builder of the shrine where a god was worshipped. Sacrifices to the gods were usually animals, but human sacrifices of prisoners of war were made in return for victory. Such sacrifices might be decided by drawing lots, so that the will of the gods might be made manifest. There might also be occasional sacrifices at funerals, and we know from one detailed account from the tenth century that a slave girl was killed to provide a bride for a warrior leader who died among Scandinavians on the Volga, far from home, and was cremated on his ship with the body of the girl beside him. This account was written by a reliable Arab scholar and diplomat who witnessed it in 921 CE. The girl was strangled and stabbed, in accordance with the rites of Odin.

Much of the literature concerned with Odin has references to the end of the worlds of gods and humankind at Ragnarok, when their enemies endeavour to bring back the cold, darkness and chaos which existed before the founding of Asgard and the setting up of the sun and the moon. First the Wolf swallows the sun, and there is a terrifying three-year winter, without light or heat. Then the foes of the gods force a way into the stronghold, and in the final battle those on both sides are destroyed, in spite of Odin's splendid army of heoes, summoned by the horn of Heimdall, and the might of Thor. The giants, along with Loki who like the monsters has broken loose from his bonds, come by sea against Asgard, while the sons of Muspell, a band of enemies associated with fire, ride across the rainbow bridge and shatter it beneath their weight. The Wolf and the Serpent advance to fulfil their destiny, although they too perish. Odin is devoured by the Wolf, which is then slain by the god's young son, while Thor destroys the World Serpent but is killed by its poison. Freyr is overcome by Surt, a giant who brings fire to destroy the earth, and the old enemies Heimdall and Loki slay one another. Fire rages over the earth, and finally the sea overwhelms it.

Such is the account given by Snorri Sturluson, based on the memorable poem *Völuspá* (Prophecy of the Seeress) in the *Poetic Edda*, believed to have been composed about 1000 CE. Here we are told also that this is not the final chapter in the earth's history. It will rise again from the sea, cleansed by fire and water, and the sons of the gods, presumably with the goddesses, will survive to establish creative order once again, while a man and woman who have been sheltered in the World Tree will emerge to repeople the earth. This powerful myth of the last days has been preserved in great clarity, and shows some striking resemblances to Iranian myths of the world's ending. It may be based on an ancient mythical conception which survived into the Viking Age through its association with the god Odin. The climate of Iceland, with its terrible volcanic eruptions, some of which took place in early medieval times and included flooding and tidal waves, gave its people the experience of the extemes of cold and heat, and may have lent a new emphasis to earlier traditions.

Irish mythology

Christianity was introduced early into Ireland, so that there is no direct literary evidence for pre-Christian myths as in Iceland, but written sources of the Christian period have preserved some material about mythological figures about whom stories were remembered. Divine characters sometimes appear as members of royal families or as outstanding heroes, and some have a good deal in common with the Norse deities, although the Celtic gods are perhaps more complex in their attributes and powers.

There are tales of the Dagda, whose name means 'Good God', and who bears some resemblance to Thor in that he is a rather primitive figure armed with a club, with abundant strength and energy and a huge appetite. The title 'good' is not based on moral virtue, but on his skills and abilities; he was expert in warfare, magic and building, and was hailed as 'Lord of Perfect Knowledge'. Like Thor with his hammer, he could not only kill with his club but also restore to life. He was renowned for his hospitality, and his cauldron was a symbol of abundance, while he was known also for his sexual vigour. Although represented as a rough and somewhat grotesque figure in the tales, he was undoubtedly a deity of great and varied powers.

Certain features are shared by the Irish god Lug and the Norse Odin, while Lug and the Germanic Wodan, Odin's predecessor, were both identified by the Romans with Mercury. Place-names show that Lug was known in Gaul, Holland and Silesia; Lyons, the capital of Gaul, was named after him, as was Luguvalium (later Carlisle) in Roman Britain. He has more inscriptions in his honour than any other Celtic deity, and there are legends of saints demolishing his temples and statues. He is a more sophisticated figure than the Dagda; his name probably means the Shining One, and he is often depicted as young and beardless. In Irish tradition he was many-skilled, excelling as smith, harper, poet, healer and craftsman, and he possessed kingly attributes, and is described as sitting in state beside the maiden who represented the sovereignty of Ireland. Like Odin, he was armed with a great spear, could give help in battle and was skilled in magic. He also fathered heroes, and the great Cu Chulainn was said to be his son. His festival, Lugnasa, was held on 1 August, and was celebrated on hill-tops in Ireland. Some have believed Lug to be a very ancient deity, going back to the time of the Indo-Europeans.

A third god remembered in Ireland who seems also to have been worshipped in Gaul was Donn, associated with death and the underworld. He plays little part in the literary sources, but is remembered in local traditions surviving into modern times. His home, House of Donn, is still said to be on a small island off the coast of Kerry, where he welcomes athletes such as footballers and hurlers who die young. He is described as a gloomy lord of the dead who also ruled the storm, and the dead were sometimes said to be seen travelling to his realm, so that he bears some resemblance to the Germanic Wodan. He is named in the literature as one of the sons of Mil who invaded Ireland and defeated the Túatha Dé, the company of the gods.

This tradition of warfare between two goups of supernatural beings is in agreement with Norse tradition of a war between the Æsir and the Vanir, but it is set in a different framework, and we are told more about the actual fighting. There are accounts in the literature of the First and Second Battles of Mag Tuired, and how the Túatha Dé finally took Lug as their leader. His spear and the sword of another god, Nuadu, from which there was no escape once it left the scabbard, proved invincible weapons. Nuadu lost a hand in the battle, but had it replaced by a silver one. Little is known of him, but he may be the same as the god Nodens, worshipped at Lydney Park in Gloucestershire in Roman times. Some scholars also stress the importance of a god Cernunnos (Horned One), which they identify with the horned figure sitting beside a stag on the Gudestrup Cauldron. This name is only known from a single inscription on an altar from Paris, and may be a title, since horns were worn by various deities as a sign of power. There is some evidence however for an earlier male god of the wild creatures, worshipped by Celtic hunters.

Another impressive deity in Irish literature is Manannan mac Lir (Son of the Sea), whose name is related to that of the Isle of Man, and who bears some resemblance to the Norse Heimdall. He was associated with a joyous underworld beneath the waves, and with voyages to enchanted islands. There are a number of tales in the literature of kings and heroes summoned to a wonderful realm across the sea, where existence is free from sorrow, death and corruption, and there are beautiful women to welcome the visitor. Here orchards bear golden apples, and these, as in Norse tradition, are said to bring the gift of eternal youth. This land has many strange names, such as Land of Promise, Land of the Young,

Land of Women or Plain of Delight. Other fantastic tales of voyages to islands of marvels have been preserved in the literature.

While there is no equivalent of the Ragnarok tradition in Irish sources, the account of the Second Batttle of Mag Tuired bears certain resemblances to it in the prophecies of disaster and destruction to come, and in both cases a desperate struggle is finally succeeded by the birth of a new age. Since the influence of Christian learning has to be taken into account in the written sources, it is not possible to determine what concepts of the ending of an age may have formed part of both Celtic and Germanic religious beliefs. There is no real evidence of borrowing on either side, but both peoples seem to look back on older traditions of creation, destruction and renewal.

As in Norse mythology, there are traces of cults of powerful goddesses in Ireland, and these are supported in later popular tradition. The figure of the Hag of Beare is particularly associated with the Beare peninsula in south-west Ireland, but legends about her survive elsewere and also in parts of Scotland, and there are strong indications that she has developed from an ancient mother goddess, linked with creation, wild nature, sovereignty, war and death. Another outstanding figure is that of Brigid, who has been partly transformed into a revered Christian saint, but must be linked with the goddess Brigantia worshipped in northern Britain at the time of the Roman invasion, who could bring victory and also healing. Brigid was associated with the welfare of flocks and herds, and such skills as weaving, brewing and butter-making, as well as poetry and traditional learning, and she may have descended from the chief goddess worshipped in Gaul whom Julius Caesar identified with Minerva.

We know the names of many goddesses worshipped by the Celtic peoples in Britain and Gaul from the monuments raised in their honour during the Roman occupation. Temples dedicated to them attracted crowds of pilgrims seeking healing, who sometimes left wooden figures behind with indications of their disabilities, as at the temple of Sequana at the source of the Seine. Some goddesses were adopted by the Romans, as was the goddess of the hot springs at Bath, and also the riding goddess Epona. taken over as patron of the Roman cavalry regiments, whose cult attracted both military men and horse-breeders. Such goddesses could be concerned with warfare as well as healing. One from Brittany had a helmet with an aggressive goose as a crest, while Boudicca, the queen of the Iceni in eastern England, is said to have appealed to a war-goddess Adraste for help in her revolt against the Romans, and to have massacred Roman women as offerings. Destructive goddesses of battle and violence are found in the Irish sagas, particularly the *Babd* and the *Morrigán*. They could stir up warfare and strike fighting men with terror, and like the Norse valkyries who also appeared on the battlefield they are associated with the birds of prey, crows and ravens which feast on the dead.

Some goddesses were linked with male gods, as was Rosmerta, shown frequently with the god Mercury, who has no regular partner in the Graeco-Roman tradition. The mother goddesses also, shown singly or as a pair but more often as three female figures who may be of different ages or character, were clearly of importance in local religious belief. Like the land-spirits of Scandinavia, they were linked with the fertility of the earth, and often depicted holding fruit (particularly apples), but also with the wellbeing of the family, symbolized by the babies they often hold in their arms. Thus both gods and goddesses remembered in Ireland fit into a wider group of Celtic deities in Britain and on the continent, although no coherent picture of a shared religion of the Celts survives.

Religions of the Celts

An important difference between the Celts and the Germans is that in Roman times the Celtic peoples in western Europe had a powerful priesthood. According to Greek and Roman writers, three important classes in Celtic society were those of druids, bards and seers. The druids, who have been compared to the Brahmins of India and the pontiffs of Rome, were said to organize sacrifices, make legal decisions and teach religious traditions, but their knowledge was not recorded in writing. They also predicted future events and interpreted the will of the gods, and a bronze ritual calendar found at Coligny in France appears to have been used to help in divination, perhaps to choose auspicious days for various activities. There are traces of a similar system of druids, bards and seers in Ireland, and references in the literature to druids advising the rulers, while Tacitus records how the Romans destroyed a number of druids on the island of Anglesey in Wales in 60 CE. The brief accounts of these undoubtedly influential figures caught the imagination of eighteenth-century writers, and there were continual attempts to romanticize and revive them.

Certainly they must have helped to shape religious beliefs, whereas among the Scandinavian peoples this appears to have been the work rather of poets, storytellers, seers and seeresses. The Germanic priests do not seem to have had recognized religious centres, but merely functioned at sacrificial rituals, and even there it was the kings who took the prominent part. The druids underwent long periods of training, and there were presumably lesser priests in the shrines set up for single or small groups of deities. The Celts had few large temples, but at those at Entremont and Roqueperteuse in southern France, established before the Roman conquest of Gaul, there were impressive statues of gods or ancestors in stone, and here heads of enemies killed in battle or captured and sacrificed were preserved. This continued to be an accepted practice among the Celts, borne out by both literary and archaeological evidence, and there are accounts in the Irish sagas of the head of a vanquished champion being treated with great honour and set up to preside over a feast. As in Scandinavia and Anglo-Saxon England, sacrificial feasts formed an important part of Celtic religious ritual, and many are described in the Irish sagas. The Irish had four main feasts throughout the year, Imbolc in February, Beltene in May, Lugnasa in August and Samhain in October, marking important points in the agricultural and farming year. Mead or ale and the cauldron holding it formed an essential element in the religious feast, and there was ritual distribution of the meat of the sacrificial boar according to the rank and prestige of those taking part, not surprisingly a frequent cause of strife. Irish literature contains accounts also of the ritual for the choosing of a king, when a bull or a horse might be sacrificed.

The small tribal territories would each have its own sacred centre, as among the Germanic peoples. The water of springs, lakes and rivers was of particular importance, and there might be places dedicated to supernatural beings close by, where offerings were left, or thrown into the water. Indeed the conditions under which Germanic and Celtic peoples lived before the acceptance of Christianity were generally similar, in spite of variations caused by the entry of Roman culture into the lives of many tribes when they became part of the Roman Empire. They were led by warrior kings, anxious to gain new and fruitful land for their people, supporting themselves by agriculture, hunting and adventurous trading by land and sea, as well as by raiding and piracy. They lived in an oral tradition which set considerable value on skills in poetry and oratory, the preservation of ancient learning and the rites of divination. It is therefore hardly surprising to find that similar patterns can be traced in their religion and myths.

RELIGION IN EVERYDAY LIFE

Although in ancient Europe religion extends over so great a time-span and most of our knowledge comes from the close of the pre-Christian period, it is probable that there was no great difference in the way which it affected the lives of the ordinary people from the time that agriculture began to be practised in the Neolithic period. Names of gods and goddesses and tales about them varied, as did local rituals, but a believer in the gods of the Viking Age need not have been wholly lost if he found himself present at a religious festival of the Bronze Age. One major change in religious practice came when the life of hunters and gatherers gave way to the establishment of settled communities growing crops and herding animals, while the second came with the introduction of Christianity.

The framework of early religion formed part of the life of the whole community under the king who ruled it, so that the early Christian missionaries found it essential to get the goodwill and support of the ruler when they entered non-Christian territories. There were no small exclusive groups, and there was no attempt to convert from the cult of one deity to another, although an individual or a family was often devoted to a particular god or goddess. Although the power of a deity was not confined to one particular sphere, certain powers were held to be suitable to call upon for special needs. Thus one of the early Christians in Iceland, Helgi the Lean, was said to continue to appeal to Thor when he needed good luck on a voyage. The women naturally turned to a goddess for help in family matters, childbirth and household skills, but worship of goddesses was by no means confined to women. Warlike leaders like Jarl Hakon of Norway might give devoted worship to a chosen goddess, while both men and women flocked to shrines of the goddesses for healing. House spirits and land spirits might also be called upon by both men and women. It was the men, however, who performed the worshipping rituals of the deities protecting the beasts of the forest and wild areas, and this continued long after farming was established. Military matters were also largely their concern, but not exclusively so; there were women leaders in Britain and Ireland who appear to have taken a leading part in battle, turning to goddesses for support. The emphasis in Old Norse literature on the strongly masculine cult of Odin, recorded by men concerned with the doings of kings, may be slightly misleading.

At the feasts marking stages of the agricultural year, sacrificial food and drink specially brewed for the occasion was shared with the gods. In Scandinavia the purpose of such feasts seems to have been to renew contact with the gods and so ensure their continued support and protection, and on such occasions all would want to take part. The blood of the sacrifice was deemed to possess great power, and might be sprinkled in the shrines of the gods, while Christians mocked at the Swedes for licking out the sacrificial bowls. Horns and hides of cattle killed for the feast were often hung up as a record, and the skulls of sacrificed animals retained. Again the drinking of ale or mead dedicated to the gods was a solemn moment, and vows might be made as the horn was passed round. Another time when people joined together in worship was when religious processions were held and symbols of the gods carried round. Again animal sacrifices might take place, and offerings be left in earth or water. Such ceremonies might be at certain times of the agricultural year, such as harvest, or on special occasions such as a victory. The rock carvings of the Bronze Age in Sweden give the impression that there were many such processions and rituals associated with divine symbols. Also, at times of calamity such as plagues among people or cattle, failure of crops, disastrous weather or defeat in battle there would be offerings to the gods to entreat their help. Work done by Ralston in nineteenth-century Russia, recording chants and ceremonies when Christian saints or biblical characters such as Elijah were evoked to bless the sowing or avert some danger, gives us some idea of local rituals in pre-Christian times.

People also came together at the funerals of kings and queens or leading persons, and the evidence of archaeology has shown how impressive such inhumation or cremation ceremonies could be. Funeral customs varied in different areas and periods, and families might have individual traditions, but the coming together for a memorable funeral was something at the heart of religion from the Neolithic period onwards. Mounds raised over the grave of the royal dead or the ashes of their funeral pyres often marked the sacred centre of a kingdom, and offerings were made to the ancestors who rested in them. Such impressive ceremonies helped to strengthen belief in an afterlife, although the literary evidence suggests that there was no general agreement as to the form which this might take. Simple ideas of a life continuing in the grave were mingled with traditions of a long and perilous journey to the land of the dead, and of a reception there by the supreme god or by one's dead kinsmen. The idea that kings and great warriors were received after death in the hall of Odin was one special conception of the afterlife developed by poets and sculptors in Scandinavia, but this was reserved for one particular class of aristocratic warrior.

The communal gatherings enabled people to keep in touch with the supernatural world and the deities who ruled it. There might also be lesser offerings of food and drink or part of the harvest, and personal offerings such as plaits of women's hair or ornaments might be thrown into water or left in the peat bogs. There is ample evidence for sacrifice of booty won in war, including horses and captives, in accordance with vows made before battle. When human sacrifice took place, the victims were mostly slaves, prisoners of war or malefactors;

however, in assessing the archaeological evidence it is not easy to differentiate between sacrifice and execution.

Links with the other world might be made during the simple pursuits of everyday life, taking place in the home, in fields and woods, or on a journey. In the Scottish Highlands Alexander Carmichael recorded prayers and appeals, to Mary, Brigid and Christ, to accompany various options. And these may well reflect earlier pre-Christian appeals and incantations. Reliance on help and protection from supernatural powers did not originate in Christian times, and was easily adapted to Christian teaching. Indeed many former religious traditions could be merged with the new practices of the church, as is evident from accounts of conversions in the Icelandic sagas. The feasts could be replaced by gatherings at Christian festivals, and the sanctity of food and drink could help towards an understanding of the mass. Lesser supernatural guardians of the past could be replaced by guardian angels and chosen saints. Even the myth of Odin hanging on the World Tree pierced by a spear, for which there is plenty of evidence for a pre-Christian origin in the hanging and stabbing of sacrificial victims, could have helped northern converts to accept the belief in the crucified Christ. The Anglo-Saxon poem *The Dream of the Rood*, in which the tree from which the cross was made speaks, and Christ is represented as a young warrior, shows how mythical concepts could come together with the new Christian teaching to inspire great religious poetry.

Communication with the Otherworld could be established in various ways. One was by dreams, in which advice or warning could be conveyed by a supernatural helper, and some of those described in the literature could come under the category of visions. Since dreams were found in the Bible, they were not disapproved of by the church, and many recorded in Icelandic literature contain vivid pre-Christian imagery. Sometimes the gods or helpful spirits appeared in dreams, and sometimes dark and sinister forms gave warnings of evil to come, while messages might also be received from the dead. Sleeping on a burial mound or on the hide of a sacrificed bull could bring significant dreams to the sleeper.

There were skilled interpreters of dreams, and men and women expert in other ways of ascertaining what the future held were important members of the community. We hear of seers and seeresses in Scandinavia and of druids in the Irish sagas. Shamanism continued among the Inuit and the Saami in the north and in Russia throughout the pre-Christian period, and must have influenced Scandinavian divination ceremonies. It was customary to turn to a god for counsel when important decisions had to be made, and the community also sought to learn by divination what sort of harvest was promised and where hunting would be profitable, as well as what the result of a conflict with an enemy would be. Both Old Norse and Old Irish literature are rich in examples of methods used by seers to gain inspiration, and poetic inspiration was linked with this and regarded as a divine gift. There was much consulting of omens, such as the movements of birds, the behaviour of sacred horses and observation of the natural world, and seers in Ireland might watch the spread of forest fires or listen to the noise of the sea.

While the outcome of chance might be governed by supernatural powers, the idea of an implacable fate was a powerful concept in the pre-Christian past. The destiny of kings was emphasized in the early heroic literature, but that of each child born was also taken seriously, and female guardians of destiny, such as the Scandinavian Norns, were held to determine this at birth. The concept of fate as a power higher even than the gods was strongly established in northern literature, and vividly expressed in the Scandinavian myth of Ragnarok.

Since there were no means of recording religious traditions in writing other than the restricted use of runic characters before the coming of Christianity, they were passed on in oral tradition, in poems about the gods and countless legends and myths related by storytellers, along with a wealth of symbols. This kept traditions alive but resulted in considerable flexibility and local variation, although the general pattern of beliefs seems to have remained constant. Contacts with the civilization of the Roman Empire and later with Christianity were bound to influence symbols and myths in the last period of pre-Christian religion from which most of our evidence is taken. Yet although much of this religion remains obscure and confusing to us now, an increasing amount of evidence can be found in the study of early literature, art and archaeology, if we are prepared to approach this with caution and humility.

Bibliography

Chippendale, C. 1983. *Stonehenge complete*. London: Thames and Hudson.

Dumézil, G. 1973. *Gods of the ancient Norsemen*, ed. E. Haugen. Berkeley: University of California press.

Davidson Ellis, H. R. 1988. *Myths and symbols of pagan Europe: early Scandinavian and Celtic religions*. Manchester: Manchester University Press.

1993. *The lost beliefs of northern Europe*. London: Routledge.

1998. *Roles of the northern goddess*. London: Routledge.

Evans, A. C. 1986. *Sutton Hoo ship burial*. London: British Museum Publications.

Green, M. 1986. *The gods of the Celts*. Gloucester: Alan Sutton.
    1995. *Celtic goddesses*. London: British Museum Press. And a number of other works by this author, on archaeology and symbolism of the Celts.

Hutton, R. 1967. *The pagan religions of the British Isles, their nature and legacy*. Oxford: Blackwell.

Mac Cana, P. 1982. *Celtic mythology*. New edn, Feltham: Newnes Press. An excellent general picture.

Näsström, B. 1995. *Freyja: the great goddess of the North*. Lund Studies in History of Religions 5. Lund: University of Lund.

OhOgain, D. 1990. *Myth, legend and romance: an encyclopaedia of Irish folk tradition*. London: Ryan Publishing. An extremely useful and reliable book on individual characters and myths.

Owen, G. R. 1981. *Rites and symbols of the Anglo-Saxons*. Newton Abbot: David and Charles.

Piggott, S. 1968. *The Druids*. Harmondsworth: Penguin. A good critical study.

Powell, T. G. E. 1958. *The Celts*. Ancient Peoples and Places. London: Thames and Hudson. Strong on archaeological side.

Rees, A. and B. 1961. *Celtic heritage: ancient tradition in Ireland and Wales*. London: Thames and Hudson.

Sjoedstedt, M. 1982. *Gods and heroes of the Celts*, trans. M. Dillon. Berkeley: University of California Press.

Turville Petre, E. O. G. 1964. *Myth and religion of the North*. London: Weidenfeld and Nicolson. Concentrates on textual evidence.

9 The Indus Civilization

GREGORY L. POSSEHL

Introduction

Ancient India's first civilization arose on the plains of the Greater Indus Valley of Pakistan and north-western India during the second half of the third millennium BCE (c. 2500–1900 BCE). This has come to be called the Indus Civilization and was the first period of urbanization in the Indian subcontinent. The great cities of the Indus Civilization were Mohenjo-daro and Harappa, both in Pakistan. Mohenjo-daro today is on the western bank of the Indus river in the province of Sindh, and Harappa, 650 km to the north-east, is on the southern bank of the Ravi river in the West Punjab. The ancient Indus peoples lived in a society with marked social classes and craft and career specialists, some of whom knew the art of writing. They engaged in long-distance trade with the Arabian Gulf, Mesopotamia, Iran, Afghanistan and central Asia.[1]

There is no reference to the Indus Civilization in the historical documentation of the subcontinent. This is a contrast to Mesopotamian civilization and Dynastic Egypt, which were noted in the Bible and other literature. But the Vedic texts of ancient India, the earliest of the subcontinent's historical literature, contain no direct reference to the Indus Civilization, and the discovery of these ancient peoples was purely through archaeological excavation (Possehl 1999: 38–154).

The chronology of the Indus Civilization is based on radiocarbon dates, confirmed by good cross-ties to the early history (Akkadian period) of Mesopotamia. Undoubted Indus artefacts (e.g. stamp seals, etched carnelian beads, pottery) have been found in Mesopotamia, and at Susa in south-western Iran. Those who read the Mesopotamian texts have deduced that the Mesopotamian place-name 'Meluhha' was their designation for the Indus Civilization. There is also a Mesopotamian cylinder seal that once belonged to an Akkadian person who was a translator of the Meluhhan language.

Table 9.1 *Chronological chart of the Indus Civilization*

Archaeological stage	Dates BCE
Post-urban Phase	*c.* 1900–1500
Indus Civilization	*c.* 2500–1900
Early Harappan–Indus Civilization Transition	*c.* 2600–2500
Early Harappan	*c.* 3200–2600
Beginnings of agriculture and pastoralism	*c.* 7000

Radiocarbon dates and cross-ties allow archaeologists to date the Indus Civilization to *c.* 2500–1900 BCE. Radiocarbon dates lead them to believe that agriculture and pastoralism begin *c.* 7000 BCE in the subcontinent. This was the principal economic base on which the Indus Civilization depended. The threshold of civilization comes in what they call the 'Early Harappan' which dates to *c.* 3200–2600 BCE. The Early Harappan–Indus Civilization Transition is a short period for which archaeologists have found the critical cultural changes that led to urbanization. By *c.* 1900 BCE the cities of Mohenjo-daro and Harappa were no longer urban centres. So, too, went the art of writing, and much of the craft and career specialization associated with the Indus Civilization. This period has come to be called the Post-urban Phase. This chronology is summarized in Table 9.1.

Geography

Settlements of the Indus Civilization are found over about a million square km. The most westerly settlement is a fortified site called Sutkagen-dor, near the border between Pakistan and Iran and close to the Arabian Sea. The site of Lothal in Gujarat anchors the south-western corner of the Indus Civilization. The north-eastern sites are found in the upper portion of the Ganga-Yamuna River Doab, mostly in Saharanpur District of Uttar Pradesh. There is one settlement at Manda in Jammu (India), and another near Ropar on the upper Sutlej river. The greatest concentration of sites is in an area in Pakistan known as Cholistan ('Desert Country'), with 185 Indus Civilization settlements closely spaced around Ganweriwala in the inland delta of the ancient Sarasvati, or Hakra river. The most northerly site is Shortughai in northern Afghanistan. It was almost certainly a trading centre.

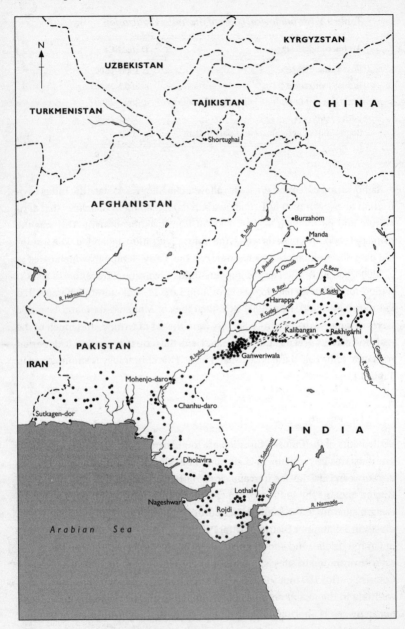

Map 9.1. Sites of the Indus Civilization.

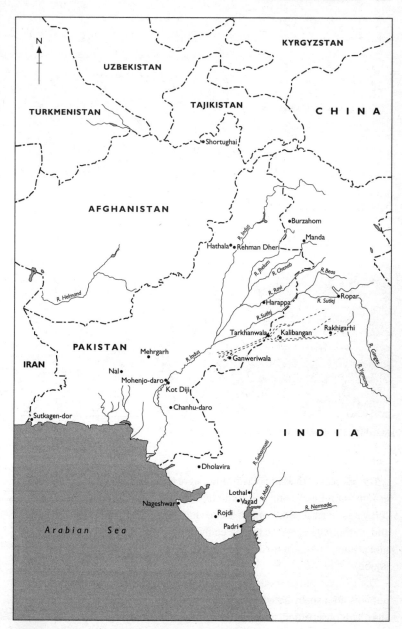

Map 9.2. Sites mentioned in the text.

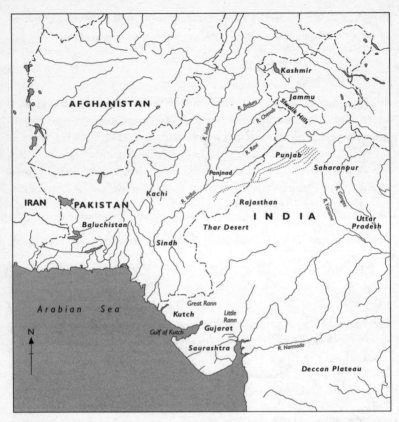

Map 9.3. Geographical places mentioned in the text.

The peoples of the Indus Civilization were farmers and herders who engaged in some hunting, fishing and gathering. They grew barley and wheat and also cultivated at least two forms of gram, chick peas, field peas, mustard, sesame and cotton. The evidence for the cultivation of rice during the Indus Civilization is poor. They also used grapes and gathered wild plants such as the Indian jujube.

The peoples of the Indus Civilization were large-scale cattle keepers. Cattle remains are usually above 50 per cent of the animal remains from excavated sites. This observation, and the cattle imagery in art, make it clear that this was the premier animal in their culture and that it is highly likely that it may have been the principal form of wealth. The Indus peoples also kept substantial numbers of water buffalo, sheep and goats.

Urban origins

The origins of the Indus Civilization are not well understood. There was a widespread Early Harappan period with four regional archaeological assemblages, but no particularly large settlements (Possehl 1999: 567–713). There is little sign of social stratification in the Early Harappan and craft specialization was not developed to a marked degree. There appears to have been a period of rapid culture change at about c. 2600–2500 BCE during which most of the institutions archaeologists associate with civilization (e.g. cities, social classes, writing, long-distance trade in luxury items) came together in the form that we now recognize as the Indus Civilization. The causes for this urbanization remain obscure.

Major settlements

There are five cities of the Indus Civilization; the two best known are Mohenjo-daro and Harappa, each about 100 ha in size. There is a third city of some 80 ha called Rakhigarhi in Haryana. This was the 'Eastern City' of the Indus Civilization and is currently under intensive excavation by the Archaeological Survey of India. The fourth city is completely untouched, in the Cholistan Desert of Pakistan. The fifth city is Dholavira. It too is some 80 ha in size. Short summaries on Mohenjo-daro and Harappa, as well as some of the other prominent Indus settlements, will serve to contextualize Indus religion.

Mohenjo-daro

Mohenjo-daro is a truly inspiring place. This is the 'city of baked brick' located on the floodplain of the Indus river, about 300 km north of the Arabian Sea coast. It was the 'premier' city of the Indus Civilization (Fig. 9.1). Since the writing system of the Indus peoples has not yet been deciphered we do not know what they called their city, or any of the others. Nor do we know what the Indus peoples called themselves.

Mohenjo-daro was first visited by an archaeologist in 1911–12, but came under systematic excavation only in 1922–23. This work continued until 1931, with the results published in several monumental works (Marshall 1931; Mackay

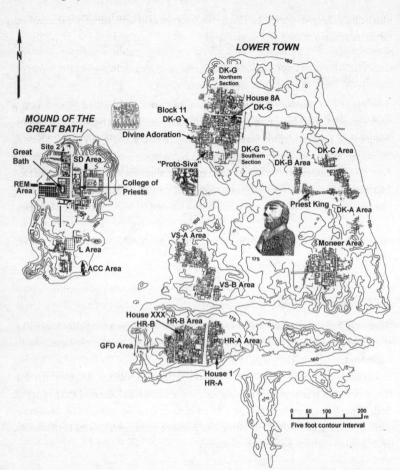

Fig. 9.1. Plan of Mohenjo-daro with principal pieces and buildings mentioned in the text. Drawn from Marshall 1931 and Mackay 1937–8, other sources and observation.

1937–38). There are two distinct mounds at Mohenjo-daro. To the west there is a high, relatively small, man-made prominence called the 'Mound of the Great Bath'. This part of the city has many impressive buildings, including what has been widely interpreted as a ritual bathing facility. Today the Lower Town is an extensive set of rolling mounds to the east of the Mound of the Great Bath, which is the area within which the main population of the city lived and worked. It is in this section of the site, about 1000 × 600 m in size, that we find the best expression of Harappan baked brick architecture, the grid town plan and the famous drainage system, connecting houses to a system of public sanitation. No one knows the size of the population at Mohenjo-daro, but estimates in the range of 20,000 – 30,000 seem to be the most reasonable.

Archaeologists have not found an Early Harappan settlement at Mohenjo-daro and the place seems to be a 'founder's city', a metropolis that was conceived and built as a single inspiration. The city was probably built during the Early Harappan–Indus Civilization Transition.

The excavation areas of Mohenjo-daro, which are used to designate the buildings and finds, are derived for the most part from the names of the excavators. Thus we have DK-Area excavated by K. N. Dikshit, HR-Area from H. Hargreaves, VS-Area from its excavator M. S. Vats, and so forth.

Harappa

The ancient city of Harappa is located on the southern bank of the Ravi, some 650 km to the north-east of Mohenjo-daro (Fig. 9.2). The city today is a huge set of rolling mounds, with the westernmost of them being quite high and steep, looming above the others. It is all quite dramatic, and unmistakable as an archaeological site. Harappa was first recorded as an ancient place in the early 1800s when it was visited by British travellers. In the middle of the nineteenth century Harappa was ravaged by brick robbers who used these materials for railway construction.

Excavation at Harappa was first undertaken in 1922–23 by D. R. Sahni of the Archaeological Survey of India. This city was settled considerably earlier than Mohenjo-daro, by the middle of the fourth millennium. There is also a substantial Early Harappan village there and then the great Indus metropolis. The site has been divided into several areas: the High Mound, also called Mound AB; Mound F to the north with a 'granary' or warehouse, husking floors and other small, regular buildings. Somewhat curiously, Harappa has not produced the kinds of insights into Indus religion that have come from Mohenjo-daro; however it has produced the same range of artefacts as Mohenjo-daro, and in a style that is virtually identical. The poor preservation of the site does not give the visitor the same sense of an ancient urban environment as one finds at Mohenjo-daro, but the two cities would have been comparable when they were inhabited.

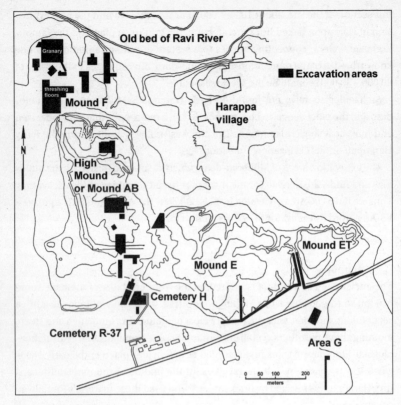

Fig. 9.2. Plan of Harappa.

Chanhu-daro

This is an Indus town located 110 km south of Mohenjo-daro. It is important for the presence of a workshop for making stamp seals and beads, and for understanding the relationship between the Indus Civilization and the Post-urban Phase in the region (Mackay 1943).

Lothal

Lothal is located in Gujarat at the head of the Gulf of Cambay. This trading centre provides an understanding of Indus Civilization trade and craftsmanship and the stratigraphic relationship between the Indus Civilization and the Post-urban

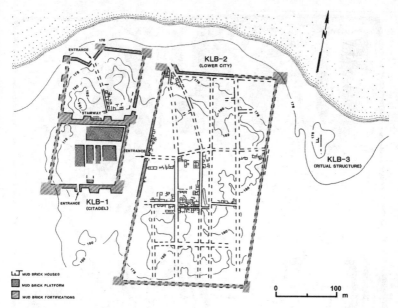

Fig. 9.3. Plan of Kalibangan.

Period in the region. The large brick-lined enclosure at the site was probably a water storage facility.

Dholavira

Located on an island in the Rann of Kutch, Dholavira was a major regional centre of the Indus Civilization. It is midway between Chanhu-daro and Lothal. At 60 ha the site was large by Indus standards. Dholavira was fortified and has a stratigraphic succession from the Early Harappan to the Indus Civilization and succeeding cultures.

Kalibangan

The Indus town of Kalibangan is very close to the present border between India and Pakistan on a now dry river, known today as the Hakra river and in antiquity as the Sarasvati (Fig. 9.3). It is a good example of a regional centre of the Indus Civilization. As a result of careful excavation it has a well-documented stratigraphic sequence from the Early Harappan to the Indus Civilization.

Fig. 9.4. An Indus stamp seal with the 'unicorn' device.

Writing

In spite of many claims to the contrary, the Indus script remains undeciphered (Possehl 1996a). The Indus peoples used a system of pictographic writing with about 400 characters according to most researchers. The most formal of the inscriptions are found on a series of stamp seals, most of which are made of steatite, a very soft stone. A majority of these seals are laid out with a line of script at the top, and an animal device below. The most frequently found animal device is a bull which perspective shows with a single horn, commonly called the 'unicorn' (Fig. 9.4). Other devises include the zebu, the Indian gaur, tigers, elephants and rhinos. There are also bar seals without devices. Writing was also done on copper-bronze tools, copper tablets, miniature tablets of shell, faience and steatite, bangles and pottery. The corpus of writing, not counting the graffiti scratched on the pottery, would come to about 3100 objects.

There are no Indus texts or writing preserved on paper, bark or other such materials. The layout of the inscriptions does not suggest a system of accounts, or lists of products. In fact, the number system, if there is one, is not a prominent feature of the corpus of texts. The inscriptions are short, from one to twenty-six characters, with an average of between five and six. This suggests that the messages on the stamp seals were used for identification: names, places, titles and the like. Graffiti on pottery could be names of owners/manufacturers and the like, as well as product identifications and places of origin/shipment. Some of the items with writing could have short incantations, sayings and the like. Some of the stamp seals and tablets seem to be narrative, or mnemonic devices, used in storytelling. Some of these suggest religious themes, which will be investigated as this chapter proceeds (Fig. 9.5).

While the script has not been demonstrably deciphered, there are some points of agreement about it, as well as some working hypotheses.

1. The script is to be read from the right to the left in stamp seal impressions.
2. The language of the inscriptions might be either of the Proto-Dravidian family or an early form of Munda, an Austro-Asiatic language found today in eastern India.
3. There is a need for a confirmed sign list. Most researchers agree that the sign counts and characteristics place it within the range of a logosyllabic system. There are too many signs for an alphabet and too few for a logographic system like Chinese, where individual words have individual characters. But there is disagreement concerning a number of important variables. What are the primary or core signs and which signs are ligatures, or combinations of these signs? What constitutes scribal and stylistic variation within the signs? Is there change in these variables over time and between places like Mohenjo-daro and Harappa?
4. The rebus principle, using the sign for a fish to stand for a more abstract notion that has the same kind of sound as the word for fish (e.g. using the image of an eye, for the first person singular 'I'), is probably the most powerful decipherment tool for cracking this writing system.

Fig. 9.5. The narrative seal of 'Divine Adoration'.

Trade and crafts

The peoples of the Indus Civilization were wide-ranging traders, within their territories of Pakistan and north-western India and with more distant places including Afghanistan, central Asia, the Iranian Plateau and Mesopotamia. Seafaring merchants of the Indus Civilization reached the Arabian Gulf and Mesopotamia, and probably the mouth of the Red Sea. The internal trade and commerce was involved with subsistence materials, such as fish, extending to raw materials such as copper, gold, silver, chert, soft grey stone, chalcedony and other semiprecious stones, lapis lazuli and shells.

The trade with Mesopotamia, which for the most part seems to have been maritime, is very well documented (Possehl 1996b). The first clue to these contacts comes from cuneiform documents, which speak of ships sailing in the Arabian Gulf, and those of Meluhha, or the Indus Civilization. These ships brought back semi-precious stones, exotic birds, timber and the like. Unfortunately we have little idea of what these shipping ventures brought to ancient India in exchange for these products. But there are many Indus artefacts in Mesopotamia, including seals, etched carnelian beads and ceramics. On the other hand, the Mesopotamian products found at Indus sites are very few.

The transformation of the Indus Civilization

The excavations at Mohenjo-daro and Harappa have demonstrated that these ancient cities were largely abandoned by 1900 BCE, at the end of the Indus period (Possehl 1997). This evidence, as well as regional archaeological exploration, indicate that Sindh and the West Punjab experienced the widespread abandonment of Indus settlements at the opening of the second millennium. But the same is not true everywhere. In Gujarat there are many settlements at the beginning of the Post-urban Phase. Rojdi, an important site in central Saurashtra, underwent a major rebuilding in the opening centuries of the second millennium that expanded the total size of the settlement by half. In the Indian Punjab, Haryana, northern Rajasthan and western Uttar Pradesh there are 216 known Indus Civilization settlements. The opening centuries of the second millennium BCE see them increase to 859: a fourfold rise. No one knows for sure the full meaning of these observations, but it does seem to indicate that the eclipse of the Indus Civilization was a regional phenomenon that did not strike all parts of the Indus world in the same way.

Older theories which hold that the cities and civilization were destroyed by invading Aryan tribes make very little sense. This is in part because there is no evidence for the sacking of any of the Indus Civilization settlements. Nor is there good chronological agreement between the date of the Vedic texts and the changes seen so graphically at Mohenjo-daro and Harappa. The proposition that a natural dam formed across the Indus river in Sind and flooded out the civilization has been widely critiqued and has been discredited.

The peoples of the Indus Civilization

Considerable attention has been given to the religion of the Indus Civilization, and not only from archaeologists. There is a core bibliography on this interesting topic (Marshall 1931: 48–78; Hiltebeitl 1978; McEvilley 1981; Parpola 1984, 1985, 1992; Allchin 1985; Atre 1987b). The best early study of Indus religion remains that done by Sir John Marshall (Marshall 1931). The term 'religion' in the context of the Indus Civilization has to be broadly defined as an institution dealing with spirits, the founding principles of which are believed to be true by the adherents, but which cannot be proved or falsified. It includes the system of belief in the 'other world' as well as in gods and goddesses. Indus Civilization mythology and astronomy/astrology are also included. Aspects of ideology, that is, the systematic knowledge and beliefs held by people about the proper nature of human life and the proper order of socio-cultural systems, also interwoven with this subject, at least in the Indus Civilization case.

The ethnicity of the Indus peoples

Some archaeologists have sought assistance in the difficult job of understanding the institutions of the Indus Civilization by turning to the history of various ethnic groups in the subcontinent. They seek to use historical inference and analogy to suggest the configuration of Indus institutions like religion. Ethnically and linguistically, the Indian subcontinent is a very complex place, but there are two huge groups that dominate the scene: the Dravidians, mostly in the south, and the Aryans, mostly in the north. If it could be settled that the Indus was a 'Dravidian civilization' then historical data and analogies to their known religious practices could assist in understanding. On the other hand, if the Indus was an 'Indo-Aryan civilization' then their history could be used in a similar way.

The Dravidians

There is no good estimate of the antiquity of the Dravidian languages in the subcontinent. They have 'always' been there. While much is known of their life and culture today, and there is a reconstruction of their ancient languages, little is known of the details of their prehistoric past. Their first written texts date to the early years of the common era, but these are devotional poetry, not historical documents. The hypothesis, or assumption, that the Indus script renders a proto-Dravidian language into written form is a well-known one, and not a bad starting point for would-be decipherers. But this does not really inform us about early Dravidian institutions.

From time to time in this chapter reference will be made to Dravidian belief or practice, but in the absence of good written texts this is little more than educated guesswork. However, the earliest of India's texts is the Rigveda, a religious document in Vedic Sanskrit of about 1000 BCE. The antiquity and richness of this text would be of immense help if it could be applied to the study of the Indus peoples.

Aryans and Indo-European languages

Sir William Jones was a noted eighteenth-century jurist and scholar of the Calcutta High Court. In 1786 he proposed a historical relationship between Sanskrit, Greek and Latin as part of his 'Third Anniversary Discourse' to the Asiatic Society of Bengal, the institution he founded.

> The *Sanscrit* [sic] language, whatever may be its antiquity, is of a wonderful structure; more perfect than *Greek*, more copious than *Latin*, and more exquisitely refined than either, yet bearing to both of them a stronger affinity, both in the roots of verbs and in the forms of grammar, than could possibly have been produced by accident; so strong indeed that no philologer could examine them all three, without believing them to have sprung from some common source, which, perhaps no longer exists; there is a similar reason, though not quite so forcible, for supporting that both the *Gothic* and the *Celtic*, though blended with a very different idiom, had the same origin with the *Sanscrit*; and the old *Persian* might be added to the same family, if this were the place for discussing any question concerning the antiquities of Persia.   (Jones 1788: 348–49)

Others had proposed this historical relationship, some as early as 1583 (Mallory 1989: 273, fn. 1). Jones had the intellectual stature to bring the idea to the notice of a large body of scholars and make it stick. Jones' insight was a huge revelation. The German philosopher Georg Wilhelm Friedrich Hegel compared Jones' linguistic discovery to the finding of a new continent. The notion that the Sanskrit of the Vedas evidenced a historical connection between the Celts, Germans, Greeks, Persians and Indians was hard to believe, but there it was.

Who is an Aryan?

The priests who composed the hymns of the Rigveda called themselves 'Arya'. Just to the west, the Iranian branch of the Indo-European languages contains this word in its cognate form 'Airyia', and the Iranian King Darius (522–486 BCE) described himself as Aryan. The term is probably confined to the Indo-Iranian languages, not Indo-European generally (Mallory 1989: 126). Calling oneself

'Aryan' was akin to a Native American calling himself a 'Sioux' or peoples of eastern India calling themselves 'Naga'. There is no evidence that the term carried with it the notion of a biological race in Vedic times.

Beginning in about the fifteenth century some German scholars began to break away from the cultural tradition that took their roots back to classical antiquity. They spoke of a

> descent from powerful rulers of earlier times who manifested their might in regions far distant from the Rhine. From these beliefs in linguistic and historical fables of widespread German political preeminence in antiquity was born the nationalism that characterized the Reformation. In that religious and political movement, Germans broke away from their mediaeval tradition of accepting a cultural debt to Latin antiquity, and the reformers came to consider themselves as self-made conquerors with historical roots inherent within their own cultural tradition of a non-Semitic, non-Latin, chosen people destined to rule the world. An original language . . . was the hallmark of the original race . . . in the minds of those nationalistic Germans in the period of the Enlightenment and early years of Romanticism.
>
> (Kennedy 1995: 34)

Friedrich Schlegel was a German statesman and novelist who knew some Sanskrit and was, of course, familiar with Jones' 'discourse'. He believed in the antiquity and splendour of Sanskrit. In 1805 he proposed that warlike tribes speaking this language left the Himalayan Mountains and conquered India, the Middle East and Europe, bringing civilization with them (Schlegel 1808): 'thus the primitive Germanic people were drawn into this Völkerwanderung of prehistory, becoming amalgamated in the process into a colony of this mysteriously driven race' (Kennedy 1995: 34; an excellent review of this problem). This theory was embraced by the German philosopher Hegel, the Norwegian Sanskritist Christian Lassen and the brothers Grimm. Even Max Müller agreed for a time and then recanted. 'These and other writers of an Aryan race concept based upon language, biology, myth and ideologies of the Germanic right of conquest were the instruments whereby the esoteric deliberations of philosophers and antiquarians entered the arena of public awareness' (Kennedy 1995: 36).

Houston Stewart Chamberlain, son-in-law of Richard Wagner, was an Englishman who moulded these concepts into the doctrine of Nordic-Teutonic racial supremacy. Chamberlain's *Foundations of the nineteenth century* appeared in

1899, and many earlier statements by other authors concerning Aryan superiority were continued by Chamberlain who preferred the term Teutons or Teutonic race. It is fair to place at the feet of Friedrich Schlegel, Houston Stewart Chamberlain and their colleagues the repugnant distortion of what an Aryan was. Their idea had its humble beginnings in Calcutta at the end of the eighteenth century in the honest, brilliant scholarship of Sir William Jones. They turned a simple designation of what a people called themselves into a race of 'supermen' and implemented the political and racist doctrines of Adolf Hitler's Third Reich.

The position taken here

The position taken in this chapter is that the Indus Civilization is neither Dravidian nor Indo-Aryan, but is itself, its own, unique configuration of culture. There were many Indus peoples, with many backgrounds and histories, speaking a variety of languages, probably from a number of language families. Many of these languages and language families must now be extinct. In the end, the question of whether the Indus Civilization is either Dravidian or Indo-Aryan fails because it is a gross oversimplification of a complex cultural and historical reality.

Sir John Marshall's position on the Indus and Aryan civilizations

Sir John Marshall was the first person to synthesize the results from early excavations at Indus Civilization sites. In one of his essays he contrasted the Indus Civilization with what we know of the life of the Aryans as it comes to us in the Rigveda (Marshall 1931: 110–12). There are some important discrepancies. The Indus peoples lived in cities, built large houses of baked brick and were intensive farmers, with some pastoralism. The Vedic peoples lived in camps, did not know of baked brick and were pastoral more than agricultural. The Indus peoples knew the art of writing. The Vedic Aryans did not know writing, or even know people who practised this art. The Indus Civilization had many settlements in the Punjab, Sindh, Baluchistan and Gujarat. Vedic life was confined to the Punjab: Sindh, Baluchistan and Gujarat were distant, shadowy places. Indus religion was iconic, Vedic religion was not. Indus religion involves what Marshall calls 'phallic worship', Vedic religion does not. In Indus religion there is evidence for balance in the worship of both male and female elements. In Vedic religion the female element is subordinate to the male, and much less prominent.

Marshall summarizes his position with this final, almost playful, observation:

we are wholly at a loss to explain how the Indo-Aryans came to relapse from the city to the village state, or how, having once evolved excellent houses of brick, they afterwards contented themselves with inferior structures of bamboo; or how, having once worshipped . . . the linga and the Mother Goddess, they ceased to do so in the Vedic Period, but returned to their worship later; or how, having once occupied Sind, they subsequently lost all memory of that country and of the Lower Indus.   (Marshall 1931: 112)

The religion of the Indus Civilization

Sir John Marshall's comments on Indus religion were perhaps the most sophisticated of his thoughts on these ancient peoples. While there are parts of Marshall's syntheses that are no longer tenable, many of the fundamentals are sound. This being the case, the structure of his approach will be used here, updated where needed, introducing collateral thoughts along the way, but sticking to his path. Marshall began his discussion with the great divisions of this Indus institution into the domains of a Great Mother Goddess and a Great Male God (Marshall 1931: 49–58).

The Great Female Goddess

The Great Mother Goddess was made manifest in female figurines and other iconography. Some of the female figurines manufactured by Indus peoples were toys, but others were votive offerings, or perhaps cult images for household shrines (Marshall 1931: 50).

Among these, the first that demand attention are a large number of female figurines of terracotta, found at both Mohenjo-daro and Harappa.[2] These are paralleled, as we shall see, by kindred examples from the neighbouring country of Baluchistan. The figurines like the woman kneading dough or the one holding a dish of cakes in her arms are probably toys, without any religious meaning.

Others with children in their arms, or pregnant may be assumed to be ex-voto offerings, perhaps with a magical significance. The great majority, however, of these figurines portray a very distinctive and generally uniform type, viz. a standing and almost nude female, wearing a band or girdle about her loins with elaborate head-dress and collar, and occasionally with ornamental cheek cones and a long necklace.   (Marshall 1931: 50)

Fig. 9.6. Figurines from the Indus Civilization that may be representative of Marshall's Female Deity.

Unfortunately there are no gender markers on many of the figurines of which Marshall speaks, but he saw parallels in mother goddess worship with western Greece and the Aegean, where he began his archaeological career working with Sir Arthur Evans at Knossos.

The evidence for mother goddess figurines in Indus Civilization religion is not particularly robust (Fig. 9.6). Just which functions the terracotta female (and male) figurines played in Indus Civilization life is open to question. It might well be that some of them were multi-functional. Based on the material record in general, female sexuality is deeply engrained in Indus Civilization religion and

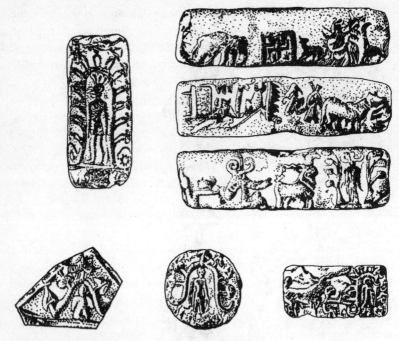

Fig. 9.7. Representations of the scene of 'Divine Adoration'.

ideology, and notice will be taken of this point as this exploration of ancient beliefs progresses.

The seal of 'Divine Adoration'

An analysis of a seal that can be called the seal of 'Divine Adoration' also may lend some insights in the Great Mother Goddess (see Figs. 9.5 and 9.7). This is an extremely interesting representation which occurs often in the corpus of Indus glyptics.

The composition of the scene of Divine Adoration suggests that it is a kind of mnemonic device for the narrative of an important story or theme in Indus culture. It is made up of several sub-scenes. The central figure, placed in the upper right-hand corner of the seal impression is a human figure standing inside a plant, with a ring base. The figure wears a tripartite head-dress and has long hair down the back.

In front of the tree and standing figure is a second human, in a head-dress and hairdo similar to the principal. But, this figure is in a kneeling posture suggesting a supplicant or worshipper. There is some justification, therefore, in thinking of the figure in the tree as a divine personage. Behind the supplicant is a goat with wide, corkscrew horns jutting out parallel to the ground.

As will be seen as this chapter develops, there is a strong dichotomy in the Indus Civilization concerning males and an association with animals and females and an association with plants. I therefore take the supplicant associated with the goat to be male and the person inside the plant to be a woman. Marshall noted: 'The nude deity appearing between the branches is very small and roughly portrayed, but the absence of any evidence of male sex, coupled with the fact that tree deities in India are usually female and that the ministrant figures on this seal also appear to be women, all point to its being a goddess rather than a god' (Marshall 1931: 64).

A line of seven attendants facing away from the goddess is at the bottom of the seal. They have lesser head-dresses and their long hair is differently displayed. Marshall wrote of them: 'The seven figures in a line at the bottom I take to be female officiants or ministrants of the goddess. The plumes on their heads might be feathers; but it is more probable that they are small branches, such as in Kafiristan are still worn on the head by officiants at the worship of [fruit] of the Himalayan pencil cedar . . . when branches are also burnt in honor of the tree spirit' (Marshall 1931: 65). Their garment, as it is portrayed, has more than a vague resemblance to modern Punjabi dress.

Some scholars have seen a sacrificial altar on this seal (Parpola 1992). This is not apparent to me, nor would I agree that the 'goat' is necessarily a sacrificial animal. The Soviets in their proposed decipherment of the Indus script made many assumptions about the presence of sacrifice in the Indus Civilization, none of which seems to be to be supported by real evidence.

Marshall wrapped this iconography in later Indian notions of the pipal tree as the 'tree of knowledge' and with tree spirits. This method has strengths and obvious weaknesses (see Parpola 1992 for another interpretation of this seal).

Seven attending figures on the seal of Divine Adoration

Seven standing figures occur in several places in Indus iconography (Fig. 9.8), the most prominent being the seal of Divine Adoration. Seven is an auspicious number in the Indian tradition and there is mention of the 'seven sisters' in the

Fig. 9.8. Two Indus objects with seven figures.

Rigveda. For example in one of the 'Sarasvati Hymns' the river is venerated as one of them:

> And dear to us among the dear, with her seven sisters Sarasvati, well-loved, has been worthy of our praise.
>
> Having filled the terrestrial regions, the broad expanse and intermediate space, may Sarasvati protect us from scorn!
>
> Having three abodes and sevenfold, making the Five Tribes to increase, she has been worthy of invocation in every contest.
>
> She who, great among them by reason of her greatness, outshines the others in splendors, most active among the active, mighty, made, like a chariot, to be a match, – Sarasvati should be lauded by the one who under-stands.   (Rigveda VI.61.10–13, after Maurer 1986: 197–8)

The geography of the Rigveda is centred on the Punjab, and we know that the reference to 'seven sisters' is to the 'seven rivers' of the region, beginning with the Indus and moving east as follows: Jhelum, Chenab, Ravi, Beas, Sutlej and Sarasvati. Given the continuities in belief that seem to mark ancient India, it is at least possible that this notion of the 'seven river sisters' came to the Vedic pundits from an Indus source.

The Great Male God

Perhaps the best-known part of Marshall's comments on Indus religion is the identification of the device on a stamp seal as a Proto-Shiva that is claimed to have been a forerunner of the Hindu deity (Fig. 9.9) (Marshall 1931: 52–6).

This seal has received a great deal of notice in discussions of Indus religion, and is undoubtedly the most important single object in this regard. The pose is one of a yogi, a feature of later Indian asceticism, and an important attribute of the later Hindu deity Shiva, who sits atop Mount Kailash in the Himalayas as the 'Mahayogi' whose contemplations are key universal elements. Marshall saw three faces to the central figure on this seal, and connected them to the three manifestations of Shiva. He also associated Shiva as the 'Lord of the Beasts' with the animals around the central figure. Shiva, per se is not a part of the Rigveda. There is a Vedic deity, Rudra ('howler', 'the terrible', 'the ruddy one'), who developed into Shiva, at least his destructive aspect, but not before 200 BCE. The seal was discovered in the north-western portion of Mohenjo-daro and would seem to date to *c.* 2250–2150 BCE. These points having been made to

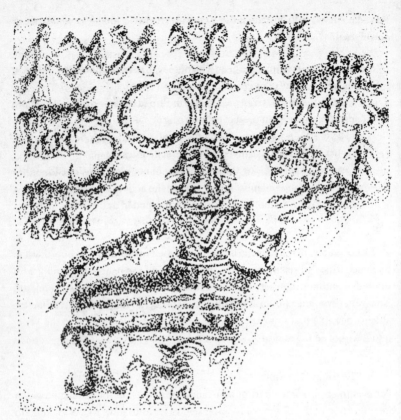

Fig. 9.9. The Proto-Shiva seal from Mohenjo-daro.

support the notice it has received, some attention to Marshall's presentation of his Proto-Shiva is in order.

Marshall properly describes this figure as being in the attitude of a practitioner of yoga. The male sits on a dais with his body erect, back straight, head full front, up and alert. His legs are bent double beneath him, the heels together, the toes down. His arms, covered with bangles, are outstretched with hands resting lightly on his knees, thumbs out. The lower limbs are bare. Marshall believed that the phallus was exposed, but some consider this to be simply a waist-band. He draws on the connection with Shiva as 'pre-eminently the prince of yogis – the typical ascetic and self-mortifier, whence his name . . . Mahayogi . . . in the course of time the yogi came to be regarded as a magician, miracle-monger and charlatan' (Marshall 1931: 53–4).

Shiva is not only the Mahayogi but also 'Lord of the Beasts'. In historical times this was thought of as the 'Lord of Cattle', but in the Vedas the name signified the master of beasts in the forest; thus the presence of wild animals on the seal would have to be interpreted as following the more ancient usage. Rudra also bore the title 'Lord of the Beasts'.

The head is surmounted by a pair of large buffalo horns meeting in a high central head-dress. Four wild animals surround the figure: elephant, rhinoceros, water buffalo and tiger. Beneath the dais are two antelopes or ibexes. Seven Indus logographs are included on the seal, but one of them, a simple human stick figure, may be out of place and not a part of the inscription.

Marshall's position on the Proto-Shiva seal can be summarized as follows:

1. The figure has three faces, and that Shiva was portrayed with three as well as with the more usual five faces comes to us from abundant examples.
2. The head is crowned with the horns of a bull. He felt that this formed a trident, Shiva's three-pronged symbol. Both the bull and the trident are characteristic emblems of Shiva.
3. The figure is in a typical yoga posture, and Shiva was and still is regarded as the Mahayogi – the great yogi.
4. He is surrounded by animals, and Shiva is the 'Lord of the Beasts'.

D. Srinivasan, in a review of this seal, notes that many authors have expressed a favourable view of Marshall's identification of the figure on seal number 420 as a Proto-Shiva (Srinivasan 1984, citing Mackay 1948; 56–7; Wheeler 1968: 105).

A critique of Marshall's Proto-Shiva

While Marshall continues to be supported by some in his interpretation, there are obvious difficulties in using specific concepts and gods of historical India to interpret the remains from the Indus Civilization. There is an opinion that the horned figure is not even human, but a very cleverly conceived pastiche of different animals (e.g. the arms seemingly covered with bangles are actually centipedes, the body is composed of two cobras!). Others have proposed that the central figure is a Proto-Brahma, a great Creator, rather than Proto-Shiva. Three other points on the Proto-Shiva seal have been made.

Fig. 9.10. Seal from Mohenjo-daro showing a water buffalo being speared.

The central figure on the Proto-Shiva represents the Buffalo God

A. Hiltebeitel has noted that the central figure on the Proto-Shiva seal is not wearing bull or cattle horns but rather those of a buffalo, the shape and ribbing being the most diagnostic features. Indian tradition is rich in mythology and symbolism concerning the Buffalo God (Mahisa) (Hiltebeitl 1978). A yogic posture, even an ithyphallic pose, would not be inconsistent with a representation of the Buffalo God, who is separate from, but deeply intertwined with, Shiva. It also seems to occur in various contexts in the Indus Civilization. There is a seal from Mohenjo-daro showing a buffalo being speared (Fig. 9.10), which can be seen as a prototypical depiction of an episode in the Indian epic the Mahabharata where the war-god kills the Buffalo Demon with a spear, or the story from an Indian epic known as the Ramayana, where Valin kills a buffalo. It could also be seen as the prototype of a Dravidian-style buffalo sacrifice, quite common among these peoples (Hiltebeitl 1978: 773–4).

The Proto-Shiva seal has on it the vehicles of later Hindu gods

Turning to other iconography on the Proto-Shiva seal, Hiltebeitel notes the surrounding animals – the elephant, rhinoceros, tiger and buffalo – and suggests that they may represent the vehicles for gods of later Indian tradition, particularly Yama, Indra, Varuna and Kubera, the Guardians or Regents of the Four Directions.[3] Two of the animals have obvious analogues as mounts: the buffalo of Yama, Regent of the south, and the elephant of Indra, Regent of the east. The rhino and the tiger present more of a problem for Hiltebeitel. In the end this is resolved by proposing that the rhinoceros is the animal of the west, an original vehicle of Varuna, and that the tiger of the seal was later replaced by the lion as the mount of Kubera, Regent of the north (Hiltebeitl 1978: 777). In the end, the lack of good analogies for the rhino and the tiger means that the proposed animal iconography on the Proto-Shiva as vehicles of the gods is not very convincing.

The central figure on the Proto-Shiva seal is a deity

The pose, demeanour and dress of the figure all combine to suggest that the central figure on the Proto-Shiva seal is a god of some sort. The figure is not clearly, entirely human, and might even be three-faced. The buffalo horn head-dress very strongly suggests an association with this animal and the Buffalo deity. The posture of the central figure on the Proto-Shiva seal is clearly posed in some way. It looks like a form of ritual discipline and is the classic pose of someone who practises yoga in later, historical times (Fig. 9.11). One expert on yoga sees this pose as possibly the first representation of a yogic position that can, in general, be called *mulabandhasana* (McEvilley 1981: 49). The corpus of Indus glyptics contains a number of representations of humans in this position. These offer sound evidence that during the Indus Civilization, or even earlier, the Indus peoples, or some group(s) of them, were engaged in the kind of ritual discipline that emerges in later India as yoga.

Yoga in later Indian tradition is said to have been founded by the sage Yajnavalkya and was later codified by Patanjali in his *Yoga Sutra*. It is a form of mental and physical discipline, a code for ascetics (Walker 1968: II, 616–17). If yoga originated in the context of the Indus Civilization then either later Hindu tradition formed its own 'origin myth' or the history of this sort of ritual discipline is more complex than might at first be suspected. It is probably the latter.

There is a clear association between the god and the buffalo based on the head-dress. The sweeping curve of the horns and the fact that the artist who carved this seal has attempted to indicate the distinctive ribbing of buffalo horns testify to this fact.

History of the water buffalo motif in the Indus region

The buffalo horn motif first appears in the Early Harappan and it is quite common there. A famous pot from the site of Kot Diji (Fig. 9.12), just across the Indus River from Mohenjo-daro, has an early representation of a buffalo with a somewhat human face. This pot seems to date from the Early Harappan–Indus Civilization Transition, within the time frame when the Indus Civilization was in the process

Fig. 9.11. Yogic postures in the Indus Civilization. 1–4. Mohenjo-daro, 5–7. Harappa.

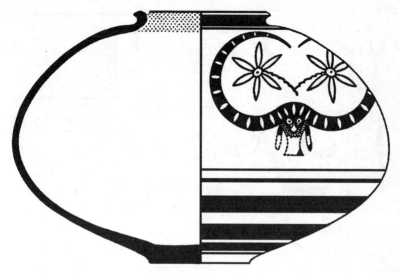

Fig. 9.12. Buffalo pot from Kot Diji.

of being born. Other good examples of this motif come from Early Harappan levels at sites in the Gomal Valley (Fig. 9.13).

There is also a very fine example of a Kot Dijian vessel found at Burzahom in Kashmir, with the buffalo horn motif (Fig. 9.14). The Burzahom pot is probably what archaeologists call 'Late Kot Dijian' (2500–1900 BCE), contemporary with the Indus Civilization.

The Proto-Shiva seal and the Kot Diji pot clearly represent the buffalo, not bulls, by virtue of the careful rendering of the ribbing on the horns. Buffalo horns and bull horns are also somewhat different in their shape. While both buffalo and cattle horns are a part of the Indus imagery, the buffalo stands out as important by virtue of the Proto-Shiva seal. The Kot Diji pot documents the development of this imagery, and presumably the religious ideas around it, in either the Early Harappan or the Early Harappan–Indus Civilization Transition. It is not a part of the imagery of the Post-urban Phase, but seems to have been preserved in the folk ways of rural communities as the cult of the Buffalo God.

Summary on the Proto-Shiva seal

The Proto-Shiva seal seems to portray an Indus deity connected with the buffalo who is practising a form of ritual discipline, probably an early form of yoga. A

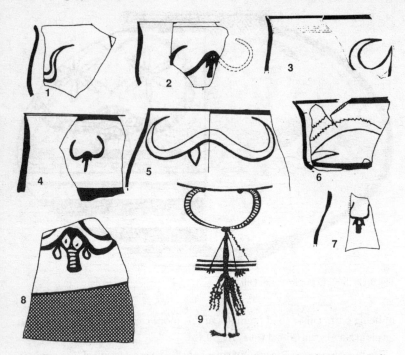

Fig. 9.13. Horns on pottery from the Gomal Valley, Pakistan and Padri, Gujarat, India. 1–7. Rehman Dheri, 8. Hatala, 9. Padri in Gujarat.

water buffalo god emerges in later Indian religion as the Buffalo God. There are few things more Indian than yoga. These observations suggest that there is some continuity between the Indus Civilization and later Indian religious beliefs and practice. The time separating the beliefs illustrated on the Proto-Shiva seal and the later Indian tradition is between one and two millennia. Moreover, during the Vedic age, neither the Buffalo God nor yoga is represented, so it seems that these parts of the Indus tradition survived among the indigenous, non-Aryan peoples of India, outside the world noted in the Vedic texts.

Continuity between the religion of the Indus Civilization and later India

The history of Indian religion is deep and complex. The Proto-Shiva seal offers hints that some aspects of later Hinduism are to be found in the Indus Civilization,

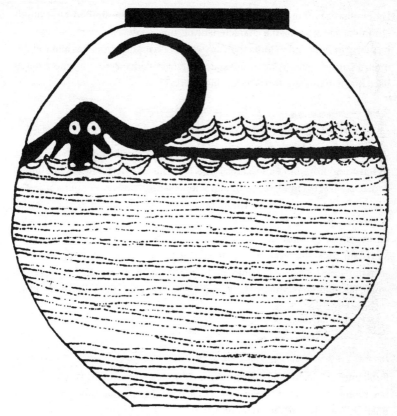

Fig. 9.14. The buffalo pot from Burzahom.

but these aspects of religion are either totally missing from the Vedic period, or weakly represented. T. McEvilley has performed a 'stratigraphic analysis' for yoga as

> a reflection of the stratification of different cultural-psychological layers in Indian religions in general: a composite primitive stratum of shamanic magic, totemic magic, and agricultural magic; possible fresh shamanic input from Central Asia at about the end of the second millennium BC (not to mention other possible outside influences); an overlay of Vedic ritualism in the middle Vedic period; and a general redefinition under the influence of idealist philosophy in the following periods. (McEvilley 1981: 77)

He emphasizes that this 'mixing of elements cannot be limited by a purely chronological scheme; the characteristic of "uneven development," which may be more pronounced in India than anywhere else in the world, has allowed this interplay of elements from various stages of religious history to continue to renew itself down to modern times' (McEvilley 1981: 77).

The 'Priest-King' as a yogi

One of the most identifiable images from the Indus Civilization is the so-called 'Priest-King' from Mohenjo-daro (Fig. 9.15). This wonderful representation of a male is only 18 cm high. We do not know that it represents either a priest or a king, let alone someone on whom these dual responsibilities were conferred. R. Chanda observed that he appears to have his half-closed eyes concentrated on the tip of his nose, a yogic pose (Mackay 1931c: 357, fn. 1, attributed to Marshall). Since the eyes are missing this is open to interpretation, but I have seen the 'Priest-King' many times and Chanda may well be correct. If he is, this would be additional evidence for a yoga-like form of ritual discipline in the Indus Civilization.

Shaktism

Fundamental to the Marshall synthesis of Indus religion is that it marks the beginning of a later Indian principal called 'shaktism', the principle of sexual dualism, a kind of 'duality in unity'.

> *Shakti* or 'energy,' is the term applied to the wife of a god, and signifies the power of a deity manifested in and through his consort. The deity and his wife represent the dual aspect of the divine unity, and together symbolize the power of the godhead. But in many cases the need for a consort or companion was satisfied by creating a practically inactive goddess who played no conspicuous part in the life of her spouse, and she was often named after the deity himself, thus: Agnayi after Agni; Brahmani after Brahman . . . On the other hand, in many instances the female deity of the divine pair was regarded as the active principle of the universe, and was often conceived of as having greater importance than the male. The principal divine couples when named conjointly were therefore named with the shakti or female name first, e.g. Radha-Krishna, Gauri-Shankar, Sita-Rama.   (Walker 1968: II, 336)

Fig. 9.15. The 'Priest-King' from Mohenjo-daro.

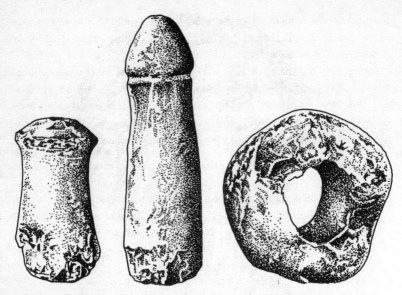

Fig. 9.16. Two phallic stones (lingas) and a yoni (on the right) from Mohenjo-daro.

In Marshall's view this primitive mother worship led to the transformation of the goddess into a personification of female energy (*shakti*) and the 'eternal productive principle', which was in turn united with the 'eternal male principle' to become the creator and 'Mother of the Universe' (Marshall 1931: 57–8).

Support for the presence of this duality in the Indus Civilization came to Marshall in the form of cult objects representing human sexuality: baetylic and phallic stones (lingas) as well as the female, yoni ring stones.

Three cults: baetyls, lingas and yonis

There are many phallic objects from sites of the Indus Age, only a few of which are crafted well enough for them to suggest the male organ. The so-called yonis could be symbolic representations of anything female. Three objects of this sort are shown in Fig. 9.16.

Baetyls, also known as omphalos or navel stones, were a more difficult proposition for Marshall. They were objects shaped much like lingas, but lacked any anatomical detail. They were just plain columnar stones, with a flat bottom and a curved top. He admitted that they too could represent the male organ, but thought that it was not likely that the Indus peoples would have some stones of this sort with anatomical detail and some without. So, those without anatomical detail were dubbed 'baetyls'.

Larger phallic and baetylic stones were intended for worship; the smaller ones were amulets to be carried on the person. Rebirth and, by implication, a pardon of sin could have been achieved by physically putting some part of the body through a yoni ring stone.

Marshall summarizes his position on this matter this way:

> I distinguish three types of cult stones at Mohenjo-daro and Harappa – the baetylic, the phallic and the *yoni* ring-stones. Each of these types is represented by numerous examples, both small and large, the former much predominating over the latter. The large specimens I take to be objects of cult worship; the smaller ones to be amulets for carrying on the person, just as miniature *lingas* and *yonis* are still commonly carried . . . but it is not unlikely that some of the smaller specimens may also have served as gamesmen. Whether these three represent three distinct cults is uncertain; but it is not unnatural to suppose that *linga* and *yoni* worship may have been associated then, as they were later under the aegis of Saivism. On the other hand, it is probable that they were originally quite distinct from baetylic worship, which is found frequently connected with the cult of the Mother Goddess among the oldest tribes, whereas phallism is rarely, if ever, found among these aboriginal people.   (Marshall 1931: 63)

The concepts Marshall deals with in this matter, and others in his discourse on Indus religion, are highly refined notions, backed by centuries, even millennia, of philosophical thought. The religious features of the Indus Civilization and those akin to them in later Indian religion should not be thought of as 'the same'. They were different, the Indus philosophical thought being comparatively unrefined. The vocabulary would have been different as well. These points call into question the wisdom of using words like 'yoga' and 'shakti', let alone 'Mother of the Universe', in describing Indus practice, since it would be wrong to believe that Indus 'shakti' was just like Hindu 'shakti' in word or in deed. Given the qualification just given, there still may be a germ of later Hinduism in the Indus Civilization. We can imagine that these beliefs and practices were retained by the decendants of the Indus peoples as a folk tradition. They came to Hinduism as these indigenous peoples interacted with the Arya as they together participated in the emergence of their religion.

Fig. 9.17. Two sealings with animals in procession, from Mohenjo-daro.

Other aspects of Indus religion

Zoolatry

There is widespread evidence for animal worship in Indus beliefs. For example, two processional sealings show animal figures carried above the crowd (Fig. 9.17). This is evidence for both public performances, with religious overtones, and the veneration of animals.

There are many portrayals of composite animals, some with three heads on one body, or tigers entwined, tigers with horns, human torsos on four-legged bodies (minotaur-like creatures), 'unicorns' with elephant trunks and 'unicorns' growing out of trees (Fig. 9.18). The 'unicorn' on the stamp seals may have been a mythical creature and not a bull at all.

How these animal, and animal/human, motifs work together is not known. But, it seems clear that the belief systems of the Indus peoples propounded all kinds of cross-breeds of beasts and humans, some with multiple heads. The iconography also admits the possibility that we are witnessing an artistic rendering of an otherwise oral form of 'another world'. Although it is comfortable to view these animal themes within the context of 'religion' or 'ideology' it is not clear that 'deity' and 'worship' should be inferred. The notion that the representations of 'unicorns' with elephant trunks were composite 'gods' may be out of place.

The swastika

The swastika is one of the most widely recognized symbols of the twentieth century. It is often viewed with apprehension because of its close association with the German Nazi Party, Aryanism and racist elitism. Actually the motif is very widespread in both time and place, being found at several ancient places in the Americas, Scandinavia, Greece, Egypt, Iran, China and, of course, ancient India. Two early representations come from south-western Iran, as seen in Fig. 9.19.

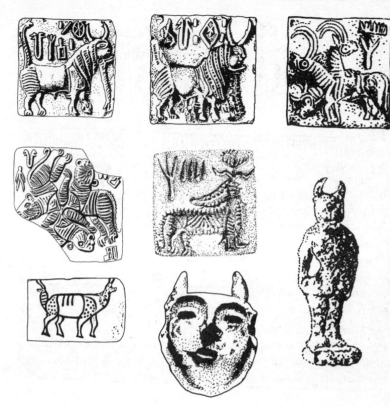

Fig. 9.18. Mythical animals in the art of the Indus Civilization.

Fig. 9.19. The swastika from Susa (*left*) and Tall-i Bakun (*right*), in south-western Iran.

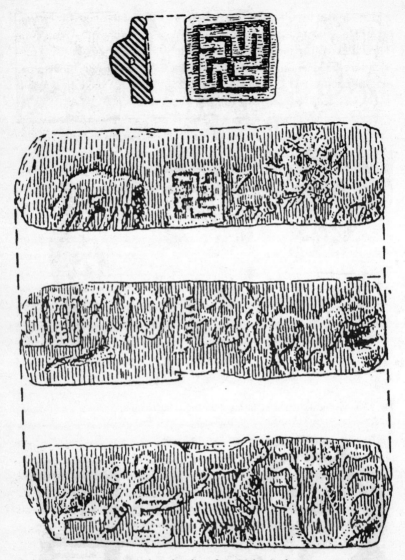

Fig. 9.20. The swastika on seals and sealings from Mohenjo-daro.

The swastika is a prominent part of the iconography of the Indus Civilization, occurring most frequently on seals and sealings, sometimes combining with other Indus religious themes. This is seen in Fig. 9.20, where the swastika is seen on a three-sided terracotta sealing with the scene of Divine Adoration on one side, the swastika and an elephant on the others. We do not know the symbolic value of this symbol during Indus times.

In historical India the swastika is a symbol that can be widely seen, and it has many associations, some of which are as follows. Hindus and Jainas use the swastika as a mark for good beginnings and it is therefore associated with door-ways, thresholds and offerings. The right-hand swastika, the one most frequently seen, is also a symbol representing the progression of the sun and the rotation of the earth. An extension of this notion is carried forward in the association of the swastika with the continued cycle of rebirth. The left-hand swastika, or *sauvastika*, is associated with darkness, magic and the goddess Kali. In Buddhism the swastika is associated with the unseen Buddha, especially his feet and path.

While the swastika is graphically a part of the Indus Civilization, and is a part of historical Indian symbolism, this continuity does not imply that the symbolic association of the later occurrences can be used to understand the Indus Civilization. There is simply too much time and opportunity for change for this supposition to be a sound one.

Mesopotamian themes in Indus iconography

Two iconographic themes that appear on Indus seals have parallels in Mesopotamian mythology; both are related to the Gilgamesh epic. The first is shown on a seal from Mohenjo-daro (Fig. 9.21). It shows a monster, half-human female, half-bull, attacking a horned tiger.

This Indus seal could be seen as portraying the story of the Mesopotamian goddess Aruru who created Ebani or Enkida as a bull-man monster to do combat with Gilgamesh, but who ultimately became his ally and fought with Gilgamesh against the wild animals (Marshall 1931: 67). The second motif is the well-documented Mesopotamian combat scene, with Gilgamesh fighting off rampant animals on either side (Fig. 9.22). The richness of this theme in Mesopotamian art, and even Near Eastern art generally, has been nicely developed and documented by Parpola (Parpola 1984).

The excavations of the so-called 'Royal Graves of Ur' produced a wealth of art. Among the most important objects to be recovered from these tombs were two

Fig. 9.21. The Ebani or Enkidu seal from Mohenjo-daro.

small sculptures, each depicting a goat standing on its hind legs, browsing in a tree (Fig. 9.23). There is a sealing from Mohenjo-daro with this scene.

Since we know that ancient India and Mesopotamia were in contact through sea trade, and possibly overland as well, it should not be surprising that some of the more powerful themes from Mesopotamian society were brought back to the Indus Valley. The notion that Indus sailors and traders, possibly even Mesopotamians themselves, brought some version of the 'Gilgamesh epic' to the cities and towns of the Greater Indus region as a part of their commerce makes good sense.

Fig. 9.22. A Gilgamesh theme seal from Mohenjo-daro.

Fig. 9.23. Goats or 'rams' in the posture of those from the Royal Graves of Ur.

The important place of water in the belief system of the Indus Civilization

Marshall deals briefly with the importance of water to the Indus peoples.

> Of the sanctity of water in the abstract, no tangible evidence has yet been found, but that water was held in great reverence and that it played a highly important part in the daily lives and religion of the citizens of Mohenjo-daro is demonstrated by the elaborate bathing establishment described in Chapter III, as well as by the universal arrangements made in private houses for the supply of water and for baths. Indeed, it is safe, I think, to affirm that in no city of antiquity was so much attention paid to this matter of bathing as in Mohenjo-daro; and we can hardly believe that the practice would have been so ubiquitous and firmly rooted there, had it not been regarded in the light of a religious duty. That such emphasis should have been laid on bathing – even at this remote age – will not come as a surprise to anyone familiar with the importance that from time immemorial the Indian has attached to ceremonial ablutions in sacred tanks, pools, and rivers.
> (Marshall 1931: 75)

Marshall is correct in drawing attention to the importance of water at Mohenjo-daro and many other Indus sites. Water, and its management, play an interesting role in the life of the Indus peoples. This is the clearest at Mohenjo-daro and M. Jansen has published a book with the English title *Mohenjo-daro: city of wells and drains, water splendor 4000 years ago*. The bathing facilities in each house inform us that washing and cleanliness were important to the Indus peoples. We have to anticipate that this involved both physical cleanliness, as well as something of a more symbolic nature. The many wells throughout the city were sources of new, pure water, essential for effective cleanliness. The drainage system served to move the effluent away from the houses and their occupants, below ground, safely out of the way and safely out of sight, in brick-lined channels that prevented massive contamination of the earth of the city.

The Great Bath is a ritual bathing facility, raised to the civic level. It is larger and more complex than the other structures, but conforms to the proposition that cleanliness of both types was an important element in the ideology of the Indus Civilization. It is interesting too that the builders of the Great Bath used elevation and distance to set it apart symbolically from the rest of Mohenjo-daro. This was an important ritual space, and one that would seem to have been reserved for the elites of the city.

Wheeler also found 'water splendour' an interesting and important feature of the Indus Civilization. He felt that the Great Bath and the 'extravagant provision for bathing' were both testimony to the importance of water in Indus life, as well as a tie to later Hinduism (Wheeler 1968: 110).

There is some suggestion from Marshall that rivers may have had sacred qualities during the Indus Civilization, as Ganga, Yamuna and Sarasvati did in historical India. There is no basis for this, other than Marshall's sense of cultural and historical continuity, and Mackay took issue with him on the point (Mackay 1948: 66).

Marshall's synthesis of Indus religion

Marshall did not ever bring Indus religion together under a single 'philosophy'. He saw the diversity of belief, and, by inference, the lack of a 'state religion'. But he was never able to bring the diverse strands of belief that he saw into a unified whole, giving us the sense of an Indus institution. We are thus left with the notion that there may have been a number of 'Indus religions', some people worshipping the great male god, others the mother goddess, or water, or the phallus, without any overarching philosophical principles involved. Sir Mortimer Wheeler was quite explicit in sensing this multiplicity of beliefs and titled a chapter in one of his works 'The Indus religions' (Wheeler 1968: 108–10).

Some other attempts to synthesize Indus religion

There are other authorities who have tried to synthesize the religion of the Indus Civilization. Many of these are politicized tracts, and although this is a legitimate form of inquiry, it is not objective scientific investigation. The first study of the latter type was undertaken by R. Chanda, a Superintendent of the Archaeological Section of the Indian Museum, Calcutta.

Ramaprasad Chandra

R. Chanda's first work on the Indus Civilization was titled *The Indus Valley in the Vedic period* (Chanda 1926). It was published just as the first major season of excavation at Mohenjo-daro was taking place, when very little was known of this civilization. Chanda's writing is anything but tentative. He concluded that there was little in the remains of the Indus Civilization to make a direct link to the Vedic Age, or to Aryan culture. Chanda also noted that there were some elements in the Indus Civilization that seem to be a part of historical India, but not so much the Vedic Age. He was not quite sure how to explain this, but there it was. Today, many scholars sense the same thing, and are making renewed attempts to explain these connections in a rational way, using anthropology and archaeology, as well as texts, as their guides.

Shubhangana Atre

S. Atre undertook a study of Indus religion as a PhD topic at Deccan College in India. This later appeared as a book (Atre 1987a). Dr Atre begins her investigation with a critique of Sir John Marshall's thoughts on Indus religion. She feels that there is little to connect the Indus Civilization to the later Hindu beliefs that Marshall draws on so freely. Atre writes: 'He also erroneously compared the *purusha* and *prakriti*; the basic elements on which the highly philosophical systems like *sankhya* are based, with shaktism and phallic worship. In reality these three systems are very tenuously connected with each other and represent three entirely different planes albeit within the bounds of modern Hinduism' (Atre 1987b: 8).

Her treatment of Indus religion is very detailed, investigating many minutiae, which is useful for those deeply interested in this topic. Her thesis deals with the mother goddess in Indus life and Atre is virtually alone in seeing the central deity on the Proto-Shiva seal as female, a 'Mistress of Animals' rather than the 'Lord of the Beasts'. 'The motifs occurring on seals and sealings constitute the only base for reconstructing the Indus pantheon and after examining them we have formed a hypothesis that the main deity of the Indus peoples was the Great Goddess of animals and vegetation' (Atre 1987a: 191). Atre argues forcefully for her position and marshals many good ideas about the 'mother goddess' aspects of Indus religion. Whether the central figure on the Proto-Shiva seal is male (my contention) or female (Atre's contention), she certainly gives us thoughts on this topic that are an alternative to Marshall, and the mainstream.

Asko Parpola

A. Parpola's research on the Indus script has led him to a parallel study of Indus religion. His research deals with themes already noted here: the pose of ritual discipline on the Proto-Shiva seal, Indus iconography in Near Eastern contexts, an interpretation of the 'seal of Divine Adoration' (Parpola 1984, 1992). The central point for Parpola's research on Indus beliefs is his study of the 'Priest-King' and his garment (Parpola 1985).

The Sky Garment

The garment worn by the 'Priest-King' is covered with a trefoil motif, found in other Indus Civilization contexts, most prominently beads. The trefoils on the garment were originally filled with a red pigment, the colour the Indus peoples always associated with this design. This motif also occurs in the west, and Wheeler says of these examples: 'The analogies from Egypt and Mesopotamia at least combine to suggest a religious and in particular an astral connotation for the motif, and support the conjecture that the Mohenjo-daro bust may portray a deity or perhaps a priest-king' (Wheeler 1968: 87).

Whatever the western parallels, Parpola sees some striking connections with Indian tradition, starting with the Rigveda. He proposes that the central figure on the Proto-Shiva seal is a representation of Varuna, the divine king *par excellence*. Varuna's garment is the *tarpya*, which is not mentioned in the Rigveda, but does appear in the later Atharvaveda. Parpola's seven references to the *tarpya* in the Atharvaveda include the use of this garment at sacrifices and royal rituals (Parpola 1985: 44–5). However, nowhere in the Atharvaveda is the *tarpya* described as a garment with the trefoil design on it, nor are there any artistic representations on which such a conclusion could be based. Parpola takes the *tarpya*, and its association with sacrifice, and suggests that the trefoils, and the circles on the robe of the 'Priest-King', are images of fireplaces, that are central to Vedic sacrifice and ritual, thereby making his connection between the garment and the design.

The inferences that Parpola makes go even farther. At one point he says:

> The initial working hypothesis of this study was that the trefoil motif on the Indus 'priest-king's' garment had an astral meaning. In the course of the investigation it has been possible to conclude that the Indus peoples imagined the stars to be heavenly fireplaces, that the trefoil probably denoted specifically one particular asterism, namely Apabharani, and moreover that the fireplace, the Apabharani, as well as the Vedic tarpya garment corresponding to the 'priest-king's' garment all symbolize the 'womb' in the Veda. Evidence of the existence of 'womb' symbolism for the trefoil motif in Indus religion seems to be given by the round pedestal of red stone from Mohenjo-daro. This has been compared to the round stand of the later Hindu lingas, representing yoni, 'womb' or 'vulva.' Covered

> with trefoils, the pedestal seems to provide external confirmation to the
> proposed meanings of the trefoil pattern, while these in turn support the
> comparison with the yoni stands.   (Parpola 1985: 101)

While Parpola has shown that he is an immensely knowledgeable scholar, and
he argues forcefully for his points, in the end the logic supporting his proposal
concerning the *tarpya* 'Sky Garment' of the 'Priest-King' is indirect, tenuous
and hard for me to accept. Since his insights into Indus religion are no more
informative than the assumptions underlying them, they are not yet convincing.
But Parpola is an imaginative scholar, and his lack of success at the moment
should not lead one to infer that he is at a dead end.

F. R. Allchin's interpretation of a seal from Chanhu-daro

E. J. H. Mackay found a rather extraordinary seal in the course of his excavations
at Chanhu-daro (Mackay 1943: pl. LI, no. 13). It shows a short-horned bull, an
Indian gaur, above a prostrate human figure (Fig. 9.24). Mackay thought that the
scene depicted a simple attack by the bull, and the human was merely attempting
a defence against the animal (Mackay 1943: 147).

F. R. Allchin has published a short study of this seal (Allchin 1985). As he sees
it, the gaur is standing on his hind legs, elevated above the human figure. The
animal's front legs are shown in excited motion. His erect penis is shown in
correct anatomical position. The figure below the gaur is less clearly shown and
consequently more difficult to interpret. Allchin and Mackay see a head-dress
to the far right bottom of the seal impression. Allchin compares the human to,
among other things, the plant-goddess inside the tree on portrayals of 'Divine
Adoration' (see Fig. 9.7). The head can be made out, but it is not clear if it is shown
in profile, with a beak-like nose, or with head turned, and both eyes apparent.
The diagonal line(s) between the gaur's forelimbs and the figure's head seem to
be an arm or arms, fending off the animal's pawing thrusts. There is a prominent
incision on the seal, shown as a line parallel and to the right of the erect penis. After
rejecting several possibilities Allchin concludes, reservedly, that this represents
an umbilical cord linking the human to the gaur. The deep diamond-shaped cut
at the base of this line is the female's sexual organ, opened to receive the animal.

The scene is one of very great dynamic and excitement: a bull about to take a
female goddess in an act of sexual aggression. But the clear appearance of her
open, exposed genitals tells us that she is a willing partner in this deed.

Fig. 9.24. The seal from Chanhu-daro with a gaur ravishing a human.

Allchin rightly rejects the notion that this scene has any serious connection to the Horse Sacrifice: both the participants are clearly alive, and there is no place for the very prominent umbilical cord in this story. Instead he turns to the Vedas and forms an interesting hypothesis concerning the scene:

> The Vedas offer a distance view of certain aspects of creation and a coherent, if mysterious, symbolic language through which related subjects are approached. One special feature is the way in which certain concepts and words stand in formal relationships to one another. As is well known, Heaven and Earth form a pair, often addressed together . . . Together they form two world-halves or bowls . . . of the Vedic universe. Heaven . . . is masculine and constitutes a primal Male element: Earth . . . is feminine and represents a primal Female equivalent. It follows that there are often references to the fatherhood of Heaven and the motherhood of Earth: for example, 'Heaven is my father . . . Earth is my great mother'.
>
> (Rigveda I, 163, 33 and also I, 89, 4; I, 85, 10–11, etc.)(Allchin 1985: 376)

Such references to Heaven and Earth are invariably linked to creation, as in: 'Heaven is my father, here is the navel that gave me birth; here is my connection (or umbilical cord), Earth is my great Mother; the womb for me was between the two bowls stretched apart; the father placed the embryo in the daughter' (Rigveda I, 164, 33) (Allchin 1985: 377). This kind of documentation continues, with selections from the Atharvaveda as well, and allows Allchin to conclude: 'in the Chanhu-daro seal we have a representation of Heaven, the bull, who is at once the consort and the father of Earth; and of Earth who is at the same time the consort of the Bull, Heaven, and the mother of the Bull, her calf; and that these themes can be understood by reference to the Creation myths found in the Atharvaveda' (Allchin 1985: 381).

There is a good fit between the iconography of this seal, which shall now be called the 'Heavenly Father–Mother Earth' seal, and the creation myths in Vedic literature that Allchin has presented. He cautions against simplistic thought about the culture historical implications of his observations: 'But having said so much, it will still be admitted that the correspondences in the present case appear to be so profound, and so harmonious, that they must have involved some kind of fairly direct culture contact' (Allchin 1985: 382).

Some thoughts on Marshall and others

The ethnic and cultural diversity which seems so clearly implied in the Early Harappan and Indus Civilization remains may be informing us that there never was a single Indus religion, but simply the sum of the belief systems of the peoples who lie behind these archaeological cultures. However, with the Indus Civilization there seems to be some level of integration, which implies intense communication throughout the Greater Indus region that would have promoted a corresponding amount of change, adjustment, synthesizing and sharing of the older, diverse beliefs of the Early Harappan stage. The emergence of the two 'Great Gods' may be a reflection of the 'Great Tradition' of the Indus Civilization.

Some insights into the nature of Indus religion, or perhaps religions, can be gained through an examination of the architecture that has been considered in this context.

Indus religious architecture

One of the more interesting observations about the Indus Civilization is that no temples have been found. Nor is there much to be said of monumental architecture with a religious function. The pyramids and temples of Dynastic Egypt and the ziggurats of Mesopotamia have no parallel in the Indus Civilization. It is clear that the Indus peoples had beliefs we can consider 'religious' but they expressed this institution in a way that was notably different from the Egyptians and Mesopotamians. Constructing huge, physical monuments to their gods and goddesses was apparently inappropriate to the Indus belief system(s). There can be little doubt, given the large urban centres, that the capability was there both in engineering skills and in the ability to mobilize a workforce. That this was not done is an important element in understanding the nature of ancient Indian civilization.

There is another contrast between Egypt and Mesopotamia and the Indus Civilization. This is the absence of palaces, the large abodes of the heads of government and their powerful associates charged with managing the fortunes of the Indus political apparatus. The possibility is that there was no single personage on whom the Indus political system focused, a king.

The tension and competition between the religious and political institutions of Egypt and Mesopotamia were a source of creativity. The construction of ever larger temples and ziggurats, funerary monuments, palaces and city walls was fuelled by this rivalry. Without suggesting that this competition was the only source of inspiration for the construction of such monuments, it was an important focus. The absence of such monuments in the Indus Civilization suggests that the fundamental organizing and operational principles of the Indus Civilization were different from those of Egypt and Mesopotamia. It does not necessarily mean that the Indus Civilization was any less complex than they were. The refined nature of Indus city life and management, their mastery of complex technologies, their writing system and ability to mobilize resources from distant lands all argue for a level of socio-cultural development at least as sophisticated as that of their neighbours to the west. The absence of temples and palaces, and other forms of monumental architecture, should not be seen as an indication that the Indus Civilization was a lesser development. The Indus Civilization is simply a good example of an alternative way in which a civilization has expressed itself. The Indus Civilization is just as convincing an expression of socio-cultural complexity as Egypt or Mesopotamia. It is just different from them, and different in some important ways, the religious and political institutions being among the most prominent.

There are several structures at Mohenjo-daro interpreted as buildings used by the Indus religious establishment. The best candidates include buildings on the Mound of the Great Bath: the Bath itself, the so-called 'College of Priests', a temple that has been said to be below the Buddhist stupa. House 1 and House XXX, as well as two buildings in the northern excavation area at Mohenjo-daro known as 'DK-G Area', have also been discussed in this context.

There are also structures that have been called 'fire-altars' at both Kalibangan and Lothal. Harappa is conspicuous for the absence of architectural remains associated with religious activities.

Religious structures on the Mound of the Great Bath

The Great Bath

The most prominent religious or ritual structure of the Indus Civilization is certainly the Great Bath at Mohenjo-daro (Fig. 9.25). It was discovered in 1925–26 by Sir John Marshall himself. This was an extraordinary event, since there was no surface indication of the Great Bath and Marshall simply chose the place for his own reasons. The size and height of the Mound of the Great Bath could have led him to believe that it would contain important architecture, and the presence of a Buddhist stupa there would have suggested that this was a religious precinct in antiquity. But still, for Marshall to go to Mohenjo-daro for one season, never having been there before, select one place to dig and find the single most important piece of architecture for an entire civilization is a remarkable feat by any standards. There are three substantive descriptions of the Great Bath composed by those who had a first-hand knowledge of the architectural complex (Figs. 9.26 and 9.27) (Marshall 1925–26: 76–80; 1931: 24–6; Mackay 1931a).

Marshall's thoughts on the function of the bath are interesting:

> For what purpose the tank in the centre of this building was intended can only be surmised. But taking all things into consideration – and particularly the position and imposing character of the building – the most plausible hypothesis seems to be that it was connected in some way with the city's religion – serving either as a bath for devotees at a neighboring shrine (and there are reasons for believing that the city's principal shrine was located in this quarter) or as a tank in which sacred fish, crocodiles or the like were kept. Sacred tanks for both of these purposes having long been a familiar feature of Indian religious life and it is likely enough that they were already in use during the Chalcolithic age.
>
> (Marshall 1925–26: 78)

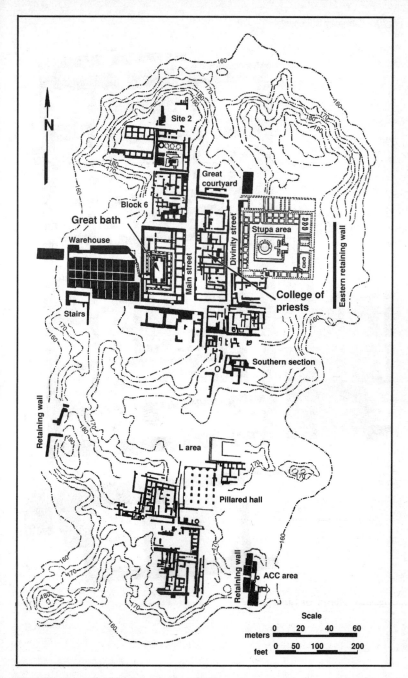

Fig. 9.25. Plan of the Mound of the Great Bath.

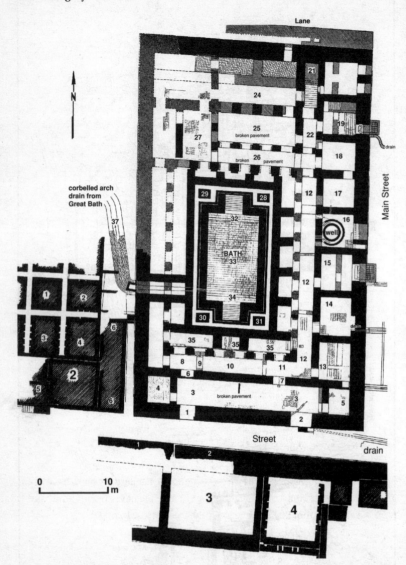

Fig. 9.26. Plan of the Great Bath.

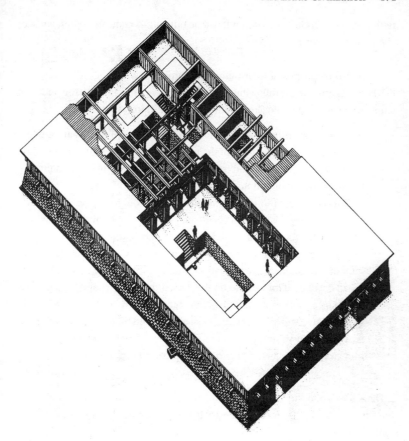

Fig. 9.27. Reconstruction of the Great Bath.

These observations are the essence of what the Great Bath seems to have been. There is one exception – the 'neighboring shrine' has never been found, and it is, as we shall see, not likely to be under the Buddhist stupa.

The College of Priests
Not much of a case can be made that Block 1 on the Mound of the Great Bath was actually a 'College of Priests' or even a residential structure. Its location, across Main Street from the Great Bath, is important, as is its size and internal complexity. It strikes many archaeologists as a place where business took place. But until there is a much clearer idea of what took place on the Mound of the Great

Bath during the Indus Civilization it will be difficult to know the significance of even this prime location.

A temple proposed to be below the stupa

E. J. H. Mackay made the following very hopeful observations about the Buddhist stupa on the Mound of the Great Bath at Mohenjo-daro:

> The Buddhist stupa of Kushan date on the Mound of the Great Bath had been built over the remains of the principal temple at Mohenjo-daro. He [J. Marshall] was prevented from excavating there for fear that removing the stupa would offend Buddhists in Burma and Sri Lanka.
>
> Three considerations suggest that this building will, on excavation, prove to be a great temple dedicated to the city's chief deity, with a surrounding complex of priestly quarters and administrative buildings. Firstly, throughout history a site once regarded as sacred has tended to remain so, and the converse may reasonably be presumed. Secondly, with a well developed trade between the ancient Indus cities and Sumer, there would be a probability of both being organized politically and socially on similar lines. Thirdly, excavation has already laid bare a number of buildings round and about the stupa mound which can hardly be interpreted otherwise than as belonging to a great priestly corporation.
>
> (Mackay 1948: 40)

His reference to the 'buildings round and about' is to the 'College of Priests', the Great Bath and the small set of eight bathing rooms to the north of the Great Bath in Block 6.

It is certainly a common practice around the world for later peoples, especially conquerors, to usurp the sacred grounds and buildings of their predecessors, thus symbolically capturing something of the essence of their past. But, the Mohenjo-daro case would presume that the Kushans knew where the ancient temple of Mohenjo-daro was located when they built their stupa. Roughly 2000 years separate the Buddhists from the Indus peoples and it seems unlikely that the Buddhists had such knowledge.

There has been considerable excavation around, even in, the Buddhist stupa area and it has produced no suggestion of a monumental building there. While the proof of this hypothesis will be in the digging, not the argumentation, there is no assurance the excavation will reveal anything, given what we already know of this part of Mohenjo-daro.

**Summary of the proposed religious structures on the Mound
of the Great Bath**

The Great Bath is the only convincing example of a ritual structure in this district of Mohenjo-daro. The 'College of Priests', across Main Street, is a very large building and propinquity suggests that whatever went on there was connected to activities at the Great Bath. The 'College of Priests' does not appear, itself, to have been a place of worship.

The Mound of the Great Bath can be thought of as highly symbolic space, built to elevate the Great Bath (and other religious architecture?) above the Indus plains, and above the ordinary, inauspicious areas of the lower town of Mohenjo-daro: a place where the religious elites practised their beliefs, using water, above and distanced from the masses of the city and the vulgar activities of daily life. It may be that the 'the city's principal shrine' that Marshall was seeking is the Great Bath itself.

Proposed temples in the lower town of Mohenjo-daro

There are four buildings in the lower town of Mohenjo-daro that have been discussed as possible temples. The first is called 'House 1', a unique structure, almost certainly not a domestic building (Fig. 9.28).

M. Jansen has written a long article on this building, or 'buildings' (Jansen 1985). The structure that we see can be quickly described. It is approached from the south, where the remains were disturbed and not completely excavated. There is an entrance corridor in the approximate centre, with separate room complexes to right and left. A circular alignment of bricks, in which a shank shell was found, is in this area and probably marks the place where a tree grew in antiquity. Straight ahead is a wall with staircases on both sides that allow access to the elevated complex of rooms which crosses the northern end of the building.

Jansen's access to original field records has enabled him to plot the find spots for twelve seals found in House 1. Special note should be made that all of the seals with devices are 'unicorns'. We also know that there was a concentration of finds (miniature vessels, faience objects) along the southern wall of the northern building.

The layout of House 1 is unique. There is nothing else like it in the Indus world. But this is the only thing that suggests that it could have been a 'temple' and that is simply not enough. It could just as easily have been a kind of 'clan house' for the 'unicorn' segment of Indus society.

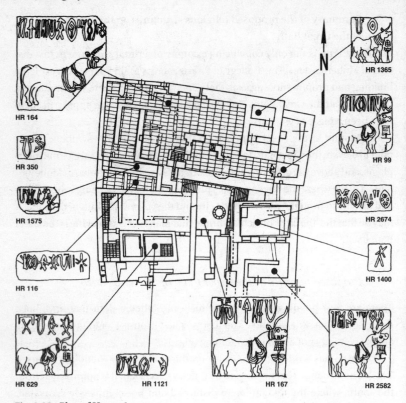

Fig. 9.28. Plan of House 1.

There is a massive building, designated House XXX, in a neighbourhood adjacent to House 1. The exterior dimensions of House XXX are about 24 × 11 m. The outer walls are some 1.37 m thick, and preserved to a height of over 2 m in places. Many of the interior rooms have no apparent entrances but are solid podia of mudbrick packing. Except for the southern rooms, associated with a well, the whole seems to have been a very solid understructure for another building, either vanished or never built, that would have been very substantial indeed.

Just as with House 1, the unique character of House XXX (its massive walls and its unusual configuration) have led some to consider it a possible religious structure (Fig. 9.29). But, once again, this is not enough to confirm such a use.

There is a building of irregular in shape in the northern area of Mohenjo-daro, called 'Block 11'. The structure has not been completely excavated but it contains

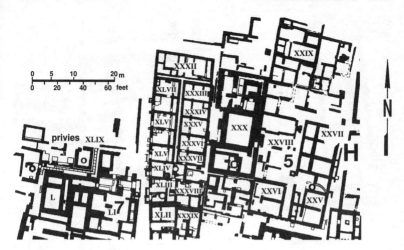

Fig. 9.29. House XXX.

a courtyard and three wells, a culvert and a water chute (Fig. 9.30). There were many modifications to Block 11 late in the history of the city. Owing to the openness of the plan, and the presence of so many water facilities, Mackay stated: 'This building seems to me to approximate more closely to our idea of a temple than any building yet excavated at Mohenjo-daro. The three wells, which are almost in a straight line, probably provided water for ablutions in the temple precincts. Not many antiquities were found within this complex beyond a few baked pottery figurines in the chambers on the south of the courtyard'(Mackay 1931b: 252). This is not very convincing, but given the proposed importance of water in the religious life of the Indus peoples it is perhaps closer than most guesses.

Block 8A is near Block 11 in the northern neighbourhoods of Mohenjo-daro. It is an 'L'-shaped structure with very solidly built walls with interior buttresses. The buttresses are unusual features at Mohenjo-daro and may have carried a second storey or a continuous gallery around the building. The entrance, 1.4 m wide, is in the south-eastern corner of the building, with a well room adjacent to the north. The general ground level of this neighbourhood was rising because of demolition and this necessitated the construction of a set of stairs down into the well room where one of the so-called 'massacre' scenes of Mohenjo-daro was found.

Block 8A is, once again, a unique structure, not like a private home (Fig. 9.31). Mackay noted the following about Block 8A:

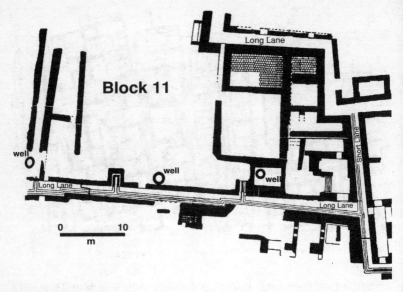

Fig. 9.30. Block 11.

There is little doubt that this was not an ordinary dwelling house. Nor, though at first I thought it was a temple, is it possible to retain that view in the complete absence of any objects of religious significance within the building or of anything in the nature of a shrine for a statue. A khan would have required store-rooms on the ground-level, to say nothing of a gateway wide enough to admit loaded animals; and the most probable explanation of this building with its well close beside the entrance seems to be that it was some kind of hostel for pilgrims or travelers.   (Mackay 1937–38: 92)

Fire-altars

Small pits filled with ash and other debris have been identified as fire-altars at the Indus sites of Kalibangan (northern Rajasthan), Lothal (Gujarat), Vagad (Gujarat) and Nageswar (Gujarat). It is not clear that all of these facilities are 'fire-altars' and their nature is controversial, as far as the study of Indus religion is concerned. Since many of the features that have been identified as 'fire-altars' may be simply hearths or small furnaces, only those from Kalibangan will be dealt with here.

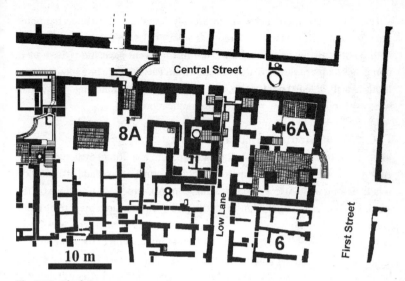

Fig. 9.31. Block 8A.

Fire-altars at Kalibangan

The Kalibangan fire-altars were found on platforms on the southern half of the High Mound there, as well as in a so-called 'Ritual Structure' (Lal 1979: 77–8). The southern half of the High Mound was made up of mudbrick platforms, oriented to the cardinal directions. On one of the platforms was a series of seven oblong depressions lined with clay. They contained ash and charcoal, besides a cylindrical or faceted clay (burnt or unburnt) pillar near the centre. Behind the pits was a north–south wall from which we can infer that the persons using them would have had to face the east, the rising sun. To the west of the pits was the lower half of a jar, embedded in the floor. It also contained ash and charcoal and seems to be associated with the pits. In the same area there were bathing pavements and a well, suggesting ablutions were performed there.

The excavator, B. B. Lal, originated the notion that these pits were 'fire-altars' and associates them with ritual ablutions that would have been performed prior to worship, something current in India among the Hindu communities. Another pit at Kalibangan, in the same area as the fire-altars, was rectangular and lined with baked bricks. It contained cattle bones and antlers, suggesting to Lal that it was used for sacrifice (Lal 1979: 78).

There is no agreement that these are literally 'fire-altars'. R. Meadow has noted that the most typical hearth at Harappa is oblong or keyhole shaped with a pillar in the centre. All that have been found during the recent excavations there are in domestic contexts, with up to three in one room. This seems to be a standard type Indus hearth, at least in the north, and could be what the Kalibangan examples were used for (R. Meadow, personal communication 1996).

The 'Ritual Structure' at Kalibangan

In addition to the 'fire-altars' at Kalibangan there is a 'Ritual Structure' to the east of the Lower Town there. This architectural complex was made of mudbrick. It is 12 m long and enclosed a large number of plastered pits, like those on the southern rhomb. Too little is known of this structure for a judgement to be made about its true function, and the final determination as to whether it was or was not a 'ritual structure' will have to await further publication of the material.

In the end the Kalibangan plastered pits have been called 'fire-altars' mostly by default: what else could they be? Without suggesting that this identification is totally incorrect, it is not a strong form of archaeological reasoning, and should be taken as a tentative conclusion, at best. There is still a chance, after all, that these were facilities for cooking and merely reflect the day-to-day life of the Indus peoples.

Religious architecture: summary

The only building, or building complex, in the Indus realm that is religious or ritual in nature is the Great Bath at Mohenjo-daro. Its location and size suggest that it was used by a small number of people in an exclusive way. The importance of distance and elevation lend this exclusiveness, water and cleanliness lend ideological importance. The purpose of the remainder of the buildings remains unclear. While House 1 is an intriguing structure, it could be seen as a seat of a political potentate as easily as a temple or seat of religious authority. House XXX is just a massive structure and could have functioned in many ways. The fire-altars at Kalibangan, and other sites, are a bit more ambiguous. On one level they are only plastered pits with ash and bone, and sometimes triangular terracotta cakes. These could be domestic hearths or furnaces. But, the groupings on the High Mound at Kalibangan do not support domestic use, and nor does the apparent concentration of them in the Kalibangan 'Ritual Structure', but the case is not yet proved.

Indus funerary practices and religion

There is little record of the funerary practices of the Indus peoples. The only substantial cemeteries for the Indus Civilization are at Harappa, Kalibangan and Lothal. There are many earlier burials at Mehrgarh (c. 7000–5000 BCE), but since they are so early they do not pertain to this discussion. The rest of the funerary evidence is found at a few settlements like Nal in Baluchistan, or the single convincing cremation site at Tarkhanwala Der in Rajasthan. It is apparent from what we know that there was a diversity of funerary practices for the Indus peoples, suggesting the kind of ethnic diversity that other remains tend to support.

There is evidence for extended supine burials in pits and coffins, much as Muslims and Christians practise this custom. The best evidence for this comes from Cemetery R-37 at Harappa, the Kalibangan cemetery (Fig. 9.32). It is also apparent that some Indus human remains were exposed to the elements and reduced to skeletons before being gathered together for final inhumation. Archaeologists call these 'fractional burials'. Evidence for this practice comes from Mohenjo-daro and Harappa during the Indus Civilization and from Nal and other Baluchi sites during the Early Harappan. The evidence for cremation is not particularly robust, Tarkhanwala Der in Rajasthan having the only convincing data. Mohenjo-daro and Harappa both produced evidence for 'post-cremation urns' that contain Indus Civilization artefacts, mostly pottery, some ash and bone, but almost none of it human.

There is a sense that the Indus peoples were somewhat casual about the care for at least some of the dead. Stray human bone and teeth are a part of the excavation records at many sites. Moreover, many of the fractional burials have remains from more than one person in them, sometimes mixing adults and children. It is therefore not possible to identify one single form of funeral and so it is not possible to draw any conclusions regarding beliefs in an afterlife.

There may be a link with later historical times in some of these practices, and these are at least worth noting here. Burial, cremation and other treatments of the dead are noted in the Rigveda. Cremation was one of the two normal methods of disposing of the dead, the other being burial. The Atharvaveda adds two further modes of disposal: 'casting out' and 'exposure'. 'Casting out' may have a parallel in the Iranian practice of placing corpses in the open to be reduced by animals

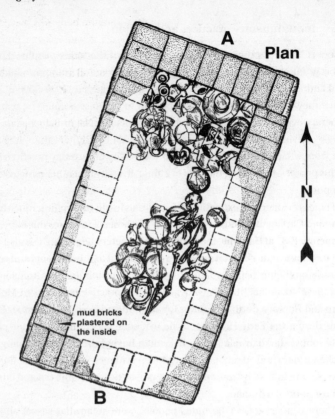

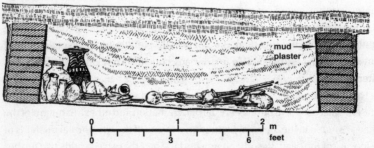

Fig. 9.32. A brick-lined grave at Kalibangan.

and birds. 'Exposure' was a form of disposal where the body was placed in an out of the way place, safe from animals and birds, to wither away. Burial was common in Vedic times, since there is an entire hymn that describes the ritual attending it. The dead man was buried apparently in full attire, with his bow in his hand.

Summary of Indus religion

The Indus Civilization was founded on an ideology, an Indus Great Tradition, fashioned in part from the heritage of the Early Harappan Stage, in part from the genius of the Indus peoples themselves. This would have been a distinctively Indus way of looking at the world, an all-encompassing philosophy of life. If this hypothesis is anywhere near correct the Indus ideology would have been both universalistic and powerful, like Hinduism, Islam and Buddhism, capable of moulding the lives of hundreds of thousands, if not millions of people. The substance of this Great Tradition would have been ideas, not buildings and arte-facts. This would have been the higher meaning of the rituals conducted at the Great Bath, or the fire-altars at Kalibangan. Of these ideas almost nothing can be said, given our present state of knowledge concerning the Indus belief system. More can be said of the artefacts that inform us about the Indus Great Tradi-tion, but in the end these just stand for something else, the search for which represents a challenge to those who study these ancient peoples. Perhaps it will take written evidence to elucidate the philosophical issues that support the Indus Great Tradition. What can be done is to make an outline description of the Indus system of beliefs, as a beginning point for understanding these peoples.

There are three themes that emerge from this investigation of Indus religion: (1) the outlines of an Indus pantheon of gods and goddesses, (2) the lack of public religious architecture which leads to the thoughts concerning the individualized nature of worship and (3) cultural continuity from the Indus Civilization into later Indian belief.

The Indus pantheon

The two great gods
A theme central to Indus religion appears to be a male–female duality. The male is best seen on the Proto-Shiva seal and the numerous other examples of this

god in Indus art. It is clear that this male deity is represented by the buffalo, not the zebu, in spite of the importance of cattle in Indus life. It appears that in some contexts a simple curve of horns was used as a symbol of the great male deity. The symbolism surrounding the male deity on the Proto-Shiva seal is exclusively animal, suggesting the use of a male god–animal relationship. The phallic objects and baetyls from some Indus sites support the reasoning behind the presence of a male deity.

The female deity emerges from the figurines but perhaps most strongly from the 'Divine Adoration' theme, with a female inside a plant, often the object of veneration from a male in front of her. The 'female god–plant' symbolism complements the 'male god–animal' relationship as a kind of opposition. The presence of yonis emphasizes the presence of the female deity in Indus life.

The 'Heavenly Father–Mother Earth' seal from Chanhu-daro can be interpreted along a number of dimensions. First, it adds documentation for the male deity, outside the context of the great yogi. It also sustains the notion that the male deity is associated with the bull, in this case the gaur, and animals generally. This seal also informs us about the presence of a female deity, associated with the earth and thereby perhaps with plants.

This male–female relationship carries with it a sense of the dualism found in the later notion of shakti. This is a particular form of energy that brings the male–female duality to one. In this sense the two deities may have been ultimately resolved into one supreme Indus deity. But this *shakti* was not something that was rendered into physical form, or not at least a form that would seem to be present in archaeological finds.

Other Indus gods

One can gather together the two great gods of the Indus Civilization as aspects of the Indus Great Tradition, but there are more representations of gods, or spirits, or god-like creatures. These are the minotaur-like creatures, half-human, half-animal, with claws on the back feet and human feet in the front, the multi-headed animals, tigers with bull horns, humans with horns, 'unicorns' with elephant trunks, perhaps 'unicorns' themselves as in the terracotta figurines from Chanhu-daro. This is the zoolatry that Marshall discusses, and constitutes what might be considered the Indus 'Little Tradition' or the opposing force of 'evil', or threat, in the Indus Great Tradition.

Indus ritual

Water appears to have been a prominent part of Indus ritual. This judgement begins with the Great Bath at Mohenjo-daro, and extends from there to the plethora of water acquisition, use and management facilities at many Indus sites. Taken together, these sources inform us that the Indus peoples had respect for cleanliness, both symbolic and physical. The Great Bath was probably the civic-level facility for water ritual. The bathing floors in the private homes were the domestic site for such ritual. The importance of water for the growth of plants, and the crops that sustained the Indus peoples, may suggest that the water ritual was affiliated with the female/plant side of the duality in the Indus Great Tradition.

Fire ritual in the Indus Civilization emerges rather poorly from the archaeological record. The best evidence for it comes from Kalibangan. Taken alone, the plastered pits with ash and bone on the High Mound there are not fully convincing as ritual facilities, since they could have been for domestic use. The poorly known 'Ritual Structure', with a concentration of these pits, separate from the town itself, is more difficult to explain in this way. But, we need to know more about the ritual structure before making a final judgement on fire ritual in the Indus context. There is a temptation, of course, to imagine fire as the opposite of water, and to place it on the male/animal side of the great Indus duality.

Religious architecture

The Indus peoples did not express their religious beliefs in monumental architecture. There are no temples, pyramids or ziggurats in the Indus world. The profoundly religious nature of so many monuments in Mesopotamia and Dynastic Egypt is a contrast of no small importance in understanding some of the fundamental differences between ancient India and the west.

The absence of ostentatious buildings and façades says nothing of a priesthood for the Indus Great Tradition, which may or may not have been present. Evidence for this class of religious practitioners emerges best from the Great Bath, in terms of thinking about who used this facility and to what end. If their 'headquarters' was, in fact, across the street in the 'College' there may have even been the hypothetical system of religious practitioners. But it is just as possible that this too was a weakly developed part of the system and that priests, if present at all, were not organized into their own hierarchy, but functioned more individually, as in Islam or Buddhism.

Given the absence of pyramids, ziggurats and great temples, and the fact that the Great Bath is a unique facility, it may be that the practice of religion was a rather individualized obligation, possibly done in the home, by family members, without a significant number of liturgical objects, like Christians praying at home, Buddhist meditation or Hindu daily devotion at a household shrine. This is perhaps the most appealing suggestion to emerge from this study of the Indus system of beliefs, because it is so harmonious with the artefactual and architectural evidence. The terracotta figurines, baetyls, lingas and yonis could all be very nicely accounted for in this view of Indus ideology.

There is some direct evidence for public performances which may have had a religious nature. This comes from the two sealings from Mohenjo-daro that show a procession, with participants carrying banners, statues of cattle and what may be models of the 'standard' that is generally found in front of the 'unicorn' on the stamp seals. These public performances, and the Great Bath, combined with the notion of household worship give us two levels of devotion, at Mohenjo-daro anyway. The apparent importance of individual worship in the Indus scheme of things is, of course, a tie to later times, and the emergence of Hinduism.

Aspects of later Indian religion begin in the Indus Civilization

There are a number of practices by the Indus peoples that provide us with evidence that certain aspects of later Indian beliefs have their roots in the Indus Civilization. The apparent importance of household worship may be one of these. Male/female duality, the symbolic value of water, the presence of yoga-like ritual discipline, a Water Buffalo Deity, the 'Heavenly Father–Mother Earth' theme all combine as evidence for some sort of cultural continuity with historical India. At the conclusion of the paper on the 'Heavenly Father–Mother Earth' seal Allchin makes the following comment:

> This should warn us against . . . any over simple attempt to derive these ideas from an Indus source. But having said so much, it must still be admitted that the correspondences in the present case appear to be so profound, and so harmonious, that they must have involved some kind of fairly direct

culture contact. Several times in recent years we have expressed our view that Indo-Aryan speaking people must have arrived in the Indus Valley during the lifetime of the mature Indus civilization, and that there must have been a period of cultural synthesis between the two very different elements. It is still not possible to say when the first Indo-Aryans arrived, nor over how long a period they continued to move into the Indus region from their earlier homelands in Central Asia, but the model of this period of cultural interaction provides in our view the most plausible indication of the medium within which the sort of cultural synthesis suggested by the Chanhu-daro seal and the Rigvedic myths could have taken place.

(Allchin 1985: 382)

Allchin is proposing that Indo-Aryans were in the Indus Valley sometime during the period 2500–1900 BCE. This is considerably earlier than the codification of the Rigveda at *c.* 1000 BCE. It has already been noted that the history and ritual in the Rigveda then is older than this. Allchin seems to be indicating that at least the germ of an idea about the 'Heavenly Father–Mother Earth' theme goes back to the third millennium BCE. This is a long time, not impossibly long, but long enough that an alternative explanation might be called for.

Following the eclipse of urbanization, the peoples of the Indus Civilization continued their way of life in a modified form, without cities, social classes, writing and long-distance trade in luxury items. Excavations at a number of sites in Punjab, Haryana, northern Rajasthan and western Uttar Pradesh give archaeologists a complete, unbroken culture historical sequence linking the Indus Civilization settlements to the North Indian Early Iron Age at *c.* 1000 BCE. This period is associated with a kind of pottery called Painted Grey Ware, which has been found at more than 700 sites in northern India and Pakistan.

These peoples continued to be farmers and herders, they made metal tools, and maintained contact among themselves to a limited extent. But there were many of them. Some degree of cultural diversity is suggested by the observation that words from languages in several language families are evidenced in the Vedic texts, including Dravidian, Sino-Tibetan, maybe even Munda, along with the base of Indo-European Sanskrit.

These post-urban folk did not write, or make seals, or even many figurines. Notions about their religion are difficult to gather. But they would have retained many of the beliefs and customs that can be thought of as a part of the Indus

Civilization. There is a strong sense that the linear descedants of the peoples of the Indus Civilization were in the Punjab in the second half of the second millennium when presence of Vedic Aryans can be documented there. It was in this 'Punjabi melting pot' that ideas about life and culture, religion and religious practice could have been shared. It is possible that the period of 'cultural synthesis' that Allchin so rightly proposes was closer to 1000 BCE than it was to 2000 BCE.

This sense of continued interaction and synthesis between the Aryans and the indigenous peoples of India can also be gained from the Atharvaveda, a book of magic, spells and incantations in verse. This text has the sentiment of simple animism and sympathetic magic, with many non-Aryan elements, and seems to reflect the beliefs of the indigenous ancient Indian tribal peoples noted in the Vedic literature.

Hinduism rightly traces its history back to the Vedas, and the Aryan poet-priests who composed them. But the Aryans did not live alone in the prehistoric Punjab. They were one ethnic group in a sea of indigenous peoples, and continued to be so until the notion of 'Aryan' as a 'tribe' or people disappeared, merged into the larger ancient Indian social order. It was within this setting that ideas were shared among these peoples and that the indigenous folk of India, some of whom traced their cultural heritage and religion back to the Indus Civilization, played a role in shaping the unfolding beliefs that emerged as Hinduism.

If this scenario is even close to being correct, then did the Indus peoples practise a form of ritual discipline they called 'yoga'? Probably not. Did their practices of ritual discipline contribute to the emergence of yoga? Probably. Did the Indus peoples have a notion of male–female synthesis called *shakti*? Probably not. Did their notions of male–female duality and possibly synthesis contribute to the emergence of the Hindu notion of *shakti*? Probably. Were the qualities of water as purifying in both a physical and a symbolic sense a part of the life of the Indus peoples? Yes. Should we trace this same belief, that appears in later Hinduism, back to the Indus Civilization? Probably.

For these, and other features of the Indus Civilization that seem to be documented as a part of life in later Indian history, the historical links were complex and multi-faceted. Ideas about religion, the cosmos and gods, ritual and belief were not passed along like a ball, complete and unchanged. The period of 'cultural synthesis' was one during which there was a sharing and shaping of ideas as a constant process of change on all sides, out of which eventually emerged several of the world's Great Traditions, Hinduism prominently among them.

Notes

1. General works on the Indus Civilization include: Allchin 1997; Possehl 1999.
2. The reader who is interested can peruse the excavation reports to find these figurines, and other material mentioned in this chapter. The principal reports are: Marshall 1931; Mackay 1937–38; Vats 1940.
3. This was first suggested by Marshall (1931: 53, fn. 1) but relegated to a footnote and never pursued.

Bibliography

Allchin, Bridget and Raymond 1997. *Origins of a civilization: the prehistory and early archaeology of South Asia.* New Delhi: Viking.

Allchin, F. R. 1985. The interpretation of a seal from Chanhu-daro and its significance for the religion of the Indus Valley. In J. Schotsmans and M. Taddei (eds.), *South Asian Archaeology 1983.* Naples: Istituto Universitario Orientale, Dipartimento di Studi Asiatici, Series Minor 23, pp. 369–84.

Atre, Shubhangana 1987a. *The archetypical mother: a systematic approach to Harappan religion.* Pune: Ravish Publishers.

1987b. Lady of beasts – the Harappan goddess. *Puratattva* 16: 7–14.

Chanda, Ramaprasad 1926. *The Indus Valley in the Vedic period.* Memoirs of the Archaeological Survey of India 31. Delhi.

Hiltebeitl, Alf 1978. The Indus Valley 'Proto-Siva', reexamined through reflections on the goddess, the buffalo, and the symbolism of vahanas. *Anthropos* 73: 767–97.

Jansen, Michael 1985. Mohenjo-daro HR-A, house 1, a temple? Analysis of an architectural structure. In J. Schotsmans and M. Taddei (eds.), *South Asian Archaeology 1983.* Naples: Istituto Universitario Orientale, Dipartimento di Studi Asiatici, Series Minor 23, pp. 157–206.

1993. *Mohenjo-daro: Stadt der Brunnen und Kanale (city of wells and drains), Wasserlexus vor 4500 Jahren (Water splendor 4500 years ago).* Dual German–English text. Bergisch Gladbach: Frontinus-Gesellschaft e. V.

Jones, Sir William 1788. The Third Anniversary Discourse: On the Hindus. *Asiatic Researches* 1: 343–55.

Kennedy, Kenneth A. R. 1995. Have Aryans been identified in the prehistoric skeletal record from South Asia? Biological anthropology and concepts of ancient races. In George Erdosy (ed.), *The Indo-Aryans of ancient South Asia: language, material culture and ethnicity.* Berlin: Walter de Gruyter, pp. 32–66.

Lal, B. B. 1979. Kalibangan and Indus Civilization. In D. P. Agrawal and Dilip Chakrabarti (eds.), *Essays in Indian protohistory*. Delhi: B. R. Publishing Corporation, pp. 65–97.

McEvilley, Thomas 1981. An archaeology of yoga. *Res* 1: 44–77.

Mackay, Ernest J. H. 1931a. L area. In Sir John Marshall (ed.), *Mohenjo-daro and the Indus Civilization*. 3 vols., London: Arthur Probsthain, pp. 151–75.

    1931b. DK area. In Sir John Marshall (ed.), *Mohenjo-daro and the Indus Civilization*. 3 vols., London: Arthur Probsthain, pp. 233–61.

    1931c. Statuary. In Sir John Marshall (ed.), *Mohenjo-daro and the Indus Civilization*. 3 vols., London: Arthur Probsthain, pp. 356–64.

    1937–38. *Further excavations at Mohenjo-daro*. 2 vols., Delhi: Government of India.

    1943. *Chanhu-daro excavations 1935–36*. New Haven: American Oriental Society, American Oriental Series 20.

    1948. *Early Indus civilizations*. 2nd edn revised by Dorothy Mackay, London: Luzac & Co.

Mallory, J. P. 1989. *In search of the Indo-Europeans: language, archaeology and myth*. New York: Thames and Hudson.

Marshall, Sir John 1925–26. Exploration, Western Circle, Mohenjo-daro. *Annual Report of the Archaeological Survey of India, 1925–26*: 72–98.

    (ed.) 1931. *Mohenjo-daro and the Indus Civilization*. 3 vols., London: Arthur Probsthain.

Maurer, Walter H. 1986. *Pinnacles of India's past: selections from the Ṛgveda*. University of Pennsylvania Studies in South Asia 2. Philadelphia: Pennsylvania University Press.

Parpola, Asko 1984. New correspondences between Harappan and Near Eastern glyptic art. In Bridget Allchin (ed.), *South Asian archaeology 1981*. Cambridge: Cambridge University Press, pp. 176–95.

    1985. The Sky-Garment: a study of the Harappan religion and its relation to the Mesopotamian and later India religion. *Studia Orientalia* 57: 8–216.

    1992. The 'fig deity seal' from Mohenjo-daro: its iconography and inscription. In Catherine Jarrige (ed.), *South Asian Archaeology 1989*. Monographs in World Archaeology 14. Madison: Prehistory Press, pp. 227–36.

Possehl, Gregory L. 1996a. *Indus Age: the writing system*. Philadelphia: University of Pennsylvania Press.

1996b. Meluhha. In Julian E. Reade (ed.), *The Indian Ocean in antiquity.*
London: Kegan Paul International in Association with the British Museum,
pp. 133–208.

1997. The transformation of the Indus Civilization. *Journal of World
Prehistory* 11(4): 425–72.

1999. *Indus Age: the beginnings.* Philadelphia: University of Pennsylvania
Press.

Schlegel, F. 1808. *Essay on the language and wisdom of the Indians.* Heidelberg:
Mohr and Zimmer.

Srinivasan, Doris 1984. Unhinging Siva from the Indus Civilization. *Journal of
the Royal Asiatic Society of Great Britain and Ireland*: 77–89.

Vats, M. S. 1940. *Excavations at Harappa.* 2 vols., Delhi: Government of India.

Walker, Benjamin 1968. *Hindu world: an encyclopedic survey of Hinduism.*
London: George Allen and Unwin.

Wheeler, Sir Mortimer 1968. *The Indus Civilization.* 3rd edn, Supplementary
Volume to the *Cambridge History of India.* Cambridge: Cambridge
University Press.

10 The religion of ancient China

EDWARD L. SHAUGHNESSY

Presuppositions

Towards the end of the nineteenth century, when China was still ruled by the last of its dynastic houses, scholars intimately familiar with China's traditional culture would have been able to write the history of ancient Chinese religion perfectly and with great assurance. Now, at the start of a new millennium, the task is considerably more difficult, and one that a modern scholar – and especially a western scholar – approaches with much less confidence. This is not at all because we know less now about either ancient China or religion than did scholars a century ago. Indeed, with respect to ancient China (by which for the purposes of this chapter I will mean the roughly thousand years from the appearance of the first historical records about 1200 BCE until the establishment of a unified Chinese empire about 200 BCE), the last hundred years have been a time of unprecedented discovery of new sources. Some of these new sources give first-hand evidence of cultural practices that were still alive or at least well known to traditional scholars. Others, however, would have dumbfounded those scholars, as they do us today. They show us a culture more colourful, more discordant, more pungent than we could have ever imagined. To try not just to describe, but also to make some sort of coherent sense, of these new sights, sounds and smells would require, ideally, the curiosity of an archaeologist, the precision of an engineer and the inspiration of an artist.

Changes in our understanding of religion also complicate the story. One hundred years ago, historians conceived of religion in ancient China in one of two aspects: either the teachings of the Masters, such as Confucius (551–479 BCE), Laozi (sixth century BCE), Mozi (c. 478–392 BCE), Mencius (c. 385–305 BCE), Zhuangzi (c. 365–285 BCE), and Xunzi (c. 316–235 BCE); or the rituals of the royal court. Today, again thanks to archaeology, we have in addition to much more evidence about this elite culture, evidence also of the life of the great mass of the people. This evidence reveals, perhaps surprisingly but perhaps not so surprisingly, that practices and beliefs that we might term religious were not rigidly stratified according to social class. Kings and philosophers were just as likely to perform divinations, consult atrologers, practise meditation or engage the services of a spirit medium as were the common people (indeed, perhaps even more so, since they had readier access). And the common people, for their part, seem to have subscribed to the same overriding world-view as their social superiors. To be sure, religion, like the culture of ancient China in general, was by no means homogeneous or monolithic; archaeology is beginning to reveal significant geographical diversities in religious expression, and with better control of the dates of their sources historians can now discern how these expressions changed over the course of time. But, based on the evidence that is currently available (and given the important role that archaeology continues to play in the study of all facets of ancient China this is by no means an empty caveat), there is little justification when talking about ancient China to use terms such as high and low religions, great and little traditions.

Sources

As suggested above, the sources available to us for the study of religion in ancient China may be generally divided into two types: traditional (the sort of evidence that was available to the nineteenth-century historian) and archaeological (that which has been discovered only in the twentieth century). Each of these two types can in turn be divided into two sub-types. The traditional evidence is almost without exception textual, but questions about the dates and authenticities of different texts require different treatments. Some texts were actually written at or about the time of the events that they describe, and thus can be used – with due caution – as primary documents. Other texts, however, were certainly written much later than the events and institutions that they purport to describe. This does not mean that what these texts say about earlier events is necessarily wrong, but it is important to realize that they were written in response to the events of their own period and that their content reflects the concerns of the later period much more directly than it does those of the earlier period. Sometimes there are disagreements among scholars over the division of these texts, but we are certainly now in a better position than ever before to determine when a text may have been written. This is due in large part to evidence discovered archaeologically in the last century. This evidence can also be divided into two general types: palaeographic (i.e. written) and artefactual or figural. Sometimes these two types are combined in a single piece (for instance, an inscribed bronze vessel), but historians usually use the evidence differently.

Traditional texts

The earliest surviving texts of ancient China were written during the Western Zhou dynasty (1045–771 BCE); they are the three main classics of the Chinese tradition: the *I Ching* or *Classic of Changes*, the *Shang shu* or *Venerated Documents* (also known as *Shu jing* or *Venerated Documents*), and the *Shi jing* or *Classic of Poetry*. Although these texts were certainly added to in later periods (and this is especially true of the *Classic of Changes* and the *Venerated Documents*), their oldest portions do give us a reasonably well-rounded picture of the religious life of the time. Over the next 500 years, many more texts were produced which have survived to the present, but in some respects they are more narrow. Other than historical texts such as the *Zuo zhuan* or *Zuo's Tradition* and the *Guo yu* or *Sayings of the States*, both of which were probably written in the fourth century BCE and both of which describe events of the preceding several centuries, most surviving texts of this later period contain the sayings and writings of the various philosophical 'masters' of the time. Examples are the *Analects* of Confucius, a compilation of Confucius' sayings and conversations with his disciples (and some sayings of the disciples themselves), edited by the disciples and by their disciples and so on over a more or less lengthy period (perhaps two centuries); the *Mozi* or *Master Mo* (many of the philosophical texts of this period are usually referred to just by the name of the putative author, with the honorific *zi* or 'master' appended to it), which seems to contain some of the earliest sustained philosophical essays, probably written late in the fifth century BCE; or the *Lü shi chunqiu* or *Mister Lü's Springs and Autumns*, written apparently over a brief period of time about 240 BCE by a group of scholars commissioned by one Lü Buwei, Chancellor of the important state of Qin. There are also some texts that were certainly written during this period, but the date of which is still debated. The most important of these is the *Laozi* or *Dao de jing (Classic of the Way and its Virtue)*. Traditional Chinese scholars dated the text to the sixth century BCE, basing this on stories – which we now recognize almost surely to be apocryphal – that Laozi was a teacher of Confucius. For the last generation or more, most western scholars, who are often sceptical of Chinese traditions, have thought the text could not have been written before about 250 BCE. However, in 1993 in a tomb dating to about

300 BCE were found bamboo strips on which was written a text very similar to the extant *Laozi*; it now seems clear that the composition of the *Laozi* – and that of several other texts as well – dates earlier than most western scholars had heretofore believed.

Of works probably written later than the time that they purport to describe, the most important – especially for ancient religion – are the three ritual texts: the *Zhou Li* or *Rites of Zhou*, the *Yi li* or *Ceremonies and Rites*, and the *Li ji* or *Record of Rites*. All three of these texts give more or less systematic accounts of government and religious practice. The *Rites of Zhou* purports to describe the early Zhou government, with sections given to different branches of the administration; among these, the third section, entitled 'Zong bo' or 'President of the Ancestral Temple', is especially important for religious officers. The *Ceremonies and Rites*, on the other hand, describes the rituals expected of a member of the *shi* class, somewhat analogous to the knights of the middle ages in the west or of the samurai class in Japan; these rites include 'capping' (the coming of age ceremony for a male), marriage, funerals and mourning, and so on. The *Record of Rites* is less systematic, but includes many definitions of ritual terms, as well as teachings explicitly attributed to Confucius. All three of these texts appeared only during the Han dynasty (202 BCE to 220 CE), and it is quite certain that the *Rites of Zhou*, for instance, was not written anywhere nearly as early as the early Western Zhou, as it is traditionally supposed to have been (its authorship being credited to the famous Duke of Zhou, who lived in the eleventh century BCE). On the other hand, it now also seems clear that all three texts derive from materials first produced well before the Han dynasty, perhaps from the fourth century BCE. Taken together, they consitute a remarkable storehouse of information concerning how people of the time thought religious rituals were supposed to be performed.

Archaeological materials

Our understanding of ancient China, and especially of the religion of the time, has been transformed by archaeology. The first great archaeological discovery came at the very end of the nineteenth century: bones and shells bearing the earliest known Chinese writing. Throughout the twentieth century, more and more such bones and shells were discovered (just the most significant pieces already number over 50,000), and these have given rise to an independent field of study: oracle-bone studies. Scholars have shown that these pieces – the scapula

494   Edward L. Shaughnessy

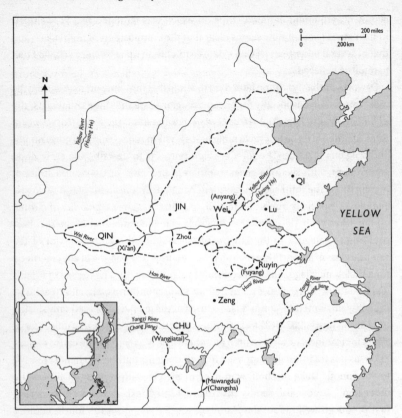

Fig. 10.1. Major states and archaeological sites of ancient China.

bones of oxen and the plastrons (i.e. the flat underbelly) of turtles – were used by the kings of the Shang dynasty (*c.* 1600–1045 BCE) in performing divinations (attempts to determine the outcome of future actions). From them we have learned virtually all that we know about the religion of the Shang dynasty, and they are particularly rich since some of the Shang kings divined about most major state affairs before undertaking them. Thus, we know of the Shang high god Shang Di or Lord on High, of nature spirits and ancestral spirits, and of sacrifices and rituals both formulaic (i.e. those performed according to a regular schedule) and also *ad hoc* (those performed only for particular purposes), and also of how Shang divination was performed and something of what the people of the time thought about divination (for which, see especially, pp. 511–12 and 526–7).

Inscribed oracle bones have also been discovered from the subsequent Western Zhou dynasty, as have numerous inscribed bronze vessels that were used in performing sacrifices to the ancestors. The inscriptions on these bronze vessels usually describe an event or events (often an audience at the royal court) that they commemorate, but they also include prayers to their ancestors seeking various types of spiritual aid (for instance, long life, sons and grandsons, and support in their service to the king). Although bronze inscriptions underwent many changes over the next several centuries (reflecting changes in the society at large), they remain the most important archaeologically recovered texts until about the fourth century BCE.

From the fourth century BCE onwards, we now have a growing corpus of textual materials written on bamboo and wooden strips. These texts range from records of divination – some that had used turtle shells and others that had used a method that produced a numerical result similar to those found in the *Classic of Changes* – to records of court cases, to almanacs of lucky and unlucky days, and even one story that describes how a man who had been convicted of a crime and then executed was returned to life after successfully pleading his innocence in the underworld (his post-resurrection report of the underworld includes such interesting advice as that ghosts dislike spitting). They also include early versions of known texts, such as the *Record of Rites*, *Laozi* and *Classic of Changes*. They have also been particularly important in showing that some traditional texts long suspected of being late forgeries do in fact derive from ancient China. Recently, bamboo strips of the third century BCE discovered at Wangjiatai in Hubei province preserve passages that match almost exactly a text known as the *Guicang* or *Returning To Be Stored* which is supposed to represent a different divination tradition from that of the *Classic of Changes*, but which has also long been supposed to have been written after the Han dynasty. This discovery shows not only that the *Returning To Be Stored* probably dates from before the Han dynasty (202 BCE to 220 CE), but also that there were competing styles of divination, even within the divination system of the *Classic of Changes*.

Important as these new texts have been for the reconstruction of all aspects of ancient Chinese civilization, and especially religion, they have been by no means the only contribution archaeology has made. The archaeology of ancient China has been overwhelmingly mortuary in nature, which is to say that most discoveries have been of and in tombs. These discoveries include most of the textual materials described above, but also other types of ritual implements either used by the deceased during his or her life or else used in the funeral ceremony. Some of these burial goods are extraordinarily beautiful. For instance, the lacquer coffin from the tomb of Lord Yi of Zeng (d. 433 BCE), depicts not only numerous fantastic creatures apparently guarding the coffin, but also windows through which the soul of the deceased might have come and gone. And the funeral banner from the tomb of Lady Dai at Mawangdui (d. *c.* 165 BCE) seems to portray the lady in three different realms of existence: as an old lady, leaning on a cane, in the middle of the banner; as the deceased in the tomb chamber under the ground (she is represented by ritual bronze vessels); and as a young woman again, at the top of the banner, sloughing off her mortal being (as a snake sloughs off its skin) and residing in the heavens between the sun (depicted with a raven) and the moon (depicted with a frog).

As depicted in the funeral ceremony for Lady Dai, bronze vessels were perhaps chief among all ritual implements. Below (pp. 521–4) we will see other ways in which artefactual evidence might be used to reconstruct religious experience, since dramatic changes in the types and numbers of ritual bronzes between the beginning and the middle of the Western Zhou dynasty (about 900 BCE) seem to indicate an important reform of the way rituals were performed. Other changes can be seen in the tombs themselves. Originally more or less simple shaft graves (i.e. a single chamber dug straight down into the ground), by the fifth century BCE tombs came to be more and more elaborate, with different rooms (some equipped with musical instruments and other secular entertainments) and eventually vaulted ceilings complete with paintings of the heavens. This perhaps suggests an important religious development that had taken place by the end of the period with which we are concerned, whereby individuals could pursue spiritual ends by and for themselves, rather than just as members of a family.

The world of ancient China

The first truly historical state of ancient China for which we have evidence is the Shang, a dynastic kingdom centred on its capital at Anyang, Henan, in the east central portion of the north China plain. Before this time, the story of China is told through either legends or archaeological discoveries. The legends include those of five ruling culture heroes who were responsible for inventions such as fire, clothing and housing, and also for cultural practices such as burial and so on; and of three other rulers – Yao, Shun and Yu – who are said to have created the forms of government, and who would subsequently become the patron saints of competing philosophers during the Warring States period (fifth to third centuries BCE). Yu seems especially to mark the end of one era and the beginning of another. Legend has it that he saved China from a flood, digging channels in the ground so that the water could flow to the sea. He also initiated the era of dynastic government. His son succeeded him to rule, establishing the first of China's traditional dynasties, the Xia. The Xia kings, all descended from Yu, are supposed to have ruled all of China until the evil last king, named Jie, was overthrown, about 1600 BCE, by the founder of the next dynasty, the Shang.

Whether there really was a Xia dynasty and, if so, just what it was like are important issues that Chinese archaeologists have sought to determine. They have discovered a distinct cultural zone in the western part of the north China plain dating to about 2000–1500 BCE, the place and time associated with the Xia in traditional histories. This is but one of numerous Neolithic and Early Bronze Age cultures that have been identified in China during the two or three millennia prior to the time of the Shang. These cultures used to be divided into two general types: a western type, known as Yangshao, characterized by painted, free-form pottery; and an eastern type, known as Longshan, with monochromatic black pottery made to exacting specifications, often with legs, spouts and/or handles. As more and more discoveries have been made (and as contemporary Chinese politics have become more and more decentralized), archaeologists have identified several other local cultures that do not fit this neat east–west divide. This picture of local diversity is also coming to characterize ancient China's historical period, despite the traditional notion that there was a single king ruling over the entire territory.

As mentioned above, according to China's traditional history the Shang was the second of these dynastic powers, but it is the first for which there are contemporary written records. These records – the oracle-bone inscriptions described above – derive from the reigns of the last nine kings of the dynasty, from roughly 1200 to 1045 BCE. These kings controlled an area perhaps 500 km east–west by an equivalent distance north–south, though their degree of control was obviously greater near the centre. This area must also have included large expanses of uninhabited territory, and also parts intermittently controlled by enemies of the Shang. In their capital at present-day Anyang (in northern Henan province near the border with Hebei province), the Shang were able to provide their kings with the trappings of a royal government. The oracle-bone inscriptions mention numerous government officers (though it would be premature to posit any sort of stable bureaucracy at this time), and archaeology has revealed large temple and residential complexes, as well as gigantic royal tombs. Although all of the royal tombs had been robbed long before the archaeologists opened them, the tomb of a royal consort discovered in 1975 gives some indication as to the riches that were available to the Shang kings: over 400 bronze vessels and implements, 600 exquisitely carved jade pieces (the jade coming from as far away as present-day Xinjiang province, well over 2000 km to the west), and over 7000 cowrie shells (a form of wealth in ancient China).

This wealth did not prove lasting for the Shang kings. By the middle of the eleventh century BCE, a new power, known as the Zhou, had arisen in the Wei River valley (present-day Shaanxi province) to the west of Shang. In 1045 BCE, the Zhou overthrew the Shang, and established themselves as rulers of most of what is today north China, especially the area through which the Yellow River flows. The Zhou kings attempted to bring under control this relatively vast area (more than double the size of the area controlled by the Shang) by deputing blood relatives to rule over the indigenous peoples and newly established Zhou colonies in the east. This patriarchal form of government was successful for three or four generations (roughly one century). Then, a combination of military defeats that stripped away the eastern territories, a gradual but inevitable weakening of the blood ties linking the Zhou king with the rulers of the local states, and also fragmentation of local families (and competition within and among them for the reduced land and resources available to them) all led to a notable restructuring of Zhou life. This restructuring manifested itself in new forms of government, social structure, religious performance, and perhaps even literature. With this great reform of the middle Western Zhou, we seem to see a society moving from what Weber would term patriarchal forms to bureaucratic ones. For instance, in the government, individuals were now appointed to offices with particular responsibilities within a more or less well-defined hierarchy. A similar development seems to have taken place in religious practice: whereas in earlier times family members had performed their own rituals, there is evidence that about this time specially trained priests and ritual celebrants began to perform rituals on behalf of the families.

Like the Shang before them, the Western Zhou too fell, though the kings managed to maintain their dynasty – in a much attenuated form – in the eastern part of their realm. In 771 BCE the Zhou capital near present-day Xi'an, Shaanxi province, fell to a combination of invading 'barbarians' from the west and disaffected members of the Zhou state (legend has it that one of the leaders of the attack on the Zhou capital was the father-in-law of the queen, who had been set aside by the king in favour of a concubine with whom he was enamoured). This fall was almost surely due also to the increasing strength of the eastern states that had originally been established as Zhou colonies. These were then to constitute the independent states of the following Eastern Zhou period (770–256 BCE). This period is also traditionally divided into two other periods: the Springs and Autumns period (722–481 BCE, named after the title of the chronicle of the state of Lu that Confucius was supposed to have edited), and the Warring States period (463–222 BCE).

Whereas the historical development of the Western Zhou period had been from a consolidated royal government towards independent local states, the tendency of the Eastern Zhou period was just the reverse. By one count, of 162 states that were in existence at the beginning of this period, only fourteen were left by the end of the Springs and Autumns period. Indeed, by the middle of the seventh century BCE, with only minor perturbations thereafter, four major powers carved up north, south, east and west China among themselves: Qi in the east, Jin in the north, Qin in the west and Chu in the south. Throughout this period, first one and then another of these states would become most powerful (Qi and Jin even being recognized by Zhou kings as 'premiers' among the states at various times), but it was not until the middle of the third century BCE that the western state of Qin finally gained supremacy of power. Over the course of twenty-five years, the last of the Qin kings, King Zheng – or as he is better known Qin Shi huangdi, the First Emperor of China – defeated all of the other states, uniting them into a centralized empire. The creation of this empire opens a new period in the history of ancient China, whether considered from the perspective of government, society, philosophy, literature or religion; trying to tell its story would probably overwhelm this chapter, and so I will leave it aside for the most part.

The social organization of religion

The oracle-bone inscriptions of the Shang dynasty show that the Shang religion was primarily a family cult. Although there is some mention of nature spirits, most of the Shang ritual activity was directed at the royal ancestors. It seems, too, that the Shang high god, Shang Di, was conceived of as a high ancestor, perhaps the first of the ancestors or even the ensemble of the ancestors. With only one or two exceptions, sacrifices to these ancestors could be performed only by members of the royal family, the king being the first among them. When the Zhou overthrew the Shang, they were able to protray their high god Tian or Heaven as an all-encompassing god, with power over but also available to all families 'under heaven'. Despite this theological universality, in practice Zhou religion remained resolutely familial. Each family had its own ancestral temple in which sacrifices – to the family's own ancestors – took place. The following inscription on one bell of a large set of bells used in the ancestral sacrifices of one family illustrates just how important the ancestors were conceived to be. The person for whom the bell was cast, a scribe at the Zhou court by the name of Xing, addresses his prayer directly to three generations of his ancestors. It is interesting that, in referring to himself, he vacillates between first person and third person address; nevertheless, it is clear that he was seeking the blessings of the ancestors for himself and his family.

Xing Zhong 1

Xing permanently morning and night in a sagely and bright manner offers filial piety to high grandfather Duke Xin, to cultured grandfather Duke Yi, and to august deceased-father Duke Ding (with this) harmonic set of bells, using (it) to summon the prior cultured men to approach and enjoy the solemn music, and using (it) to make offering for longevity and to beseech an eternal mandate, extensively blessed wealth, and pure favors. Would that the august ancestors and deceased-father and High (Ancestor?) in response abundantly and piercingly be watchful on high. *P'iong-p'iong, dz'iwan-dz'iwan, d'iong-d'iong*! Impress rich and many blessings and broadly open Xing's body to increases in eternal mandate and embrace and give me abundant and variform blessings. May Xing for ten-thousand years be even-horned and resplendently glorious in offering rites without limit to the cultured spirits and to glorify (their) blessings, thereby securing glory to Xing's person. Eternally will I treasure it!

(*Yin Zhou jinwen jicheng* 246)

Other inscriptions on vessels cast for Xing or for other members of his family indicate that his 'high grandfather Duke Xin' was the founder of a branch lineage of the family. As families became more and more fragmented towards the end of the Western Zhou, and especially into the Eastern Zhou period, the ancestors seem to have lost some of their potency vis-à-vis the living. Whereas virtually all inscribed Western Zhou bronze vessels are dedicated to one ancestor or another, by the seventh and sixth centuries BCE very few inscriptions mention ancestors at all (by one count, only eleven of 341 Eastern Zhou inscriptions are dedicated to ancestors). Instead, the inscriptions seem designed primarily to show off the accomplishments of the person for whom the vessel was cast. This is perhaps consistent with a general trend among the government officers and intellectuals of the period to 'honour the worthy'. By the end of the Springs and Autumns period, there is a noticeable decline in the number of high-ranking government officers who come from noble families. Their places were taken by individuals, largely drawn from the ranks of the *shi* class, who had demonstrated special aptitudes and training. Much of this training must have come from private teachers such as Confucius and Mozi, who at just this time were collecting about them more or less extensive groups of disciples.

At least some of those disciples who did not find employment in the government continued to live communally with their fellow disciples. The followers of Confucius divided into several different sects after his death, and seem to have been employed as itinerant ritualists, expert especially at funeral rites. Mozi's followers banded into small armies that offered their services to besieged cities, as a practical application of Mozi's doctrine against offensive warfare. These sorts of doctrinal sects may have given rise to the great religious communities that eventually arose in China in the second century CE. Unfortunately, the social organization of religion in the intervening period is still unclear, and this must remain as merely conjecture.

The trend towards individuality and 'honouring the worthy' in the Springs and Autumns period also revealed itself in the religious expression of the time. Not all religious experience was communal. Many now sought individual mystical union with the Dao or Way. The *Laozi* describes the sage as one who is self-contained.

> Without stirring abroad
> One can know the whole world;
> Without looking out of the window
> One can see the way of heaven.
> The further one goes
> The less one knows.
> Therefore the sage knows without having to stir,
> Identifies without having to see,
> Accomplishes without having to act.[1]

Indeed, there seems even to have been a change in the understanding of what 'spirit' (*shen*) is, at least on the part of some. In the Shang and Zhou periods, spirits were deceased ancestors who continued to influence events in the world. By the Warring States period, spirit had become a power that could be internalized, that could be concentrated in one's own person.

There is evidence that some people achieved these mystical experiences by way of practices akin to yoga and/or meditation. Some of these practices probably originated in self-cultivation techniques valued, at least at first, for their physical benefits. A jade block from about 300 BCE is inscribed with a nine-step rhymed instruction for how to breathe; it is referred to as 'moving the vapour (*qi*)'.

> Swallowing, it moves;
> Moving, it extends;
> Extending, it descends;
> Descending, it stabilizes;
> Stabilizing, it solidifies;
> Solidifying, it sprouts;
> Sprouting, it grows;
> Growing, it returns;
> Returning, it is Heaven.

The last stage of these instructions reveals that this breathing technique had religious implications as well as physical benefits. Another text from just about the same time that also seems to describe breathing techniques allows more of these religious implications to be seen. The 'Nei ye' or 'Inner Achievement' chapter of the *Guanzi* or *Master Guan* contains the following passage.

> Concentrate the vapor as a spirit, and the ten-thousand things will exist completely (within you). Can you concentrate; can you be one? Can you not perform turtle-shell and milfoil divination and yet know the auspicious and ominous? Can you stop? Can you cease? Can you not seek it in others and yet obtain it in yourself?

It was perhaps these practices, 'concentrating the vapour as a spirit', that gave rise about this time (fourth and third centuries BCE) to cults of 'immortals' (literally 'men on mountains') who withdrew from society and went off to cultivate their inner being. The *Zhuangzi*, the most evocative of all texts from this period, provides the following description of these immortals.

The religion of ancient China   **503**

> The Perfect man is godlike. Though the great swamps blaze, they cannot burn him; though the great rivers freeze, they cannot chill him; though swift lightning splits the hills and howling gales shake the sea, they cannot frighten him. A man like this rides the clouds and mist, straddles the sun and moon, and wanders beyond the four seas. Even life and death have no effect on him, much less the rules of profit and loss![2]

The appearance of the individual quest probably marks the most significant development in the religious experience of ancient China. Yet, even by the end of the period under consideration in this chapter, religion remained overwhelmingly communal – primarily within the family. This is doubtless related to the world-view of the time, which saw all life as interrelated. To withdraw from society, to live outside of relationships, would be to go counter to the way of the world.

The world-view of ancient China

Early correlative thought

It is very common to characterize early Chinese thought as being based in a view of the world that correlates natural phenomena with events in the human realm. Although this sort of correlative thought was not systematized until the fourth or third century BCE, it almost surely underlies much of the intellectual and cultural expression of earlier periods as well. For example, we can suppose – as later Chinese texts do – that when King Wen of Zhou began his rule in 1099 BCE and declared his kingship in 1057 BCE, thus nominally establishing the Zhou dynasty, he saw his 'mandate of heaven' to have been portended by a spectacular and very rare conjunction of the five visible planets that took place in May of 1059 BCE. Similarly, when the Western Zhou dynasty was coming to its end, an equally rare succession of lunar eclipses (15 January 783 BCE, 4 January and 24 December 782 BCE), followed by a solar eclipse (4 June 781 BCE), and then in the very next year by an apparently spectacular earthquake in the Zhou capital area, led the poets of the day to envision the crumbling of their own moral and political order.

The Beginning of the Tenth Month (*Classic of Poetry*, Mao 194)

At the beginning of the tenth month,
The first day *xinmao* (day 28 in the Chinese cycle of sixty),

The sun was eclipsed,
Again a great calamity.
That moon was diminished,
This sun is diminshed.
Now for these people below,
Again, a great woe.

The sun and the moon announce the balefulness,
Not using their paths.
The four states are without government,
Not using their worthies.
For that moon to be eclipsed,
Then is common.
For this sun to be eclipsed,
Wherein is the immorality!

Flashing and flashing the thunder and lightning,
Neither calm nor assured.
The hundred rivers bubble and leap,
The mountains and hills crumble and fall.
The high cliffs become valleys,
The deep valleys become peaks.
Woe to the people of today,
Why has no one taken warning!

(Here and where no other name given, translator Shaughnessy)

Terrestrial phenomena did not need to be so startling as an earthquake to be portentous. Thus, when Confucius encouraged his disciples to study the *Classic of Poetry* for, among other reasons, 'the more to recognize the names of birds and animals, plants and trees' (*Analects* 19/9), his interest was almost surely not pedantically biological. Instead, he believed that birds and animals, plants and trees partake of the same world order as do the affairs of, for instance, family members and statesmen. Some animals are crafty, while others can be tamed; some plants are bitter, while others can bring about a smile and even more. Knowing their names, and thus understanding their natures, leads to a better understanding of the human realm as well. By paying careful enough attention to nature, one can literally hear it sing out its advice, as in the following early poem.

Chopping Wood (*Classic of Poetry*, Mao 165)

Chopping wood, *ding ding*,
A bird chirps *ying ying*.
Coming out of the dark valley,
Moving to the lofty tree.
Ying its chirp,
Seeking its friend's sound.
Look at that bird,
Even it seeks its friend's sound.
How much more so should not a man
Seek a friend!
Internalize it, hear it;
In the end, it will be harmonious and peaceful.

'Hear it', indeed, for it may be phrased in a very human language. The first poem in the *Classic of Poetry*, entitled 'The *Join*ing Osprey' (Mao 1), begins with an excellent example of a poetic style, referred to in traditional Chinese literary criticism as *xing* or 'evocation', in which a stanza is composed of two parallel couplets, the first describing some thing or event in the natural world and the second a corresponding person or event in the human world.

> *Join, join* cries the osprey
> On the river's isle.
> Delicate is the young girl,
> A fine match for the lord.

According to traditional Chinese zoology, the osprey is supposed to be a bird that mates for life, and so well evokes romantic relations between a lord and a suitable woman. Just as the osprey here is 'on the river's isle', implying that it is separated from its mate (the Chinese word for 'river' is part of an extended word family that includes many words for 'separation', thus perhaps 'the watery cleaver'), so too the lord is portrayed as not yet having joined with the woman. But he hears the osprey calling to its mate with the sound *guan guan*, understanding the sound to be the Chinese word *guan*, which means 'to join'. Thus, the bird call links the two couplets, and in so doing bridges the divide between the natural and human realms.

As we will go on to see in the section on divination below (pp. 525–32), poetry was linked to various forms of divination, both formally and conceptually.

Indeed, in the Zhou dynasty, the same officers responsible for poetry (the *shi* or 'scribes') were also responsible for, among other things, divination and astronomy. But poetry is important for more than just its formal relations; by giving expression to the linkage – the correlation – between the natural and human realms, one can divine from the poetry something of the spirit of ancient China. One of the western world's great interpreters of ancient China, Marcel Granet (1884–1940), used the evocations of ancient Chinese poetry to describe what this spirit meant to the people of the time.

> They experienced the presence of a tutelary power whose sanctity sprang from every corner of the landscape, blessed forces which they strove to capture in every way. Holy was the place, sacred the slopes of the valley they climbed and descended, the stream they crossed with their skirts tucked up, the blooming flowers they plucked, the ferns, the bushes, the white elms, the great oaks and the wood they took from them: the lit bonfires, the scents of the nosegays, the spring water in which they dipped themselves, and the wind that dried them as they came from bathing, all had virtues, unlimited virtues; all was a promise given to all hopes. And the animals which teemed and also held their seasonal assemblies, grasshoppers gathering under the grass, the arrested flights of birds of passage, ospreys gathered together on sandy islets, wild geese calling to one another in the woods, all were part of the festival and shared in the holiness of the place and the moment. Their calls, their chases, were signals, emblems, a language in which men heard an echo of their own emotions. They felt themselves strong by their harmony with the natural world.[3]

The rise of Five Processes systems

Nature was intelligible to man because – apart from abnormal phenomena such as eclipses and earthquakes that required the expert knowledge of diviners – it was basically regular and predictable. The circuit of the year is perhaps the best example of nature's predictability. Star gazers knew that at the beginning of February the horns of the dragon constellation (α Virginis) would appear in the eastern sky at dusk; that by mid-summer the entirety of that constellation (which included also virtually all of what in the west has been grouped as Scorpio) would be arrayed across the southern sky; that in the autumn it would sink, head first, below the western horizon; and that in winter the dragon would not be visible at all in the night sky. On earth, trees and plants would correspond with the movements of the dragon: coming out in spring, coming to full flower in summer, being ready for harvest in autumn, and hibernating in the winter. It is not hard to see that the four seasons would offer a ready categorization for nature's varieties. It is perhaps also not hard to imagine how the seasons might be correlated with another fourfold categorization of the world: the four directions. That the dragon constellation, like the sun, came out in the east, flourished in the south, and culminated in the west, served to correlate the east with spring, south with summer, west with autumn, and north – where the sun does not reach – with the dead of winter.

The regularity of the stars and seasons early on gave rise to almanacs telling people what to do when. Probably the earliest of these is yet another poem in the *Classic of Poetry*, this one entitled 'The Seventh Month'. It is a lengthy poem that begins with the ebbing of the Fire Star (i.e. Antares, the Heart of the Dragon constellation), and proceeds to describe events – both natural and human – associated with the various months of the year. Here it will be possible to translate only two stanzas, taken from different parts of the poem.

The Seventh Month (*Classic of Poetry*, Mao 154)

In the seventh month the Fire ebbs;
In the ninth month we give out coats.
As the spring days carry warmth,
There is the cry of the oriole.
The girls clutching their fine baskets,
Follow those narrow paths
To pluck the tender mulberry leaves.
As the spring days grow longer,
They gather the white aster in bunches.
The girls' hearts are pained and sad,
Until with their men together they return.
...
In the fifth month the locusts move their legs,
In the sixth month the grasshoppers shake their wings.
In the seventh month in the fields,
In the eighth month under the eaves,

> In the ninth month on the windows,
> In the tenth month the cricket
> Enters under our bed.
> Plugging up the holes and smoking out the rats,
> Blocking up the openings and sealing the windows,
> We call to our wives and children,
> Saying 'For the changing of the year,
> Enter the house and stay put.'

Over the next several centuries, the folk wisdom in this poem came to be categorized into rules for life and, especially, rules for government. One of the earliest such manuals of government is in another chapter of the *Guanzi* (the text mentioned above with respect to its chapter 'Nei ye' or 'Inner Achievement'). In a chapter entitled 'The Four Seasons', we find specific activities appropriate to each season. The text begins by noting: 'Commands have their seasons; if there were no seasons, then it would be necessary to observe and follow whence the heavens come, but with the five vastnesses and six murkinesses, who could know it?' However, thanks to the sages of the past, the seasonal commands had already been catalogued and been made available in this text. The commands for spring are as follows.

> The eastern quadrant is designated to the stars; its season is spring; its breath is the wind. The wind generates wood and bone. Its virtues are joy and growth which are emitted in moderation. Make seasonal its activities and commands: repair and clean the places of the spirits, and respectfully pray that decay be blocked; venerate the upright *yang*, put in order the dikes, hoe and plant the fields, erect bridges, repair canals, roof the houses and fix the plumbing; resolve grievances and pardon the guilty, bringing into communication the four quarters. Then the soft breezes and sweet rains will come, the hundred families will be long-lived, and the hundred insects will be abundant. This is called the virtue of the stars. The stars control the emission of the winds. This is why if in spring you enact the governances of winter then there will be exhaustion; if you enact the governances of autumn, then there will be frost; if you enact the governances of summer, then there will be desires. This is why in the third month of spring, on the *jia* and *yi* days, you issue the five governances, the first of which is caring for youths and orphans and releasing the guilty; the second of which is bestowing ranks and rewards; the third of which

is repairing canals when the ice has thawed and returning men who have absconded; the fourth of which is called levelling the precipices, repairing the boundary markers, and erecting the field rows; and the fifth of which is called not killing the young animals and not plucking flowers and cutting stems. If these five governances are timely, then the spring rains will come.

The final portion of this passage points towards one of the most important developments in early Chinese cosmology: the correlation of the archaic fourfold categorization scheme with a new fivefold scheme that would come to dominate all Chinese world-views by the third century BCE. The process by which this development came about is both simple and complex. The simple explanation (and we will have to be satisfied with it here, since the complex explanation would take far too much space) is that the centre was added to the four directions to give five orientations. These were then correlated with five natural elements – Wood, Fire, Earth, Metal and Water – that were considered to be the basic building blocks of nature, but building blocks that were constantly in flux (whence the Chinese term for them, *xing*, which means 'steps' or 'moving', and thus is perhaps best translated as 'processes'). Their movements could be either by way of generation (Wood generates Fire, Fire generates Earth [as ashes], Earth generates Metal, Metal generates Water [turning fluid when heated], and Water in turn generates Wood) or by way of conquest (Metal conquers Wood, Wood conquers Water [containing it], Water conquers Fire, and Fire conquers Earth). Once these five elemental processes were enumerated, it was then a natural step to extend their correlations to all the various aspects of life, correlations almost as complex as life itself. Table 10.1 gives just a few of these correlations.[4] The connection between this fivefold categorization of the world and the religious life of ancient China may not be immediately apparent, but since – by the end of the period with which we are concerned in this chapter – it underlay virtually all understandings of the way the world was structured, it is important to have at least some sense of it also to appreciate developments in religion. We will see several manifestations of this system when we go on to consider the practice of divination in ancient China.

Religious experience in ancient China

The mechanistic nature of the Five Processes categorization scheme described above does not mean that there were not experiences in ancient China apart

Table 10.1 *The Five Processes system*

	Wood	**Fire**	**Earth**	**Metal**	**Water**
Seasons	Spring	Summer	–	Autumn	Winter
Directions	East	South	Centre	West	North
Tastes	Sour	Bitter	Sweet	Acrid	Salty
Smells	Goatish	Burning	Fragrant	Rank	Rotten
Numbers	8	7	5	9	6
Heavens	Stars	Sun	Earth	Constellations	Moon
Planets	Jupiter	Mars	Saturn	Venus	Mercury
Weather	Wind	Heat	Thunder	Cold	Rain
States (China)	Qi	Chu	Zhou	Jin	Yan
Ministries	Farming	War	Capital	Justice	Works
Colours	Green	Red	Yellow	White	Black
Animals	Fishes	Birds	Man	Mammals	Insects
Domestic An.	Sheep	Fowl	Ox	Dog	Pig
Grains	Wheat	Beans	Panicled millet	Hemp	Millet
Viscera	Spleen	Lungs	Heart	Kidney	Liver
Body parts	Muscles	Veins	Flesh	Skin and hair	Bones
Organs	Eyes	Tongue	Mouth	Nose	Ears
Emotions	Anger	Joy	Desire	Sorrow	Fear

from the regular cycle of phenomenal life. Indeed, in all periods of ancient China, people from kings to the common man could call upon a wide variety of gods to intervene on their behalf in the working of the world. They communicated with these gods through numerous rituals. Some of these rituals were systematic, such as sacrifices to the ancestors and seasonal celebrations; others were impromptu, such as divinations before undertaking many activities or exorcisms in the event of illness or other misfortune. Most of the rituals were performed communally (many, such as those of the ancestral cult, within the family), serving thus as important means of social organization and expression. Ironically, however, so important were these rituals that many of the philosophers of the Warring States period came to regard them also as the foundation of individual moral development. In the following section, we will consider in turn some of the gods of ancient China, the ancestor cult, types of rituals and attitudes towards ritual, and then finally just one among the many types of religious practices available to the people of the time.

The gods of ancient China

An increasing abundance of goods placed in tombs throughout China's Neolithic period (roughly 5000–2000 BCE) probably attests to a rich religious experience, including numerous gods. But it is only with the first written records, the oracle-bone inscriptions of the Shang dynasty, that we can begin to put names to them and to describe their particular powers. As we might expect, there were various nature gods, such as the mountain-god Yue or the river-god He, but their powers were distinctly limited; in fact, even before the dynasty came to a close, divinations about and sacrifices to these nature gods were discontinued. Throughout the Shang dynasty, it is clear that for the Shang kings – and it is important to note that virtually all of the Shang oracle-bone inscriptions that we have derive from divinations performed on behalf of the Shang kings – the most important supernatural powers were their own royal ancestors. Again and again we read of the kings' concern that their ancestors were influencing events in the mortal world, and of the kings' own attempts to influence the ancestors. Thus, on one occasion when King Wu Ding (d. *c.* 1189 BCE) was suffering from a toothache, he divined to determine whether it were his father, King Xiao Yi, who was the cause of it.

> Divining: 'There is a sick tooth; it is not Father Yi who is harming (it).'
>
> (*Heji* 13646)

It seems that the more recently deceased an ancestor was the more malevolent he could be (ancestresses, too, were occasionally divined about, but they seem to have been less powerful). Sacrifices could be made to propitiate these ancestors, with divinations made too about the potential efficacy of these sacrifices. Thus, the same King Wu Ding divined about sacrificing a cow to his three royal uncles (all elder brothers of his father King Xiao Yi, and thus also referred to as 'father').

> Divining: 'We will offer to Xiang Jia, Father Geng, and Father Xin one cow.'
>
> (*Heji* 6647f)

As ancestors became more distant, their interventions seem to have become more postive. There are numerous divinations about the king either hosting or visiting the high ancestors (many Chinese words pertaining to communication were originally indistinct as to direction). The following divination is a complete example, containing a preface indicating the day and performer of the divination, the 'charge' or topic of the divination proper, the king's prognostication of it, and a subsequent verification indicating that the king's prognostication was indeed accurate.

> Crack-making on *guiwei* (day 20), (the diviner) Que divining: 'On *jiashen* (day 21) the king will host (or visit) the sun of (high ancestor) Shang Jia.' The king prognosticated saying: 'Auspicious; (I) will host (or visit).' He really did host (or visit) (it).   (*Heji* 1248f)

This divination points to a significant aspect of all of the Shang ancestors: they were associated with (and named for) one of the days in the Chinese ten-day week (*jia, yi, bing, ding, wu, ji, geng, xin, ren, gui*, the days in turn being represented by one of ten suns that took turns illuminating the daytime heavens) and they received cult on their own individual days. In the case of this particular divination, ancestor Shang Jia was hosted (or visited) by the king (again, King Wu Ding) on the day *jiashen*, the second of six *jia* days.

  While Shang Jia was the high ancestor of the Shang kings, there was one power above even him: the high god Di. It is unclear what sort of god Di was (or, perhaps, were, since one of the more plausible explanations is that Di was a collection of all of the ancestors), but his powers were certainly considerable. He had power to send down the wind and rain and good harvests, to approve city building, and to assist in warfare, among other powers. The following inscriptions give some indication of his over-arching power. In the case of these inscriptions, I will quote both the (grammatically) positive and negative charges, a paired divination style characteristic of the divinations performed for King Wu Ding.

> Divining: 'The king should let it be Zhi Guo with whom he allies to attack the Bafang, (for if he does) Di will give us aid.'
>
> 'The king ought not let it be Zhi Guo with whom he allies to attack the Bafang, (for if he does) Di may not give us aid.'   (*Heji* 6473f)
>
> Crack-making on *renzi* (day 49), Zheng divining: 'We may make a city, (for if we do) Di will not obstruct it but will approve.' Third month.
>
> Crack-making on *guichou* (day 50), Zheng divining: 'We ought not make a city, (for if we do not) Di will approve.'   (*Heji* 14206f)

Curiously, despite his great power, Di was never the recipient of sacrifices from the Shang kings.

  Towards the end of the Shang period, a second high god appears in the historical record. This was Tian or Heaven. Unlike Di, who seems to have been a god only for the Shang people (and perhaps only for their kings, who, as mentioned above, may have considered themselves to be descended from him), Heaven was associated with the Zhou people. The Zhou lived to the west of the Shang, and by the end of the Shang period had come to be their major competitors in what is now north China. One of the earliest references to Heaven, albeit in a much later source (the *Shi ji* or *Records of the Historian* of Sima Qian (145–86 BCE)), purports to date to the reign of the Shang king Wu Yi (r. *c.* 1131–1117). Sima Qian's account reads as follows:

> Thearch Wu Yi was without the Way. He made a stick figure and called it the god of Heaven. He had a race with it, commanding a man to run against it. The god of Heaven did not win, and then he mocked and ridiculed it. (On another occasion), he made a leather pouch, filled it with blood, hung it up and shot it, commanding that he had shot Heaven.

It seems clear that in addition to political differences that eventually led the Zhou to conquer the Shang, bringing the Shang dynasty to an end about 1045 BCE, the Zhou and their god Heaven also belonged to a different religious tradition.

In sources dating from after the Zhou conquest of Shang, the only further mention of Di comes in propaganda speeches purportedly given by the Zhou rulers to the conquered people of Shang. The 'Many Sires' ('Duo shi') chapter of the *Venerated Documents* (*Shang shu*) quotes the Duke of Zhou as giving the following explanation for the Shang defeat.

> It was also Heaven that grandly established, protected, and ruled the Shang. What is more, none of the Shang kings dared to neglect Di, and none did not match it with Heaven's grace. Now this last successor king greatly lacked illumination with respect to Heaven; how much the less could you say that he had heard and considered the former kings' diligence for their house. He made greatly licentious his dissoluteness, and did not look back upon Heaven's lustre and the people's blessings. It was this one that Di on High did not protect but sent down such a great loss as this. It was Heaven that did not give or make bright its virtue, and in the loss of all the little and great countries of the four quarters there were none that did not stand accused in their guilt.

The Zhou made the case that Di was but a family god, his power extending only to the Shang royal family. Heaven, on the other hand, was a universal god. Just as the great vault of heaven covered all of the four quarters, so too could Heaven serve as the god of all the people of the four quarters.

As in the case of Di, it is difficult to specify too clearly the nature of Heaven. Like Di, it also had, or came to have, certain anthropomorphic qualities. The most important of these was its role as the ancestor of the Zhou kings, who by shortly after the Zhou conquest came routinely to be called 'Son of Heaven' (*tianzi*). It was also the bestower of the Mandate of Heaven (*tian ming*) that was seen by the Zhou people to legitimate their right to rule. These two aspects are both on display in the following bronze inscription (the *Da Yu ding*), which probably dates to the year 981 BCE and which records a Zhou king's address to his tutor Yu.

> The king said to the effect: 'Yu, illustrious King Wen received Heaven's great mandate. At (the time) King Wu succeeded Wen and made the country, (he) ridded its evil, extending to the four quarters, and governed their people. Among the managers of affairs, he suppressed wine; none dared to get flushed. Having offerings and sacrifices, none dared to get drunk. Therefore, heaven respectfully looked down and treated (him) as a son, and greatly protected the former kings . . . have the four quarters.'
>
> (*Yin Zhou jinwen jicheng* 2837)

The Mandate of Heaven would in turn become one of the Zhou dynasty's greatest gifts to Chinese posterity, underwriting all subsequent notions of political legitimacy.

However, Heaven never lost its natural characteristics. As mentioned above, p. 503, the Zhou people saw the Mandate of Heaven literally illuminated in the heavens above: the great conjunction of the five visible planets in the year 1059 BCE. The heavens were also the abode of other lesser gods, known from somewhat later sources. For instance, the *Zuo zhuan* or *Zuo's Tradition*, a historical source from the fourth century BCE, preserves the following story set in the year 541 BCE (first year of Duke Zhao).

> The lord of Jin was ill, and the Elder of Zheng sent Gongsun Qiao to Jin to pay him a visit and to ask about the illness. But Shu Xiang asked him about it, saying 'As for our lord's illness, the diviners say that Shichen (Substance Submerging) and Taitai (Terrace Nag) are hexing him, but none of the scribes know them; dare I ask who these gods are?' Zi Chan said

'In antiquity, the emperor Gao Xin had two sons, the elder named Ebo (Obstruction the Elder) and the younger named Shichen (Substance Submerging). They lived in a vast forest, but couldn't abide each other, daily seeking out shields and battle-axes with which to attack each other. The succeeding emperor (Yao) did not approve and moved Obstruction the Elder to the Mound of Shang to preside over (the constellation) Chronogram (Antares and Scorpio). The men of Shang have based themselves on this, and thus Chronogram is the Shang star. He moved Substance Submerging to the Great Xia (the area of the state of Jin) to preside over the star Triaster (Orion). The men of Tang have based themselves on this, in order to serve the Xia and the Shang.'

The account continues with much of interest for the history and interpretation of divination and medicine in ancient China. But for our present purposes, the important thing to note is that the two gods Ebo (Obstruction the Elder) and Shichen (Substance Submerging) are simply the constellations known in the west as Scorpio and Orion. Their banishment to the east and west respectively is but a mythic explanation of the natural fact that the two constellations never appear together in the night sky: as Scorpio arises in the east, the constellation Orion sets (or, in Chinese mythological and astronomical terminology, 'submerges') in the west. It is interesting too that their mutual antagonism, to the extent of seeking out weapons to do battle with each other, finds a counterpart in the Greek myth of the god Orion, who after doing battle with a giant scorpion plunged into the sea.

By the end of the ancient period in China, another astral deity had metamorphosed into the singular high god Tai Yi (Grand One), 'the most exalted of the spirits of Heaven', in the words of a memorial presented to the Han emperor Wu (r. 140–87 BCE). Tai Yi referred to the topmost of a group of four stars in an inverted Y-shape (this shape being very similar to the Chinese character *tai* or 'grand') located just above the Northern Dipper. It seems originally to have governed military campaigns, as demonstrated by its use decorating the blade of a dagger-axe from the Warring States period. By 112 BCE Emperor Wu had established two different altars dedicated to Tai Yi to conduct the state's most important sacrifices. In the *Records of the Historian* of Sima Qian, who was Grand Scribe during the reign of Emperor Wu, there is the following account of a ritual performed at the outset of a military campaign in that same year.

(Emperor Wu) was about to launch an attack on Nan Yue, and offered prayers for success to Tai Yi. A banner painted with the sun, moon, the Northern Dipper, and the Ascending Dragon served as the Tai Yi spear, and was called the Numinous Flag. While performing the prayer for success in battle, the Grand Scribe raised the flag and pointed it at the country to be attacked.

Just such a banner as that used in this ritual was discovered in a tomb dating to 168 BCE at Mawangdui, Changsha, Hunan. It is a painting on silk that is labelled 'Diagram for Repelling Weapons'. Here Tai Yi appears, this time in a quasi anthropomophic form but one that still retains the shape of an inverted Y, in the top middle of the diagram, with the Rain Master to his right, the Thunder Lord to his left, four 'warrior disciples' beneath him, and three dragons forming a triangle beneath him. These three dragons probably represent the three stars just below the Tai Yi star, and one of them is probably the Ascending Dragon depicted on the 'Numinous Flag' used in Emperor Wu's military ritual described above. That flag also included the sun, the moon and the Northern Dipper. It is clear that Tai Yi was never far removed from his original residence at the very top of the heavens.

One should not conclude from the gods described above that all gods in ancient China resided in the heavens. Indeed, gods were all about. Just as in the Shang dynasty, the mountains and rivers continued to have their individual gods. Plants were imbued with special powers to harm or to heal. Animals need not be as fantastic as dragons to be regarded as gods. And humans of all sorts had apotheosized into ghosts and spirits. Although A. C. Graham, the foremost western historian of early Chinese thought, could write 'The tendency throughout the classical age [i.e. 500–200 BCE] is to ignore the spirits of the dead and of the mountains and rivers after paying them their customary respects, and to regard Heaven as an impersonal power responsible for everything outside human control',[5] it was really his own tendency to ignore the spirits; for the people of the time, the spirits – of every sort – were far too much a part of everything to be ignored.

The ancestor cult

If asked to specify the single most important feature of Chinese culture, most Chinese people – whether in traditional times or today – would probably point to their veneration for their ancestors. As described above, the earliest written records in China describe sacrifices made by the Shang kings to their ancestors. By the end of the Shang dynasty, sacrifices dedicated to the ancestors were so regular that one cycle of sacrifices filled a 360-day year. Five different types of sacrifices were offered in sequence throughout the ten-day weeks, first to Shang Jia, then to Bao Yi, Bao Bing, Bao Ding, and so on (recall that the Shang week was in the sequence *jia, yi, bing, ding, wu, ji, geng, xin, ren, gui*). An example of an oracle-bone divination from one of the last reigns of the Shang dynasty mentions one of these sacrifices.

> *Guichou* (day 50), the king crack-making: 'In the next ten-day week there will be no trouble.' The king prognosticated and said: 'Auspicious.' In the fifth month, *jiayin* (day 51), the *yong* sacrifice to Da Jia.   (*Yingcang* 2505)

By this time, not only were the five sacrifices formulaic, but also divination itself had become largely a matter of routine: on the tenth day of the week, the king divined the simple formula 'In the next ten-day week there will be no trouble', and then issued the unvarying prognostication 'auspicious'.

When the Zhou overthrew the Shang, the Zhou rulers argued to the Shang people that one of the reasons they did so was because the last Shang king had become lax in his performance of the sacrifices, perhaps alluding to this routinization of the ancestral cult.

> Then it was because your last king of Shang was lazy, sloppy in his government, and impure in his sacrifices, that Heaven sent down this loss.
>
> ('Duo fang', *Venerated documents*)

The Zhou were anything but lax in their sacrifices to their ancestors. They cast thousands of ritual bronze vessels, many of them ending with the inscribed prayer that the vessel be used to make offerings to the deceased grandfathers and fathers. The term used to indicate these offerings is *xiao*, usually translated as filial piety. The earliest Chinese dictionary, *Shuo wen jie zi* (Explanations of pictographs and interpretations of composite graphs), completed in the early second century CE, explains that the character is composed of the element for an elderly (or deceased) father written above that for child: '*Xiao* means to excel at serving one's father and mother. It comes from a simplification of the graph for elderly (or deceased) father and that for child. It means that the child holds up (i.e. supports) the elderly.'

No one, not even the Zhou kings (perhaps especially not the Zhou kings), was exempt from obligations to his ancestors. One of the very few bronze vessels made on behalf of a reigning Zhou king illustrates well the continuing relationship with one's ancestors. This vessel, the *Hu gui*, discovered in 1980, was made for King Li (r. 857–842 BCE), who refers to himself in the inscription by his personal name Hu. The inscription includes a long prayer to his ancestors (curiously stating that they lived in the court of the god Di).

> Hu makes (this) giant sacrificial treasured *gui*-tureen, with which vigorously to aid my august cultured and valorous grandfather and deceased father. May they approach the prior cultured men, may they constantly be in the court of Di on High, ascending and descending, continuously visited with the august Di on High's great and felicitous mandate, with which commandingly to protect our family, my position and Hu's person.
>
> (*Yin Zhou jinwen jicheng* 4317)

Already in the Western Zhou dynasty, the understanding of *xiao* or filial piety seems to have evolved from the offering of sacrifices to one's deceased ancestors into an ethical notion of proper attitude or conduct towards one's parents, whether they were dead or alive. It was further extended to include reciprocal obligations, in which the father also had explicit responsibility for his son. The 'Kang gao', one of the documents contained in the *Venerated Documents*, includes the following instruction from the Duke of Zhou to his younger brother.

> Feng, of the prime evils and great obtusenesses, what could be worse than not being filial and not being right-like (i.e., responsible)? If a son does not respectfully fulfil his father's service, he greatly wounds his deceased father's heart; with the father who is not able to treat his son as a son, then he sickens his son; with the younger brother who does not consider the lustre of Heaven, then he is not able to honour his elder brother; with the elder brother who likewise does not consider and pity his younger brother, this is to be greatly not right-like (i.e., irresponsible) with respect to the younger brother.

By the time of Confucius, or at least no later than his early disciples, *xiao* or filial piety had coalesced into perhaps the core Confucian virtue. Several maxims regarding the need for filial piety to be internalized are attributed to Confucius in the second book of the *Analects*.

> Meng Yizi asked about being filial. The Master answered, 'Never fail to comply.'
>
> Fan Chi was driving. The Master told him about the interview, saying, 'Mengsun asked me about being filial. I answered, "Never fail to comply."'
>
> Fan Chi asked, 'What does that mean?'
>
> The Master said, 'When your parents are alive, comply with the rites in serving them; when they die, comply with the rites in burying them; comply with the rites in sacrificing to them.'   (*Analects* 2/5)

> Meng Wubo asked about being filial. The Master said, 'Give your father and mother no other cause for anxiety than illness.'   (*Analects* 2/6)

> Zi You asked about being filial. The Master said, 'Nowadays for a man to be filial means no more than that he is able to provide his parents with food. Even hounds and horses are, in some way, provided with food. If a man shows no reverence, where is the difference?'   (*Analects* 2/7)

> Zi Xia asked about being filial. The Master said, 'What is difficult to manage is the expression on one's face. As for the young taking on the burden when there is work to be done or letting the old enjoy the wine and the food when these are available, that hardly deserves to be called filial.'   (*Analects* 2/8)[6]

Another saying of Confucius specifies an important ritual practice: the need for a son to mourn the death of his father (and also other relatives) for three full years.

> The Master said, 'If, for three years, a man makes no changes to his father's ways, he can be said to be a good son.'   (*Analects* 4/20)

In later times, there were precise codes for how to carry out this ritual mourning. Whether these codes were already in effect at the time of Confucius, or even earlier – as another of his sayings (*Analects* 14/40) would suggest – is not clear. But there can be no doubt that the ancestor cult was an essential social institution and that filial piety was its most important individual manifestation.

Rituals and ritual

The first saying of Confucius quoted above has already indicated to us the premier role played by ritual in the social and religious life of ancient China: 'When your parents are alive, comply with the rites in serving them; when they die, comply with the rites in burying them; comply with the rites in sacrificing to them.' Confucius probably had in mind a code of ritual such as that preserved for us in the *Yili* or *Ceremonies and Rites* or the *Liji* or *Record of Rites*. When this code came to be defined is also unclear, the handbook-like nature of these texts making them very difficult to date with any confidence. However, as we will see below, archaeology is now providing some material evidence to suggest that formal ritual institutions, if not actual codes, were coming into practice in the middle of the Western Zhou dynasty, around 900 BCE.

We have already seen that even in the Shang the sacrifices to the ancestors had already been made routine. However, there were other sacrifices that suggest a concurrent diversity of religious expression, at least for the earlier period during the reign of King Wu Ding (*c.* 1200 BCE). Oracle-bone inscriptions contain references to a wide variety of types of sacrifices, as well as objects of sacrifice. A list of just the most frequent types of sacrifice would have to include 'cleaving' (the oracle-bone character for which graphically portrays something split into two halves), 'burning', 'drowning' (especially in the case of offerings made to the god of the River) and 'beheading'; the objects of sacrifice regularly included multiples of oxen, sheep, pigs and also humans. The practice of human sacrifice during the Shang period is attested both in the records of the oracle-bone inscriptions (e.g., 'Crack-making on *yimao* [day 52], Xing divining: "The king will host [or visit] Grandfather Yi, and will offer up fifteen decapitated Qiang [enemies of the Shang] and will cleave penned-sheep, for if he does there will be no fault." In the twelfth month' (*Heji* 22551)) and in pits excavated at Anyang containing rows of skeletons carefully lined up, and all headless.

Human sacrifice is most characteristic of the Shang, but it did not end with the Shang. Although there is little or no evidence for human sacrifice in the Western Zhou (there is a record that some Shang noblemen were executed, perhaps 'sacrificed', after the Zhou conquest of Shang), there is an account of human offering at a later period, upon the death of Duke Mu of Qin (r. 659–621 BCE), that has been immortalized by a poem included in the *Classic of Poetry*. The poem describes three noblemen of Qin on their way to the grave to follow their deceased ruler in death. The first of three similar stanzas pertains to the first of the three noblemen.

Yellow Bird (*Classic of Poetry*, Mao 131)

Flying past each other the yellow birds,
Stopping on the thornbush.
Who follows Duke Mu?

> Zi Ju Yanxi.
> It is this Yanxi,
> Who is unique among a hundred fellows.
> Overlooking that pit,
> So terrified his trembling.
> That blue Heaven
> Destroys our finest men.
> Oh, if he could be ransomed,
> His person would be worth a hundred men.

A century or so later, Confucius is said to have criticized even the practice of putting pottery figurines of humans into tombs, because it preserved the attitude, if not the actual bloodshed, of human sacrifice.

> When Confucius said, 'The inventor of burial figurines in human form deserves not to have any progeny,' he was condemning him for the use of something modelled after the human form.   (*Mencius* 1A/4[7])

But even for Confucius, his aversion to human sacrifice did not extend to a general avoidance of bloodletting. When one of his favourite disciples, Zi Gong, proposed doing away with sacrificing a sheep in the monthly ritual marking the new moon, Confucius refused to go along with the change, remarking: 'You love the sheep, but I love the rite' (*Analects*, 3/17).

For the Western Zhou dynasty, not only is there little or no evidence of human sacrifice, there is very little evidence of many sacrifices outside of the ancestor cult. This is almost certainly due to the types of sources we have available for the period. Unlike the oracle-bone divinations of the Shang period, which were often performed just before a sacrifice, bronze inscriptions, which constitute the primary palaeographic source for the Western Zhou, usually are more bureaucratic in content (though I should hasten to add that these inscriptions too show that the vessels on which they were written were intended primarily for use in sacrifice). Likewise, the documents of the *Venerated Documents* and the poems of the *Classic of Poetry* that date to the period, though occasionally mentioning sacrifices, are generally more concerned with government or social relationships. However, some scholars have recently argued that changes in the sorts of ritual vessels used during the Western Zhou reveal important changes in the way ritual was conducted. This is an important insight with far-ranging implications for the development of Chinese religious and social institutions.

In the early Western Zhou period, families produced relatively small sets of ritual vessels, usually fewer than ten in number. These vessels were decorated with very fine and intricate designs. To appreciate this decor fully, it is necessary to view it from as close as possible. And since all of the vessels in the set would have been grouped together on a single small altar (examples of which have also been discovered archaeologically), it would have been possible for all of the members of the family to gather around the altar to perform the sacrifices to the ancestors together. The earliest poems in the *Classic of Poetry*, which date to the same period as these small, intricately decorated sets of bronze vessels, are liturgical hymns sung in the performance of sacrifices to the ancestors. They too show that these sacrifices were celebrated (perhaps a better word would be concelebrated) by actual members of the family. The following poem, 'It Is Heaven's Mandate', ends with a prayer (marked by the word 'may') explicitly stated with a plural 'we.'

It Is Heaven's Mandate (*Classic of Poetry*, Mao 267)

It is Heaven's mandate;
Oh, stately, is it unending!
Wuhu, illustrious!
The purity of King Wen's virtue
Approaches to shower down upon us.
May we receive it;
Quickly help us, King Wen's great grandsons, to make it steadfast.

Towards the middle of the Western Zhou period, sets of ritual vessels underwent striking changes in their composition, number and ornamentation. A set of thirty-nine vessels and bells were cast for a single individual, a man named Weibo Xing, who was active at the Zhou court in the first half of the ninth century BCE. At least three features are immediately apparent from this set of ritual vessels. First, the number of vessels included in the set is obviously far greater than that in the earlier sets. Second, the ornamentation is generally simpler, more geometrical, and taken together almost monotonous. And third, there are now multiple vessels of each different vessel type, often ranked in graduated size. The considerable differences between this set and the early Western Zhou set of ritual vessels surely suggest that there must have been considerable differences also in the performance of rituals in the two periods.

A reconstruction of how these vessels were placed in the ancestral temple gives a hint as to what these differences in performance may have been. The thirty-nine vessels in the Weibo Xing group would doubtless have been arrayed in a row across a lengthy altar (this would have been essential in the case of the bells, since the different sizes produced different tones). To appreciate the grandeur of the display, it would have been necessary to view it from some distance; if one were to draw near to one end of the altar to view more closely the vessels there, then the vessels at the other end would be out of sight. Besides, the ornamentation on any single vessel would not repay closer scrutiny. This perhaps suggests that there was a ritual specialist, a priest, who performed the sacrifices at the altar, while the family members for whom the sacrifice was being performed observed from a distance. Yet another poem in the *Classic of Poetry*, 'There are Blind Drummers', probably written about the time that Weibo Xing was active at court, describes just this sort of scene.

> There are blind drummers, there are blind drummers
> In the court of Zhou.
> Erecting stands, erecting racks
> With high flanges and mounted wings.
> The echo-drums, kettle-drums, suspended drums,
> Little-drums, chimes, rattles, and clappers
> Being ready then are played.
> The pan-pipes and flutes are all raised:
> *Huang-huang*, their sound.
> Solemn and harmonizing the concordant sound.
> The prior ancestors hear this.
> Our guests arrive and stop,
> Long viewing their performance.

This scene, with guests viewing a performance, confirms the separation between the performer, the ritual specialist or priest, and the audience, probably including the family members.

This change in the way rituals were performed would also come to have important social ramifications. Probably by the end of the Western Zhou period, and certainly no later than the early Springs and Autumns period, there developed sumptuary codes governing the number of vessels members of different classes of society would be entitled to use. According to the most commonly cited code, the king (i.e. the 'Son of Heaven') was entitled to use nine *ding*-cauldrons, the feudal lords seven, the great officers (*dafu*) five, and the sires (*shi*) three. Archaeological evidence confirms that sets of vessels placed in tombs were graduated in these numbers, and many scholars use the number of vessels in the tomb to determine the social rank of the deceased. While there clearly was an association between the number of ritual vessels and social rank, it would seem unwise to draw too strict a parallel; it has often enough been the case that someone would arrogate a rank higher than that to which he was entitled. For instance, Confucius criticized the warlord leaders of his own state of Lu for using eight ranks of dancers in their ceremonies, the number to which only the king was entitled (*Analects*, 3/1).

Disciples of Confucius not only served as ritual experts (as mentioned above, p. 501, some at least among them earned their livelihood by presiding at funerals), but also philosophized about ritual, treating it as the foundation of education and moral development. Xunzi (*c.* 315–235 BCE), in particular, put ritual above all else, dedicating one chapter of his book *Xunzi* to a discussion of it ('A Discussion of Rites'). He provided both abstract discussion and also specific instructions.

> What is the origin of ritual? I reply: man is born with desires. If his desires are not satisfied for him, he cannot but seek some means to satisfy them himself. If there are no limits and degrees to his seeking, then he will inevitably fall to wrangling with other men. From wrangling comes disorder and from disorder comes exhaustion. The ancient kings hated such disorder, and therefore they established ritual principles in order to curb it, to train men's desires and to provide for their satisfaction. They saw to it that desires did not overextend the means for their satisfaction, and material goods did not fall short of what was desired. Thus both desires and goods were looked after and satisfied. This is the origin of rites.[8]

With respect to the mourning rites for the dead, he argued:

> What is the purpose of the three-year mourning period? I reply: it is a form which has been set up after consideration of the emotions involved; it is an adornment to the group and a means of distinguishing the duties owed to near or distant relatives, eminent or humble. It can neither be lengthened nor shortened. It is a method that can neither be circumvented nor changed. When a wound is deep, it takes many days to heal; where there is great pain, the recovery is slow. I have said that the three-year

mourning period is a form set up after consideration of the emotions involved, because at such a time the pain of grief is most intense. The mourning garments and the cane of the mourner, the hut where he lives, the gruel he eats, the twig mat and pillow of earth he sleeps on – these are the adornments of the intense pain of his grief.[9]

It is no exaggeration to say that rituals and ritual are the foundation of Chinese social intercourse.

One variety of religious experience: divination

In an overview such as this, it is difficult even to touch on all aspects of ancient Chinese religious experience, much less to trace all of their developments in detail. No matter who the historian, the ancestor cult and ritual would certainly be featured, as they have been here. A discussion of the gods is both intrinsically important, and perhaps even more important for comparative purposes. Other general topics deserving of detailed discussion with respect to ancient Chinese religion might include at least the afterlife, astrology, demons, divination, ethics, exorcism, fate, iconography, life passages, magic, meditation, mediums, mythology, possession, shamanism, spirit flights, temples and tombs. The choice of which among these to discuss will depend at least in part on the expertise and interest of the individual historian. For the purposes of this chapter, rather than saying a little bit about all or even just several of these topics I prefer instead to focus on just one of them: divination. This approach offers the advantage of being able to survey in some detail the development of at least one variety of religious experience. And divination as a topic offers several advantages. First, we have already encountered divination in the form of Shang oracle bones above, and it will be good to follow up that early practice. Second, evidence for it is available in a number of different sources and genres, both traditional and archaeological. Third, it was a practice resorted to by people of all social classes and all periods throughout the length of ancient Chinese history, so it is possible through its various permutations and manifestations to see certain important differences and changes in the way the people of the time conceived of the world around them. Fourth and finally, divination also gave rise to the *Classic of Changes* (or *I ching*), a book barely mentioned so far in this chapter but one so important for all aspects of Chinese culture that no history of Chinese religion – for any period – could neglect it; by focusing on the development of divination we will be able to introduce the fundamental notions of the *Classic of Changes*.

Because we have already had the opportunity above to examine several different oracle-bone divinations from the Shang dynasty, here it will suffice to introduce just two further examples, one from the reign of King Wu Ding (*c.* 1200 BCE) and one from near the end of the dynasty about 150 years later. In the course of this period, important changes took place both in the format of the divinations and also, apparently, in the Shang conception of divination. Among the divinations we have already seen was one example of a positive–negative paired divination from the reign of King Wu Ding. The following is another example of this most complete type of inscription. It shows the king's concern for his consort, Consort Hao, who was about to give birth.

> Crack-making on *renyin* (day 39), (diviner) Que divining: 'Consort Hao will give birth and it will be advantageous.' On *renchen* (day 29) cleaving into *guisi* (day 30), she gave birth; it was a girl.   (*Heji* 6948a)

> Crack-making on *renyin* (day 39), (diviner) Que divining: 'Consort Hao will give birth but it will not perhaps be advantageous.' The king prognosticated and said: 'Pray that it not be advantageous. If it is advantageous, it will not be auspicious; it is in breach. Like this, then she will die.'
>
>   (*Heji* 14001a)

There are at least three things to note about this divination, at least for our purposes here. First, the positive–negative nature of the two 'charges' (i.e. the topic of divination as announced to the turtle shell) would seem to be akin to the daisy-petal style of divination performed by young children: 'She loves me', 'She loves me not.' Although in some respects the combination of the two statements constitutes a type of questioning, there is no doubt that the diviner hoped for only one of the two results, and hoped too that his performance of divination could help to bring about that result. In the case of the Shang king's divination about his consort's birthgiving, it is clear that he hoped the result would be 'advantageous'. Second, the topic of the divination here is completely impromptu, addressed to a particular event in the life of the king. Third, the king's prognostication is of danger; the king seems to have been literally in awe of the spirits.

By the end of the Shang dynasty, something of a theological constriction took place in the Shang kings' performance of divination. No longer was the broad range of royal life open to determination, nor were negative consequences entertained. Instead, divinations were routinely performed on *gui* days, the tenth and final day of the Shang ten-day week, announcing the desire that there be no misfortune in the coming week. Also unlike the earlier divinations of King Wu Ding in which the king often anticipated baleful results, now the king's prognostications were uniformly auspicious. The following inscription is just one of literally thousands of virtually identical examples.

> On *guiwei* (day 20), the king made a crack and divined: 'In the coming ten-day week there will be no misfortune.' The king prognosticated and said: 'Auspicious.' In the fourth month.   (*Heji* 35400)

The last thing to notice about this divination inscription – and perhaps the most important thing – is that the topic of the divination is conceptually positive; there is now no negative pair. It seems that by this point the Shang king did not even entertain the notion that the future could be negative.

The Zhou people too performed oracle-bone divination, though the number of turtle shells (and the Zhou seem to have used only turtle shells in this form of divination) that has been discovered so far is far smaller for the Zhou period than for the Shang. The inscriptions on these shells are generally similar to those of the Shang, yet they also display certain important Zhou innovations. Among these, perhaps the most important is the routine phrasing of the divination in the form of a prayer, as seen in the following example.

> On *guisi* (day 30), divining at the temple of the cultured and martial Di Yi: 'The king will summon and sacrifice to Cheng Tang, performing a caldron exorcism of the two surrendered women; he will offer the blood of three rams and three sows. May it be correct.'   (H11:1)

The Zhou oracle bones are generally too fragmentary to shed much light on their divinational context, but one complete turtle shell seems to suggest that Zhou divination, somewhat like that of the early Shang, entailed a two-step procedure. However, in this case the second Zhou divination seems perhaps to have been an elaboration of the first – a way to specify the result. This shell includes five discrete inscriptions, two of which are related in this way.

> 1a. May it lead to an eternal end.
> 1b. May it lead to a beneficent mandate.
> 2. The Protector determines about the palace; auspicious.
> 3a. Use this omen to catch the wife.
> 3b. This omen is also that this one is missing.   (H31:1)

As we will see in divinations from later contexts, this two-stage divination process seems to have become a standard feature.

Finally, these Zhou oracle-bone inscriptions perhaps also reflect, even if only indirectly, the Zhou use of milfoil divination (milfoil, also known as yarrow, is a type of plant that produces numerous long narrow stalks, which were used in China as counting rods). Milfoil divination is the form of divination associated with the *Classic of Changes*. Several of these shell fragments, as also a number of Zhou bronze vessels, contain groupings of numerals, almost always in sets of six. Although it is unclear just how these numerals should be interpreted, it does seem likely, that they were produced in the course of milfoil divination akin to that with which the *Classic of Changes* was used.

Unfortunately, milfoil does not survive long burial the way that shells and bones do, and thus the milfoil divination of the early Zhou period has not left any other trace besides the *Classic of Changes* itself. However, an important discovery in 1987 of divination records from near the end of the Zhou dynasty shows that both both turtle-shell divination and milfoil divination were used in similar contexts and interpreted in similar ways. These records were written on bamboo strips found in the tomb of one Zuoyin Tuo, apparently an administrator of the southern state of Chu who died in 316 BCE. The divinations were performed during the last year of his life in an attempt to determine how to alleviate a life-threatening illness from which he was suffering. The first of the divinations quoted below, using turtle-shell divination, was performed in the fifth month of 317 BCE, while the second, using milfoil divination resulting in a pair of sets of six numerals, perhaps the original form of hexagrams (the sixty-four groupings of six solid or broken lines, such as ☷ or ☵, that are the basis of the *Classic of Changes* were expressed), was performed in the fourth month of 316 BCE. In both cases, the divinations involved two stages, the first, producing an initial prognostication – a 'long-term determination' that seems invariably to have diagnosed certain problems, and then a second, exorcistic rite intended to resolve those problems. The first divination record reads:

> It was the year that the emissary Wu Cheng from East Zhou returned to serve in the capital Ying (317 BCE); in the Summer Presentation month (i.e., the fifth month of the Chu calendar), on the day *yichou* (day 2), Ke Jia used the Long Model (turtle shell) to divine on behalf of Zuoyin Tuo: 'In exiting and entering to wait upon the king, from this Summer Presentation month until the next full year's Summer Presentation month, throughout the year

would that his body have no trouble.' Prognosticating it, the long-term determination is auspicious, but there is a little anxiety in his body, and there are some incongruities without. For these reasons, they exorcised it, offering prayer to the Chu ancestors Lao Tong, Zhu Rong, and Yu Yin, to each one sheep; 'May it attack and resolve his guiltlessness.' Ke Jia prognosticated it, saying: 'Auspicious.'

The second divination, though apparently using the different medium of milfoil divination, produced a formally similar record.

It was the year that the Great Supervisor of the Horse Shao Zhi dispatched the Chu state's troops and infantry to rescue Fu (316 BCE); in the Formal Presentation month (i.e., the fourth month of the Chu calendar), on the day *jimao* (day 16), Wu Sheng used the Assisting Virtue (stalks) to divine on behalf of Zuoyin Tuo: 'In exiting and entering to attend the king, from this Formal Presentation month until the next full year's Formal Presentation month, throughout the year would that his body have no trouble': 1-8-1-1-8-1 1-8-8-1-1-8. Prognosticating it, the long-term determination is auspicious, but there is a little anxiety in the palace chambers' infirmary. For this reason, they exorcised it, offering prayers to the Palace Lord's Earth Altar, one ram; offering prayers to the road, one white dog, and wine to drink; and killing at the main gate one white dog. Wu Sheng prognosticated it, saying: 'Auspicious.'

While this second pair of divinations performed on behalf of Zuoyin Tuo appears to have resulted in hexagrams of the type found in the *Classic of Changes*), it does not tell us how the *Classic of Changes* was used in divination. Indeed, no archeological evidence yet discovered seems to provide this information. However, there are accounts of divination in the traditional literary record that, when reconsidered in the light of the sorts of archeological discoveries discussed above, may tell us both how such divinations were performed and even how they influenced the form of the *Classic of Changes* itself.

Probably the most complete description of divination using the *Classic of Changes* that we have from the Zhou dynasty is found in the *Zuo's Tradition*. It purports to recount a divination performed in the year 535 BCE on behalf of Duke Xiang of Wei to determine which of his two sons should succeed him as duke of Wei.

The wife of Duke Xiang of Wei had no son, but his concubine Zhou Ge bore to him Meng Zhi. Kong Chengzi (the grand minister of Wei) dreamt that Kangshu (i.e., the first lord of Wei) told him to establish Yuan (Primary) . . . Zhou Ge bore him a second son and named him Yuan. The feet of Meng Zhi were disabled so that he was feeble in walking. Kong Chengzi used the *Zhou Changes* (i.e., the *Classic of Changes*) to divine it by milfoil, saying: 'Would that Yuan enjoy the state of Wei and preside over its altars.' He met the hexagram *Zhun* ☲☳. He next said: 'I want to establish Zhi; would that he be capable of enjoying it.' He met the *Bi* ☶☷ (line) of *Zhun* ☲☳ (i.e., the bottom line of *Zhun* hexagram). He showed these to Scribe Chao. Scribe Chao said: '"Primary receipt" (*yuan heng*); what further doubt can there be?' Chengzi said: 'Is it not said of the elder?' (Scribe Chao) replied: 'Kangshu named him (i.e., Yuan), so that he can be said to be the elder. And Meng is not a complete man (because of his disability); he will not be placed in the ancestral temple and cannot be said to be the elder. Moreover, its omen-statement says: "Beneficial to establish a lord." If the heir were auspicious, what need would there be to "establish" one. To "establish" is not to inherit. The two hexagrams both say it. The younger one should be established.'

This interesting passage suggests three distinct features about divination using the *Classic of Changes*. First, just as with turtle-shell divination, the topic of the divination was expressed in the form of a 'charge', a statement indicating a desire on behalf of the person for whom the divination was being performed. Second, the divination involved two stages, in this case the first resulting in a single hexagram (the hexagram statement of which is quoted) and the second resulting in one of the lines of that same hexagram (the line statement of which is quoted). And third, as we might expect, it is the hexagram and line statements of the *Classic of Changes* that are quoted that provide the basis for the prognostication.

Most hexagram and line statements of the *Classic of Changes* are similar to the results of this pair of divinations: the hexagram statement of *Zhun* hexagram reads 'Primary receipt; beneficial to divine; do not herewith have any traveling; beneficial to establish a lord', while the '*Bi* ☶☷ (line) of *Zhun* ☲☳' (i.e., its bottom or Initial Nine line, the line by which the hexagram picture of *Bi* ☶☷ differs from that of *Zhun* ☲☳) reads 'The boulder is secure: beneficial to perform a residential divination; beneficial to establish a lord.' How these statements may have originally been composed is still more or less a mystery. Even their meaning has often been unclear enough to keep commentators engaged in attempting to explain them for the last two thousand years.

Another archaeological discovery of recent times, the tomb of Xiahou Zao, the Lord of Ruyin, who died in 165 BCE, unearthed in Fuyang, Anhui in 1977, reveals how the *Classic of Changes* could be used as a divination manual, perhaps even by those who did not understand at all the original meaning of the text itself. The materials from Fuyang were written on bamboo strips. Although they are extremely fragmentary (the bamboo having broken into small pieces), they can be reconstructed in part. They generally include a line statement from the *Classic of Changes*, and then general results pertaining to various possible topics of divination. The following example is typical.

> '[Nine in the Third: Lying belligerents in the grass: ascending the high hillock, for three years they do not] arise': divining about one who is guilty: ominous; divining about battling enemies: the strong will not get their will; divining about the sick: if they do not die then they will be discarded.

In the *Classic of Changes*, the line statement 'Lying belligerents in the grass: ascending the high hillock, for three years they do not arise' is attached to the third line of *Tongren* hexagram. Although it would seem to be no clearer than 'The boulder is secure' of *Zhun* hexagram, this divination manual provides a ready interpretation for almost any topic, whether it be about a criminal case, warfare, or sickness. With a manual such as this, divination no longer required a diviner with special skills or insight. It became available to all.

Tutrtle-shell and milfoil divination were by means the only types of divination used in ancient China. Other types included divination by dreams, by listening to the songs of children, by observing the behaviour of animals, and many others. As might be expected, the planets and stars were particularly important in divining future events. Also discovered in the tomb of Xiahou Zao was an instrument, usually referred to as a 'cosmic board' (*shi*), that was used to track the stars. The instrument is composed of two pieces: a square bottom board (representing earth), about the outside of which are written the names of the twenty-eight lunar lodges of Chinese astronomy. Inside of this, in two different rows, are written the names of the heavenly stems and the earthly branches, the constituent components of the Chinese cycle of sixty, used for counting days. On top of this square board was placed a round disk (representing heaven). It too has the twenty-eight lunar lodges written around its perimeter, correlated with the twelve months of the year. In the middle of the disk, corresponding to the top of heaven, are the seven stars of the Northern Dipper. Apparently this round heaven disk would be rotated on the square earth board to indicate the correlation between the stars and the months and the days.

The use of this cosmic board must have involved numerological calculations concerning days, which Daybooks (*rishu*) discovered in many tombs from throughout ancient China show to have had particular natures. Like the divination manual based on the *Classic of Changes* that was found in the tomb of Xiahou Zao, these Daybooks provide formulaic results for many different topics. They differ only in that the results pertain to types of days rather than to line statements in the *Classic of Changes*. The following example is typical:

> Breakthrough days: beneficial for raising troops, for setting out on campaign, for meeting with people; when making offerings high and low, all will be beneficial; beneficial for the birth of a son; if it be a daughter, she will leave the country. (*Shuihudi* 736)

Other entries in the Daybooks show that particular days in the ten-day week were lucky or unlucky for various activities. For instance, according to this same daybook, an audience held at dawn on a *yin* day would result in anger while a similarly timed audience on a *mao* day would have an agreeable result, and an evening audience on a *zi* day would result in praise but one on a *chou* day would bring blame.

These Daybooks are the precursors to almanacs found throughout later Chinese history, and still very common today wherever there are Chinese communities. Like these almanacs, the Daybooks were doubtless intended for use by a wide variety of people in the society of their time, the third and second centuries BCE. This is perhaps the most important development in the practice of divination from the time of Shang dynasty oracle-bone divination. The underlying conception of divination – that there is a necessary correlation between the natural and human worlds – was still the same. But by this time it had become a worldview, and a world, accessible to all. No longer did one need to be a king, or the lord of a state or even an officer of the court, as in the Zhou dynasty divinations discussed above, to be able to fathom the workings of the spirit world.

Whether in terms of institutional or intellectual history, China's ancient period is generally regarded as coming to an end in 221 BCE, the year that the state of Qin succeeded in conquering the last of the other independent states. This year marks a convenient dividing line in the study of Chinese religion too. Together with its newly centralized government, the onset of the imperial age brought also the first manifestations of mass religious organizations. By the first century of the common era, Buddhism had made its way into China proper, apparently by way of the Silk Roads of Central Asia. A century later, messianic religious states professing belief in an ultimate Dao (Tao) were founded in both eastern and western parts of the empire. Over the millennia to come, these two religions, Buddhism and Daoism (Taoism), would develop in numerous different ways. Buddhism itself would divide into at least four major sects (Pure Land, Tiantai, Huayan, and Chan (better known in the West as Zen, the Japanese pronunciation)), while Daoism would include two separate traditions (Lingbao and Shangqing). Throughout the long middle period of Chinese history, virtually every Chinese person would have had some experience of – and often a great deal of experience of – both of these religions. Other religions such as Islam and Christianity would also come to be introduced into China, and would attract numerous believers, though not nearly so many as Buddhism and Daoism. It can be stated with certainty that the early European view of China as being a land devoid of religion was very much mistaken. Indeed, so full is the history of later Chinese religion that it is properly the subject of another volume.

I hope to have shown that the subject of this chapter – the history of ancient Chinese religion – was very full, certainly much richer and much more complicated than scholars a century ago might have imagined. Although definable religions such as Buddhism and Daoism had not yet formed, the archaeological discoveries of the twentieth century, from the oracle-bone inscriptions of the thirteenth century BCE through the Daybooks of the third century BCE, have shown that since the beginning of recorded history the Chinese were keenly interested in spiritual matters.

Notes

1. D. C. Lau (trans.), *Lao Tzu: Tao Te Ching* (Harmondsworth: Penguin Books, 1963), p. 108.
2. Burton Watson (trans.), *The complete works of Chuang Tzu* (New York: Columbia University Press, 1970), p. 46.
3. Marcel Granet, *The religion of the Chinese people*, trans. Maurice Freedman (Oxford: Basil Blackwell, 1975), pp. 41–2.
4. Adapted from Joseph Needham, *Science and civilisation in China*, vol. 3: *Mathematics and the sciences of the Heavens and the Earth* (Cambridge: Cambridge University Press, 1959), pp. 262–3.

5. A. C. Graham, *Disputers of the Tao: philosophical argument in ancient China* (La Salle, IL: Open Court Press, 1989), p. 47.
6. For these translations (modified for romanization), see D. C. Lau (trans.), *Confucius, The Analects (Lun yü)* (Harmondsworth: Penguin Books, 1979), pp. 63–4.
7. D. C. Lau (trans.), *Mencius* (Harmondsworth: Penguin Books, 1970), p. 52.
8. Burton Watson (trans.), *Hsün Tzu: basic writings* (New York: Columbia University Press, 1963), p. 89.
9. Ibid., pp. 105–6.

Bibliography

Bilsky, Lester 1975. *The state religion of ancient China.* 2 vols., Taipei: The Chinese Association for Folklore. One of the few attempts to describe systematically the religion of ancient China, this book is nevertheless limited by its traditional approach.

Chang, Kwang-chih 1976. *Early Chinese civilization: anthropological perspectives.* Cambridge, MA: Harvard University Press. A collection of essays by the leading western interpreter of Chinese archaeology, this introduces his provocative views on the social organization of the Shang dynasty, and on shamanism, among other topics related to the religion of ancient China.

Eno, Robert 1990. *The Confucian creation of Heaven.* Albany, NY: SUNY Press. A provocative interpretation of Confucius and his followers, portraying them in a distinctly religious context.

Falkenhausen, Lothar von 1993. *Suspended music: chime-bells in the culture of Bronze Age China.* Berkeley: University of California Press. Although only tangentially related to the study of religion (music played an important role in the performance of Chinese ritual), this is an excellent survey of archaeological evidence dating from the tenth through the fifth centuries BCE.

Fingarette, Herbert 1972. *Confucius: the secular as sacred.* New York: Harper and Row. A path-breaking religious interpretation of Confucius that has stirred discussion for a generation now.

Fong, Wen (ed.) 1980. *The great Bronze Age of China: an exhibition from the People's Republic of China.* New York: Metropolitan Museum of Art. This is still the most convenient and authoritative introduction to Chinese archaeology, particularly for the dramatic discoveries of the 1970s.

Graham, A. C. 1989. *Disputers of the Tao: philosophical argument in ancient China*. La Salle, IL: Open Court Press. A fine survey of the intellectual history of ancient China by the acknowledged master of the field.

Granet, Marcel 1968. *La pensée chinoise* [1934]; rpt. Paris: Albin Michel. Granet's masterpiece: even well over seventy years after its publication this work is still fresh. What is more, unlike most books in the field, its view of ancient China seems to find corroboration with each new archaeological discovery. Those who cannot read French but wish to gain some idea as to Granet's approach will find useful his *The religion of the Chinese people*, trans. Maurice Freedman (Oxford: Basil Blackwell, 1975).

Harper, Donald 1998. *Early Chinese medical literature: the Mawangdui medical manuscripts*. London: Kegan Paul. Not at all limited to medicine; the introduction to this book provides a magisterial survey of archaeological discoveries from the fourth to second centuries BCE by the leading scholar in the field.

Keightley, David N. 1978. *Sources of Shang history: the oracle-bone inscriptions of Bronze Age China*. Berkeley: University of California Press. This remains, more than twenty years after its writing, the best introduction to Shang dynasty divination with oracle bones. Those wishing to read Keightley's conclusions regarding religion without reading through all of the technical discussion of this book will find interesting his 'The religious commitment: Shang theology and the genesis of Chinese political culture', *History of Religions* 17 (1978): 211–24, and 'Shang divination and metaphysics', *Philosophy East & West* 38 (1988): 367–97.

Loewe, Michael 1994. *Divination, mythology and monarchy in Han China*. Cambridge: Cambridge University Press. A collection of essays, many of them touching on points related to religion, by the west's leading authority on the Han dynasty.

  (ed.) 1993. *Early Chinese texts: a bibliographical guide*. Berkeley: The Society for the Study of Early China and the Institute of East Asian Studies, University of California. An indispensable handbook to sixty-four books dating to China's ancient period, it provides descriptions of contents, discussions of authenticity, and also lists of translations into western languages.

Loewe, Michael and Edward L. Shaughnessy (eds.) 1999. *The Cambridge history of ancient China: from the beginnings of civilization to 221 B.C.*. New York: Cambridge University Press. This is the best overview of the history of ancient China; it includes essays by most of the leading scholars in the field and incorporates all of the recent archaeological discoveries.

Lopez, Donald S. Jr. (ed.) 1996. *Religions of China in practice*. Princeton, NJ: Princeton University Press. A general sourcebook for the religions of China, with sections on oracle-bone inscriptions, inner cultivation traditions, spirit flights, exorcisms and state sacrifices in ancient China.

Overmyer, Daniel (ed.) 1995. Chinese religion: the state of the field. *Journal of Asian Studies* 54.1: 124–8. This bibliographic survey includes essays on the Neolithic and Shang periods (by David Keightley), the Western Zhou (by Edward Shaughnessy), the Springs and Autumns (by Constance Cook) and the Warring States and Han (by Donald Harper).

Poo, Mu-chou 1998. *In search of personal welfare: a view of ancient Chinese religion*. Albany, NY: State University of New York Press. The most recent systematic survey of ancient Chinese religion, it is particularly good on mantic practices of the Warring States period, including especially the *Rishu* or Daybooks.

Shaughnessy, Edward L. 1997a. *Before Confucius: studies in the creation of the Chinese classics*. Albany, NY: SUNY Press. A collection of essays discussing how the earliest of the Chinese classics, the *Changes*, *Documents* and *Poetry*, may have come to be written.

Shaughnessy, Edward L. (ed.) 1997b. *New sources of early Chinese history: an introduction to the reading of inscriptions and manuscripts*. Berkeley: The Society for the Study of Early China and the Institute of East Asian Studies, University of California. Does for archaeologically discovered texts what *Early Chinese texts: a bibliographical guide* does for traditional texts, providing concise introductions to the various genres of materials.

11 Aztec and Inca civilizations

Introduction

The Aztec and Inca civilizations of the Americas rivalled their Old World counterparts in the size of their cities and the degree of influence over geographical areas. They were radically different from one another. Yet they are united by the fact that they both interacted directly with Europeans. It was out of this traumatic contact situation that came American culture which transformed the world.

Because of the contentious nature of the contact between cultures during the 'Age of Discovery', or that period immediately following 1492, surprisingly little of a certain factual nature can be said about the inner religious dimensions of Aztec and Inca civilizations. Indeed more can be discovered about these civilizations by examining them with reference to European civilizations. It is the gaps between various understandings of 'religion' that take us a long way towards understanding ancient America.

In the languages of neither the Aztecs (Nahuatl) nor the Incas (Quechua) is there a word equivalent to 'religion'. In these civilizations there are no 'religious' institutions which are autonomous to other political or economic institutions. But if one looks to the literal meaning of 'religion' from the Latin 'ligare', which means 'to bind', then there is ample evidence of 'religion' among the Aztecs and Incas. But its emphasis is on a ceremonial 'binding together' rather than on textual 'binding together'. Therefore the character of religion in the Americas was very different from its character in Europe and the Old World. The *binding* feature of Aztec and Inca urban existence was the constant emphasis on their cities as primarily ceremonial centres. The political and economic functions of Tenochtitlan for the Aztecs and Cuzco for the Incas were secondary to their ceremonial function.

Another way in which 'religion' is an understandable concept among ancient American civilizations is in the sense of religion as orientation. According to

Map 11.1. The cultural areas of the Aztec, Mayas and Incas with sites discussed in the chapter.

Long's definition (1986: 7), religion is orientation in the ultimate sense of how one comes to terms with the ultimate significance of one's place in the world. For the Aztecs and Incas this religious sense of orientation can be taken literally in terms of how they situated themselves with reference to seen and unseen material realities.

There is no direct textual record written by the Aztec people, however, that reveals to the scholar the deepest religious meanings of ancient American civilizations. Instead evidence of these religions come to us through the sixteenth-century contact between the Spanish and the Aztec and Inca civilizations. Even though the Americas contained a number of urban civilizations through time, it is best to begin with the Aztecs and Incas who made direct contact with Europeans. It is significant, therefore, that what are currently regarded as the 'religions' of the Aztecs and Incas have been created in the popular and scholarly imaginations. But the creative endeavour of imagining these splendid civilizations does not imply that our current formulations are uninteresting, or wrong. Rather, scholars of ancient American civilizations ply their imaginations on various kinds of source materials to comprehend the inner dimensions of these cultures. The academic study of ancient American religions, more than the study of other ancient religions, is a process of sifting and filtering various kinds of evidence.

The Aztecs and Incas in the popular and scholarly imaginations

Academic interest in the Aztec and Inca civilizations has been consistent since contact with Europeans in the sixteenth century. But the reasons for that interest have changed dramatically. In the early colonial period the interest that Catholic priests had in these peoples' traditions and their language was directly connected with missionization. During the later colonial period often religious understandings were connected with legal issues related to land transfers or ceremonial customs. In the eighteenth and nineteenth centuries there was speculation that these civilizations were connected with Old World ones. This generated intense interest among early archaeologists. In the twentieth century there was a general celebration of these civilizations in the art, theatre and literature of Latin America. In Mexico and Peru, for example, there is the general recognition that the Aztec and Inca cultures contributed directly to the current formulation of those countries' unique cultural identity. This understanding continues in spite of the fact that current Nahuatl- and Quechua-speaking people, as well as other indigenous people throughout the Americas, are among the most despised and disadvantaged.

What follows is an account of current scholarly understandings of Mesoamerican (i.e. those civilizations of 'Central America' which predate, include and follow the Aztecs) and Inca civilizations. It will serve as a general history from which to conceptualize the religious dimensions of these civilizations.

The Olmecs: 'mother culture'

Olmec is a Nahuatl word that means 'people of the rubber trees'. The Olmecs had an urban civilization which developed in the lowlands of Mexico in southern Vera Cruz and western Tabasco near the Gulf of Mexico about 1800 BCE. Reference to the rubber trees ties this civilization to its place of origin. The principal features of these cities were pyramid structures, which served as focal points of ceremonial life. As there are no surviving written records from these people, what is known of these religions comes solely from archaeological evidence. Over several decades of excavations scholars have had to imagine rigorously what the religious life of the Olmecs was like. Above all else it is clear that what is distinctive about Mesoamerica (i.e. ceremonial pyramidal architecture, ancestor cult and veneration of food plants) came into being with the Olmecs, leading the Mexican artist and scholar Miguel Covarrubias to characterize this as the 'mother culture'.

The intensification of agriculture made possible the rise of Olmec civilization. Most important was the development of maize. Olmec religion, therefore, was an extension of agricultural practices. Ceremonies would follow the agricultural cycles of rainy and dry seasons. Emphasis seems to have been placed on the hydrological cycles, on the spiritual dimensions of seeds and particularly on planting. For example, at San Lorenzo a jaguar mosaic floor was discovered. The jaguar motif, which persisted throughout Mesomerica up until the Aztec period, was associated with the 'earth lord' symbolism. When the tile floor was removed another similar jaguar mosaic was discovered underneath. When that floor was removed another was discovered, and so on down to a depth of 10 m. This indicates that the Olmec built architecture that was interior to the earth, thereby emphasizing the importance of the underworld in the regeneration of life.

Striking features of Olmec art and iconography are the giant basalt heads, which stand about 2 m high and often weigh 80 tonnes and would have been transported over several kilometres. Because these heads often have a highly individual character it has been hypothesized that they were created to represent deceased Olmec rulers, indicating that ancestor worship held an important place in Olmec religion. Worship of important dead rulers was an important feature of the processes by which the Olmec bound themselves together. But the stone heads also indicate a connection to the earth similar to the jaguar mosaic floors. While the heads are above ground the body of the ancestor is directly associated with the earth; or was the earth. As with other Native American civilizations, ancestors were directly connected with agricultural processes. The Olmecs initiated a pattern for rulership in Mesoamerica in which the leader of the city was seen as being directly responsible, in life and death, for maintaining agricultural fertility, thereby promoting the health and well-being of his people.

Ceremonial buildings were designed to replicate the local landscape. The Olmecs were the first in the Americas to build pyramids. Unlike the Egyptians, the Olmec used pyramids as ceremonial platforms, which would often duplicate the mountainous topography on the horizon. In addition there is evidence that the design of the urban centre was associated with the movements of the sun and moon as well as other planets and constellations. The ceremonial spaces of the Olmecs were designed so as to integrate a range of natural phenomena. According to Wheatley, this urban design was to promote an 'intimate parallelism' between microcosmic and macrocosmic patterns. The Olmecs were interested in integrating their existence with the larger cosmos in order to promote life through ceremonial activity.

Since their discovery the Olmecs have fascinated the modern world. However, many in both popular and scholarly communities have insisted that this advance could not have been indigenous to the New World. There is a tremendous range of suggested places from which the Olmec are supposed to have come, including Egypt, ancient Israel (being one of the lost tribes), Africa, Polynesia, Northern Asia and Outer Space. Some of these hypotheses are more likely than others. What is clear is that we will never know for sure if the Olmecs originated from another place or, if so, exactly where that place may have been. What is clear, however, is that the Olmecs themselves did not emphasize their having come from another place, in their religious ceremonies. Instead they consistently emphasized their being situated in their own place. What is more, their ceremonial buildings and activities served to highlight the importance and meaning of being in their place, through an association with agriculture and ancestors. In spite of the fact that the Olmecs had the first urban civilization, therefore, their ceremonies emphasized an indigenous sensibility. It is in this sense of an indigenous urban existence that

542   Philip P. Arnold

Fig. 11.1. The city of Teotihuacan looking south from the top of the Temple of the Moon along the Street of the Dead. Temple of the Sun is to the left. Photograph by the author.

the Olmecs are the 'mother civilization' which truly characterized the religions of ancient American civilization.

The great city of Teotihuacan

Perhaps the most impressive pre-Columbian site in Central America is Teotihuacan (Fig. 11.1). The pyramids of the Sun and Moon are familiar images on travel posters and brochures beckoning tourists to visit the wonders of central Mexico (Fig. 11.2). The remains of the once great city of Teotihuacan (100–700 CE) give the viewer a sense of its having once been the centre of the world.

As impressive as it is, however, very little is known of Teotihuacan's builders or inhabitants. As with the Olmecs, archaeology is the only means for understanding the religion of Teotihuacan. There is currently no knowledge of the ethnicity or language of its creators. This very lack of knowledge has tended to promote a fascination with the site. Teotihuacan was named by the Aztecs, and means 'Place of the Gods'. It figures prominently in Aztec (1325–1521 CE) creation myths (see below) and there is evidence that they performed ceremonies, which may have included human sacrifice at this place. Like the modern traveller to this site,

Fig. 11.2. The Temple of the Sun at Teotihuacan. Photograph by the author.

the Aztecs were impressed with its magnitude and splendour. In addition to archaeological evidence, therefore, much of the current fascination and understanding of the site comes through the Spanish contact with the Aztecs. As a mythic centre Teotihuacan is perhaps more important than it was when originally occupied.

There are important clues to the ceremonial life of the inhabitants of Teotihuacan, which are embedded in its urban design and architecture. As is the case throughout ancient America, the meanings of these remains are constantly transforming with new excavations and discoveries. For example, for most of the twentieth century it was thought that the Pyramid of the Sun and the Pyramid of the Moon, the principal ceremonial structures of Teotihuacan, were dedicated to a solar and lunar cult. Now, as a result of different interpretations and more thorough excavations from the 1970s to the 1990s, scholars think that its central cultic structure was water and cave, or underworld, symbolism. The cardinal orientation of the city thus seems to be associated with water and the movement of important celestial bodies, including the sun, the moon and the Pleiades. The major axis of the city, called the Street of the Dead, connects the pyramids of the Sun and the Moon. It is actually a series of ascending ceremonial platforms which probably featured various rituals.

Teotihuacan has been excavated intermittently since the 1930s. In the 1960s an extensive mapping project of the region by Millon yielded some very important information: first, that the city was much bigger than once thought (at its peak around 700 CE as many as 200,000 people may have lived there); second, that its structure was very uniform, following a rigid, near cardinal orientation. Even the river, which bisects the city, was rerouted to follow the grid design.

Aspects of the city layout indicate the Teotihuacanos' religious orientation. In the 1970s Aveni discovered that the alignment of the city corresponds with the setting of the Pleiades on the horizon at the beginning of the rainy season. That the Teotihuacanos knew about the correspondence of the Pleiades star constellation and the beginning of the rainy season is indicated by a series of 'pecked crosses', which are an arrangement of small indentations carved in a plaster floor or rock. These markings are numerically related to the agricultural calendar and are located in Teotihuacan at strategic locations for viewing celestial events.

These disparate data collected throughout the twentieth century indicate that Teotihuacan was designed and built with reference to the movement of water, which was so important to agricultural life, and therefore to the success of the city itself. But water was intimately connected with the movement of the stars and the local geographical features, which in turn were integrated into the urban design.

As mentioned above, as a result of recent excavations around the Pyramid of the Sun and the Quetzalcoatl pyramid at the southern end of the Street of the Dead, scholars now think that Teotihuacan was primarily dedicated to material exchanges between human and divine beings. It is now thought that while the obsidian trade (a volcanic glass used in the manufacturing war clubs) may have been responsible for Teotihuacan's rise to prominence in Mesoamerica, it was its ceremonial emphasis on water and food symbolism that made up its core religious values.

Two important deities, Quetzalcoatl (the plumed serpent) and Tlaloc (the deity of rain and fertility), first appear at Teotihuacan (Fig. 11.3). These are Nahuatl names given to them by the Aztecs but they have probably continuously exerted a religious influence throughout Mesoamerica up until the present time. Quetzalcoatl was a significant figure in the myth/history of the Toltecs and images of Tlaloc appear in the Maya area. Both of these illustrate the dominant influence of Teotihuacan in shaping the urban landscape of Mesoamerica.

Fig. 11.3. Tlaloc brazier from the Templo Mayor. Photograph by the author.

Mythic Tollans

Just as the Olmecs and Teotihuacan dramatically influenced the Mesoamerican world, likewise the mythic stature of Tollan continues to organize our understanding of the cultures of central Mexico. Tollan is associated with the pre-Columbian site of Tula in central Mexico where the Toltecs held dominance (900–1100 CE).

As the ideal city, Tollan became the model for rulers throughout Mesoamerica. It therefore had less importance as the specific site of Tula and more influence as a model upon which rested urban authority through its ceremonial functions.

The mythic status of Tollan and the ideal capital ruled by the priest-king is of primary importance. According to these myths the priest Quetzalcoatl once ruled in a peaceful kingdom. Unlike his rivals, Quetzalcoatl was said to sacrifice only butterflies and was loved by his subjects. The trickster figure Tezcatlipoca was his rival who magically duped Quetzalcoatl into getting intoxicated and sleeping with his sister. Ashamed and dejected Quetzalcoatl left his kingdom, sailing across the sea to the east. But before he left he swore that he would return to assume his throne once again.

The Aztecs embraced the myth of Quetzalcoatl so as to authorize their rise to prominence in the Valley of Mexico. Their 'tlatoani', or 'principal speakers' such as Motecuzuma, understood that their power rested squarely with the mythic structure of Tollan.

The peaceful Mayas

One of the most enduring misconceptions regarding the Mayas over most of the twentieth century was that they were a peaceful, non-violent people who passively watched the sky. This perspective was perpetrated by a few Mesoamericanists of the previous generation and held sway into the 1970s. Currently Maya scholars have a much different perception. Now the Mayas are seen as people continuously defending their urban centres from conquerors and also raiding other groups for sacrifices to their gods. As discussed below, the Mayas were often involved in brutal ceremonies of torture, sacrifice and autosacrifice to legitimate their connections with deities and ancestors.

The Maya area covers the lowlands of Mexico, the Yucatan peninsula and areas of Guatemala, Belize and El Salvador. What scholars refer to as the Maya was actually not a single cultural group at all but a tremendously diverse group of city-states with different languages and ceremonial complexes, which span a long time period (300–1400 CE). Ceremonies held at these urban settings were particular to each city, in part through their leaders, and the ancestors of their leaders, who played principal roles in the rituals. The number of cities is unknown, but in general Maya scholars think that there was a classical period, associated with sites such as Tikal, Yaxchilan, Palenque, Uxmal and Copan. After the collapse of the classic Maya period there was a post-classic renaissance in northern Yucatan. The site of Chichen Itza is most commonly associated with the post-classic return of the Maya.

Of the religious innovations of the Mayas during the classical period the calendar is perhaps the most well known. Indeed the depth of Maya knowledge of celestial bodies, mathematics and the calendar has tended to exacerbate the view that they were a peaceful people. Observations of the planets and stars were associated with the migration of the seasons. As at Teotihuacan, the Maya urban centres integrated their concern with agricultural cycles into their urban design and ceremonial events. In particular, observations of the planet Venus played a central role in determining the 'long count' calendar. The disappearance and reappearance of Venus would be recorded in multi-year counts – as in the Dresden Codex, which could integrate Venus cycles with the cycles of the sun and moon, as well as other planets and star constellations.

The classic Mayas also developed an elaborate system of writing. Deciphering these icons is currently one of the most exciting areas of research in Mesoamerican studies. Icons were inscribed onto stelae, or stone megaliths, which, as at Tikal, were set upright in the ceremonial plaza. Stelae communicate a wide variety of messages but principally contain stories which link the activity of the ruling family with mythic founders and deities. Some have a historical character while others are more mythic in nature, but this distinction, while important for modern civilizations, seems to have been much less important for the Mayas.

Notable examples of these stelae are the sarcophagus stone of Pacal at Palenque, the tablets at the Temple of the Cross at Palenque, and the depictions of the rulers Shield Jaguar and Lady Xoc at Yaxchilan. These three depictions of rulers will serve as entry into the religious cosmology of the classic Mayas.

Central to Mesoamerican tradition is the ritual use of the human body as an instrument for interacting with the unseen forces responsible for material life. This is most clear with the Mayas as it comes to us through their inscriptions. The sarcophagus lid of Lord Pacal's tomb is a powerful example of the role of the ruler as ancestor. The image on the tomb captures the moment of death. From Pacal's body sprouts an enormous tree just as he descends into the jaws of the earth lord. Trees, just as mountains in the central Mexican cities of Teotihuacan and Tollan, played the role of the world centre connecting celestial, earthly and underworldly spheres. The Mayas more clearly articulated that the ruler's body was intimately involved with the maintenance of the cosmos. In life and death the ruler was the intermediary between human and otherworldly realms.

Maintaining good relationships with the underworld, or Xibalba, was of utmost importance for the Mayas. The Popal Vuh, or the *Book of Council*, of the Quiché Maya states that the deities of the underworld were the originators of maize and other agricultural produce. Hero twins made an arduous journey to the underworld and were captured by the deities of darkness. By means of their ball-playing skills the twins escaped Xibalba with the agricultural goods.

The importance of the connection between agriculture and Xibalba is demonstrated in urban design. Ball courts are a prominent attribute of the ceremonial precinct in both the central Mexican and Maya areas and were the sites of elaborate ceremonial drama. Teams were selected on their abilities to move the solid rubber ball deftly with their feet and hips. The teams scored when the ball was flung through vertically arranged hoops mounted on the side walls. Spectators would also be involved in the game, sometimes wagering all their worldly belongings on a team. The winners of the game were sometimes sacrificed. As well as its connection with Xibalba, the east–west orientation of the ball courts also indicates that there was solar symbolism associated with the game.

The succession of rulers was of great importance to the Maya urban structure. Tablets from the Temple of the Cross at Palenque portray the accession of Chan-Bahlum, who was the son of Pacal. Pacal and Chan-Bahlum face one another on either side of the tablet. Pacal is portrayed as already having died. Between the rulers is the cosmic tree, which is perched atop the earth lord who is graphically characterized as a monster. This image, therefore, is similar to Pacal's sarcophagus lid in style and substance. This time, however, the intention is of ceremoniously authorizing the status of his son, Chan-Bahlum. There were undoubtedly ongoing ceremonial occasions to emphasize and legitimate the succession of Maya rulers. As with the ball courts, the prominent place of these monuments at the centre of the ceremonial precincts testifies to their importance in the maintenance of urban life.

The lintels of Yaxchilan of Shield Jaguar and Lady Xoc underscore the ceremonial responsibilities of Maya rulers as intermediaries between human and sacred beings. In the first lintel Shield Jaguar is standing over Lady Xoc, who is pulling a rope of thorns through her tongue. Maya rulers were often required to let their own blood, or perform autosacrifice, to re-establish ordered relationships with the gods. The second lintel portrays a vision that resulted as the consequence of Lady Xoc's autosacrifice. Out of the burnt offering of paper soaked with her own blood rises a vision serpent. From this creature's mouth comes a deity who forcefully imparts his message to the ruler. There were several reasons why rulers were required to let their own blood. First, it was understood to be the mortar of the cosmos. The body and blood of rulers symbolized the ordered workings of the city – which was a reflection of the cosmos. Second, the blood of rulers was seen as re-establishing proper relationships with sky and underworld beings. These rituals of self-sacrifice substantiated a Maya ruler's authority as an intermediary between human beings and deities of water, land, etc. The ruler was also seen as an intermediary between the urban population and ancestors, who were important for maintaining a sense of community. Third, the ruler would let blood as a method for attaining a vision. Attaining knowledge of the unseen world of the deities and ancestors was a constant source of activity. Divination was intensely practised throughout Mesoamerica in pre-Columbian times and is still practised among Maya people.

Although the Mayas were astute in their development of art, writing, astronomy, mathematics, agriculture, sports, architecture, etc., they could not now be regarded as a 'peaceful' people. Unlike scholars of the 1940s, current scholars are careful not to confuse the sophistication of their culture with their temperament. As with other civilizations, the urban cultures of the Mayas resulted from the violent rendering of the world. This resulted in the collapse of their cities well before the coming of Europeans. The most accepted hypothesis for the Mayas' collapse is that their jungle environment could not support the continuing increase in population pressure. Yet the Mayas remain as an exceptional pre-Columbian culture.

The bloody Aztecs

While the Mayas were generally regarded over the last century as 'peaceful', the Aztecs on the other hand have been seen as developing one of the most violent cultures in the world. As with the Mayas, these assumptions about the Aztecs have been overemphasized by those who have wanted to demonize them for various reasons.

The Aztec (1325–1521 CE) rise to prominence in central Mexico was relatively late among Mesoamerican cultures. The Aztecs authorized their presence in central Mexico by accentuating the similarities of their culture to those of Olmec, Teotihuacan and Tollan. The languages and ethnicity of the people who lived in these places is unknown. In fact most of what is currently known of the pre-Aztec cultures of central Mexico is filtered through the Aztec conceptions of these people. For example, many of the place-names, such as Teotihuacan and Tula, are Nahuatl words. Also the Aztecs performed their own archaeological explorations and held important ceremonies at these sites.

The etymology of the word 'Aztec' is a reference to the story of their migration as a tribe, called the Mexica, from an unknown land north of central Mexico. Nahuatl, the language of the Aztecs, is part of a family of languages called Uto-Aztecan. It seems that the Aztecs indeed originated in the north because Nahuatl is similar to the Hopi, Huichol, Ute and Paiute languages. This land was called 'Aztlan', or the place of the seven caves. From that place the Aztecs emerged out of the earth, then wandered southward. They were despised and distrusted by those with whom they came into contact. As they wandered they were led by a group of priests who were attempting to divine signs from Huitzilopochtli, 'Hummingbird on the left', who was their tribal deity. After a long time of being driven from place to place the Aztecs sought refuge in the marshy cane fields in the middle of Lake Texcoco. Throughout the Valley of Mexico there were enormous salt and sweet water lakes which were a major food resource for the residents. There the priests saw an eagle with a snake in its beak perched on a cactus, which grew out of a rock in the middle of the lake. The eagle was a manifestation of Huitzilopochtli and associated with the sun. This is the 'hierophany', or manifestation of the sacred, which founded the Aztec capital city of Tenochtitlan.

The legacy of the Aztec remains is due to the fact that Tenochtitlan lies beneath Mexico City. Pre-Columbian artefacts are unearthed by virtually every public works project. The significance of Aztec culture for Mexico is exemplified by the hierophany of Tenochtitlan's founding being depicted on the flag. In 1978 electrical workers uncovered an elaborately carved stone near the great Cathedral and the Zocalo, the central square of Mexico City. They tried to cover-up the find because it would delay their work, but it was eventually reported and led to the most important Aztec excavation. The workers had discovered the now famous Coyoxauhqui stone, which lay at the base of the steps of the Templo Mayor, the central temple structure of Tenochtitlan. The Templo Mayor was built and rebuilt by each new ruler of the Mexica, who was called the 'tlatoani' (i.e. principal speaker). From 1325 to 1521 the temple was enlarged and rededicated on the spot where Huitzilopochtli descended onto the cactus in the middle of Lake Texcoco. The discovery and excavation of the temple radically transformed the scholarly and popular understanding of Aztec civilization.

Although there were written descriptions of the temple it had not been seen since Cortés destroyed Tenochtitlan in 1521. As with the other parts of the city, the Spanish conquistadors levelled the Templo Mayor with cannon fire. For them the temple symbolized the heathen worship of the Aztecs. They used the cut stone of the temple to construct what is now the oldest part of the National Cathedral nearby to the west. The Templo Mayor survives as a series of bases from successive rebuilding stages. When a new temple was to be erected the old one was carefully buried under the new structure. By the sixteenth century, therefore, the Templo Mayor was an enormous pyramid.

The Templo Mayor functioned as a ceremonial platform. The Nahuatl term for city is 'altepetl' ('Water Mountain') and refers to the dominant temple which occupied the centre of every city, town and hamlet. For Mesoamericans, includ-ing the Aztecs, the city was defined by its central temple. When a town was cap-tured by the Aztecs, for example, that event was iconographically represented by the temple having been toppled and set on fire. But the term 'altepetl' also indicates that the central temple, like the Pyramid of the Sun at Teotihuacan and the cosmic tree for the Mayas, was a vertical axis that connected human beings with the sky and the underworld. Mountains were understood to be containers of water. Either too little or too much water could be devastating for agricultural success. As we have seen at other sites in Mesoamerica, the intimate relation-ships between various aspects of material life were directly involved in the urban planning and the ceremonies.

The Templo Mayor is actually two temples in one structure. The southern side of the temple is dedicated to Huitzilopochtli, the tribal god of the Aztecs, and the northern side is dedicated to Tlaloc, the god of rain and fertility whose earliest appearance is at Teotihuacan. The bifurcated structure is extremely rare among Mesoamerican cities; only one other bifurcated temple is known. While the Aztecs conquered an enormous area stretching from the Pacific to the Atlantic, they did not seem as interested in imposing their religious structures on sub-ject peoples. Rather they were interested in the flow of tribute to Tenochtitlan. This is dramatized by the absence of similar bifurcated temples throughout their conquered region.

The dominant status of Huitzilopochtli at the Templo Mayor was not surprising to researchers. What was surprising was the absence of images of the god. In fact no iconographical representations of Huitzilopochtli were found at the site. Yet as Matos Moctezuma, the archaeologist responsible for the excavations, has said, it was Huitzilopochtli who oversaw the imperial designs of the Aztecs. As god of the sun Huitzilopochtli was venerated at the Templo Mayor with sacrifices and other offerings. Like the sun he was omnipresent, but at the same time he was a uniquely Aztec deity. Scholars have been quick to point out that the absence of images of Huitzilopochtli at the Templo Mayor should not be seen as symptomatic of his significance for the Aztecs. Instead he may have been of great significance as a *deus otiosus*, a god obscured, or remote.

Unlike Huitzilopochtli, the presence of Tlaloc at the Templo Mayor is ubi-quitous. For Broda this indicates that the Aztecs perceived the Templo Mayor as a symbol of absolute fertility. As with the ceremonial centres of Teotihua-can, the Aztecs saw their principal temple as an 'altepetl', a 'water mountain', which established the proper connection between human and divine beings for purposes of agricultural success. Huitzilopochtli was the solar god but also the Mexica deity of war and tribute. Tlaloc was the water and fertility god and a pan-Mesoamerican deity of agriculture. In the bifurcated Templo Mayor, therefore, the Aztec venerated deities who symbolized the material well-being of the city of Tenochtitlan.

The Aztecs adopted Tlaloc as their own deity and thereby authorized their presence in the Valley of Mexico. Thousands of figurines and statues were found at the Templo Mayor, as well as numerous other artefacts associated with water and fertility. The richest source of Tlaloc material is the offering boxes, which have been found throughout the site and are associated with all phases of the temple's construction. For Lopéz Luján, an archaeologist who has worked intensively with the offering boxes, the profusion of Tlaloc material can be 'read' like a book. The various layers of these boxes were intended to represent the different layers of the cosmos. In addition these layers indicate how Aztec ceremonial life unfolded.

Offering box no. 48, for example, is a particularly rich example. At the bottom of the box are various shells and corals from both Atlantic and Pacific oceans. They are laid out in an east–west direction, tracing the path of the sun. Above that were found various objects including jaguar skeletons, beads, figurines of various gods, and jars which symbolize the temple as a container of water. Above these objects were the entire skeletons of forty-two children below the ages of 7, with a corresponding number of Tlaloc figurines capping off the box. This offering was dated to 1454 when there was a very serious multi-year drought in Central Mexico. In desperation the Aztecs propitiated the deities of rain, principal of them being Tlaloc, to bring rain.

The Aztecs are famous, perhaps infamous, for their use of human sacrifice. These sacrificial rites have held a powerful place in the European imagination, and at certain points in the last 500 years they have assumed mythic proportions. Incidents of human sacrifice in the New World were often emphasized and exaggerated by Europeans in order to justify their colonial operations in the Americas. It is important to note, however, that the Spanish killed millions more people than did the Aztecs. This is particularly ironic given that the intention of the Spanish, as with other Europeans in the New World, was to spread a religion of love. The 'Black Legend' of the Spanish brutality perperated by Bartolomé de Las Casas in 1550 was promoted by the Protestant cultures of northern Europe. Protestants wished to demonize the Spanish Catholics by emphasizing the atrocities throughout the Americas. As horrific as Aztec human sacrifice was they killed far fewer people in the course of a given agricultural year than did the Spanish.

The phenomenon of human sacrifice is no different from similar offering rites. In an exchange economy of relationships with the deities human sacrifice is the gift among all gifts. Even so, the descriptions of these rites that have survived through the conquest of Tenochtitlan seem to indicate that even among Mesoamerican cultures, who were no strangers to human sacrifice, the Aztecs were known to be particularly bloody in their sacrificial rites. Since the scholarly view of the Mayas has been altered since the 1950s their counterparts in central Mexico look more similar and less bloody than they had done.

The imperial Incas

As far as scholars can tell, there was no contact between the cultures of Mesoamerica and Peru. There is some evidence that each had knowledge of the existence of the other but there was no formal interaction. For example, according to Wheatley Mesoamerican and Peruvian civilizations are two of the seven locations of primary urban generation. This indicates that over the course of their long development each had little direct knowledge of the other's existence.

And yet there are a number of similarities between Mesoamerican and Inca civilizations. Both were organized around central ceremonial cities, both had powerful rulers at the centre of their social organization; and both have been regarded as imperialistic in the domination of their respective regions.

Cuzco was the centre of the Inca empire (1200–1533 CE). At its zenith the Incas exerted influence over an area that extended from Ecuador to Chile. Like Mesoamerican cities, at its centre was a notable temple called the Temple of the Sun. The Inca, or ruler, was responsible for maintenance of the ceremonies. The extent of Inca influence covered a vast area. They developed a series of roads that radiated out from Cuzco in all directions. Along these roads would travel various sorts of people with tribute that flowed into the Inca centre.

From 1525 to 1532 two moieties of the empire were at war. The civil war was between two Incas (the term Inca is the title for both the empire and the ruler), Atahualpa and Huascar. Atahualpa eventually won back the rule but was overthrown by Pizarro, the conquistador from Spain, in 1533.

As with the Aztecs, what is known of the Incas comes to us primarily through contact with the Spanish. Their descriptions of the city of Cuzco are very similar to those of Tenochtitlan in that they tend to emphasize them as paradisiacal.

These accounts also emphasize the imperial character of the Inca capital. But there is evidence to suggest that the Incas were not imperial in the same sense as were the Spanish. In areas that were once dominated by the Incas several native languages were spoken that predate Quechua, or the language of the Inca. Aymara, for example, is still spoken in mountain villages of Bolivia while Quechua and Spanish are spoken in the lower areas. As with the Aztecs, the Incas tended to allow for a cultural plurality in areas that they controlled and were not interested in missionization as an instrument of social control. This stands in marked contrast with the Spanish, and other European empires, which emphasized the necessity of cultural uniformity with respect to language and religion.

The Incas were primarily concerned with tribute payments and not with imperial control of the hinterlands. Tribute was utilized in a gift exchange economy, as among the Mesoamericans. At the centre of this economy were the gifts given to the deities of the sun, water, the creator god Viracocha, and the moon goddess, as well as numerous other gods.

The sources

Pre-Columbian 'texts': the primary sources

Texts

The irony of an investigation of the 'primary' texts of the civilizations of the Americas is that they are ciphers that cannot be entirely comprehended by the scholarly community. At the outset we must acknowledge that the interpretation and investigation of these documents is a continuous enterprise that will never be completed. Part of the problem of comprehensibility has to do with the composition of the texts themselves, and whether or not they should be characterized as 'texts'. In the case of Aztec and Maya material there is a basis for referring to these documents as texts. In the Inca case, however, 'weaving' might be more appropriate than 'text'.

Another dilemma is that virtually all of the pre-Columbian texts were destroyed in bonfires set by Catholic missionaries in the sixteenth century. This action was taken in order that conversion to Christianity would not be compromised by the continuing worship of ancient deities. About sixteen pre-Columbian texts survived the blazes because they were sent back to Europe as curiosities and these texts are housed in libraries primarily in Italy, France, England and Spain.

Fig. 11.4. The frontispiece of the Fejérváry Mayer, which depicts the Aztec cosmology.

The circuitous routes of these documents to their present locations are adventure stories in themselves. Interpretation of the primary texts, therefore, is involved with the phenomenon of cultural contact between Old and New Worlds. Although they were created by pre-Columbian people, the range of possible meanings of these texts has been transformed by the conquest and colonial periods. The primary texts that have survived come from a variety of cultural areas but their meanings have been associated with Aztec and Inca civilizations.

In Tenochtitlan there were probably several thousand books of painted images, like the Fejérváry Mayer (Fig. 11.4), that were used in a variety of ceremonial contexts. Some of these occasions were of a public nature for the entire community and some were for individual households, such as at naming or birth ceremonies. These texts were housed in libraries of the calmecac, or the schools for training priests. It is likely that they were utilized by experts who were trained to 'read' them by appealing to other material forces such as the flow of blood in the body or climatological activity. In other words these texts were used in a manner that more closely resembled ritual activity than our present understanding of 'reading'. For the most part they served as the focal point of divinatory activity and would be consulted to ascertain whether or not an offering or a question for the deity was successfully received.

The most significant inroads towards interpreting Mesoamerican texts have been made by art historians rather than linguists, since the ancient cultures of the Americas created texts which were largely based in painted images. While some phonetic elements were paired with images these texts tended to cluster information around images. Reading the text thus required a high degree of cultural knowledge and sophistication. This is particularly true regarding Maya epigraphic texts because they use images, and in order to read them one must keep a large number of images in mind. This is in contrast to a phonetic symbolic system, such as the alphabet.

The primary texts, therefore, tell us less about the facts of Aztec life and more about how they perceived their interaction with the hidden dimensions of the cosmos. Most of the surviving texts are articulations of the tonalpohualli, or the divinatory calendar of 260 days, and the 365-day agricultural calendar. The former was used throughout Mesoamerica. There are various theories of why a 260-day calendar was chosen. Some suggest that this count is close to particular cycles of Venus, but many agree that 260 days is close to nine months, or the human gestation period, given the centrality of the human body to all Aztec ceremonial activity.

Maya diviners continue to utilize the tonalpohualli. According to Tedlock, who was trained as a diviner, the 'reader' of the days utilizes the pulses of blood in his/her own body to understand the messages contained in the calendar.

Inca primary 'texts', called quipu, are composed of knotted cords which either radiate outward from a central cord ring or are strung along a rope (Fig. 11.5). Multicoloured cords and knots recount to the reader stories, histories and numerical arrangements. In particular the knots of the quipus may correspond to particular sites called huacas that are connected by invisible sight lines, called ceques, situated throughout the surrounding landscape. These knotted cords trace out the ceque/huaca system which maps the interrelationships between the movement of celestial phenomena with reference to features of the landscape. Thus they were also linked closely with ceremonies. These 'texts' may have been used to record calendrical information that would have been used on particular cere- monial occasions, but, unlike the Mesoamerican texts, they do not seem to have been used in divinatory activities. They also numerically record various features of celestial phenomena or tribute. How to 'read' these 'texts' is the source of much debate since, like the codices of central Mexico, they record information to be used in a ritual or performative occasion. Recently thirty-two quipus were found in a cave in north-eastern Peru and the possibility now exists, therefore,

Fig. 11.5. Quipu expert from Guamán Poma de Ayala.

that these can be compared with written accounts of the conquest in order to 'crack the code' of the Inca. Like the discovery of the Rosetta Stone in 1799 and the advances in Maya scholarship since the 1970s, Inca scholars may well be able to 'read' quipus in the near future (Urton 1981).

The texts of the Aztec and the Inca emphasized counting, celestial phenomena and ceremonial activity, but some were also used to keep track of tribute flowing into each of the ceremonial centres. They were meant to be used with reference to a particular landscape by those who had the ability to 'read' them. Unlike the books of the European intellectual tradition, interpretations of these texts was very much embedded in their physical location and the orientation of the reader. They present the scholar with some significant interpretive challenges.

Archaeology

The other primary source of information about ancient civilizations of the Americas is the archaeological record. Both the Aztecs and the Incas left considerable physical remnants which are constantly being unearthed and assessed. One of the most exciting aspects of studying these civilizations is that new finds are regularly revealed and, as a consequence, our understanding of them is radically transformed.

The Templo Mayor and other ceremonial sites, such as the ceremonial complexes at Cholula, have undergone intensive scrutiny over several years but questions regarding who built them persist. Cholula was a very important religious centre that was continuously occupied from the late Olmec through the Aztec period, and yet very little is known about why this city lasted so long or the nature of its influence in the Mesoamerican world. Some have referred to it as the 'Rome' of the New World. Its pyramid is the largest in the world by volume and it was home to a diversity of temples, but it is difficult to assess their importance because currently a Catholic church sits atop the pyramid, which now looks like a large hill. This is also the case with other temples in the area. Cholula thus raises the dilemma of the degree to which one compromises the current religious building to discover more about those underneath.

The Templo Mayor presented archaeologists with the difficulties of urban excavations. It sits in the centre of one of the most densely populated cities in the world, just north of the Presidential Palace and east of the National Cathedral of Mexico. Fortunately the few colonial ruins that lay atop the Templo Mayor could be moved or worked around in some fashion. A museum was built to house the vast array of objects taken from the site. Because, like the texts, it was destroyed by the Spanish, the reconstruction of the pyramid has been a laborious and complex process of educated speculations about how it must have looked 500 years ago.

The nature of the archaeological enterprise in urban contexts has yielded critical information regarding ancient American civilizations but also increases the number of questions. This is also the case in more remote sites such as Teotihuacan, Tula and Malinalco, as well as numerous lowland sites. Because these sites have been intensively excavated over several generations by scholars who had their own intellectual agendas, the records often create more confusion. In addition the interpretation of pre-Columbian sites is intimately connected with Mexican cultural identity. For example, in their rush to get the site ready for a national commemoration of the revolution in the early twentieth century, Teotihuacan was originally excavated with dynamite. Further, several of these sites are tourist destinations, the most famous including Tula, Chichen Itza, Tikal, Teotihuacan, Xochimilco Xochicalco (Fig. 11.6) and the Templo Mayor. Excavations of tourist areas tend to focus on reconstruction of the sites as they once were, which means that they are building projects as much as they are excavations.

Less dramatic, but just as significant, has been the interpretive shift in American archaeology called the New Archaeology. Since the 1950s fewer monumental buildings have been excavated and interest has concentrated on generating a better understanding of how common people lived in these cities. House mounds rather than ceremonial builds and chinampa fields rather than palace courtyards have been the focus of archaeological labours. This has yielded a fuller picture of the whole spectrum of life from ruler to citizen. The New Archaeology has likewise given us a glimpse of the religion of common people. Often the ethnic identity of a community can be traced through their altar or figurine styles. By emphasizing new questions associated with common people, which would have been regarded as peripheral a century ago, archaeologists have given us a better understanding of the totality of urban life.

The central urban position of the Templo Mayor has led to interesting cultural innovations. When Rigoberta Menchú won the 1992 Nobel Peace Prize she decided to house the medal in the Templo Mayor Museum rather than take it to her home in southern Mexico. Outside the site there are numerous vendors of Aztec-like goods, book stalls, musicians and dancers, and various political groups have information booths in order to lobby for the rights of indigenous people of Mexico.

The Inca were highly skilled stone workers. The temples at Cuzco and, 80 km north, the city of Machu Picchu were crafted from very hard stone. No mortar was used in their construction and yet the joints between stones are so tight that not even the blade of a knife can be inserted between them. Currently some scholars think that Machu Picchu was a kind of agricultural testing outpost in the Andes where varieties of potato and cereal crops could be genetically selected at high altitude: the numerous terraces and fields at the site are too small to support a large population. In addition to tribute it was agricultural success that ensured the continuation of the Inca empire.

The breathtaking location of Machu Picchu has attracted large numbers of travellers; its location has generated numerous interpretations of Inca religion and civilization. As with the Templo Mayor, the site demands the imaginative labours of the tourist, the activist and the scholar. Excavations in areas where

Fig. 11.6. Ball court at Xochicalco. Photograph by the author.

people, for various reasons, have intense interest in the discoveries yield further questions, further interpretations, and therefore further meanings. The significance of the ancient civilizations of the Americas is never finished. The archaeological record offers us important clues which have to be reconsidered every time someone puts in a new sewer line.

Ethnography

To the list of 'primary sources' should be added the indigenous people of Mexico, Guatemala, Belize, Peru, Bolivia and other countries. It is estimated that 2 to 3 million people in central Mexico speak Nahuatl, with a comparable number speaking native languages, mostly Maya, in the lowlands of Mexico; thirty-two different languages are spoken in Mexico. About 10 million native people in Peru, close to half of the population, are Quechua and Aymara speakers. Many of these communities continue to practise versions of the ceremonies of their ancestors, and even though these practices of present-day native people are not directly connected with those of pre-Columbian people they can nevertheless be regarded as a primary source. Ethnographic 'upstreaming' (i.e. utilizing ethnographic information to evaluate other 'primary' sources) helps overcome some of the problems associated with textual and archaeological resources and often gives scholars insights into the practices of ancient people. Ethnographies tend to inform us about the religious practices of common people rather than about those of ruling classes.

A single example is the Mesoamerican understanding and use of paper. In the Codex Mendosa, a text that was created after the conquest but in a pre-Columbian style, paper is shown as a major tribute item that came into Tenochtitlan. Literally tons of paper were transfered to the Aztecs from subject territories. Given that the Aztecs did not write books in the conventional European sense, the question emerges of what the Aztecs were doing with all that paper.

According to ethnographies, among the Otomi (Galinier 1983) and other contemporary Nahuatl speakers (Sandstrom 1991) paper is a very important ritual object that is used to propitiate deities associated with water, seeds and ancestors, as well as a host of other deities. The manufacture of paper is sometimes done by shamans, and ritual specialists cut the paper into the shapes of deities to arrange on altars. With this knowledge one can revisit the primary texts with a new understanding of the ritual use of paper. Ethnographic knowledge highlights other important aspects of the primary sources in ways that promote new understandings of these ancient civilizations.

Colonial texts, the secondary sources

Priestly writings

Many of the most important resources for understanding pre-Columbian civilizations were generated by the conquerors. Of course this presents us with another ironic situation. They are similar to the primary sources in that colonial texts still tend to obscure the religious world-views of the Aztecs or the Incas. However, they are dissimilar in that colonial texts nevertheless are generally written in such a way as to present the pre-Columbian past as wholly comprehensible. There is a tendency of colonial writers to speak with an expert knowledge that camouflages the real gaps between colonial and indigenous cultures.

In central Mexico very soon after the fall of Tenochtitlan there was a flurry of intellectual activity generated by various Catholic orders to learn native languages and codify them in grammars and dictionaries. These texts would then be used to translate official church doctrine, create catechisms or give sermons in Nahuatl. There were also writings intended to record various aspects of the life of the Indians. Both of these endeavours, the linguistic and the ethnographic, were carried out in order to facilitate the conversion of native communities.

As a consequence of these labours Nahuatl became the lingua franca of New Spain (i.e. Mexico). Significant amounts of colonial court records having to do with land transactions and inheritance disputes, for example, were recorded in Nahuatl. The written form of Nahuatl used during the colonial period had been transformed into an alphabetic and phonetic form by Catholic priests.

The most important figure in generating this colonial record of pre-Columbian cultures was Fray Bernardino de Sahagún. He was a Franciscan monk who came to Mexico soon after it became New Spain in 1521, after the fall of Tenochtitlan. He dedicated his intellectual talents to learning Nahuatl, a project that was already underway. Over approximately a forty-year period, from 1530 to 1570, Sahagún collected information related to all facets of Aztec life. The most complete record of this work is *The general history of the things of New Spain*, commonly referred to as *The Florentine Codex*. It is currently housed in the Laurentian Library in Florence, Italy. The *Florentine* is an encyclopaedic work in thirteen volumes which covers pre-Columbian understandings of the gods, ceremonies, moral philosophy, the natural world and the conquest.

The work is ahead of its time in that Sahagún dispassionately records the totality of Aztec culture in a systematic and detailed fashion. Sahagún's method has earned him the title of the 'father of American ethnography'. But very little is known about Sahagún the man. This information could help scholars understand why he approached the descriptive task the way that he did, the consequence of which was to create a new way of interacting with other civilizations and cultures.

There were many other priests who wrote about the Aztecs, including the Dominican Fray Diego Durán. Durán's insights are valuable in that he was born and reared in New Spain and was in constant contact with Nahuatl-speaking people and thus had a familiarity with Aztec customs. What Sahagún and Durán share is an extreme antagonism towards Aztec religion as well as towards the figurehead of the religion – the Aztec priest. Although Sahagún does not dwell on his prejudice he does begin and end each volume of the *Florentine* with a diatribe against the false religion he is setting out to record. Durán is less disciplined about attacking what he sees as diabolic in Aztec tradition and frequently editorializes in the midst of his writing about the Aztecs.

The interpretive dilemma is, therefore, how to know when to filter out the prejudice of the priestly writings in attempting to look at the civilizations that pre-dated their creation. Even though priestly writings, written in a post-Columbian world, constitute a very important resource in understanding pre-Columbian cultures, how reliable are they when their authors were so firmly dedicated to eradication of those same cultures? This is an even more vexing problem when dealing with the topic of religion.

As alluded to above, one of the most glaring omissions from these texts is the Aztec priest. In the *Florentine* there are only scant, even cryptic references to these religious leaders because they were considered by Catholic priests as the arch-enemy of the promotion of Christianity in the New World. Yet the priesthood of Mesoamerica was an institution which developed over the course of millennia and, had we known more about it, could have significantly impacted upon our appreciation of religious innovation.

Accounts of the Conquistadores

Both Cortés and Pizarro were in direct contact with the Aztecs and the Incas respectively. Their writings, therefore, are key secondary sources for knowing about these people. In Mexico it is also the case that one of Cortés' men, Bernal Diaz de Castillo, wrote an important text several years after the fall of Tenochtitlan.

Both Cortés and Pizarro, however, were keenly aware of their positions as agents of the crown. Moreover, both were very ambitious and so wanted to present their actions in the best possible light. In his letters to the Spanish monarch, Cortés tends to emphasize the wonders of his discoveries in the New World and the need for someone to be appointed Viceroy of the New World, such as himself, who would be most able to bring the riches to the king most effectively. Pizarro speaks similarly of the Inca cities and the possibilities of gold extraction. These men had a keen eye for what use their 'discoveries' might have for Spain and were therefore less curious about what they actually saw. This is unfortunate but understandable given the military cunning of both of them.

Being a foot soldier with little or nothing to lose, Diaz del Castillo on the other hand had nothing to gain immediately from the conquest. It is in his writing that we can begin to appreciate the first impressions of Tenochtitlan as a paradisal place from the perspective of a complete outsider. His account was written long after the conquest and is therefore subject to the problems of memory.

Native narratives

There are a few accounts of pre-Columbian life written by prominent native authors. These authors are significant in that they would have had to have sufficient means to re-educate themselves in a Spanish system. Notable among them is Felipe Guaman Poma de Ayala, who chronicled the Inca world together with its conquest by the Spanish. As with Sahagún, Guaman Poma's life story is difficult to assess. He was born very close to the time of the conquest of Cuzco and lived most of his life in Spain. He completely dedicated himself to the task of writing about the Incas and their demise. He characterized his writing as weeping about the end of the world. His account is perhaps the most valuable for our gaining entrance into the Inca world in that his perspective represents the native view. His account is also from the perspective of someone who underwent the transition from an Incan to a Spanish world-view in the scope of a single lifetime.

Other native authors set down in writing family histories and mythic narratives. Often these were recorded by the once ruling-class families who, during the colonial era, still had some legal title to land and aristocratic status in the courts. Many of these texts were written as attempts to legitimate one's connection to an ancestor to ensure survival under the Spanish crown.

When reading the secondary sources to understand pre-Columbian cultures one is constantly aware of the various interpretive agendas at work. To compound the problem, however, there is the generally remote nature of the primary evidence. The work of interpreting pre-Columbian American civilization requires an ability of the scholar to weigh and integrate a great variety of evidence. None of the texts, experiences or physical evidence is adequate in itself. In attempting to interpret these civilizations the scholar must be continually aware of the profound trauma of the conquest.

With that does not come a demoralization that nothing certain can be understood of these cultures. On the contrary, the dexterity required in sifting various kinds of evidence can be satisfying in that new discoveries tend to emerge out of old material once thought to be completely and finally known. The imaginative abilities of the scholar to sort through various types of evidence can yield important new angles with which to view these ancient civilizations. Below are some examples of how different kinds of evidence can come together in order to help us understand Aztec and Inca mythic and ceremonial life.

Religion and ritual life

For both the Aztecs and the Incas, understandings of how the cosmos was created were directly related to their ceremonial life. This section will utilize a variety of primary and secondary source materials to relate their distinctive creation myths and connect those with ritual activities. Central to both cases were their respective perspectives on the human body and the necessity of giving back to the deities a measure of life that humans have been given. Both cultures emphasized rituals involving human sacrifice to establish cosmological order.

The Aztecs

The Aztecs lived in an age known as the Fifth Sun. It was preceded by four previous suns which were all known by their destruction. The creation of the Fifth Sun took place at Teotihuacan, the 'city of the gods'. It was there, in total darkness, that two gods agreed to throw themselves into the fire to create the new sun. The first was a boastful and handsome deity and the second was a sickly deity. The first could not summon the courage to throw himself into the firepit, however, so the creation was in jeopardy. The sickly god, Nanahuatzin, eagerly threw himself into the fire. After his autosacrifice the other deities all threw themselves into the fire, thereby ensuring that the sun would rise again and the Fifth Age would begin (Read 1998).

Central to the Aztec cosmogony is the willing sacrifice of the gods to usher in the new sun. Likewise it was understood that human beings also had the responsibility to perform autosacrifices at regular intervals of time to keep the sun moving. The relationship between human sacrifice and movement of time is strongly emphasized in the myth of the birth of Huitzilopochtli, the god of the sun.

Once the mother of the earth, Coatlicue ('serpent skirt'), was sweeping out the temple at the top of 'altepetl', or the sacred 'water mountain'. A small ball of feathers fell down from the sky and Coatlicue caught it and tucked it into her blouse. After this she immediately became pregnant. Her daughter the moon, Coyoxauhqui, and her sons, called the 400 Southerners, were enraged that their mother should get pregnant in such a scandalous way and not have a proper husband. Coyoxauhqui and her brothers, the 400 Southerners, decided that they would kill their mother. With their battle gear they marched up altepetl and the sound of their approach frightened their mother. But deep within her womb she heard a calming voice which assured her that there was nothing to fear. A little while later she again heard the approaching army of her children and again she heard the calming voice from her womb telling her that everything was as it was supposed to be. Just as Coyoxauhqui and the 400 Southerners were about to break into the temple Huitzilopochtli sprang from his mother's womb in full battle array and decapitated his sister Coyoxaugqui. Her body then fell down altepetl and became dismembered in the process. She came to rest at the bottom of the hill but was broken into pieces. As for the 400 Southerners, Huitzilopochtli chased them, scattering them to lands far away.

This myth takes place at the Templo Mayor. It also accounts for why the Coyoxauhqui stone, the find that initiated the excavation in 1978, would have been found at the bottom of the Huitzilopochtli side of the temple. The myth also recounts daybreak, at which time the sun is born from the earth (at the horizon) and the moon and stars (i.e. the 400 Southerners) are vanquished. As with the creation myth of the Fifth Sun, this story emphasizes the importance of human death in perpetuating the cosmic order.

The mythic theme of human sacrifice as an integral part of the temporal order of the cosmos is a common one in Aztec ritual. A particularly important ritual event, however, was the New Fire Ceremony, or 2 Reed. It took place every fifty-two years, which was the number of years required for the 260-day divinatory calendar and the 365-day agricultural calendars to be resynchronized with one another. The resynchronization took place on the day named 2 Reed and was thus the name of the ceremony. It took place on a hill south of Tenochtitlan now called the Hill of the Star. Before the ceremony all fires were extinguished throughout the entire Aztec area. Clay pots which were fired in furnaces were broken and children were hidden in granaries to prevent their being turned into mice during this dangerous moment of chaos. A sacrificial victim was led to the spot on the hill by the priests of Tenochtitlan. At midnight, or when the star constellation of the Pleiades was directly overhead, the priests laid the victim on a stone, cut open his chest and offered the blood to the deities. In his chest cavity the priest lit a new fire. The fire was then distributed to everyone throughout the empire.

From the perspective of the Aztec mythology this ritual restored a temporal structure by giving the sun human blood. Thus, the two calendars were restored from the chaos of darkness.

The Incas

The creator deity of the Incas was Viracocha (Sea of Fat). Viracocha was the eternal creator of all beings on the earth. His other titles named him as the 'foundation of the earth' and its lord. He is also associated with the Milky Way. His position in the cosmos, therefore, was above all celestial and earthly phenomena. Yet he was continually involved with his companions who oversaw various areas of the creation. A temple at Cuzco was dedicated to Viracocha. In it was a statue in human form which was said to be made of gold and about the size of a ten-year-old boy.

Out of the south-east, the direction from which the sun was born, Viracocha came walking towards the north-west with two of his companions. As he walked over the land he named things. It was through the act of walking and naming that the world was created. He had previously drawn the images of the things he had named on the island at Lake Titicaca. At that place he used the images to rehearse his cosmogonic sojourn. He then ascended into the high sky, or heaven. Important for the creation story is that where Viracocha rehearsed his creation and where he eventually departed from the earth have a specific geographical referent.

Cuzco was arranged into moieties, which were then divided again to become associated with the four cardinal directions. Further subdividing the Inca capital were some 400 divisions of holy sites, called ceques. These lines continued to the farthest extent of the empire. Care for these sites was assigned to be the work of a social group. Thus religious and social organization was maintained through the ceque system. The festival of Capac hucha required the sacrifice of children to the deities of rain and fertility. The group responsible for giving the children to the Incas either sent them to the centre via the ceque line or would walk to their homeland from Cuzco along the ceque line. In the latter case the children would then be sacrificed at a home huaca, or holy site.

During fertility ceremonies at Cuzco the Inca ruler was required to open the ground using a planting stick. His activity reproduced the activities of Viracocha. In addition mummies of previous Inca rulers would be carried on litters over the ceremonial planting grounds. It was understood that the movement of the rulers' desiccated bodies had a fertilizing effect on the land.

Contemporary Aymara-speaking groups in Bolivia still have an oral memory of these traditions. Always known to be capable diviners, these groups recall having served the Incas in the capacity of litter-bearers. The Inca practice of mummification was seen as removing fat from the body. For current groups the soul is directly connected with the liquids of the body. The mummified body of the Inca ruler and the bodies of children, therefore, would have had associations with the seeds and the fructifying ability of fat, or bodily energy. Today the indigenous people still use the fat of animals in various rituals associated with planting and healing.

In addition, the ceque lines are reminiscent of the creative labours of Viracocha. The Inca ceque/huaca system, their division of the empire into moieties and cardinal directions, and their intricate system of roads were all associated with the cosmogonic sojourn of Viracocha.

Survivals of ancient civilized religions in Latin American Catholicism

Aztec and Inca religions have not disappeared but, after the trauma of colonialism, have adapted themselves to the religious conditions of the New World. Estimates of current numbers of indigenous people in Mexico and Peru vary, but in both countries they constitute a major portion of the population, if not the majority. Their social status has not much improved since the colonial period in spite of the fact that the ancient civilizations from which they have descended are a source of profound nationalistic pride. There is therefore a wide variety of indigenous movements in Mexico and Peru which have been connected with other indigenous people from throughout the Americas and the rest of the world. It is precisely the indigenous emphasis of contemporary groups in interpreting their ancient urban roots that unites their religious innovations since the conquest by Spain.

Throughout Latin America, beginning soon after the conquest, there have been several apparitions of the Virgin Mary, who appears as a 'black' or Indian Virgin. Prominent among these 'hierophanies' is the Virgin of Guadalupe (Fig. 11.7). Since as early as 1540 she has been the symbol of Mexican identity as a creative combination of pre-Columbian and Catholic world-views. In 1531, which was just ten years after the fall of Tenochtitlan, a Nahuatl-speaking man named Juan Diego was walking by a hill called Tepeyac. At the hill he encountered the dark-skinned Virgin Mary who sternly instructed him to go to see the archbishop of Mexico and have him build a cathedral at that site in her honour. When Juan Diego went to the archbishop's palace he was rejected by the guards. As he walked home by Tepeyac he again encountered the Virgin and she instructed him to pick some flowers that were miraculously blooming out of season. Juan Diego gathered the flowers in his cloak, which was a native Aztec garment, and carried them back to the archbishop's palace. This time the guards wanted to see what Juan Diego was concealing in his cloak. In the scuffle they all discovered that an image of the Virgin of Guadalupe was magically formed on Juan Diego's cloak. The apparition was recognized as the Virgin of Guadalupe in Spain, where there have been other Marian apparitions .

Recently the miracle of the Virgin of Guadalupe was recognized by the Vatican. In December each year millions of Mexicans crawl on their knees to the Basilica erected on Tepeyac in veneration of the Virgin's appearance at that site. But the site of Tepeyac was also where an important Aztec female deity was worshipped. In pre-Columbian times Tonantzin, which means 'Our Honoured Mother', was associated with the great salt and fresh water lakes that surrounded the Aztec capital. Tonantzin is still a title used by Nahuatl-speaking people to refer to the Virgin of Guadalupe.

From an Aztec point of view the apparition of the Virgin forms the basis of what could be seen as a movement to *indigenize* Catholicism in the New World, that is, to connect the phenomenon of the religious life of the Old World with the Aztec tradition. From the church's point of view, however, the acceptance of the apparition as genuine is a strategy which brings the Aztecs into the church by embracing the new symbolic language at the site of old rituals. In this sense the Virgin of Guadalupe is similar to the building of the church on top of the pyramid at Cholula, as discussed above. The phenomenon of Catholic symbols replacing or overlying pre-Columbian religious forms is a regular occurrence throughout Latin America (Fig. 11.8).

Fig. 11.7. The image of the Virgin of Guadalupe which was said to have miraculously appeared on the cloak of Juan Diego in 1531.

Fig. 11.8. A Catholic church on top of the Mesoamerican pyramid at Cholula, Mexico.
Photograph by the author.

Another important area in which to appreciate the survival of indigenous traditions throughout Latin America is the ceremonies to the dead. As we have discussed already, the ancestors and the dead played an important role in pre-Columbian traditions. They continue to do so through 'Day of the Dead' ceremonies in Mexico and feasts of the dead in Peru. Both of these ceremonial occasions have been integrated into the Catholic liturgical calendar as 'All Souls Day', which takes place on 2 November. In Mexico the Day of the Dead involves creating an altar to the ancestors and hosting an all-night feast in the village cemetery. These are elaborate celebrations which often involve the entire extended family. In pre-Columbian times a similar feast, called Tepeilhuitl (Festival of the Mountains), was held which also included the construction of family altars and feasting.

Quechua- and Aymara-speaking people in Bolivia hold a similar celebration (Bastien 1978). Among Andean people altars are constructed in the shape of a mountain, which they understand to be a living being. Upon death, part of the human soul enters the earth and begins a journey to the top of the mountain. In their sojourn the souls are responsible for good harvests, and the connection between agricultural success and the ancestors is common throughout Latin America. From the top of the mountain body the soul can be reborn into the human community once again. Day of the Dead festivities in rural Bolivian communities are intended to assist the dead in the journey back to the living.

There are numerous ways in which pre-Columbian world-views continue to exert an influence on indigenous people today. The roles of the stars, the underworld and divination in ceremonies, frequently associated with the Catholic church, are often direct continuations of Aztec and Inca practices.

Conclusion: the legacy of cultural contact

Descendants of the Aztecs and the Incas continue to emphasize the indigenous quality of their ceremonial lives. As with pre-Columbian cultures, the native people of Latin America connect religion to how they meaningfully inhabit their material worlds. There is a persistence of the civilizations of ancient America in spite of the trauma of colonial conquest.

This cultural persistence is due to an understanding of 'religion' as a mode of expression which binds a human community to the hidden dimensions of material existence. As with their ancestors, the indigenous people of today perform rituals that orient their communities to ultimate conditions of existence. Even though they had no specific words to express the concept, the ancient civilizations of the Americas practised something that we modern people would understand as 'religion'.

The Aztecs and Incas present scholars with a distinctive, and often disturbing, case that calls into question our current understandings and interpretations of religion. The pre-Columbian worlds of the Aztecs and Incas have been worked on by the scholarly and popular imaginations over the last 500 years. They continue to exert an important influence on modern-day conceptions of 'civilization' and 'religion'. With each new archaeological discovery we revisit our presumptions about these civilizations. In this way the Aztecs and the Incas continue to influence the development of culture in ways analogous to the civilizations of the Old World.

Bibliography

Arnold, Philip P. 1999. *Eating landscape: the Aztec and European occupation of Tlalocan*. Niwot: University Press of Colorado. A description of the ritual landscape of the Aztec in comparison with Spanish understandings of the New World.

Aveni, Anthony F. 1980. *Sky watchers of ancient Mexico*. Austin: University of Texas Press. A classic text of ancient Mesoamerican calendar systems.

Bastien, Joseph W. 1978. *Mountain of the condor: metaphor and ritual in an Andean ayllu*. Prospect Heights, IL: Waveland Press. A classic anthropological study of contemporary people of Bolivia.

Boone, Elizabeth and Walter Mignolo (eds.) 1994. *Writing without words: alternative literacies in Mesoamerica and the Andes*. Durham, NC: Duke University Press. This text examines the relationship between text and art throughout the ancient Mesoamerican and Inca worlds.

Broda, Johanna 1971. Las fiestas Aztecas de los dioses de la lluvia: una reconstrucción según las fuentes del siglo XVI. *Revista Española de Antropología Americana* 6: 245–327. An invaluable study of the fertility cult among the Aztecs.

Brotherston, Gordon 1978. *Image of the New World: the American continent portrayed in native texts*. London: Thames and Hudson. A comprehensive survey of native texts from throughout the Americas.

Burkhart, Louise M. 1989. *The slippery earth: Nahua Christian moral dialogue in sixteenth century Mexico*. Tucson: University of Arizona Press. A detailed look at the relationship between pre-Columbian and Spanish worlds as revealed through their distinctive understandings of the world.

Carrasco, Davíd 1982. *Quetzalcoatl and the irony of empire: myths and prophecies in the Aztec tradition*. Chicago: University of Chicago Press. This examines the famous story of Quetzalcoatl and Cortés' use of the myth to topple the Aztec empire.

1990. *Religions of Mesoamerica: cosmovision and ceremonial centers*. San Francisco: Harper and Row. A useful textbook regarding the phenomenon of religion in pre-Columbian Mexico.

Cobo, Fray Bernabé 1990. *Inca religion and customs*, trans. and ed. Roland Hamilton. Austin: University of Texas Press. A primary source which describes Inca life from a contemporary perspective.

Diaz del Castillo, Bernal 1956. *The discovery and conquest of Mexico, 1517–1521*, trans. A. P. Maudslay. New York: Farrar, Straus, and Cudahy. Castillo was a soldier in Cortés' army and this text gives a gritty portrayal of the fall of the Aztec empire.

574 Philip P. Arnold

Durán, Fray Diego 1971. *Book of the gods and rites and the ancient calendar*, ed. and trans. Fernando Horcasitas and Doris Heyden. Norman: University of Oklahoma Press. This is a primary text written by a priest in Mexico from the sixteenth century.

Galinier, Jacques 1983. *Pueblos de la Sierra Madre: etnografía de la Communidad Otomí*. Mexico City: Instituto Nacional Indigenista. An account of a contemporary indigenous group from Mexico which is helpful when thinking about Mesoamerican religion.

Guamán Poma de Ayala, Felipe 1981. *El primer nueva corónica y buen gobierno*, ed. John V. Murra and Rolena Adorno, trans. Jorge L. Urioste. Mexico City: Siglo Veintiuno. This is written from the point of view of an Inca nobleman who is trying to get readers to appreciate his pre-Spanish heritage.

Las Casas, Bartolomé de 1992. *The devastation of the Indies, a brief account*, trans. Herma Briffault, intro. Bill M. Donovan. Baltimore, MD: Johns Hopkins University Press. This text is the source of the Black Legend of Spanish injustices in the New World. Las Casas was a priest who is still widely regarded as the defender of the Indian.

Long, Charles H. 1986. *Significations: signs, symbols, and images in the interpretation of religion*. Philadelphia, PA: Fortress Press. Long is one of the most important theorists in the comparative study of religion. He emphasizes the importance of culture contact as a vehicle for understanding the American experience.

López Austin, Alfredo 1988. *The human body and ideology: concepts of the ancient Nahuas*, 2 vols., trans. Thelma and Bernard Ortiz de Montellano. Salt Lake City: University of Utah Press. A thorough analysis of the connections between the human body and the cosmos in Mesoamerica.

López Luján, Leonardo 1994. *The offerings of the Templo Mayor of Tenochtitlan*, trans. Bernard and Thelma Ortiz de Montellano. Niwot: University Press of Colorado. A detailed survey of the findings at the Templo Mayor and a convincing analysis of their meaning.

Matos Moctezuma, Eduardo 1995. *Life and death in the Templo Mayor*, trans. Bernard and Thelma Ortiz de Montellano. Niwot: University Press of Colorado. This is written by the director of the Templo Mayor excavation and he successfully integrates the importance of the site into the Aztec cosmology.

Nicholson, Henry B. 1971. Religion in prehispanic central Mexico. In *Handbook of Middle American Indians: guide to the ethnohistorical sources*, vol. 11, ed. R. Wauchope. Austin: University of Texas Press. pp. 395–445. A clear and concise description of Mesoamerican deities.

Nutini, Hugo G. 1998. *Todos Santos in rural Tlaxcala: a syncretic, expressive and symbolic analysis of the Cult of the Dead*. Princeton, NJ: Princeton University Press. This is a very good account of the annual ceremonies to the dead and their importance in a contemporary Nahua-speaking community.

Ortiz de Montellano, Bernard R. 1990. *Aztec medicine, health, and nutrition*. New Brunswick, NJ: Rutgers University Press. Often health and religion were two sides of the same coin in Mesoamerica. This is written by an anthropologist who also has command of both Mesoamerican texts and medical knowledge.

Read, Kay Almere 1998. *Time and sacrifice in the Aztec cosmos*. Bloomington: Indiana University Press. An analysis of the relationship between the calendar and human sacrifice in the Aztec empire.

Sahagún, Fray Bernardino de 1951–82. *Florentine Codex: general history of the things of New Spain*, 13 parts, ed. and trans. Arthur J. O. Anderson and Charles E. Dibble. Salt Lake City: University of Utah Press. Sahagún's text is the single most important and complete primary source on Mesoamerican culture.

Sandstrom, Alan R. 1991. *Corn is our blood: culture and ethnic identity in a contemporary Aztec Indian village*. Norman: University of Oklahoma Press. An invaluable look at the ritual life of modern Nahuatl-speaking people of Mexico.

Schele, Linda and Mary Ellen Miller 1986. *The blood of kings: dynasty and ritual in Maya art*. New York: George Braziller. A classic account of kingly succession among the Maya.

Sullivan, Lawrence E. 1988. *Icanchu's drum: an orientation to meaning in South American religions*. New York: Macmillian. An exhaustive exploration of the religions of the entire South American continent.

Tedlock, Barbara 1982. *Time and the Highland Maya*. Albuquerque: University of New Mexico Press. A personal account of her journey as a Maya shaman apprentice.

Todorov, Tzvetan 1984. *The conquest of America*, trans. Richard Howard. New York: Harper Torchbooks. Written by a linguist, this offers a critical analysis of the contact between Spanish and Mesoamerican worlds.

Urton, Gary 1981. *At the crossroads of the earth and sky: an Andean cosmology*. Austin: University of Texas Press. A classic account of a Quechua-speaking group of people and their ongoing relationship to the stars.

van der Loo, Peter 1987. *Codices costumbres continuidad: un estudio de la religión Mesoamericana*. Leiden: Indiaanse Studies 2, Archeologisch Centrum RU. Demonstrates the importance of pre-Columbian texts for contemporary Nahuatl-speaking people of Mexico.

Zuidema, R. Thomas 1964. *The ceque system of Cuzco: the social organization of the capital of the Inca*. International Archives of Ethnography, Supplement to vol. 50. Leiden: E. J. Brill. A classic study of the ceque system (or a system of invisible, radial lines) that emanated from the centre of the Inca empire.

Index

read more (Ⓟ)

PENGUIN REFERENCE LIBRARY

THE PENGUIN HANDBOOK OF LIVING RELIGIONS

EDITED BY JOHN R HINNELLS

'Excellent … This whole book is a joy to read'
The Times Higher Education Supplement

Religion is more relevant than ever. From Islam to fundamentalism to the Kabbalah, faith is never far from the headlines, making our understanding of it utterly crucial. *The Penguin Handbook of Living Religions* is designed with this in mind. Crammed with charts, maps and diagrams, it comprises lengthy enlightening chapters on all of today's major religions, from Hinduism to Christianity to Baha'ism, as well as additional essays on cross-cultural areas, such as gender and spirituality. Each chapter represents a book's worth of information on all twenty-first century religions, featuring detailed discussion of the history, culture and practices of each. Comprehensive, informative and compiled by a team of leading international scholars, it includes discussion of modern developments and recent scholarship.

- Explains the sources and history of the world's religions, from Buddhism, Christianity, Hinduism, Islam, Sikhism and Zoroastrianism to regional groups in Africa, China and Japan

- Describes different doctrines, practices and teachings, including rites of passage and specific rituals

- Explores the role of gender and diaspora in modern religion

ONLY PENGUIN GIVES YOU MORE